MCTS®
Microsoft™ SQL Server 2005
Implementation and Maintenance
Study Guide
(Exam 70–431)

MCTS®
Microsoft™ SQL Server 2005
Implementation and Maintenance
Study Guide
(Exam 70-431)

Joseph L. Jorden

Dandy Weyn

Wiley Publishing, Inc.

Acquisitions and Development Editor: Maureen Adams
Technical Editors: Marcellus Duffy and Marilyn Miller-White
Production Editor: Daria Meoli
Copy Editor: Kim Wimpsett
Production Manager: Tim Tate
Vice President and Executive Group Publisher: Richard Swadley
Vice President and Executive Publisher: Joseph B. Wikert
Vice President and Publisher: Neil Edde
Permissions Editor: Shannon Walters
Media Development Specialist: Steven Kurdirka
Book Designer: Judy Fung
Compositor and Illustrator: Jeffrey Wilson, Happenstance Type-O-Rama
Proofreader: Nancy Riddiough
Indexer: Ted Laux
Cover Designer: Archer Design

ISBN-13: 978-0-470-02565-9
ISBN-10: 0-470-02565-4

Sybex®
An Imprint of
WILEY

To Our Valued Readers:

Thank you for looking to Sybex for your Microsoft SQL Server 2005 certification exam prep needs. The Sybex team at Wiley is proud of its reputation for providing certification candidates with the practical knowledge and skills needed to succeed in the highly competitive IT workplace. Just as Microsoft Learning is committed to establishing measurable standards for certifying individuals who design and maintain SQL Server 2005 systems, Sybex is committed to providing those individuals with the skills needed to meet those standards.

The authors and editors have worked hard to ensure that the Study Guide you hold in your hands is comprehensive, in-depth, and pedagogically sound. We're confident that this book will exceed the demanding standards of the certification marketplace and help you, the SQL Server 2005 certification candidate, succeed in your endeavors.

As always, your feedback is important to us. If you believe you've identified an error in the book, please visit the Customer Support section of the Wiley web site. Or if you have general comments or suggestions, feel free to drop me a line directly at nedde@wiley.com. At Sybex we're continually striving to meet the needs of individuals preparing for certification exams.

Good luck in pursuit of your SQL Server 2005 certification!

Neil Edde
Vice President & Publisher
Sybex, an Imprint of John Wiley & Sons

Acknowledgments

Like all the books I've written and tech edited for Sybex over the years, this has been quite a ride. A lot of work goes into these books, and it is not all from the authors. When it comes time for accolades, the first person who comes to mind is our acquisitions editor, Maureen Adams. She got the ball rolling and kept it rolling the whole time. I would also like to thank the production editor, Daria Meoli; the copy editor, Kim Wimpsett; and the tech editors, Marcellus Duffy and Marilyn Miller-White for all their hard work in making the book a success.

I owe my friends and family a special thanks because they supported me throughout my writing odyssey even though they didn't quite understand what it was that I was writing about. First, my family: Mary (a.k.a. Mom); Buddy and Shelly Jorden; and Janet, Colin, and Leian McBroom—thanks to all of you. Also, when I started to lose my sanity, there were those who helped me look for it (we'll find it yet!): I have to thank Zerick Campbell (Big Daddy Z); his lovely and talented wife, Tanya; and the boys, Jostin and Brenton. Thanks to everyone at Jelly Belly; there is no better place to work than a candy company. For all the laughs I have to thank Nick Saechow—you rock (insert noun here)! Special thanks to Jyles McDonald for working with me all those early mornings; let's do it again sometime. Most important, though, thanks to my wife, Rachelle Jorden, for her patience and understanding as I wrote yet another book. Finally, thanks to all of you for reading this work. May it serve you well. —Joseph L. Jorden

From my part, I want to thank Joseph L. Jorden for his dedication and support as an experienced writer. I would not have been able to complete this work without the support of our acquisitions editor, Maureen Adams. Thanks, Maureen—you had so much patience with me. A special thanks goes to Cristian Lefter, who supplied a lot of questions and additional tech review for this book; I am really looking forward to writing a book together one day.

Thanks also to all my friends for their support, and please let's not forget my mom and stepdad! Unfortunately, I spent a lot of time writing instead of playing tour guide on their first U.S. visit.

A special thanks to my special friend and fellow MCT Paul Silva. Thanks, Paul, for taking care, for being concerned when I got stressed, and for being such a close friend. Also, thanks to the entire Microsoft Certified Trainer community, who gave me the opportunity to train on SQL Server 2005 and harden my skills on the product by all the interesting questions they devised.

And thanks to all of you reading this, and congratulations on your interest in becoming a Microsoft Certified Technology Specialist on SQL Server 2005. Finally, a big thank you to the Microsoft SQL Server product team members who made this product so successful and built all these cool features. —Dandy Weyn

About the Authors

Joseph L. Jorden (MCP, MCSE, MCTS) is the Lead Developer for Jelly Belly Candy Company where he spends a great deal of his time developing database applications and assisting the DBA with SQL Server administration tasks. Joseph was one of the first 100 people to achieve the MCSE+I certification from Microsoft and one of the first 2,000 people to earn the MCSE certification on Windows 2000. Joseph also spent a few years as an MCT during which time he taught Microsoft Official Curriculum courses on SQL Server 6.5, 7.0, and 2000. He has spoken at PASS conferences and Comdex about SQL Server and computing subjects. Joseph has also written a number of articles for various publications, and he has written and tech edited several books for Sybex, most of them on the subject of SQL Server.

Dandy Weyn is a SQL Server technologist, born and raised in Belgium, Europe. He started working with databases by the age of 16, when he sold his first commercial database application on dBASE III. He worked with various non-Microsoft relational databases before he switched to SQL Server 6.5. Dandy has more than 10 years' experience in relational database design and training. He started his own company in 2000 and has been trained using all Microsoft Official Curriculum targeting Microsoft certification since NT 4.0.

Although he is based in Belgium, Dandy spends most of his time in the United States, where the past couple of years he trained in the Microsoft Partner Readiness Channel and delivered workshops and seminars all over the country. In 2005 Dandy trained more than 1,000 people on SQL Server and has been to more than 30 cities in North America to broadcast his passion for SQL Server 2005.

For his early training on SQL Server 2005 in the MCT community, by organizing Train the Trainer events, he was awarded with a Microsoft Certified Trainer Community Leader title. For the past couple of years Dandy was also part of the team that structures and organizes the hands-on labs at premier conferences as Microsoft Tech-Ed. In 2005 he presented instructor-led hands-on labs at the Microsoft World Wide Partner Conference, and he developed courseware for the Microsoft Partner Readiness Channel. In 2006 Dandy delivered seminars for Microsoft Kenya and Microsoft Portugal and again provided his knowledge as Technical Learning Guide at Microsoft Tech-Ed. Besides being current with the new SQL Server 2005 certification, he also has MCSA, MCDBA, MCDST, and MCSE certifications. Dandy is a frequent poster in database forums and is also founder of a new SQL Server community site (www.ilikesql.com).

Contents at a Glance

Contents

Introduction

Microsoft's new generation of certifications emphasizes not only your proficiency with a specific technology but also tests whether you have the skills needed to perform a specific role. The Microsoft Certified Technology Specialist: SQL Server 2005 exam tests whether you know how to use SQL Server 2005 not only in theory but in practice. This makes the Microsoft Certified Technology Specialist: SQL Server 2005 certification a powerful credential for career advancement.

Obtaining this certificate has only one exam requirement, 70-431TS: Microsoft SQL Server 2005—Implementation and Maintenance. We developed this book primarily to give you the information you need to prepare for this exam. But don't put the book away after you pass; it will serve as a valuable reference during your career as a SQL Server 2005 professional.

Introducing the Microsoft Certified Technology Specialist Program

Since the inception of its certification program, Microsoft has certified millions of people. Over the years, Microsoft has learned what it takes to help people show their skills through certification. Based on that experience, Microsoft has introduced a new generation of certifications:

- Microsoft Certified Technology Specialist (MCTS)
- Microsoft Certified IT Professional (MCITP)
- Microsoft Certified Professional Developer (MCPD)
- Microsoft Certified Architect (MCA)

The MCTS certification program is designed to validate core technology and product skills for a specific product. It helps you prove you are capable of implementing, building, troubleshooting, and debugging that product.

The new generation of exams offers a shorter certification path than previous iterations. For example, to become a Microsoft Certified Database Administrator, you have to pass four exams. To obtain an MCTS certification, you need to pass only one exam.

How Do You Become Certified on SQL Server 2005?

As mentioned, you have to pass only one test to gain certification, but attaining a Microsoft certification has always been a challenge. In the past, students have been able to acquire detailed exam information—even most of the exam questions—from online "brain dumps" and third-party "cram" books or software products. This is no longer the case.

To ensure that a Microsoft certification really means something, Microsoft has taken strong steps to protect the security and integrity of its certification tracks. Now prospective candidates must complete a course of study that develops detailed knowledge about a wide range of topics. It supplies them with the true skills needed, derived from working with SQL Server 2005.

The SQL Server 2005 certification programs are heavily weighted toward hands-on skills and experience. Microsoft has stated that "nearly half of the core required exams' content demands that the candidate have troubleshooting skills acquired through hands-on experience and working knowledge."

Fortunately, if you are willing to dedicate the time and effort to learn SQL Server 2005, you can prepare yourself well for the exams by using the proper tools. By working through this book, you can successfully meet the exam requirements to pass the SQL Server 2005—Implementation and Maintenance exam.

This book is part of a complete series of study guides published by Sybex, an imprint of Wiley. Please visit the Sybex website at www.sybex.com and the Wiley website at www.wiley.com for complete program and product details.

Registering for the Exam

You may take the Microsoft exams at any of more than 1,000 Authorized Prometric Testing Centers (APTCs) and VUE testing centers around the world. For the location of a testing center near you, call Prometric at 800-755-EXAM (755-3926), or call VUE at 888-837-8616. Outside the United States and Canada, contact your local Prometric or VUE registration center.

Find out the number of the exam you want to take (70-431 for the SQL Server 2005—Implementation and Maintenance exam), and then register with Prometric or VUE. At this point, you will be asked for advance payment for the exam. The exams vary in price depending on the country in which you take them. You can schedule exams up to six weeks in advance or as late as one working day prior to the date of the exam. You can cancel or reschedule your exam if you contact the center at least two working days prior to the exam. Same-day registration is available in some locations, subject to space availability. Where same-day registration is available, you must register a minimum of two hours before test time.

You may also register for your exams online at www.prometric.com or www.vue.com.

When you schedule the exam, you will be provided with instructions regarding appointment and cancellation procedures, information about ID requirements, and information about the testing center location. In addition, you will receive a registration and payment confirmation letter from Prometric or VUE.

Microsoft requires certification candidates to accept the terms of a nondisclosure agreement before taking certification exams.

Taking the SQL Server 2005—Implementation and Maintenance Exam

The SQL Server 2005—Implementation and Maintenance exam covers concepts and skills related to implementing and managing SQL Server 2005. It emphasizes the following elements of server management:

- Installing and configuring SQL Server 2005
- Implementing high availability and disaster recovery

- Supporting data consumers
- Maintaining databases
- Monitoring and troubleshooting SQL Server performance
- Creating and implementing database objects

This exam will test your knowledge of every facet of SQL Server 2005 implementation and maintenance, including tuning and configuring, creating databases and objects, backing up and restoring databases, managing security, and supporting end users. To pass the test, you need to fully understand these topics. Careful study of this book, along with hands-on experience, will help you prepare for this exam.

 Microsoft provides exam objectives to give you a general overview of possible areas of coverage on the Microsoft exams. Keep in mind, however, that exam objectives are subject to change at any time without prior notice and at Microsoft's sole discretion. Please visit Microsoft's Learning website (www.microsoft.com/learning) for the most current listing of exam objectives.

Types of Exam Questions

In an effort to both refine the testing process and protect the quality of its certifications, Microsoft has focused its exams on real experience and hands-on proficiency. The test places a greater emphasis on your past working environments and responsibilities and less emphasis on how well you can memorize. In fact, Microsoft says an MCTS candidate should have at least one year of hands-on experience.

 Microsoft will accomplish its goal of protecting the exams' integrity by regularly adding and removing exam questions, limiting the number of questions that any individual sees in a beta exam, and adding new exam elements.

 The 70-431 exam covers a set of precise objectives. We have written this book about these objectives and requirements for the Microsoft exam. When you take the exam, you will see approximately 52 questions, although the number of questions might be subject to change. At the end of an exam, you will get your exam score, pointing out your level of knowledge on each topic and your exam score total with a pass or a fail.

Exam questions may be in a variety of formats. Depending on which exam you take, you'll see multiple-choice questions, select-and-place questions, and prioritize-a-list questions:

Multiple-choice questions   Multiple-choice questions come in two main forms. One is a straightforward question followed by several possible answers, of which one or more is correct.

The other type of multiple-choice question is more complex and based on a specific scenario. The scenario may focus on several areas or objectives.

Select-and-place questions   Select-and-place exam questions involve graphical elements that you must manipulate to successfully answer the question. A typical diagram will show computers and other components next to boxes that contain the text "Place here." The labels for the boxes represent various computer roles on a network, such as a print server and a file server. Based on information given for each computer, you are asked to select each label and place it in the correct box. You need to place *all* the labels correctly. No credit is given for the question if you correctly label only some of the boxes.

Prioritize-a-list questions   In the prioritize-a-list questions, you might be asked to put a series of steps in order by dragging items from boxes on the left to boxes on the right and placing them in the correct order. One other type requires that you drag an item from the left and place it under an item in a column on the right.

For more information on the various exam question types, go to www.microsoft.com/learning.

Microsoft will regularly add and remove questions from the exams. This is called *item seeding*. It is part of the effort to make it more difficult for individuals to merely memorize exam questions that previous test takers gave them.

Tips for Taking the Exam

Here are some general tips for achieving success on your certification exam:

- Arrive early at the exam center so you can relax and review your study materials. During this final review, you can look over tables and lists of exam-related information.

- Read the questions carefully. Don't be tempted to jump to an early conclusion. Make sure you know *exactly* what the question is asking.

- For questions you're not sure about, use a process of elimination to get rid of the obviously incorrect answers first. This improves your odds of selecting the correct answer when you need to make an educated guess.

What's in the Book?

When writing this book, we took into account not only what you need to know to pass the exam but what you need to know to take what you've learned and apply it in the real world. Each book contains the following:

Objective-by-objective coverage of the topics you need to know   Each chapter lists the objectives covered in that chapter.

The topics covered in this study guide map directly to Microsoft's official exam objectives. Each exam objective is covered completely.

Assessment test   Directly following this introduction is an assessment test that you should take before starting to read the book. It is designed to help you determine how much you already know about SQL Server 2005. Each question is tied to a topic discussed in the book. Using the results of the assessment test, you can figure out the areas where you need to focus your study. Of course, we do recommend you read the entire book.

Exam essentials   To highlight what you learn, you'll find a list of essential topics at the end of each chapter. This "Exam Essentials" section briefly highlights the topics that need your particular attention as you prepare for the exam.

Glossary   Throughout each chapter, you will be introduced to important terms and concepts you will need to know for the exam. These terms appear in *italic* within the chapters, and at the end of the book, a detailed glossary gives definitions for these terms, as well as other general terms you should know.

Review questions, complete with detailed explanations   Each chapter is followed by a set of review questions that test what you learned in the chapter. The questions are written with the exam in mind, meaning they are designed to have the same look and feel as what you'll see on the exam. Question types are just like the exam, including multiple-choice, select-and-place, and prioritize-a-list questions.

Hands-on exercises   In each chapter, you'll find exercises designed to give you the important hands-on experience that is critical for your exam preparation. The exercises support the topics of the chapter, and they walk you through the steps necessary to perform a particular function.

Case studies and real-world scenarios   Because reading a book isn't enough for you to learn how to apply these topics in your everyday duties, we have provided case studies and real-world scenarios in special sidebars. These explain when and why a particular solution would make sense in a working environment you'd actually encounter.

Interactive CD   Every Sybex study guide comes with a CD complete with additional questions, flash cards for use with an interactive device, a Windows simulation program, and the book in electronic format. Details are in the following section.

What's on the Book's CD?

With this new member of our best-selling Study Guide series, we are including quite an array of training resources. The CD offers numerous simulations, bonus exams, and flash cards to help you study for the exam. We have also included the complete contents of the book in electronic form. You'll find the following resources on the book's CD:

The Sybex e-book   Many people like the convenience of being able to carry their whole study guide on a CD. They also like being able to search the text via computer to find specific information quickly and easily. For these reasons, the entire contents of this study guide are supplied on the CD in PDF. We've also included Adobe Acrobat Reader, which provides the interface for the PDF contents as well as the search capabilities.

The Sybex test engine   This is a collection of multiple-choice questions that will help you prepare for your exam. You'll find sets of questions:

- Two bonus exams designed to simulate the actual live exam.
- All the questions from the study guide, presented in a test engine for your review. You can review questions by chapter or by objective, or you can take a random test.
- The assessment test.

Sybex flash cards for PCs and handheld devices   The "flash card" style of question offers an effective way to quickly and efficiently test your understanding of the fundamental concepts covered in the exam. The Sybex flash card set consists of 150 questions presented in a special engine developed specifically for the Study Guide series.

Chapter exercise files   In some of the hands-on exercises, the authors have provided sample files so you can better follow along and enhance your SQL 2005 skills. These chapter files are included on the CD.

Because of the high demand for a product that will run on handheld devices, we have also developed a version of the flash cards that you can take with you on your hand held device.

How Do You Use This Book?

This book provides a solid foundation for the serious effort of preparing for the exam. To best benefit from this book, you may want to use the following study method:

1. Read each chapter carefully. Do your best to fully understand the information.

2. Complete all hands-on exercises in the chapter, referring to the text as necessary so you understand each step you take. Install the evaluation version of SQL Server, and get some experience with the product.

Use an evaluation version of SQL Server Enterprise Edition (which can be downloaded from www.microsoft.com/sql) instead of Express Edition because Express Edition does not have all the features discussed in this book.

3. Answer the review questions at the end of each chapter. If you prefer to answer the questions in a timed and graded format, install the Edge Tests from the CD that accompanies this book and answer the chapter questions there instead of in the book.

4. Note which questions you did not understand, and study the corresponding sections of the book again.

5. Make sure you complete the entire book.

6. Before taking the exam, go through the review questions, bonus exams, flash cards, and so on, included on the CD that accompanies this book.

To learn all the material covered in this book, you will need to study regularly and with discipline. Try to set aside the same time every day to study, and select a comfortable and quiet place in which to do it. If you work hard, you will be surprised at how quickly you learn this material. Good luck!

Hardware and Software Requirements

You should verify that your computer meets the minimum requirements for installing SQL Server 2005. We suggest that your computer meet or exceed the recommended requirements for a more enjoyable experience.

Assessment Test

1. You have a custom application that employees use to manage product data. They often search for products based on the product description, so you decide to implement full-text search. What version of SQL Server can you use to support this? (Choose all that apply.)

   A. Express Edition

   B. Workgroup Edition

   C. Standard Edition

   D. Enterprise Edition

2. When installing SQL Server 2005, you choose the Dictionary Order, Case-Sensitive, for Use with 1252 Character Set SQL Collation setting. Now your application developers are complaining that their applications require case-insensitive collation. How can you switch to the correct character set?

   A. Change the character set using SQL Server Configuration Manager.

   B. Run the `sp_server_settings ('sort', 'ci')` system stored procedure.

   C. Run the `DBCC ChangeSort('ci')` command.

   D. Reinstall SQL Server 2005 with the correct sort order and collation.

3. You are going to upgrade to SQL Server 2005, and you plan to use Reporting Services. You need to be able to create data-driven subscriptions. What version of SQL Server can you use? (Choose all that apply.)

   A. Express Edition

   B. Workgroup Edition

   C. Standard Edition

   D. Enterprise Edition

4. You are the administrator of a SQL Server 2005 server that contains a development database. Your developers are concerned only with recovering the database schema in the event of a disaster, not the data. You are concerned with saving as much disk space as possible, and you do not want to back up anything unnecessarily. What recovery model should you use?

   A. Simple

   B. Bulk-Logged

   C. Full

5. You are creating a new table for your manufacturing department that will be used to store vendor data. This is the schema:

Name	Datatype
ID	Int
Name	Varchar(50)
Address	Varchar(50)
City	Varchar(20)
State	Char(2)
PostalCode	Char(9)

This table has a clustered index in the ID column. The department expects to have about 1,000,000 rows in this new table at any given time. How much space will it take?

A. 85KB

B. 8.5MB

C. 85MB

D. 850MB

6. You have created a table with a fill factor of 90 percent. How many bytes per page are reserved for future input?

A. 7,286

B. 1,620

C. 810

D. 405

7. You have created a view with the following code:

```
CREATE VIEW PayRate
AS
SELECT FirstName, LastName, Phone, Pay
FROM HumanResources.dbo.Employees
```

What changes do you need to make to this code to make this view indexable?

A. No changes are needed; the view is already indexable.

B. Change the code to look like this:

```
CREATE VIEW PayRate WITH SCHEMABINDING
AS
SELECT FirstName, LastName, Phone, Pay
FROM HumanResources.dbo.Employees
```

C. Change the code to look like this:

```
CREATE VIEW PayRate WITH SCHEMABINDING
AS
SELECT FirstName, LastName, Phone, Pay
FROM dbo.Employees
```

D. Change the code to look like this:

```
CREATE VIEW PayRate
AS
SELECT FirstName, LastName, Phone, Pay
FROM dbo.Employees
```

8. You have a table that contains employee data. One of the columns, named PayRate, contains the pay rate for each employee. You need to partition the table into three divisions, one for employees that make less than 65,000, one for employees that make 65,001 to 85,000, and one for employees that make 85,0001 and higher. Which function should you use?

A. Use the following:

```
CREATE PARTITION FUNCTION pfSalary (money)
AS RANGE RIGHT FOR VALUES (65000,85000);
```

B. Use the following:

```
CREATE PARTITION FUNCTION pfSalary (money)
AS RANGE RIGHT FOR VALUES (65001,85001);
```

C. Use the following:

```
CREATE PARTITION FUNCTION pfSalary (money)
AS RANGE LEFT FOR VALUES (65000,85000);
```

D. Use the following:

```
CREATE PARTITION FUNCTION pfSalary (money)
AS RANGE LEFT FOR VALUES (65001,85001);
```

9. You have a table that contains information about your products. One of the columns in this table, named description, is a varchar(max) column that contains a large amount of text describing each product. When a customer calls, your users want to make sure they find all the products that might fit the customers' needs, so they need to be able to search for products using phrases instead of just single words. How can you accommodate this?

A. Create a full-text index on the column.

B. Create a clustered index on the column.

C. Create a nonclustered index on the column.

D. You can't accommodate this because SQL Server does not allow users to search for phrases.

10. You have a table that contains sales data. This table is updated frequently throughout the day, so you need to ensure that there is enough free space in the leaf nodes of the index to insert new data. How should you create the index to make sure 10 percent of each leaf node is reserved for new data?

A. Create the index using the PAD_INDEX(10) function.

B. Create the index with a 10 percent fill factor.

C. Create the index with a 90 percent fill factor.

D. Do nothing; SQL Server leaves 10 percent of each index page open by default.

11. You have several developers on staff who need to be able to create objects in the development database as part of their regular duties. They should not be able to modify anything other than the database schema and the data in the database. What is the most efficient and secure way to give the developers the permissions they need?

A. Add them to the db_owner fixed database role.

B. Add them to the db_ddladmin fixed database role.

C. Add them to the sysadmin fixed server role.

D. Grant each developer the permission to create objects in the database separately, and instruct them to create objects as DBO.

12. You need to delegate the authority to add users to a database to one of your assistant DBAs. What group should you make this DBA a member of so that they can add users to the database and no more?

A. db_owner

B. db_accessadmin

C. db_securityadmin

D. db_ddladmin

13. You are performing maintenance on one of your databases, so you run the following query against the database to find the index fragmentation:

```
USE AdventureWorks;
SELECT INDEX_ID, AVG_FRAGMENTATION_IN_PERCENT
FROM sys.dm_db_index_physical_stats (db_id(),
```

```
object_id('Sales.SalesOrderDetail'),
 1, null, 'LIMITED');
```

You receive this result:

```
INDEX_ID    AVG_FRAGMENTATION_IN_PERCENT
1                   31.06
```

Assuming that index 1 is named PK_IDX_Sales with a fill factor of 75 percent, what should you do to optimize this index?

A. ALTER INDEX ALL ON Sales.SalesOrderDetail REBUILD WITH (FILLFACTOR = 75, ONLINE = ON, STATISTICS_NORECOMPUTE = ON)

B. ALTER INDEX PK_IDX_Sales ON Sales.SalesOrderDetail REORGANIZE

C. ALTER INDEX PK_IDX_Sales ON Sales.SalesOrderDetail REBUILD WITH (FILLFAC-TOR = 75, ONLINE = ON, STATISTICS_NORECOMPUTE = ON)

D. ALTER INDEX ALL ON Sales.SalesOrderDetail REORGANIZE

14. You've just successfully upgraded one of your old SQL Server systems from SQL Server 2000 to SQL Server 2005. Everything seems to be running fine, but some of your users start complaining they are seeing some strange values in some of the queries they run against several of the databases. It looks like some of the columns now contain larger numbers than expected. What should you run to fix this?

A. DBCC CHECKDB WITH ESTIMATEONLY

B. DBCC CHECKDB WITH DATA_PURITY

C. DBCC CHECKDB WITH PHYSICAL_ONLY

D. DBCC CHECKDB WITH REPAIR_REBUILD

15. Your company has hired several temporary workers to help inventory your products for the annual inventory process. Because these users are new to the system, management is concerned that they might enter incorrect information, so they want to be able to roll the database back to a specific point in time if incorrect data is found. To accomplish this, you decide to set the recovery model of the database to Full and perform full backups of the database every night and transaction log backups every three hours during the day. Is this the correct solution?

A. This is the correct solution.

B. No, the recovery model should be set to Simple.

C. No, you need to perform differential backups to use a point-in-time restore.

D. No, you need to back up the transaction logs at least once an hour to use point-in-time restores.

16. You have a database that is used to store sales information and is set to use the Full recovery model. You perform a full backup of the entire database once a week on Saturday. You perform a differential backup every night Monday through Friday at 9 p.m. and transaction log backups every hour starting at 6 a.m. until 6 p.m. On Thursday at 1 p.m., as soon as you get back from lunch, you find that the database is down. Which backup should you restore first to bring the database back online?

   A. Restore the differential backup from Monday.

   B. Restore the differential backup from Tuesday.

   C. Restore the differential backup from Wednesday.

   D. Restore the most recent transaction log backup.

   E. Restore the full backup from last Saturday.

17. You are the administrator of a SQL Server 2005 server located in San Francisco. That server contains a sales database that needs to be replicated to your satellite offices in New York, Chicago, and Ontario, which are connected via a partial T1 connection that consistently runs at 70 percent capacity. Each of the offices contains a single SQL Server that can handle the load of subscribing to a publication but little more. Your sales associates make frequent changes to the database that the users in the satellite offices need to see with very little delay. Which replication model should you use?

   A. Central subscriber/multiple publishers

   B. Multiple publishers/multiple subscribers

   C. Central publisher/central distributor

   D. Remote distribution

18. You are the administrator of a SQL Server 2005 server located in San Francisco. That server contains a sales database that needs to be replicated to your satellite offices in New York, Chicago, and Ontario, which are connected via a partial T1 connection that consistently runs at 70 percent capacity. Each of the offices contains a single SQL Server that can handle the load of subscribing to a publication but little more. Your sales associates make frequent changes to the database that the users in the satellite offices need to see with very little delay. Which replication model should you use?

   A. Merge

   B. Transactional

   C. Snapshot

   D. Transactional with updating subscribers

   E. Snapshot with updating subscribers

19. Your SQL Server resides in a different building on the campus where you work, and you are not always able to get there quickly when there is a problem with the server. You need to be able to connect to the dedicated administrator connection from your desktop. What should you do to enable this?

    A. Use `sp_configure 'remote admin connections', 1`.

    B. Use `sp_configure 'remote DAC', 1`.

    C. Use `sp_configure 'remote admin connections', 0`.

    D. Nothing; you can access the DAC remotely by default.

20. You want to make sure your SQL Server is running as efficiently as possible, which includes making sure queries are not taking an inordinately long time to complete. You decide to run Profiler to capture all the activity on the server, but what template should you use to create a trace that tells you how long queries take to complete?

    A. TSQL

    B. TSQL_SPs

    C. TSQL_Duration

    D. TSQL_Replay

    E. Tuning

Answers to Assessment Test

1. B, C, D.   Only Workgroup Edition, Standard Edition, and Enterprise Edition support full-text search. See Chapter 1 for more information.

2. D.   The only way to change the sort order and collation is to reinstall SQL Server. Neither sp_server_settings ('sort', 'ci') nor DBCC ChangeSort('ci') exists. See Chapter 1 for more information.

3. D.   Only Enterprise Edition supports data-driven subscriptions in Reporting Services. See Chapter 1 for more information.

4. A.   Simple will allow you to recover the database up to the last full backup; any data after that will be lost. This is the best model to use for development databases because you will be able to recover the database schema in the event of a disaster and because you will not be backing up transactions from the transaction log unnecessarily. See Chapter 2 for more information.

5. C.   The three fixed-length columns added together are 4 + 2 + 9 = 15 bytes. The variable columns take up 2 + (3 × 2) + 50 = 58 bytes. The null bitmap is 2 + ((6 + 7) Π 8) = 3.625, or 3 bytes. The total row size is 15 + 58 + 3 + 4 = 80 bytes. Each page holds 8,096 Π (80 + 2) = 98 rows per page. The total pages in the database is 1,000,000 Π 96 = 10,417 pages. Each page is 8,192 bytes. Therefore, the table takes 85,336,064 bytes, or about 85MB. See Chapter 2 for more information.

6. B.   A fill factor of 90 percent reserves 10 percent of each page for future input. With a default of 8,096 bytes available per page, that makes 810 bytes of reserved space per page. See Chapter 2 for more information.

7. C.   You need the SCHEMABINDING option on a view that you intend to index, but you cannot have three-part notation. You must create indexed views using only two-part notation; no three- or four-part notation is allowed. See Chapter 3 for more information.

8. C.   The LEFT range gives you three partitions: 0–65,000; 65,001–85,000; and 85,001 and higher. A RIGHT range would give you 0–64,999; 65,000–84,999; and 85,000 and higher. See Chapter 3 for more information.

9. A.   Full-text indexes are perfect for columns that have nothing but large amounts of text. You can create this index and query it for phrases instead of just single words like a standard SELECT query. Clustered and nonclustered indexes do not affect the way text columns are searched. See Chapter 4 for more information.

10. C.   Specifying a fill factor of 70 percent tells SQL Server to fill the index up to 70 percent, leaving 30 percent open. Also, PAD_INDEX(30) is not a valid option; the only valid parameters for PAD_INDEX are on and off. See Chapter 4 for more information.

11. B.   Adding users to the db_ddladmin role is the most secure way to accomplish this goal. Adding them to the db_owner role would grant them too much authority over the database and would not maintain strict security. Adding them to the sysadmin fixed server role would give them authority at the server level, which you do not want. See Chapter 6 for more information.

12. B. The db_accessadmin role gives users the permission to add new users to a database. The db_owner role gives the user authority to do whatever they want in the database. The db_securityadmin role allows a user to add users to groups, and the db_ddladmin role allows a user to make changes to the database structure. See Chapter 6 for more information.

13. C. Ten percent or less fragmentation requires no action because it is acceptable. On the other hand, 10 to 30 percent requires an index reorganization, and higher than 30 percent requires a rebuild. This is 31 percent fragmented, so it should be rebuilt; however, you do not want to rebuild all the indexes—just the one that is fragmented—so ALTER INDEX ALL is not required. See Chapter 10 for more information.

14. C. Because the users are saying they are getting bigger numbers than expected, it is possible the data was corrupted in the database. The DATA_PURITY clause of the DBCC command is especially for fixing problems with tables that are returning unexpected results, such as returning int when it should return smallint, and it is useful only for databases that have been upgraded. PHYSICAL_ONLY checks the physical structure of a database that you suspect might be corrupt. The ESTIMATE_ONLY option tells you how much space the operation will consume in tempdb. The REPAIR_REBUILD option is used to repair errors, but not errors resulting from an upgrade. See Chapter 10 for more information.

15. A. To perform point-in-time restores, you need to back up the transaction log, which you are doing with this solution. You would not be able to back up the transaction log using the Simple recovery model, so that option would not work, and differential backups would not give you the ability to perform a point-in-time restore. See Chapter 11 for more information.

16. F. The first backup you need to restore in any scenario is the last full backup. No other backups can be restored until the last full backup has been restored. See Chapter 11 for more information.

17. C. The models that involve multiple publishers obviously won't work here because you have only one publisher. You could use the remote distributor model, but there is no need because you have plenty of bandwidth and limited server resources. This makes the central publisher/central distributor the most logical choice. See Chapter 12 for more information.

18. B. Because the entire database does not change every day, you do not need to use the snapshot replication model. Also, the snapshot replication model would use a great deal more bandwidth than transactional. Because the subscribers do not need to update their copy of the data, you do not need the added complexity of merging or updating subscribers. Also, your remote users can handle a limited amount of delay, so immediate updating is not required. That makes transactional replication the best choice. See Chapter 12 for more information.

19. A. By default, the DAC is not available over the network; you must set the remote admin connections option to 1 by using the sp_configure stored procedure. Setting it to 0 will disable remote connections. Also, remote DAC is not a valid option. See Chapter 14 for more information.

20. C. The TSQL_Duration template was made just for this purpose. This template contains everything you need to find out how long it takes for queries to complete. See Chapter 14 for more information.

Chapter

1

Installing Microsoft SQL Server 2005

MICROSOFT EXAM OBJECTIVES COVERED IN THIS CHAPTER:

- ✓ Verify prerequisites.
- ✓ Upgrade from an earlier version of SQL Server.
- ✓ Create an instance.

Remember the first time you bought a bicycle? You probably just got a box full of bicycle parts from the store with a label on the front that read "some assembly required." If you're like most people, you probably set the instruction booklet somewhere on the floor and just started picking out parts that looked like they should fit together. In the end, you probably had something that didn't even remotely resemble the bicycle you saw on the showroom floor and an overpowering desire to read the assembly instructions.

SQL Server 2005 should have a label right on the box that says "some assembly required" just to remind you to read the instructions first, not last. Just like with the first bicycle you bought, with SQL Server if you read the instructions after the install, you will end up with a mess. This mess is not easy to clean up, though; in some instances, you may even need to reinstall SQL Server.

In this chapter, we will present the instructions for installing SQL Server 2005 so that you need do it only once. We'll start by covering the prerequisites, explaining the required hardware and software that need to be in place before you begin the install procedure. Then we'll move into installing SQL Server, covering each step of the Setup Wizard and pointing out topics that require special attention. Since you might be upgrading from a previous version of SQL Server, we'll also walk you through the upgrade process. Finally, since not all installs go perfectly, we'll provide some troubleshooting techniques to ensure that SQL Server gets up and running.

Meeting the Prerequisites

You will need a few pieces in place on your machine before you will be able to install SQL Server 2005, the first of which is Internet Explorer (IE) 6.0 Service Pack 1 (SP1) or newer. Many people see this requirement and instantly think SQL Server requires IE to serve data. That is not the case. The only parts of SQL Server 2005 that require IE are the Microsoft Management Console (discussed later in this book) and Books Online (BOL).

You must also be certain your machine meets the minimum hardware requirements before you can install SQL Server 2005. Otherwise, SQL Server may run very slowly, or not at all. Each edition of SQL Server has a different set of hardware requirements. Table 1.1 lists the hardware requirements for the Express Edition, Table 1.2 lists the Workgroup Edition requirements, and Table 1.3 lists the Standard Edition, Developer Edition, and Enterprise Edition requirements.

TABLE 1.1   Express Edition Requirements

Component	32-bit
Processor	600 megahertz (MHz) Pentium III–compatible or faster processor; 1 gigahertz (GHz) or faster processor recommended
Memory	192 megabytes (MB) of random access memory (RAM) or more; 512MB or more recommended
Disk drive	CD or DVD drive
Hard disk space	Approximately 350MB of available hard disk space for the recommended installation with approximately 425MB of additional space for SQL Server BOL, SQL Server Mobile BOL, and sample databases
Operating system	Windows XP with SP2 or newer; Windows 2000 Server with SP4 or newer; Windows Server 2003 Standard Edition, Enterprise Edition, or Datacenter Edition with SP1 or newer; Windows Small Business Server 2003 with SP1 or newer

TABLE 1.2   Workgroup Edition Requirements

Component	32-bit
Processor	600MHz Pentium III–compatible or faster processor; 1GHz or faster processor recommended
Memory	512MB of RAM or more; 1GB or more recommended
Disk drive	CD or DVD drive
Hard disk space	Approximately 350MB of available hard disk space for the recommended installation with approximately 425MB of additional space for SQL Server BOL, SQL Server Mobile BOL, and sample databases
Operating system	Microsoft Windows 2000 Server with SP4 or newer; Windows 2000 Professional Edition with SP4 or newer; Windows XP with SP2 or newer; Windows Server 2003 Enterprise Edition, Standard Edition, or Datacenter Edition with SP1 or newer; Windows Small Business Server 2003 with SP1 or newer

TABLE 1.3   Developer/Standard/Enterprise Edition Requirements

Component	32-bit	x64	Itanium
Processor	600MHz Pentium III–compatible or faster processor; 1GHz or faster processor recommended	1GHz AMD Opteron, AMD Athlon 64, Intel Xeon with Intel EM64T support, Intel Pentium IV with EM64T support processor	1GHz Itanium or faster processor
Memory	512MB of RAM or more; 1GB or more recommended	512MB of RAM or more; 1GB or more recommended	512MB of RAM or more; 1GB or more recommended
Disk drive	CD or DVD drive	CD or DVD drive	CD or DVD drive
Hard disk space	Approximately 350MB of available hard disk space for the recommended installation with approximately 425MB of additional space for SQL Server BOL, SQL Server Mobile BOL, and sample databases	Approximately 350MB of available hard disk space for the recommended installation with approximately 425MB of additional space for SQL Server BOL, SQL Server Mobile BOL, and sample databases	Approximately 350MB of available hard disk space for the recommended installation with approximately 425MB of additional space for SQL Server BOL, SQL Server Mobile BOL, and sample databases
Operating system	Microsoft Windows 2000 Server with SP4 or newer; Windows 2000 Professional Edition with SP4 or newer; Windows XP with SP2 or newer; Windows Server 2003 Enterprise Edition, Standard Edition, or Datacenter Edition with SP1 or newer; Windows Small Business Server 2003 with SP1 or newer	Microsoft Windows Server 2003 Standard x64 Edition, Enterprise x64 Edition, or Datacenter x64 Edition with SP1 or newer; Windows XP Professional x64 Edition or newer	Microsoft Windows Server 2003 Enterprise Edition or Datacenter Edition for Itanium-based systems with SP1 or newer

At this point you are probably wondering why there are so many versions of SQL Server 2005 and which one is right for you. The following discussion compares the versions and shows you what each edition does:

Express Edition   Express Edition supports one central processing unit (CPU), supports up to 1GB of RAM, and has a maximum database size of 4GB. It does not have full 64-bit support, but it will run on 64-bit operating systems using the Windows-on-Windows (WOW) technology.

Workgroup Edition   Workgroup Edition supports two CPUs, supports up to 3GB of RAM, and has no maximum database size limit. It does not have full 64-bit support, but it will run on 64-bit operating systems using the WOW technology. In addition, this edition provides backup log-shipping, full-text search, the SQL Server Agent scheduling service, and the Report Builder.

Standard Edition   Standard Edition supports four CPUs, supports as much RAM as the operating system (OS) can support, and has no maximum database size limit. It has full 64-bit support. In addition to all the features that Workgroup Edition provides, Standard Edition has database mirroring, failover clustering, the Database Tuning Advisor, Notification Services, Integration Services with basic transforms, and Hypertext Transfer Protocol (HTTP) endpoints.

Enterprise/Developer Edition   These two editions support as many CPUs as the OS allows, support as much RAM as the OS can support, and have no maximum database size limit. They have full 64-bit support. In addition to all the features that the Standard Edition and Workgroup Edition provide, these editions offer partitioning, parallel index operations, indexed views, online indexing and restoration, fast recovery, Integration Services advanced transforms, Oracle replication, the scale-out of report servers, and data-driven subscriptions (for Reporting Services).

Now you have the hardware and OS in place, but you have still more to consider before you can install SQL Server.

Preparing to Install

Before you actually install SQL Server, which you'll do in Exercise 1.1, you'll need to understand a few topics, so in this section we'll discuss some of the decisions you need to make before installing.

Choosing Default Instances or Named Instances

One of the first choices you need to make is whether this SQL Server is the default instance or a *named instance*. That may seem a bit confusing if you are new to SQL Server; *named instances* are essentially like running multiple SQL Servers on one machine. The most common time to run multiple instances is when you need to run multiple versions of SQL Server but you have limited hardware resources. By using this method you can have SQL Server 2005 running as a named instance and SQL Server 7.0 or 2000 running as the default instance. Your client machines will see two distinct SQL Servers on the network, even though they are both running on the same machine.

The default instance is selected by default (no pun intended) and should be left that way for the first installation of SQL Server on a machine. Subsequent installations on the same machine can be given installation names of up to 16 characters. Clients will then use this new name to refer to the new instance.

Choosing Service Accounts

When you first turn on your Windows machine and try to use it, you are presented with a dialog box that asks you for a username and password. That username and password give you access to the machine (and the network) with whatever privileges your administrator has seen fit to assign. Many services, such as programs running in the background, require a user account just like you do. This special user account, called a *service account*, gives the service access to the machine and network with the privileges it requires to get its work done.

The SQL Server services require a user account to run, so you need to pick one of three types, as shown in Table 1.4.

TABLE 1.4   Service Account Comparison

Type	Limitations	Advantages
Built-in system account	You will not be able to communicate with other SQL Servers over the network.	Easy to set up since you don't need to create a user account
Local user account	You will not be able to communicate with other SQL Servers over the network.	Allows you to control the service permissions without allowing network access
Domain user account	None, but slightly more difficult to configure than the other two because a network administrator must create and configure the accounts.	Allows you to communicate fully with other network machines, including SQL Servers and e-mail servers

If you opt to use a user account (local or domain), you must first create it using the appropriate tool for your operating system. If you create only one account to be used by both SQL Server and SQL Server Agent services (discussed later in this book), then you must add the user account to the Administrators local group; otherwise, replication (also discussed later in this book) will not function properly. If you decide you want greater control over the security on your network, then you can add two separate accounts, one for the SQL Server service and one for the SQL Server Agent service. A good reason to do this is that only the SQL Server Agent service really requires administrative authority; the other can get by just fine as a standard user.

Selecting an Authentication Mode

Another important decision is which *authentication mode* to use. Chapter 6 discusses authentication modes in detail, but it is good to know a little about them for setup purposes. To access SQL Server, your users need to log in to the server. And to log in to the server, they need an account. The type of account they use depends upon the authentication mode that is set. If you select Windows Authentication Mode, then only clients that have an Active Directory account will be able to access the system. If you have other clients (like Novell or Unix), then you should select Mixed Mode.

You can change the authentication mode at any time after installation; in other words, if you choose the wrong one for your needs, it is OK.

Choosing a Collation Setting

In versions of SQL Server prior to SQL Server 2000, it was necessary to choose a character set, a sort order, and a Unicode collation setting. In SQL Server 2005, these three entities have been combined to form the *collation setting*. You can choose from two collation settings: SQL Collation and Windows Collation.

SQL Collation is for backward compatibility with older versions of SQL Server and does not control Unicode character storage. If you need to replicate with older versions of SQL Server or you will be switching between SQL Server 2005 and SQL Server 7.0 and older, then you should use SQL Collation. If you are installing SQL Server 2005 on a machine with an older version of SQL installed, then the setup program will detect the necessary collation for you; otherwise, you need to select the proper collation.

Windows Collation uses the collation (code page, sort order, and so on) of the underlying operating system and controls Unicode and non-Unicode sorting and storage. If you choose Windows Collation, then you have two more issues to worry about: the collation designator and the sort order.

Selecting a Collation Designator

As you read this book, you see the characters as lines, curves, and various shapes. If you read Cyrillic, then you see different shapes for the characters than someone reading German or English. Computers need to read and interpret characters just like we do; the only problem is that computers don't see them as various shapes—they see them as different combinations of 1s and 0s. It makes sense then that if your computer is storing German data, it must store different characters, or combinations of 1s and 0s, than an English server stores. How these characters are stored is controlled by the *collation designator*.

If you decide to use Windows Collation, then it is best to use the collation of the underlying operating system; for example, if you are running a German server, then you will most likely choose a German collation designator. The easiest way to find your collation designator is to look in the Control Panel under the regional options; you should use the locale displayed there as your collation designator. The most common selection is Latin1_General.

Selecting a Sort Order

All the data you are storing on your server must be sorted from time to time, usually during queries or indexing (discussed later in this book). We sort it because looking at a mass of unsorted data is hard on the brain, whereas looking at a nicely ordered report of data is pleasing to the eye. The *sort order* defines how SQL sorts and compares your data during queries or indexing. This sort order is the second part of the collation setting.

Several sort options are available. The default sort order is case, accent, kana, and width insensitive. This means SQL Server will not pay attention to case or special character marks when sorting, when indexing, or when performing queries. Some options can change this behavior, and if you are familiar with previous versions of SQL Server, then you will want to pay attention because they have changed:

Binary   Using the default sort order, SQL Server will view characters as characters; by using binary, SQL Server will view characters as binary representations. This is the fastest sort order available, but it is case, accent, and kana sensitive.

Binary code point   This works much the same as binary sorting but has some additional functionality. This sort order uses Unicode code points when sorting, which allows SQL Server to sort on the locale as well as the data. This means English data would be sorted separately from Japanese data stored as Unicode. This too is case, accent, and kana sensitive.

Case sensitive   This simply tells SQL Server to use dictionary sort order and pay attention to case.

Accent sensitive   This tells SQL Server to use dictionary order and pay attention to accent marks.

Kana sensitive   This tells SQL Server to use dictionary order and pay attention to kana marks, which are used in many Asian languages.

Width sensitive   This tells SQL Server to treat single-byte characters and double-byte characters as different characters.

Here's the catch: once you have installed SQL Server, you cannot change the collation setting. To change it, you must reinstall SQL Server and rebuild all your databases. So, choose wisely; it is usually best to use the default sort setting of case insensitivity and build sensitivity into your applications if you need it.

Upgrading from a Previous Version

You can directly upgrade to SQL Server 2005 from SQL Server 2000 SP3 or SQL Server 7.0 SP4. Most of the upgrade operations are handled during setup, so you don't need to run any special wizard or installation program. To make sure you are completely prepared, though, you need to run the Upgrade Advisor.

To use the Upgrade Advisor, you first need to install the .NET Framework 2.0 and then install the Upgrade Advisor. The first time you run the Upgrade Advisor, you should run the Analysis Wizard, which will analyze various parts of your existing SQL Server installation and let you know whether they are ready for upgrade (see Figure 1.1).

FIGURE 1.1   The Upgrade Advisor welcome screen

Specifically, the Analysis Wizard checks the following:

- Database engine
- Analysis Services
- Notification Services
- Reporting Services
- Data Transformation Services (now called SQL Server Integration Services, or SSIS)

The wizard generates a report based on its findings, which you can view using the Upgrade Advisor Report Viewer (see Figure 1.2). Anything marked with a green icon is ready to upgrade. A yellow icon indicates a potential problem that can usually be fixed after the upgrade is complete. Anything marked with a red icon needs to be fixed before an upgrade can take place.

FIGURE 1.2   The Upgrade Advisor Report Viewer shows you potential problems to fix before upgrading.

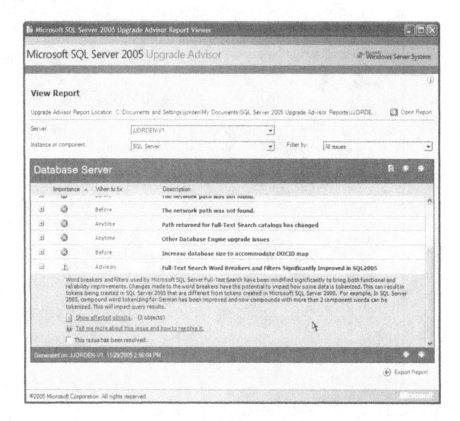

Once you've made sure your system meets all the requirements and you make all the necessary decisions about setup, you are ready to install SQL Server 2005.

Installing SQL Server 2005

Now you are ready to install SQL Server 2005 on your own machine. Follow the steps in Exercise 1.1 to do so (these steps are for installing the Standard Edition, but the steps are similar for all editions).

Installing SQL Server 2005

1. Create a user account named SqlServer, and make it a member of the Administrators local group. You can perform this task using one of these tools: on a Windows member server or on Windows XP use Computer Management, and on a Windows domain controller use Active Directory Users and Computers.

2. Insert the SQL Server CD, and wait for the automenu to open.

3. Under Install, click Server Components, Tools, Books Online, and Samples.

4. You then will be asked to read and agree with the end user license agreement (EULA); check the box to agree, and click Next.

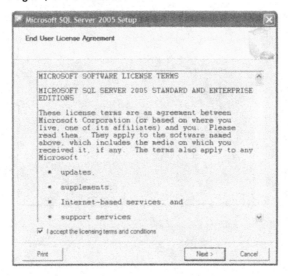

5. If your machine does not have all the prerequisites installed, the setup will install them for you at this time. Click Install if you are asked to do so. When complete, click Next.

6. Next you will see a screen telling you that the setup is inspecting your system's configuration again, and then the welcome screen appears. Click Next to continue.

7. Another, more in-depth, system configuration screen appears letting you know whether any configuration settings will prevent SQL Server from being installed. Errors (marked with a red icon) need to be repaired before you can continue. Warnings (yellow icon) can optionally be repaired and will not prevent SQL Server from installing. Once you have made any needed changes, click Next.

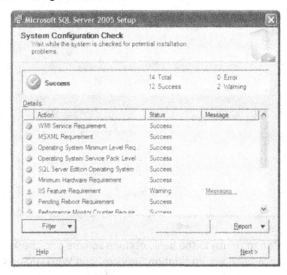

8. After a few configuration setting screens, you will be asked for your product key. Enter it, and click Next.

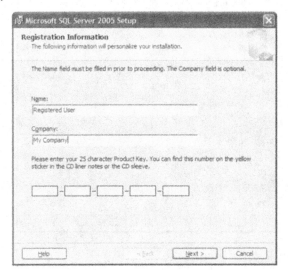

EXERCISE 1.1 *(continued)*

9. On the next screen, you need to select the components you want to install. Click the Advanced button to view the advanced options for the setup.

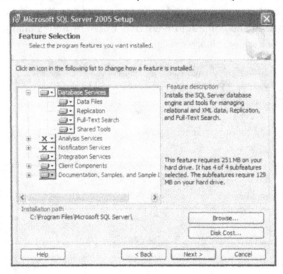

10. Click the Back button to return to the basic options screen, and check the boxes next to SQL Server Database Services, Integration Services, and Workstation Components, Books Online, and Development Tools. Then click Next.

11. On the Instance Name screen, choose Default Instance, and click Next (you'll install a named instance in the next exercise).

12. On the next screen, enter the account information for the service account you created in step 1. You will be using the same account for each service in this exercise. When finished, click Next.

13. On the Authentication Mode screen, select Mixed Mode, enter a password for the sa account, and click Next.

14. Select the Latin1_General collation designator on the next screen, and click Next.

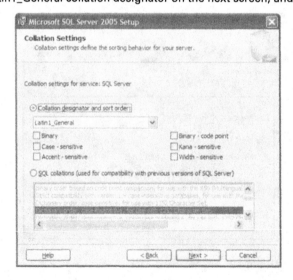

15. On the following screen, you can select to send error and feature usage information directly to Microsoft. This setting is entirely up to you, but you will not be checking it here. So, leave the defaults, and click Next.

16. On the Ready to Install screen, you can review your settings and then click Install.

17. The setup progress appears during the install process. When the setup is finished (which may take several minutes), click Next.

18. The final screen gives you an installation report, letting you know whether any errors occurred and reminding you of any post-installation steps to take. Click Finish to complete your install.

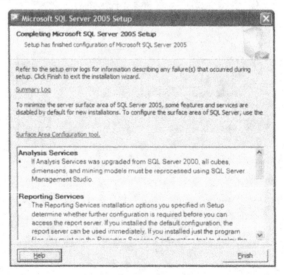

19. Reboot your system if requested to do so.

Now that you have SQL installed, you should make sure it is running. Go to Start ➢ All Programs ➢ Microsoft SQL Server 2005 ➢ Configuration Tools ➢ SQL Server Configuration Manager. Select SQL Server 2005 Services, and check the icons. If the icon next to SQL Server (MSSQLServer) service is green, then your installation is a success (see Figure 1.3).

FIGURE 1.3   Check the SQL Server Configuration Manager to see whether your services are running after install.

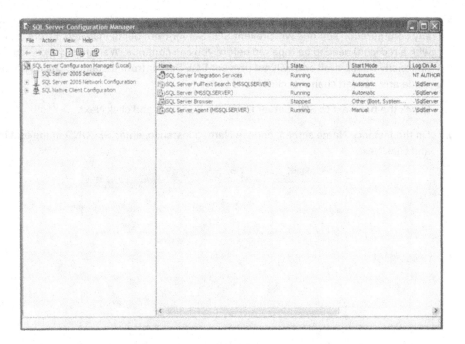

Installing a Second Instance

Because SQL Server 2005 has the capability of running multiple instances of itself on the same machine, it is a good idea to try installing more than one instance. In Exercise 1.2, you will create a second instance of SQL Server on the same machine using a different sort order.

EXERCISE 1.2

Installing a Named Instance of SQL Server 2005

1. Insert the SQL Server 2005 CD, and wait for the automenu to open.

2. Under Install, click Server Components, Tools, Books Online, and Samples.

EXERCISE 1.2 *(continued)*

3. You then will be asked to read and agree with the EULA; check the box to agree, and click Next.

4. Next you should see a screen telling you that the setup is inspecting your system's configuration again, and then the welcome screen appears. Click Next to continue.

5. Another, more in-depth, system configuration screen appears letting you know whether any configuration settings will prevent SQL Server from being installed. Errors (marked with a red icon) need to be repaired before you can continue. Warnings (yellow icon) can optionally be repaired and will not prevent SQL Server from installing. Once you have made any needed changes, click Next.

6. Check the box next to SQL Server Database Services, and click Next.

7. On the Instance Name screen, choose Named Instance, enter **SECOND** in the text box, and click Next.

8. On the next screen, enter the account information for the service account you created in step 1 of Exercise 1.1. You will use the same account for each service in this exercise. When finished, click Next.

9. On the Authentication Mode screen, select Mixed Mode, enter a password for the sa account, and click Next.

10. Select the Dictionary Order, Case-Insensitive, for Use with 1252 Character Set option in the SQL Collations list, and click Next.

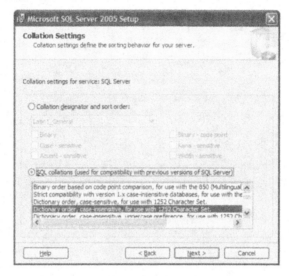

11. On the following screen, you can select to send error and feature usage information directly to Microsoft. This setting is entirely up to you, but you will not be checking it here. So, leave the defaults, and click Next.

12. On the Ready to Install screen, you can review your settings and then click Install.

13. The setup progress appears during the install process. When the setup is finished (which may take several minutes), click Next.

14. The final screen gives you an installation report, letting you know whether any errors occurred and reminding you of any post-installation steps to take. Click Finish to complete your install.

15. Reboot your system if requested to do so.

You can now test the second instance of SQL Server using the same method for testing the default instance. Go to Start ➢ All Programs ➢ Microsoft SQL Server 2005 ➢ Configuration Tools ➢ SQL Server Configuration Manager. Select SQL Server 2005 Services, and refer to the icons. If the icon next to SQL Server (Second) instance is green, then your installation is a success (see Figure 1.4).

FIGURE 1.4   Check the SQL Server Configuration Manager to see whether your services are running for the SECOND instance.

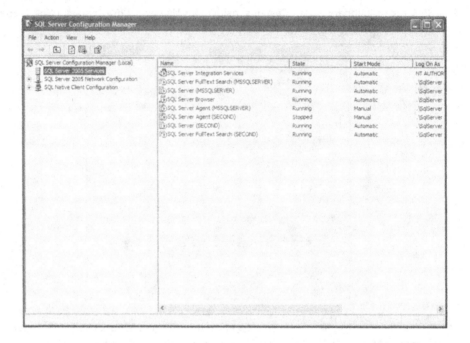

Troubleshooting the Installation

If it turns out that your install failed, you can take a few steps to troubleshoot it. The first place to check when you have problems is in the Windows Event Viewer. SQL will log any problems it encounters in the Application log, so check there first. If you find a problem, then you can take the error number and some of the text of the message and look them up on the Microsoft support website (http://support.microsoft.com/support) or in TechNet.

If you do not find the source of your ailments in the Event Viewer, then navigate to X:\Program Files\Microsoft SQL Server\90\Setup Bootstrap\LOG, open the Summary.txt file, and check for error messages. If that doesn't help, then open the SQLSetupxxxx.cab file. If that CAB file does not exist, then open the SQLSetupxxxx_ComputerName_Core.log file. If you saw an error during the graphical portion of the setup process, you can also check the SQLSetupxxxx_ComputerName_WI.log file. Also, you can check the SQLSetupxxxx_ComputerName_SQL.log file. In any of these SQLSetupxxxx files, you can perform a search for the phrase *UE 3*, which is short for Return Value 3, which means an error occurred.

Summary

This chapter explained the ins and outs of the installation process. First you learned the prerequisites of each of the five editions of SQL Server. Those editions are:

- Express
- Workgroup
- Standard
- Enterprise
- Developer

After learning the prerequisites you found out that there are some decisions to make before running the installation. First you need to decide whether to install a named instance or a default instance. If you already have a default instance of SQL Server installed on the machine then you must install a named instance.

Next you learned that you need to choose the right service accounts for the services to run under. Service accounts allow services to log on as a Windows user and inherit all of that users permissions on the machine and the network.

You also discovered that you need to choose the right authentication mode, which dictates how users log in to the SQL Server instance. Windows Only mode only allows users with Windows accounts to access SQL Server while Mixed Mode allows access to users with Windows accounts and SQL Server accounts.

You also learned about choosing the right collation setting. The collation setting tells SQL Server how to store characters in tables. Each language has an collation setting that works best.

Next you installed a default instance and a second instance of SQL Server 2005 on your system. Finally you learned how to troubleshoot setup if anything goes awry.

Exam Essentials

Know the prerequisites.   Know the system prerequisites, how much memory you need, how fast a processor you need, and which operating system version is best.

Understand the Upgrade Advisor.   Know how to use the Upgrade Advisor and how to read the report it produces. You especially need to know when an upgrade is going to fail based on the Upgrade Advisor's report.

Review Questions

1. You have a machine that has an 800MHz Pentium III processor with 256MB of RAM and a 400GB hard drive running Windows Server 2000 SP4. Which editions of SQL Server 2005 can you install? (Choose all that apply.)

    A. Express Edition

    B. Workgroup Edition

    C. Standard Edition

    D. Enterprise Edition

    E. Developer Edition

2. One of your third-party applications has been certified to run on SQL Server 2000 but not 2005. Your company has just bought a new application that requires SQL Server 2005 to run. How can you run both of these applications with minimal overhead?

    A. Buy a second server, and install SQL Server 2005 on the new machine.

    B. You can't run both applications; you will have to wait until the older application is certified to run on SQL Server 2005.

    C. Install SQL Server 2005 as a named instance, and configure your new application to use the new instance.

    D. Install SQL Server 2005 as the default instance, and configure your new application to use the new instance.

3. You are installing a new SQL Server 2005 instance on a machine in a small peer-to-peer network. You will not be performing replication, so SQL Server will not need to communicate with other servers over the network. You need to be able to change the service account's password every six months per company policy. Which service account type should you use?

    A. Built-in system account

    B. Local system account

    C. Domain account

4. One of the databases you will be using on your new SQL Server holds data in several different languages, including U.S. English, German, and Italian. When your users search the data, they may be looking for information in any of the available languages. You want to be able to sort through data as quickly as possible, and you are not concerned with sensitivity. Which sort order is best?

    A. Binary

    B. Binary code point

    C. Binary without the case-sensitivity option

    D. Binary code point without the case-sensitivity option

5. You have a machine that has a 3.2GHz Pentium Xeon processor with 4GB of RAM and a 320GB hard drive running Windows 2003 Enterprise Edition. Which editions of SQL Server 2005 can you install? (Choose all that apply.)

   A. Express Edition

   B. Workgroup Edition

   C. Standard Edition

   D. Enterprise Edition

   E. Developer Edition

6. Your company has decided it is time to upgrade to SQL Server 2005. You currently run SQL Server 7.0 SP3. What do you need to do before you can upgrade?

   A. Nothing; you can upgrade directly to SQL Server 2005.

   B. Upgrade to SQL Server 2000, and then you can upgrade to SQL Server 2005.

   C. Upgrade to SQL Server 2000, install SQL Server 2000 SP3, and then upgrade to SQL Server 2005.

   D. Install SQL Server 7.0 SP 4, and then upgrade to SQL Server 2005.

7. When you run the Upgrade Advisor, you get a report with a warning telling you "Full-Text Search Word Breakers and Filters Significantly Improved in SQL2005." What do you need to do before upgrading?

   A. Uninstall full-text search on your machine, and rerun the Upgrade Advisor.

   B. Nothing; you can install without modification.

   C. Uninstall full-text search, and do not rerun the Upgrade Advisor.

   D. Run the Upgrade Advisor with the /NoFTSCheck option.

8. You are installing a new SQL Server 2005 instance on a machine in a large network with several Active Directory domains across the country. You need to replicate data between several SQL Servers. Which service account type should you use?

   A. Built-in system account

   B. Local system account

   C. Domain account

9. You have a wide variety of clients on your network that need access to SQL Server. Many of these run Unix with Samba, which allows them to use an Active Directory account to access resources on the Windows domain. Several others use Mac clients with the AppleTalk protocol for accessing the network. The remaining clients are Windows 98 and XP Professional clients. Which authentication mode setting should you select when installing SQL Server?

   A. Windows Authentication Mode

   B. Mixed Mode

10. You have a machine that has a 1GHz AMD Opteron processor with 512MB of RAM and a 400GB hard drive running Windows 2003 Standard x64 Edition. Management wants to make sure the new software will take full advantage of the hardware. Which editions of SQL Server 2005 can you install? (Choose all that apply.)

    A. Express Edition

    B. Workgroup Edition

    C. Standard Edition

    D. Enterprise Edition

11. You are going to upgrade to SQL Server 2005, and you want to employ a two-node failover cluster for high availability. What version of SQL Server can you use? (Choose all that apply.)

    A. Express Edition

    B. Workgroup Edition

    C. Standard Edition

    D. Enterprise Edition

12. You are going to upgrade to SQL Server 2005. Your company has several Oracle servers, and you need to be able to synchronize the data between your SQL Server and Oracle databases using replication. What version of SQL Server can you use? (Choose all that apply.)

    A. Express Edition

    B. Workgroup Edition

    C. Standard Edition

    D. Enterprise Edition

13. One of the databases you will be using on your new SQL Server holds data in several different languages, including U.S. English, German, and Italian. Users will primarily search for data in their own language but occasionally search for data in other languages. You want to be able to sort through data as quickly as possible, and you are not concerned with sensitivity. Which sort order is best?

    A. Binary

    B. Binary code point

    C. Binary without the case-sensitivity option

    D. Binary code point without the case-sensitivity option

14. Your company has an Active Directory domain with primarily Windows XP and Windows 2000 Professional clients, all of which have Active Directory accounts. You have a few Unix clients that do not have Active Directory accounts. Only your Windows-based clients will need access to your SQL Server. Which authentication mode setting should you select when installing SQL Server?

    A. Windows Authentication Mode

    B. Mixed Mode

15. When installing SQL Server 2005, you meant to use the default SQL Collation setting (the Dictionary Order, Case-Insensitive, for Use with 1252 Character Set option); instead, you chose the case-sensitive version by accident. What should you do to switch to the correct character set?

A. Change the character set using SQL Server Configuration Manager.

B. Run the `sp_change_collation` system stored procedure.

C. Reinstall SQL Server 2005 with the correct sort order and collation.

D. Run the `sp_change_sort` system stored procedure.

16. Your installation of SQL Server 2005 has failed. Where is the first place you should look to find clues about the cause?

A. The System log in the Event Viewer

B. The `Summary.txt` file

C. The `SQLSetupxxxx_ComputerName_Core.log` file

D. The Application log in the Event Viewer

17. You are going to upgrade to SQL Server 2005, and you want to use full-text search for many of your applications. What version of SQL Server can you use? (Choose all that apply.)

A. Express Edition

B. Workgroup Edition

C. Standard Edition

D. Enterprise Edition

18. You are installing a new SQL Server 2005 instance on a machine in a small network. This is the only SQL Server on the network, and you want to make administration as simple as possible. Which service account type should you use?

A. Built-in system account

B. Local system account

C. Domain account

19. You are installing a new server with SQL Server 2005. Your sister company runs SQL Server 7.0 SP4. You need to replicate data between the two servers regularly. What collation setting should you use?

A. Windows Collation

B. SQL Collation

20. Your installation of SQL Server has failed, giving you a graphical error message, which you wrote down and misplaced. Can you find the error message again?

A. Graphical error messages are not recorded during setup.

B. Graphical error messages are recorded in the `Summary.txt` file.

C. Graphical error messages are recorded in the `SQLSetupxxxx_ComputerName_Core.log` file.

D. Graphical error messages are recorded in the `SQLSetupxxxx_ComputerName_WI.log` file.

Answers to Review Questions

1.   A. The only edition that can run reliably on this machine is the Express Edition, which requires a minimum of 192MB RAM.

2.   C. The option with the least administrative overhead and lowest cost is to install 2005 as a named instance. You can't install it as the default instance without uninstalling SQL Server 2000 first.

3.   B. You can't use a domain account because there is no domain, and you can't change the password for the built-in system account, so the only choice here is a local system account.

4.   A. Because your users might be looking for data in any language, you do not need the language-specific capability provided by binary code point. With both binary sort orders, case sensitivity is mandatory and cannot be shut off.

5.   A, B, C, D, E. This machine can easily handle any edition of SQL Server 2005.

6.   D. You can upgrade to SQL Server 2005 from SQL Server 7.0 SP 4 but not from SQL Server 7.0 SP3.

7.   B. Most warnings will not prevent you from upgrading to SQL Server, and the "Full-Text Search Word Breakers and Filters Significantly Improved in SQL2005" message is just informing you that full-text search will work a little differently after the upgrade. Also, the /NoFTSCheck option doesn't exist.

8.   C. You must use a domain account because it is the only type that will allow SQL Server to communicate with other servers over the network.

9.   B. Your Mac clients will not be able to access SQL Server when you select Windows Authentication Mode because they do not have Windows domain accounts, so you need to select Mixed Mode.

10.   C, D. Although Workgroup Edition and Express Edition will run on a 64-bit machine, they run in 32-bit mode only using the WOW technology. So, only Standard Edition, Enterprise Edition, and Developer Edition will take full advantage of the hardware.

11.   C, D. Only Standard Edition and Enterprise Edition support failover clustering, and Standard Edition will support a maximum of two nodes on the cluster.

12.   D. Enterprise Edition is the only edition that supports Oracle replication.

13.   B. Because your users are primarily looking for data in their own language, then it is best to use the language-specific capability provided by binary code point. With both binary sort orders, case sensitivity is mandatory and cannot be shut off.

14.   A. Because all the clients that need access to your SQL Server have Active Directory accounts, you should select Windows Authentication Mode.

15. C. The only way to change the sort order and collation is to reinstall SQL Server. Neither `sp_change_collation` nor `sp_change_sort` exist.

16. D. The first place to look for clues is in the Application log because all the steps taken by the setup process are logged there.

17. B, C, D. Only Workgroup Edition, Standard Edition, and Enterprise Edition support full-text search.

18. A. The built-in system account is the easiest to maintain because you do not need to control the password for it (in fact, you can't). Also, you do not need to communicate with other servers over the network, so a domain account is unnecessary.

19. B. To replicate with versions of SQL Server older than 2000, you need to select the SQL Collation setting.

20. D. Graphical error messages are all logged in the `SQLSetupxxxx_ComputerName_WI.log` file.

Chapter 2

Creating and Configuring Databases

MICROSOFT EXAM OBJECTIVES COVERED IN THIS CHAPTER:

✓ Configure log files and data files.

✓ Choose a recovery model for the database.

SQL Server 2005 uses two types of files to store your database information: one or more database files and one or more transaction log files. As an administrator, it is your responsibility to create and maintain these files. As part of your role as a database creator, you must decide how large to make these database files and what type of growth characteristics they should have as well as their physical placement on your system.

This chapter will examine these topics in more detail, first covering some planning issues and then explaining how to create a database and transaction log. You'll then learn how to manage these database objects by altering their various configuration options and by removing them from SQL Server. The chapter will also discuss database filegroups, which are used for optimizing file access and backups.

Planning Your Database

Before you create a database, you need to know some important facts. You need to know how large to make the database and how much growth to expect. Then you need to think about the physical location for the database files. To make an informed decision in these matters, it is helpful to understand how memory is allocated in SQL Server. In this section, we will talk about how your database is created, where you should place the database, and what the different internal memory management structures are.

Introducing Database Files

In SQL Server 2005, a new user database is really a copy of the Model database. Everything in the Model database will show up in your newly created database. Once the copy of the database has been made, it expands to the requested size. When you create a database in SQL Server 2005, you must specify at least one file to store the data and hold your system tables and another file to hold the transaction log.

Databases can comprise up to three file types. *Primary data files* have a default extension of .mdf. If you create a database that spans multiple data files, then *secondary data files* are used, which have a default filename extension of .ndf. The *transaction log* is stored in one or more files, with a default .ldf extension. Additional transaction log files, however, don't change their extensions. You should remember several important facts about your data and log files:

- It is recommended that you create the data and log files on a storage area network (SAN), iSCSI-based network, or locally attached drive.

- Only one database is allowed per data file, but a single database can span multiple data files.

- Transaction logs must reside in their own file; they can also span multiple log files.
- SQL Server fills the database files in a filegroup proportionally. This means if you have two data files, one with 100MB free and one with 200MB free, SQL Server will allocate one extent from the first file and two extents from the second file when writing data. In this manner, you can eliminate "hot spots" and reduce contention in high-volume Online Transaction Processing (OLTP) environments.
- Transaction log files are not filled proportionally; instead, they fill each log file to capacity before continuing to the next log file.
- When you create a database and don't specify a transaction log size, the transaction log will be resized to 25 percent of the size of your data files.

It is suggested that you place your transaction logs on separate physical hard drives. In this manner, you can recover your data up to the second in the event of a media failure.

Why have multiple data files? This technique, as opposed to just enlarging your current database files, has certain advantages and disadvantages. The main disadvantage of multiple database files is administration. You need to be aware of these different files, their locations, and their use. The main advantage is that you can place these files on separate physical hard disks (if you are not using striping), avoiding the creation of hot spots and thereby improving performance. When you use database files, you can back up individual database files rather than the whole database in one session. If you also take advantage of filegroups, you can improve performance by explicitly placing tables on one filegroup and the indexes for those tables on a separate filegroup. A *filegroup* is a logical grouping of database files used for performance and to improve administration on very large databases (VLDBs)—usually in the hundreds of gigabyte or terabyte range. We will discuss filegroups in the next section.

When you create a database, you are allocating hard disk space for both the data and the transaction log. You can store your data files using a variety of methods, depending on your hardware and software.

Introducing Filegroups

You can logically group database files into a *filegroup*. Using filegroups, you can explicitly place database objects into a particular set of database files. For example, you can separate tables and their nonclustered indexes into separate filegroups. This can improve performance, because modifications to the table can be written to both the table and the index at the same time. This can be especially useful if you are not using striping with parity (RAID-5). Another advantage of filegroups is the ability to back up only a single filegroup at a time. This can be extremely useful for a VLDB, because the sheer size of the database could make backing up an extremely time-consuming process. Yet another advantage is the ability to mark the filegroup and all data in the files that are part of it as either read-only or read-write. There are really only two disadvantages to using filegroups. The first is the administration that is involved in keeping track of the files in the filegroup and the database objects that are placed in them. The other is that if you are working with a smaller database and have RAID-5 implemented, you may not be improving performance.

The two basic filegroups in SQL Server 2005 are the primary, or default, filegroup that is created with every database and the user-defined filegroups created for a particular database. The primary filegroup will always contain the primary data file and any other files that are not specifically created in a user-defined filegroup. You can create additional filegroups using the ALTER DATABASE command or Management Studio.

Filegroups have several rules you should follow when you are working with them:

- The first (or primary) data file must reside in the primary filegroup.

- All system files must be placed in the primary filegroup.

- A file cannot be a member of more than one filegroup at a time.

- Filegroups can be allocated indexes, tables, text, ntext, and image data.

- New data pages are not automatically allocated to user-defined filegroups if the primary filegroup runs out of space.

If you place tables in one filegroup and their corresponding indexes in a different filegroup, you must back up the two filegroups as a single unit—they cannot be backed up separately.

Deciding on Database File Placement

Placing database files in the appropriate location is highly dependent on your available hardware and software. You have to follow few hard-and-fast rules when it comes to databases. In fact, the only definite rule is that of design. The more thoroughly you plan and design your system, the less work it will be later, which is why it is so important to develop a good capacity plan.

When you are attempting to decide where to place your database files, you should keep several issues in mind. This includes planning for growth, communication, fault-tolerance, reliability, and speed.

Among the several measures you can take to ensure the reliability and consistency of your database—each with its own features and drawbacks—are the different levels of Redundant Array of Inexpensive Disks (RAID).

Unlike previous versions of SQL Server, it is possible to create network-based files (files stored on another server or network-attached storage) by using trace flag 1807.

Introducing RAID-0

RAID-0 uses disk striping; that is, it writes data across multiple hard disk partitions in what is called a *stripe set*. This can greatly improve speed because multiple hard disks are working at the same time. You can implement RAID-0 through the use of Windows Server software or third-party hardware. Although RAID-0 gives you the best speed, it does not provide any fault-tolerance. If one of the hard disks in the stripe set is damaged, you lose all of your data. Because of the lack of fault-tolerance, Microsoft doesn't recommend storing any of your SQL Server data on RAID-0 volumes.

Introducing RAID-1

RAID-1 uses disk mirroring. *Disk mirroring* actually writes your information to disk twice— once to the primary file and once to the mirror. This gives you excellent fault-tolerance, but it is fairly slow, because you must write to disk twice. Windows Server allows you to implement RAID-1 with a single controller, or you can use a controller for each drive in the mirror, commonly referred to as *disk duplexing*. This is the recommended place for storing your transaction logs because RAID-1 gives fast sequential write speed (writing data in sequence on the disk rather than jumping from one empty spot to the next), a requirement for transaction logs.

Introducing RAID-5

RAID-5—striping with parity—writes data to the hard disk in stripe sets. Parity checksums will be written across all disks in the stripe set. This gives you excellent fault-tolerance as well as excellent speed with a reasonable amount of overhead. You can use the parity checksums to re-create information lost if a single disk in the stripe set fails. If more than one disk in the stripe set fails, however, you will lose all your data. Although Windows Server supports RAID-5 in a software implementation, a hardware implementation is faster and more reliable, and we suggest you use it if you can afford it. Microsoft recommends storing your data files on this type of RAID because data files require fast read speed as opposed to transaction logs, which need fast write speed.

Introducing RAID-10

You should use RAID-10 (sometimes referred to as RAID 0+1) in mission-critical systems that require 24/7 uptime and the fastest possible access. RAID-10 implements striping with parity as in RAID-5 and then mirrors the stripe sets. So, you get the incredible speed and fault-tolerance, but RAID-10 has a drawback. With this type of RAID you get the added expense of using more than twice the disk space of RAID-1. Then again, we are talking about a situation that can afford no SQL Server downtime.

Unless you can afford a RAID-10 array, Microsoft suggests a combination of RAID-5 and RAID-1. In this scenario, you place your data files on the RAID-5 array for speed and redundancy. You place your transaction log files on the RAID-1 drives so they can be mirrored.

File Placement

Many companies have a substantial budget for the information technology (IT) department and can therefore afford more expensive hardware. If this is the case where you work, you may want to budget for a hardware-based RAID solution or a SAN that provides RAID capabilities. This provides a number of benefits; most noticeably, hardware-based RAID off-loads processing from the CPU to the RAID controller, speeding up your system. Another benefit of the hardware-based RAID system is that this is the only way to get RAID-10, which offers a great deal more fault-tolerance than the other types of RAID discussed in this chapter. The drawback to using a separate RAID controller is that you must *not* use a caching controller unless it is specifically designed for a database server. Such a controller will have a battery backup so that in the event of a crash or power spike, data is not lost.

Quite often in the real world, though, money is tight and there is just no budget for lots of hardware. That is when you need to decide where to put your files using the RAID capabilities built into Windows Server: RAID-0, RAID-1, and RAID-5.

RAID-0 gives no fault-tolerance and therefore is not a good choice for data protection. RAID-1 is a mirror of two disks that are duplicates of each other. This type of RAID protection is great for transaction logs because they require fast sequential writes (writes placed in sequence on the disk). RAID-5 is a stripe set with parity and does not offer fast sequential writes, but it is very fast at reading. This makes RAID-5 perfect for data files because SQL Server uses lazy writes to write to the database. This means SQL Server will write to the database when it gets the chance. You need to be able to read from it as fast as you can, though, to service user needs.

If you are faced with the choice, you should use one mirror for the operating system and binary files, another mirror for transaction logs, and a RAID-5 array for data files. Because of the expense involved, however, you may not be able to afford this configuration. In that case, you can place the binary files, OS, and transaction logs on the same mirror and the data files on a RAID-5 array.

Creating Data Storage Structures

SQL Server 2005 has two main types of storage structures: extents and pages.

Introducing Extents

An *extent* is a block of eight pages totaling 64KB in size. Because the extent is the basic unit of allocation for tables and indexes and all objects are saved in a table of some kind, all objects are stored in extents. SQL Server has two types of extents:

Uniform   In uniform extents, all eight pages are used by the same object.

Mixed   Mixed extents are used by objects that are too small to take up eight pages, so more than one object is stored in the extent.

When a table or an index needs additional storage space, another extent is allocated to that object. A new extent will generally not be allocated for a table or index until all pages on that extent have been used. This process of allocating extents rather than individual pages to objects serves two useful purposes.

First, the time-consuming process of allocation takes place in one batch rather than forcing each allocation to occur whenever a new page is needed. Second, it forces the pages allocated to an object to be at least somewhat contiguous. If pages were allocated directly, on an as-needed basis, then pages belonging to a single object would not be next to each other in the data file. Page 1 might belong to table 1, page 2 might belong to index 3, page 3 might belong to table 5, and so on. This is called *fragmentation* (which we will discuss more later in this book). Fragmentation can have a significant negative impact on performance. When pages for a single object are contiguous, though, reads and writes can occur much more quickly.

Introducing Pages

At the most fundamental level, everything in SQL Server is stored on an 8KB *page*. The page is the one common denominator for all objects in SQL Server. Many types of pages exist, but every page has some factors in common. Pages are always 8KB in size and always have a header, leaving about 8,060 bytes of usable space on every page.

SQL Server has eight primary types of pages:

Data pages   Data pages hold the actual database records. The data page is 8,192 bytes, but only 8,060 of those bytes are available for data storage because a header at the beginning of each data page contains information about the page itself. Rows are not allowed to span more than one page, but if you have variable-length columns that exceed this limit, you can move them to a page in the ROW_OVERFLOW_DATA allocation unit (more on this later in this chapter).

Index pages   Index pages store the index keys and levels making up the entire index tree. Unlike data pages, you have no limit for the total number of entries you can make on an index page.

Text/image pages   Text and image pages hold the actual data associated with text, ntext, and image datatypes. When a text field is saved, the record will contain a 16-byte pointer to a linked list of text pages that hold the actual text data. Only the 16-byte pointer inside the record is counted against the 8,060-byte record-size limit.

Global Allocation Map pages   The Global Allocation Map (GAM) page type keeps track of which extents in a data file are allocated and which are still available.

Index Allocation Map pages   Index Allocation Map (IAM) pages keep track of what an extent is being used for—specifically, to which table or index the extent has been allocated.

Page Free Space pages   This is not an empty page; rather, it is a special type of page that keeps track of free space on all the other pages in the database. Each Page Free Space page can keep track of the amount of free space of up to 8,000 other pages.

Bulk Changed Map pages   This page contains information about other pages that have been modified by bulk operations (such as BULK INSERT) since the last BACKUP LOG statement.

Differential Changed Map pages   This page contains information about other pages that have changes since the last BACKUP DATABASE statement.

In previous versions of SQL Server, you were limited to a hard 8,096-byte length limit for data rows. In SQL Server 2005, this limit has been relaxed for variable-length columns by the introduction of ROW_OVERFLOW_DATA. This means if you have a table with variable-length columns whose length exceeds the 8,096-byte limit, the variable-length columns will be moved from the page that contains the table to the ROW_OVERFLOW_DATA area, and only a 24-byte pointer will be left behind. This happens when an insert or update is performed that increases the record past the 8,096-byte limit. If a subsequent update is performed that decreases the row size, then the data is returned to the original page.

> The 8,096-byte restriction does not apply to the large object datatypes: varchar(max), nvarchar(max), varbinary(max), text, image, and xml. It applies only to varchar, nvarchar, varbinary, sql_variant, or common language runtime (CLR) user-defined datatypes.

The page is the smallest unit of input/output (I/O) in SQL Server. Every time data is either read from or written to a database, this occurs in page units. Most of the time this reading and writing is actually going back and forth between the data cache and disk. The data cache is divided into 8KB buffers, intended solely for the purpose of holding 8KB pages. This is an important part of database capacity planning.

Estimating Storage Requirements

All storage space in SQL Server is preallocated. Databases can be both expanded and contracted. This raises an interesting question for you as a database administrator. How large should your databases be? They need to be large enough to accommodate your data needs without having to expand shortly after being created, but making them too large will waste disk space. When estimating storage requirements, you must go to the basic level of data storage: the table and the index. This section explains how you can estimate storage space by using these objects.

Estimating Table Storage Requirements

Tables are really nothing more than templates specifying how data is to be stored. All data stored in a table must adhere to a datatype. You can follow a specific process to estimate the space required by a table:

1. Calculate the space used by a single row of the table.
2. Calculate the number of rows that will fit on one page.
3. Estimate the number of rows the table will hold.
4. Calculate the total number of pages that will be required to hold these rows.

Calculating Row Size

Datatypes have various shapes and sizes and give you incredible control over how your data is stored. Table 2.1 lists some of the most common (but not all available) datatypes.

TABLE 2.1   Datatypes and Sizes

Datatype Name	Description	Size
TinyInt	Integer from 0 to 255	1 byte
SmallInt	Integer from -32,768 to 32,767	2 bytes
Int	Integer from -2,147,483,648 to 2,147,483,647	4 bytes
Real	1- to 7-digit precision, floating-point	4 bytes
Float	8- to15-digit precision, floating-point	8 bytes
Small-datetime	1/1/1900 to 6/6/2079 with accuracy to the minute	4 bytes
Datetime	1/1/100 to 12/31/9999 with accuracy to 3.33 milliseconds	8 bytes
Smallmoney	4-byte integer with 4-digit scale	4 bytes
Money	8-byte integer with 4-digit scale	8 bytes
Char	Character data	1 byte per character

When calculating storage requirements for a table, you simply add the storage requirements for each datatype in the table plus the additional overhead. This will give you the total space that is occupied by a single row. For example, if a table in a database has three fields defined as char(10), int, and money, you could calculate the storage space required for each row as follows:

- Char(10) = 10 bytes
- Varchar(20)
- Varchar(10)
- Int = 4 bytes
- Money = 8 bytes

Each row also has a small amount of overhead, called the *null bitmap* (because it is used to maintain nullable data). Here is the calculation to find the size of the null bitmap:

```
null_bitmap = 2 + ((number of columns + 7) ÷ 8)
```

So, to find the amount of overhead for this table, the calculation is $2 + ((4 + 7) \div 8) = 3.375$. Throwing out the remainder, you get 3 bytes of overhead for the table.

Now you need to know how much space to allocate for the variable-length columns. Here is the formula:

```
variable_datasize = 2 + (num_variable_columns × 2) + max_varchar_size
```

So, to calculate the space for the variable-length columns, you use this: $2 + (2 \times 2) + 20 = 26$. So, the variable-length columns should take 26 bytes out of the table (not 30 as you might expect from the sizes of the columns).

The last step is to figure out the total row size, which you can do using this calculation:

```
Row_Size = Fixed_Data_Size + Variable_Data_Size + Null_Bitmap + Row_Header
```

Because the row header is always 4, you can use this to calculate the table size: $22 + 26 + 3 + 4 = 55$. Therefore, each row in the table takes 55 bytes.

Calculating Rows per Page

Once you have a number indicating the total bytes used per row, you can easily calculate the number of rows that will fit on a single page. Because every page is 8KB in size and has a header, about 8,096 bytes are free for storing data. You can calculate the total number of rows per page as follows:

```
8096 ÷ (RowSize + 2)
```

The resulting value is truncated to an integer.

In this example, each row requires 55 bytes of space to store. Therefore, you can calculate the rows per page as $8,096 \div (55 + 2) = 142$.

> Like you did here, you'll need to round down to the nearest whole number when performing these calculations because a row cannot be split between two pages.

Special Considerations

When calculating rows per page, you will need to consider some additional factors. Remember that rows can never cross pages. If a page does not have enough space to complete the row, the entire row will be placed on the next page. This is why you had to round down the result of your calculation.

In addition, the number of rows that can fit on one page may also depend on a *fill factor* that is used for the clustered index. *Fill factor* is a way of keeping the page from becoming 100 percent full when the index is created. Using a fill factor may reduce the amount of space used on a page when the index is built, but since fill factor is not maintained, the space will be eventually used.

As an example, if a clustered index were built on the example table with a fill factor of 75 percent, the data would be reorganized such that the data pages would be only 75 percent full. This means that instead of 8,096 bytes free on each page, you could use only 6,072 bytes.

Estimating the Number of Rows for the Table

Estimating the number of rows used in your table has no secret formula. You have to know your data to estimate how many rows your table will eventually hold. When you make this estimate, try to consider—as well as possible—how large you expect your table to grow. If you do not allow for this growth in your estimates, you will need to expand the database. That would make this exercise in projecting storage requirements a somewhat wasted effort.

Calculating the Number of Pages Needed

Calculating the number of pages needed is another simple calculation, as long as you have reliable figures for the number of rows per page and the number of rows you expect the table to hold. The calculation is the number of rows in the table divided by the number of rows per page. Here, the result will be rounded up to the nearest whole number (again, this is because a row cannot span pages).

In the previous example, you saw that 142 rows would fit in a single page of the table. If you expected this table to eventually hold 1,000,000 records, the calculation would be as follows:

1. $1,000,000 \div 142 = 7,042.25$.

2.   Round the value up to 7,043 pages.

Now multiply the number of pages by the actual size of a page (8,192 bytes), and you get 57,696,256 bytes, or about 58MB. Add a little bit of space for possible unexpected growth (in other words, maybe you end up with 1,100,000 rows), and you are ready to proceed to the next table.

Estimating Index Storage Requirements

Indexes in SQL Server are stored in a B-Tree format; that is, you can think of an index as a large tree. You can also think of an index as a table with a pyramid on top of it. The ultimate concept here is that every index has a single entry point: the root of the tree or the apex of the pyramid.

When estimating storage requirements, you can think of the base of this pyramid as a table. You go through a similar process in estimating the "leaf" level of an index as you would in estimating the storage requirements of a table. Although the process is similar, a few issues are important to consider:

- You are adding the datatypes of the index keys, not the data rows.
- Clustered indexes use the data page as the leaf level. You do not need to add storage requirements for a clustered-index leaf level.

The toughest part of estimating the size of an index is estimating the size and number of levels you will have in your index. Although you can use a fairly long and complex series of calculations to determine this exactly, we usually find it sufficient to add 35 percent of the leaf-level space estimated for the other levels of the index.

Creating and Configuring Databases

In this section, we will explain how to create and configure databases.

Creating a Database

You can create a database in SQL Server in two ways. You can use the CREATE DATABASE statement in a Transact-SQL (T-SQL) query, or you can use the graphical tools in Management Studio. Using the graphical tools is by far the easier of the two methods, so in Exercise 2.1 you will create a database named Sybex using Management Studio. You will have two data files, each 3MB in size, with a FILEGROWTH of 1MB and a maximum size of 20MB. You will also create a transaction log with a size of 1MB, a FILEGROWTH of 1MB, and no maximum size.

EXERCISE 2.1

Creating a Database Using Management Studio

1. Start Management Studio by selecting Start ➤ Programs ➤ Microsoft SQL Server 2005 ➤ Management Studio.

2. Connect to your SQL Server.

3. Expand your Databases folder as shown here:

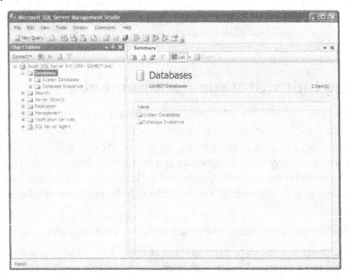

4. Right-click either the Databases folder in the console tree or the white space in the right pane, and choose New Database from the context menu.

5. You should now see the General page of the Database properties sheet. Enter the database name **Sybex**, and leave the owner as <default>.

6. In the data files grid, in the logical name column, change the name of the primary data file to **Sybex_data**. Use the default location for the file, and make sure the initial size is 3.

7. Click the ellipsis button (the one with three periods) in the Autogrowth column for the Sybex_data file; then, in the dialog box that pops up, select the Restricted File Growth (MB) radio button, and restrict the file growth to 20MB then click OK.

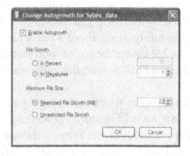

8. To add the secondary data file, click the Add button, and change the logical name of the new file to **Sybex_Data2**. Here too use the default location for the file, and make sure the initial size is 3.

9. Restrict the file growth to a maximum of 20MB for Sybex_Data2 by clicking the ellipsis button in the Autogrowth column.

10. Leave all of the defaults for the Sybex_log file.

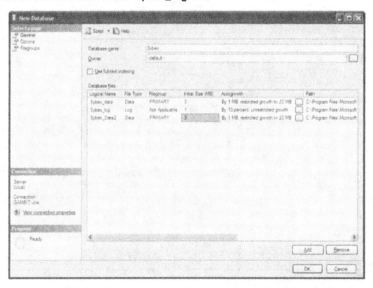

11. Click OK when you are finished. You should now have a new Sybex database.

Gathering Information about Your Database

Using Management Studio, you can gather a wealth of information about your databases. This includes the size of the database, its current capacity, any options currently set, and so on.

When you select a database in Management Studio, you will see a button with a green notebook icon labeled Report in the summary pane. When you click this button, you will see a variety of reports that you can use to gather information. The report in Figure 2.1 shows what the Disk Usage report looks like.

You can also use system stored procedures to gather information about your database. The sp_helpdb stored procedure used by itself will give you information about all databases in your SQL Server. You can gather information about a particular database by using the database name as a parameter. Figure 2.2 shows the sp_helpdb stored procedure and its result set.

Notice that the Sybex database is 7MB in size; this is the size of both of the data files and the log file combined.

If you switch to the Sybex database (by selecting it from the available databases drop-down list on the toolbar) and run the sp_helpfile stored procedure, you can gather information about the data and log files that are used for the Sybex database (see Figure 2.3).

As you can see from Figure 2.3, you can gather information about file sizes and locations, the filegroups they are members of, and the database file usage (either data or log).

FIGURE 2.1   The Disk Usage report shows you how much disk space a database is using.

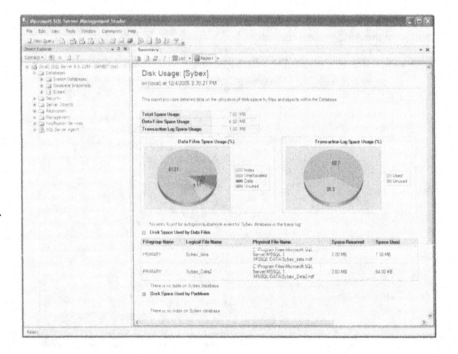

FIGURE 2.2   The sp_helpdb stored procedure

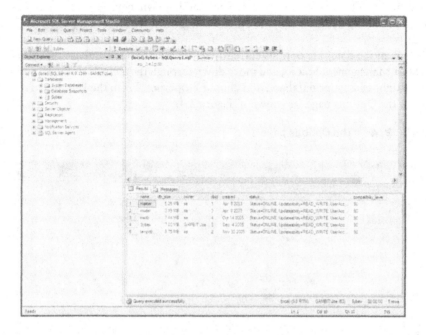

FIGURE 2.3   The sp_helpfile stored procedure

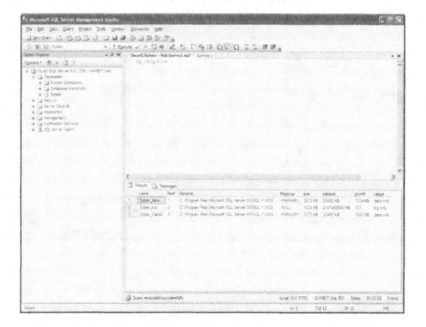

Setting Database Options

Database options allow you to specify how your database will behave in given situations. You can view and modify database options using Management Studio or the ALTER DATABASE statement.

Let's look at the database options currently set on your Sybex database that you created earlier. Start Management Studio, and move down through the console tree until you see your database. Right-click your database, and choose Properties. From the Database Properties sheet, click the Options page, as shown in Figure 2.4.

FIGURE 2.4   The Options page

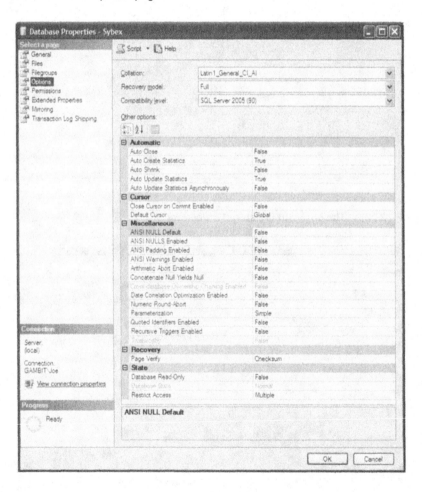

You can set a number of options on this page:

Collation   This is the collation designator for the database. We discuss collation in more detail in Chapter 1, but essentially this tells SQL Server what language the data in this database is and whether it is case sensitive.

Recovery Model   You can choose from three recovery models, which we'll discuss later in this chapter.

Compatibility Level   This option will change the way a database behaves so it is compatible with previous versions of SQL Server. The three levels of compatibility are SQL Server 7.0 (70), SQL Server 2000 (80), and SQL Server 2005 (90).

Auto Close   This option safely closes your database when the last user has exited from it. This can be a useful option for optimization on databases that are infrequently accessed because it decreases the amount of resources that SQL Server needs to consume in order to maintain user information and locks. This should not be set on databases that are accessed on a frequent basis because the overhead of opening the database can outweigh the benefits of closing the database in the first place.

Auto Create Statistics   This option will automatically generate statistics on the distribution of values found in your columns. The SQL Server Query Optimizer uses these statistics to determine the best method to run a particular query.

Auto Shrink   This option will automatically shrink both data and log files. Log files will be shrunk after a backup of the log has been made. Data files will be shrunk when a periodic check of the database finds that the database has more than 25 percent of its assigned space free. Your database will then be shrunk to a size that leaves 25 percent free.

Auto Update Statistics   This option works with the Auto Create Statistics option. As you make changes to the data in your database, the statistics will be less and less accurate. This option periodically updates those statistics.

Auto Update Statistics Asynchronously   This option works with the Auto Create Statistics option. As you make changes to the data in your database, the statistics will be less and less accurate. This option periodically updates those statistics.

Close Cursor on Commit Enabled   When this option is set to true, any cursor that is open will be closed when the transaction that opened it is committed or rolled back. When false, the cursor will stay open when the transaction is committed and will be closed only when the transaction is rolled back.

Default Cursor   This specifies whether cursors are global or local by default.

ANSI NULL Default   This option specifies the default setting for ANSI NULL comparisons. When this is on, any query that compares a value with a null returns a 0. When off, any query that compares a value with a null returns a null value.

ANSI NULLS Enabled   This specifies whether ANSI NULLS are on or off for the database.

ANSI Padding Enabled   When this option is set to true, if you store data in a column that is less than the column width, then the remaining data is filled in with trailing blanks. When set to false, any remaining data is trimmed off.

ANSI Warnings Enabled   When set to true, a warning is generated when a null value is used in an aggregate function (like SUM or AVG). When false, no warning is generated.

Arithmetic Abort Enabled   When this is set to on, a divide-by-zero error will cause a query to terminate. If this is off, the query will continue but a message is displayed.

Concatenate Null Yields Null   This option specifies that anything you concatenate to a null value will return a null value.

Date Correlation Optimization Enabled   When this option is set to on, SQL Server maintains statistics between any two tables in the database that are linked by a FOREIGN KEY constraint and have datetime columns. When it is set to off, correlation statistics are not maintained.

Numeric Round-Abort   When this is on, a loss of precision will generate an error message. When it is off, a message will not be generated.

Parameterization   When this is set to Simple, SQL Server may choose to replace some of the literal values in a query with a parameter, but you have no control over what is changed into a parameter. When set to Forced, all literal values are replaced with a parameter.

Quoted Identifiers Enabled   This option allows you to use double quotation marks as part of a SQL Server identifier (object name). This can be useful in situations in which you have identifiers that are also SQL Server reserved words.

Recursive Triggers Enabled   This option allows recursive triggers to fire. Recursive triggers occur when one trigger fires a trigger on another table, which in turn fires another trigger on the originating table.

Page Verify   This option controls how SQL Server verifies the validity of each page in the database. This setting has three options:

None   No verification takes place.

Checksum   A mathematical calculation is run against all of the data on the page and the value (called the *checksum*) is stored in the header. When the mathematical calculation is run again, if the result does not match the checksum value, then the page is damaged.

TornPageDetection   The smallest unit of data SQL Server works with is 8KB, but the smallest unit of data that is written to disk is 512 bytes. This means parts of a page may not be written to disk, a condition known as a *torn page*. This option allows SQL Server to detect when this problem occurs. It is not as accurate as checksum, but it can be faster.

Database Read-Only   When true, this option marks the database as read-only. No changes to the database will be allowed. This is usually set to speed up access to archival data that will never be written to.

Restrict Access   This option has three possible settings:

Multiple   Everyone with permissions can access the database. This is the default setting.

Single   Only one user at a time can access the database and with only a single connection. This is used primarily when you are restoring or renaming databases, because only one person, you, should be in the database during these activities. Make sure no one is using the database when you set this option.

Restricted   Only members of db_owner, dbcreator, and sysadmin security roles have access to this database when this option is selected. This option is used during development or when you need to change the structure of one of the objects in the database and do not want anyone to access the new objects until you are done.

That is a lot of options, but one in particular requires special attention: Recovery Model. This is because the model you choose affects how fast your backups are and how effectively you can restore data after a crash. You can choose from three models:

Simple   The transaction log is used for very little in this recovery model. In fact, almost nothing is recorded in the log. This means any database set to use this model can be recovered only up to the last backup. Any changes made to your database after the last backup was performed will be lost because they are not recorded in the transaction log. This model is a good choice for development databases where most data is test data that does not need to be restored after a crash. It is also a good choice for databases that are not changed often, such as an OLAP database.

Bulk-Logged   This model records much more information in the transaction log than the Simple model. Bulk operations such as SELECT INTO, BCP, BULK INSERT, CREATE INDEX, and text and ntext operations are the only information not recorded. This means you can recover most of the data in the event of a crash; only bulk operations may be lost. You can set this option just before performing a bulk-insert operation to speed up the bulk insert. You need to back up your database immediately after performing bulk operations if this option is selected because everything that is inserted during this time is not in the transaction log so it will all be lost if the database crashes before the next backup.

Full   This is the default option, which records every operation against the database in the transaction log. Using this model, you will be able to recover your database up to the minute of a crash. This is a good option for most production databases because it offers the highest level of protection.

Case Study: Increasing Disk Capacity

To illustrate the points in this chapter, consider what the AlsoRann company did with its databases. AlsoRann is a small company of about 300 employees with offices on both coasts of the United States. The company started out with a single database server located in its home office on the West Coast. AlsoRann didn't have many databases to start with, but the one you're most interested in is the Sales database. The Sales database, as the name implies, stores sales information. It contains a product catalog table, a customer information table, orders tables, and the like.

The company needed to figure out how much space the database would take up on its system before it even created the database because the company had limited resources on the server and needed to know beforehand if the database would require a new hard drive. Using the math from this chapter, AlsoRann discovered that the database would use approximately 1GB of hard disk space within six months. This was fine because the company would store the disk on a mirrored 40GB hard disk.

However, after about one year, AlsoRann's sales skyrocketed, and the Sales database grew at a much faster rate than anticipated. Because all of the company's databases were stored on the same 40GB drive, the Sales database was quickly running out of room to grow; therefore, Also-Rann had to install a second disk array and expand the database onto the new disk. AlsoRann did this by creating a secondary data file on the new array (configured as a RAID-5 array), that allowed the database to expand.

Summary

There is much more to data storage in SQL Server than meets the eye. The SQL Server data storage structure is more than just a file or a collection of files. It is an entire internal architecture designed for one purpose alone: to extract and modify your data as quickly and efficiently as possible. In this chapter, we covered many aspects of data storage:

- We defined databases and the files they are made of, including the following:
  - The primary data file has an `.mdf` extension and is used to hold data.
  - Secondary data files have an `.ndf` extension and are used to hold data.
  - Log files have an `.ldf` extension and are used to store transactions before they are written to the database so that the database can be recovered in the event of an emergency.
- We looked at the various RAID levels you can use for fault-tolerance and performance:
  - RAID-1 is used primarily for transaction logs.
  - RAID-5 should be used for your databases.
  - RAID-10 (also called RAID 0+1) can be used for either data or logs, but it is more expensive and available only as a third-party hardware solution.
- You learned how to estimate the size of a data file before creating it.
- You learned how to create databases using Management Studio.
- You learned about the recovery models, what they do, and when to use each one.

Exam Essentials

Know how to create databases.   Know how to create databases because that is what SQL Server is all about: storing data in databases.

Understand your files.   Understand how big to make your files and where those files should be placed.

Know your recovery models.   Know how each recovery model functions and what they allow you to restore.

Review Questions

1. You are a SQL Server 2005 administrator. You have a server with a database named Commerce that will be used to store sales transactions. The database must be available at all times and must be as fast as possible. Your server is configured as follows:

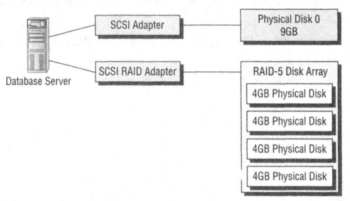

Where should you place your database and transaction logs for maximum speed and fault-tolerance?

A. Place the transaction log on physical disk 0 and the data file on the RAID-5 disk array.

B. Place the transaction log on the RAID-5 disk array and the data file on physical disk 0.

C. Place the transaction log and the data file on physical disk 0.

D. Place the transaction log and the data file on the RAID-5 disk array.

2. You have created a table with the following columns:

Name	Datatype
ID	Int
FirstName	Char(25)
Lastname	Char(25)
Address	Char(50)
City	Char(20)
State	Char(2)
ZipCode	Char(5)

Approximately how much space will this table require on disk if it has 1,000,000 rows?

A. 150MB

B. 162MB

C. 144MB

D. 207MB

3. You have just installed two new 40GB hard disks in your server that you are going to use to hold a database named Inventory. You need to add, update, and delete data as fast as possible. How should you configure these hard disks? (Choose two.)

A. Configure the hard disks as a RAID-1 array.

B. Configure the hard disks as a RAID-0 array.

C. Configure the hard disks as a RAID-5 array.

D. Configure the hard disks as two independent drives.

E. Place the data files and log files on the same volume.

F. Place the data file on the first volume and the log file on the second volume.

4. You are about to bring a new server online, and you want the most efficient disk configuration possible for your new system. Select the proper RAID array to place your files on for optimum performance and fault-tolerance. Choose from RAID-1, RAID-2, RAID-0, and RAID-5:

RAID 0

RAID 1

RAID 2

RAID 5

OS/Binaries
Data files
Transaction

5. You are creating an Inventory database that requires 6GB of data space and 2GB of log space. Your servers' hard disks are configured as follows:

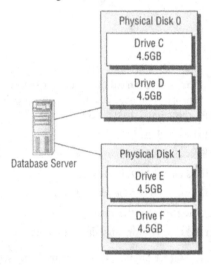

Your OS files are on the C drive. You want to maximize performance. What should you do?

A. Add a 1GB log to drive C, a 1GB log to drive D, a 3GB data file to drive E, and a 3GB data file to drive F.

B. Add a 1GB log to drive E, a 1GB log to drive F, a 3GB data file to drive E, and a 3GB data file to drive F.

C. Add a 2GB log to drive D, a 3GB data file to drive E, and a 3GB data file to drive F.

D. Add a 2GB log to drive F, a 3GB data file to drive D, and a 3GB data file to drive E.

6. You are the administrator of a SQL Server 2005 server that contains a development database. Your developers are not concerned with recovering any of the data in the database in the event of an emergency, and they want to keep the transaction log from accidentally filling up. What recovery model should you use?

A. Simple

B. Bulk-Logged

C. Full

7. You need to configure your system for optimum access to a 1.5TB database. Approximately half of the tables are used primarily for writing; the rest are used primarily for reading and generating reports. How can you optimize this database for the fastest access?

   A. Place the log file and data file on the same disk so the system has to work from only one disk.

   B. Create two log files and place each on a separate disk while leaving the data file on a single disk array.

   C. Place the files that are used for reading in one filegroup and the files that are used primarily for writing in a second filegroup on another disk array.

   D. Limit the number of users who can access the database at once.

8. Which statement about placing tables and indexes in filegroups is true?

   A. Tables and their corresponding indexes must be placed in the same filegroup.

   B. Tables and their corresponding indexes must be placed in separate filegroups.

   C. Tables and indexes that are placed in separate filegroups must be backed up together.

   D. Tables and indexes that are placed in separate filegroups cannot be backed up together.

9. You are creating a new database for your accounting department that will have the following tables:

Receivables

Name	Datatype
ID	Int
VendorID	Int
BalanceDue	Money
DateDue	Datetime

Payables

Name	Datatype
ID	Int
VendorID	Int
BalanceDue	Money
DateDue	Datetime
Terms	Char(50)
PrevBalance	Float

Vendors

Name	Datatype
ID	Int
Name	Varchar(50)
Address	Varchar(50)
City	Varchar(20)
State	Char(2)
PostalCode	Char(9)

Each table has a clustered index in the ID column. The Vendors table has a nonclustered index on the Name column. The Accounting department expects to have about 2,000,000 rows in the Vendors table; 5,000 rows in the Receivables table; and 2,500 rows in the Payables table at any given time. How much space will the Receivables table take?

A. 15MB

B. 150MB

C. 15KB

D. 150KB

10. In the scenario from question 9, how much space will the Payables table take?

A. 21MB

B. 21KB

C. 112MB

D. 112KB

11. In the scenario from question 9, how much space will the Vendors table take?

A. 167MB

B. 185KB

C. 200MB

D. 156MB

12. In the scenario from question 9, how big should you make the Accounting data file?

A. 300MB

B. 230MB

C. 180MB

D. 150MB

13. In the scenario from question 9, how big should you make the Accounting transaction log?

    A. 36MB

    B. 60MB

    C. 100MB

    D. 57MB

14. Your company has just installed a new storage area network, and you have been asked for the best RAID model to use for your databases. You need optimum speed and reliability. How should you configure these hard disks?

    A. Configure the hard disks as a RAID-1 array for data and a RAID-5 array for logs.

    B. Configure the hard disks as a RAID-0 array for data and a RAID-5 array for logs.

    C. Configure the hard disks as a RAID-5 array for both data and logs.

    D. Configure the hard disks as two RAID-10 arrays for both data and logs.

15. You need to import a large amount of data into a table in one of your production databases using a BULK INSERT statement. Put these steps in the correct order for optimum speed and reliability.

    A. Set the database to use the Full recovery model.

    B. Set the database to use the Bulk-Logged recovery model.

    C. Set the database to use the Simple recovery model.

    D. Back up the database.

    E. Run the BULK INSERT statement.

16. Your servers' hard disks are filling to capacity, and your database is running out of space. You do not have money in the budget for more disk space right now, but you do have plenty of disk space on one of your file servers. Can SQL Server use this disk space for database files?

    A. Yes, just create secondary data files on the remote server using the UNC filename convention (*server**share**filename*.ext); no other configuration is necessary.

    B. Yes, just turn on trace flag 1807, and then create secondary data files on the remote server using the UNC filename convention (*server**share**filename*.ext).

    C. Yes, just turn on trace flag 3205, and then create secondary data files on the remote server using the UNC filename convention (*server**share**filename*.ext).

    D. No, SQL Server cannot use remote drives for database file storage.

17. You have created a table with the following columns:

Name	Datatype
ID	Int
Description	Varchar(27)
Price	Money
Instock	Bit
VendorID	Int

Approximately how much space will this table require on disk if it has 100,000 rows?

A. 150MB

B. 162MB

C. 144MB

D. 207MB

18. You have created a table with a fill factor of 80 percent. How many bytes per page are reserved for future input?

A. 6,476

B. 1,620

C. 2,640

D. 3,126

19. You have just created a database with a 500MB data file. How big will the transaction log be by default?

A. 130MB

B. 120MB

C. 125MB

D. 225MB

20. Which of these page types is used to store information about changes to the database since the last BACKUP DATABASE statement was executed?

A. Index Allocation Map page

B. Global Allocation Map page

C. Differential Changed Map page

D. Data page

E. Page Free Space page

F. Index page

G. Bulk Changed Map page

H. Text/image page

Answers to Review Questions

1. D. Both the data and log files should be placed on the RAID-5 array because it is the only array that offers fault-tolerance. Physical disk 0 is just a disk with no fault-tolerance whatsoever.

2. C. A record in this table is 131 bytes long with 3 bytes of null bitmap space and a 4-byte row header, which equates to 57 records per page. At 1,000,000 records, that is 17,544 pages (1,000,000 ÷ 57 rounded up). Multiply 17,544 by the full size of a page (8,192 bytes with overhead), and you get 143,720,448, or approximately 144MB.

3. D, F. Because you want to perform write operations as fast as possible, a mirror is not going to work for you because the write speed is very slow. And because you do not have enough disks, you cannot create a RAID-5 array (it requires three at least). RAID-0 is out of the question because of the complete lack of fault-tolerance, so the best option is to create two independent disks and put the log and data files on separate disks. That way if you lose one, you can still recover data from the other.

4.

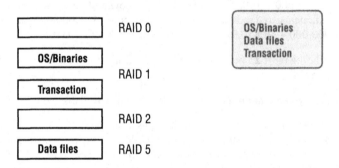

OS and Binaries should be on a mirror. Transaction logs should be on a mirror because they need the sequential write speed that a mirror provides. Data files should be on a stripe set with parity for the read speed it provides.

5. C. The best strategy is to place the log file on drive D and the data files on E and F. That way, all of them can grow if necessary, the transaction log and data files are separate, and the OS is on its own partition.

6. A. Simple will allow you to recover the database up to the last full backup; any data after that will be lost. This is the best model to use for development databases because the developers do not need to recover the data in the database, and they need to keep the transaction logs from filling up.

7. C. To specify which disk you want to place an object on, you must create a filegroup and then specify which filegroup to place the object in at the time it is created.

8. C. Tables and indexes can be placed in separate filegroups, but if you do that, they must be backed up as a unit.

9. D. The int datatype is 4 bytes, and datetime and money datatypes are both 8 bytes, so the size of the columns added together is 4 + 4 + 8 + 8 = 24 bytes. The null bitmap is 2 + ((4 + 7) ÷ 8) = 3.375, or 3 bytes. The total row size is 24 + 3 = 27 bytes. Each page holds 8,096 ÷ (27 + 2) = 279 rows per page. The total pages in the database are 5,000 ÷ 279 = 18 pages. Each page is 8,192 bytes. Therefore, the table takes 147,456bytes, or about 150KB.

10. B. The int datatype is 4 bytes; datetime, money, and float are 8 bytes; and char(50) is 50 bytes. Therefore, the size of the columns added together is 4 + 4 + 8 + 8 + 50 + 8 = 82 bytes. The null bitmap is 2 + ((6 + 7) ÷ 8) = 3.625, or 3 bytes. The total row size is 82 + 3 = 85 bytes. Each page holds 8,096 ÷ (85 + 2) = 93 rows per page. The total pages in the database are 2,500 ÷ 93 = 27 pages. Each page is 8,192 bytes. Therefore, the table takes 221,184 bytes, or about 216KB.

11. A. The three fixed-length columns added together are 4 + 2 + 9 = 15 bytes. The variable columns take up 2 + (3 × 2) + 50 = 58 bytes. The null bitmap is 2 + ((6 + 7) ÷ 8) = 3.625, or 3 bytes. The total row size is 15 + 58 + 3 + 4 = 80 bytes. Each page holds 8,096 ÷ (80 + 2) = 98 rows per page. The total pages in the database is 2,000,000 ÷ 98 = 20,408 pages. Each page is 8,192 bytes. Therefore, the table takes 170,663,936 bytes, or about 167MB.

12. B. This is a simple calculation. Just add the estimated size of the tables (in bytes) like this: 171,000,000 + 212,000 + 100,000 = 171,312,000. Now add about 35 percent of the size of the tables with nonclustered indexes, which is 35 percent of 171,000,000, or 59,850,000, and you get 171,000,000 + 59,850,000 = 230,850,000, or about 230MB.

13. D. The size of the log file is 25 percent of the size of the data file for a standard OLTP database, so it should be 57MB.

14. D. RAID-10 gives you optimum speed and reliability. If it is available, you should use it.

15. B, E, A, D. Before you insert the data, you should set the database to use the Bulk-Logged recovery model because it is fastest for inserting bulk data. Next, since this is a production database, it is safe to assume that it was using the Full recovery model, so don't forget to set it back to Full. Finally, after running the statement you need to back up the database because you will lose your bulk-imported data if the database crashes before your next scheduled backup.

16. B. Yes, you can use the remote drives by enabling trace flag 1807. Trace flag 3205 does exist, but it is for disabling hardware compression for tape drives.

17. C. A record in this table is 131 bytes long with 3 bytes of null bitmap space and a 4-byte row header, which equates to 57 records per page. At 1,000,000 records, that is 17,544 pages (1,000,000 ÷ 57 rounded up). Multiply 17,544 by the full size of a page (8,192 bytes with overhead), and you get 143,720,448, or approximately 144MB.

18. B. A fill factor of 80 percent reserves 20 percent of each page for future input. With a default of 8,096 bytes available per page, that makes 1,620 bytes of reserved space per page.

19. C. The default transaction log size is 25 percent of the data file size.

20. C. The Differential Changed Map page stores information about changes to the data since the last BACKUP DATABASE statement was executed. The Bulk Changed Map page holds data about changes to the database since the last BACKUP LOG statement was executed.

Chapter

3

Working with Tables and Views

MICROSOFT EXAM OBJECTIVES COVERED IN THIS CHAPTER:

✓ **Implement a table.**

- Specify column details.
- Specify the filegroup.
- Specify a partition scheme when creating a table.
- Specify a transaction.

✓ **Implement a view.**

- Create an indexed view.
- Create an updateable view.

It is safe to say that you probably have a dresser for storing your clothes. How does that dresser function? Does it have just one huge drawer into which you stuff all your clothes? Probably not. Most dressers have multiple drawers so you can organize your clothes. If all your clothes were stuffed into a single drawer, then you would have a great deal of trouble finding them when you need them, and they would be a wrinkled mess when you finally did find what you need.

Your data is like the clothes in this analogy—you don't want to just dump them all in one drawer, so to speak, which is why your dresser (the database) has several drawers for holding data. These drawers are tables. Inside the database, you have several tables that hold the various types of data you need to store. Just like you have a shirt drawer for shirts and a pants drawer for pants in your dresser, you would have a Customers table for your customer data and a separate Products table for product information.

In this chapter, we will discuss tables. We'll cover all the various parts of a table and then show how to create them. Then we'll cover views, which are database objects that can be used to look at the data in your tables from different angles, so to speak.

Before you can actually create any tables in your database, though, you must plan how they will look and function. The first section deals with just that—planning tables.

Planning Tables

Tables are the objects in the database that you use to hold all your data. As shown in Figure 3.1, tables consist of two basic objects, fields and records:

Fields   Fields contain a certain type of information such as last name or ZIP code. They're also referred to as *columns*.

Records   A record is a group of related fields containing information about a single entity (such as a person) that spans all the fields. Records are also referred to as *rows*.

You should grab a piece of paper and a pencil for the first phase of creating your tables, because it's much easier to create them when you can see them drawn in front of you, rather than trying to remember all the details involved. You should first decide what fields should be in your table.

FIGURE 3.1   Tables consist of fields and records.

The Fname Field

Fname	Lname	Address	City	State	Zip
Varchar(20)	Varchar(20)	Varchar(50)	Varchar(20)	Varchar(2)	Varchar(5)
Tom	Smith	111 Main	New York	NY	11101
Janet	McBroom	715 3rd	Phoenix	AZ	85034
Shane	Travis	816 Star	Chicago	IL	21563
John	Thomas	3035 1st	Sacramento	CA	94305

Fname Has a Datatype of Varchar(20) → points to Varchar(20)

The "Shane Travis" Record, Number 3 → points to Shane

If you're creating a Customer table, for example, you may want it to contain each customer's first and last names, address, phone and fax numbers, and customer ID number. When you create these fields, it's best to make them as specific as possible. Instead of creating a name field for a customer's first and last names, for instance, you should create a first-name field and a last-name field. This will make it easier to search your database for a specific customer later, because you need to search only on the last name instead of on the first and last name combined. The same is true for the address—separate it into street address, city, state, and ZIP code fields. This will make it easier to find customers who live in certain cities or ZIP codes, or even to find a specific customer based on address alone. Once you have defined the most specific fields possible, you're ready to pick datatypes for your fields.

Introducing Built-in Datatypes

Each field in a table has a specific datatype, which restricts the type of data that can be inserted. For example, if you create a field with a datatype of int (short for *integer*, which is a whole number [a number with no decimal point]), you won't be able to store characters (A–Z) or symbols (such as %, *, or #) in that field because SQL Server allows only numbers to be stored in int fields. In Figure 3.1, you can see the datatypes listed in the second row (note that datatypes don't show up as records—the figure is showing the datatypes merely for readability). You'll notice that all the fields in this table are either char or varchar (short for *character* and *variable character*, respectively), which means you can store characters in these fields as well as symbols and numbers. However, if numbers are stored in these fields, you won't be able to perform mathematical functions on them directly because SQL Server sees them as characters, not numbers.

Several of these datatypes deal with Unicode data, which is used to store up to 65,536 different characters, as opposed to the standard ANSI character sets, which store 256 characters.

Bit   This can contain only a 1 or a 0 as a value (or null, which is no value). It's useful as a status bit—on/off, yes/no, or true/false, for example.

Int   This can contain integer (or whole number) data from -2^{31} ($-2,147,483,648$) through $2^{31} - 1$ ($2,147,483,647$). It takes 4 bytes of hard disk space to store and is useful for storing large numbers that you'll use in mathematical functions.

Bigint   This datatype includes integer data from -2^{63} ($-9,223,372,036,854,775,808$) through $2^{63} - 1$ ($9,223,372,036,854,775,807$). It takes 8 bytes of hard disk space to store and is useful for extremely large numbers that won't fit in an int field.

Smallint   This datatype includes integer data from -2^{15} ($-32,768$) through $2^{15} - 1$ ($32,767$). It takes 2 bytes of hard disk space to store and is useful for slightly smaller numbers than you would store in an int field, because smallint takes less space than int.

Tinyint   This datatype includes integer data from 0 through 255. It takes 1 byte of space on the disk and is limited in usefulness since it stores values only up to 255. Tinyint may be useful for something like a product code when you have fewer than 255 products.

Decimal   This datatype includes fixed-precision and scale-numeric data from $-10^{38} - 1$ through $10^{38} - 1$ (for comparison, this is a 1 with 38 zeros following it). It uses two parameters: precision and scale. *Precision* is the total count of digits that can be stored in the field, and *scale* is the number of digits that can be stored to the right of the decimal point. Thus, if you have a precision of 5 and a scale of 2, your field has the format 111.22. You should use this type when you're storing partial numbers (numbers with a decimal point).

Numeric   This is a synonym for decimal—they're one and the same.

Money   This datatype includes monetary data values from -2^{63} ($-922,337,203,685,477.5808$) through $2^{63} - 1$ ($922,337,203,685,477.5807$), with accuracy to a ten-thousandth of a monetary unit. It takes 8 bytes of hard disk space to store and is useful for storing sums of money larger than 214,748.3647.

Smallmoney   This datatype includes monetary data values from $-214,748.3648$ through $214,748.3647$, with accuracy to a ten-thousandth of a monetary unit. It takes 4 bytes of space and is useful for storing smaller sums of money than would be stored in a money field.

Float   This datatype includes floating-precision number data from $-1.79E + 308$ through $1.79E + 308$. Some numbers don't end after the decimal point—pi is a fine example. For such numbers, you must approximate the end, which is what float does. For example, if you set a datatype of float(2), pi will be stored as 3.14, with only two numbers after the decimal point.

Real   This datatype includes floating precision number data from $-3.40E + 38$ through $3.40E + 38$. This is a quick way of saying float(24)—it's a floating type with 24 numbers represented after the decimal point.

Datetime   This datatype includes date and time data from January 1, 1753, through December 31, 9999, with values rounded to increments of .000, .003, or .007 seconds. This takes 8 bytes of space on the hard disk and should be used when you need to track specific dates and times.

Smalldatetime This datatype includes date and time data from January 1, 1900, through June 6, 2079, with an accuracy of one minute. It takes only 4 bytes of disk space and should be used for less specific dates and times than would be stored in datetime.

Timestamp This is used to stamp a record with the time when the record is inserted and every time it's updated thereafter. This datatype is useful for tracking changes to your data.

Uniqueidentifier The NEWID() function is used to create globally unique identifiers that might appear as follows: 6F9619FF-8B86-D011-B42D-00C04FC964FF. These unique numbers can be stored in the uniqueidentifier type field; they may be useful for creating tracking numbers or serial numbers that have no possible way of being duplicated.

Char This datatype includes fixed-length, non-Unicode character data with a maximum length of 8,000 characters. It's useful for character data that will always be the same length, such as a State field, which will contain only two characters in every record. This uses the same amount of space on disk no matter how many characters are actually stored in the field. For example, char(5) always uses 5 bytes of space, even if only two characters are stored in the field.

Varchar This datatype includes variable-length, non-Unicode data with a maximum of 8,000 characters. It's useful when the data won't always be the same length, such as in a first-name field where each name has a different number of characters. This uses less disk space when fewer characters appear in the field. For example, if you have a field of varchar(20) but you're storing a name with only 10 characters, the field will take up only 10 bytes of space, not 20. This field will accept a maximum of 20 characters.

Varchar(max) This is just like the varchar datatype; but with a size of (max) specified, the datatype can hold $2^{31} - 1$ (2,147,483,67) bytes of data.

Nchar This datatype includes fixed-length, Unicode data with a maximum length of 4,000 characters. Like all Unicode datatypes, it's useful for storing small amounts of text that will be read by clients that use different languages (that is, some using Spanish and some using German).

Nvarchar This datatype includes variable-length, Unicode data with a maximum length of 4,000 characters. It's the same as nchar except that nvarchar uses less disk space when there are fewer characters.

Nvarchar(max) This is just like nvarchar; but when the (max) size is specified, the datatype holds $2^{31} - 1$ (2,147,483,67) bytes of data.

Binary This datatype includes fixed-length, binary data with a maximum length of 8,000 bytes. It's interpreted as a string of bits (for example, 11011001011) and is useful for storing anything that looks better in binary or hexadecimal shorthand, such as a security identifier.

Varbinary This datatype includes variable-length, binary data with a maximum length of 8,000 bytes. It's just like binary, except that varbinary uses less hard disk space when fewer bits are stored in the field.

Varbinary(max) This has the same attributes as the varbinary datatype; but when the (max) size is declared, the datatype can hold $2^{31} - 1$ (2,147,483,67) bytes of data. This is useful for storing binary objects such as JPEG image files or Microsoft Word documents.

Xml   This datatype stores entire Extensible Markup Language (XML) documents or fragments (a document that is missing the top-level element).

Identity   This isn't actually a datatype, but it serves an important role. It's a property, usually used in conjunction with the int datatype, and it's used to increment the value of the column each time a new record is inserted. For example, the first record in the table would have an identity value of 1, and the next would be 2, then 3, and so on.

Sql_variant   Like identity, this isn't an actual datatype per se, but it actually lets you store values of different datatypes. The only values it cannot store are varchar(max), nvarchar(max), text, image, sql_variant, varbinary(max), xml, ntext, timestamp, and user-defined datatypes.

> The text, ntext, and image datatypes have been deprecated in this version of SQL Server. You should replace these with varchar(max), nvarchar(max), and varbinary(max).

Table and Cursor Datatypes

You can't assign two other datatypes to a column: table and cursor. You can use these two datatypes only as variables:

Cursor   Queries in SQL Server return a complete set of rows for an application to use. Sometimes the application can't work with the resulting set of rows as a whole, so it requests a *cursor*, which is a subset of the original recordset with some added features (such as the ability to move back and forth between records or to position on a specific row). The cursor datatype allows you to return a cursor from a stored procedure. You can also store a cursor in a variable. However, you can't store a cursor in a table using this datatype.

Table   This datatype returns tables from stored procedures or stores tables in variables for later processing. You can't use this datatype to store a table in a column of another table, however.

When you're adding these datatypes, you must specify any required parameters. For example, if you're creating a field to hold state abbreviations, you need to specify char(2) and then the appropriate constraints (discussed later in this chapter) to ensure that users enter only valid state abbreviations. Finally, you include a default that will add data to the fields if your users forget.

Introducing Computed Columns

Along with these built-in datatypes, you can create *computed columns*, which are special columns that don't contain any data of their own but display the output of an expression performed on data in other columns of the table. For example, in the AdventureWorks sample database, the

TotalDue column of the Sales.SalesOrderHeader table is a computed column. It contains no data of its own but displays the values of the Subtotal + TaxAmt + Freight columns as a single value.

 You can also create your own datatype, called a *user-defined datatype*. We'll discuss this in more detail in Chapter 5.

Creating Tables

In Chapter 2, you created a database named Sybex. In this section, you'll create three tables in that Sybex database. The first table, cleverly named Customers, will store customer information such as name, address, customer ID, and so on. The next table, which you'll call Orders, will contain order detail information such as an order number, product ID, and quantity ordered. Finally, the Products table will contain such product information as the name of the product, the product ID, and whether the product is in stock. Table 3.1, Table 3.2, and Table 3.3 list (on paper, just as it should be) the properties of the three tables.

TABLE 3.1   Products Table Fields

Field Name	Datatype	Contains
ProdID	Int, identity	A unique ID number for each product that can be referenced in other tables to avoid data duplication
Description	Nvarchar(100)	A brief text description of the product
InStock	Int	The amount of product in stock

TABLE 3.2   Customers Table Fields

Field Name	Datatype	Contains
CustID	Int, identity	A unique number for each customer that can be referenced in other tables
Fname	Nvarchar(20)	The customer's first name
Lname	Nvarchar(20)	The customer's last name
Address	Nvarchar(50)	The customer's street address

TABLE 3.2   Customers Table Fields *(continued)*

Field Name	Datatype	Contains
City	Nvarchar(20)	The city where the customer lives
State	Nchar(2)	The state where the customer lives
Zip	Nchar(5)	The customer's ZIP code
Phone	Nchar(10)	The customer's phone number without hyphens or parentheses (to save space, these will be displayed but not stored)

TABLE 3.3   Orders Table Fields

Field Name	Datatype	Contains
CustID	Int	References the customer number stored in the Customers table so you don't need to duplicate the customer information for each order placed
ProdID	Int	References the Products table so you don't need to duplicate product information
Qty	Int	The amount of products sold for an order
OrdDate	Smalldatetime	The date and time the order was placed

In Exercise 3.1 you'll create the Products table in the Sybex database.

EXERCISE 3.1

Creating the Products Table

1. Open SQL Server Management Studio. In Object Explorer, expand *Server* ➢ Databases ➢ Sybex.

2. Right-click the Tables icon, and select New Table to open the Table Designer.

3. In the first row, under Column Name, enter **ProdID**.

4. Just to the right of that, under Data Type, select Int.

5. Make certain Allow Nulls isn't checked. The field can be completely void of data if this option is checked, and you don't want that here.

6. In the bottom half of the screen, under Column Properties and in the Table Designer section, expand Identity Specification, and then change (Is Identity) to Yes.

7. Just under ProdID, in the second row under Column Name, enter **Description**.

8. Just to the right of that, under Data Type, enter **nvarchar(100)**.

9. Make certain Allow Nulls is cleared.

10. Under Column Name in the third row, enter **InStock**.

11. Under Data Type, select Int.

12. Uncheck Allow Nulls.

13. Click the Save button on the left side of the toolbar (it looks like a floppy disk).

14. In the Choose Name box that pops up, enter **Products**.

15. Close the Table Designer by clicking the *X* in the upper-right corner of the window.

With the Products table in place, you're ready to create the Customers table. Let's do that in Exercise 3.2.

EXERCISE 3.2

Creating the Customers Table

1. Right-click the Tables icon, and select New Table to open the Table Designer.

2. In the first row, under Column Name, enter **CustID**.

3. Under Data Type, select Int.

4. Make certain Allow Nulls isn't checked.

5. Under Column Properties and in the Table Designer section, expand Identity Specification, and then change (Is Identity) to Yes.

6. Just under CustID, in the second row under Column Name, enter **Fname**.

7. Just to the right of that, under Data Type, enter **nvarchar(20)**.

8. Make certain Allow Nulls is unchecked.

9. Using the parameters displayed earlier, fill in the information for the remaining columns. Don't allow nulls in any of the fields.

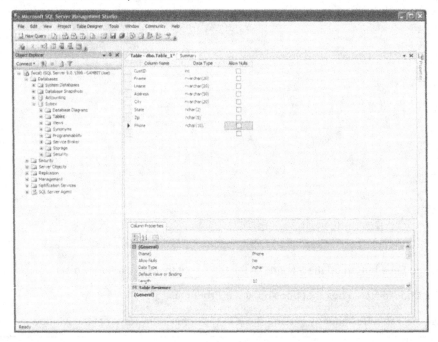

10. Click the Save button.

11. In the Choose Name box that pops up, enter **Customers**.

12. Close the Table Designer.

Now let's follow the same steps to create the Orders table in Exercise 3.3.

EXERCISE 3.3

Creating the Orders Table

1. Right-click the Tables icon, and select New Table to open the Table Designer.

2. In the first row, under Column Name, enter **CustID**.

3. Under Data Type, select Int.

4. Make certain Allow Nulls isn't checked.

5. This won't be an identity column like it was in the Customers table, so don't make any changes to the Identity Specification settings.

6. Just under CustID and in the second row under Column Name, enter **ProdID** with a datatype of int. Don't change the Identity Specification settings. Don't allow null values.

7. Just below ProdID, create a field named **Qty** with a datatype of int that doesn't allow nulls.

8. Create a column named **OrdDate** with a datatype of smalldatetime. Don't allow null values.

9. Click the Save button.

10. In the Choose Name box that pops up, enter **Orders**.

EXERCISE 3.3 *(continued)*

11. Close the Table Designer.

To verify that all three of your tables exist, expand Tables under the Sybex database—you should see the three tables you created (you may need to right-click the Tables icon and select Refresh to see the tables).

With all three of these tables in place, you're almost ready to unleash the users. Before you can allow the users to start working with the tables, though, you must further restrict what they can enter.

Restricting the Data

When you first create a table, it's wide open to your users. It's true they can't violate datatype restrictions by entering characters in an int type field and the like, but that is really the only restriction. It's safe to say you probably want more restrictions than that. For example, you probably don't want your users to enter XZ for a state abbreviation in a State field (because XZ isn't a valid abbreviation), and you don't want them entering numbers for someone's first name. You need to restrict what your users can enter in your fields, which you can do by using constraints.

Introducing Constraints

You can use three types of constraints in SQL Server: check constraints, default constraints, and unique constraints.

Using Check Constraints

A *check constraint* is a T-SQL statement that is linked to a field. Check constraints restrict the data that is accepted in the field even if the data is of the correct datatype. For example, the Zip field in the Customers table is the nchar datatype, which means it could technically accept letters. This can be a problem, because in the United States no ZIP codes contain letters (ZIP codes with letters are generally referred to as *postal codes*); so, you need to keep users from entering letters in the Zip field. In Exercise 3.4, you will create the check constraint that will accomplish this.

EXERCISE 3.4

Creating the Valid ZIP Code Constraint

1. In Object Explorer, expand the Sybex database ➢ Tables ➢ dbo.Customers.

2. Right-click Constraints, and click New Constraint.

3. In the New Constraint dialog box, enter **CK_Zip** in the (Name) text box.

4. In the Description text box, enter **Check for valid zip codes**.

5. To create a constraint that will accept only five numbers that can be zero through nine, enter the following code in the Expression text box:

   ```
   (zip like '[0-9][0-9][0-9][0-9][0-9]')
   ```

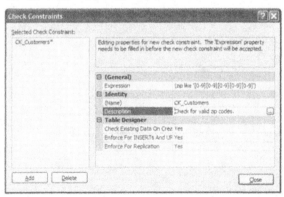

6. Click Close.

7. Click the Save button at the top left of the toolbar.

8. Close the Table Designer (which was opened when you started to create the constraint).

To test the new constraint you just created, let's enter some new records into the table by using the INSERT statement you will learn more about in Chapter 7. You will test your constraint in Exercise 3.5.

Testing Your Constraint

1. In SQL Server Management Studio, click the New Query button.

2. Enter the following code into the query window:

    ```
    USE Sybex

    INSERT customers

    VALUES ('Gary','McKee','111 Main','Palm Springs','CA',

    ➡'94312','7605551212')
    ```

3. Click the Execute button just above the query window to execute the query, and notice the successful results.

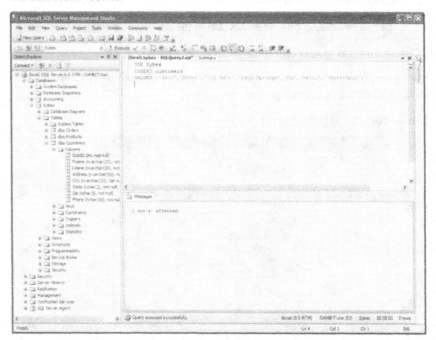

4. To see the new record, click the New Query button, and execute the following code:

```
SELECT * FROM customers
```

5. Notice that the record now exists with a CustID of 1 (because of the identity property discussed earlier, which automatically added the number for you).

6. To test the check constraint by adding characters in the Zip field, click the New Query button, and execute the following code (note the letters in the Zip field):

```
USE Sybex

INSERT customers

VALUES ('Amanda','Smith','817 3rd','Chicago','IL',
```
➡ 'AAB1C','8015551212')

7. Notice in the results pane that the query violated a constraint and so failed.

> You may have used *rules* in the past to do the work of check constraints. Rules are slated to be removed from future versions of SQL Server, so you should convert all your existing rules to check constraints.

It's easy to see how the check constraint can be a powerful ally against entering wrong data—all you need to do is figure out what data belongs in your column and create a constraint instructing SQL Server not to accept anything else. Check constraints serve no purpose if your users simply forget to enter data in a column, though—that is why default constraints exist.

Using Default Constraints

If users leave fields blank by not including them in the INSERT or UPDATE statement that they use to add or modify a record, *default constraints* fill in those fields. This can be a big time-saver in a data-entry department if you use it correctly.

For example, suppose most of your clientele live in California and your data-entry people must enter **CA** for every new customer they enter. That may not seem like much work, but if you have a sizable customer base, those two characters can add up to a lot of typing. By using a default constraint, your users can leave the State field intentionally blank, and SQL Server will fill it in.

You can't use default constraints in a few places, though:

- Defaults can't be used on columns with the timestamp datatype.

- Defaults can't be used on IDENTITY columns. IDENTITY columns contain a number that is automatically incremented with each new record.

- Defaults can't be used on columns with the ROWGUIDCOL property set. ROWGUIDCOL indicates that the column is a globally unique identifier (GUID) column for the table.

To demonstrate the capabilities of default constraints, let's create one on the Customers table in Exercise 3.6.

EXERCISE 3.6

Creating a Default Constraint

1. Open SQL Server Management Studio. In Object Explorer, expand *Server* ➤ Databases ➤ Sybex ➤ Tables ➤ dbo.Customers ➤ Columns.

2. Right-click the State column, and click Modify.

3. In the bottom half of the screen, in the Default Value or Binding text box, type **'CA'** (with the single quotes).

4. Click the Save button, and exit the Table Designer.

5. To test the default, click the New Query button in SQL Server Management Studio. Select New SQL Server Query, and connect with Windows Authentication if requested.

6. Enter and execute the following code:

```
USE Sybex

INSERT customers (fname, lname, address, city,

➥zip, phone)

VALUES ('Tom','Smith','609 Georgia','Fresno',

➥'33405','5105551212')
```

7. To verify that CA was entered in the State field, select Query ➢ New Query with Current Connection.

8. Enter and execute the following code:

```
SELECT * FROM customers
```

9. Notice that the Tom Smith record has CA in the State field.

Using Unique Constraints

You should use a *unique constraint* when you need to ensure that no duplicate values can be added to a field. A good example of a field that might require a unique constraint is a Social Security number field, because all the values contained therein need to be unique. Because you don't have a perfect candidate for a unique constraint in your tables, you'll come as close as you can by creating a unique constraint on the Phone field in Exercise 3.7.

You now know how to protect the data that is entered in your tables by enforcing domain and entity integrity, but you still have one more area of integrity to consider. You need to know how to protect related data that is stored in separate tables by enforcing referential integrity.

Creating a Unique Constraint

1. In SQL Server Management Studio, click the New Query button.

2. Select Sybex in the database drop-down list on the toolbar.

3. Enter and execute the following code:

```
ALTER TABLE customers

ADD CONSTRAINT CK_Phone

UNIQUE (Phone)
```

4. To test your new constraint, click the New Query button, and execute the following code to add a new record to the Customers table:

```
USE Sybex

INSERT customers

VALUES ('Shane','Travis','806 Star','Phoenix','AZ',

➡'85202','6021112222')
```

5. Click the New Query button, and try entering another customer with the same phone number by entering and executing the following:

```
USE Sybex

INSERT customers

VALUES ('Janet','McBroom','5403 Western','Tempe','AZ',

➡'85103','6021112222')
```

6. Notice that this fails, with a message that the UNIQUE_KEY constraint was violated by the duplicate phone number.

Partitioning Tables

Tables in SQL Server can range from small, having only a single record, to huge, with millions of records. These large tables can be difficult for users to work with simply because of their sheer size. To make them smaller without losing any data, you can *partition* your tables.

Partitioning tables works just like it sounds: you cut tables into multiple sections that can be stored and accessed independently without the users' knowledge. Suppose you have a table that contains order information, and the table has about 50 million rows. That may seem like a big table, but such a size isn't uncommon. To partition this table, you first need to decide on a partition column and a range of values for the column. In a table of order data, you probably have an order date column, which is an excellent candidate. The range can be any value you like; but since you want to make the most current orders easily accessible, you may want to set the range at anything older than a year. Now you can use the partition column and range to create a *partition function*, which SQL Server will use to spread the data across the partitions.

You create partition functions using the CREATE PARTITION FUNCTION statement. You can use this to create two types of ranges: left and right. The difference is simple really; take this code, for example:

```
CREATE PARTITION FUNCTION pfQty (int)
AS RANGE LEFT FOR VALUES (50,100)
```

This code creates three partitions that divide a table based on integer values of a column. Here is how it divides:

Partition 1	Partition 2	Partition 3
Col <= 50	col > 50 and <= 100	col > 100

To create a right range, just use this code:

```
CREATE PARTITION FUNCTION pfQty (int)
AS RANGE LEFT FOR VALUES (50,100)
```

This divides the table in this way:

Partition 1	Partition 2	Partition 3
Col < 50	col >= 50 and < 100	col >= 100

After you figure out how to divvy up the table, you need to decide where to keep the partitioned data physically; this is called the *partition schema*. You can keep archived data on one hard disk and current data on another disk by storing the partitions in separate filegroups, which can be assigned to different disks.

If you are going to divide current data from archive data, you will want to put the current data on the fastest disks you have because it is accessed more frequently. Also, you may want to mark the archive filegroup as read-only. This will speed up access because SQL Server does not place write locks on a read-only filegroup.

Once you have planned your partitions, you can create partitioned tables using the methods already discussed in this chapter.

In Exercise 3.8, you will create a partition function and scheme for the Orders table. The partition will be based on the OrdDate column and will separate current orders from archive orders. Anything in the last 30 days will be considered current.

EXERCISE 3.8

Creating a Partition Function and Scheme

1. In SQL Server Management Studio, right-click the Sybex database, and click Properties.

2. On the Filegroups page, click the Add button.

3. In the Name box, enter **TestPF1**.

4. Click Add again, and in the Name box, enter **TestPF2**.

5. Click Add again, and in the Name Box, enter **TestPF3**.

6. Click OK.

7. Select Sybex from the drop-down list on the toolbar.

8. Open a new query window, and execute the following code to create the partition function:

   ```
   CREATE PARTITION FUNCTION pfOrders (smalldatetime)

   AS RANGE LEFT FOR VALUES ((Getdate() - 30)
   ```

9. To create a partition scheme based on this function, execute this code:

   ```
   CREATE PARTITION SCHEME pfOrders

   AS PARTITION pfOrders

   TO (TestPF1, TestPF2, TestPF3);
   ```

Now that you have a better understanding of tables, you are ready to start working with views.

 Some good examples are the TransactionHistory and TransactionHistory-Archive tables in the AdventureWorks database, which are partitioned on the ModifiedDate field.

Understanding Views

It's an interesting challenge to describe views. Microsoft describes a view as either a virtual table or a stored SELECT query, but you might want to try thinking of it as being like a television set. When you watch television, you generally see people engaged in various activities. However, are any of these people actually *inside* your television set? Maybe when you were younger you thought so, but now you know those people are many miles away in a studio. You're seeing people who aren't really there—you're viewing a representation of them.

Views work in much the same way. *Views* represent the data that is stored in a table, just the way a television set represents people who are in a studio. Of course, a view has more advantages than just looking at the data stored in a table. For instance, you may want to see only a subset of records in a large table, or you may want to see data from multiple tables in a single query. Both of these are good reasons to use a view.

In Exercise 3.9, you will create a view that displays only those records in a table that have 398 as the first three characters of the phone number. Because you do not have many records in the Sybex database, you will use the AdventureWorks sample database.

EXERCISE 3.9

Creating the Contacts_in_398 View

1. Open SQL Server Management Studio by selecting it from the SQL Server 2005 group under Programs on your Start menu, and connect with Windows Authentication if requested.

2. In Object Explorer, expand *Server* ➢ Databases ➢ AdventureWorks, then right-click Views, and finally select New View.

3. In the Add Table dialog box, select Contact (Person), and click Add.

4. Click Close, which opens the View Designer.

5. In the T-SQL syntax editor text box, under the column grid, enter the following:

   SELECT LastName, FirstName, Phone

   FROM Person.Contact

   WHERE (Phone LIKE '398%')

6. Click the Execute button (the red exclamation point) on the toolbar to test the query.

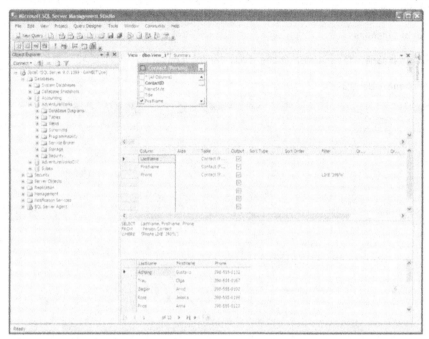

7. Choose File ➢ Save View - dbo.View_1.

8. In the Choose Name dialog box, enter **Contacts_in_398**, and click OK.

9. To test the view, click the New Query button, and execute the following code:

```
USE AdventureWorks
```

```
SELECT * FROM dbo.Contacts_in_398
```

10. To verify that the results are accurate, open a new query, and execute the code used to create the view:

USE AdventureWorks

SELECT lastname, firstname, phone from Person.Contact

WHERE phone LIKE '398%'

Notice that the view and the SELECT query in Exercise 3.9 returned the same results—but which was easier to query? The view was far easier to query because it took less code. However, the requirements for your view may change over time, so you may need to modify the view to reflect those requirements. You can see the power and flexibility that a view can give you—but there is even more. You can use views to modify your data, as well.

Modifying Data through a View

Not only can you use views to retrieve data, but you can also modify data through them—inserting, updating, and deleting records. If you decide to use views to make changes to your data, keep these points in mind:

- If you use a view to modify data, the modification can affect only one base table at a time. This means if a view presents data from two tables, you can write a statement that will update only one of those tables—if your statement tries to update both tables, you'll get an error message.

- You can't modify data in a view that uses aggregate functions. Aggregates are functions that return a summary value of some kind, such as SUM() or AVG(). If you try to modify such a view, you'll get an error.

- You saw earlier that views don't necessarily present all the fields in a table; you may see only a few. If you try to insert a record into a view that doesn't show all fields, you could run into a problem. Some of the fields that aren't shown in the view may not accept null values, but you can't insert a value into those fields if they aren't represented in the view. Because you can't insert values in those fields and they don't allow null values, your insert will fail. You can still use such a view for UPDATEs and DELETEs, though.

To overcome these limitations, you need to use INSTEAD OF triggers, which are discussed in Chapter 5.

To modify data through a view, you need to create a view that will allow you to modify data. You don't have one yet, because the view you've been working on thus far doesn't contain enough columns from any of its base tables to allow modifications; so, you need to create a simpler view, which you will do in Exercise 3.10.

EXERCISE 3.10

Creating an Updateable View

1. Open SQL Server Management Studio by selecting it from the SQL Server 2005 group under Programs on your Start menu, and connect with Windows Authentication if requested.

2. In Object Explorer, expand *Server* ➢ Databases ➢ AdventureWorks, right-click Views, and select New View.

3. In the Add Table dialog box, select Location (Production), and click Add.

4. Click Close to open the View Designer.

5. In the Transact-SQL syntax editor text box, enter the following:

SELECT Name, CostRate, Availability

FROM Production.Location

```
SELECT Name, CostRate, Availability from Production.Location
```

EXERCISE 3.10 *(continued)*

6. Choose File ➤ Save View - dbo.View_1.

7. In the Choose Name box, enter **Update_Product_Location**.

8. To test your view, open a new query, and execute the following code:

   USE AdventureWorks

   SELECT * FROM dbo.Update_Product_Location

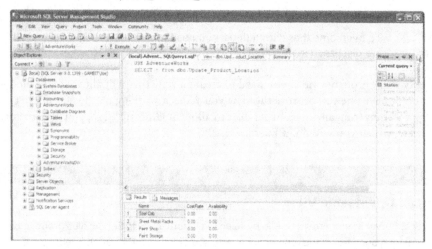

9. Now that you're sure the view is working the way you want, you'll create a new record. Open a new SQL Server query, and then enter and execute the following code:

   USE AdventureWorks

   INSERT dbo.Update_Product_Location

   VALUES ('Update Test Tool',55.00,10)

10. To verify that the record was inserted and that you can see it in the view, execute the following code in the query window:

    USE AdventureWorks

    SELECT * FROM dbo.Update_Product_Location

    WHERE Name = 'Update Test Tool'

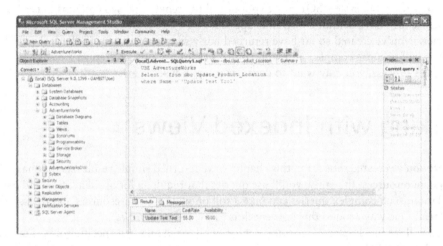

11. To view the data as it was inserted into the base table, enter and execute the following code in the query window:

USE AdventureWorks

SELECT * FROM Production.Location

WHERE Name = 'Update Test Tool'

When you look at the result set from the dbo.Update_Product_Location view, you should see only three columns, all filled in. When you look at the base table, though, you'll see five columns, all filled in. When you modified the view, you inserted values for only the three columns that were available—SQL Server populated the remaining two columns in the base table because they have default constraints applied.

The views you've created so far have returned fairly simple result sets; in the real world, your views will be more complex and will require a lot of resources to return a result set. To optimize this process, you may want to consider using indexed views.

Working with Indexed Views

The views you've created thus far in this chapter have returned simple result sets that haven't taxed system resources. In reality, you'll use queries that require a lot of calculation and data manipulation; such complex queries can take a toll on your system resources and thus slow your system. One way around this bottleneck is to use indexed views.

As you will see in Chapter 4, an *index* is a list of all the values in a specific column of one of your tables that SQL Server can reference to speed up data access. One type of index is called a *clustered index*; it physically arranges the data in a table so that the data conforms to the parameters of the index. A clustered index works a great deal like a dictionary, which physically arranges words so you can skip right to them. To make data access faster on a complex view, you can create a clustered index on the view.

When you create a clustered index on a view, the result set returned by the view is stored in the database the same way a table with a clustered index is stored, meaning the result set of the view is stored as an entirely separate object in the database and doesn't have to be regenerated (or materialized) every time someone runs a SELECT query against it. However, don't jump in and start creating clustered indexes on all your views just yet; we'll discuss a few considerations first.

For a complete discussion of indexes, please refer to Chapter 4.

Using indexes on complex views has its benefits, the first being performance. Every time a view is queried, SQL Server must materialize the view. *Materialization* is the process of performing all the JOINs and calculations necessary to return a result set to the user. If the view is complex (requires a large number of calculations and JOINs), indexing it can speed up access because the result set will never need to be materialized—it will exist in the database as a separate object, and SQL Server can call it whenever it's queried.

Another advantage to indexing a view is the way the Query Optimizer treats indexed views. The *Query Optimizer* is the component in SQL Server that analyzes your queries, compares them with available indexes, and decides which index will return a result set the fastest. Once you've indexed a view, the Query Optimizer considers this view in all future queries no matter what you're querying. This means queries on other tables may benefit from the index you create on the view.

The bad part about indexing a view is the overhead it incurs on the system. First, indexed views take up disk space because they're stored as separate objects in the database that look just like tables with a clustered index. Because clustered indexes store the actual data rather than just a pointer to the data in the base tables, they require extra disk space. For example, if you create a view that displays the Firstname, Lastname, and Extension columns from an Employees table and subsequently place a clustered index on that view, the Firstname, Lastname, and Extension columns will be duplicated in the database.

Another consideration is the way the indexed view is updated. When you first create an indexed view, it's based on the data that exists at the time of the indexing. When you update the tables the view is based on, though, the indexed view is immediately updated to reflect the changes to the base table. This means if you create an indexed view on a table and then make changes to the records in that table, SQL Server will automatically update the view at the same time. So if you have an indexed view on a table, the modifications are doubled and so is the system overhead.

If you decide your database would benefit from an indexed view, the tables and view itself must adhere to a few restrictions:

- The ANSI_NULLS and QUOTED_IDENTIFIER options must be turned on when the view is created. To do this, use the sp_dboption stored procedure:

  ```
  Sp_dboption 'ANSI_NULLS', TRUE
  Sp_dboption 'QUOTED_IDENTIFIER', TRUE
  ```

- The ANSI_NULLS option must have been turned on during the creation of all the tables that are referenced by the view.

- The view can't reference other views, only tables.

- Any user-defined function's data access property must be NO SQL, and external access property must be NO.

- All the tables referenced by the view must be in the same database as the view and must have the same owner as the view.

- The view must be created with the SCHEMABINDING option. This option prohibits the schema of the base tables from being changed (adding or dropping a column, for instance). If the tables can be changed, the indexed view may be rendered useless. To change the tables, you must first drop the indexed view.

- Any user-defined functions referenced in the view must have been created with the SCHEMABINDING option as well.

- All objects in the view must be referenced by their two-part names: *owner.object*. No one-, three-, or four-part names are allowed.

- SQL Server has two types of functions: *deterministic* functions return the same value each time they're invoked with the same arguments, and *nondeterministic* functions return different values when they're invoked with the same arguments. DATEADD, for example, returns the same result each time you execute it with the same arguments. GETDATE, however, returns a different value each time you execute it with the same arguments, making it nondeterministic. Any functions referenced in an indexed view must be deterministic.

- The SELECT statement that is used to create the view must follow these restrictions:

  - Column names must be explicitly stated in the SELECT statement; you can't use * or *tablename.** to access columns.

  - You may not reference a column twice in the SELECT statement unless all references, or all but one reference, to the column are made in a complex expression. For example, the following is illegal:

    ```
    SELECT qty, orderid, qty
    ```

    However, the following is legal:

    ```
    SELECT qty, orderid, SUM(qty)
    ```

  - You may not use a derived table that comes from using a SELECT statement encased in parentheses in the FROM clause of a SELECT statement.

  - You can't use ROWSET, UNION, TOP, ORDER BY, DISTINCT, COUNT(*), COMPUTE, or COMPUTE BY.

  - Subqueries and outer or self JOINs can't be used.

  - The AVG, MAX, MIN, STDEV, STDEVP, VAR, and VARP aggregate functions aren't allowed in the SELECT statement. If you need the functionality they provide, consider replacing them with either SUM() or COUNT_BIG().

  - A SUM() that references a nullable expression isn't allowed.

  - A Common Language Specification (CLS) user-defined function can only appear in the SELECT list of the view, it can't be used in WHERE or JOIN clauses.

  - CONTAINS and FREETEXT aren't allowed in the SELECT statement.

  - If you use GROUP BY, you can't use HAVING, ROLLUP, or CUBE, and you must use COUNT_ BIG() in the select list.

All the aggregate and string functions in SQL Server 2005 are considered deterministic.

That is an abundance of restrictions, but each one is necessary to keep the indexed view functioning. With all the considerations out of the way, you can create your own indexed view in Exercise 3.11.

EXERCISE 3.11

Creating an Indexed View

1. Open SQL Server Management Studio, and connect using Windows Authentication if requested.

2. Click the New Query button, and select New SQL Server Query. Connect using Windows Authentication if requested.

3. Create a view similar to dbo.Contacts_in_398 but without the XML column and ORDER BY and TOP clauses. Add the ContactID field and SCHEMABINDING so that the view can be indexed on the ContactID field, which is unique. To do all this, enter and execute the following code:

   SET QUOTED_IDENTIFIER ON

   go

   CREATE VIEW [Person].[Indexed_Contacts_in_398]

   ➥WITH SCHEMABINDING

   AS

   SELECT c.ContactID, title as [Title],

   ➥lastname as [Last Name], firstname as [First Name],

   ➥phone as [Phone Number], c3.cardtype as [Card Type]

   FROM Person.Contact c

   JOIN Sales.ContactCreditCard c2

   ➥ON c.ContactID = c2.ContactID

   JOIN Sales.CreditCard c3

   ➥ON c2.CreditCardID = c3.CreditCardID

   ➥WHERE phone LIKE '398%'

4. To test the Person.Indexed_Contacts_in_398 view, enter and execute the following query:

   USE [AdventureWorks]

   SELECT * FROM Person.Indexed_Contacts_in_398

EXERCISE 3.11 *(continued)*

5. Now you'll create an index on the ContactID column, because it's unique. To do that, open a new query window, and execute this code:

```
USE [AdventureWorks]

CREATE UNIQUE CLUSTERED INDEX

Cl_Indexed_View

➥ON Person.Indexed_Contacts_in_398(ContactID)
```

6. To make sure your index has been created, right-click Views under AdventureWorks in Object Explorer, and click Refresh.

7. Next, expand Views ➢ Person.Indexed_Contacts_in_398 ➢ Indexes. You should see the new Cl_Indexed_View index listed.

8. To test the indexed view, execute this code:

```
USE [AdventureWorks]

SELECT * FROM Person.Indexed_Contacts_in_398
```

This query obviously isn't too complex, but it does give a simple method for demonstrating the mechanics of creating a clustered index on a view. In the real world, this process will be much more complex, so weigh the benefits carefully before implementing this solution.

Case Study: Creating a Product Catalog Table

Let's visit our friends at the AlsoRann company again. When they needed to set up a sales database, the first thing we did was break out the pencil and paper and have them sit down in a conference room so we could draw the tables (OK, we used a whiteboard, but it still counts). We decided to create several tables, including a product catalog table.

The product catalog table would contain information about the products AlsoRann has for sale. Naturally they would need to store the product name, description, and price, but we needed more. Each product had to be uniquely identified in the table so that it would be easier to find in a query, and because the manufacturer's product ID was unique, we decided to store it as well. We also thought it would be a good idea to keep a record of how many of each item was in stock, so we added a column for that as well. The product ID and name were not a set length, so we decided to use a variable-length datatype. The Description field needed to hold a lot of text, because the marketing guys were a bit long-winded. The Price column obviously needed to be money and the InStock column was numeric, so we ended up with a product catalog table that looked like this:

ProductID	ProductName	Description	Price	InStock
Varchar(20)	Varchar(50)	Varchar(max)	Money	Int

The company wanted to make sure the value in the InStock field could never be less than zero, because that just didn't make sense from a business standpoint. The problem was that the int datatype allows negative numbers. To prevent users from entering a negative number, we added a check constraint to the InStock column that did not allow numbers less than 0 to be entered into that column.

Summary

As you can see, creating and managing tables involves a great deal of information. Here is a brief synopsis of what this chapter covered:

Planning tables   You learned you must sit down with a pencil and paper to draw the tables before you create them. You need to decide what the tables will contain, making the tables as specific as possible. You also learned that tables consist of fields (which contain a specific type of data) and rows (an entity in the table that spans all fields). Each of the fields in the table has a specific datatype that restricts the type of data it can hold—a field with an int datatype can't hold character data, for example. Then you learned you can create your own datatypes that are just system datatypes with all the required parameters presupplied.

Creating tables   You learned the mechanics of creating the tables in the database—there's not a lot to it, but it's still an important topic.

Restricting the data   You learned that tables are wide open to just about any kind of data when they're first created. The only restriction is that users can't violate the datatype of a field; other than that, the tables are fair game. To restrict what data your users can enter in a field, you learned how to create default, check, and unique constraints.

Then you learned what a view is. Much like a television set doesn't actually contain people, your view doesn't actually contain any data—it's just another means of seeing the data in the table. After that, you actually created a simple view based on a single table.

Next you learned how to use views to modify data. Don't forget that modifying data through a view has a few caveats:

- You can't modify more than one table at a time through a view.

- If your view is based on aggregate functions, you can't use it to modify data.

- If your view is based on a table that contains fields that don't allow null values yet your view doesn't display those fields, then you won't be able to insert new data. You can update and delete data, though.

Then you discovered you can index views. Doing so is particularly useful if your view is complex, because it can take a while to materialize. If you create an index on a view, SQL Server won't need to materialize the view every time someone queries it, because the result set is stored in the database the same way a table with a clustered index is stored. Just remember that creating and maintaining indexed views has many caveats—so make certain you absolutely need them.

Exam Essentials

Know your datatypes.   Be familiar with the built-in datatypes, and know when to use each one. For example, it is fairly obvious when you should use varchar instead of float, but it may not be as obvious when you need to use smallmoney versus money. If you are familiar with the datatypes, you will know when each datatype is appropriate.

Know your constraints.   Understand the constraints discussed in this chapter. Check constraints restrict the data a user is allowed to enter in a column even though the datatype does not restrict the data. Default constraints fill in data for you automatically when you do not specify a value while inserting a new record. Unique constraints prevent users from accidentally inserting duplicate records.

Understand table partitions.   Partitioning tables allows you to break a table into multiple pieces stored in separate files on multiple disks. To partition a table, you need to select a column, create a partition function, and then create a partition scheme. The partition function can be a LEFT or RIGHT range, so make sure you know how to choose.

Understand tables and views.   It sounds basic, but you should know what tables and views are. A table is a collection of fields and records (or rows and columns) that SQL Server uses to store and organize data. Views do not actually contain data; they are used to display the data stored in tables in a different format.

Know how to index a view.   Views can be indexed to speed up query times, but they have a number of caveats. Review the list of considerations for indexing a view earlier in this chapter, and make sure you are familiar with them.

Know how to make an updateable view.   You can update the underlying tables used to create a view, but you need to consider a few issues. If you use a view to modify data, the modification can affect only one base table at a time. You can't modify data in a view that uses aggregate functions, such as SUM() or AVG(). If you try to insert a record into a view that doesn't show all fields and any of those missing fields do not accept null values, the insert will fail. You can still use such a view for UPDATEs and DELETEs, though.

Review Questions

1. You have a table in you database that looks like this:

ProductName	Description	Quantity	InStock	VendorID
Datatype: varchar(50)	Datatype: varchar(100)	Datatype: int	Datatype: bit	Datatype: uniqueidentifier
Screwdriver	Use with screws	500	1	AD5A83CD-AB64-CA25-B23E-A1C54DF584A1
Hammer	Use with nails	350	1	7D1A87FC-7D2A-20FC-A52C-10F2B1C38F2C
Wrench	Use with bolts	0	0	6F9619FF-8B86-D011-B42D-00C04FC964FF

   What is the ProductName object?

   A. A record

   B. A field

   C. A datatype

   D. A view

2. In the table from question 1, what is the line that contains all of the data about screwdrivers called?

   A. A record

   B. A field

   C. A datatype

   D. A view

3. In the table from question 1, which values can the InStock field contain?

   A. Dates

   B. Numbers

   C. Text

   D. 0s and 1s

4. Suppose you want to add a column to the table from question 1 that contains the price of the product. None of your products will cost more than $300. What datatype should you use?

   A. Int

   B. Money

   C. Smallmoney

   D. Float

   E. Real

5. You have a table in you database that looks like this:

CustID	FirstName	LastName	Address	City	State	ZipCode	Phone
Datatype: int, identity	Datatype: varchar(20)	Datatype: varchar(20)	Datatype: varchar(50)	Datatype: varchar(20)	Datatype: char(2)	Datatype: char(5)	Datatype: char(10)
1	Bob	Jones	500 N. Main	Fresno	CA	94905	1115551212
2	Sally	Smith	205 E. 3rd	Chicago	IL	65201	2225551212
3	Andy	Thompson	718 Oak	Portland	OR	98716	3335551212

How can you prevent your users from entering invalid state abbreviations (like XZ) in the State field?

A. Create a default constraint.

B. Create a unique constraint.

C. Create a check constraint.

D. There is no way to prevent this.

6. In the table from question 5, assuming that most of your new customers are coming from California, what can you do to save time for users entering new customer records?

A. Create a default constraint on the State field.

B. Create a unique constraint on the State field.

C. Create a check constraint on the State field.

D. You can't do anything.

7. In the table from question 5, you want to make sure the CustID field is automatically incremented and filled in when a new customer is added to the table. What do you need to do?

A. Create a default constraint on the CustID field.

B. Create a unique constraint on the CustID field.

C. Create a check constraint on the CustID field.

D. You do not need to make any changes to the table.

8. In the table from question 5, your users need an easy way to display only the first name, last name, and phone number for customers in the 222 area code. What should you have them do?

A. Use this query on the table:
    `SELECT * FROM customers WHERE phone LIKE '222%'`

B. Use this query on the table:
    `SELECT firstname, lastname, phone FROM customers`
    `➥WHERE phone like '222%'`

C. Create a view based on the table using this query:
    `SELECT * FROM customers WHERE phone LIKE '222%'`
    Then have users query the view.

D. Create a view based on the table using this query:
    `SELECT firstname, lastname, phone FROM customers`
    `➥WHERE phone like '222%'`
    Then have users query the view.

9. You need to create a new view, and you are planning on using this code:

```
CREATE VIEW Contacts_in_222
AS
SELECT c.ContactID, title as [Title], lastname as [Last
➥Name], firstname as [First Name], phone as [Phone Number],
➥c3.cardtype as [Card Type]
FROM Person.Contact c
JOIN Sales.ContactCreditCard c2 on c.ContactID = c2.ContactID
JOIN Sales.CreditCard c3 on c2.CreditCardID = c3.CreditCardID
➥WHERE phone LIKE '222%'
```

You may need to index this view later to improve performance. What changes, if any, do you need to make to this code to be able to index the view later?

A. No changes are necessary.

B. Change the code to this:

```
CREATE VIEW Contacts_in_222 WITH SCHEMABINDING
AS
SELECT c.ContactID, title as [Title], lastname as
➥[Last Name], firstname as [First Name], phone as [Phone
➥Number], c3.cardtype as [Card Type]
FROM Person.Contact c
JOIN Sales.ContactCreditCard c2 on c.ContactID =
➥c2.ContactID

JOIN Sales.CreditCard c3 on c2.CreditCardID =
➥c3.CreditCardID

WHERE phone LIKE '222%'
```

C. Change the code to this:

```
CREATE VIEW Contacts_in_222 WITH INDEXABLE
AS
SELECT c.ContactID, title as [Title], lastname as
➥[Last Name], firstname as [First Name], phone as [Phone
➥Number], c3.cardtype as [Card Type]

FROM Person.Contact c

JOIN Sales.ContactCreditCard c2 on c.ContactID =
➥c2.ContactID

JOIN Sales.CreditCard c3 on c2.CreditCardID =
➥c3.CreditCardID

WHERE phone LIKE '222%'
```

D. Change the code to this:

```
CREATE VIEW Contacts_in_222 WITH TABLEBINDING
AS
SELECT c.ContactID, title as [Title], lastname as
➥[Last Name], firstname as [First Name], phone as [Phone
➥Number], c3.cardtype as [Card Type]

FROM Person.Contact c
JOIN Sales.ContactCreditCard c2 on c.ContactID =
➥c2.ContactID

JOIN Sales.CreditCard c3 on c2.CreditCardID =
➥c3.CreditCardID

WHERE phone LIKE '222%'
```

10. You need to create a new view, and you are planning on using this code:

```
CREATE VIEW Contacts_in_222 WITH SCHEMABINDING
AS
SELECT c.ContactID, title as [Title], lastname as [Last
➥Name], firstname as [First Name], phone as [Phone Number], c3.*

FROM Person.Contact c
JOIN Sales.ContactCreditCard c2 on c.ContactID = c2.ContactID
➥
JOIN Sales.CreditCard c3 on c2.CreditCardID = c3.CreditCardID
➥
WHERE phone LIKE '222%'
```

You may need to index this view later to improve performance. What changes, if any, do you need to make to this code to be able to index the view later?

A. No changes are necessary.

B. Change the code to this:

```
CREATE VIEW Contacts_in_222 WITH SCHEMABINDING, SELECTALL
AS
SELECT c.ContactID, title as [Title], lastname as
➥[Last Name], firstname as [First Name], phone as [Phone
➥Number], c3.*

FROM Person.Contact c
JOIN Sales.ContactCreditCard c2 on c.ContactID =
➥c2.ContactID

JOIN Sales.CreditCard c3 on c2.CreditCardID =
➥c3.CreditCardID

WHERE phone LIKE '222%'
```

C. Change the code to this:
```
CREATE VIEW Contacts_in_222 WITH SCHEMABINDING
AS
SELECT c.ContactID, title as [Title], lastname as
➡[Last Name], firstname as [First Name], phone as [Phone
➡Number], c3.[*]

FROM Person.Contact c
JOIN Sales.ContactCreditCard c2 on c.ContactID =
➡c2.ContactID

JOIN Sales.CreditCard c3 on c2.CreditCardID =
➡c3.CreditCardID

WHERE phone LIKE '222%'
```

D. Change the code to this:
```
CREATE VIEW Contacts_in_222 WITH SCHEMABINDING
AS
SELECT c.ContactID, title as [Title], lastname as
➡[Last Name], firstname as [First Name], phone as [Phone
➡Number], c3.CreditCardType as [Card Type]

FROM Person.Contact c
JOIN Sales.ContactCreditCard c2 on c.ContactID =
➡c2.ContactID

JOIN Sales.CreditCard c3 on c2.CreditCardID =
➡c3.CreditCardID

WHERE phone LIKE '222%'
```

11. You have a table that looks like this:

EmpID	FirstName	LastName	Address	City	State	ZipCode	Phone	SSN	Pay
Datatype: int, identity not nullable	Datatype: varchar(20) not nullable	Datatype: varchar(20) not nullable	Datatype: varchar(50) not nullable	Datatype: varchar(20) not nullable	Datatype: char(2) not nullable	Datatype: char(5) not nullable	Datatype: char(10) not nullable	Datatype: char(9) not nullable	Datatype: Money nullable
1	John	Jackson	20 N. 2nd	Oakland	CA	94905	1115551212	111223333	50,000.00
2	Jane	Samuels	37 S. Elm	Springfield	IL	65201	2225551212	444556666	65,000.00
3	Tom	Johnson	256 Park	Quahog	RI	05102	3335551212	777889999	45,000.00

You need to make sure the users entering new employees do not accidentally enter the same employee twice. What can you do?

A. Create a unique constraint on the FirstName and LastName fields.

B. Create a unique constraint on the EmpID field.

C. Create a unique constraint on the SSN field.

D. Create a unique constraint on the phone field.

12. Using the table from question 11, you need to create a view that allows users to add new employees. You want them to be able to add all the information except the pay rate. What changes do you need to make to the table to accomplish this?

    A. Add a default constraint to the Pay column with a value of 0.00.

    B. Change the Pay column so it is not nullable, and add a default constraint with a value of 0.00.

    C. Change all the columns to nullable,

    D. Do nothing; the table is fine as is.

13. Using the table from question 11, you need to create a view that allows users to update the FirstName, LastName, Phone, and Pay columns. The code to create the view looks like this:

```
CREATE VIEW Update_Pay WITH SCHEMABINDING
AS
SELECT FirstName, LastName, Phone, Pay
FROM HumanResources.Employees
```

    Users complain they cannot use the new view to add new employees. Why does this fail?

    A. Some columns in the table are not nullable, so the view can't be used to insert new records.

    B. The EmpID column was not included in the view, so the view can't be used to insert new records.

    C. WITH SCHEMABINDING can't be used on an updateable view, so the view can't be used to insert new records.

    D. Columns with the money datatype, such as the Pay column, can't be used in updateable views, so the view can't be used to insert new records.

14. Using the table from question 11, you need to partition the table into three divisions, one for employees that make less than 50,000, one for employees that make 50,001 to 70,000, and one for employees that make 70,0001 and higher. Place the following steps in order to create a partition for this table.

    A. Create a partition scheme.

    B. Create a partition function.

    C. Add filegroups to the database.

    D. Choose a partition column and value.

15. Using the table from question 11, you need to partition the table into three divisions, one for employees that make less than 50,000, one for employees that make 50,001 to 70,000, and one for employees that make 70,0001 and higher. Which function should you use?

A. Use the following:
```
CREATE PARTITION FUNCTION pfSalary (money)
AS RANGE LEFT FOR VALUES (50000,70000);
```

B. Use the following:
```
CREATE PARTITION FUNCTION pfSalary (money)
AS RANGE LEFT FOR VALUES (50001,70001);
```

C. Use the following:
```
CREATE PARTITION FUNCTION pfSalary (money)
AS RANGE RIGHT FOR VALUES (50000,70000);
```

D. Use the following:
```
CREATE PARTITION FUNCTION pfSalary (money)
AS RANGE RIGHT FOR VALUES (50001,70001);
```

16. Using the table from question 11, you need to partition the table into three divisions, one for employees who make less than 49,000, one for employees who make 50,000 to 69,999, and one for employees who make 70,0000 and higher. Which function should you use?

A. Use the following:
```
CREATE PARTITION FUNCTION pfSalary (money)
AS RANGE LEFT FOR VALUES (50000,70000);
```

B. Use the following:
```
CREATE PARTITION FUNCTION pfSalary (money)
AS RANGE LEFT FOR VALUES (50001,70001);
```

C. Use the following:
```
CREATE PARTITION FUNCTION pfSalary (money)
AS RANGE RIGHT FOR VALUES (50000,70000);
```

D. Use the following:
```
CREATE PARTITION FUNCTION pfSalary (money)
AS RANGE RIGHT FOR VALUES (50001,70001);
```

17. You have created a view that your users need to use to update records in one of your tables. The code to create the view looks like this:
```
CREATE VIEW ProductCost WITH SCHEMABINDING
AS
SELECT ProdID, Cost, Qty, SUM(qty * cost) FROM Products
```

What do you need to change on this view to make it updateable?

A. Nothing, the view is updateable as is.

B. Change the code to look like this:
```
CREATE VIEW ProductCost
AS
SELECT ProdID, Cost, Qty, SUM(qty * cost) FROM Products
```

C. Change the code to look like this:
```
CREATE VIEW ProductCost WITH ALLOWAGREGATES
AS
SELECT ProdID, Cost, Qty, SUM(qty * cost) FROM Products
```

D. Change the code to look like this:
```
CREATE VIEW ProductCost WITH SCHEMABINDING
AS
SELECT ProdID, Cost, Qty FROM Products
```

18. You have created a view with the following code:
```
CREATE VIEW Update_Pay WITH SCHEMABINDING
AS
SELECT FirstName, LastName, Phone, Pay
FROM HumanResources.dbo.Employees
```

What changes do you need to make to this code to make this view indexable?

A. No changes are needed; the view is already indexable.

B. Change the code to look like this:
```
CREATE VIEW Update_Pay WITH SCHEMABINDING
AS
SELECT FirstName, LastName, Phone, Pay
FROM HumanResources.dbo.Employees
```

C. Change the code to look like this:
```
CREATE VIEW Update_Pay WITH SCHEMABINDING
AS
SELECT FirstName, LastName, Phone, Pay
FROM HumanResources.dbo.Employees
```

D. Change the code to look like this:
```
CREATE VIEW Update_Pay
AS
SELECT FirstName, LastName, Phone, Pay
FROM HumanResources.Employees
```

19. Which datatype is best suited for storing large images (greater than 8KB)?

A. Varchar(max)

B. Varbinary(max)

C. Binary

D. Image

20. You have created a view with the following code:
```
CREATE VIEW Get_Pay WITH SCHEMABINDING
AS
SELECT FirstName, LastName, Phone, Pay, GetDate()
FROM HumanResources.Employees
```

What changes do you need to make to this code to make this view indexable?

A. Change the code to look like this:
```
CREATE VIEW Get_Pay WITH SCHEMABINDING
AS
SELECT FirstName, LastName, Phone, Pay
FROM HumanResources.Employees
```

B. Change the code to look like this:
```
CREATE VIEW Get_Pay
AS
SELECT FirstName, LastName, Phone, Pay, GetDate()
FROM HumanResources.Employees
```

C. Change the code to look like this:
```
CREATE VIEW Get_Pay WITH SCHEMABINDING
AS
SELECT FirstName, LastName, Phone, Pay, GetDate()
FROM HumanResources.dbo.Employees
```

D. No changes are needed; the view is already indexable.

Answers to Review Questions

1. B. Tables consist of fields and records. Fields contain a certain type of information such as last name or ZIP code. A record is a group of related fields containing information about a single entity (such as a person) that spans all the fields. ProductName is a field that contains the name of the product for each record in the table.

2. A. Tables consist of fields and records. Fields contain a certain type of information such as last name or ZIP code. A record is a group of related fields containing information about a single entity (such as a person) that spans all the fields. The line that contains all of the records about screwdrivers is therefore a record.

3. D. Datatypes restrict the type of data that can be inserted in a column. The InStock column has the bit datatype assigned, which means only 0s and 1s can be stored in that column.

4. C. This new column would be best suited for smallmoney. Int allows only whole numbers so it would not allow change (in other words, $1.50 would not work). Float would work OK, but it is not meant for storing currency. Money is meant for storing currency, but it is best suited to values larger than 214,748.3647. So, because you are selling products valued at less that $300, it is best to use smallmoney.

5. C. Check constraints restrict the data that is accepted in the field even if the data is of the correct datatype. So, you can use a check constraint to prevent users from entering invalid state abbreviations.

6. A. Default constraints specify what value to use in a column when the user does not specify a value. So by using a default constraint, your users would not have to enter a state value when adding a new customer unless that customer is not from California.

7. D. The CustID column is an identity column, which means every time a new record is inserted, the value in the CustID column is automatically incremented and inserted for you. In fact, you can't add a constraint to the CustID column because it is an identity column.

8. D. t is much faster for the users to query a view in this case because there is less code. You do not want to use the SELECT * statement because that returns all fields from the table and you need only FirstName, LastName, and Phone.

9. B. To index a view, you must use the SCHEMABINDING option, which prevents the underlying table from being changed unless the schema bound view is dropped first. Also, TABLEBINDING and INDEXABLE are not actual options.

10. D. You can't index a view that has CreditCardType in the SELECT statement; all columns must be called out specifically. Also, SELECTALL is not an actual option.

11. C. The SSN field is the most likely candidate for a unique constraint because more than one employee may have the same first and last names, and if two employees live together, they would have the same phone number. The EmpID field is an identity field, so it is unique for each record already and therefore does not require a unique constraint.

12. D. To create an updateable view that will allow users to insert new records with everything except the Pay column, you do not need to make any changes because the Pay column is nullable; therefore, your users do not have to insert a value in the Pay column when inserting a new record.

13. A. Several non-nullable columns appear in the underlying table, so when users try to insert a new record, SQL Server expects values for all of the non-nullable columns. Since this view does not display all these columns, the view can't be used to insert new records. It can be used to update existing records, though.

14. D, C, B, A. First, you have to plan the partition and choose a column. Next, you need to make sure you have enough filegroups in the database to handle the partitions. After you have that, you can create a partition function, and then you can create the partition scheme.

15. A. The LEFT range gives you three partitions: 0–50,000; 50,001–70,000; and 70,001 and higher. A RIGHT range would give you 0–49999; 50,000–69,999; and 70,000 and higher.

16. C. The RIGHT range give you three partitions, 0–49,999; 50,000–69,999; and 70,000 and higher. A LEFT range would give you 0–49,999; 50,000–69,999; and 70,000 and higher.

17. D. Aggregate functions, such as SUM() and AVG(), are not allowed in updateable views, so you have to remove SUM(qty * cost). Also, ALLOWAGREGATES is not a valid option.

18. C. You need the SCHEMABINDING option on a view that you intend to index, but you cannot have three-part notation. You must create indexed views using only two-part notation; no three- or four-part notation is allowed.

19. B. Varbinary(max) holds 2,147,483,67 bytes of data, so it is well suited for large images. Varchar(max) is used only for holding large amounts of text, binary is used for holding small objects (smaller than 8KB), and image has been deprecated, so it can no longer be used.

20. A. You need the SCHEMABINDING option on a view that you intend to index, and three-part notation is not allowed. Nondeterministic functions return a different value every time they are called; deterministic functions return the same value every time they are called. Nondeterministic functions such as GETDATE() can't be used in a view you intend to index.

Chapter

4

Performing Indexing and Full-Text Searching

MICROSOFT EXAM OBJECTIVES COVERED IN THIS CHAPTER:

✓ **Implement indexes.**

- Specify the filegroup.
- Specify the index type.
- Specify relational index options.
- Specify columns.
- Specify a partition scheme when creating an index.
- Create an online index by using an ONLINE argument.

✓ **Implement a full-text search.**

- Create a catalog.
- Create an index.
- Specify a full-text population method.

If you wanted to look up *triggers* in this book, how would you go about it? First you would look in the index in the back of the book for the word *triggers,* which is listed alphabetically under the *T* section. Once you located the entry, you would reference the page number next to *triggers* and find the description you needed rather quickly. However, suppose this book had no organization—no index, no table of contents, not even chapters or page numbers. How would you find *triggers* then? You would have to scan the entire book, page by page, until you found what you sought—a painfully slow process. SQL Server tables work much the same way.

When you first create a table and start inserting data, the table has no organization whatsoever—information is inserted on a first-come, first-served basis. When you want to find a specific record later, SQL Server has to look through every record in the table to find the record you need. That is called a *table scan*, and it can slow the database server considerably. Because you need fast access to your data, you need to add organization to the tables that contain that data, much like this book is organized with chapters, page numbers, and indexes.

To add organization to tables, you need to understand indexing. In this chapter, we'll discuss the two different types of indexes, clustered and nonclustered, and how they work to accelerate data access. We'll also show you how, when, and where to create these indexes so they provide the utmost proficiency in data retrieval.

Before you can truly understand how indexes accelerate data access, though, you must understand the index architecture.

Understanding Index Architecture

In Chapter 2, you learned that SQL Server stores data on the hard disk in 8KB pages inside the database files. By default, these pages and the data they contain aren't organized in any way. To bring order to this chaos, you must create an index. Once you've done so, you have index pages as well as data pages. The data pages contain the information that users have inserted in the tables, and the index pages store a list of all the values in an indexed column (called *key values*) along with a pointer to the location of the record that contains that value in the indexed table. For example, if you have an index on a LastName column, a key value might be Smith 520617—this indicates that the first record with a value of Smith in the LastName field is on extent 52, page 6, record number 17 (an *extent* is a collection of eight contiguous pages in a data file).

You can create two types of indexes on a table: clustered and nonclustered. Which type should you use and where? To answer that question accurately, you need to understand how SQL Server stores and accesses data when no index exists—this type of table is called a *heap*.

Understanding Heaps

Have you ever been in one of those cities that has streets broken up by canals, highways, and sundry obstructions? Every time you're about to find the address you need, the street ends because of an obstacle of some sort. To continue your search for your destination, you have to refer to your map to find out where the street begins on the other side. The worse the street is broken up, the more often you refer to your map to find the next section of street.

Tables with no clustered index in place, called *heaps*, are a great deal like those broken streets. SQL Server stores tables on disk by allocating one extent (eight contiguous 8KB pages) at a time in the database file. When one extent fills with data, another is allotted. These extents, however, aren't physically next to each other in the database file; they're scattered about much like a street that keeps starting and stopping. That is part of what makes data access on a heap so slow—much like you need to keep accessing your map to find various sections of the street you're on, SQL Server needs to access a map to find various extents of the table it's searching.

Suppose, for instance, that you're searching for a record named Adams in a Customers table. The Customers table may be quite sizable, so SQL Server needs to find all the extents that belong to that table in the database file before it can even think of searching for Adams. To find those extents, SQL Server must query the sysindexes table.

Don't let the name fool you: even though this table is generally used to store index information, every table in your database has an entry in the sysindexes table, whether or not the particular table has an index in place. If your table is a heap (such as this Customers table), it has a record in the sysindexes table with a value of 0 in the indid (index identifier) column. Once SQL Server finds the record for the Customers table in the sysindexes table and reads a 0 in the indid column, SQL Server looks specifically at the FirstIAM column.

The FirstIAM column tells SQL Server exactly where the first IAM page is in the database. Much like the street map you use to find various sections of a street, the IAM is what SQL Server must use to find various extents of a heap, as depicted in Figure 4.1. This IAM is the only thing that links pages together in a heap; without the IAM page, SQL Server would need to scan every page in the database file to find one table—just like you would have to drive every street in town to find a single address if you had no street map.

Even with this IAM page, data access is generally slower than if your table were indexed. Think of it this way: if there were no break in the street on which you were searching for an address, it would be much easier and faster to find your destination. However, because the street is broken up, you must constantly refer to your map to find the next section of street. In the same fashion, SQL Server must constantly refer to the IAM page to find the next extent of a table to continue searching for data. This process of scanning the IAM page and then scanning each extent of the table for the record needed is called a *table scan*. You can see what a table scan looks like by completing Exercise 4.1.

EXERCISE 4.1

Generating a Table Scan

1. Open SQL Server Management Studio, and connect using Windows Authentication.

2. To force SQL Server to perform a table scan, you need to delete an index (which you'll re-create later in this chapter). In Object Explorer, expand *Server* ➢ Databases ➢ AdventureWorks ➢ Tables.

3. Right-click HumanResources.EmployeePayHistory, and select Modify.

4. Right-click the EmployeeID column, and click Remove Primary Key.

5. Click the Save button on the toolbar.

6. Open a new query and enter, but do not execute, the following code:

    ```
    USE AdventureWorks

    SELECT * FROM HumanResources.EmployeePayHistory
    ```

7. On the Query menu, click Display Estimated Execution Plan. This will show you how SQL Server goes about finding your data.

8. Scroll down to the bottom of the results pane, and hover over the Table Scan icon to view the cost of the scan—this tells you how much CPU time the scan took (in milliseconds).

FIGURE 4.1   To find all the pages associated with a table, SQL Server must reference the IAM page.

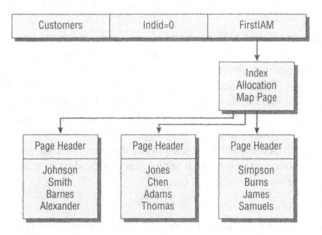

Table scans can slow your system, but they don't always. In fact, table scans can be faster than indexed access if your table is small (about one extent in size). If you create an index on such a small table, SQL Server must read the index pages and then the table pages. It would be faster just to scan the table and be done with it. So, on small tables, a heap is preferable. On larger tables, though, you need to avoid table scans—to do that, you should understand indexes. We'll start by looking into clustered indexes.

Estimating the Size of a Table in Extents

Chapter 2 discusses this in more detail, but here is a brief overview. To estimate the size of a table in extents, do the following:

1.   Calculate the size of a record in the table.

2.   Divide 8,092 by the result from step 1.

3.   Divide the number of estimated rows by the result from step 2.

4.   Divide the result from step 3 by 8—you'll have the number of extents your table occupies.

Understanding Clustered Indexes

Clustered indexes physically rearrange the data that users insert in your tables. The arrangement of a clustered index on disk can easily be compared to that in a dictionary, because they both use the same storage paradigm. If you needed to look up a word in the dictionary—for example, *satellite*—how would you do it? You would turn right to the *S* section of the dictionary and continue through the alphabetically arranged list until you found the word *satellite*. The process is similar with a clustered index; a clustered index on a LastName column would place *Adams* physically before *Burns* in the database file. This way, SQL Server can more easily pinpoint the exact data pages it wants.

It might help to visualize an index in SQL Server as an upside-down tree. In fact, the index structure is called a *B-tree* (binary-tree) structure. At the top of the B-tree structure, you find the *root page*; it contains information about the location of other pages further down the line called *intermediate-level pages*. These intermediate-level pages contain yet more key values that can point to still other intermediate-level pages or data pages. The pages at the bottom of a clustered index, the *leaf pages*, contain the actual data, which is physically arranged on disk to conform to the constraints of the index.

Data access on a clustered index is a little more complex than just looking for letters or numbers in the data pages, though—the way SQL Server accesses the data in this structure is similar to a global positioning system (GPS) in a car.

> You can have only one clustered index per table because clustered indexes physically rearrange the data in the indexed table.

Accessing Data with a Clustered Index

If you've never had the opportunity to drive a car that is equipped with a GPS map guidance system, you're missing quite an interesting experience. The GPS system is a computerized map that is designed to guide you while you're driving. It looks like a small computer screen that rests on a gooseneck pole between the driver and passenger in the front seat, much like a gear-shift in a standard transmission car. The interesting feature of this map is that it talks you through the directions—"Turn left one quarter mile ahead," "Turn right at the next intersection," and so on. When it's finished speaking to you, you're at the destination you desire.

In this analogy, the beginning point of your journey is the root page of the clustered index. Each of the twists and turns you take in your journey is an intermediate level of the clustered index, and each one is important in getting to your destination. Finally, the destination in your journey is the leaf level of the index, the data itself. However, because SQL Server doesn't use GPS, what is the map?

When you perform a query on a column that is part of a clustered index (by using a SELECT statement), SQL Server must refer to the sysindexes table where every table has a record. Tables with a clustered index have a value of 1 in the indid column (unlike heaps, which have a value of 0). Once the record has been located, SQL Server looks at the root column, which contains the location of the root page of the clustered index.

When SQL Server locates the root page of the index, it begins to search for your data. If you're searching for *Smith*, for example, SQL Server searches through the entire root page looking for an entry for *Smith*. Since the data you're seeking is toward the bottom of the table, SQL Server most likely won't find *Smith* in the root page. What it will find at the bottom of the root page is a link to the next intermediate-level page in the chain.

Each page in the clustered index has pointers, or links, to the index page just before it and the index page just after it. Having these links built into the index pages eliminates the need for the IAM pages that heaps require. This speeds up data access because you don't need to keep referring to the IAM pages—you move right to the next index page in the chain, much like in the GPS analogy where you follow the computer's voice to the next turn in your route.

SQL Server then looks through each intermediate-level page, where it may be redirected to another intermediate-level page or finally to the leaf level. The leaf level in a clustered index is the end destination—the data you requested in your SELECT query. If you've requested one record, that single record found at the leaf level is displayed.

Suppose, though, that you've requested a range of data (for example, *Smith* through *Quincy*). Because the data has been physically rearranged, as soon as SQL Server has located the first value in the search, it can read each subsequent record until it reaches *Quincy*. SQL Server has no need to keep referring to the root and intermediate-level pages to find subsequent data. This makes a clustered index an excellent choice for columns where you're constantly searching for ranges of data or columns with low selectivity. *Selectivity* is the number of duplicate values in a column; low selectivity means a column has many duplicate values. For example, a LastName column may contain several hundred records with a value of Smith, which means it has low selectivity, whereas a PhoneNumber column should have few records with duplicate values, meaning it has high selectivity. The whole process looks a lot like Figure 4.2.

FIGURE 4.2   The data in a table with a clustered index is physically rearranged for ease of location.

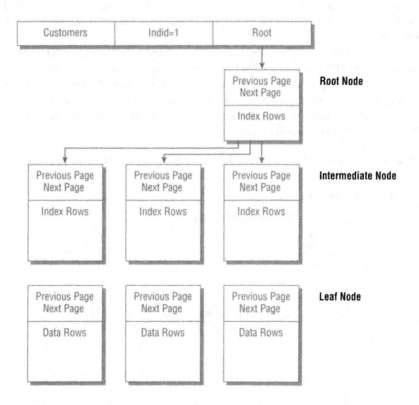

You now know how SQL Server accesses data via a clustered index, but there is more to it than that. Now you need to understand how that data gets there in the first place and what happens if it changes.

Modifying Data with a Clustered Index

To access data on a table with a clustered index, you use a standard SELECT statement—there is nothing special about it. Modifying data with a clustered index is the same—you use standard INSERT, UPDATE, and DELETE statements. What makes this process intriguing is the way SQL Server has to store your data; it must be physically rearranged to conform to the clustered index parameters.

On a heap, the data is inserted at the end of the table, which is the bottom of the last data page. If there is no room on any of the data pages, SQL Server allocates a new extent and starts filling it with data. Because you've told SQL Server to physically rearrange your data by creating a clustered index, SQL Server no longer has the freedom to stuff data wherever room exists. The data must physically be placed in order. To help SQL Server accomplish this, you need to leave a little room at the end of each data page on a clustered index. This blank space is referred to as the *fill factor*.

Setting the fill factor on a clustered index tells SQL Server to leave blank space at the end of each data page so it has room to insert new data. For example, suppose you have a clustered index on a LastName column and you want to add a new customer with a last name of *Chen*, which needs to be placed on one of the data pages containing the C data. SQL Server must put this record on the C page; with a fill factor specified, you'll have room at the end of the page to insert this new data. Without a fill factor, the C page may fill entirely, and there will be no room for *Chen*.

You specify the fill factor when you create the clustered index, and you can change it later if you want. A higher fill factor gives less room, and a lower fill factor gives more room. If you specify a fill factor of 70, for example, the data page is filled with 70 percent data and 30 percent blank space (as shown in Figure 4.3). If you specify 100, the data page is filled to nearly 100 percent, with room for only one record at the bottom of the page (it seems strange, but that's how SQL Server views 100 percent full).

FIGURE 4.3   Set the fill factor to leave blank space for new data in your pages.

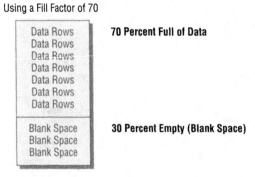

Using a Fill Factor of 70

70 Percent Full of Data

30 Percent Empty (Blank Space)

SQL Server doesn't automatically maintain the fill factor, though. This means your data pages can and will fill to capacity eventually. What happens when a data page fills completely?

When you need to insert data into a page that has become completely full, SQL Server performs a *page split*. This means SQL Server takes approximately half the data from the full page and moves it to an empty page, thus creating two half-full pages (or two half-empty pages, depending on how you look at it). Now you have plenty of room for the new data, but you have to contend with a new problem. Remember that this clustered index is a doubly linked list, with each page having a link to the page before it and a link to the page after it. So, when SQL Server splits a page, it must also update the headers at the top of each page to reflect the new location of the data that has been moved. Because this new page can be anywhere in the database file, the links on the pages don't necessarily point to the next physical page on the disk. A link may point to a different extent altogether, which can slow the system.

For example, if you have inserted a new record named *Chen* into the database but your C page is full, SQL Server will perform a page split. Half the data is moved to a new page to make room for the *Chen* record, but the new page for the data that has been moved isn't in line anymore. Take a look at Figure 4.4 to better understand what can happen.

Notice that before the page split (as shown in Figure 4.4), all the pages were neatly lined up—page 99 pointed to page 100, page 100 pointed to page 101, and so on. Then after the page split, some of the data had to be moved from page 100 to page 102. Now page 102 comes directly after 100 in the linked list. This means when you search for data, SQL Server will need to jump from page 99 to page 100, from page 100 to page 102, from page 102 back to page 101, and then from page 101 to page 103. You can see how that might slow the system down, so you need to configure the fill factor to avoid excessive page splits.

FIGURE 4.4   Page splits move half the data from a full page to a new page to make room for more data.

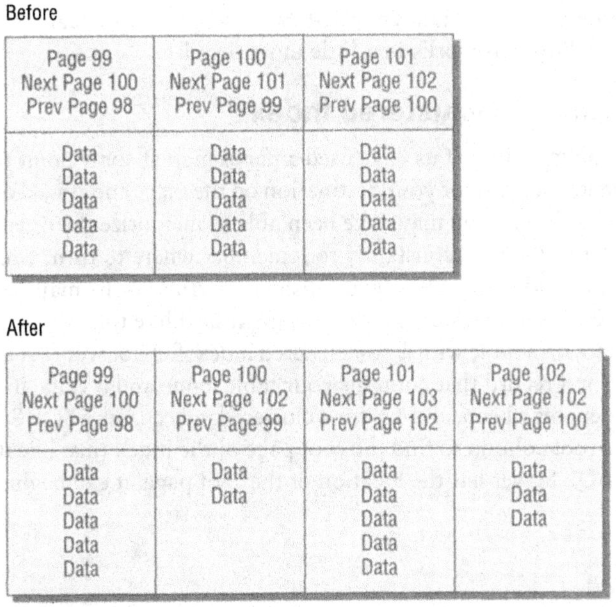

Before

Page 99	Page 100	Page 101
Next Page 100	Next Page 101	Next Page 102
Prev Page 98	Prev Page 99	Prev Page 100
Data	Data	Data
Data	Data	Data
Data	Data	Data
Data	Data	Data
Data	Data	Data

After

Page 99	Page 100	Page 101	Page 102
Next Page 100	Next Page 102	Next Page 103	Next Page 102
Prev Page 98	Prev Page 99	Prev Page 102	Prev Page 100
Data	Data	Data	Data
Data	Data	Data	Data
Data		Data	Data
Data		Data	
Data		Data	

The term *excessive* is subjective when discussing page splits, though. In an environment where data is used primarily for reading, such as a decision support services environment, you'll want to use a high fill factor (less free space). This high fill factor will ensure that data is read from fewer pages in the database file. You should use a lower fill factor (more free space) in environments that have a lot of INSERT traffic. This lower fill factor will cut down on page splits and increase write performance.

Now that you have a better understanding of the inner workings of a clustered index, you're probably ready to create one for each column of your table—but please don't try to do that just yet (even if you want to, you're limited to one clustered index per table). Before you find out where and how to create indexes, you need to learn about nonclustered indexes.

Understanding Nonclustered Indexes

Like its clustered cousin, the *nonclustered index* is a B-tree structure having a root page, intermediate levels, and a leaf level. However, two major differences separate the index types. The first is that the leaf level of the nonclustered index doesn't contain the actual data; it contains pointers to the data that is stored in data pages. The second big difference is that the nonclustered index doesn't physically rearrange the data. It's much like the difference between a dictionary and an index at the back of a topically arranged book.

A clustered index is much like a dictionary in that the data contained therein is physically arranged to meet the constraints of the index. So if you wanted to find *triggers* in a dictionary, you would turn to the *T* section and find your way from there. A nonclustered index is more like the index at the back of a book. If you wanted to find *triggers* in this book, you couldn't turn to the *T* section of the book and look for *triggers* because there is no *T* section to turn to, as there is in a dictionary. Instead, you turn to the back of the book and refer to the index, which does have a *T* section. Once you locate *triggers* in the index, you turn to the page number listed to find the information you need. If you're searching for a range of data, you must constantly refer to the index to find the data you need, because most of the data is contained on different pages. Let's see how this works in a little more detail.

Accessing Data with a Nonclustered Index

Let's return to the map analogy. Most of us have used a paper map at some point to locate a destination. You unfolded it, searched for your destination on the map, and traced out a route to get there. If the route was simple, you may have been able to memorize the directions, but most times you had to refer to the map constantly to remember where to turn, what street names you were looking for, and so on. Once you finished referring to the map, you were probably at your destination. A nonclustered index is a great deal like this.

When you search for data on a table with a nonclustered index, SQL Server first queries the sysindexes table looking for a record that contains your table name and a value in the indid column from 2 to 251 (0 denotes a heap, and 1 is for a clustered index). Once SQL Server finds this record, it looks at the root column to find the root page of the index (just like it did with a clustered index). Once SQL Server has the location of the root page, it can begin searching for your data.

If you're searching for *Smith,* for example, SQL Server looks through the root page to find *Smith;* if it isn't there, the server finds the highest value in the root page and follows that pointer to the next intermediate-level page. SQL Server keeps following the intermediate-level links until it finds *Smith* in the leaf level. This is another difference between clustered and non-clustered indexes: the leaf level in a nonclustered index doesn't contain the actual data you seek. The leaf level contains a pointer to the data, which is contained in a separate data page—much like the index at the back of a book doesn't have a description of what you're looking for but refers you to a different page of the book.

If you're searching for a single value, SQL Server needs to search the index only once because the pointer at the leaf level directs SQL Server right to the data. If you're looking for a range of values, though, SQL Server must refer to the index repeatedly to locate the key value for each record in the range you're trying to find. This means you should use nonclustered indexes on columns in which you seldom search for ranges of data or columns with high selectivity. As mentioned previously in this chapter, selectivity is the number of duplicate values in a column; low selectivity means a column contains many duplicate values, and high selectivity means a column contains few duplicate values.

Once SQL Server finds the leaf level it needs, it can use the pointer to find the data page that contains *Smith;* how SQL Server finds the data page depends on whether you have a clustered index in place yet.

If you're searching a nonclustered index that is based on a heap (a table with no clustered index in place), SQL Server uses the pointer in the leaf-level page to jump right to the data page and return your data (as shown in Figure 4.5).

If your table has a clustered index in place, the nonclustered index leaf level doesn't contain a pointer directly to the data; rather, it contains a pointer to the clustered index key value, as shown in Figure 4.6. This means once SQL Server is done searching your nonclustered index, it has to traverse your clustered index as well. Why on Earth would you want to search two indexes to come up with a single value? Wouldn't one index be faster? Not necessarily—the secret lies in updating the data.

Modifying Data with a Nonclustered Index

The commands used to modify data here aren't anything special—you use the standard T-SQL statements (INSERT, UPDATE, and DELETE) to accomplish these tasks. The interesting part is how SQL Server stores the data.

When inserting data using a nonclustered index on a heap, SQL Server doesn't have much work to do. It stuffs the data wherever it finds room and adds a new key value that points to the new record of the associated index pages. The process becomes a bit more complex when you throw a clustered index into the equation.

When you insert data into a table with a nonclustered and a clustered index in place, SQL Server physically inserts the data where it belongs in the order of the clustered index and updates the key values of the nonclustered index to point to the key values of the clustered index. When one of the data pages becomes full and you still have more data to insert, a page split occurs: half the records on the full page are moved to a new page to make room for more data. This process of page splitting is why the key values of the nonclustered index point to the clustered index instead of the data pages themselves.

When you're using a nonclustered index without a clustered index in place, each index page contains key values that point to the data. This pointer contains the location of the extent and the page and record number of the data being sought. If a page split occurred and the nonclustered index didn't use clustered index key values, then all the key values for the data that had been moved would be incorrect because all the pointers would be wrong. The entire nonclustered index would need to be rebuilt to reflect the changes. However, because the nonclustered index references the clustered index key values (not the actual data), all the pointers in the nonclustered index will be correct even after a page split has occurred, and the nonclustered index won't need to be rebuilt. That is why you reference the key values of a clustered index in a nonclustered index.

FIGURE 4.5   When you're using a nonclustered index on a heap, the leaf page contains a pointer to the data, not the data itself.

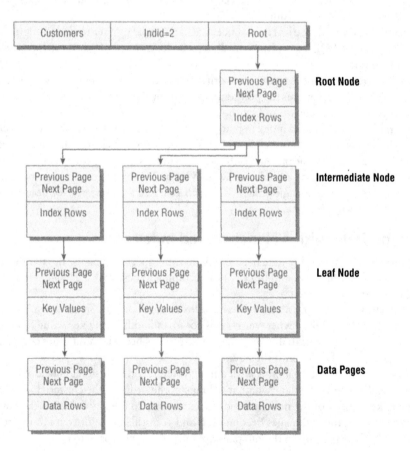

FIGURE 4.6   When you're using a nonclustered index on a clustered index, the leaf page contains a pointer to the clustered index value.

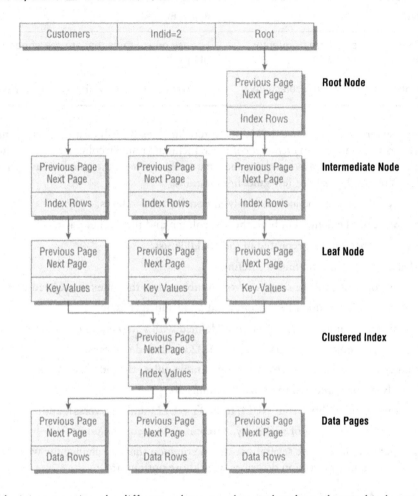

Table 4.1 summarizes the differences between clustered and nonclustered indexes.

TABLE 4.1   Differences between Clustered and Nonclustered Indexes

Clustered	Nonclustered
Only 1 allowed per table	Up to 249 allowed per table
Physically rearranges the data in the table to conform to the index constraints	Creates a separate list of key values with pointers to the location of the data in the data pages

TABLE 4.1 Differences between Clustered and Nonclustered Indexes *(continued)*

Clustered	Nonclustered
For use on columns that are frequently searched for ranges of data	For use on columns that are searched for single values
For use on columns with low selectivity	For use on columns with high selectivity

In SQL Server 2005, you can extend nonclustered indexes to include nonkey columns. This is referred to as an index with *included columns*. Including nonkey columns in a nonclustered index can significantly improve performance in queries where all the columns are included in the index. You need to keep a few guidelines in mind:

- Nonkey columns can be included only in nonclustered indexes.
- Columns can't be defined in both the key column and the INCLUDE list.
- Column names can't be repeated in the INCLUDE list.
- At least one key column must be defined.
- Nonkey columns can't be dropped from a table unless the index is dropped first.
- A column can't be both a key column and an included column.
- You must have at least one key column defined with a maximum of 16 key columns.
- You can have only up to a maximum of 1,023 included columns.
- Nonkey columns can't be dropped from a table unless the index is dropped first.
- The only changes allowed to nonkey columns are
    - changing nullability (from NULL to NOT NULL, and vice versa), and
    - increasing the length of varbinary, varchar, or nvarchar columns.

Both types of indexes have several options in common that can change the way the index functions. The following section describes what those options are.

Setting Relational Options

Clustered and nonclustered indexes share common options that can change the way the index works:

PAD_INDEX When this option is set to ON, the percentage of free space that is specified by the fill factor is applied to the intermediate-level pages of the index. When this is OFF, the intermediate-level pages are filled to the point that there is room for one new record.

FILLFACTOR This specifies how full the database engine should make each page during index creation or rebuild. Valid values are from 0 to 100. Values of 0 and 100 are the same in that they both tell the database engine to fill the page to capacity, leaving room for only one new record. Any other value specifies the amount of space to use for data; for instance, a fill factor of 70 tells the database engine to fill the page to 70 percent full with 30 percent free space.

Partitioned Indexes

As discussed in Chapter 3, tables can be partitioned for performance and storage reasons; well, so can indexes. It's usually best to partition a table and then create an index on the table so that SQL Server can partition the index for you based on the partition function and schema of the table. However, you can partition indexes separately. This is useful in the following cases:

- The base table isn't partitioned.

- Your index key is unique but doesn't contain the partition column of the table.

- You want the base table to participate in collocated JOINs with more tables using different JOIN columns.

If you decide you need to partition your index separately, then you need to keep the following in mind:

- The arguments of the partition function for the table and index must have the same datatype. For example, if your table is partitioned on a datetime column, your index must be partitioned on a datetime column.

- Your table and index must define the same number of partitions.

- The table and index must have the same partition boundaries.

SORT_IN_TEMPDB   When SQL Server builds an index, it must perform a sort on the table during the build. Setting this option to ON tells SQL Server to store the results of this intermediate sort in TempDB. This can speed up index creation if TempDB is on a different set of hard disks, but it also takes more disk space than OFF. Setting this option to OFF tells SQL Server to store the intermediate sort results in the same database as the table being indexed.

IGNORE_DUP_KEY   This option tells SQL Server what to do when it encounters a duplicate value while creating a unique index. OFF tells SQL Server to issue an error message and stop building the entire index. ON tells SQL Server to issue a warning message and that only the record with the duplicate value will fail. This can't be set to ON for XML indexes or indexes created on a view.

STATISTICS_NORECOMPUTE   For the query optimizer to work correctly, it must know what indexes are available and what data those indexes cover. That information is referred to as *statistics*. By default this option is OFF, which means SQL Server will automatically recompute statistics to keep them up-to-date. Setting this option to ON tells SQL Server not to update statistics, in which case you must do it yourself. You can turn this on when you want to schedule recomputation after-hours so it does not interfere with normal read-write operations.

DROP_EXISTING   Setting this option to ON allows you to create a new index with the same name as an existing index. If this option is OFF and you try to create a new index with the same name as an existing index, you will get an error. This is useful after making a large amount of changes (perhaps after a BULK INSERT operation) that may require you to re-create your index to reflect the changes to the underlying data.

ONLINE   In SQL Server 2005 Enterprise Edition, this option states whether the underlying tables and indexes are available for queries and data modification while indexing operations are taking place. This has two available settings:

OFF   Table locks are applied for the duration of the index operation. Clustered index operations acquire a schema lock, which prevents all user access to the underlying table for the duration of the index operation. Nonclustered operations acquire a shared lock on the table that allows for read operations but prevents data modification.

ON   Long-term table locks are not held for the duration of the index operation with this setting. During the main phase of the operation, SQL Server will first acquire an intent share lock, which allows queries and data modifications. Then SQL Server acquires a shared lock at the start of the index operation and quickly releases it. If a nonclustered index is being created, SQL Server will acquire a shared lock again at the end of the operation. If a clustered index is being created or dropped, or a nonclustered index is being rebuilt, SQL Server acquires a schema modification lock at the end of the operation. ONLINE can't be set to ON for indexes created on local temporary tables (tables whose names start with the # character).

ALLOW_ROW_LOCKS   Setting this to ON allows SQL Server to use row locks on an index. OFF does not allow row locks to be used.

ALLOW_PAGE_LOCKS   Setting this to ON allows SQL Server to use page locks on an index. OFF does not allow page locks to be used.

MAXDOP   SQL Server is capable of using multiple processors when executing a query. This option tells SQL Server how many processors it is allowed to use, or rather it sets the maximum degree or parallelism. Setting this to 1 prevents parallel plan execution, so only one processor is used. Anything greater than 1 sets the number of processors that SQL Server can use (in other words, 5 tells SQL Server to use as many as five processors). A setting of 0 tells SQL Server that it can use all available processors when querying this index; this is the default setting.

Now that you know when and where to create both types of indexes, you only need to know how to create them. In the next section, we'll cover the mechanics of creating indexes.

Creating Indexes

After all the work of planning your indexes, creating them is a breeze. You'll create a simple index on the HumanResources.EmployeePayHistory table of the AdventureWorks database in Exercise 4.2.

You can see how easy it is to create an index this way. If you want to make this a nonclustered index, all you need to do is leave the Create as Clustered box unchecked. There's nothing to it—the hard part is deciding what to index, as discussed earlier. Now you are ready for a more advanced use of indexes. The next section covers how to work with primary keys.

Using Primary Keys

A *primary key* ensures that each of the records in your table is unique in some way. It does this by creating a special type of index called a *unique index*. An index is ordinarily used to speed up access to data by reading all of the values in a column and keeping an organized list of where the record that contains that value is located in the table. A unique index not only generates that list, but it does not allow duplicate values to be stored in the index. If a user tries to enter a duplicate value in the indexed field, the unique index will return an error, and the data modification will fail.

EXERCISE 4.2

Creating an Index

1. Open SQL Server Management Studio, and connect using Windows Authentication.

2. Expand your server in Object Explorer, and then choose Databases ➢ AdventureWorks ➢ Tables ➢ HumanResources.EmployeePayHistory.

3. Right-click Indexes, and select New Index.

4. Limber up your typing fingers, and in the Index Name box, enter **idx_ModifiedDate**.

5. Select Nonclustered for the Index Type option.

6. Click the Add button next to the Index Key Columns grid.

7. Select the boxes next to the ModifiedDate column.

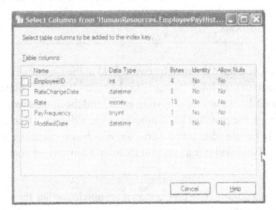

EXERCISE 4.2 *(continued)*

8. Click OK to return to the New Index dialog box.

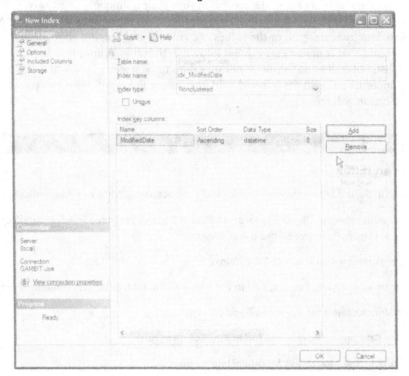

9. Click OK to create the index.

Suppose, for instance, you have defined the custid field in the Customers table as a primary key and that you have a customer with ID 1 already in the table. If one of your users tried to create another customer with ID 1, they would receive an error, and the update would be rejected because custid 1 is already listed in the primary key's unique index. Of course this is just for example, because your custid field has the identity property set, which automatically assigns a number with each new record inserted and will not allow you to enter a number of your own design.

    When a column can be used as a unique identifier for a row (such as an identity column), it is referred to as a *surrogate* or *candidate key*.

The primary key should consist of a column (or columns) that contains unique values. This makes an identity column the perfect candidate for becoming a primary key, because the values contained therein are unique by definition. If you do not have an identity column, make sure to choose a column, or combination of columns, in which each value is unique. The choice here is easy; in Exercise 4.1, you deleted the primary key for the HumanResources.EmployeePay-History table of the AdventureWorks database. In Exercise 4.3, you'll re-create that index using Management Studio.

EXERCISE 4.3

Creating a Primary Key

1. Open SQL Server Management Studio by selecting it from the SQL Server 2005 group in Programs on your Start menu, and connect using Windows Authentication.

2. In Object Explorer, expand Databases ➢ AdventureWorks ➢ Tables.

3. Right-click the HumanResources.EmployeePayHistory table, and select Modify.

4. Hold down the Shift key, and click the EmployeeID and RateChangeDate columns.

5. Right-click EmployeeID under Column Name, and select Set Primary Key. Notice that just to the left of both fields, a small key icon now denotes that this is the primary key.

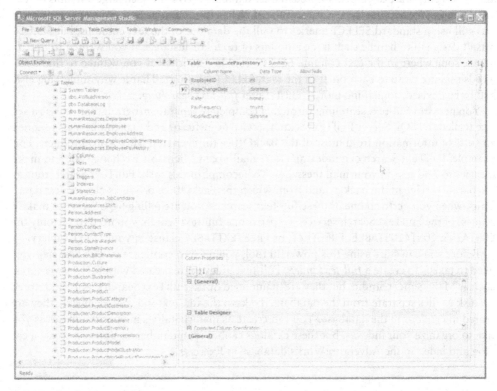

6. When you click the Save icon on the toolbar, SQL Server will create a new unique index, which ensures that no duplicate values can be entered in the custid field.

7. Close the Table Designer.

You can use primary keys with foreign keys to relate two tables on a common column. Foreign key relationships are beyond the scope of this book, so for a complete discussion of foreign key relationships, see *Mastering SQL Server 2005* (Sybex, 2006).

The index types discussed so far are great for most types of data, but not all. For larger datatypes, you have full-text search.

Using Full-Text Searching

People generally stored small amounts of data in their tables when databases first came into use. As time went on, however, people figured out that databases are excellent containers for all sorts of data, including massive amounts of text. Many companies, in fact, have entire libraries of corporate documents stored in their databases. To store such large amounts of text in a database, the text datatype was formulated. When this datatype first came out, everybody was still using standard SELECT queries to pull the data out of the text columns, but SELECT wasn't designed to handle such large amounts of text. For instance, if you wanted to find a phrase somewhere in the text column, SELECT couldn't do it. Or if you wanted to find two words that are close to each other in the text, SELECT fell short. That is why something else had to be devised, something more robust. Enter *full-text searching*.

You perform full-text searching through a completely separate program that runs as a service (called the SQL Server FullText Search service or msftesq) and that can be used to index all sorts of information from most of the BackOffice (or even non-Microsoft) products. For example, FullText Search can index an entire mailbox in Microsoft Exchange 2003 to make it easier to find text in your mail messages. To accomplish this task, FullText Search runs as a separate service in the background from which the BackOffice products can request data. Thus, when you perform one of these full-text searches, you are telling SQL Server to make a request of the FullText Search service. To perform a full-text search, you need to use only the CONTAINS, CONTAINSTABLE, FREETEXT, or FREETEXTTABLE clause in your SELECT query.

Before you can start using this powerful tool, you need to configure it. The first step you need to take is to create a *full-text index*. Full-text indexes are created with SQL Server tools, such as Management Studio, but they are maintained by the FullText Search service and stored on disk as files separate from the database. To keep the full-text indexes organized, they are stored in *catalogs* in the database. You can create as many catalogs in your databases as you like to organize your indexes, but these catalogs cannot span databases. You will create a catalog and index in the AdventureWorks database in Exercise 4.4.

You can find a detailed discussion of CONTAINS, CONTAINSTABLE, FREETEXT, and FREETEXTTABLE in *Mastering SQL Server 2005* (Sybex, 2006).

EXERCISE 4.4

Creating a Full-Text Catalog and Index

1. Open SQL Server Management Studio, and in Object Explorer expand Databases ➢ AdventureWorks ➢ Tables.

2. Right-click Production.Document, move to Full-Text Index, and click Define Full-Text Index.

3. On the first screen of the Full-Text Indexing Wizard, click Next.

4. Each table on which you create a full-text index must already have a unique index associated with it for full-text searching to work. In this instance, select the default PK_Document_DocumentID index, and click Next.

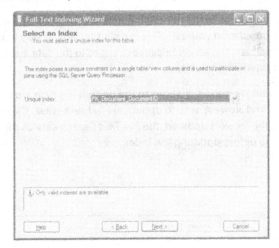

5. On the next screen, you are asked which column you want to full-text index. Document-Summary is the only nvarchar(max) column in the table, so it is the best candidate; select it here by checking the box next to it, and click Next.

6. On the next screen, you are asked when you want changes to the full-text index applied. These are your options:

Automatically means that the full-text index is updated with every change made to the table. This is the fastest, easiest way to keep full-text indexes up-to-date, but it can tax the server because it means changes to the table and index take place all at once.

Manually means changes to the underlying data are maintained, but you will have to schedule index population yourself. This is a slightly slower way to update the index, but it is not as taxing on the server because changes to the data are maintained but the index is not updated immediately.

Do Not Track Changes means changes to the underlying data are not tracked. This is the least taxing, and slowest, way to update the full-text index. Changes are not maintained so when the index is updated, the FullText Search service must read the entire table for changes before updating the index.

7. Choose Automatically, and click Next.

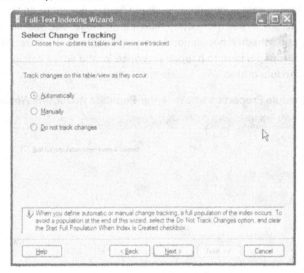

8. The next screen asks you to select a catalog. You'll need to create a new one here, because there are none available. In the Name field, enter **AdventureWorks Catalog**. You can also select a filegroup to place the catalog on; leave this as default, and click Next.

EXERCISE 4.4 *(continued)*

9. On the next screen, you are asked to create a schedule for automatically repopulating the full-text index. If your data is frequently updated, you will want to do this more often, maybe once a day. If it is read more often than it is changed, you should repopulate less frequently. You can schedule population for a single table or an entire catalog at a time. Here, you will set repopulation to happen just once for the entire catalog by clicking the New Catalog Schedule button.

10. On the New Schedule Properties screen, enter **Populate AdventureWorks**, and click OK.

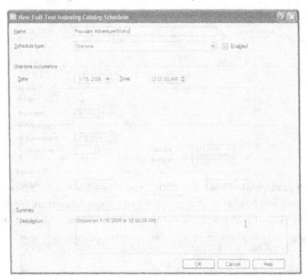

11. When you are taken back to the Full-Text Indexing Wizard, click Next.

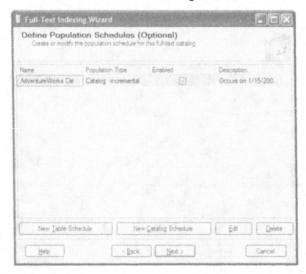

12. On the final screen of the wizard, you are given a summary of the choices you have made. Click Finish to create the index.

13. To see your new catalog and index, in Object Explorer expand the AdventureWorks ➢ Storage ➢ Full Text Catalogs.

14. Double-click the AdventureWorks catalog to open its properties.

15. Click Cancel to close the Properties window.

Now that you have a fully populated full-text index, you will be able to start querying it using full-text clauses.

Case Study: Indexing Product Catalog Tables

Let's revisit the AlsoRann company. When we first started working with the AlsoRann company, they already had an e-commerce website up and running. They had their entire product catalog on the website, and they were taking close to 400 orders every week.

When they first launched the site, everything ran fairly quickly; users could click the link for the product they wanted to see, and it would come right up. As the site grew and more products were added, the site started to slow down—so much so that users actually started to complain. Of course, many factors were involved, but one of the biggest problems was the indexes, or rather, lack of indexes, on the catalog tables.

You see, all of AlsoRann's competitors already had websites up when AlsoRann developed its website, so they wanted it up in a hurry. Therefore, they didn't pay enough attention to indexing on their catalog tables. When there were only a few queries against a small table, it seemed to work fine; however, when there were lots of queries against a larger table, the site slowed down.

The fix, at least for the catalog table, was simple. First, we had to look at the table schema:

ProdID	VendorID	ProdName	ProdDesc	Price	InStock
Int	int	varchar(100)	varchar(max)	money	int

Then we had to look at the queries against the table. The most popular was the following:

```
SELECT ProdName, ProdDesc, Price FROM ProdCatalog
➥WHERE Price BETWEEN('10.00' and '20.00')
```

Of course, there were different price ranges, but the query was essentially the same every time. When creating indexes for a table, you need to index the columns in the WHERE clause, in this case, the Price column. So we had the index column candidate, now we needed the type. Because customers were always querying for a range of data, the logical choice was a clustered index.

With this new index in place, we were able to cut the response time nearly in half for the product catalog pages on the website.

Summary

You first learned in this chapter how SQL Server accesses and stores data when no index is in place. Without a clustered index, the table is called a *heap*, and the data is stored on a first-come, first-served basis. When accessing this data, SQL Server must perform a table scan, which means SQL Server must read every record in the table to find the data you're seeking. This can make data access slow on larger tables; but on smaller tables that are about one extent in size, table scans can be faster than indexing.

Next you learned how to accelerate data access by using indexes. The first index you looked at was the clustered index. This type of index physically rearranges the data in the database file. This property makes the clustered index ideal for columns that are constantly being searched for ranges of data and that have low selectivity, meaning several duplicate values.

Next came nonclustered indexes. These indexes don't physically rearrange the data in the database but rather create pointers to the actual data. This type of index is best suited to high-selectivity tables (few duplicate values) where single records are desired rather than ranges. Then you learned how to create indexes using SQL Server Management Studio.

Finally, you found that full-text searching could greatly enhance SELECT queries by allowing you to find words or phrases in your text fields.

With this newfound knowledge about indexing, you'll be able to speed up data access for your users. However, what if you don't want your users to see all the data in the tables? In the next chapter, we'll show you how to limit the data available to your users by using views.

Exam Essentials

Know the difference between clustered and nonclustered indexes. Know the difference between clustered and nonclustered indexes. Clustered indexes physically rearrange the data in a table to match the definition of the index. Nonclustered indexes are separate objects in the database that refer to the original table, without rearranging the table in any way.

Understand full-text indexing. Understand what full-text indexing is for and how to manage it. Full-text indexing runs as a separate service and is used to search columns of text for phrases instead of just single words. You have to repopulate the index occasionally to keep it up-to-date with the underlying table. SQL Server can do this for you automatically if you want.

Know the relational options for creating indexes. In the "Setting Relational Options" section, you learned about the different relational options and what they do. Familiarize yourself with these options for the exam.

Review Questions

1. You have a table that holds customer data as shown here:

ID	FirstName	LastName	Address	City	State	PostalCode	Phone
1	John	Jones	402 Main	San Jose	CA	94602	1112223333
2	Andrea	Elliott	301 N. 3rd	Anchorage	AK	99508	4445556666
3	Bob	Simpson	2058 Oak	Fresno	CA	96105	7778889999
4	Dan	Rosman	502 Winchester	Fairfield	CA	94533	1114447777

Which of these columns has the lowest selectivity?

A. State

B. Phone

C. FirstName

D. LastName

2. In the table from question 1, your users frequently query the database for phone numbers based on the customer's last name. For example, the query to find the phone number for the customer with the last name of Simpson would look like this:

```
SELECT FirstName, LastName, Phone
➡FROM Customers WHERE LastName = 'Simpson'
```

You are going to create an index on the LastName column, and there are no existing indexes in place on the table. What type of index should it be, and why?

A. Clustered, because the lastname column has low selectivity

B. Nonclustered, because the lastname column has low selectivity

C. Clustered, because the lastname column has high selectivity

D. Nonclustered, because the lastname column has high selectivity

3. You need to create a nonclustered index on one of your tables. You want to make certain that 30 percent of each index page is left open so there is enough room to insert new leaf nodes in the index when new records are inserted into the table. How should you create the index?

A. Create the index with a 30 percent fill factor.

B. Create the index with a 70 percent fill factor.

C. Create the index using the OPENSPACE(30) function.

D. Do nothing; SQL Server leaves 30 percent of each index page open by default.

4. You have a large table that is in use 24/7. You need to be able to perform maintenance on the indexes on this table, but you can't take the table offline to perform the maintenance. What can you do to make the table available while performing index operations?

   A. Create the index with UPDATEABLE = ON.

   B. Create the index with ONLINE = ON.

   C. Create the index with MAXDOP = 0.

   D. You can't do anything; the table will not be available during index operations.

5. Which versions of SQL Server allow you to create an ONLINE index? (Choose all that apply.)

   A. Express Edition

   B. Workgroup Edition

   C. Standard Edition

   D. Enterprise Edition

6. You have a table that contains information about books you sell. One of the columns is a varchar(max) column that contains a large amount of text describing each book. You want to be able to query the data in this column for phrases instead of just single words. What can you do?

   A. Create a clustered index on the column.

   B. Create a nonclustered index on the column.

   C. Create a full-text index on the column.

   D. Create an ONLINE index on the column.

7. You have a SQL Server 2005 that houses a busy database containing your company's product catalog. This table is being queried all the time, and although your server can handle the current load, you are not sure if it can handle the load of a full-text index population. You need to create a full-text index on the table, but you want to populate it manually, off-hours. You do not want any impact on performance during working hours. What should you do?

   A. When creating the full-text index, tell SQL Server to automatically apply changes to the index.

   B. When creating the full-text index, tell SQL Server to manually apply changes to the index.

   C. When creating the full-text index, tell SQL Server not to track changes on the table.

   D. Do nothing; SQL Server populates full-text indexes off-hours by default.

8. You have a server with several hard disk sets; all of your system databases, including TempDB, Master, and Model, are on one disk set, and a user database that you will be updating is on a disk set of its own. You need to create an index on a large table, and you want to make it as fast as possible. You are not worried about system resources such as disk space, processor time, or memory used. What can you do to create this index as fast as possible?

   A. Create the index with MAXDOP = 0.

   B. Create the index with STATISTICS_NORECOMPUTE = ON.

   C. Create the index with SORT_IN_TEMPDB = ON.

   D. Create the index with PAD_INDEX = ON.

9. You have a table containing product information that your users query frequently. They specifically use this query most often:

```
SELECT Name, Description, Vendor, InStock, Price
➥FROM Products where Name = 'name'
```

You have a nonclustered index on this table on the Name column, but your users are complaining that the query is still too slow. What can you do to speed it up?

A. Modify the index to include the Description, Vendor, InStock, and Price columns as non-key columns.

B. Create a new nonclustered index on the Description, Vendor, InStock, and Price columns.

C. Create a new clustered index on the Description, Vendor, InStock, and Price columns.

D. You can't do anything to speed up this query.

10. You have a SQL Server 2005 that houses a busy database containing your company's product catalog. This table is being queried all the time, and although your server can handle the current load, you are not sure if it can handle the extra load of recalculating index statistics. What can you do to minimize the overhead required to recalculate index statistics?

A. Create the index with ALLOW_ROW_LOCKS = ON.

B. Create the index with ALLOW_PAGE_LOCKS = ON.

C. Create the index with STATISTICS_NORECOMPUTE = ON.

D. Create the index with SORT_IN_TEMPDB = ON.

11. You have a table containing employee information that your users query frequently. They specifically use this query most often:

```
SELECT FirstName, LastName, Address, Phone
➥FROM Employees WHERE SSN = 'ssn'
```

You have a clustered index on this table on the SSN column, but your users are complaining that the query is still too slow. What can you do to speed it up?

A. Modify the index to include the FirstName, LastName, Address, and Phone columns as nonkey columns.

B. Create a new nonclustered index on the FirstName, LastName, Address, and Phone columns.

C. Create a new clustered index on the FirstName, LastName, Address, and Phone columns.

D. You can't do anything to speed up this query.

12. You have a machine with eight processors, 12GB of RAM, and a RAID-5 hard disk array. You want SQL Server to query indexes as fast as possible, so you decide to let SQL Server use all available processors when querying data. What setting do you need to use to configure this?

A. MAXDOP = 0.

B. MAXDOP = 1.

C. MAXDOP = ALL.

D. None; SQL Server will use all processors by default.

13. You have a SQL Server 2005 that houses your company's product catalog database. You need to create and maintain a full-text index on the table. The server has more than enough system resources, and you want to make this index as easy as possible to maintain. What should you do?

A. When creating the full-text index, tell SQL Server to automatically apply changes to the index.

B. When creating the full-text index, tell SQL Server to manually apply changes to the index.

C. When creating the full-text index, tell SQL Server not to track changes on the table.

D. Do nothing; SQL Server automatically populates full-text by default.

14. You work for a small company that has a limited budget for servers. One of your main servers has eight processors. To conserve hardware resources, you decide to run SQL Server and SharePoint Services on this machine, which means you need to limit the resources SQL Server uses while running queries. What can you do to configure SQL Server to use only four of the available processors when querying an index?

A. Set MAXDOP = 4.

B. Set MAXDOP = 0.

C. Set MAXDOP = 1.

D. You can't do anything; SQL Server uses all available processors for every query.

15. You have created a clustered index on a table with a fill factor of 72 percent. When a data page in this index fills to capacity, what happens?

A. SQL Server moves 25 percent of the data to a new data page to maintain the fill factor and make room for new data.

B. SQL Server moves 75 percent of the data to a new data page to maintain the fill factor and make room for new data.

C. SQL Server moves 50 percent of the data to a new data page to make room for new data.

D. SQL Server starts filling a new page and leaves the current pages intact.

16. You have a large table with several thousand rows of product data. You have just imported a whole new catalog of seasonal data that has changed most of the data in the products table. You have a nonclustered index on the table that is now out-of-date. You need to bring it back up-to-date quickly. What can you do?

A. Re-create the index using STATISTICS_NORECOMPUTE = ON.

B. Re-create the index using DROP_EXISTING = ON.

C. Drop the existing index manually, and re-create it.

D. Do nothing; SQL Server will bring the index back up-to-date automatically.

17. You have a table with customer information that is updated frequently. You need to create an index on this table, but you need to make sure there is enough room at every level of the index for the constant influx of new records. What can you do to accomplish this goal? (Choose all that apply.)

 A. Create the index with FILLFACTOR = 0.

 B. Create the index with FILLFACTOR = 70.

 C. Create the index with PAD_INDEX = ON.

 D. Create the index with PAD_INDEX = OFF.

18. You have a table that contains employee information. Human Resources frequently queries this table using a query similar to the following:

```
SELECT FirstName, LastName, Address, Phone
➡FROM Employees WHERE SSN = 'ssn'
```

You need to create an index to speed up this query. What type should you create?

 A. Create a clustered index on the SSN column.

 B. Create a nonclustered index on the SSN column.

 C. Create a full-text index on the SSN column.

19. You have a table that contains product data. The table has a column that contains the product ID but because of some data entry problems, several of the products have been entered more than once. You need to create a clustered unique index on the product table. How can you do this with duplicate data in the column?

 A. Create the index with ONERROR=CONTINUE.

 B. Create the index with IGNORE_DUP_KEY = ON.

 C. Create the index with IGNORE_DUP_KEY = OFF.

 D. You will have to manually remove the duplicate values before creating the index.

20. When monitoring SQL Server using Profiler, you find many table scans are being performed on the Orders table in your sales database. What should you do?

 A. Create a clustered or nonclustered index on the table.

 B. Create a clustered or nonclustered index with IGNORE_DUP_KEY = ON.

 C. Create a full-text index on the table.

 D. Do nothing; table scans are normal on heavily used tables.

Answers to Review Questions

1. A. Selectivity is the number of duplicate values in a column; low selectivity means the column has many duplicate values. In this case, the State column has the lowest selectivity.

2. A. Selectivity is the number of duplicate values in a column; low selectivity means the column has many duplicate values. Clustered indexes physically rearrange the data in the table, arranging the records so they are in sequence. This makes the LastName column a good candidate for a clustered index because your users are searching for a range of values in the LastName column.

3. B. Specifying a fill factor of 70 percent tells SQL Server to fill the index up to 70 percent, leaving 30 percent open. Also, OPENSPACE(30) is not a valid function.

4. B. If you have SQL Server 2005 Enterprise Edition, you can create the index with ONLINE = ON to allow users to modify data during index operations. MAXDOP tells SQL Server how many processors it can use while querying an index, and UPDATEABLE is not a valid option.

5. D. Only Enterprise Edition will allow you to use ONLINE indexes. Developer Edition will also allow ONLINE indexes, but it is not licensed to be used in a production environment, so it is not listed as an option.

6. C. Full-text indexes are perfect for columns that have nothing but large amounts of text. You can create this index and query it for phrases instead of just single words like a standard SELECT query. Clustered and nonclustered indexes, ONLINE or not, do not affect the way text columns are searched.

7. C. To incur the least amount of overhead, you need to tell SQL Server not to track changes when updates are made to the table. You will be able to apply all updates to the index yourself manually whenever you like, usually by scheduling a job with the SQL Agent. Telling SQL Server to automatically track and apply changes incurs the most amount of overhead because all updates are applied to the index immediately. Manually tells SQL Server to track changes to the table but not to update the full-text index so it does not incur as much overhead as the automatic setting, but it incurs more overhead than not tracking changes at all.

8. C. MAXDOP tells SQL Server how many processors it can use when querying the index. STATISTICS_NORECOMPUTE tells SQL Server not to automatically update statistics after the index has been created. PAD_INDEX works with FILLFACTOR to keep a percent of intermediate page space free. SORT_IN_TEMPDB tells SQL Server to store the results of the intermediate sort that it generates in TempDB. This can speed up the creation of an index when TempDB is on a separate disk from the database containing the new index.

9. A. You can include the remaining columns in the query as nonkey columns in the index. This can significantly increase performance on the query.

10. C. To incur the least amount of overhead, you need to tell SQL Server not automatically recomputed statistics. You can do this yourself by scheduling a job to run after-hours to update the statistics.

11. D. You already have a clustered index on this table, so you can't create another one. You can't add nonkey columns to a clustered index. Adding a new nonclustered index on the remaining columns will not do any good because they are not in the WHERE clause, so your users will just have to deal with slowness until you can upgrade the hardware.

12. D. MAXDOP = 1 tells SQL Server to use only one processor when querying an index. MAXDOP = 0 would accomplish your goal of using all processors; however, because this is the default setting, you are not required to use it, and you do not need to add any clauses. Also, MAXDOP = ALL is not a valid setting.

13. A. Telling SQL Server to automatically track and apply changes is the easiest way to maintain a full-text index because SQL Server will handle maintenance for you. This method incurs the most amount of overhead because all updates are applied to the index immediately, but your server can handle it in this instance. Manually tells SQL Server to track changes to the table but not to update the full-text index so it does not incur as much overhead as the automatic setting, but it incurs more overhead than not tracking changes at all. Telling SQL Server not to track changes when updates are made to the table would require the most administration because you would need to apply all updates to the index yourself manually.

14. A. Setting MAXDOP to 4 instructs SQL Server to use only four processors when querying the index. A setting of 0 allows SQL Server to use all available processors, and a setting of 1 permits the use of only a single processor.

15. C. When a page fills to capacity, SQL Server moves half of the data to a new page to make room for more data. This is called a *page split*. SQL Server does not maintain the fill factor automatically; it is reset only when the index is rebuilt.

16. B. The fastest way to bring the index back up-to-date is to re-create it using the DROP_ EXISTING clause. This tells SQL Server to drop the existing index and create it again using the same properties as the original index. If you drop the index yourself and create it again, you will need to specify all the properties over again. STATISTICS_NORECOMPUTE = ON tells SQL Server not to automatically recompute statistics about the index; it has no effect on how quickly the index is brought back up-to-date in this case.

17. B, C. A FILLFACTOR of 0 tells SQL Server to fill the index pages to capacity, leaving room for only one new record. PAD_INDEX = OFF does the same thing for intermediate-level pages. Setting the FILLFACTOR to 70 percent tells SQL Server to fill the pages to 70 percent full, and setting PAD_INDEX = ON tells SQL Server to apply the FILLFACTOR setting to the intermediate pages, in this case filling them to 70 percent full.

18. B. Each employee has a unique Social Security number, so this query will search only for a single record, not a range of records. Clustered indexes are best for searching for a range of data; nonclustered indexes are best when you will be returning a single value. A full-text index is useful for searching for phrases in a column of text; it has no bearing on this query whatsoever.

19. B. If you set IGNORE_DUP_KEY = ON, then SQL Server will create the index in spite of the duplicate values, but the duplicated records will not be included in the index. If you set IGNORE_ DUP_KEY = OFF, then the SQL Server will not create the index because of the duplicated records. Also, ONERROR=CONTINUE is not a valid option.

20. A. A table scan occurs when someone queries a table that does not have an index; they slow down the server and need to be fixed. To avoid table scans, create a clustered or nonclustered index on the table; no relational clauses are required. A full-text index will not stop table scans from occurring.

Chapter 5

Introducing More Database Objects

MICROSOFT EXAM OBJECTIVES COVERED IN THIS CHAPTER:

✓ **Implement stored procedures.**

- Create a stored procedure.
- Recompile a stored procedure.

✓ **Implement triggers.**

- Create a trigger.
- Create DDL triggers for responding to database structure changes.
- Identify recursive triggers.
- Identify nested triggers.
- Identify transaction triggers.

✓ **Implement functions.**

- Create a function.
- Identify deterministic versus nondeterministic functions.

✓ **Create user-defined types.**

- Create a Transact-SQL user-defined type.
- Create a CLR user-defined type.

Databases consist of more than just tables and relational data; inside the data files are objects such as views, stored procedures, triggers, functions, indexes, and more. For example, to implement business logic within the database, you can create stored procedures and triggers and even use functions to perform calculations or manipulations on your data. You can use these objects to improve the performance of the database, help secure the database, and implement business logic within the database.

It is important to know how you put all these pieces together, because every single item in SQL Server 2005 has its purpose. Since the integration of the *.NET CLR* in SQL Server 2005, you have full-featured tools intended for specific purposes. For example, the addition of the .NET Framework hosted inside the SQL Server process allows you to create custom assemblies containing managed code procedures, user-defined types, triggers, and managed code functions. These various capabilities all have their best practices and usage guidelines.

In this chapter, we'll explain the database objects we haven't covered yet. We'll start by covering stored procedures and their functionality. Then we'll move into triggers and show how to work with functions. We'll cover how to create triggers and determine their scope, and then we'll introduce user-defined types. Since it is important to understand when you are going to use managed code versus T-SQL, we'll focus on best practices for the two approaches and when to use which implementation.

Introducing Stored Procedures

Stored procedures in SQL Server are similar to the procedures you write in other programming languages. Specifically, a *stored procedure* is a predefined batch of code that is stored as an object in the database. In SQL Server you have various types of stored procedures, and we'll cover them in the following sections.

A stored procedure has the ability to accept parameters but doesn't necessarily need to use parameters. Within a stored procedure, you can use almost all T-SQL statements, except another CREATE PROCEDURE statement.

Understanding the Types of Stored Procedures

SQL Server consists of several types of procedures:

- System stored procedures
- T-SQL stored procedures

- CLR procedures
- Extended stored procedures

Introducing System Stored Procedures

You can perform a lot of administrative tasks within SQL Server by using built-in system stored procedures. These stored procedures have been predefined within a database to perform maintenance and management activities, such as sending an email message from within a T-SQL batch or providing system information about an object stored in a database. Most system stored procedures start with an SP_ prefix, so it is recommended that when you create a user-defined procedure, you don't use the SP_ prefix. In SQL Server 2005, system stored procedures are physically stored in the Resource database; logically they will appear in the sys schema of a user database (see Chapter 6 for more information).

You can view the system stored procedures and all the other programmable objects using Object Explorer in SQL Server Management Studio, as displayed in Figure 5.1.

The Resource database is a hidden system database that contains the physical storage for most SQL Server system database objects such as internal tables and system stored procedures.

FIGURE 5.1   System stored procedures in Object Explorer

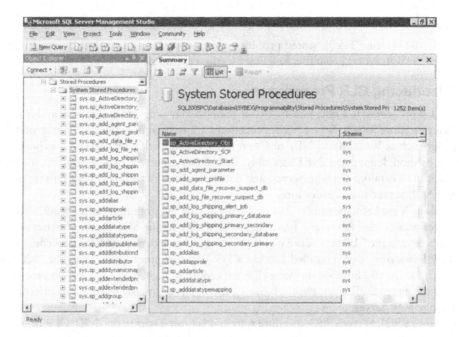

Introducing T-SQL Stored Procedures

Stored procedures are intended to encapsulate code that will be reused, so a *T-SQL stored procedure* is a batch of T-SQL statements stored within SQL Server as a database object. T-SQL stored procedures can, but don't necessarily have to, accept parameters for input, and they can return various output parameters.

T-SQL stored procedures provide the following benefits:

- Reduced network traffic

  - They're centrally stored on the server, so you get reduced network traffic instead of passing the entire T-SQL batch from the client application.

- Permission-based execution

  - To execute a T-SQL stored procedure, you need to have valid permissions. This gives you the ability to hide the complexity of the database but also allows you to have EXECUTE permission on the stored procedure without needing access to the underlying objects.

  - In SQL Server 2005 you can specify the security context in which a stored procedure must run (OWNER/CALLER/USER).

- Code reusability

  - When a T-SQL stored procedure is executed, the procedure will be compiled and stored in cache for later retrieval

- Security

  - A T-SQL stored procedure is a good way to prevent *SQL injection attacks*.

  - By creating T-SQL stored procedures with parameters, you restrict access to the full T-SQL syntax, resulting in a more secure environment.

Introducing CLR Procedures

A *CLR procedure* is a reference to a CLR method that supports parameters and is cataloged as a procedure in SQL Server. CLR procedures are written in a .NET CLR interpretable language such as Visual Basic .NET or C#. A .NET Framework CLR method is exposed to SQL as a method defined in a .NET assembly. Before you can use a CLR procedure, the assembly needs to be cataloged in SQL Server, and the method within the assembly needs to be exposed as a SQL Server stored procedure.

Using Visual Studio, you can automatically deploy the stored procedure from within a SQL Server project. (See Exercise 5.1 later in this chapter.) Within SQL Server, the user who references or calls the CLR procedure won't see any difference between a CLR procedure call and a T-SQL procedure call; it is called, just like a T-SQL stored procedure is, using the EXEC keyword.

The scope and functionality of a CLR procedure is huge. You can create a procedure that uses the entire .NET Framework, meaning it will allow you to get access to external objects outside SQL Server.

Since a SQL Server CLR procedure runs and is hosted within the .NET CLR, it is common to use CLR or *managed procedures* for complex calculations and for access to objects such as the network or file system.

Introducing Extended Stored Procedures

In previous editions of SQL Server, extended stored procedures were frequently used to provide access to objects or methods that run outside the SQL Server process. However, in future versions of SQL Server, extended stored procedures will be removed, so you should instead use a CLR procedure, which will generally give you better execution and performance. The best practice is to rewrite the extended stored procedure in a managed code procedure because of additional security.

Creating Stored Procedures

To create a stored procedure, of course the code you will use will depend on the type of procedure you are creating (managed or T-SQL). A T-SQL stored procedure follows the syntax covered in the next section. To create a CLR stored procedure, you will use a development tool such as Visual Studio. The actual syntax in Visual Studio will then depend on the language in which you program (covering the syntax to create managed stored procedure is out of scope for the exam certification).

Creating a T-SQL Stored Procedure

You can create a stored procedure by using the CREATE PROCEDURE syntax:

```
CREATE { PROC | PROCEDURE }
➥[schema_name.] procedure_name [ ; number ]
    [ { @parameter [ type_schema_name. ] data_type }
        [ VARYING ] [ = default ] [ [ OUT [ PUT ]
    ] [ ,...n ]
[ WITH <procedure_option> [ ,...n ]
[ FOR REPLICATION ]
AS { <sql_statement> [;][ ...n ] | <method_specifier> }
[;]
<procedure_option> ::=
    [ ENCRYPTION ]
    [ RECOMPILE ]
    [ EXECUTE_AS_Clause ]

<sql_statement> ::=
{ [ BEGIN ] statements [ END ] }

<method_specifier> ::=
EXTERNAL NAME assembly_name.class_name.method_name
```

A stored procedure can contain one or more parameters, and you must supply the value when the stored procedure is called, except if a default value is provided or the value is set by another parameter.

The easiest ways to create a T-SQL stored procedure are by starting a new database query in Microsoft SQL Server Management Studio, by using a predefined template from Template Explorer (see Figure 5.2), or by starting with an empty database query.

FIGURE 5.2   Using a predefined template from Template Explorer

Let's look at a basic procedure example. In the following example, you'll create a procedure that will convert an amount in U.S. dollars to euros, using a fixed currency conversion rate:

```
CREATE PROCEDURE STP_USD_to_EUR (@USD money)
AS BEGIN
    Select @USD / 1.10
END
```

To execute the stored procedure, call the stored procedure using the EXEC statement:

```
EXEC STP_USD_to_EUR 500
```

This returns the following result set:

```
454.54545454
```

Instead of writing this example as a stored procedure you an also write it as a user defined function, which in this example might be a preferred method. See Exercise 5.3 where the same example is written as a user defined function.

Creating and Deploying a CLR Procedure

You write a CLR or managed code procedure in a CLR-supported language such as Visual Basic .NET or C#. From within Visual Studio 2005, you can create a SQL Server project as displayed in Figure 5.3.

FIGURE 5.3   A CLR code procedure

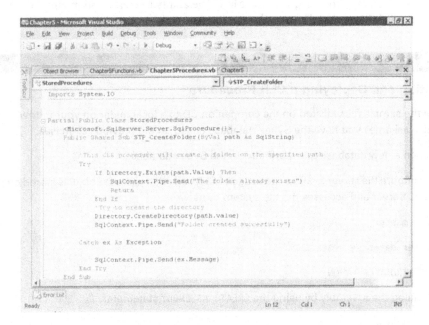

When a project is deployed to SQL Server, the assembly or DLL file will be cataloged in the SQL database. These objects are displayable by querying the `sys.assemblies` system view. However, it is possible to deploy a solution from within Visual Studio 2005. It is common for a database administrator to catalog the assembly and then create procedures from the methods exposed within the library (DLL or assembly).

Enabling the Server for CLR Support

Before being able to use CLR managed objects, you first need to enable the server for CLR support. The CLR integration is a feature; it can be enabled or disabled.

You do this by executing the following syntax:

```
sp_configure 'clr_enabled',1
reconfigure
```

When a call to a CLR procedure is made without having the CLR enabled, an error message that says the .NET Framework is not enabled will appear.

The steps involved to use CLR-integrated functionality are as follows:

1. Enable CLR support on the server.

2. Catalog the assembly within the database.

3. Create the procedure from the assembly.

Figure 5.3 displayed an example of a CLR procedure written in Visual Basic. Since you did not install Visual Studio 2005, you don't have the ability to create and manipulate the code; however, you will catalog the procedure in Exercise 5.1.

EXERCISE 5.1

Creating and Deploying a CLR Procedure

Install the sample files located on the companion CD to a local folder on your C drive. This exercise assumes you have the Sybex database based on the previous exercises.

1. Open a new database query window in the Sybex database.

2. Configure the server to allow the usage of CLR code that accesses objects stored outside SQL Server and accesses the file system or network:

   USE master

   alter database sybex

   SET TRUSTWORTHY ON

3. Catalog the assembly by using the CREATE ASSEMBLY statement:

   USE SYBEX

   CREATE ASSEMBLY CHAPTER5

   FROM 'C:\SYBEX\70-431\Chapter 5\SourceCode\Chapter5\bin\Chapter5.dll'

   WITH PERMISSION_SET = EXTERNAL_ACCESS

4. After you have cataloged the assembly, create a stored procedure that references the assembly and method:

   CREATE PROCEDURE [dbo].[STP_Createfolder]

   @foldername [nvarchar](200) OUTPUT WITH EXECUTE AS CALLER

   AS EXTERNAL NAME [Chapter5].[Chapter5.StoredProcedures].[Createfolder]

5. Test the stored procedure by using the EXEC statement:

   EXEC STP_Createfolder 'c:\CHAPTER5'

6. You might get an error message that states that .NET Framework is disabled, like so:

Msg 6263, Level 16, State 1, Line 2

Execution of user code in the .NET Framework is disabled. Enable "clr enabled" configuration option.

If you receive this error message, you need to enable the CLR by executing the following code after configuring the stored procedure again:

```
sp_configure 'clr_enabled',1
```

```
reconfigure
```

7. Next, try to create the folder again:

```
EXEC STP_Createfolder 'c:\CHAPTER5'
```

8. This will result in the following:

```
The folder is created successfully
```

Create Assembly Permissions

When cataloging an assembly, you have the ability to specify what security the assembly needs in SQL Server. You do this by assigning the permission using the WITH PERMISSION_SET option on the assembly. The permissions you can set are as follows:

- SAFE: Only safe code that runs inside the SQL process can be executed.

- EXTERNAL_ACCESS: The managed code needs access to files, networks, environmental variables, and the registry.

- UNSAFE: The managed code needs access to the Win32 subsystem, or unrestricted access to resources, both within and outside an instance of SQL Server.

Recompiling Stored Procedures

When a stored procedure executes for the first time, the query execution plan will be calculated and stored in a cache. Every subsequent run of a stored procedure will use the same execution plan. If an underlying table used by the stored procedure is modified, it will invalidate the cache and force the stored procedure to *recompile*. When a new index is added to a table or a table has been updated extensively, however, the optimization of the stored procedure and query execution plan are not recalculated before the next time the stored procedure is compiled. Therefore, it might be useful to force the stored procedure to recompile. If a stored procedure based on its parameters should generate different execution plans, you can create the stored procedure WITH RECOMPILE option. This will force the stored procedure to recompile on every execution.

Another way to force a stored procedure to recompile on the next execution is by executing the sp_recompile system stored procedure.

Creating a stored procedure WITH RECOMPILE option will force the stored procedure to recompile. However, this option is not used frequently because it slows down the execution of a stored procedure.

Introducing Triggers

SQL Server has different options to implement business logic and data integrity. You have the option to implement constraints, or you can achieve your requirements by implementing *triggers*.

A trigger has the same functionality as a stored procedure; it consists of a predefined set of T-SQL code that will execute. A stored procedure is called by using an EXECUTE statement, but a trigger will fire automatically when the event where it is defined occurs; it can never be called directly.

When combining triggers and constraints on a table, the constraints will fire before the trigger does. If a constraint violation occurs, the trigger won't fire. The constraint is proactive, and the trigger is reactive.

Understanding the Types of Triggers

In SQL Server 2005 you have two types of triggers:

- Data Manipulation Language (DML) triggers
- Data Definition Language (DDL) triggers

DML triggers existed in previous editions of SQL Server, but DDL triggers are one of the key new features that will ease your work when logging or even when manipulating DDL instructions.

In the following sections, you'll take a look at each of these trigger types.

Understanding DML Triggers

DML triggers execute automatically when a DML action (insert, delete, update) is executed against a table or a view. Within a trigger you have the ability to work with the data affected by the DML statement along with the original data.

By default, triggers in SQL Server are AFTER triggers, which means the trigger executes after the statement that triggered it completes.

> On a table, you can create multiple triggers for the same action. The order triggers are fired in is determined by the `sp_settriggerorder` stored procedure.

Understanding How a DML Trigger Works

When performing a trigger action, two special tables are used within the trigger action: the inserted and the deleted table. These tables are managed by SQL Server and will be used to affect the DML statement. You will use these tables in various situations when you want to look at the rows affected by an insert, delete, or update statement.

Understanding How an *INSERT* Trigger Works

Figure 5.4 shows how an INSERT trigger works. During a transaction, the inserted data will be available in a table called *inserted*. Within the trigger action, you have the ability to retrieve and manipulate values inside that inserted table.

FIGURE 5.4   How an INSERT trigger works

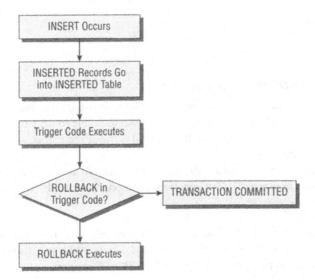

The inserted table will have a copy of all the affected rows during an INSERT statement. This is where you have the ability to interfere or interact with the records inserted.

Since the default behavior of a trigger is an AFTER action, you need to perform a rollback of the transaction if you don't want to perform the insert action.

Understanding How a *DELETE* Trigger Works

In the case of a DELETE statement, the deleted statement will have a copy of all the affected rows during that action. Again, if you don't want to perform the actual delete, you need to roll back the transaction. Figure 5.5 shows how a DELETE trigger works with the deleted table.

FIGURE 5.5   How a DELETE trigger works

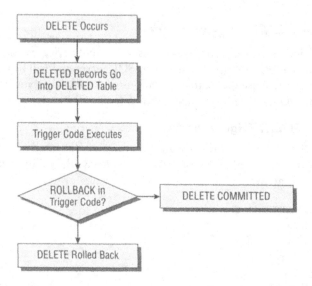

Understanding How an *UPDATE* Trigger Works

You probably would assume for an UPDATE trigger there would be an updated table, but there isn't.

The UPDATE statement will use the deleted table and the inserted table to keep track of the records that have been modified. The OLD status will be loaded in the deleted table, and the NEW status will be saved in the inserted table.

Often these tables are joined to provide you with a result set of the old and new value of an update action. Figure 5.6 shows how an UPDATE trigger uses the inserted and the deleted statement.

Using *INSTEAD OF* Triggers

Since an AFTER trigger works after the actual action already took place, if you want to avoid or revert this, you need to roll back the transaction. Since SQL Server 2000, you also have the ability to work more or less proactively by performing INSTEAD OF triggers.

As you can assume from its name, you perform a different task with INSTEAD OF performing the actual DML statement. Figure 5.7 shows you how an INSTEAD OF trigger does not perform the actual action but does something else instead.

FIGURE 5.6 How an UPDATE trigger works

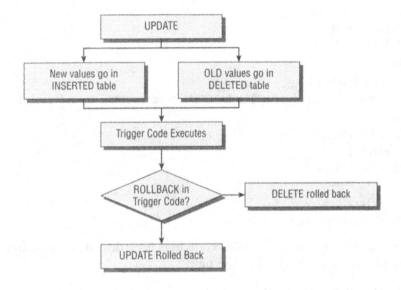

FIGURE 5.7 INSTEAD OF trigger

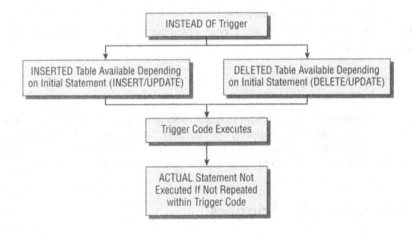

Creating a DML Trigger

The following shows how to create a DML trigger:

```
CREATE TRIGGER [ schema_name . ]trigger_name
ON { table | view }
[ WITH <dml_trigger_option> [ ,...n ] ]
{ FOR | AFTER | INSTEAD OF }
{ [ INSERT ] [ , ] [ UPDATE ] [ , ] [ DELETE ] }
[ WITH APPEND ]
[ NOT FOR REPLICATION ]
AS { sql_statement  [ ; ] [ ...n ] | EXTERNAL NAME <method specifier [ ; ] > }

<dml_trigger_option> ::=
    [ ENCRYPTION ]
    [ EXECUTE AS Clause ]

<method_specifier> ::=
    assembly_name.class_name.method_name
```

The following trigger example will block records from being deleted on the products table if more than one record is deleted at the same time:

```
CREATE TRIGGER trg_delete on products FOR DELETE
AS
BEGIN
 If (select count(*) from deleted) > 1
 RAISERROR ('You can not delete more than one record at the same time',16,1)
 ROLLBACK TRANSACTION
END
```

Raiserror is a statement that will raise an error message that consists of an error severity level and a state identifier. Severity levels from 0 through 18 can be specified by any user. Severity levels from 19 through 25 can only be specified by members of the **sysadmin** fixed server role.

Understanding DDL Triggers

In SQL Server 2005, you also have the ability to create *DDL triggers*. The cool feature of DDL *triggers* is that you can now log every CREATE TABLE and any other type of DDL event. This means you have the ability to allow the execution of DDL only under special conditions or circumstances and furthermore, it is in your power to roll back the DDL statement.

Understanding How a DDL Trigger Works

A DDL trigger executes automatically like any other trigger, and it fires when a certain action occurs, in this case a DDL statement. DDL triggers are often used to protect your production environment from issuing certain DDL statements, and they can provide auditing and logging of specific DDL statements in a database.

Creating a DDL Trigger

To create a DDL trigger, you use the CREATE TRIGGER statement, which is the same as when adding a DML trigger. The difference will be for the object you specify it on, which could be the database or the server. Here's an example:

```
CREATE TRIGGER trigger_name
ON { ALL SERVER | DATABASE }
[ WITH <ddl_trigger_option> [ ,...n ] ]
{ FOR | AFTER } { event_type | event_group } [ ,...n ]
AS { sql_statement  [ ; ] [ ...n ] |
EXTERNAL NAME < method specifier >  [ ; ] }

<ddl_trigger_option> ::=
    [ ENCRYPTION ]
    [ EXECUTE AS Clause ]

<method_specifier> ::=
    assembly_name.class_name.method_name
```

The following trigger will block you from executing a CREATE or DROP table statement and will fire only within the database it is creating:

```
CREATE TRIGGER trg_block_droptable_altertable
ON DATABASE
FOR DROP_TABLE, ALTER_TABLE
AS
    PRINT 'You can not drop or alter tables'
    ROLLBACK
```

Triggers generally have their scope inside the database; however, you can create them on the server level as well. This allows you to fire triggers on server events, such as the creation of databases.

Understanding DDL Trigger Events and Scope

Since DDL triggers are new to SQL Server, it is important to understand their scope. DDL events can be categorized into different scopes—a database scope or a server scope. This means in the CREATE TRIGGER statement ON DATABASE | SERVER, you can specify the event only if it is declared within the scope. The following two lists show the possible events that can be triggered on the server scope and the events that can be triggered on the database scope. These are the DDL trigger events that can be defined on the server scope:

- **DDL_SERVER_LEVEL_EVENTS:** CREATE_DATABASE, ALTER_DATABASE, DROP_DATABASE
  - **DDL_ENDPOINT_EVENTS:** CREATE_ENDPOINT, ALTER_ENDPOINT, DROP_ENDPOINT
  - **DDL_SERVER_SECURITY_EVENTS:**
    - **DDL_LOGIN_EVENTS:** CREATE_LOGIN, ALTER_LOGIN, DROP_LOGIN
    - **DDL_GDR_SERVER_EVENTS:** GRANT_SERVER, DENY_SERVER, REVOKE_SERVER
    - **DDL_AUTHORIZATION_SERVER_EVENTS:** ALTER_AUTHORIZATION_SERVER

These are the trigger events that can be defined on the database scope:

- **DDL_DATABASE_LEVEL_EVENTS:**
  - **DDL_TABLE_VIEW_EVENTS:**
    - **DDL_TABLE_EVENTS:** CREATE_TABLE, ALTER_TABLE, DROP_TABLE
    - **DDL_VIEW_EVENTS:** CREATE_VIEW, ALTER_VIEW, DROP_VIEW
    - **DDL_INDEX_EVENTS:** CREATE_INDEX, DROP_INDEX, ALTER_INDEX, CREATE_ XML_INDEX
    - **DDL_STATISTICS_EVENTS:** CREATE_STATISTICS, UPDATE_STATISTICS, DROP_STATISTICS
    - **DDL_SYNONYM_EVENTS:** CREATE_SYNONYM, DROP_SYNONYM
    - **DDL_FUNCTION_EVENTS:** CREATE_FUNCTION, ALTER_FUNCTION, DROP_FUNCTION
    - **DDL_PROCEDURE_EVENTS:** CREATE_PROCEDURE, DROP_PROCEDURE, ALTER_PROCEDURE
    - **DDL_TRIGGER_EVENTS:** CREATE_TRIGGER, DROP_TRIGGER, ALTER_TRIGGER
    - **DDL_EVENT_NOTIFICATION_EVENTS:** CREATE_EVENT_NOTIFICATION, DROP_EVENT_NOTIFICATION
    - **DDL_ASSEMBLY_EVENTS:** CREATE_ASSEMBLY, ALTER_ASSEMBLY, DROP_ASSEMBLY
    - **DDL_TYPE_EVENTS:** CREATE_TYPE, DROP_TYPE
  - **DDL_DATABASE_SECURITY_EVENTS:**
    - **DDL_CERTIFICATE_EVENTS:** CREATE_CERTIFICATE, ALTER_CERTIFICATE, DROP_CERTIFICATE
    - **DDL_USER_EVENTS:** CREATE_USER, DROP_USER, ALTER_USER
    - **DDL_ROLE_EVENTS:** CREATE_ROLE, ALTER_ROLE, DROP_ROLE
    - **DDL_APPLICATION_ROLE_EVENTS:** CREATE_APPLICATION_ROLE, ALTER_ APPLICATION_ROLE, DROP_APPLICATION_ROLE

- DDL_SCHEMA_EVENTS: CREATE_SCHEMA, ALTER_SCHEMA, DROP_SCHEMA
- DDL_GDR_DATABASE_EVENTS: GRANT_DATABASE, DENY_DATABASE, REVOKE_DATABASE
- DDL_AUTHORIZATION_DATABASE_EVENTS: ALTER_AUTHORIZATION_ DATABASE
- DDL_SSB_EVENTS:
  - DDL_MESSAGE_TYPE_EVENTS: CREATE_MSGTYPE, ALTER_MSGTYPE, DROP_MSGTYPE
  - DDL_CONTRACT_EVENTS: CREATE_CONTRACT, DROP_CONTRACT
  - DDL_QUEUE_EVENTS: CREATE_QUEUE, ALTER_QUEUE, DROP_QUEUE
  - DDL_SERVICE_EVENTS: CREATE_SERVICE, DROP_SERVICE, ALTER_SERVICE
  - DDL_ROUTE_EVENTS: CREATE_ROUTE, DROP_ROUTE, ALTER_ROUTE
  - DDL_REMOTE_SERVICE_BINDING_EVENTS: CREATE_REMOTE_SERVICE_ BINDING, ALTER_REMOTE_SERVICE_BINDING, DROP_REMOTE_SERVICE_BINDING
  - DDL_XML_SCHEMA_COLLECTION_EVENTS: CREATE_XML_SCHEMA_ COLLECTION, ALTER_XML_SCHEMA_COLLECTION, DROP_XML_SCHEMA_COLLECTION
- DDL_PARTITION_EVENTS:
  - DDL_PARTITION_FUNCTION_EVENTS: CREATE_PARTITION_FUNCTION, ALTER_PARTITION_FUNCTION, DROP_PARTITION_FUNCTION
  - DDL_PARTITION_SCHEME_EVENTS: CREATE_PARTITION_SCHEME, ALTER_ PARTITION_SCHEME, DROP_PARTITION_SCHEME

It is important to have a clear understanding of the capabilities of DDL triggers. In Exercise 5.2, you will create and test the functionality of a DDL trigger and will log the actual statement in a log table.

EXERCISE 5.2

Creating a DDL Trigger

1. Open a new database query window on the Sybex database.

2. Create a trigger on the database that will roll back every DDL event:

    ```
    CREATE TRIGGER trg_block_ddl ON DATABASE

    FOR DDL_DATABASE_LEVEL_EVENTS

    AS

      RAISERROR ('Database locked for DDL events',16,1)

      ROLLBACK TRANSACTION
    ```

EXERCISE 5.2 *(continued)*

3. Test the trigger functionality by creating a table:

```
CREATE TABLE test (testid int)
```

4. Drop the existing trigger:

```
DROP TRIGGER trg_block_ddl ON DATABASE
```

Understanding Trigger Recursion and Nesting

When working with triggers, you can force one trigger to execute a trigger event on another or on the same table. This means these trigger events will be fired within another trigger action and will thus nest them.

Nested triggers   SQL Server supports the *nesting* of triggers up to a maximum of 32 levels. *Nesting* means that when a trigger is fired, it will also cause another trigger to be fired and thus nest them.

If a trigger creates an infinitive loop, the nesting level of 32 will be exceeded and the trigger will cancel with an error message. You can disable trigger nesting by using a system stored procedure with the nested trigger option. For example:

```
SP_CONFIGURE 'nested_triggers',0
RECONFIGURE
```

This statement will block trigger nesting but also block indirect recursion.

Recursive triggers   When a trigger fires and performs a statement that will cause the same trigger to fire, recursion will occur. SQL Server has two types of recursion:

Direct recursion   Direct recursion occurs when the trigger TRIGGER1 fires on a table, which will perform a statement in the trigger that will cause the same trigger, TRIGGER1, to fire again.

Indirect recursion   Indirect recursion occurs when the trigger TRIGGER1 fires on a table and performs a statement inside the trigger that will cause another trigger, TRIGGER2, to fire on a different table. TRIGGER2 causes TRIGGER1 to fire again.

This is like playing tennis: you hit the ball, and your opponent hits the ball back.

Blocking recursion   You can block direct recursion only by issuing the RECURSIVE_ TRIGGERS option. You can block indirect recursion only by blocking nested triggers.

By default, recursion is disabled; you can enable recursion by using an ALTER DATABASE statement or by specifying the options on the database configuration page. For example:

```
ALTER DATABASE databasename
SET RECURSIVE_TRIGGERS ON | OFF
```

Understanding Disabling Triggers

To prevent a trigger from firing, you can use DISABLE to disable it. In the case of a DML trigger, you have two options to disable a trigger; you can use an ALTER TABLE statement or use a DISABLE TRIGGER statement. For example:

```
DISABLE TRIGGER { [ schema . ] trigger_name
 [ ,...n ] | ALL }
ON { object_name | DATABASE | ALL SERVER } [ ; ]
```

Understanding Event Notifications

Another way of implementing event monitoring instead of using DDL triggers is by creating *event notifications*. Event notifications use SQL Server Broker architecture, which is covered in later in this book. Event notifications submit the event to a SQL Server Service Broker service by submitting it to a queue.

To better understand the difference between event notifications and triggers, see the following:

Triggers	Event Notifications
Executes on DDL or DML statements	Notifies on DDL or DML statements but also trace events
Contains the execution code in the trigger	Submits to a SQL Server Broker architecture
Has fewer options on the server level	Allows most of the database scope events to be defined on server level too

The syntax for creating event notifications looks similar as creating a DDL trigger but directly logs to a broker service. Therefore, the first step when configuring event notification is setting up a SQL Server Service Broker architecture. Chapter 9 covers this in detail.

Understanding Event Notifications DDL Events and Scope

The DDL events that can occur in a SQL Server environment can be logged by *event notifications* at both the database and server levels. Different from DDL triggers, event notifications can also manage trace events and log them to a broker server.

Event notifications certainly have more capabilities in terms of monitoring than DDL triggers have. You can also put most of the DDL events on both the server and the database scope.

These are the DDL events on server scope that can be used with event notifications:

- **DDL_SERVER_LEVEL_EVENTS:** CREATE_DATABASE, ALTER_DATABASE, DROP_DATABASE
    - **DDL_ENDPOINT_EVENTS:** CREATE_ENDPOINT, ALTER_ENDPOINT, DROP_ENDPOINT

- **DDL_SERVER_SECURITY_EVENTS:**
  - **DDL_LOGIN_EVENTS:** CREATE_LOGIN, ALTER_LOGIN, DROP_LOGIN
  - **DDL_GDR_SERVER_EVENTS:** GRANT_SERVER, DENY_SERVER, REVOKE_SERVER
  - **DDL_AUTHORIZATION_SERVER_EVENTS:** ALTER_AUTHORIZATION_SERVER

These are the DDL events on server and database scope that can be used with event notifications:

- **DDL_DATABASE_LEVEL_EVENTS:**
  - **DDL_TABLE_VIEW_EVENTS:**
    - **DDL_TABLE_EVENTS:** CREATE_TABLE, ALTER_TABLE, DROP_TABLE
    - **DDL_VIEW_EVENTS:** CREATE_VIEW, ALTER_VIEW, DROP_VIEW
    - **DDL_INDEX_EVENTS:** CREATE_INDEX, DROP_INDEX, ALTER_INDEX, CREATE_ XML_INDEX
    - **DDL_STATISTICS_EVENTS:** CREATE_STATISTICS, UPDATE_STATISTICS, DROP_STATISTICS
  - **DDL_SYNONYM_EVENTS:** CREATE_SYNONYM, DROP_SYNONYM
  - **DDL_FUNCTION_EVENTS:** CREATE_FUNCTION, ALTER_FUNCTION, DROP_FUNCTION
  - **DDL_PROCEDURE_EVENTS:** CREATE_PROCEDURE, DROP_PROCEDURE, A LTER_PROCEDURE
  - **DDL_TRIGGER_EVENTS:** CREATE_TRIGGER, DROP_TRIGGER, ALTER_TRIGGER
  - **DDL_EVENT_NOTIFICATION_EVENTS:** CREATE_EVENT_NOTIFICATION, DROP_EVENT_NOTIFICATION
  - **DDL_ASSEMBLY_EVENTS:** CREATE_ASSEMBLY, ALTER_ASSEMBLY, DROP_ASSEMBLY
  - **DDL_TYPE_EVENTS:** CREATE_TYPE, DROP_TYPE
  - **DDL_DATABASE_SECURITY_EVENTS:**
    - **DDL_CERTIFICATE_EVENTS:** CREATE_CERTIFICATE, ALTER_CERTIFICATE, DROP_CERTIFICATE
    - **DDL_USER_EVENTS:** CREATE_USER, DROP_USER, ALTER_USER
    - **DDL_ROLE_EVENTS:** CREATE_ROLE, ALTER_ROLE, DROP_ROLE
    - **DDL_APPLICATION_ROLE_EVENTS:** CREATE_APPLICATION_ROLE, ALTER_APPLICATION_ROLE, DROP_APPLICATION_ROLE
    - **DDL_SCHEMA_EVENTS:** CREATE_SCHEMA, ALTER_SCHEMA, DROP_SCHEMA
    - **DDL_GDR_DATABASE_EVENTS:** GRANT_DATABASE, DENY_DATABASE, REVOKE_DATABASE
    - **DDL_AUTHORIZATION_DATABASE_EVENTS:** ALTER_AUTHORIZATION_ DATABASE

- **DDL_SSB_EVENTS:**
  - **DDL_MESSAGE_TYPE_EVENTS:** CREATE_MSGTYPE, ALTER_MSGTYPE, DROP_MSGTYPE
  - **DDL_CONTRACT_EVENTS:** CREATE_CONTRACT, DROP_CONTRACT
  - **DDL_QUEUE_EVENTS:** CREATE_QUEUE, ALTER_QUEUE, DROP_QUEUE
  - **DDL_SERVICE_EVENTS:** CREATE_SERVICE, DROP_SERVICE, ALTER_SERVICE
  - **DDL_ROUTE_EVENTS:** CREATE_ROUTE, DROP_ROUTE, ALTER_ROUTE
  - **DDL_REMOTE_SERVICE_BINDING_EVENTS:** CREATE_REMOTE_SERVICE_ BINDING, ALTER_REMOTE_SERVICE_BINDING, DROP_REMOTE_SERVICE_BINDING
- **DDL_XML_SCHEMA_COLLECTION_EVENTS:** CREATE_XML_SCHEMA_ COLLECTION, ALTER_XML_SCHEMA_COLLECTION, DROP_XML_SCHEMA_COLLECTION
- **DDL_PARTITION_EVENTS:**
  - **DDL_PARTITION_FUNCTION_EVENTS:** CREATE_PARTITION_FUNCTION, ALTER_PARTITION_FUNCTION, DROP_PARTITION_FUNCTION
  - **DDL_PARTITION_SCHEME_EVENTS:** CREATE_PARTITION_SCHEME, ALTER_ PARTITION_SCHEME, DROP_PARTITION_SCHEME

Event notifications provide you with a way to be notified about certain trace events that can be monitored.

These are the trace events that can be used with event notifications:

- **TRC_ALL_EVENTS:**
- **TRC_CURSORS**
- **TRC_DATABASE:**
  - DATA_FILE_AUTO_GROW
  - DATA_FILE_AUTO_SHRINK
  - DATABASE_MIRRORING_STATE_CHANGE
  - LOG_FILE_AUTO_GROW
  - LOG_FILE_AUTO_SHRINK
- **TRC_ERRORS_AND_WARNINGS:**
  - BLOCKED_PROCESS_REPORT
  - ERRORLOG
  - EVENTLOG
  - EXCEPTION
  - EXCHANGE_SPILL_EVENT
  - EXECUTION_WARNINGS
  - HASH_WARNING

- MISSING_COLUMN_STATISTICS
- MISSING_JOIN_PREDICATE
- SORT_WARNINGS
- USER_ERROR_MESSAGE
- **TRC_LOCKS:**
  - DEADLOCK_GRAPH
  - LOCK_DEADLOCK
  - LOCK_DEADLOCK_CHAIN
  - LOCK_ESCALATION
- **TRC_OBJECTS:**
  - OBJECT_ALTERED
  - OBJECT_CREATED
  - OBJECT_DELETED
- **TRC_PERFORMANCE:**
  - SHOW_PLAN_ALL_FOR_QUERY_COMPILE
  - SHOW_PLAN_XML_FOR_QUERY_COMPILE
- **TRC_SCANS**
- **TRC_SECURITY_AUDIT:**
  - AUDIT__SCHEMA_OBJECT_GDR_EVENT
  - AUDIT_ADD_DB_USER_EVENT
  - AUDIT_ADD_LINKED_SERVER
  - AUDIT_ADD_LOGIN_TO_SERVER_ROLE_EVENT
  - AUDIT_ADD_MEMBER_TO_DB_ROLE_EVENT
  - AUDIT_ADD_ROLE_EVENT
  - AUDIT_ADDLOGIN_EVENT
  - AUDIT_APP_ROLE_CHANGE_PASSWORD_EVENT
  - AUDIT_BACKUP/RESTORE_EVENT
  - AUDIT_CHANGE_AUDIT_EVENT
  - AUDIT_CHANGE_DATABASE_OWNER
  - AUDIT_CHANGE_USERS_LOGIN
  - AUDIT_CREDENTIAL_EVENT
  - AUDIT_DATABASE_CONNECTION_EVENT
  - AUDIT_DATABASE_MANAGEMENT_EVENT
  - AUDIT_DATABASE_OBJECT_ACCESS_EVENT

- AUDIT_DATABASE_OBJECT_GDR_EVENT
- AUDIT_DATABASE_OBJECT_MANAGEMENT_EVENT
- AUDIT_DATABASE_OBJECT_TAKE_OWNERSHIP_EVENT
- AUDIT_DATABASE_OPERATION_EVENT
- AUDIT_DATABASE_PRINCIPAL_IMPERSONATION_EVENT
- AUDIT_DATABASE_PRINCIPAL_MANAGEMENT_EVENT
- AUDIT_DATABASE_SCOPE_GDR_EVENT
- AUDIT_DBCC_EVENT
- AUDIT_LOGIN
- AUDIT_LOGIN_CHANGE_PASSWORD_EVENT
- AUDIT_LOGIN_CHANGE_PROPERTY_EVENT
- AUDIT_LOGIN_FAILED
- AUDIT_LOGIN_GDR_EVENT
- AUDIT_LOGOUT
- AUDIT_PARTITION_FUNCTION_PERMISSION_EVENT
- AUDIT_PARTITION_SCHEME_PERMISSION_EVENT
- AUDIT_SCHEMA_OBJECT_ACCESS_EVENT
- AUDIT_SCHEMA_OBJECT_MANAGEMENT_EVENT
- AUDIT_SCHEMA_OBJECT_TAKE_OWNERSHIP_EVENT
- AUDIT_SERVER_ALTER_TRACE_EVENT
- AUDIT_SERVER_EVENTNOTIFICATION_EVENT
- AUDIT_SERVER_OBJECT_GDR_EVENT
- AUDIT_SERVER_OBJECT_MANAGEMENT_EVENT
- AUDIT_SERVER_OBJECT_TAKE_OWNERSHIP_EVENT
- AUDIT_SERVER_OPERATION_EVENT
- AUDIT_SERVER_PRINCIPAL_IMPERSONATION_EVENT
- AUDIT_SERVER_PRINCIPAL_MANAGEMENT_EVENT
- AUDIT_SERVER_SCOPE_GDR_EVENT
- **TRC_DEPRECATION:**
  - DEPRECATION_ANNOUNCEMENT
  - DEPRECATION_FINAL_SUPPORT
- **TRC_SERVER:**
  - SERVER_MEMORY_CHANGE

- TRACE_FILE_CLOSE
- MOUNT_TAPE
- TRC_SESSIONS
- TRC_STORED_PROCEDURES:
    - SP_CACHEMISS
    - SP_CACHEINSERT
    - SP_CACHEREMOVE
    - SP_RECOMPILE
- TRC_TRANSACTION
- TRC_USER_CONFIGURABLE:
    - USERCONFIGURABLE_0
    - USERCONFIGURABLE_1
    - USERCONFIGURABLE_2
    - USERCONFIGURABLE_3
    - USERCONFIGURABLE_4
    - USERCONFIGURABLE_5
    - USERCONFIGURABLE_6
    - USERCONFIGURABLE_7
    - USERCONFIGURABLE_8
    - USERCONFIGURABLE_9
- TRC_OLEDB:
    - OLEDB_ERRORS
- TRC_BROKER
- TRC_FULL_TEXT:
    - FT_CRAWL_STARTED
    - FT_CRAWL_STOPPED
    - FT_CRAWL_ABORTED
- TRC_PROGRESS_REPORT

Creating an Event Notification

To create an event notification, you use the CREATE EVENT NOTIFICATION syntax. In the following example, an event notification is generated for a login event on the server level.

Here's the code syntax:

```
CREATE EVENT NOTIFICATION event_notification_name
ON { SERVER | DATABASE | QUEUE queue_name }
```

```
[ WITH FAN_IN ]
FOR { event_type | event_group } [ ,...n ]
TO SERVICE 'broker_service' ,
 { 'broker_instance_specifier' | 'current database' }
[ ; ]
```

For example:

```
CREATE EVENT NOTIFICATION Evt_logins
ON SERVER
FOR AUDIT_LOGIN TO SERVICE 'EVENTLOGSERVICE'
```

 In order for event notifications services to log to a Service Broker, the broker service has to be configured first. This means that the necessary contracts, queues, and message types have to be created. To find out more about SQL Server Broker Service see Chapter 9.

Introducing Eventdata Collection

The EVENTDATA( ) function gives you access to all the information that is gathered in a DDL trigger or during event notifications. This function is extremely useful to perform tracing and monitoring on the actual event or the DDL trigger that executed. The EVENTDATA( ) function returns an Extensible Markup Language (XML) result set in the following structure:

```
<EVENT_INSTANCE>
    <EventType>type</EventType>
    <PostTime>date-time</PostTime>
    <SPID>spid</SPID>
    <ServerName>name</ServerName>
    <LoginName>name</LoginName>
    <UserName>name</UserName>
    <DatabaseName>name</DatabaseName>
    <SchemaName>name</SchemaName>
    <ObjectName>name</ObjectName>
    <ObjectType>type</ObjectType>
    <TSQLCommand>command</TSQLCommand>
</EVENT_INSTANCE>
```

To retrieve a scalar datatype, you need to decompose the XML result set into relational data. In Chapter 8, we will show you how to work with XML data in SQL Server 2005 and how you can return XML data in T-SQL and scalar data.

Introducing Functions

SQL Server functions are similar to functions you write in any programming languages. A function is a piece of code or routine that accepts parameters and is stored as an object in SQL Server. SQL Server will always return a result or result set from a function.

One of the key differences between functions and stored procedures is that a function can be called within a SELECT statement or even a WHERE clause, while a stored procedure is called by using an EXECUTE procedure statement.

Understanding the Types of Functions

SQL Server consists of several types of functions

- Scalar functions
- Table-valued functions
- Built-in functions
- CLR functions

In the following sections, we'll cover each of these functions.

Using Scalar Functions

A *scalar function* returns a single data value as defined in the CREATE FUNCTION statement. The value returned is defined by the RETURN statement. For example:

```
CREATE FUNCTION [ schema_name. ] function_name
( [ { @parameter_name [ AS ]
[ type_schema_name. ]
 parameter_data_type
    [ = default ] }
    [ ,...n ]
  ]
)
RETURNS return_data_type
    [ WITH <function_option> [ ,...n ] ]
    [ AS ]
    BEGIN
                function_body
        RETURN scalar_expression
    END
[ ; ]
```

In Exercise 5.3, you'll create a scalar user defined function that will convert U.S. dollars to euros.

EXERCISE 5.3

Creating a Scalar User-Defined Function

1. Open a new database query window on the Sybex database.

2. Create a user-defined function by using the following syntax:

```
USE SYBEX

CREATE FUNCTION fn_Dollar_to_Euro(@dollar money)

returns money

as

begin

  declare @result money

  set @result = @dollar /1.10

  return @result

end
```

3. Test the user-defined function:

```
select dbo.fn_Dollar_to_Euro (50)
```

Introducing Table-Valued Functions

A *table-valued function* returns a table datatype result set, using scalar dataypes as defined in the CREATE FUNCTION statement. The value return is defined by the RETURN statement. The table-valued functions could be an alternative to a view, since they provide more capabilities and logic than is possible within a view.

Given its structure, a table-valued function can also be a powerful alternative to a stored procedure. A key benefit is that a table-valued function can be referenced in the FROM clause of a T-SQL batch.

Introducing Built-in Functions

Be careful when you create your own user-defined functions or CLR functions. Specifically, you have to keep in mind that a lot of built-in functionality and functions are predefined in

SQL Server. Rewriting or redefining your own would not only be a waste of time but also probably be a waste of performance when it comes to execution.

You can categorize these functions as shown in the Table 5.1.

TABLE 5.1 SQL Server 2005 Function Categories

Function Category	Description
Aggregate functions	Functions that perform aggregations, such as COUNT, SUM, MIN, MAX, DISTINCT, and AVERAGE
Configuration functions	Scalar functions that return information about configuration settings such as @@SERVERNAME and @@VERSION
Cryptographic functions	Functions that perform encryption and decryption as well as the validation of signatures, such as ENCRYPTBYKEY and DECRYPTBYKEY
Cursor functions	Functions that return information about the status of a cursor such as CURSOR_STATUS and @@FETCH_STATUS
Date and time functions	Functions that manipulate date and time, such as DATEADD, DATEDIFF, and GETDATE
Mathematical functions	Functions for trigonometric, geometric, and other numeric operations such as ABS, RAND, SIN, and SQUARE
Metadata functions	Functions that return information about the attributes of databases and database objects such as DB_NAME and COL_NAME
Ranking functions	Nondeterministic functions that return a ranking value, such as RANK, DENSE_RANK, and ROW_NUMBER
Rowset functions	Functions that return the rowsets that can be used in the place of a table reference in a T-SQL statement such as OPENROWSET and CONTAINSTABLE
Security functions	Functions that return information about users and roles
String functions	Functions that perform string manipulations such as QUOTENAME and SUBSTRING
System functions	Functions that perform various system-level functions such as COALESCE and SCOPE_IDENTITY

TABLE 5.1   SQL Server 2005 Function Categories *(continued)*

Function Category	Description
System statistical functions	Functions that return information about the performance of SQL Server such as @@CPU_BUSY
Text and image functions	Functions that change text and image values

Introducing CLR Functions

In the same way you can write managed code procedures, you now can also write a user-defined function in any .NET programming language. Also, in the same way as with the scalar or a table-valued T-SQL function, a managed code function can be scalar or table-valued. One excellent example of the implementation of a CLR scalar-valued function is a real-time currency conversion. It is possible within the managed procedure to get access to a web service, get the most recent currency conversion data, and use that within the scalar-valued CLR function.

Enabling CLR

Before you can use a managed function, you first need to enable CLR support on the server. You can do this by executing the following syntax:

```
sp_configure 'clr_enabled',1
reconfigure
```

When a call to a CLR function is made without having the CLR enabled, an error message that says the .NET Framework is not enabled will appear.

A CLR function is also useful in an environment where you want to have access to the operating system. The following example, written in VB .NET, performs an operating system call to determine the current computer's IP address:

```
Imports System
Imports System.Data
Imports System.Data.SqlClient
Imports System.Data.SqlTypes
Imports Microsoft.SqlServer.Server
Imports System.Net
Imports System.Runtime.InteropServices
```

```
Partial Public Class UserDefinedFunctions
    <Microsoft.SqlServer.Server.SqlFunction
➥(name:="GetIP", fillrowmethodname:="FillIpRow", tabledefinition:="ipaddress
nvarchar(20)")> _
        Public Shared Function GetIP(ByVal servername As SqlString) As
IEnumerable
    Dim hostname As IPHostEntry
    hostname = Dns.GetHostEntry(servername.Value)
    ' Resolve is obsolete
    Return hostname.AddressList
    End Function


    Public Shared Sub FillIpRow(ByVal o As Object, <Out()> ByRef ip As
SqlString)
        ip = o.ToString
    End Sub
End Class
```

In Exercise 5.4, you'll create a CLR user-defined function.

EXERCISE 5.4

Creating a CLR User-Defined Function

1. Open a new database query window on the Sybex database.

2. Create a user-defined function by using the following syntax:

USE SYBEX

CREATE ASSEMBLY CHAPTER5

FROM

 'C:\SYBEX\70-431\Chapter 5\SourceCode\Chapter5\bin\Chapter5.dll'

WITH PERMISSION_SET = EXTERNAL_ACCESS

If you cataloged the assembly in a previous exercise, you will get an error message that the assembly is already cataloged:

CREATE FUNCTION [dbo].[GetIP]

(@servername [nvarchar](4000))

RETURNS TABLE ([IPaddress] [nvarchar](20))

AS

EXTERNAL NAME

[Chapter5].[Chapter5.UserDefinedFunctions].[GetIP]

3. Test the CLR user-defined function:

SELECT * FROM [SYBEX].[dbo].[GetIP] ('localhost')

Introducing Deterministic and Nondeterministic Functions

SQL Server marks a function as *deterministic or nondeterministic*. A *deterministic function* always returns the same result given a specific input value. For example, a conversion function that transforms a temperature from Fahrenheit to Celsius is deterministic because given an input value, it will always return the same result set.

You can create an index on a computed column if a function is deterministic. This means whenever the row is updated, the index will also be updated, and you could gain a lot of query performance when using the function in a query expression.

User-defined functions are deterministic when the function is the following:

- Schema bound

- Defined with only deterministic user-defined or built-in functions

> As with managed procedures, you use CLR functions to perform complex calculations or conversions that are outside the scope of a data-centric environment or to create functionality that scopes outside of SQL Server and cannot be resolved within a T-SQL function.

All functions are deterministic or nondeterministic:

- Deterministic functions always return the same result any time they are called with a specific set of input values.

- Nondeterministic functions may return different results each time they are called with a specific set of input values.

Whether a function is deterministic or nondeterministic is called the *determinism* of the function. A function needs to be deterministic in order to be able to create an index on the computed column or on the view definition where the function is used.

SCHEMA BINDING binds the function to the object that it references. All attempts to drop the object referenced by a schema bound function will fail. To create a function with the WITH SCHEMABINDING option, the following must be true:

- All views and user-defined functions referenced by the function must be schema bound as well.

- All objects referenced by the function must be in the same database.

Introducing User-Defined Types

In Chapter 3 you learned how to work with datatypes. Sometimes it might be useful to create your own datatypes in order to streamline your business environment and use a common method for referring to specific data. Before SQL Server 2005, you had the ability to create your own datatypes in T-SQL. We'll cover the limitations of working with user-defined datatypes.

A strong benefit of using managed code, as you already learned by creating managed procedures and CLR functions, is that it will also give you the ability to create a complex datatype and define its own methods and properties on it.

Creating T-SQL User-Defined Types

You define a *user-defined type* in SQL Server 2005 by using a CREATE TYPE or a SP_ADDTYPE. The type you create always needs to match with a system-defined type, and you have the ability to set the length and NOT NULL option:

```
sp_addtype [ @typename = ] type,
    [ @phystype = ] system_data_type
    [ , [ @nulltype = ] 'null_type' ]
    [ , [ @owner = ] 'owner_name' ]
```

Here's an example:

```
EXEC sp_addtype ssn, 'VARCHAR(11)', 'NOT NULL'
```

Using T-SQL user-defined types will make creating a table easier because you don't need to repeat the entire column definition, as you will discover in Exercise 5.5.

EXERCISE 5.5

Creating a T-SQL User-Defined Type

1. Open a new database query window on the Sybex database.

2. Create a user-defined type by using the following syntax:

   ```
   EXEC sp_addtype ssn, 'VARCHAR(11)', 'NOT NULL'
   ```

3. Use the defined type in a CREATE TABLE statement:

   ```
   CREATE TABLE employees

   (EmployeeID int identity (1,1),
   ```

```
Employeename nvarchar(200),

DepartmentID int,

EmployeeSSN ssn)
```

T-SQL user-defined types are not used frequently because of their limitations. You don't have the ability to alter the type if it is used in a table definition.

Because a T-SQL datatype always maps to an existing system datatype, it is often referred to as an *alias type*.

Creating CLR User-Defined Types

Working with managed code datatypes or CLR user-defined types adds a new dimension to how you will work with SQL Server 2005. In Chapter 3 you learned how to work with system datatypes. A user-defined type is a CLR class that will have reference types and value types.

User-defined types contain multiple elements and are useful in environments to indicate geospatial data, to indicate date and time functionality, or even to perform data encryption or object-oriented storage.

Since we already covered the implementation of managed procedures and functions, you know that you first need to catalog the assembly and create the datatype by using a CREATE STATEMENT in which you reference the assembly:

```
CREATE TYPE [ schema_name. ] type_name
{
    FROM base_type
    [ ( precision [ , scale ] ) ]
    [ NULL | NOT NULL ]
    | EXTERNAL NAME assembly_name [ .class_name ]
} [ ; ]
```

Here's a code example:

```
CREATE TYPE Distance
EXTERNAL NAME
Distances.[Sybex.Samples.UserDefinedTypes.Distance];
```

Getting More CLR Functionality

Besides creating a CLR function, you also can create user-defined aggregates. This gives you the ability to group and summarize functions using managed code that then can be used within a SQL view or query.

A good example is the "sum by sales region" referenced in the following case study. For advanced functionality, you can also create a CLR trigger, which could be used in environments where you want to add trigger functionality that needs complex calculation or access to web services, the file system, or objects outside SQL Server.

Just like being able to create managed stored procedures and functions, you also can create a managed code trigger. This is, however, used only to perform complex trigger code on the data for the given trigger action.

 Real World Scenario

Case Study: Implementing SQL Server Database Objects

The XYZ company ships orders from pharmaceutical companies to customers all over the world. The company implemented SQL Server 2005 within its business environment. To retrieve the current location of the packages, the company uses GPS-tracking devices on its trucks. Every five minutes the company receives the exact GPS position from its delivery trucks and uses a customized application to track the destination to the customer.

To calculate and work with the GPS position, data that is sent by the devices is stored in SQL Server 2005 as a CLR-defined datatype. This gives the company the flexibility to perform complex calculations on the positioned data and find out the best routing, keeping in mind the detour information it receives from a web service.

For traffic information, the company consults a third-party web service. To better integrate within its application, the XYZ company uses a managed stored procedure that retrieves the information from the web service.

When an order is delivered at the customer location, the delivery note and entire tracking information about the delivery to the customer are both stored in a history table. Because there is no information that requires calculations and all the data retrieval can be managed using standard T-SQL, T-SQL triggers are implemented to transfer the data to history table.

Since some of the products that are shipped by XYZ are confidential, access to the data is exposed only by using stored procedures to avoid SQL injection over the web-based interface.

Summary

In this chapter, we covered several database objects you need to know. It's important to understand the benefits of the capabilities you have with managed code and T-SQL. You have to keep in mind, however, that every object has its own best practices and purpose.

Triggers provide the capability to automatically execute code when an event occurs; this can be a DDL event (such as `CREATE TABLE` and `UPDATE_STATISTICS`) or a DML event such as the insertion of records in a table.

Since the integration of the .NET Framework in SQL Server 2005, most of the extended stored procedures will benefit from being rewritten in a database upgrade phase.

Exam Essentials

Understand how to create a stored procedure.   Know how to create a T-SQL stored procedure with parameters, and be able to identify a valid create procedure syntax.

Identify the differences between stored procedures and functions.   Understand the functional difference between a stored procedure and a function.

Understand T-SQL versus CLR-managed code.   Understand when to use T-SQL over CLR-managed code in order to be able to identify the best implementation method.

Understand DDL triggers and DML triggers.   Understand the functional difference in triggers and when to use DDL triggers. Also, be familiar with the syntax of creating DDL and DML triggers, know how triggers are executed, and be able to determine their scope. It's important to know how triggers can be nested and how recursion can be blocked/enabled.

Know functions.   You need to understand the functional difference between the different types of functions, as well as built-in functions. It is also important to know when to use CLR user-defined functions over T-SQL functions. When working with functions, it is important to know when a function is deterministic or nondeterministic.

Review Questions

1. You are the database administrator of your company. One of your company's applications should maintain data integrity and return custom error messages when the entry data is incorrect. How can you achieve that with minimum effort?

   A. Add check constraints to necessary columns.

   B. Use a DDL trigger.

   C. Use a CLR trigger.

   D. Use a DML trigger.

2. Your company has a CRM application. Some contacts are imported directly from email messages, and sometimes the import fails. You investigate the problem and find out that the cause is a check constraint that validates a column called PhoneNumber. The constraint rejects all phone numbers that contain dashes or parentheses. How can you solve the problem without modifying the check constraint?

   A. Create an additional check constraint that would remove non-numeric characters.

   B. Create a DML AFTER trigger to remove non-numeric characters.

   C. Create a DML INSTEAD OF trigger to remove non-numeric characters.

   D. Create a DML FOR trigger to remove non-numeric characters.

3. You need to create a trigger for auditing the creation of new tables in a database named Test. You need to record the login name, the username, the command text, and the time. Which code can you use?

   A. Use the following:

```
USE Test
GO
CREATE TRIGGER audit_CREATE_TABLE
ON DATABASE
FOR CREATE_TABLE
AS
INSERT tblAudit(
                    PostTime
                    ,LoginName
                    ,UserName
                    ,SQLText)
VALUES (GETDATE(), SYSTEM_USER, CURRENT_USER,
EVENTDATA().value
('(/EVENT_INSTANCE/TSQLCommand)[1]',
➡'nvarchar(2000)'))
RETURN;
GO
```

   B. Use the following:

```
USE Test
GO
CREATE TRIGGER audit_CREATE_TABLE
ON DATABASE
FOR CREATE_TABLE
AS
INSERT tblAudit(
                    PostTime
                    ,LoginName
                    ,UserName
                    ,SQLText)
                VALUES (GETDATE(), SYSTEM_USER, CURRENT_USER,
```

```
EVENTDATA().value
('(/EVENT_INSTANCE/EventType)[1]',
 ➡'nvarchar(2000)'))
RETURN;
GO
```

C. Use the following:

```
USE Test
GO
CREATE TRIGGER audit_CREATE_TABLE
ON DATABASE
FOR CREATE_TABLE
AS
INSERT tblAudit(
                PostTime
                ,LoginName
                ,UserName
                ,SQLText)
           VALUES (GETDATE(), SYSTEM_USER, CURRENT_USER,
EVENTDATA().query
('(/EVENT_INSTANCE/TSQLCommand)[1]',
 ➡'nvarchar(2000)'))
RETURN;
GO
```

D. Use the following:

```
USE Test
           GO
CREATE TRIGGER audit_CREATE_TABLE
ON DATABASE
FOR DDL_DATABASE_LEVEL_EVENTS
AS
INSERT tblAudit(
                PostTime
                ,LoginName
                ,UserName
                ,SQLText)
```

```
         VALUES (GETDATE(), SYSTEM_USER, CURRENT_USER,
EVENTDATA().value
 ('(/EVENT_INSTANCE/EventType)[1]',
➡'nvarchar(2000)'))
RETURN;
GO
```

4. You need to disable all modifications for a reporting database named CompanyReports. Which code can you use?

   A. Use the following:

   ```
   CREATE TRIGGER PreventModifications
   ON DATABASE
   FOR DDL_DATABASE_LEVEL_EVENTS
   AS
   INSERT tblAudit(
               PostTime
               ,LoginName
               ,UserName
               ,SQLText
               )
   VALUES (GETDATE(), SYSTEM_USER, CURRENT_USER,
   EVENTDATA().value ('(/EVENT_INSTANCE/EventType)[1]', 'nvarchar(2000)'))

   RETURN;
   GO
   ```

   B. Use the following:

   ```
   CREATE TRIGGER PreventModifications
   ON DATABASE
   FOR DDL_DATABASE_LEVEL_EVENTS
   AS
   RAISERROR
    ('You are not allowed to modify this production database.', 16, -1)
   ROLLBACK
   RETURN;
   GO
   ```

C. Use the following:

```
CREATE TRIGGER PreventModifications
ON DATABASE
FOR DDL_DATABASE_LEVEL_EVENTS
AS
RAISERROR
 ('You are not allowed to modify this production database.', 16, -1)
ROLLBACK
RETURN;
GO
```

D. Use the following:

```
CREATE TRIGGER PreventModifications
ON DATABASE
FOR CREATE_TABLE
AS
RAISERROR
('You are not allowed to modify this production database.', 16, -1)
ROLLBACK
RETURN;
GO
```

5. You need to determine whether a function named **fnTest** from the sales schema is deterministic. Which code can you use?

A. Use the following:

```
SELECT
OBJECTPROPERTY(OBJECT_ID('sales.fnTest'),
➥ 'IsDeterministic');
GO
```

B. Use the following:

```
SELECT
OBJECTPROPERTY(OBJECT_ID('sales.fnTest'),
➥ 'Deterministic');
GO
```

C. Use the following:

```
SELECT
TYPEPROPERTY(OBJECT_ID('sales.fnTest'),
➥ 'IsDeterministic');
GO
```

D. Use the following:

```
SELECT
TYPEPROPERTY(OBJECT_ID('sales.fnTest'),
➥'Deterministic');
GO
```

6. You need to create a clustered index on a view. Which functions can be used inside the view definition? (Choose all that apply.)

   A. AVG()

   B. RAND()

   C. RAND(1000)

   D. GETDATE()

7. You need to determine the nesting level of a DDL trigger named `AuditUpdates`. Which code can you use?

   A. Use the following:

   ```
   SELECT
   TRIGGER_NESTLEVEL(OBJECT_ID('AuditUpdates'),
     ➥'AFTER', 'DML');
   GO
   ```

   B. Use the following:

   ```
   SELECT
   TRIGGER_NESTLEVEL(( SELECT object_id FROM sys.triggers
   WHERE name = 'AuditUpdates'), 'AFTER', 'DML' );
   GO
   ```

   C. Use the following:

   ```
   SELECT
   TRIGGER_NESTLEVEL(OBJECT_ID('AuditUpdates'),
     ➥'AFTER', 'DDL' );
   GO
   ```

   D. Use the following:

   ```
   SELECT
   TRIGGER_NESTLEVEL(( SELECT object_id FROM sys.triggers
   WHERE name = 'AuditUpdates'), 'AFTER', 'DDL' );
   GO
   ```

8. You create a DML trigger to audit the updates of a table. You need to prevent the trigger from nesting more than three levels. How can you accomplish that?

   A. Using `sp_configure`, set the nested triggers server option to 0.

   B. Using `ALTER DATABASE`, disable the `RECURSIVE_TRIGGERS` option.

   C. Use the following code inside your trigger:

   ```
   IF ((SELECT TRIGGER_NESTLEVEL()) > 3 ) RETURN
   ```

   D. Use the following code inside your trigger:

   ```
   IF ((SELECT TRIGGER_NESTLEVEL()) > 2 ) RETURN
   ```

9. Your database server is configured using the default settings, and the user databases have the default options. One of your applications updates a table named tblCustomers. The update fires a trigger named `UpdateCustomerDetails` that will modify the tblCustomerDetails table. The modification of table tblCustomerDetails fires a trigger named `UpdateCustomer` that will modify the tblCustomers table. This behavior generates recursion. Which option allows this behavior?

   A. The `RECURSIVE_TRIGGERS` database option set to `ON`

   B. The `RECURSIVE_TRIGGERS` database option set to `OFF`

   C. The nested triggers' server configuration option set to 0

   D. The nested triggers' server configuration option set to 1

10. One of your applications updates a table named tblOrders. The update fires a trigger named `UpdateOrderDate` that will modify the tblOrders table by setting a date column. The modification of table tblOrders will fire the `UpdateOrderDate` trigger again. How can you prevent the `UpdateOrderDate` trigger from firing again? (Choose all that apply.)

    A. Use `sp_configure` to set the nested triggers' server option to 0.

    B. Use `ALTER DATABASE`, and disable the `RECURSIVE_TRIGGERS` option.

    C. Insert the following code as the beginning of your trigger:

    ```
    IF ((SELECT TRIGGER_NESTLEVEL()) > 1 ) RETURN
    ```

    D. Insert the following code as the beginning of your trigger:

    ```
    IF ((SELECT TRIGGER_NESTLEVEL()) = 1 ) RETURN
    ```

11. You created a complex stored procedure for a tax application. Monitoring the performance of your stored procedure, you have noticed that it is recompiled on each execution. The cause of recompilation is a simple query statement. How can you optimize the performance of your stored procedure with minimum effort?

    A. Create an additional stored procedure, and include the query that causes the recompilation. Call the new stored procedure from the new one.

    B. Use the `sp_recompile` system stored procedure to force the recompilation of your stored procedure the next time it runs.

    C. Modify your stored procedure, and include the `WITH RECOMPILE` option in its definition.

    D. Add the `RECOMPILE` query hint to the query statement that causes the recompilation.

12. You need to recompile one of your stored procedures each time it is running. How can you achieve that? (Choose all that apply.)

   A. Use the `sp_recompile` system stored procedure.

   B. Modify your stored procedure, and include the `WITH RECOMPILE` option in its definition.

   C. Specify the `WITH RECOMPILE` option when you execute the stored procedure.

   D. Add the `RECOMPILE` query hint to one of the stored procedure statements.

13. You need to decide on a datatype for storing geospacial data to perform GPS positioning. Which datatype seems to be the most suitable for storing GPS position data that requires complex calculation methods?

   A. Use a T-SQL user-defined type.

   B. Use a system-provided image datatype.

   C. Use a CLR-created datatype.

   D. Use an XML datatype.

14. You implemented a trigger that blocks and restricts the creation of tables in the production database. To create an additional table, you need to temporarily remove the DDL trigger. How can you perform this with the least administrative effort?

   A. `ALTER TABLE`

   B. `DISABLE TRIGGER`

   C. `SP_CONFIGURE 'block_triggers',0`

   D. `DROP TRIGGER`

15. You need to catalog an assembly that requires access to a remote web service to retrieve currency data. What permission set do you need to define when cataloging the assembly?

   A. `CREATE ASSEMBLY...WITH PERMISSION_SET = SAFE`

   B. `CREATE ASSEMBLY...WITH PERMISSION_SET = EXTERNAL_ACCESS`

   C. `CREATE ASSEMBLY...WITH PERMISSION_SET = UNSAFE`

   D. `CREATE ASSEMBLY...WITH PERMISSION_SET = OWNER`

16. You need to create a stored procedure that inserts a square value of a given integer. What is the best way to accomplish this?

   A. Create a CLR-managed code procedure.

   B. Use a built-in function inside a T-SQL stored procedure.

   C. Use a managed code function inside a T-SQL stored procedure.

   D. Create a user-defined datatype.

17. Your network administration department asks you to monitor SQL Server for successful and failed logon attempts and log it in a table. How can you achieve this result?

A. Create a DDL trigger on the server level to log all the events to a table.

B. Create a DML trigger on the server level to log all the events to a table.

C. Create a DDL trigger on the server level to log to a service broker.

D. Create an event notification to log to a service broker.

18. When executing a stored procedure, you get the error message, "Execution of user code in the .NET Framework is disabled. Enable 'clr enabled' configuration option." What statement do you need to execute to get the stored procedure to execute?

A. `sp_configure 'clr_enabled', 1`

B. `sp_configure 'clr_enabled',0`

C. `sp_dboption 'clr_enabled',0`

D. `sp_dboption 'clr_enabled',1`

19. You are required to log every change to the customer data in a separate table named customer_history. How can you achieve this?

A. Create a DML trigger on the customer table.

B. Create a DDL trigger on the customer table.

C. Use database snapshots.

D. Use database mirroring.

20. After creating some triggers on a table, you realized that they execute in the wrong order. What can you do to have the triggers executing in the right order?

A. Drop the triggers, and re-create them in the corresponding order.

B. Use the `sp_settriggerorder` system stored procedure.

C. Execute an `ALTER TABLE` statement with `ALTER TRIGGER` to change the trigger order.

D. Create the triggers with _x where x is the trigger order number.

Answers to Review Questions

1. **D.** A Data Manipulation Language (DML) trigger is the best solution. It can validate entry data and return custom error messages. Option A is incorrect because check constraints would not allow you to return custom error messages, though they can maintain data integrity. Option B is incorrect because a DDL trigger responds to objects' modifications, and in this case you are interested in data modifications. Option C can be used but with a greater amount of work.

2. **C.** An INSTEAD OF trigger will be executed before constraint processing. Options B and D are incorrect because an AFTER trigger (which is the same as a FOR trigger) will be executed after constraint processing, so they will not prevent the error generated by the check constraint. Option A cannot solve the problem.

3. **A.** The EVENTDATA function returns for a CREATE_TABLE event the following result:

```
<EVENT_INSTANCE>
<EventType>CREATE_TABLE</EventType>
<PostTime>2005-1208T16:14:10.077</PostTime>
<SPID>51</SPID>
<ServerName>MyServer</ServerName>
<LoginName>MyServer\Administrator</LoginName>
<UserName>dbo</UserName>
<DatabaseName>test</DatabaseName>
<SchemaName>dbo</SchemaName>
<ObjectName>TestTable</ObjectName>
<ObjectType>TABLE</ObjectType>
<TSQLCommand><SetOptions ANSI_NULLS="ON"
➥ANSI_NULL_DEFAULT="ON" ANSI_PADDING="ON" QUOTED_IDENTIFIER="ON"
ENCRYPTED="FALSE"/>
➥<CommandText>create table TestTable (i int)&#x0D;
</CommandText>
</TSQLCommand>
</EVENT_INSTANCE>
```

   Option B is incorrect because you need to save the T-SQL command executed, not the type of command. Option C is incorrect because you need to use the value method, not the query method. Option D is incorrect because you want to audit just the creation of tables, not all events.

4. **C.** The trigger has to be created in CompanyReports database and has to respond to all DDL events (that's why the DDL_DATABASE_LEVEL_EVENTS option is needed). The ROLLBACK is used to cancel any DDL statement.

5. A. The OBJECTPROPERTY function with the ObjectId of the function and IsDeterministic as arguments is the solution. Option B is incorrect because there is no Deterministic argument. Options C and D are incorrect because the TYPEPROPERTY function returns information about a datatype.

6. A, C. You need to use only deterministic functions. RAND is deterministic only when a seed is specified, and GETDATE is nondeterministic. A and C are correct because AVG() and RAND(1000) are deterministic.

7. D. The TRIGGER_NESTLEVEL function can receive as arguments the ObjectId of the trigger, the trigger type, and the trigger event category. The OBJECTPROPERTY function will not return an ObjectId for a DDL trigger, so you need to obtain its ObjectId from sys.triggers. Options A and C are incorrect because the OBJECT_ID function will return NULL in this case. Option B is incorrect because the trigger category is DDL, not DML.

8. C. The TRIGGER_NESTLEVEL function will return the total number of triggers on the call stack when no parameters are supplied. Option A is incorrect because the RECURSIVE_TRIGGERS setting prevents direct recursions. Option B is incorrect because it will prevent all nested triggers. Option D is incorrect because it has an incorrect value specified for the nesting level.

9. D. In this case, you have indirect recursion. The RECURSIVE_TRIGGERS setting prevents only direct recursions and by default is set to OFF. In this case, the RECURSIVE_TRIGGERS setting has no effect. To disable indirect recursion, you should set the nested triggers server option to 0 by using sp_configure. By default, the nested triggers' server option is set to 1, allowing AFTER triggers to cascade to as many as 32 levels. Options A and B are incorrect because the RECURSIVE_TRIGGERS setting has no effect for indirect recursion. Option C is incorrect because the default value for the nested triggers' server option is set to 1.

10. A, B, C. All three options will prevent the trigger from running more than once. D is incorrect because the code will exit from the trigger without running the update of the date column. The trigger code should be executed once.

11. D. You can obtain the best performance with minimum effort by recompiling just a statement and not the complete stored procedure. Option A is also a solution but requires greater effort. Options B and C would not solve the problem.

12. B, C. Both options will cause the stored procedure to be recompiled each time it is executed. Option A is incorrect because it will cause the stored procedure to be recompiled the next time it is run. Option D is incorrect because only the statement with the RECOMPILE query hint will be recompiled.

13. C. Since the datatype requires calculations and is a complex datatype, it needs to be created as a CLR datatype. Option A is incorrect because a T-SQL user-defined type is an alias to an existing system datatype, which is not suitable in this scenario. Image data is definitely not an option since we are storing GPS location data. XML data would work; however, the preference is to work with a CLR datatype because of the methods and calculations on the data.

14. B. To temporarily disable a trigger, you execute the DISABLE TRIGGER statement. A DROP TRIGGER statement will force you to re-create the trigger, but it will require more effort than temporary disabling a trigger. The SP_CONFIGURE block trigger option does not exist. The ALTER TABLE statement would allow you to temporarily disable a trigger as well but takes more administrative effort.

15. B. When requiring access to a web service, you catalog the assembly as EXTERNAL_ACCESS. You will not be able to catalog the assembly as safe, since you require access over the network/Internet. PERMISSION_SET = OWNER does not exist.

16. B. SQL Server has a built-in function, SQUARE, that will perform this action. Since you need to use a stored procedure, you use a built-in function inside a stored procedure. Creating a managed code procedure or function would cause too much system overhead since the calculation can easily be done within T-SQL. Creating a user-defined datatype will not provide the functionality required.

17. D. You cannot audit login events by creating DDL or DML triggers; the only option is to use an event notification service trace event that logs the logins to a service broker that uses the AUDIT_LOGIN event trace data.

18. A. You need to execute the sp_configure statement with option 1 to enable the CLR; option 0 disables it. sp_dboption is a system stored procedure that is used to configure database options. The use of CLR functionality is a server setting, so db_option cannot be used.

19. A. You need to create a DML trigger on the customer table that will join the inserted and deleted table and insert those modified records in the customer_history table. Creating a database snapshot will record all changes made to any table in a snapshot database and will not store any intermediate results since the snapshot was created. Database mirroring is a high-availability feature that will not provide the required result.

20. B. You need to use the sp_settriggerorder stored procedure to define the trigger order. Dropping the triggers and creating them in the necessary order will not achieve the desired results and will be too much effort. ALTER TABLE does not have an option to change the trigger order. Creating the triggers with the _x option does not specify a trigger order.

Chapter

6

Implementing Security in SQL Server 2005

MICROSOFT EXAM OBJECTIVES COVERED IN THIS CHAPTER:

✓ **Configure SQL Server security.**

- Configure server security principals.
- Configure database securables.
- Configure encryption.

✓ **Configure linked servers by using SQL Server Management Studio (SSMS).**

- Identify the external data source.
- Identify the characteristics of the data source.
- Identify the security model of the data source.

✓ **Creating and Implementing Database Objects.**

- Assign permissions to a role for tables.
- Assign permissions to a role or schema for a view.
- Assign permissions to a role for a stored procedure.

Protecting information—guarding access to an organization's data—is much like protecting a physical structure. For example, imagine you own a business and the building that houses it. You don't want the general public to gain access to your building—only you and your employees should have access. However, you also need restrictions on the areas to which your employees have access. Because only accountants should have access to the accounting department and almost no one should have access to your office, you must implement various security systems.

Protecting SQL Server is like protecting your company's building: no one gets in unless they're granted access, and once users are inside, various security systems keep prying eyes out of sensitive areas. In this chapter, we'll discuss the methods used to apply security to SQL Server.

Understanding Security Modes

To continue the business analogy, for your employees to gain access to the building, they need some sort of key, whether a metal key or an electronic access card. For your users to gain access to SQL Server, you need to give them a key as well. The type of key you give them largely depends on the type of lock—authentication mode—you use.

An *authentication mode* is how SQL Server processes usernames and passwords. SQL Server 2005 provides two such modes: Windows Authentication and Mixed.

Using Windows Authentication Mode

With this mode, a user can sit down at their computer, log in to the Windows domain, and gain access to SQL Server using the Kerberos security protocol. Although an in-depth discussion of Kerberos is beyond the scope of this book, here is a brief overview of how this security protocol works:

1. When the user logs in, Windows performs a Domain Name System (DNS) lookup to locate a key distribution center (KDC).
2. The user's machine logs in to the domain.
3. The KDC issues a special security token called a *ticket-granting ticket* (TGT) to the user.
4. To access the SQL Server, the user's machine presents the TGT to SQL Server; if the ticket is accepted, the user is allowed access.

It may be easier to think of Kerberos security as a trip to the carnival. If you've ever been to a carnival and seen all the rides, you probably know that to get on one of those rides, you need a ticket. You must buy that ticket from a counter at the gate of the carnival. Once you have tickets in hand, you can give them to the ride operators and enjoy yourself on the rides.

In Kerberos security, the services, such as SQL Server, would be the rides you want to access; but to use the services, you need to present a ticket. The ticket you present is the TGT you received from the KDC at login time, so you can think of the KDC as the counter at the carnival that sells the tickets. Once you have this TGT, you can access any services to which you've been given permission, including SQL Server 2005.

The main advantage of Windows Authentication mode is that users don't have to remember multiple usernames and passwords. This vastly increases security, because there is less danger of users writing down their passwords and storing them in an unsafe place (such as a sticky note on their monitor). This mode also gives you tighter reign over security, because you can apply Windows password policies, which perform such tasks as expiring passwords, requiring a minimum length for passwords, keeping a history of passwords, and so on.

One of the disadvantages is that only users with Windows accounts can open a *trusted* connection to SQL Server. This means someone such as a Novell client can't use Windows Authentication mode because they don't have a Windows account. If you have such clients, you'll need to implement Mixed mode.

Using Mixed Mode

Mixed mode allows both Windows Authentication and SQL Server Authentication. SQL Server Authentication works as follows:

1. The user logs in to their network, Windows or otherwise.

2. The user opens a *nontrusted* connection to SQL Server using a username and password other than those used to gain network access. It's called a *nontrusted* connection because SQL Server doesn't trust the operating system to verify the user's password.

3. SQL Server matches the username and password entered by the user to an entry in the syslogins table.

The primary advantage is that anyone can gain access to SQL Server using Mixed mode. Mac users, Novell users, Unix users, and the like, can gain access. You could also consider this to be a second layer of security, because if someone hacks into the network in Mixed mode, it doesn't mean they have automatically hacked into SQL Server at the same time.

Ironically, multiple passwords can be a problem as well as an advantage. Consider that users will have one username and password to log in to the network and a completely separate username and password to gain access to SQL Server. When users have multiple sets of credentials, they tend to write them down and thus breach the security system you have worked so hard to set up.

Setting the Authentication Mode

As an administrator, you'll probably set the authentication mode no more than once: at installation time. The only other time you might need to change the authentication mode would be if changes were made to your network. For example, if you set your SQL Server to Windows Authentication mode and needed to include Macintosh clients, you would need to change to Mixed mode.

It's interesting to note that although you can perform most tasks in SQL Server through either SQL Server Management Studio or T-SQL, setting the authentication mode is one of the rare tasks you can do only through SQL Server Management Studio. Exercise 6.1 takes you through setting the authentication mode.

Now that you've set the proper authentication mode, it's time to give your users a key to your building with SQL Server logins.

EXERCISE 6.1

Setting the Authentication Mode

1. Open SQL Server Management Studio by selecting it from the SQL Server 2005 group under Programs on the Start menu, then right-click your server in Object Explorer, and select Properties.

2. Select the Security page.

3. In the Server Authentication section, select SQL Server and Windows Authentication Mode. Doing so sets you to Mixed mode for the rest of the exercises.

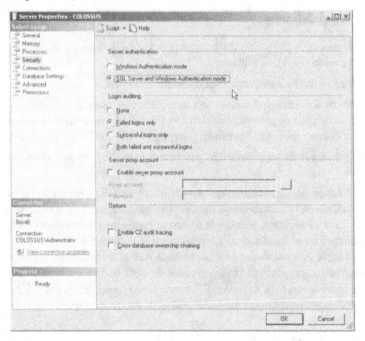

4. Click OK to close the Server Properties dialog box.

Understanding SQL Server Logins

Once you've decided what type of lock (authentication mode) to use on your building, you can start handing out keys so your employees can gain access. A real key gives your employees access to the building as a whole but to none of the resources (such as filing cabinets) inside. In the same way, a SQL Server key—a *login*—gives your users access to SQL Server as a whole but not to the resources (such as databases) inside. If you're a member of the sysadmin or securityadmin fixed server role (discussed later in this chapter), you can create one of two types of logins: standard logins (such as the metal key in the analogy) and Windows logins (such as the newer electronic access card).

Using Standard Logins

You learned earlier in this chapter that only clients with a Windows account can make trusted connections to SQL Server (where SQL Server trusts Windows to validate the user's password). If the user (such as a Macintosh or Novell client) for whom you're creating a login can't make a trusted connection, you must create a standard login for them. In Exercise 6.2, you'll create two standard logins that will be used later in the chapter.

 Although you can create standard logins in Windows Authentication mode, you won't be able to use them. If you try, SQL Server will ignore you and use your Windows credentials instead.

EXERCISE 6.2

Creating Standard Logins

1. Open SQL Server Management Studio, and expand your server by clicking the + sign next to the icon named after your server.

2. Expand Security, and then expand Logins.

3. Right-click Logins, and select New Login.

4. Select the SQL Server Authentication radio button.

5. In the Login Name box, type **SmithB**.

6. In the Password text box, type **Password1** (remember, passwords are case sensitive).

7. In the Confirm Password text box, type **Password1** again.

8. For the Default Database option, select AdventureWorks as the default database.

EXERCISE 6.2 *(continued)*

9. Uncheck the User Must Change Password at Next Login box.

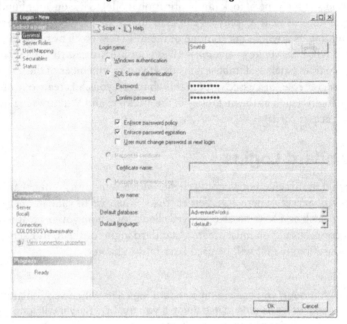

10. On the User Mapping page, check the Map box next to AdventureWorks to give your user access to the default database.

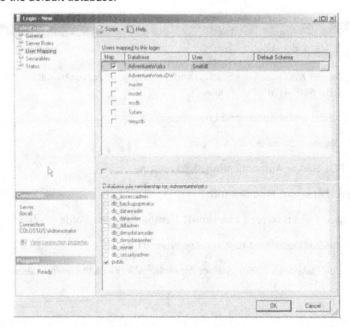

11. Click OK to create your new login.

12. Right-click Logins, and select New Login.

13. Select the SQL Server Authentication radio button.

14. In the Login Name box, type **GibsonH**.

15. In the Password text box, type **Password1**.

16. In the Confirm Password text box, type **Password1**.

17. For the Default Database option, select AdventureWorks as the default database.

18. Uncheck the User Must Change Password at Next Login box.

19. Don't check the Permit box next to AdventureWorks on the User Mapping page. You'll create a database user account later in this chapter.

20. Click OK to create your new login.

21. To test the SmithB login, click the New Query button in SQL Server Management Studio.

22. Click the Change Connection button on the toolbar.

23. In the dialog box that pops up, select SQL Server Authentication from the Authentication drop-down list.

24. In the Login Name box, type **SmithB**.

25. In the Password box, type **Password1**.

26. Click Connect to connect to AdventureWorks.

Using Windows Logins

Creating Windows logins isn't much different from creating standard logins. Although standard logins apply to only one user, however, a Windows login can be mapped to one of the following:

- A single user
- A Windows group an administrator has created
- A Windows built-in group (for example, Administrators)

Before you create a Windows login, you must decide to which of these three you want to map it. Generally you'll map to a group you've created. Doing so will help you a great deal in later administration. For example, suppose you have an Accounting database to which all 50 of your accountants require access. You could create a separate login for each of them, which would require you to manage 50 SQL Server logins. On the other hand, if you create a Windows group for these 50 accountants and map your SQL Server login to this group, you'll have only one SQL Server login to manage.

The first step in creating Windows logins is to create user accounts in the operating system. In Exercise 6.3, you'll create some user accounts and groups.

EXERCISE 6.3

Creating Windows Accounts

1. Open Computer Management in the Administrative Tools group under Programs on the Start menu, expand Local Users and Groups, click Users, and then select Action ➢ New User.

2. Create six new users with the criteria from the following list:

Username	Description	Password	Must Change	Never Expires
MorrisL	IT	Password1	Deselect	Select
RosmanD	Administration	Password1	Deselect	Select
JohnsonK	Accounting	Password1	Deselect	Select
JonesB	Accounting	Password1	Deselect	Select
ChenJ	Sales	Password1	Deselect	Select
SamuelsR	Sales	Password1	Deselect	Select

3. While in Computer Management, create a Local group called **Accounting**.

4. Add the new users you just created whose Description value is Accounting.

5. While still in Computer Management, create a Local group named **Sales**.

6. Add all the users whose Description value is Sales.

7. Open Local Security Policy from the Administrative Tools group under Programs on the Start menu.

EXERCISE 6.3 *(continued)*

8. Expand Local Policies, and click User Rights Assignment.

9. Double-click the Allow Log on Locally right, and click Add User or Group.

10. Select the Everyone group, click OK, and then click OK again. (On a production machine this is not a best practice; this is only for this exercise.)

11. Close the Local Policies tool, and open SQL Server Management Studio.

With your user accounts and groups created, you're ready to create SQL Server logins that map to these accounts, as described in Exercise 6.4.

EXERCISE 6.4

Creating SQL Server Logins for Windows Accounts

1. Open SQL Server Management Studio, and expand your server by clicking the + sign next to the icon named after your server.

2. Expand Security, and expand Logins.

3. Right-click Logins, and select New Login.

4. In the Login Name box, type *Sqldomain***Accounting** (the name of the Local group created earlier).

5. For the Default Database option, select AdventureWorks as the default database.

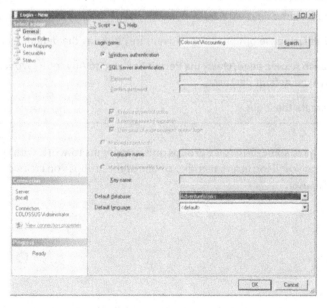

6. On the User Mapping page, check the Map box next to AdventureWorks to give your user access to the default database.

7. Click OK to create the login.

8. Right-click Logins, and select New Login.

9. In the Login name box, type **Sqldomain\Sales** (the name of the Local group created earlier).

10. For the Default Database option, select AdventureWorks as the default database.

11. On the User Mapping page, check the Map box next to AdventureWorks to give your user access to the default database.

12. Click OK to create the login.

13. Right-click Logins, and select New Login.

14. Fill in the Login Name field with **Sqldomain\RosmanD**.

15. For the Default Database option, select AdventureWorks as the default database.

16. On the Database Access page, check the Permit box next to AdventureWorks to give your user access to the default database.

17. Click OK to create the login.

18. Right-click Logins, and select New Login.

19. Fill in the Login Name field with **Sqldomain\MorrisL**.

20. For the Default Database option, select AdventureWorks as the default database.

21. On the Database Access page, check the Permit box next to AdventureWorks to give your user access to the default database.

22. Click OK to create the login.

Now that you have some Windows groups and user logins to work with, you'll test them in Exercise 6.5. First you'll log in as a member of one of the groups you created, and then you'll log in as a specific user.

EXERCISE 6.5

Testing SQL Server Logins for Windows Accounts

1. Log out of Windows, and log back in as JonesB.

2. Open a new SQL Server query in SQL Server Management Studio, and select Windows Authentication from the Authentication drop-down list.

3. Close SQL Server Management Studio, log out of Windows, and log back in as RosmanD.

4. Open a new SQL Server query in SQL Server Management Studio, and select Windows Authentication from the Authentication drop-down list.

Understanding the Items Common to All Logins

You may have noticed that some features are common to all the logins you created.

The first is the default database. When users first log in to SQL Server, they connect to the default database. If you don't set the default database, this is the master—which isn't the best place for your users to get started. You should change that to a different database; for example, change it to the Accounting database if you're working with an accounting user. You can also set a default language, which won't need frequent changing, because the default is the server's language. You can set a different language here for users who require it.

In all types of logins, you can grant database access at create time. On the User Mapping page of the SQL Server Management Studio New Login dialog box, all you need to do is select the database to which this login requires access; doing so automatically creates a database user account, like you did for the AdventureWorks database in the previous set of exercises.

 If you create a Windows login using sp_grantlogin, you can't set the default database or language.

In addition, you can add users to a fixed server role at the time you create them; you do this on the Server Roles tab in SQL Server Management Studio. The next section discussed fixed server roles—limitations on access.

Understanding Fixed Server Roles

Back to the business analogy: as the owner, when you walk into your building, you're allowed to do whatever you want (after all, you own it). When members of the accounting department walk in, however, they're limited in what they can do. For example, they aren't allowed to take keys away from other workers, but they may be allowed to do other administrative tasks, such as sign checks.

That is what *fixed server roles* are used for—to limit the amount of administrative access a user has once logged in to SQL Server. Some users may be allowed to do whatever they want, whereas other users may be able only to manage security. You can assign users any of eight server roles. The following list starts at the highest level and describes the administrative access granted:

sysadmin   Members of the sysadmin role have the authority to perform any task in SQL Server. Be careful whom you assign to this role, because people who are unfamiliar with SQL Server can accidentally create serious problems. This role is only for the database administrators (DBAs).

serveradmin   These users can set serverwide configuration options, such as how much memory SQL Server can use or how much information to send over the network in a single frame. They can also shut down the server. If you make your assistant DBAs members of this role, you can relieve yourself of some of the administrative burden.

setupadmin   Members here can install replication and manage extended stored procedures (these can perform actions not native to SQL Server). Give this role to the assistant DBAs as well.

securityadmin   These users manage security issues such as creating and deleting logins, reading the audit logs, and granting users permission to create databases. This too is a good role for assistant DBAs.

processadmin   SQL Server is capable of multitasking; that is, SQL Server can perform more than one task at a time by executing multiple processes. For instance, SQL Server might spawn one process for writing to the cache and another for reading from the cache. A member of the processadmin group can end (or *kill*, as it's called in SQL Server) a process. This is another good role for assistant DBAs and developers. Developers especially need to kill processes that may have been triggered by an improperly designed query or stored procedure.

dbcreator   These users can create and make changes to databases. This may be a good role for assistant DBAs as well as developers (who should be warned against creating unnecessary databases and wasting server space).

diskadmin   These users manage files on disk. They perform actions such as mirroring databases and adding backup devices. Assistant DBAs should be members of this role.

bulkadmin   Members of this role can execute the BULK INSERT statement, which allows them to import data into SQL Server databases from text files. Assistant DBAs should be members of this role.

Now you'll apply this knowledge by assigning some users to fixed server roles, thereby limiting their administrative authority. You'll do this in Exercise 6.6.

If you don't want users to have any administrative authority, don't assign them to a server role. This limits them to being normal users.

EXERCISE 6.6

Adding Logins to Fixed Server Roles

1. Open SQL Server Management Studio by selecting it from the SQL Server 2005 group under Programs on the Start menu, expand Security, and expand Server Roles.

2. Double-click Sysadmin Server Role to open its properties.

3. Click Add, click Browse, check the *SqlDomain*\MorrisL box, click OK, and then click OK again.

4. MorrisL should now appear in the Role Members list.

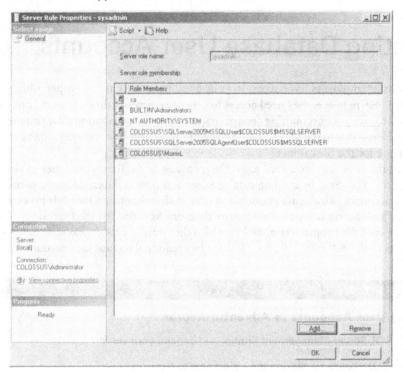

5. Click OK to exit the Server Role Properties dialog box.

6. Double-click Serveradmin Server Role Properties.

7. Click Add, enter **GibsonH**, and click OK.

8. Click OK to exit the Server Role Properties dialog box.

WARNING BUILTIN\Administrators is automatically made a member of the sysadmin server role, giving SQL Server administrative rights to all of your Windows administrators. Because not all of your Windows administrators should have these rights, you may want to create a SQLAdmins group in Windows, add your SQL Server administrators to that group, and make the group a member of the sysadmin role. Afterward you should remove BUILTIN\Administrators from the sysadmin role.

You're ready to grant your users access to the databases that reside on your SQL Server by creating database user accounts.

Creating Database User Accounts

Now that your employees have access to your building as well as the proper administrative access once they're inside, they need access to other resources to do their work. For example, if you want to give your accounting department access to the accounting files, you need to give them a new key—one to the file cabinet. Your employees now have two keys, one for the front door and one for the file cabinet.

In much the same way, you need to give users access to databases once they have logged in to SQL Server. You do so by creating database user accounts and then assigning permissions to those user accounts (we discuss permissions later in this chapter). Once this process is complete, your SQL Server users also have more than one key, one for the front door (the login) and one for each file cabinet (database) to which they need access. In Exercise 6.7, you'll give users access to the AdventureWorks database by creating database user accounts.

EXERCISE 6.7

Creating User Accounts in AdventureWorks

1. Open SQL Server Management Studio, and expand your server.

2. Expand Databases by clicking the + sign next to the icon.

3. Expand the AdventureWorks database.

4. Expand Security, and click the Users icon.

5. Right-click Users, and select New User.

6. Click the ellipsis button next to the Login Name box, and click Browse. View all the available names; note that only logins you've already created are available.

7. Check the GibsonH box, and click OK twice.

8. Enter **GibsonH** in the User Name box and **dbo** in the Default Schema box.

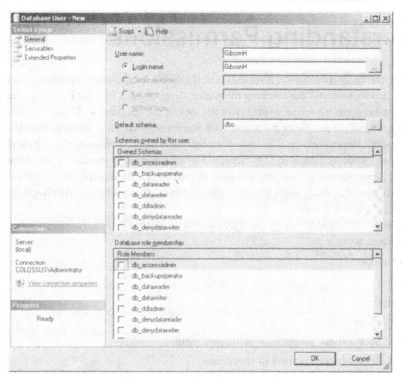

9. Click OK to create the GibsonH database user account.

You may have noticed that two user accounts already exist in your databases when they are first created: DBO and guest. Members of the sysadmin fixed server role automatically become the database owner (DBO) user in every database on the system. In this way, they can perform all the necessary administrative functions in the databases, such as adding users and creating tables. *Guest user* is a catchall database user account for people who have a SQL Server login but not a user account in the database. These users can log in to the server as themselves and access any database where they don't have a user account. The guest account should be limited in function, because anybody with a SQL Server login can use it.

Whenever a member of the sysadmin fixed server role creates an object (such as a table), it isn't owned by that login. It's owned by the DBO. If GibsonH created a table, the table wouldn't be referred to as GibsonH.table but as dbo.table instead.

Now that you've created user accounts for everyone, you need to restrict what those users are capable of doing with the database. You do so by assigning permissions directly to the users or adding the users to a database role with a predefined set of permissions.

Understanding Permissions

To continue the business analogy, it would be unthinkable for the sales department to go to the accounting department and start writing themselves large checks. In most businesses today, the sales department doesn't have permission to even look at the checkbook. To take the analogy one step further, not all the people in the accounting department have full access to the checkbook; some have permission to only read from it, whereas others have permission to write checks from it.

You see the same situation in SQL Server. Not all your users should be able to access the accounting department's or human resources department's databases, because they contain sensitive information. Even users who are allowed in to these sensitive databases should not necessarily be given full access.

Any object to which SQL Server regulates access is referred to as a *securable*. Securables can fall under three scopes:

- Server scope
  - Server
  - Endpoint
  - SQL Server login
  - SQL Server login mapped to Windows login
  - SQL Server login mapped to certificate
  - SQL Server login mapped to asymmetric key
- Database scope
  - Database users
  - Database users mapped to Windows login
  - Database users mapped to certificate
  - Database users mapped to asymmetric key
  - Database roles
  - Application roles
  - Assemblies
  - Message type
  - Service contract
  - Service
  - Full-text catalog
  - DDL events
  - Schema

- Schema scope
  - Table
  - View
  - Function
  - Procedure
  - Queue
  - Type
  - Rule
  - Default
  - Synonym
  - Aggregate

You secure all these objects by applying permissions.

Applying Statement Permissions

In your building, do you allow the contractors who constructed it to come in and use your files, copiers, and various other resources? No, you gave them permission to construct the building initially and make renovations over time—but not to use the files and other such resources inside.

In SQL Server, this constraint is akin to granting the contractors *statement permissions*. Statement permissions have nothing to do with the actual data; they allow users to create the structure that holds the data. It's important not to grant these permissions haphazardly, because doing so can lead to such problems as broken ownership chains (discussed later) and wasted server resources. It's best to restrict statement permissions to DBAs, assistant DBAs, and developers. Exercise 6.8 demonstrates the mechanics of applying the following statement permissions:

- Create Database
- Create Table
- Create View
- Create Procedure
- Create Index
- Create Rule
- Create Default

 When you create a new database, a record is added to the sysdatabases system table, which is stored in the master database. Therefore, the CREATE DATABASE statement can be granted on the master database only.

EXERCISE 6.8

Applying Statement Permissions

1. To prepare SQL Server for the following exercises, you need to remove all permissions from the public role, because the existing permissions will interfere with your work. Open a new SQL Server query in SQL Server Management Studio, and execute the following query. (You may see a warning that says, "The ALL permission is deprecated and maintained only for compatibility. It DOES NOT imply ALL permissions defined on the entity." You can safely ignore this.)

   USE AdventureWorks

   REVOKE ALL from public

2. Close the query window, and don't save the changes.

3. In Object Explorer, expand your server, and then expand Databases.

4. Right-click the AdventureWorks database, and select Properties.

5. In the Properties dialog box, select the Permissions page.

6. Grant RosmanD the Create Table permission by selecting RosmanD in the Users or Roles list and checking the Grant box next to Create Table.

7. Grant Accounting the permissions called Backup Database and Backup Log.

8. If the guest user has any permissions granted, remove them by unchecking the boxes. Click OK to apply your changes.

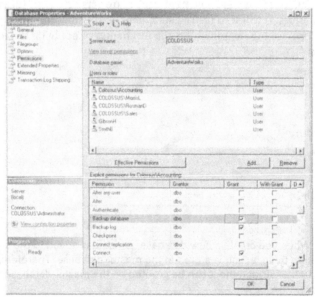

9. Log out of Windows, and log back in as JonesB.

10. Open a new SQL Server query in SQL Server Management Studio, connect using Windows Authentication, and type the following query:

```
USE AdventureWorks

CREATE TABLE Statement1

(column1    varchar(5)    not null,

column2    varchar(10)    not null)
```

11. From the Query drop-down menu, select Execute Query. Notice that the query is unsuccessful because JonesB (a member of the Accounting group) doesn't have permission to create a table.

12. Close SQL Server Management Studio, log out of Windows, and log back in as RosmanD.

13. Open a new SQL Server query in SQL Server Management Studio, and enter and execute the code from step 10 again. This time it's successful, because RosmanD has permission to create tables.

Applying Object Permissions

Once the structure exists to hold the data, you need to give users permission to start working with the data in the databases, which is accomplished by granting *object permissions* to your users. Using object permissions, you can control who is allowed to read from, write to, or otherwise manipulate your data. The 12 object permissions are as follows:

Control   This permission gives the principal ownership-like capabilities on the object and all objects under it in the hierarchy. For example, if you grant a user Control permission on the database, then they have Control permission on all the objects in the database, such as tables and views.

Alter   This permission allows users to create, alter, and drop the securable and any object under it in the hierarchy. The only property they can't change is ownership.

Take Ownership   This allows the user to take ownership of an object.

Impersonate   This permission allows one login or user to impersonate another.

Create   As the name implies, this permission lets a user create objects.

View Definition   This permission allows users to see the T-SQL syntax that was used to create the object being secured.

Select   When granted, this permission allows users to read data from the table or view. When granted at the column level, it lets users read from a single column.

Insert   This permission allows users to insert new rows into a table.

Update   This permission lets users modify existing data in a table but not add new rows to or delete existing rows from a table. When this permission is granted on a column, users can modify data in that single column.

Delete   This permission allows users to remove rows from a table.

References   Tables can be linked together on a common column with a foreign key relationship, which is designed to protect data across tables. When two tables are linked with a foreign key, this permission allows the user to select data from the primary table without having the Select permission on the foreign table.

Execute   This permission allows users to execute the stored procedure where the permission is applied.

You'll now get some hands-on experience with applying and testing object permissions in Exercise 6.9.

EXERCISE 6.9

Applying and Testing Object Permissions

1. Open SQL Server Management Studio, expand your server, expand Databases, expand AdventureWorks, and then expand Tables.

2. Right-click Person.Address, and select Properties.

3. On the Permissions page, add *Sqldomain***\Sales** and **SmithB** under the Users or Roles list.

4. Select *SqlDomain*\Sales in the Users or Roles list, and grant Sales the Select permission by checking the Grant box next to Select.

5. Select SmithB in the Users or Roles list, and grant SmithB the Select permission by checking the Grant box next to Select.

EXERCISE 6.9 *(continued)*

6. If the guest user has any permissions granted, remove them by clicking each one until all check boxes are clear.

7. Click OK, and close SQL Server Management Studio.

8. Log out of Windows, and log back in as JonesB.

9. Open a new SQL Server query in SQL Server Management Studio, and connect using Windows Authentication.

10. Execute the following query (it fails because Accounting doesn't have Select permission):

    USE AdventureWorks

    SELECT * FROM authors

11. Close SQL Server Management Studio, and repeat steps 8 through 10 but for ChenJ. The query succeeds this time because Sales (of which ChenJ is a member) has Select permission.

12. Log out of Windows, and log back in as yourself.

Although granting permissions to single users is useful from time to time, it's better, faster, and easier to apply permissions en masse. This requires understanding database roles.

Understanding Database Roles

Continuing the business analogy, your accountants need to write corporate checks. You could give them permission to do so in one of two ways. First, you could give each of the accountants their own checkbook drawn from a single account with permission to write checks from it. That would be an accounting nightmare—trying to keep track of all the checks that had been written during the month. A better way to accomplish this is to get one corporate account with one checkbook and give the accountants as a group permission to write checks from that one book.

In SQL Server, when several users need permission to access a database, it's much easier to give them all permissions as a group rather than try to manage each user separately. That is what database roles are for—granting permissions to groups of database users, rather than granting permissions to each database user separately. You have three types of database roles to consider: fixed, custom, and application.

Using Fixed Database Roles

Fixed database roles have permissions already applied; that is, all you have to do is add users to these roles, and the users inherit the associated permissions. (This is different from custom database roles, as you'll see later.) You can use several fixed database roles in SQL Server to grant permissions:

db_owner   Members of this role can do everything the members of the other roles can do as well as some administrative functions.

db_accessadmin   These users have the authority to say who gets access to the database by adding or removing users.

db_datareader   Members here can read data from any table in the database.

db_datawriter   These users can add, change, and delete data from all the tables in the database.

db_ddladmin   DDL administrators can issue all DDL commands; this allows them to create, modify, or change database objects without viewing the data inside.

db_securityadmin   Members here can add and remove users from database roles, and they can manage statement and object permissions.

db_backupoperator   These users can back up the database.

db_denydatareader   Members can't read the data in the database, but they can make schema changes (for example, adding a column to a table).

db_denydatawriter   These users can't make changes to the data in the database, but they're allowed to read the data.

public   The purpose of this group is to grant users a default set of permissions in the database. All database users automatically join this group and can't be removed.

WARNING   Because all database users are automatically members of the public database role, you need to be cautious about the permissions assigned to the role.

It's time to limit the administrative authority of your users once they gain access to the database by adding them to fixed database roles, which you will do in Exercise 6.10.

EXERCISE 6.10

Adding Users to Fixed Database Roles

1. Open SQL Server Management Studio, expand your server, expand Databases, and then expand AdventureWorks.

2. Expand Security, then Roles, and then Database Roles.

3. Right-click db_denydatawriter, and select Properties.

4. Click Add.

5. Type **SmithB** in the Enter Object Names to Select box, and click OK.

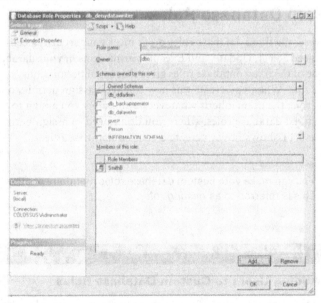

6. Click OK again to return to SQL Server Management Studio.

7. Right-click db_denydatareader, and select Properties.

8. Click Add.

9. Type **GibsonH** in the Enter Object Names to Select box, and click OK.

10. Open a new SQL Server query in SQL Server Management Studio, and connect using SQL Server Authentication.

11. In the User Name box, type **SmithB**; in the Password box, type **Password1**.

12. The following query tries to update information in the HumanResources.Department table; it fails because SmithB is a member of the db_denydatawriter role:

    ```
    INSERT INTO HumanResources.Department

    (DepartmentID, Name, GroupName, ModifiedDate)

    values (200, 'Test','TestGroup',GetDate())
    ```

13. Close the query window.

Fixed database roles cover many—but not all—of the situations that require permissions to be assigned to users. That is why you need to understand custom database roles.

Using Custom Database Roles

Sometimes, of course, the fixed database roles don't meet your security needs. You may have several users who need Select, Update, and Execute permissions in your database and nothing more. Because none of the fixed database roles gives that set of permissions, you need to create a *custom database role*. When you create this new role, you assign permissions to it and then assign users to the role; the users inherit whatever permissions you assign to that role. This is different from the fixed database roles, where you don't need to assign permissions, but just add users. Exercise 6.11 shows how to create a custom database role.

You can make your custom database roles members of other database roles. This is referred to as *nesting roles*.

Creating and Adding Users to Custom Database Roles

1. Open SQL Server Management Studio, expand your server, expand Databases, and then expand AdventureWorks.

2. Expand Security and then Roles.

3. Right-click Database Roles, and select New Database Role.

4. In the Role Name box, type **SelectOnly**, and enter **dbo** in the Owner box.

5. Add *Sqldomain*\RosmanD to the Role Members list.

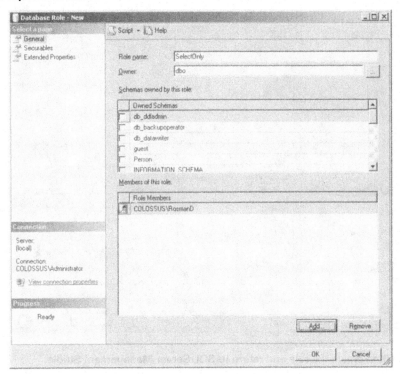

6. On the Securables page, click Add under the Securables list box, select the Specific Objects radio button, and click OK.

7. Click the Objects Type button, select Tables, and click OK.

8. Click Browse, check the HumanResources.Department box, and click OK; then click OK again.

9. In the Explicit Permissions for HumanResources.Department list, check the Grant box next to Select, and click OK.

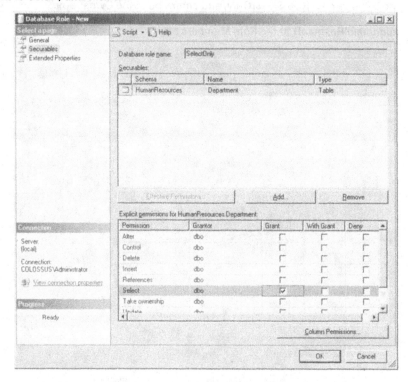

10. Click OK to create the role and return to SQL Server Management Studio.

11. Close all programs, log off Windows, and log back in as RosmanD.

12. Open a new SQL Server query in SQL Server Management Studio, and connect using Windows Authentication.

13. Notice that the following query succeeds because RosmanD is a member of the new SelectOnly role:

```
USE AdventureWorks

SELECT * FROM HumanResources.Department
```

EXERCISE 6.11 *(continued)*

14. Now notice the failure of the next query because RosmanD is a member of a role that is allowed to select only:

```
INSERT INTO HumanResources.Department

(DepartmentID, Name, GroupName, ModifiedDate)

values (200, 'Test','TestGroup',GetDate())
```

15. Close all programs, log out of Windows, and log back in as yourself.

The final database role—the application role—grants you a great deal of authority over which applications can be used to work with the data in your databases.

Using Application Roles

Suppose your HR department uses a custom program to access its database and you don't want the HR employees using any other program for fear of damaging the data. You can set this level of security by using an *application role*. With this special role, your users can't access data using just their SQL Server login and database account; they must use the proper application. Here is how it works:

1. Create an application role, and assign it permissions.

2. Users open the approved application and are logged in to SQL Server.

3. To enable the application role, the application executes the `sp_setapprole` stored procedure (which is written into the application at design time).

Once the application role is enabled, SQL Server no longer sees users as themselves; it sees users as the application and grants them application role permissions. You'll create and test an application role in Exercise 6.12.

EXERCISE 6.12

Creating and Testing an Application Role

1. Open SQL Server Management Studio, and expand Databases, then AdventureWorks, and then Security.

2. Right-click Application Roles, and select New Application Role.

3. In the Role Name box, type **EntAppRole**.

4. Enter **dbo** in the Default Schema box.

5. In the Password and Confirm Password boxes, type **Password1**.

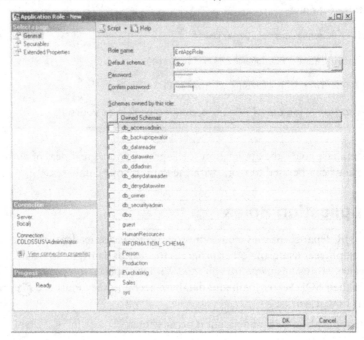

6. On the Securables page, click Add under the Securables list box, select the Specific Objects radio button, and click OK.

7. Click the Objects Type button, select Tables, and click OK.

8. Click Browse, check the HumanResources.Department box, and click OK; then click OK again.

9. In the Explicit Permissions for HumanResources.Department list, check the Grant box next to Select, and click OK.

10. Open a new SQL Server query in SQL Server Management Studio, and connect using SQL Authentication with **GibsonH** as the username and **Password1** as the password.

11. Notice that the following query fails because GibsonH has been denied Select permissions because of the membership in the db_denydatareader database role:

```
USE AdventureWorks

SELECT * FROM HumanResources.Departments
```

12. To activate the application role, execute the following query:

```
sp_setapprole @rolename='EntAppRole',

@password='Password1'
```

13. Clear the query window, and don't save the changes; repeat step 11 without opening a new query, and notice that the query is successful this time. This is because SQL Server now sees you as EntAppRole, which has Select permission.

14. Close the query window.

Understanding Permission States

All the permissions in SQL Server can exist in one of three states: granted, revoked, or denied.

Granting a Permission

Granting allows users to use a specific permission. For instance, if you grant SmithB Select permission on a table, SmithB can read the table's data. You know a permission has been granted when the Allow check box is selected next to the permission in the permissions list.

Revoking a Permission

A *revoked* permission isn't specifically granted, but a user can inherit the permission if it has been granted to another role of which they are a member. That is, if you revoke the Select permission from SmithB, SmithB can't use it. If, however, SmithB is a member of a role that has been granted Select permission, SmithB can read the data just as if SmithB had the Select permission. A permission is revoked when neither the Allow nor Deny box is selected next to a permission.

Denying a Permission

If you *deny* a permission, the user doesn't get the permission—no matter what. If you deny SmithB Select permission on a table, even if SmithB is a member of a role with Select permission, SmithB can't read the data. You know a permission has been denied when the Deny box is checked next to the permission in the permissions list.

In Exercise 6.13, you'll get some hands-on experience with changing the states of permissions and witnessing the effects.

EXERCISE 6.13

Testing Permission States

1. Open SQL Server Management Studio, and expand your server, then Databases, then AdventureWorks, and then Security.

2. Expand Users, right-click SmithB, and select Properties.

3. On the Securables page, click Add under the Securables list box, select the Specific Objects radio button, and click OK.

4. Click the Objects Type button, select Tables, and click OK.

5. Click Browse, check the HumanResources.Department box, and click OK.

6. In the Explicit Permissions for HumanResources.Department list, check the Grant box next to Select, and click OK.

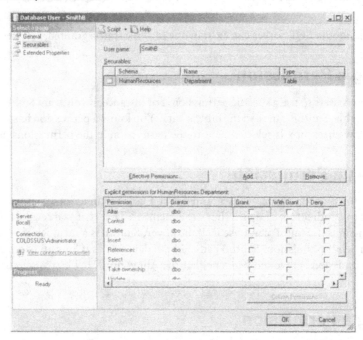

7. Open a new SQL Server query, and connect as SmithB using SQL Server Authentication.

8. Execute the following query. It's successful because SmithB has Select permission on the HumanResources.Department table:

```
USE AdventureWorks

SELECT * FROM HumanResources.Department
```

9. Right-click SmithB under Users in the AdventureWorks database, and select Properties.

10. On the Securables page, click Add under the Securables list box, select the Specific Objects radio button, and click OK.

11. Click the Objects Type button, select Tables, and click OK.

12. Click Browse, check the HumanResources.Department box, and click OK.

13. In the Explicit Permissions for HumanResources.Department list, uncheck the Grant box next to Select, and click OK.

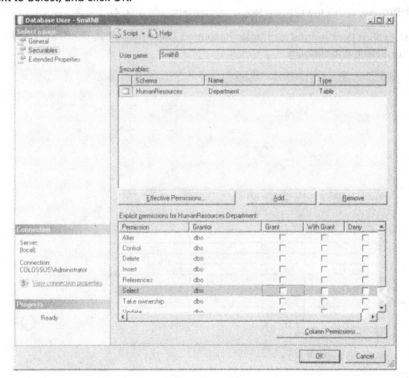

14. Return to the query window, and execute the query in step 8. It fails because SmithB doesn't have explicit Select permission.

15. Right-click SmithB under Users in the AdventureWorks database, and select Properties.

16. Under Role Membership, check the box next to the db_datareader role.

17. Return to the query window, and rerun the query from step 8. Now it's successful, because SmithB has inherited the Select permission from the db_datareader role and doesn't need to have it explicitly applied.

18. Right-click SmithB under Users in the AdventureWorks database, and select Properties.

19. On the Securables page, click Add under the Securables list box, select the Specific Objects radio button, and click OK.

20. Click the Objects Type button, select Tables, and click OK.

21. Click Browse, check the HumanResources.Department box, and click OK.

22. In the Explicit Permissions for HumanResources.Department list, check the Deny box next to Select, and click OK.

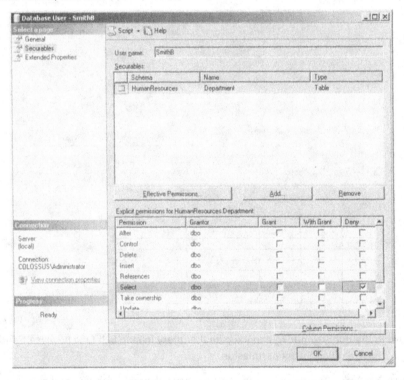

23. Return to the query window, and again run the query from step 8. It fails this time because you've specifically denied SmithB access; therefore, SmithB can no longer inherit the Select permission from the db_datareader role.

24. Right-click SmithB under Users in the AdventureWorks database, and select Properties.

25. Under Role Membership, uncheck the box next to the db_datareader role.

26. On the Securables page, click Add under the Securables list box, select the Specific Objects radio button, and click OK.

27. Click the Objects Type button, select Tables, and click OK.

28. Click Browse, check the HumanResources.Department box, and click OK.

29. In the Explicit Permissions for HumanResources.Department list, uncheck the Deny box next to Select, and click OK.

With a better understanding of how and where permissions are applied, you'll look into one of the problems generated when permissions are applied improperly: the broken ownership chain.

Introducing Ownership Chains

In the physical world, people own objects that they can do with as they please, including lending or giving them to others. SQL Server understands this concept of ownership. When users create an object, they own that object and can do whatever they want with it. For example, if RosmanD creates a table, RosmanD can assign permissions as needed, granting access only to those users deemed worthy. This is a good thing until you consider what is known as an *ownership chain*.

An object that is on loan still belongs to the owner; the person who has borrowed it must ask the owner for permission before allowing another person to use it. Acting without such permission would be like a *broken ownership chain*.

Suppose that RosmanD creates a table and grants permissions on that table to Accounting (as shown in Figure 6.1). Then one of the members of Accounting creates a view based on that table and grants Select permission to SmithB. Can SmithB select the data from that view? No, SmithB cannot select the data from that view, because the ownership chain has been broken. SQL Server checks permissions on an underlying object (in this case, the table) only when the owner changes. Therefore, if RosmanD had created both the table and the view, there would be no problem, because SQL Server would check only the permissions on the view. Because the owner changed from Accounting (who owned the view) to RosmanD (who owned the table), SQL Server needed to check the permissions on both the view and the table.

FIGURE 6.1   When objects that rely on each other have different owners, it's called a broken ownership chain.

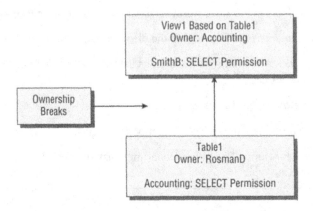

How can you avoid broken ownership chains? The first way that may come to mind is to make everyone who needs to create objects a member of the sysadmin fixed server role; then everything they create is owned by the DBO user rather than by the login. For example, because MorrisL is a member of the sysadmin fixed server role, everything MorrisL creates in any database is owned by the DBO, not MorrisL. Although this is technically possible, it's a poor method because it grants a great deal of administrative privilege over the server to people who don't need such privilege.

A much better way to avoid broken ownership chains is to make all the users who need to create objects members of either the db_owner fixed database role or the db_ddladmin fixed database role. Then, if they need to create objects, they can specify the owner as DBO (for example, CREATE TABLE dbo.*table_name*). This way, the DBO owns all objects in the database, and because the ownership never changes, SQL Server never needs to check any underlying permissions.

Don't forget that members of the db_owner role can do whatever they like with a database, whereas db_ddladmins have limited authority. Therefore, you may want to use db_ddladmin in most instances.

When a db_owner or db_ddladmin member creates an object as another user, it can be any database user, not just the DBO.

Now you have a good understanding of local security, but what if you have to access data on more than one server? The next section covers how to implement security in a distributed environment.

Introducing Linked Server Security

Let's return to the business analogy: your business is prospering, and you have expanded into two buildings. Your employees need access to resources in both buildings, which means you need to give your users a key to the new place.

You have the same concerns when your resources are spread across multiple SQL Servers; your users may need access to resources on multiple servers. This is especially true of something called a *distributed query*, which returns result sets from databases on multiple servers; the remote servers in the query are called *linked servers*. Although you may wonder why you would want to perform distributed queries when you can replicate the data between servers (Chapter 12 discusses replication), you may have practical reasons for doing the former. Don't forget that because SQL Server is designed to store terabytes of data, some of your databases may grow to several hundred megabytes in size—and you don't want to replicate several hundred megabytes under normal circumstances.

The first step in configuring your server to perform distributed queries is to inform SQL Server that it will be talking to other database servers by running the `sp_addlinkedserver` stored procedure. The procedure to link to a server named AccountingSQL looks something like this:

```
sp_addlinkedserver @server='AccountingSQL', @provider='SQL Server'
```

Your users can then run distributed queries by specifying two different servers in the query. The query `SELECT * FROM SQLServer.AdventureWorks.HumanResources.Employee,` `AccountingSQL.AdventureWorks.HumanResources.Employee` accesses data from both the SQLServer server (the server the user is logged in to, or the sending server) and the AccountingSQL server (the remote server) in the same result set.

The security issue here is that the sending server must log in to the remote server on behalf of the user to gain access to the data. SQL Server can use one of two methods to send this security information: security account delegation or linked server login mapping. If your users have logged in using Windows Authentication and all the servers in the query are capable of understanding Windows domain security, you can use account delegation. Here's how it works:

1. If the servers are in different domains, you must make certain the appropriate Windows trust relationships are in place. The remote server's domain must trust the sending server's domain. If you're using only Windows domains, the trust relationships are automatically created for you.

2. Add a Windows login to the sending server for the user to log in with.

3. Add the same account to the remote server.

4. Create a user account for the login in the remote server's database, and assign permissions.

5. When the user executes the distributed query, SQL Server sends the user's Windows security credentials to the remote server, allowing access.

If you have users who access SQL Server with standard logins or if some of the servers don't participate in Windows domain security, you'll need to add a *linked login*. Here's how to do it:

1. On the remote server, create a standard login, and assign the necessary permissions.

2. On the sending server, map a local login to the remote login using the `sp_addlinkedsrvlogin` stored procedure. To map all local logins to the remote login RemUser, type the following:

```
sp_addlinkedsrvlogin @rmtsrvname='AccountingSQL',
@useself=FALSE, @locallogin=NULL, @rmtuser='RemUser', @rmtpassword='Password1'
```

3. When a user executes a distributed query, the sending server logs in to the AccountingSQL (remote) server as RemUser with a password of Password1.

You can put another layer, encryption, on top of all this security.

Introducing Encryption

Thus far, you've seen how to protect your data from intruders by granting access and applying permissions to objects. But when someone legitimately accesses the server and starts transferring data, it travels over the network. If you need really robust security, you can go as far as to encrypt the data as it travels between the client and the server over the network. That way, if anyone is reading your network traffic, they will not be able to interpret the data.

To encrypt your connections to SQL Server, you first need to get a certificate. Covering how to obtain and install a certificate is beyond the scope of this book, but you can get one from one of the major vendors such as VeriSign, or you can install Windows Certificate services and supply your own. Once you have a certificate, you need to install it on the server. Here are the steps to do that:

1. If you run the SQL Server service as Local System, then log in to the server as an administrator. If you are using a service account, then log in to the server as the service account.

2. On the Start menu, click Run; then in the Open box, type **MMC**, and click OK.

3. In the Microsoft Management Console (MMC), on the File menu, click Add/Remove Snap-in.

4. In the Add/Remove Snap-in dialog box, click Add.

5. In the Add Standalone Snap-in dialog box, click Certificates; then click Add.

6. In the Certificates Snap-in dialog box, click Computer account, and then click Finish.

7. In the Add Standalone Snap-in dialog box, click Close.

8. In the Add/Remove Snap-in dialog box, click OK.

9. In the Certificates Snap-in dialog box, expand Certificates, expand Personal, and then right-click Certificates; then point to All Tasks, and finally click Import.

10. Complete the Certificate Import Wizard to add a certificate to the computer, and close the MMC.

After you have installed your certificate on the server, you need to configure the server to accept encrypted connections. Here is how to do that:

1. In SQL Server Configuration Manager, expand SQL Server 2005 Network Configuration, right-click Protocols for <server instance>, and then select Properties.

2. In the Protocols for <instance name> Properties dialog box, on the Certificate tab, select the desired certificate from the Certificate drop-down list, and then click OK.

3. On the Flags tab, in the ForceEncryption box, select Yes, and then click OK to close the dialog box.

4. Restart the SQL Server service.

Finally, you need to configure the clients to request encrypted connections to the server. Here's how:

1. In SQL Server Configuration Manager, expand SQL Server 2005 Network Configuration, right-click Protocols for <server instance>, and then select Properties.

2. In the Protocols for <instance name> Properties dialog box, on the Certificate tab, select the desired certificate from the Certificate drop-down list, and then click OK.

3. On the Flags tab, in the ForceEncryption box, select Yes, and then click OK to close the dialog box.

4. Restart the SQL Server service.

Creating a Security Plan

Suppose you have just been hired as database administrator for AlsoRann, a small company that relies heavily on its SQL Server. A great deal of the data on the SQL Server is proprietary and therefore must be secured. You realize, however, that jumping right in and randomly applying permissions to databases is going to result in a mess—if not a disaster—so you take a more logical approach: you develop a security plan.

Creating a good security plan is always the first step in applying security to any type of system. Here are a few issues you should consider in your plan:

Type of users   If all your users support trusted connections, you can use Windows accounts. If you have the authority to create groups in Windows, you may be able to create Windows groups and then create logins for those groups rather than creating individual accounts. If not all your users support trusted connections (such as Novell or Macintosh), you need to use Mixed mode authentication and create some standard logins.

Fixed server roles   Once you have given users access to SQL Server, how much administrative power, if any, should they be given? If your users need administrative authority, add them to one of the fixed server roles; if not, you don't need to add them.

Database access   Once your users are logged in, to which databases do they have access? It's highly unlikely that every user needs a user account in every database.

Type of access   Once the user has a database user account, how much authority do they have in the database? For example, can all users read and write, or is a subset of users allowed only to read?

Group permissions   It's usually best to apply permissions to database roles and then add users to those roles. Every system has exceptions, though; you may need to apply some permissions directly to users, especially those who need to be denied access to a resource.

Object creation   Figure out who needs the authority to create objects, such as tables and views, and group them in either the db_owner role or the db_ddladmin role. Doing this allows users to create objects as the DBO instead of as themselves. In this way, you can avoid broken ownership chains.

Public role permissions   Remember that all database user accounts are members of the public role and can't be removed. Whatever permissions the public role has are given to your users, so limit the permissions on the Public group.

Guest access   Do you want users with no database user account to be able to access databases through a guest account? For some databases, such as a catalog, this may be acceptable. In general, however, this can be considered a security risk and should not be used on all databases.

Table 6.1 shows the employees of AlsoRann and its security needs.

TABLE 6.1   The Employees of AlsoRann

Name	Windows Group	Department	Network	Admin	Permissions
SmithB	N/A	Service	Novell	None	Read, no Write
GibsonH	N/A	Development	Novell	Server Configuration	Write, Create, no Read
RosmanD	None	Administration	Windows	None	Select, Insert, Update
MorrisL	None	IT	Windows	All	All
JohnsonK	Accounting	Accounting	Windows	None	Read, Write
JonesB	Accounting	Accounting	Windows	None	Read, Write
ChenJ	Sales	Sales	Windows	None	Read, Update
SamuelsR	Sales	Sales	Windows	None	Read, Update

You may notice that AlsoRann has two Novell network users. This means you need to create at least two standard logins and implement Mixed mode authentication.

Next, some of the users—specifically, Accounting and Sales—are already grouped together in Windows. Rather than create accounts for each member of these departments, you can instead add a Windows group login for the whole lot of them. Because RosmanD and MorrisL aren't members of a Windows group, they need Windows user logins.

Next, look at the administrative rights that each user needs over the system. Because GibsonH needs to be able to configure server settings such as memory use, you should add GibsonH to the serveradmin fixed server role. Because MorrisL needs full administrative access to the entire system, you should add MorrisL to the sysadmin fixed server role.

To make this example easier to comprehend, AlsoRann has only one database. Look at the permissions that everyone needs on that database. As a customer service rep, SmithB needs permission to read the data but not to write any data; the db_denydatawriter fixed database role fits those needs well.

As a developer, GibsonH needs permission to create objects in the database, but GibsonH should not be able to read the data. Make GibsonH a member of the db_ddladmin role so they can create objects as DBO and avoid broken ownership chains. You could make GibsonH a member of the db_owner group and achieve the same effect, but then GibsonH would be able to do anything in the database, including read the data.

RosmanD needs to be able to select, insert, and update data, but RosmanD should not be able to delete any data. No fixed database role grants these three permissions together. You could apply all these permissions directly to RosmanD, but what if you hire more people who need the same permissions? It might be a better idea to create a custom database role; grant that role the Select, Insert, and Update permissions, and then make RosmanD a member of that role. The same is true of the Sales group, which needs permission to read and update; those members require a custom role.

For Accounting, it will be easiest just to add those members to the db_datareader and db_datawriter roles; this way, they will receive permissions to read and write to the database. MorrisL doesn't need to be a member of any role; because MorrisL is a member of the sysadmin fixed server role, MorrisL is automatically considered the DBO in every database on the server.

In the real world, of course, a security plan isn't going to be nearly this simple. You'll have hundreds, if not thousands, of users to deal with from a variety of networks, and each user needs different permissions. To sum up, although developing a security plan is probably more work than the actual implementation, you can't do without it.

Summary

SQL Server 2005 has a sophisticated security system that allows you to carefully implement your security plan. SQL Server can operate in Mixed security mode, which means Windows users and groups can be given access directly to SQL Server, or you can create separate, unique accounts that reside only in SQL Server. If SQL Server is running in Windows Authentication mode, every user must first connect with a preauthorized Windows account.

Case Study: Configuring Server Security at AlsoRann

When AlsoRann first installed SQL Server, the management realized that security was going to be extremely important, so they needed help devising a security plan.

The first issue we addressed was the security mode. Because all the users connecting to SQL Server would be using Windows XP, we decided to use Windows Authentication mode. This would allow AlsoRann to manage passwords in a single place with a unified policy. Next we needed to know what roles to put the users in, if any. AlsoRann had two DBAs, so we put both of them in the sysadmins fixed server role and removed the BUILTIN administrators group. This allowed the DBAs — and only the DBAs — to have administrative access to SQL Server. We decided to put the assistant DBA in the SecurityAdmin, ProcessAdmin, and BulkAdmin roles to alleviate some of the load from the DBAs.

It didn't make sense to create a login for each user in the company because many of the users required similar permissions, so we decided to create Windows groups for each department (such as accounting, sales, and marketing) and add the users Windows accounts to these groups. We then created a login for each Windows group in SQL Server to give the users the ability to connect.

A few special users needed different permissions on the server (managers and executives mostly), so we decided it was easiest to give them each an individual login. Also, five contract workers in the accounting department did not need access, so we created a group in Windows named Contractors and added all the contractors to that group. We then created a SQL Server login and denied access to this group so they would never be able to connect.

This chapter examined the processes of creating and managing logins, groups, and users. You learned how to create a Standard login and a Windows user or group login using SQL Server Management Studio or T-SQL, and you learned when each type is appropriate. If you have a well-designed security plan that incorporates growth, managing your user base can be a painless task.

To limit administrative access to SQL Server at the server level, you learned you can add users to a fixed server role. To limit access in a specific database, you can add users to a database role, and if one of the fixed database roles isn't to your liking, you can create your own. You can even go as far as to limit access to specific applications by creating an application role.

Each database in SQL Server 2005 has its own independent permissions. We looked at the two types of user permissions: statement permissions, which are used to create or change the data structure, and object permissions, which manipulate data. Remember that statement permissions can't be granted to other users.

The next section in this chapter described the database hierarchy. We looked at the permissions available to the most powerful users—the sysadmins—down through the lower-level database users.

You then learned about chains of ownership. These are created when you grant permissions to others on objects you own. Adding more users who create dependent objects creates broken ownership chains, which can become complex and tricky to manage. You learned how to predict the permissions available to users at different locations within these ownership chains. You also learned that to avoid the broken ownership chains, you can add your users to either the db_owner database role or the db_ddladmin database role and have your users create objects as the DBO.

You can grant permissions to database users as well as database roles. When a user is added to a role, they inherit the permissions of the role, including the public role, of which everyone is a member. The only exception is when the user has been denied permission, because Deny takes precedence over any other right, no matter the level at which the permission was granted.

We then covered remote and linked servers and showed how you need to set up security needs to make remote queries work. We finished with a look at linked server security and applications.

Exam Essentials

Know the differences in authentication modes.   Know when to use Mixed mode versus Windows Authentication mode. Mixed mode allows users who do not have an Active Directory account, such as Novell or Unix users, to access the SQL Server. Windows Authentication mode allows only users with Active Directory accounts to access SQL Server.

Understand your roles.   Be familiar with the various fixed server and database roles and what they can be used for in the real world. You also need to know when to create a custom database role instead of using the built-in roles. A good example is if you need to allow users to insert, update, and select on a table but they are not allowed to delete. No built-in role that allows this, so you would need a custom role.

Know your permissions.   Know what the permissions are and what they are for as well as how to assign them. Don't forget that two types of permissions exist, object and statement. Object permissions control a user's ability to create or modify database objects, such as tables and views. Statement permissions control a user's ability to manipulate data using statements such as SELECT or INSERT.

Review Questions

1. Jason is a member of a Windows group named Sales that has been granted access to SQL Server via a Windows group account in SQL Server. Jason should not have access to SQL Server, but he needs the permissions afforded the Sales group on other servers. How can you remedy this?

   A. Create a new Windows group named SQL_Sales, and add everyone but Jason to the group. Next, grant access to the SQL_Sales group by creating a group account in SQL Server, and then remove the Sales group account from SQL Server.

   B. Create a login on the SQL Server specifically for Jason, and deny the account access.

   C. Delete the Sales group login, and create separate accounts for everyone except Jason.

   D. Remove Jason from the Sales group in Windows, and grant him all the necessary permissions separately on all other servers on the network.

2. A shown in Figure 6.2, one of your users has created a table (John.table1) and granted Samantha Select permission on the table. Samantha, however, does not need to see all the data in the table so she creates a view (Samantha.view1). Thomas now wants access to Samantha's view, so Samantha grants Thomas Select permission on the view. What happens when Thomas tries to select from the view?

FIGURE 6.2   View permissions

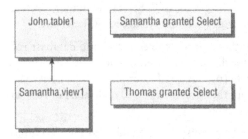

   A. Thomas can select from the view because he has been granted permissions on the view directly.

   B. Thomas cannot select from the view because he does not have permission on the underlying table and the ownership chain is broken.

   C. Thomas can select from the view because Samantha granted him permission on the view and she has permission on the underlying table.

   D. Thomas can select, but he receives an error message stating that he does not have permission on the underlying table.

3. Your SQL Server 2005 system stores information about suppliers in the Suppliers table. Table 6.2 shows the security for the table. Joe is a member of the Administration and Marketing roles in the database, and he needs to be able to perform inserts, updates, and deletes on the table. Which command should you use to give him these permissions?

TABLE 6.2   Permissions for Suppliers

Name	Select	Insert	Update	Delete
Administration	Granted	Granted	Granted	Granted
Marketing	Granted	Denied	Denied	Denied
Joe	Granted	Granted	Granted	Granted
Public	Granted	Granted	Granted	Granted

A. Use `sp_droprolemember 'Public', 'Joe'`.

B. Use `sp_droprolemember 'Marketing', 'Joe'`.

C. Use `sp_droprolemember 'Administration', 'Joe'`.

D. Do nothing; Joe already has these permissions.

4. You are the administrator of a SQL Server system that contains databases named Marketing and Sales. Amanda has a Windows account that has been granted a login to the SQL Server, and she has been given access to the Marketing database. Now she needs view and edit permissions on the Sales database as well. What T-SQL statements should you execute?

A. Use the following: `GRANT ALL ON Sales TO 'Amanda'`

B. Use the following: `EXEC sp_addrolemember 'db_datareader', 'Amanda'`
`EXEC sp_addrolemember 'db_datawriter','Amanda'`

C. Use the following: `GRANT SELECT ON Sales TO 'Amanda'`
`GRANT INSERT ON Sales TO 'Amanda'`
`GRANT UPDATE ON Sales TO 'Amanda'`

D. Use the following: `EXEC sp_grantaccess 'Amanda', 'AmandaU'`
`GO`
`EXEC sp_addrolemember 'db_datareader', 'AmandaU'`
`EXEC sp_addrolemember 'db_datawriter','AmandaU'`

5. Andrea is a member of the Sales and Marketing roles in your database. She needs Select, Insert, and Update permissions on your table. With security configured as shown here, how can you grant her the necessary permissions?

Select	Insert	Update	
Marketing	Revoked	Granted	Granted
Sales	Denied	Revoked	Revoked
Public	Granted	Revoked	Revoked

A. Add an account for Andrea, and grant it the necessary permissions.

B. Grant Select permission to the marketing role.

C. Grant Insert and Update permissions to the public role.

D. Remove Andrea from the sales role.

6. Two developers named IversonB and JacksonT need to be able to create objects in the Inventory database as part of their regular duties. You need to give them the ability to create these objects without giving them too much authority on the server. What is the most secure way to do this?

A. Add IversonB and JacksonT to the db_owner fixed database role, and instruct them to create objects as DBO.

B. Add IversonB and JacksonT to the db_ddladmin fixed database role, and instruct them to create objects as DBO.

C. Add IversonB and JacksonT to the sysadmin fixed server role, and instruct them to create objects as DBO.

D. Grant IversonB and JacksonT the permission to create objects in the database separately, and instruct them to create objects as DBO.

7. You need to grant Robert permission to modify employee phone numbers in the Employees table, but you do not want him to be able to modify any other data in the table. What is the best way to accomplish this?

A. Grant Robert Update permission on the Phone Number column of the table, and do not grant him permissions on any other column.

B. Create a view that contains only the Phone Number column, and grant Robert Update permission on the view.

C. Create a stored procedure to change the phone number, and grant Robert Execute permission on the stored procedure.

D. Create triggers on the table that reject any updates from Robert on columns other than the Phone Number column.

8. You have spent a great deal of money and effort to create a custom accounting program in Visual Basic that is designed to meet some specific needs of your company. You find that some of your users are still accessing your database through other methods such as Microsoft Excel and Query Analyzer, and this is causing problems with the integrity of your database. How can you fix this problem?

   A. Create a filter in Profiler that will reject access by all programs except your custom program.

   B. Create an account for your new application, and have all your users log in to SQL using that account. Then remove permissions from any remaining user accounts in the database.

   C. Create an application role for the account, and grant it the necessary permissions. Then add all the users in the database to the application role.

   D. Create an application role, and grant it the necessary permissions in the database. Then remove any permissions for your users in the database, and hard-code the `sp_activateapprole` stored procedure into your application to activate the role.

9. You have just created a new Windows account (Domain\BobH) for a new employee. You create a new SQL login for BobH using the command `sp_addlogin 'domain\BobH', 'password', 'accounting'`, but Bob is now complaining he cannot access SQL Server when he logs in with his Windows account. Why not?

   A. You need to configure the SQL Server to allow trusted accounts by using the command `sp_configure 'allow trusted connections', '1'`.

   B. The `sp_addlogin` command creates standard login accounts, not mapped login accounts. You need to map Bob's account to a SQL login with the `sp_grantlogin` stored procedure.

   C. Bob is not using the right network library to log in with a trusted account. Set the network library to Named Pipes, Multiprotocol, or TCP/IP.

   D. Bob's SQL Server account password does not match his Windows account password. Change one of the two so they match.

10. You are the administrator of a SQL Server system that contains a database named Accounting. To maintain strict security on the database, you want to make sure users do not have any default permissions when their account is first created. What should you do?

    A. Remove users from the public role, and add them back on an as-needed basis.

    B. In Enterprise Manager, remove all of the permissions from the public role by clicking each box until it is cleared.

    C. Execute the REVOKE ALL FROM PUBLIC command in Query Analyzer while using your database.

    D. Do nothing; no default permissions are granted to users when they are first created.

11. You have the authority to create both Windows accounts and SQL logins and roles on your network. You have a Windows server that contains a shared folder called Administration and a shared folder called Marketing. On your SQL Server database you have a database called Marketing. Ten of your users will be working on a short-term project together; all of them require the same access to the Marketing database on the SQL Server and the Marketing folder on the Windows server, but only four of them are allowed access to the Administration folder on the Windows server. What is the best way to grant these users access to the database resources?

    A. Add all the users to a Windows group, and map a SQL Server login to the new group. Then grant permissions to the group login.

    B. Create separate Windows logins for each user, and add them to a custom database role. Then assign permissions to the database role.

    C. Create a separate Windows login for each user, and grant permissions on the database to each user login.

    D. Create one login for all the users to log in with, and grant that user account permissions on the database.

12. You have several SQL Servers in your organization that participate in linked server queries with security configured as shown in Figure 6.3. BobH is complaining that the linked server queries are not working. Why can't BobH use linked server queries?

FIGURE 6.3   Linked server permissions

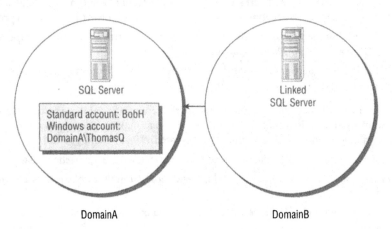

A. The server was not added as a linked server with the `sp_addlinkedserver` stored procedure.

B. The remote server has not been configured to accept incoming queries from other servers. You must configure it by setting the `ALLOW LINKED QUERIES` option to 1 using the `sp_configure` stored procedure.

C. BobH uses a standard account, so you need to map a linked server login for BobH by executing `sp_addlinkedsrvlogin` on the destination server.

D. The users who cannot access the linked server use standard logins, so you need to map a linked server login by executing `sp_addlinkedsrvlogin` on the local server.

13. You have just installed a new SQL Server on your network, and you want to make sure no Windows administrator has administrative access on the SQL Server until receiving the proper training. What should you do to keep a Windows administrator from trying to administer the new SQL Server and possibly damaging it?

A. Remove the BUILTIN\Administrators account from SQL Server. Then create a SQL-Admins group in Windows, and add all the SQL administrators to the new group. Finally, create a login mapped to the SQLAdmins group, and add it to the sysadmins role.

B. Create a separate login for each of your Windows administrators, and deny access for each of their logins.

C. Remove BUILTIN\Administrators from the sysadmins role, and create separate logins for each of the SQL administrators. Then add each separate login to the sysadmins role.

D. Do nothing; the Windows administrators do not have administrative access in SQL Server by default.

14. You are setting up a kiosk in a library that hundreds of people will access every month. You want to make sure visitors to the library have access to read data from the SQL Server, but they should not be able to change any of the data. You need to accomplish this with the least administrative overhead possible. What should you do?

A. Create a Windows account named Kiosk, and map a SQL login to that account. Then create a database user account for Kiosk, and add it to the db_denydatawriter and db_datareader roles. Finally, have all the library patrons log in to the computer system as Kiosk.

B. Enable the guest account in Windows, and map a SQL login to it. Then create a guest database user account, and add it to the db_denydatawriter and db_datareader roles.

C. Enable the guest user account in Windows. No guest login or database accounts need to be created in SQL Server because they already exist. Add the guest account to the db_denydatawriter and db_datareader roles.

D. Enable the guest user account in Windows, and map it to a SQL login. No database user account named guest will need to be created because it already exists in each database. Add the guest account to the db_denydatawriter and db_datareader roles.

15. You want to be able to use email, replication, and other interserver services with SQL Server. When you install SQL Server, what type of account should you use?

A. The local server account

B. A local account

C. A domain account with administrative privileges

D. A domain account with no administrative access

16. You need to create a new login account for one of your Unix users named WoodsJ. What command would you use to do this?

A. sp_addlogin 'WoodsJ', 'password', 'pubs'

B. sp_grantlogin 'WoodsJ', 'password', 'pubs'

C. sp_createlogin 'WoodsJ', 'password', 'pubs'

D. sp_makelogin 'WoodsJ', 'password', 'pubs'

17. You have an HR database that all users will be allowed to read from to obtain information, but only the HR department should be able to read from and update the data in the database. What is the easiest and most secure way for you to ensure this?

A. Add all the users who are not in the HR department to the db_datareader database role, and add all the users from the HR department to a custom database role that allows them all modification and selection permissions.

B. Add all the users who are not in the HR department to the db_datareader and db_deny-datawriter database roles, and add all the users from the HR department to the db_data-reader and db_datawriter database roles.

C. Add all the users who are not in the HR department to the db_datareader and db_deny-datawriter database roles, and add all the users from the HR department to the db_data-modifier database role.

D. Add all the users who are not in the HR department to the db_datareader and db_deny-datawriter database roles, and add all the users from the HR department to the db_owner database role.

18. You have a number of users in your customer service department who need Select, Insert, and Update permissions, but they should not be able to delete—only managers should have the permission to delete data. How can you ensure that only managers can delete data and users can only perform the tasks listed?

A. Add the users to the db_datareader and db_datawriter roles, and add the managers to the db_datadeleter role.

B. Add the users to the db_datareader role and the managers to the db_datawriter role.

C. Add the users to a custom role that allows only Select, Insert, and Update permissions and the managers to a custom role that allows them to read and modify data.

D. Add the users to a custom role that allows only Select, Insert, and Update permissions and the managers to the db_datareader and db_datawriter roles.

19. You are the administrator of a SQL Server system that will be used only for development access; the server will have no production databases on the server whatsoever. All your developers need to be able to create databases and objects inside the databases, such as tables, views, and so on. Which roles should they be added to at the server and database levels to accommodate these needs?

    A. sysadmins at the server level and db_owner at the database level

    B. sysadmins at the server level and db_ddladmins at the database level

    C. db_creator at the server level and db_ddladmin at the database level

    D. db_creator at the server level and db_owner at the database level

20. You are the administrator of a SQL Server system that will contain marketing, sales, and production data. Each of these departments is contained in a Windows group named after the department. Each of these departments should be able to read and modify their own data, but they should not be able to read or modify the data of other departments. You need to configure the server so it meets security requirements with minimal administrative overhead and resource consumption. What should you do? (Choose all that apply.)

    A. Create a single database for all the departments to share.

    B. Create a separate database for each department.

    C. Create a named instance of SQL Server for each department.

    D. Create a Windows Authenticated login for each department.

    E. Map each group to the sysadmin fixed server role.

    F. Map each user account to the db_datareader and db_datawriter database roles.

    G. Grant each of the database users Select, Insert, Update, and Delete permissions in the database.

    H. Create database user accounts for each department in the database.

Answers to Review Questions

1. B. The best way to accomplish this is to create a separate SQL login for Jason and deny it access. This way Jason can still be a member of the Sales group, with all of the associated access rights, but not get access to SQL Server.

2. B. Because the ownership chain is broken, Thomas cannot select from the view unless he is granted Select permission on the underlying table (John.table1).

3. B. Marketing has been denied the Select, Update, and Insert permissions, and this overrides any other permission settings. So, even though Joe has been specifically granted these permissions, he cannot use them because he is a member of a group that has been denied the permissions. The only way to get the permissions for him is to remove him from the group that has been denied these permissions.

4. D. To give Amanda access to another database, you first need to create a user account in the database, and then the easiest way to give her the necessary permissions is to add her to roles that already have the permissions assigned.

5. D. Removing Andrea from the sales role will give her the permissions she needs. She will inherit the Select permission from the public role and the Insert and Update permissions from the marketing role. None of the other options would work because as long as Andrea is a member of Sales, she would be denied the Select permission because Sales has been denied the permission.

6. B. Adding users to the db_ddladmin role is the most secure way to accomplish this goal. Adding them to the db_owner or sysadmin role would grant them too much authority over the database and would not maintain strict security. Having them create objects as DBO will avoid broken ownership chains as well.

7. C. Column-level permissions are possible in SQL Server 2005, but they are hard to maintain and rarely the answer to security problems. You could use a view, but it is not usually best to create a view for just a single column. Creating a stored procedure and granting Robert Execute permission is the best way to fix this issue.

8. D. In this case, you need to create an application role and activate it through your Visual Basic code. This will cause SQL Server to see all your users as the application role and grant them all of the rights and permissions of that role.

9. B. You must use `sp_grantlogin` to map a SQL Server login to a Windows login. The `sp_addlogin` stored procedure creates standard logins.

10. C. Users cannot be removed from the public role, which has every permission granted by default. The easiest way to remove these permissions is with the `REVOKE ALL FROM PUBLIC` command.

11. B. Because the users do not need access to the same resources on the Windows servers, you have no reason to create a Windows group for them. Because so few users are here, it is easiest to create user accounts for each user and add them to a custom database role.

12. D. For users who use standard logins to access a linked server, you need to map a local login to a login on the remote server using the `sp_addlinkedsrvlogin` command.

13. A. The most secure and easiest way to accomplish this task is to remove the Windows Administrators group from the SQL Server and add a new group of your own creation in its place. You do not actually have to remove the login entirely; however, because you have no use for it afterward, you don't need to keep it around.

14. D. Creating a user account especially for this application is possible but hard to manage, especially when a database user account already exists for each database. Therefore, creating a user login for the guest account is the easiest way to allow access to the kiosk.

15. C. If you want to perform replication, your SQL Server Agent service needs to log in with administrative access. All other interserver services (such as email) need at least a domain account with access to the requested services.

16. A. Because this is a Unix user, you know the user does not have a Windows account against which to be verified. You must use `sp_addlogin` as opposed to `sp_grantlogin`, which is used only for mapping to Windows accounts. The other two stored procedures do not exist.

17. B. Users can be members of more than one group, so it is easiest to add the members of HR to the db_datareader and db_datawriter roles and add everyone else to the db_datareader role to grant the permission to read data and to the db_denydatawriter role to deny them the permission to modify data.

18. D. No fixed database role allows the permissions that the users need, but the managers need the permissions that are allowed by the db_datareader and db_datawriter roles. Therefore, you need to use fixed roles for the managers and custom roles for the users.

19. C. The db_creator membership will give the developers just enough permission to create databases at the server level, and db_ddladmins will give them just enough permission to create objects in the databases they create. The sysadmin and db_owner roles will give them too much permission and therefore allow for lax security.

20. B, D, F, H. In this instance, you should create a separate database for each of the departments so they do not have access to the other departments' data. You also need to create a login for each of the groups and then create a database user account in the corresponding database for each login. Finally, add the accounts to the db_datareader and db_datawriter roles.

Chapter

7

Working with Relational Data

MICROSOFT EXAM OBJECTIVES COVERED IN THIS CHAPTER:

✓ **Retrieve data to support ad hoc and recurring queries.**

- Construct SQL queries to return data.
- Format the results of SQL queries.
- Identify collation details.

✓ **Manipulate relational data.**

- Insert, update, and delete data.
- Handle exceptions and errors.
- Manage transactions.

✓ **Import and export data from a file.**

- Set a database to the bulk-logged recovery model to avoid inflating the transaction log.
- Run the bcp utility.
- Perform a bulk-insert task.
- Import bulk XML data using the OPENROWSET function.
- Copy data from one table to another by using the SQL Server 2005 Integration Services (SSIS) Import and Export Wizard.

Several steps take place when representing relational data to the user. For instance, data can come from heterogeneous sources, and often data needs to be transferred while maintaining transactional consistency. In this chapter, you will learn how SQL Server handles transactions and how you can influence SQL Server by using implicit transactions. You will also learn how to import data using different data manipulation tools such as the bcp utility and a helpful SQL Server component called SQL Server Integration Services (SSIS).

When working with data, you often need to know how to import or export data and how to return data in various formats. When inserting large amounts of data, it is important to also know how to optimize the transaction log without minimizing the impact of the bulk insert logging. You can format data to represent it in a different way by using built-in functions and formatting options.

Understanding and Using Transactions

To help you understand how SQL Server handles and works with transactions to perform data manipulations (via *DML*), this section will cover how data is inserted and allocated in memory before the data is written into the transaction log and then how it is applied to the database data files. When performing data manipulations, SQL Server records all changes made in the transaction log to allow any changes to be undone (rolled back) or redone (rolled forward) in case of a system failure.

When updating or inserting a record into a database, the record is first allocated in buffer memory, and the buffer manager guarantees that the transaction log is written before the changes to the database file are written. It does this by keeping track of a log position using a log sequence number (LSN).

At certain intervals SQL Server will issue a *checkpoint* in the transaction log that will issue a write from the transaction log to the data file. Depending on the setting of the transaction log defined in the database recovery model, the transaction log will keep the committed and written records in the transaction log or truncate the log. Figure 7.1 shows this entire process.

This process of working with the transaction log and recording actions in the transaction log before applying them to the actual data files allows SQL Server to recover from failures in case of an unexpected shutdown; this is known as *autorecovery*.

The autorecovery process will check the database to see what the last-issued checkpoint and written LSN was and will then write all committed records from the transaction log that were not recorded yet in the data file to the data file. This process is a rollforward. Different from other database systems such as Oracle, SQL Server automatically issues a transaction (autocommitted) on every statement, so you don't need to explicitly commit these transactions.

FIGURE 7.1   SQL Server transactional processing

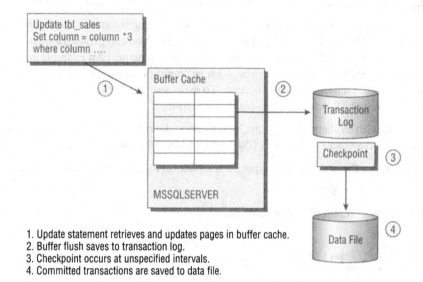

1. Update statement retrieves and updates pages in buffer cache.
2. Buffer flush saves to transaction log.
3. Checkpoint occurs at unspecified intervals.
4. Committed transactions are saved to data file.

In the next section, you'll learn the difference between implicit and explicit transactions.

Executing Implicit and Explicit Transactions

By default SQL Server automatically commits a transaction to the database and every transaction is handled as a single process. When you perform a query that issues a DML statement (insert/update/delete), SQL Server will automatically commit the transaction by recording an LSN in the transaction log. Because this process occurs without any explicit request from you to confirm the action, this is called an autocommit.

When working with transactions SQL Server supports two types of transactions: implicit and explicit.

When using implicit transactions you will need to commit every statement to the database after executed. The difference between an implicit transaction and autocommitted transaction is that you still need to COMMIT the transaction by the end of the statement.

In order to group transactions together as one single unit, you will have to use explicit transactions. For example, when you transfer money from one bank account to another using a transaction, you want the action to take place on both of the accounts at the same time; to guarantee that this occurs, you have to perform an explicit transaction. An explicit transaction occurs when the statement you issue is preceded by a BEGIN TRAN or BEGIN TRANSACTION statement. You can group transactions since some of the database actions you want to perform belong together. An example is a money transfer from one account to the other; you want to commit the entire transaction only when the account updates on both accounts succeed. To make sure these transactions execute as one single block or not at all, you use an explicit transaction.

When working with explicit transactions, you identify the transactions by using a BEGIN TRANSACTION and a COMMIT TRANSACTION or ROLLBACK TRANSACTION statement.

Explicit transactions An explicit transaction occurs when the statement you issue is preceded by a BEGIN TRAN or BEGIN TRANSACTION statement. You can group transactions since some of the database actions you want to perform belong together. An example is a money transfer from one account to the other; you want to commit the entire transaction only when the account updates on both accounts succeed. To make sure these transactions execute as one single block or not at all, you use an explicit transaction.

When working with explicit transactions, you identify the transactions by using a BEGIN TRANSACTION and a COMMIT TRANSACTION or ROLLBACK TRANSACTION statement.

Figure 7.2 displays the process of grouping a transaction logically based upon transactional consistency.

FIGURE 7.2 Transactional consistency

Committing and Rolling Back

When you want to confirm a transaction, you issue a COMMIT TRANSACTION statement. This will close the open statements and confirm the grouped DML statements. If you don't want a transaction to occur, you issue a ROLLBACK TRANSACTION statement.

For example, say you want to delete a customer in your Customers database; however, before you delete the customer, you want to insert the customer details into a history table and commit the deletion only if the insert into the temporary table succeeded. Figure 7.3 shows this process. Your decision whether to roll back or commit a transaction depends upon error handling; we'll discuss this further in the "Introducing Error Handling" section.

A typical transaction block looks like this:

```
BEGIN TRANSACTION
--actions
COMMIT TRANSACTION
```

SQL Server supports the *nesting* of transactions; in other words, within a transaction, another transaction can be called. When *nesting transactions,* the outer transaction will determine when the inner transaction is committed. However, this allows you to partially commit and roll back some of the transactions within an outer transaction block. Figure 7.4 shows a typical nested transaction process.

You can monitor transactions in SQL Server using the @@TRANCOUNT variable, which will show you the number of open transactions.

FIGURE 7.3   Transaction handling

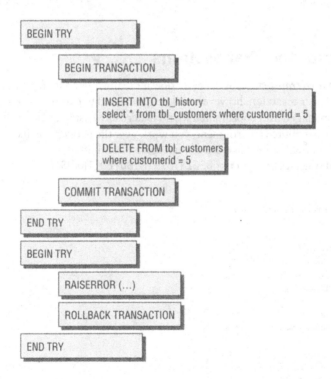

FIGURE 7.4 Nested transactions

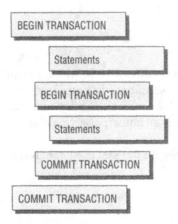

Executing Distributed Transactions

When executing a *distributed transaction*, SQL Server doesn't really differ a lot from executing an explicit transaction. The transaction, however, will be considered to execute over a remote connection and will be managed and coordinated by the Microsoft Distributed Transaction Coordinator (DTC). In a distributed environment, you work over the network segment, so the execution of the transaction will take place using a two-phase commit.

To start a distributed transaction, you use BEGIN DISTRIBUTED TRANSACTION, as displayed in Figure 7.5.

FIGURE 7.5 Distributed transactions

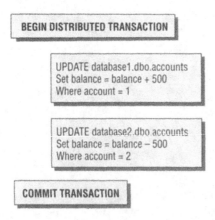

Populating Tables

When populating tables by inserting data, you will discover that data can come from various sources. One of these sources could be an application where you would use INSERT/UPDATE/ DELETE statements to populate and manipulate the data you store in a SQL Server database. However, various options and data coming from heterogeneous environments can end up and be stored in SQL Server as their final storage destination. Therefore, it is important to identify the appropriate methods for inserting this data in the most common and preferable way.

One of these could be by using BULK INSERT statements to populate and load data from a file system; another might be the insertion of data using complex data transformations.

You can import data using the following:

- BULK INSERT statements
- The bcp utility
- Data transformations using SSIS

We will cover the various options in the next sections.

Importing Data Using Bulk Insert

A BULK INSERT statement loads a data file into the database using a user-specified format, without forcing the execution of the constraints defined on the destination object.

The key strength of a BULK INSERT statement is that you can also specify what will be the field terminator and the row terminator because they are configured in the source file to perform the bulk inserts. However, when performing a BULK INSERT statement, you need to make sure the data retrieved from the source file matches the columns in the table into which you are inserting. The following code sample uses the pipe (|) as a field terminator and |\n as a row terminator:

```
BULK INSERT Sybex.dbo.Airportcodes
   FROM 'd:\Files\Airportcodes.tbl'
   WITH
      (
         FIELDTERMINATOR =' |',
         ROWTERMINATOR =' |\n'
      )
```

The following is the full syntax of the BULK INSERT statement:

```
BULK INSERT
   [ database_name . [ schema_name ] .
   | schema_name . ] [ table_name | view_name ]
     FROM 'data_file'
     [ WITH
     (
```

```
[ [ , ] BATCHSIZE = batch_size ]
[ [ , ] CHECK_CONSTRAINTS ]
[ [ , ] CODEPAGE = { 'ACP' | 'OEM' | 'RAW' | 'code_page' } ]
[ [ , ] DATA FILETYPE  =
   { 'char' | 'native'| 'widechar' | 'widenative' } ]
[ [ , ] FIELDTERMINATOR = 'field_terminator' ]
[ [ , ] FIRSTROW  =first_row ]
[ [ , ] FIRE_TRIGGERS ]
[ [ , ] FORMATFILE = 'format_file_path' ]
[ [ , ] KEEPIDENTITY ]
[ [ , ] KEEPNULLS ]
[ [ , ] KILOBYTES_PER_BATCH =kilobytes_per_batch ]
[ [ , ] LASTROW = last_row ]
[ [ , ] MAXERRORS = max_errors ]
[ [ , ] ORDER ( { column [ ASC | DESC ] } [ ,...n ] ) ]
[ [ , ] ROWS_PER_BATCH = rows_per_batch ]
[ [ , ] ROWTERMINATOR = 'row_terminator' ]
[ [ , ] TABLOCK ]
[ [ , ] ERRORFILE = 'file_name' ]
)]
```

Importing Data Using the *bcp* Utility

The bcp utility, a command-line tool, is commonly used for importing and exporting data by performing bulk imports/exports of data. The utility allows you to do the following:

- You can bulk export data from a table to a file.
- You can bulk export data from a query to a file.
- You can bulk import data into SQL Server.
- You can create format files.

The bcp utility is a command prompt tool that requires the necessary switches to specify the datatype of the data file, and you can create a format file based upon the questions that the bcp tool asks you when you don't specify a format file. Here's the syntax:

```
bcp {[[database_name.][owner].]
{table_name | view_name} | "query"}
    {in | out | queryout | format} data_file
    [-mmax_errors] [-fformat_file] [-x] [-eerr_file]
    [-Ffirst_row] [-Llast_row] [-bbatch_size]
    [-n] [-c] [-w] [-N] [-V (60 | 65 | 70 | 80)] [-6]
    [-q] [-C { ACP | OEM | RAW | code_page } ]
    [-tfield_term][-rrow_term] [-iinput_file]
    [-ooutput_file] [-apacket_size]
```

```
[-Sserver_name[\instance_name]]
 [-Ulogin_id] [-Ppassword]
    [-T] [-v] [-R] [-k] [-E] [-h"hint [,...n]"]
```

To create a format file, you use the format argument in the bcp command. You use the in parameter to import data, and you use the out parameter to export from a table or view. However, when you want to export from a query, you need to use the queryout option.

In Exercise 7.1 you will learn how to import a list of countries into a country table in the Sybex database using the bcp utility.

EXERCISE 7.1

Importing Data from a Text File Using *bcp*

1. Open a new database query window in SQL Management Studio.

2. Type the following syntax to create the countries table:

    USE SYBEX

    CREATE TABLE countries

    (countrycode char(2), Countryname varchar(50))

3. After you execute the CREATE TABLE statement (by clicking the Execute button or pressing the F5 function key), you can close SQL Management Studio.

4. Open a command prompt window, and change the directory location to c:\sybex\Chapter7.

5. You will now use the bcp utility to import data from a text file by typing the following command:

    bcp sybex.dbo.countries

    ➡in countries.txt -f countries.fmt -T

6. When you execute this command, you will get the following result set:

    Starting copy...

    4 rows copied.

    Network packet size (bytes): 4096

    Clock Time (ms.): total   1

7. Now use the sqlcmd command to verify that the records have successfully been inserted using the bcp utility:

    sqlcmd -E -Q "select * from sybex.dbo.countries"

8. This results in the following:

```
countrycode countryname

----------- ------------------------------

BE          Belgium

CA          Canada

US          USA

FR          France


(4 rows affected)
```

9. Close the command prompt window.

Copying Data Using SSIS

In SQL Server 2000 a commonly used tool to import and export data was the SQL Server 2000 DTS Wizard. SQL Server 2005 provides a new extract/transfer/load (ETL) platform: SSIS. With SSIS you have the ability to import and export data from heterogeneous sources to various destinations. The toolset provides you with extensive data transformations.

SSIS integrates with SQL Server Business Intelligence Development Studio and allows you to use a package designer or a wizard to import and export data while setting custom transformations. It works with data adapters that allow you to transfer data from any source to basically any destination. A package can connect to relational databases by using .NET and OLE DB providers and to many databases by using ODBC drivers. You can also connect to flat files, Excel files, and Analysis Services projects.

SSIS is a tool that is often used to populate data marts and data warehouses. Figure 7.6 shows you the SSIS window that consists of a Data Flow panel and a Control Flow panel where the entire data transfer is specified.

With its extensive data transformation capabilities and record manipulations that can be performed inside an SSIS package, you should consider using SSIS as a high-performance ETL tool, which allows you to perform complex data transformations often required in an ETL process. The benefit of SSIS over bcp and bulk inserts is that you can work with transactions; in addition, you have many more options for transferring data and performing custom data mapping.

In Exercise 7.2 you will open an SSIS package to import data from an Excel spreadsheet to a SQL Server 2005 database.

FIGURE 7.6   SSIS interface

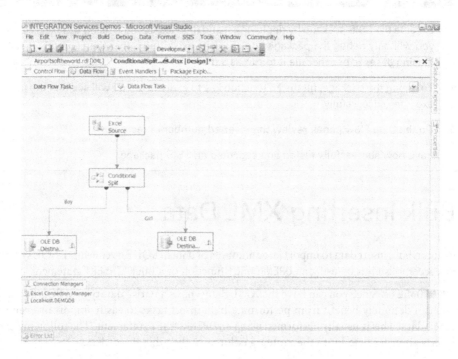

EXERCISE 7.2

Using SSIS

SSIS provides a graphical interface that allows you to transfer data from multiple sources to many destinations using complex manipulations. In this exercise, you will work with an SSIS package that will transfer data from a single Excel spreadsheet to SQL Server but that splits the source data into two tables. You'll manage this by using a conditional split, which is one of the new features of SSIS.

1. Open an existing package, and review its content.

2. In the Sybex\Chapter7\SSIS folder on this book's CD, double-click DemoSolution.ssln.

3. View the Data Flow panel:

    a. On the Data Flow panel, view the data coming from the Excel spreadsheet.

    b. On the Data Flow panel, view the two data sources going to SQL Server 2005.

4.   Execute the SSIS package by deploying it and then executing it using dtsexec. However, you will only debug the package and check its execution rather than compile it and run it using dtsexec or schedule it to run as a job.

5.   To debug the package, hit the F5 function key to execute it. You will see that the package executes successfully.

6.   On the Data Flow panel, review the inserted number of records.

You have now successfully tested and executed an SSIS package.

Bulk Inserting XML Data

You can bulk insert data to import large amounts of data in SQL Server using T-SQL syntax. You can accomplish this by using an OPENROWSET function or a BULK INSERT statement.

OPENROWSET   Since you can have the XML datatype as a native datatype in SQL Server 2005, you can definitely benefit from performing bulk insert tasks to easily import or even update XML data. This is usually performed using an OPENROWSET statement. The following example inserts an order detail into the xmldata column of the table tbl_orders:

```
INSERT INTO Tbl_orders(Xmldata)
SELECT * FROM OPENROWSET(
    BULK 'c:\Sybex\OpenRowsetXmldata.xml',
    SINGLE_BLOB) AS x
```

Of course, you also have the possibility of updating existing data using the BULK INSERT statement, as shown here:

```
UPDATE tbl_orders
SET Xmldata =(
SELECT * FROM OPENROWSET(
    BULK 'C:\Sybex\OpenRowsetXMLdata.xml',
            SINGLE_BLOB
) AS x
)
WHERE RowID = 1
GO
```

Besides being able to use the OPENROWSET to insert XML data, you can also use it to retrieve data from different OLE DB or ODBC providers using the full OPENROWSET syntax:

```
OPENROWSET
( { 'provider_name' ,
{ 'datasource' ; 'user_id' ; 'password'
  | 'provider_string' }
    , {   [ catalog. ] [ schema. ] object
      | 'query'
    }
  | BULK 'data_file' ,
      { FORMATFILE = 'format_file_path'
[ <bulk_options> ]
      | SINGLE_BLOB | SINGLE_CLOB | SINGLE_NCLOB }
} )


<bulk_options> ::=
    [ , CODEPAGE = { 'ACP' | 'OEM'
  | 'RAW' | 'code_page' } ]
    [ , ERRORFILE = 'file_name' ]
    [ , FIRSTROW = first_row ]
    [ , LASTROW = last_row ]
    [ , MAXERRORS = maximum_errors ]
    [ , ROWS_PER_BATCH = rows_per_batch ]
```

BULK INSERT   Another option for inserting XML data is to use the BULK INSERT statement, covered earlier in this chapter; this allows you to specify that the format file be in an XML format.

Supporting the Bulk-Logged Recovery Model

Choosing a Full database recovery model would have a big impact on the transaction log when performing BULK INSERT statements. To have less impact on the transaction log, you can implement the *Bulk-Logged recovery model*.

In contrast to the Full recovery model, the *Bulk-Logged* model logs bulk operations in a minimal mode. This allows the *Bulk-Logged* model to protect against media failures and provide the best performance and least log space usage.

When setting the Bulk-Logged recovery model, you can recover from a full backup only in total, that is, without performing a point-in-time recovery. When performing a log backup, you will also require access to the data files that contain the bulk-logged transactions, because the Bulk-Logged recovery model does not insert the actual transactions in the transaction log; it just keeps track of them. This means when data files in the Bulk-Logged recovery model are not accessible, you will not be able to perform any log backup.

To set the Bulk-Logged recovery model, you can use the ALTER database statement, as shown here:

```
ALTER DATABASE SYBEX SET RECOVERY BULK_LOGGED
```

Of course, you can also alter the database settings by using SQL Server Management Studio, as displayed in Figure 7.7.

FIGURE 7.7   Setting the Bulk-Logged recovery model

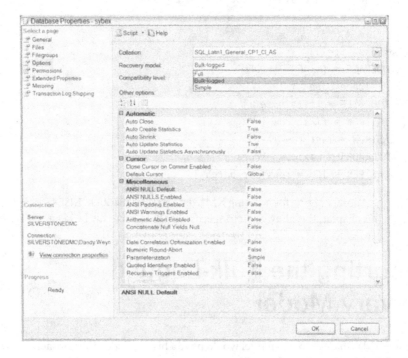

> ### ⊕ **Real World Scenario**
>
> #### Case Study: Working with Heterogeneous Data
>
> The XYZ company ships orders from pharmaceutical companies to customers all over the world. The company implemented SQL Server 2005 within its business environment. Since the company also works with a lot of third-party companies, it frequently needs to import data to and export data from SQL Server.
>
> Some of the data the company retrieves is in the form of XML files. This data can easily be imported into the system using a BULK INSERT statement.
>
> However, to map data and present it to some of XYZ's customers and co-workers in the industry, XYZ needs to perform complex data migrations to streamline the data to the target servers. For the advanced data migrations, the company uses SSIS packages that are scheduled to run multiple times a week.
>
> In the execution of the package flow, the company sends informational messages out by email to inform the database administrators about the execution steps in the packages.

Supporting Different Collation Types and Orders When Querying Data

When querying data, you sometimes need to return the data in a different format than what you want it to be returned in. For instance, the data could be returned as follows:

- In a different format
- In a different order
- In a different collation

To format data, you have several functions you can apply to a query; for example, you can apply the CONVERT function to convert between datatypes, or you can format datetime options, as shown here:

```
-- This example will display a string with
-- the current date displayed as: Today is mm/dd/yyyy
select 'Today is ' + convert(varchar,getdate(),101) as Currentdate
```

Formatting and Converting Datatypes

We already mentioned that you'll often need to convert and modify data. SQL Server offers an extensive set of functions you can use to perform conversions and formatting. You can categorize these functions into groups:

Aggregate functions   These perform operations that combine multiple values into one value by grouping, summarizing, or averaging the values. The aggregate functions include the following:

AVG	MIN
CHECKSUM	STDEV
CHECKSUM_AGG	STDEVP
COUNT	SUM
COUNT_BIG	VAR
GROUPING	VARP
MAX	

Configuration functions   Scalar functions return information about configuration settings. Configuration functions include functions such as server_name() and db_name(), which will give you information about server and database configurations, respectively.

Cryptographic functions   These functions support encryption, decryption, digital signing, and the validation of digital signatures. SQL Server 2005 supports the encryption and decryption of data using EncryptbyKey and DecryptbyKey functions. SQL Server Books Online will give you a full overview of the functionality of these functions.

Cursor functions   These return information about the status of a cursor.

Date and time functions   Date and time functions provide you with the capability to manipulate and calculate with dates and time values. Table 7.1 describes the date and time functions.

Mathematical functions   These perform trigonometric, geometric, and other numeric operations. The functions are as follows:

ABS	LOG10
ACOS	PI
ASIN	POWER
ATAN	RADIANS
ATN2	RAND
CEILING	ROUND

COS	SIGN
COT	SIN
DEGREES	SQRT
EXP	SQUARE
FLOOR	TAN
LOG	

TABLE 7.1   Date and Time Functions

Function	Description
DATEADD	Returns a new datetime value based on adding an interval to the specified date.
DATEDIFF	Returns the number of date and time boundaries crossed between two specified dates.
DATENAME	Returns a character string representing the specified date name of the specified date.
DATEPART	Returns an integer that represents the specified date part of the specified date.
DAY	Returns an integer representing the day part of the specified date.
GETDATE	Returns the current system date and time in the SQL Server 2005 standard internal format for datetime values.
GETUTCDATE	Returns the datetime value representing the current UTC (Coordinated Universal Time). The current UTC is derived from the current local time and the time zone setting in the operating system of the computer on which the instance of Microsoft SQL Server is running.
MONTH	Returns an integer that represents the month part of a specified date.
YEAR	Returns an integer that represents the year part of a specified date.

Metadata functions   These return information about the attributes of databases and database objects.

Ranking functions   These are nondeterministic functions that return a ranking value for each row in a partition. Ranking functions are new to SQL Server 2005 and allow you to use a rank or a row number within a result set. Table 7.2 describes the ranking functions.

TABLE 7.2   Ranking Functions

Function	Description
RANK	Returns the rank of each row within the partition of a result set. The rank of a row is 1 plus the number of ranks that come before the row in question.
DENSE_RANK	Returns the rank of rows within the partition of a result set, without any gaps in the ranking. The rank of a row is 1 plus the number of distinct ranks that come before the row in question.
ROW_NUMBER	Returns the sequential number of a row within a partition of a result set, starting at 1 for the first row in each partition.
NTILE	Distributes the rows in an ordered partition into a specified number of groups. The groups are numbered, starting at 1. For each row, NTILE returns the number of the group to which the row belongs.

Rowset functions   These return the rowsets that can be used in place of a table reference in a T-SQL statement.

Security functions   These return information about users and roles.

String functions   These change char, varchar, nchar, nvarchar, binary, and varbinary values. Table 7.3 describes the string functions.

TABLE 7.3   String Functions

Function	Description
ASCII	Returns the ASCII value of a character
CHAR	Returns the character value of an integer
CHARINDEX	Returns the position where a character appears in the provided string set
DIFFERENCE	Returns an integer value that indicates the difference between the SOUNDEX values of two character expressions
LEFT	Returns the left part of a character string with the specified number of characters
LEN	Returns the number of characters of the specified string expression, excluding trailing blanks
LOWER	Returns the lowercase value of a given string

TABLE 7.3   String Functions *(continued)*

Function	Description
LTRIM	Returns the string value without leading blanks
NCHAR	Returns the Unicode character with the specified integer code, as defined by the Unicode standard
PATINDEX	Returns the starting position of the first occurrence of a pattern in a specified expression
QUOTENAME	Puts the string value in a given quoted notation
REPLACE	Replaces the first occurrence in the string value
REPLICATE	Replicates a character set a given number of times
REVERSE	Reverses the string
RIGHT	Returns an *x* number of rightmost values of a string
RTRIM	Returns the string value excluding trailing blanks
SOUNDEX	Returns a four-character (SOUNDEX) code to evaluate the similarity of two strings
SPACE	Returns the number of spaces provided
STR	Converts the provided datatype in a string value
STUFF	Deletes a specified length of characters and inserts another set of characters at a specified starting point
SUBSTRING	Returns a subset of the string value
UNICODE	Returns the integer value, as defined by the Unicode standard, for the first character of the input expression
UPPER	Returns the uppercase value of a given string

System functions   These operate on or report on various system-level options and objects. Table 7.4 describes the system functions.

System statistical functions   These return information about the performance of SQL Server.

Text and image functions   These change text and image data values.

TABLE 7.4   System Functions

Function	Description
APP_NAME	Returns the application name for the current session if set by the application.
CASE expression	Evaluates the expression in a multivalued IF statement.
CAST and CONVERT	Explicitly converts an expression of one datatype to another.
COALESCE	Returns the first non-null expression among its arguments.
COLLATIONPROPERTY	Returns the property of a specified collation.
COLUMNS_UPDATED	Returns a varbinary bit pattern that indicates the columns in a table or view that were inserted or updated. COLUMNS_UPDATED is used anywhere inside the body of a T-SQL INSERT or UPDATE trigger to test whether the trigger should execute certain actions.
CURRENT_TIMESTAMP	Returns the current date and time.
CURRENT_USER	Returns the name of the current user.
DATALENGTH	Returns the number of bytes used to represent any expression.
@@ERROR	Returns the error number for the last T-SQL statement executed.
ERROR_LINE	Returns the line number at which an error occurred that caused the CATCH block of a TRY…CATCH construct to be run.
ERROR_MESSAGE	Returns the message text of the error that caused the CATCH block of a TRY…CATCH construct to be run.
ERROR_NUMBER	Returns the error number of the error that caused the CATCH block of a TRY…CATCH construct to be run.
ERROR_STATE (T-SQL)	Returns the state number of the error that caused the CATCH block of a TRY…CATCH construct to be run.
fn_helpcollations	Returns a list of all the collations supported by Microsoft SQL Server 2005.
fn_servershareddrives	Returns the names of shared drives used by the clustered server.
fn_virtualfilestats	Returns I/O statistics for database files, including log files.

TABLE 7.4   System Functions *(continued)*

Function	Description
GETANSINULL	Returns the default nullability for the database for this session.
HOST_ID	Returns the workstation identification number.
HOST_NAME	Returns the workstation name.
IDENT_CURRENT	Returns the last identity value generated for a specified table or view in any session and any scope.
IDENT_INCR	Returns the increment value of an identity.
IDENT_SEED	Returns the seed value that was specified on an identity column
@@IDENTITY	Returns the last-inserted identity value.
IDENTITY (Function)	Used only in a SELECT statement with an INTO table clause to insert an identity column into a new table.
ISDATE	Determines whether an input expression is a valid date.
ISNULL	Determines whether an input value is null.
ISNUMERIC	Determines whether an input value is numeric.
NEWID	Generates a new GUID.
NULLIF	Returns null if two expressions are equal.
PARSENAME	Returns the specified part of an object name.
@@TRANCOUNT	Counts the currently opened transactions.
UPDATE()	Validates to true if a column is updated.
USER_NAME (T-SQL)	Returns the username.

Casting and Converting

When working with data, often you'll want to represent data in a different format or explicitly convert data to a different datatype.

In the following example, you have two integers that you want to calculate with; say you want to divide 5 by 2. What should this result in? Well that depends; a logical answer is that 5 divided by 2 returns 2.5, right? But what happens if you run the following example in a query?

```
Declare @col1 int
Declare @col2 int
Declare @result decimal (9,2)
Set @col1 = 5
Set @col2 = 2
Set @result = @col1 / @col2
print @result
```

Something happens that you probably didn't expect...your result set is 2.0.

What is the story behind this? It is called *datatype precedence*. Every datatype in SQL Server gets a certain ranking or priority. So, if you combine two integers together in a calculation, your result set will be an integer as well.

Now in the previous example, the @result variable is declared as a decimal. So the calculation with the integer will take place, and then it will be stored in a decimal column, which is why the result set gives 2.0 instead of the expected 2.5.

To do the conversion appropriately, you need to cast or convert one of the integer datatypes to a decimal first. The CAST and CONVERT functions will basically return the same result but have different notation.

This is the CAST syntax:

```
CAST ( expression AS data_type [ (length ) ])
```

This is the CONVERT syntax:

```
CONVERT ( data_type [ ( length ) ] , expression [ , style ] )
```

This means if you want to modify the statement from the previous example to get the required result set, you can use CAST or CONVERT. The following example shows you the CAST function:

```
Declare @col1 int
Declare @col2 int
Declare @result decimal (9,2)
Set @col1 = 5
Set @col2 = 2
Set @result = cast(@col1 as decimal(9,2)) / @col2
print @result
```

Of course, you can also write this using CONVERT:

```
Declare @col1 int
Declare @col2 int
Declare @result decimal (9,2)
Set @col1 = 5
Set @col2 = 2
Set @result = convert(decimal(9,2),@col1) / @col2
print @result
```

We prefer to use CAST instead of convert because it is more readable, but there is initially no difference. However, you should use CONVERT when playing around with dates. With the CONVERT function you can specify the style in which you want to present a date. Table 7.5 shows the most common styles used with the CONVERT function.

So if you want to represent the current date as a varchar with only the date part, your statement will look like this:

```
Select convert(varchar,getdate(),101)
```

> **NOTE**   When converting datatypes, you can use the CAST function or the CONVERT function. This will allow you to explicitly convert two datatypes. CONVERT and CAST provide the same features, but with CONVERT you have the ability to return a date in a certain format by specifying the style.

TABLE 7.5   Common Styles Used with the CONVERT Function

Style	Example
101	mm/dd/yyyy
102	yy.mm.dd
103	dd/mm/yy
104	dd.mm.yy
105	dd-mm-yy
106	dd mon yy
107	Mon dd, yy
108	hh:mm:ss

Understanding Datatype Precedence

As already mentioned, datatypes have a certain order, or *precedence*. This means when combining datatypes, implicit data conversion will occur, and the datatype with the highest rank has priority.

When working with datatypes and returning query results, it is important to understand the datatype precedence, which is displayed in order here:

1. Ssql_variant
2. Xml
3. Datetime
4. Smalldatetime
5. Float
6. Real
7. Decimal
8. Money
9. Smallmoney
10. Bigint
11. Int
12. Smallint
13. Tinyint
14. Bit
15. Ntext
16. Text
17. Image
18. Timestamp
19. Uniqueidentifier
20. Nvarchar
21. Nchar
22. Varchar
23. Char
24. Varbinary
25. Binary (lowest)

Datatype precedence is often forgotten in application code as well, which of course could result in unexpected result sets.

Understanding Collations

Collations are used within databases in order to display and store an international character set, based on business requirements. When returning data, you have the ability to retrieve the data in a collation type different from how it was stored. When working with these multiple collations, you can invoke the COLLATE keyword and then specify the collation type you prefer to use. You can use the COLLATE keyword in various ways and at several levels:

COLLATE on database creation   You can use the COLLATE clause of the CREATE DATABASE or ALTER DATABASE statement to specify the default collation of the database. You can also specify a collation when you create a database using SQL Server Management Studio. If you do not specify a collation, the database is assigned the default collation of the instance of SQL Server.

COLLATE on table creation   You can specify *collations* for each varchar or char column using the COLLATE clause in the CREATE TABLE or ALTER TABLE statement. You can also specify a collation when you create a table using SQL Server Management Studio. If you do not specify a collation, the column is assigned the default collation of the database.

COLLATE by casting or expression   You can use the COLLATE clause to cast an expression to a certain collation. You can assign the COLLATE clause to any ORDER BY or comparison state-ment, as listed in the example here:

```
use adventureworks
Select firstname, lastname from person.contact
ORDER BY lastname COLLATE Latin1_General_BIN
```

Collations supported by SQL 2005   SQL Server 2005 supports more than 1,000 collation types, so it is important to know whether the data you want to retrieve needs to match a cer-tain collation.

To view an overview of existing collation types, since you have to reference them by name in SQL Server 2005, use SQL Server Books Online or the fn_collations() function, as in select * from fn_helpcollations().

Introducing Error Handling

SQL Server 2005 has greatly improved error handling capabilities when compared to other database platforms. In the following sections, you will learn how to use various error handling techniques and methods that are available within SQL Server. This includes everything from implementing a TRY...CATCH block as used within various programming languages such as Visual Basic and C# to creating user-defined error messages that can be raised from within a T-SQL batch.

SQL Server also uses various application variables that will provide you detailed information about the actual occurred error. It is important to understand how to create and work with error messages and how to suppress and handle potential errors within a T-SQL batch. We'll cover the RAISERROR statement first.

Using *RAISERROR*

RAISERROR allows you to raise custom error messages, based on a predefined error or a user-defined error messages. You can use the RAISERROR statement in a T-SQL batch based on the error's severity level.

The code syntax for the RAISERROR statement is as follows:

```
RAISERROR ( { msg_id | msg_str | @local_variable }
    { ,severity ,state }
    [ ,argument [ ,...n ] ] )
    [ WITH option [ ,...n ] ]
```

The message displayed can be a predefined error message that is called by the message_id or can be a message string that you pass to the statement, as shown here:

```
RAISERROR ('This is message',1,1)
```

The *severity level* identifies the level of error. Any user can specify levels from 0 to 18, and only members of the sysadmin roles can execute levels from 19 to 25. When you specify a severity level from 19 to 25, you also need to set the WITH LOG option to log in the Application log. If you specify a severity level from 20 to 25, SQL Server will immediately stop executing code and even close the client connection.

The values and settings that are generated by the RAISERROR statement are defined in the ERROR_LINE, ERROR_MESSAGE, ERROR_NUMBER, ERROR_PROCEDURE, ERROR_MESSAGE, ERROR_SEVERITY, and ERROR_STATE system functions. The @@ERROR global variable contains the error number.

When RAISERROR is executed with a severity of 11 or greater, it will transfer control to the CATCH block when executed in a TRY block. You can find more information about how to use the TRY...CATCH block in the "Using *TRY...CATCH* Blocks" section of this chapter.

You can also use the RAISERROR statement to raise a user-defined error number, such as RAISERROR (50001,10,1).

Using @@*ERROR*

The @@ERROR system variable returns an error number if the previously executed statement encountered an error. @@ERROR is cleared and reset on every executed statement, and therefore it is important to check its value at the end of every statement.

The @@ERROR statement was a frequently used statement in SQL Server 2000; however, by using SQL Server 2005, you can now benefit from using the TRY...CATCH block, which provides enhanced error logging and error handling.

The @@ERROR is often used in the following context:

```
-- perform a certain action
If @@ERROR = 0
Begin
    -- The previous statement executed successfully
end
```

When working with the @@ERROR variable, it is always better to first assign the error to a variable and work with the variable, since @@ERROR will be reset on every single statement (and that includes an IF clause).

Using Error Messages

Error messages and error handling have always been a problem in T-SQL; therefore, you should be happy that a lot of changes have occurred to the way error handling takes place in SQL Server 2005. You can now benefit from additional system functions that provide detailed information about the occurred error. However, these will be available only within the TRY...CATCH block.

ERROR_LINE   Returns the line number at which an error occurred that caused the CATCH block of a TRY...CATCH construct to be run

ERROR_MESSAGE   Returns the message text of the error that caused the CATCH block of a TRY...CATCH construct to be run

ERROR_NUMBER   Returns the error number of the error that caused the CATCH block of a TRY...CATCH construct to be run

ERROR_PROCEDURE   Returns the name of the stored procedure or trigger where an error occurred that caused the CATCH block of a TRY...CATCH construct to be run

ERROR_MESSAGE   Returns the message text of the error that caused the CATCH block of a TRY...CATCH construct to be run

ERROR_SEVERITY   Returns the severity of the error that caused the CATCH block of a TRY...CATCH construct to be run

ERROR_STATE   Returns the state number of the error that caused the CATCH block of a TRY...CATCH construct to be run

So, in SQL Server 2005, error handling is something you do by using a TRY...CATCH block, and it really is our favorite way of handling errors because of its great functionality. If you worked with @@ERROR, you will really like the way this is implemented.

Using *TRY...CATCH* Blocks

As mentioned, TRY...CATCH blocks are a great way to implement error handling in SQL Server 2005. These blocks work the same as (or very similarly to) any programming language that uses a TRY...CATCH construct, and they will catch every error that has a severity level greater than 10 but not cause any termination in the database connection.

How do they work? You type the corresponding statements you want to execute in the TRY block, and you handle it in the CATCH block. A TRY...CATCH block looks like this:

```
BEGIN TRY
     { sql_statement | statement_block }
END TRY
BEGIN CATCH
     { sql_statement | statement_block }
END CATCH
[ ; ]
```

When the code in the CATCH block completes, the control is passed back to the actual statement after END CATCH. Any error that is caught in the CATCH block is not returned to the application, and therefore you probably want to implement an error handler that uses a RAISERROR or PRINT statement within the block.

Now you'll learn how to invoke a TRY...CATCH block. For this example, say you want to execute an easy calculation. To do that, you will create two variables and assign them a value:

```
Declare @var1 int
Declare @var2 int
Declare @result int
Set @var1 = 10
Set @var2 = 5
BEGIN TRY
Set @result = @var1 / @var2
Print @result
END TRY
BEGIN CATCH
Select error_number() as ErrorNumber,
error_message() as ErrorMessage
END CATCH
```

This example results in 2.

However, if you assign the variable var2 a value of 0, the statement will jump into the CATCH block because of a division-by-zero error and return the error number and message:

```
Declare @var1 int
Declare @var2 int
Declare @result int
Set @var1 = 10
Set @var2 = 0
BEGIN TRY
Set @result = @var1 / @var2
Print @result
END TRY
BEGIN CATCH
Select error_number() as ErrorNumber,
error_message() as ErrorMessage
END CATCH
```

 It is considered to be a best practice to always include error handling within your SQL batches and stored procedures.

In Exercise 7.3 you will implement a TRY...CATCH error handling method to prevent a logical application error—a division-by-zero error message.

EXERCISE 7.3

Working with a TRY...CATCH Block

1. Type the following code in a new query window:

   ```
   Declare @col1 int

   Declare @col2 int

   Declare @result decimal (9,2)

   Set @col1 = 5

   Set @col2 = 2

   Set @result = convert(decimal(9,2),@col1) / @col2

   print @result
   ```

2. When you execute the previous code, you get a result set of 2.5.

EXERCISE 7.3 *(continued)*

3. Modify the code as follows:

    ```
    Declare @col1 int

    Declare @col2 int

    Declare @result decimal (9,2)

    Set @col1 = 5

    Set @col2 = 0

    Set @result = convert(decimal(9,2),@col1) / @col2

    print @result
    ```

4. When you execute the previous code, you will get an error message stating you cannot divide by zero. Your next step is to prevent this error message from occurring by adding a TRY...CATCH block. Modify the code to display this:

    ```
    BEGIN TRY

    Declare @col1 int

    Declare @col2 int

    Declare @result decimal (9,2)

    Set @col1 = 5

    Set @col2 = 0

    Set @result = convert(decimal(9,2),@col1) / @col2

    print @result

    END TRY

    BEGIN CATCH

    Select error_message(), error_number()

    END CATCH
    ```

You have now prevented the error.

Real World Scenario

Case Study: Transferring Data

The XYZ company often needs to import data from many suppliers into its own product database. All these subscribers provide their information in different formats.

One of the suppliers submits its data in the form of easy-to-use and easy-to-import XML files that are sent by email and never require difficult manipulations of data. To support the import of these files, the database administrator of the XYZ company decided to extract the files onto the file system and then use a BULK INSERT statement to import the data in the database. Since the amount of data that is sent from that supplier could seriously impact the transactions running and will create serious transaction logging, the database recovery model is set to Bulk-Logged in order to minimize the impact on the transaction log.

Another supplier formats its data in an Excel spreadsheet, which contains multiple sheets with information that need to be imported.

Since the data that is sent contains only updates to an original file that was imported earlier, every single product that is sold by that supplier, and thus listed in that Excel spreadsheet, needs to be checked, validated, and imported into the XYZ company's database. This is managed by using an SSIS package that will first look for the existence of an imported product to update its information. When a product does not appear in the existing database, it will then be added to the products table.

Every error that occurs using the SSIS package will be handled in the SSIS package by putting it on an exception list.

Since XYZ is using SSIS, it can now also better serve customers when one of them requires a subset of data in Excel format. XYZ uses the Export Wizard capabilities of SSIS in order to meet those customer requests.

Switching to SQL Server 2005 also provided XYZ with a solution to some of the common problems it encountered during the execution of SQL Server statements. When executing the SQL Server batches, often the statements failed because of logical errors based on a user's input of variables in stored procedures. Now when an error occurs, XYZ uses the TRY...CATCH block in T-SQL. Every error that occurs is now better handled and logged using the new error handling methods and functions.

Summary

In this chapter you learned how to work with relational data in terms of importing and exporting data. An interesting capability of SQL Server is the various methods you can use to bulk import or even export data to the file system using command-line utilities such as bcp or the BULK INSERT statement.

SSIS is the ETL tool you use to perform advanced data migrations and specify data workflows with custom scripting and transformations. The power of this tool is that you can use heterogeneous data sources and destinations.

The error handling in SQL Server 2005 is one of the best error handling capabilities so far in the SQL language because it implements a TRY...CATCH block just as it does in programming languages such as Visual Basic and C#. Since SQL Server 2005, you can now really easily retrieve the error message, which was a bit more difficult in SQL Server 2000.

Working with transactions allows you to roll back or cancel a transaction to execute in case of a certain event or condition or even roll back multiple grouped statements in a distributed environment.

SQL Server 2005 supports various recovery models, and the most common—but also the one with the biggest transaction log size—is the Full recovery model. However, if you perform large amounts of batch and bulk inserts, it might be useful not to set the recovery model to Full and instead use the Bulk-Logged recovery model.

Exam Essentials

Understand and be able to use transactions.   You need to truly understand how transactions work and how you can enforce an explicit transaction within a SQL batch. It is also important to understand how distributed transactions work and how you can implement error handling within the transactional processing.

Know how to identify collations.   You need to understand that SQL Server uses collations to play around with different sort orders and character sets within the database. Collations can be designed on a database level but also implemented with the table creation—or even enforced by explicitly casting or converting to a different collation type.

Understand how to handle exceptions and errors.   The main focus on error handling should be on how to implement a TRY...CATCH block and roll back transactions within the error handling. You need to be familiar with the new methods in error handling and how to use their syntax.

Be able to run the bcp utility.   The bcp utility has several options, including creating a format file and specifying your input or output result based on a table or a query. It is important you are able to identify the correct syntax to use to perform various bcp statements.

Know how to import and export data. You need to have a good understanding of how to import and export data by using BULK INSERT statements or even by using the OPENROWSET function. You also can use advanced ETL features with SSIS, and you need to be able to identify what tool to use for each purpose.

Understand how to configure database recovery models. When configuring database recovery models, you need to fully understand that a BULK INSERT statement has a huge impact on the size of your transaction log when defined in a Full recovery model. Therefore, you must be able to identify when to use a Bulk-Logged recovery model to minimize the impact on the transaction log and transaction log performance.

Know how to format query results. When working with queries, it is important to understand datatype conversion and the various functions that can be used within T-SQL to format a query layout.

Review Questions

1. You use the bcp utility to import data during nonworking hours. After importing data into the database, you execute a full backup statement. You need to ensure that the impact on the database during the insert is reduced to a minimum. Which of the following options can help you achieve that?

   A. Set the recovery model to Full.

   B. Set the recovery model to Simple.

   C. Set the recovery model to Bulk-Logged.

   D. Back up the transaction log while performing the inserts.

2. You import data periodically using the BULK INSERT statement for a database that is involved in log shipping. You need to minimize the time taken by the import operations. Which actions can you take?

   A. Set the recovery model to Bulk-Logged.

   B. Set the recovery model to Simple.

   C. Set the recovery model to Full.

   D. Do not import data in parallel.

3. Which of the following parameters of the bcp utility allows you to copy data from a query?

   A. in

   B. out

   C. queryout

   D. format

4. You need to bulk import and bulk export data from a SQL Server database. Which methods can you use? (Select all that apply.)

   A. Use the bcp utility.

   B. Use the BULK INSERT statement.

   C. Use the INSERT ... SELECT * FROM OPENROWSET(BULK...) statement.

   D. Use SSIS.

5. Which of the following are true about bulk insert task of SSIS? (Select all that apply.)

   A. You can use the bulk insert task to transfer data directly from other database management systems.

   B. The destination for the bulk insert task must be a table or view in a SQL Server database.

   C. You can use a format file in the bulk insert task.

   D. If the destination table or view already contains data, the new data will replace the existing data when the bulk insert task runs.

6. Which of the following is not a step for configuring a bulk insert task?

   A. Specify whether to check constraints or keep nulls when data is inserted.

   B. Specify the destination SQL Server database and the table or view.

   C. Define the format used by the bulk insert task.

   D. Set up an execute SQL task to delete existing data.

7. You want to create an SSIS package that copies data from a source to a destination. You want to run the package after you create it. Which is the simplest method to accomplish that?

   A. Use Business Intelligence Development Studio, and start the SQL Server Import and Export Wizard from an SSIS project.

   B. Use SQL Server Management Studio, and start the SQL Server Import and Export Wizard.

   C. Create the package in SSIS Designer.

   D. Use a bulk insert task.

8. Which of the following data sources can the SQL Server Import and Export Wizard use? (Select all that apply.)

   A. .NET providers

   B. SQL Server

   C. Flat files

   D. Excel

9. You want to use a TRY...CATCH block to capture error information. Which functions can be used to get information about the error? (Select all that apply.)

   A. ERROR_NUMBER()

   B. ERROR_MESSAGE()

   C. ERROR_SEVERITY()

   D. DERROR_PROCEDURE()

10. You are writing the code for a stored procedure. Inside your stored procedure you open an explicit transaction. You want to terminate the entire transaction if a T-SQL statement raises a runtime error. How can you do this automatically?

    A. Use SET XACT_ABORT ON inside your stored procedure.

    B. Use a TRY...CATCH block.

    C. Use RAISERROR.

    D. Use SET IMPLICIT_TRANSACTIONS OFF inside your stored procedure.

11. You want to start a distributed transaction using MS DTC. Which statement can you use?

    A. BEGIN DISTRIBUTED TRAN

    B. BEGIN TRAN

    C. SAVE TRAN

    D. ROLLBACK TRAN

12. You are designing several DML queries. As a part of the testing process, you want to get more information about the rows affected by these queries. Which method can you use with minimum effort?

    A. Create DML triggers on affected tables.

    B. Create DDL triggers.

    C. Use the OUTPUT clause.

    D. Use the @@ROWCOUNT.

13. You have several large tables in your database. You want to delete all rows from these tables. How can you achieve that in the fastest way?

    A. Use a TRUNCATE TABLE statement.

    B. Use a DELETE statement.

    C. Change the recovery model of your database to Simple.

    D. Change the recovery model of your database to Full.

14. One of your stored procedures contains a JOIN statement between two nvarchar columns from two tables having different collations. When you run the stored procedure, you obtain an error. How can you make the stored procedure work with a minimum amount of effort?

    A. Use the COLLATE keyword to convert one of the columns to the collation of the other column.

    B. Alter one of the tables, and use the same collations as for the other column.

    C. Alter both tables, and choose a common collation for both columns.

    D. Use a temporary table.

15. Which of the following operators and functions are collation sensitive? (Select all that apply.)

    A. The MAX operator

    B. UNION ALL

    C. CHARINDEX

    D. REPLACE

16. You have a query that returns a list with employees. You want to add a column to your query that will display a sequential number for identification purposes. Which of the following functions can be used?

    A. The RANK function

    B. The DENSE_RANK function

    C. The ROW_NUMBER function

    D. The NTILE function

17. Which options are available in SQL Server 2005 to limit the number of rows returned by a query? (Select all that apply.)

   A. The TOP operator

   B. The TABLESAMPLE clause

   C. The SET ROWCOUNT statement

   D. The @@ROWCOUNT function

18. What options to retrieve metadata are available in SQL Server? (Select all that apply.)

   A. Catalog views

   B. Dynamic management views

   C. Dynamic management functions

   D. Information schema views

19. You have a query that displays a list of products. You want to make the results more readable for the product names. Which code can help you?

   A. Use this:
   ```
   SELECT CAST(ProdName AS char(32)) AS ProductName
   FROM Sales.Products.
   ```

   B. Use this:
   ```
   SELECT CAST(ProdName AS varchar(32)) AS ProductName
   FROM Sales.Products.
   ```

   C. Use this:
   ```
   SELECT CAST(ProdName AS nvarchar(32)) AS ProductName
   FROM Sales.Products.
   ```

   D. Use this:
   ```
   SELECT ProdName
   FROM Sales.Products.
   ```

20. You want to convert a string to XML datatype and remove insignificant spaces. Which code can you use? (Select all that apply.)

   A. SELECT CONVERT(XML, '<root> <element/> </root>')

   B. SELECT CONVERT(XML, '<root> <element/> </root>',1)

   C. SELECT CONVERT(XML, '<root> <element/> </root>',0)

   D. SELECT CAST('<root> <element/> </root>' AS XML)

Answers to Review Questions

1. C. In this case, the Bulk-Logged recovery model is the appropriate model because it will minimize logging on the transaction log and thus reduce the impact of the transaction log. If you are already taking a backup, you can assume everything is on a backup after you execute the statement.

2. A. In this case, the Bulk-Logged recovery model is the appropriate model, and having log shipping will require either a Full recovery model or a Bulk-Logged recovery model. Importing data from multiple clients in parallel can give you better performance.

3. C. The queryout parameter specified as the direction for the bulk copy operation will allow you to copy data from a query.

4. A, D. The other options allow just bulk importing of data.

5. B, C. You cannot import data directly from other database management systems. You must export data to a text file first. If the destination table or view already contains data, the new data will be appended to the existing data when the bulk insert task runs.

6. D. You can optionally use an execute SQL task to delete existing data. However, this has nothing to do with configuring a bulk insert task.

7. B. The simplest method is to use the SQL Server Import and Export Wizard. If you start it from SQL Server Management Studio, you can run the package in the last step of the wizard.

8. A, B, C, D. All options specified can be data sources for the SQL Server Import and Export Wizard.

9. A, B, C, D. All these options are error functions that can be used for additional information about an error inside a TRY...CATCH block.

10. A. Only the first option will give you the intended result. When SET XACT_ABORT is ON, if a Transact-SQL statement raises a run-time error, the entire transaction is terminated and rolled back. When SET XACT_ABORT is OFF, in some cases only the Transact-SQL statement that raised the error is rolled back and the transaction continues processing.

11. A. To start a distributed transaction, you need to use a BEGIN DISTRIBUTED TRAN statement.

12. C. The OUTPUT clause will give more information about the rows affected by an INSERT, UPDATE, or DELETE statement.

13. A. The TRUNCATE statement is not logged, so it will be faster than a DELETE statement.

14. A. The simplest method is to cast one of the columns to the other's collation.

15. A, C, D. The UNION ALL statement is collation insensitive.

16. C. You should use the ROW_NUMBER function because this function will automatically add a sequential number to every result set returned.

17. A, B, C. The `@@ROWCOUNT` function returns the number of rows affected by the last statement, and it is not a correct answer.

18. A, B, C, D. All options allow you to query metadata.

19. A. Casting the ProdName column to char(32) will make the results more readable.

20. A, C, D. Option B preserves insignificant spaces.

Chapter

8

Working with XML Data

MICROSOFT EXAM OBJECTIVES COVERED IN THIS CHAPTER:

✓ **Manage XML data.**

- Identify the specific structure needed by a consumer.
- Retrieve XML data.
- Modify XML data.
- Convert between XML data and relational data.
- Create an XML index.
- Load an XML schema.

The introduction of XML as a native datatype could be considered one of the top-ten significant changes to SQL Server. In previous versions of SQL Server, storing XML data and retrieving it were possible but not in the same way or as extensively as you can do it with SQL Server 2005.

In this chapter, you will get a better understanding of how XML is used within SQL Server 2005. You'll learn how you, as a database administrator, can work with the xml datatype to store, retrieve, query, and optimize data storage. Since SQL Server 2005 now offers extensive XML capabilities, you will need to understand all of the ways you can work with XML data.

Understanding XML Data

When storing XML data, you can store the data as varchar or text data, you can decompose the data in relational data, or you can store the data as a native xml datatype:

Storing XML as varchar or text data   When storing XML as varchar or text data, you will lose most of its representation. You will not be able to perform schema validation on the XML data, and you won't be able to perform XML queries on the data.

Decomposing XML data in relational data   When decomposing XML data in relational data, you will shred the XML document into relational data and use a FOR XML clause with the SELECT statement to retrieve an XML structure from the relational data you store in the database.

This way of storing XML and retrieving content in a database is how it was frequently done in SQL Server 2000. To support the retrieval of XML data from relational storage, SQL Server 2005 has made some enhancements to the FOR XML clause, which will be covered later in this chapter.

Storing as a native xml datatype   Since SQL Server 2005 supports XML as a true datatype, you can now benefit from that by storing XML natively inside the database. Think about the big benefits you get from this. You have the ability to store and retrieve XML in a flexible way, and you have the opportunity to query inside the XML data using *XQuery* expressions, which gives you the benefits of indexes.

The *xml datatype* in SQL Server 2005 is one of its major product features. It is important you understand XML, since not only can you work with XML data but it is all over the database, going from the Eventdata collection to the ability to store entire XML documents or fragments of data in the database.

Using the xml Datatype

You can use the xml datatype in many ways; it is comparable to using any other SQL Server datatype. For example, this is how you use it in variable declarations:

```
DECLARE @xmltype XML
SET @xmltype = '<ROOT><Publisher>Sybex</Publisher></ROOT>'
```

And this is how you use it in table declarations:

```
CREATE Table Publishers
(PublisherID int, PublisherName varchar(50),
 Publishercontactdetails XML)
```

Of course, you can also use xml datatypes in stored procedures as parameters and many other options. SQL Server is flexible in the way you work with the XML data; you have the ability to store both typed and untyped XML in the database.

In Exercise 8.1 you will create a table that contains an XML column. You will also insert some records into the table.

EXERCISE 8.1

Creating a Table Containing an XML Column

1. Create a table with an XML column:

    ```
    CREATE Table Publishers

    (PublisherID int, PublisherName varchar(50),

     Publishercontactdetails XML)
    ```

2. Insert valid XML in the table:

    ```
    insert into publishers

    values (1,'Sybex','<ROOT><Publisher>
     Sybex An Imprint of Wiley</Publisher></ROOT> ')
    ```

3. Insert valid XML in the table:

    ```
    insert into publishers

    values (1,'Sybex','<invalid>Wrong Format>')
    ```

4. The previous INSERT statement will result in an error message:

    ```
    Msg 102, Level 15, State 1, Line 2

    Incorrect syntax near '<invalid>Wrong Format>'.
    ```

Using Untyped XML

When using *untyped XML*, you can store XML in the database in any form, as long as it is well-formed XML. This means that upon defining an XML column and inserting or assigning a value to the XML column, a check will occur to see whether the data you are about to insert matches the XML standard, without validating it against an XML schema.

A single XML column can take up to 2GB of storage, so you have a robust datatype to work with, rather than storing the data in text or varchar data as you could do with previous editions of SQL Server. The danger, of course, is that instead of coming up with an organized relational database model (and, yes, you should not forget that SQL Server 2005 is a relational database), people might "over XML" their databases and basically put whatever they can think of in an XML column.

You have to be cautious in doing this; everything has its best practices, and in the eyes of a DBA you are very naughty if you declare too many XML columns in your database instead of choosing a nice relational structure. Now, as DBAs, we strongly believe in the cool things you can do with this datatype in terms of data archiving and in creating a flexible data model.

Because of its structure, when using *untyped XML*, you can store any form of XML data inside the database without verifying it and match the data with an XML schema.

 Real World Scenario

Working with the xml Datatype to Ease a Relational Model and Optimize Database Performance

A sports company runs a web application where customers are able to buy sport items online. All the products the company sells have a different set of properties that need to be searchable by the customers.

If you want to buy a pair of sport shoes, for example, you want to be able to search by brand, size, color, or some other properties. If you want to buy a tennis racket, you will want to search using different properties, and when you want to buy that nice sports outfit, you'll care about size, color, and so on. Finally, a box with tennis balls will have different properties than a set of sport socks.

Now, how would you define all this in a relational database? It would definitely need a complex relational model and a lot of multiple table querying (think about that JOIN syntax) in order to represent or even retrieve the information. The solution to this will be XML data storage because you can really benefit from the flexible structure you have with storing data in XML.

In this case, you would define one XML column that would be associated with the article or product and that would contain all properties you can assign to a product.

The table definition from the real-life scenario might look like this:

```
CREATE TABLE articles
(articleID int, ArticleName varchar(50),
 Articleproperties XML)
```

This will provide a much more flexible way to store this kind of data, and the key benefit is that if you need to query it, instead of just representing it, you can use one of the SQL Server XML methods to retrieve the data (as a scalar type or even as XML).

Of course, when storing data in XML, you need to have a good method to retrieve that information as well. And that is something you will accomplish by using various query methods where you will learn not only how to retrieve XML data but also how to *decompose* XML data into relational information.

Using Typed XML

If you want to validate XML with an XML schema, you can specify an XML schema validation when creating or defining the xml datatype. You do this by just referring to the XML schema, which you initially need to store and catalog in the SQL database. XML that is validated by an XML schema is called *typed XML*.

We often refer to XML *schema validation* as putting a check constraint on a scalar datatype, since it performs a check on the values you provide. In next section, we will teach you how to work with XML Schema collections and how to store the schema in SQL Server 2005.

How do you create a datatype with schema validation? It's easy:

```
Declare @xmldata XML (schema.xmlschemacollection)
```

In the previous example, you will need to determine whether the XML schema has already been stored inside the database; otherwise, you need to "catalog" it first.

The xml datatype adds a new level of storing XML data inside SQL Server and does this in a way where complex data structures can easily be converted to an xml datatype. You can think about using the xml datatype not only for storing XML for XML purposes but also to create undefined relational structures.

This would break down relational information in such a way that it would easily resolve real-world problems where you are unable to create a nice relational model or come up with an optimized relational design.

Working with XML Schema

When an xml datatype is assigned to a Schema collection, it is called *typed XML*, and you will not be able to insert any column that doesn't match the schema definition. This can be useful in environments where the XML data you are providing and storing in the database needs to match a strict definition such as, for example, an invoice. And that is exactly where you would use the xml datatype, since on some of the structured data you would not perform heavy queries and just would want to represent the data in its whole.

Storing Typed XML Data

A broker company provides highly skilled and qualified IT professionals to enterprise custom-ers all over the world. To streamline and use a uniform set of résumés that the company can send out from the IT professionals, the company was originally using a Microsoft Word doc-ument as a template. The company asked all the IT professionals to provide their information and skills inside the résumé template.

One of the key problems the company had was that it also needed to create an entire structure of relational data to be able to search within the profiles/résumés. So within that company, initially a lot of data was stored twice but in two formats. When an IT professional submitted a new résumé, someone entered part of that information as keywords in a relational database application to support the search capabilities.

When the company switched to SQL Server 2005, it redesigned its approach of entering and providing this information. The key power the company has now is that it can store the résumé data in its native XML format directly in the database, without performing any manual action.

Because of the nature of the xml datatype and the query search capabilities, now data can eas-ily be loaded, stored, and retrieved using XML-specific query methods.

To use XML Schema collections in the database and associate them with variables and col-umns of the xml datatype, SQL Server uses the **CREATE XML SCHEMA** statement:

```
CREATE XML SCHEMA COLLECTION ProductDetails AS
'<xsd:schema targetNamespace=
"http://schemas.sybex.com/sqlserver/2006/01/70-431
➥ /ProductDetails"
    xmlns=
"http://schemas.sybex.com/sqlserver/2006/01/70-431
➥ /ProductDetails"
    elementFormDefault="qualified"
    xmlns:xsd="http://www.w3.org/2001/XMLSchema" >
    <xsd:element name="Packagetype"  >
        <xsd:complexType>
            <xsd:sequence>
                <xsd:element name="PackageUnit"
➥ type="xsd:string"  />
                <xsd:element name="PackageDescription" type="xsd:string"  />
            </xsd:sequence>
        </xsd:complexType>
    </xsd:element>
</xsd:schema>
    '

;
```

After the XML Schema collection is cataloged, you can retrieve information about it by using the XML_schema_namespace function, as shown in the following example. This example shows you the schema of the cataloged XML Schema collection called Productdetails as it was cataloged in the dbo schema:

```
SELECT xml_schema_namespace(N'dbo',N'ProductDetails')
```

Now once the schema is defined, you can use it and refer to it in a CREATE TABLE or even a declare XML statement. The following is an example of how to define a variable as an xml datatype:

```
declare @Packagetype xml (Productdetails)
set @packagetype = '<Publisher>Sybex</Publisher>'
select @packagetype
```

This results in an error message since it does not validate the schema definition, and it produces the following error:

```
Msg 6913, Level 16, State 1, Line 2
XML Validation:
 Declaration not found for element 'Publisher'.
 Location: /*:Publisher[1]
```

A better solution is to provide a value that matches the schema definition:

```
DECLARE @var XML(Productdetails)
SET @var =
 '<Packagetype xmlns="http://schemas.sybex.com/sqlserver
 /2006/01/70-431/ProductDetails
 <PackageUnit>Box</PackageUnit>
<PackageDescription>Carton Box</PackageDescription>
 </Packagetype>'
```

The previous example used a unique name to name the XML namespace. That is a best practice, but of course you can make the example easier by performing something like this:

```
CREATE XML SCHEMA COLLECTION Countries AS '
<schema xmlns="http://www.w3.org/2001/XMLSchema">
 <element name="root">
  <complexType>
   <sequence>
    <element name="Country" type="string"/>
    <element name="Code" type="string"/>
   </sequence>
  </complexType>
 </element>
</schema>'
```

```
declare @xml xml (Countries)
set @xml =
'<root><Country>Belgium</Country><Code>BEL</Code></root>'
```

And you can use this in a table definition as well:

```
CREATE table students
(studentid int identity(1,1),
studentname varchar(50), Country xml (countries))
```

An INSERT statement such as the following one would definitely succeed:

```
Insert into students (studentname, country)
    values ('Joe', '<root><Country>United States</Country><Code>USA</Code>
➥</root>')
```

 To work with XML schemas, the schema needs to be loaded into the database before you can reference it. To catalog a schema inside the SQL Server database, you use the CREATE XML SCHEMA COLLECTION statement.

Querying XML Data

Because of the hierarchical structure inside XML data, you can use query methods to retrieve information and search for data in an xml datatype. The new datatype is an object that comes with its own methods that allow you to retrieve information from the XML data you stored in the database. The XML methods you can use to retrieve data from an xml datatype are as follows:

query method   Returns a fragment of untyped XML

value method   Returns XML data as a scalar datatype

exists method   Checks whether a certain node exists in the XML data

nodes method   Returns a single column rowset of nodes from the XML column

We will discuss these methods in the next sections, where we will show you each method's functionality with an example.

Using the *query* Method

On the XML column, you have to specify the query method in order to return a certain value from a table. The following example shows you how you can return a value from within an XML column:

```
select country.query ('/root/Country') from students
```

This will result in the following partial result set but will return a fragment of untyped XML:

```
<Country>Belgium</Country>
<Country>United States</Country>
```

However, if you want to retrieve only the values, you can also use the data function.

You will use this query method to retrieve fragments of XML data and return them as an XML value. If you want to return data in a scalar datatype, you will have to use the value method, as described in the next section.

To get just the value of the matching element, you can use the data function:

```
select country.query ('data(/root/Code)') from students
```

In this case, the result set will appear as follows:

```
BEL
USA
...
```

 You use the query method to decompose XML data into a relational data result set.

Using the *value* Method

The value *method* works much like the query method and is invoked in the same way. The difference is that the value method will accept an additional parameter to determine the resulting scalar datatype. The value is returned as an instance of that type.

The following example will return a scalar int datatype, using the xml value method:

```
declare @myDoc xml
declare @ProdID int
set @myDoc = '<Root>
<ProductDescription ProductID="500"
ProductName="SQL Server 2005">
<Editions>
  <Edition>Standard</Edition>
  <MaximumCPU>4</MaximumCPU>
</Editions>
</ProductDescription>
</Root>'
```

```
select @mydoc.value
('(/Root/ProductDescription/@ProductID)[1]', 'int')
```

```
results in:
500
```

Remember that you must declare the namespace of the document if the source column is a typed XML column.

Casting and Converting to XML

The xml datatype is about the highest in the datatype precedence. This means when XML is used in expressions with other datatypes, implicit conversion to the xml datatype will occur.

To avoid implicit conversion and conversion errors, it is a best practice to use the CONVERT or CAST function to explicitly convert to the destination datatype.

Using the *exist* Method

The exist *method* takes an expression that selects a single node within the XML document and returns either True (bit value 1) if the node exists or False (bit value 0) if it does not. If the source column is a typed XML column and the element contains null, the method returns NULL instead. Therefore, the following query will return True for all items where the student has country details:

```
select country.exist ('/root/Country') from students
```

You can also use the exist method in the where clause of a statement:

```
select * from students where
country.exist ('/root/Country') = 1
```

Using the *modify* Method

Oh my, this is going to blow away a lot of you DBAs who have no experience with XML, because if you consider an XML column to be a text or varchar field, you may be amazed by how you can use XML data in SQL Server 2005.

The modify *method* consists of three substatements:

- INSERT
- DELETE
- REPLACE

Now, what makes these statements so useful? Instead of working with the entire XML structure, loading the document, and then performing updates or modifications, you can use the modify method to manipulate the current XML data stored in a table. This will provide you with strong and powerful statements that give you the opportunity to manipulate XML data inside the XML column; for example, you could modify a specific value in an order line stored in an XML column.

Remember that in a typed XML column, the resulting XML document, after executing the XML/DML statement, must conform to the schema for the column. If not, the update will fail, and an error will be raised. As an example, the following code deletes the product node that has an attribute id="501" in an XML document:

```
UPDATE @xml
SET xmlcol.modify('delete /root/product[@id="501"]')
```

To insert a new node or fragment of XML, you use an INSERT statement. The syntax for this is as follows:

```
xml-column.modify('insert new-content
{as first | as last}  into | before | after
xpath-expression')
```

Using the *nodes* Method

The previous sections covered the query, value, exist, and modify methods that are exposed by the new xml datatype in SQL Server 2005. Using the nodes *method,* you can extract data from an XML document and use that to generate subnodes that can be used for various purposes, such as, for example, to create new content or insert content into new tables.

If you have, for example, an XML document that contains a list of airport codes per country, you would be able to use the nodes mode to create a new table where each rowset becomes a row in the table.

Suppose you have an XML document that looks like this:

```
DECLARE @x xml
SET @x='<Root>      <row id="1"><Airportcode>EWR </Airportcode>
<Airportname>Newark</Airportname></row>
    <row id="2"><Airportcode>LGA</Airportcode></row>
    <row id="3" />
</Root>'
```

When executing the following nodes query, you will return relational data to which you should apply the XML value method in order to truly decompose it into a relational value:

```
SELECT T.c.query('.') AS result
FROM    @x.nodes('/Root/row') T(c)
go
```

This will result in the following:

```
Result
--------------------
<row id="1"><Airportcode>EWR</Airportcode><Airportname>Newark
</Airportname></row>
<row id="2"><Airportcode>LGA</Airportcode></row>
<row id="3" />
```

In the following example, you will apply the value method to the result set returned by the nodes method:

```
SELECT T.c.value('@id','int') as id,
       T.c.query('Airportcode') as Airportcode
FROM   @x.nodes('/Root/row') T(c)
```

You will get the following result set returned:

```
Id          Airportcode
-----------------------------------------
1           <Airportcode>EWR</Airportcode>
2           <Airportcode>LGA</Airportcode>
3
```

In the previous result set, however, you'll probably notice that ID 3 does not have an airport code. If you want to filter out these records, you can use the exists method to see whether a row exists, as mentioned earlier in this chapter:

```
SELECT T.c.value('@id','int') as id,
       T.c.query('Airportcode') as Airportcode
FROM   @x.nodes('/Root/row') T(c)
WHERE T.c.exist('Airportcode') = 1;
```

In the XML methods we have covered, two methods, value and exists, will return a scalar result set.

The XML method query will always return an XML fragment. exists checks whether a certain node exists inside the XML document you are querying and will therefore always return a bit datatype.

Real World Scenario

Decomposing xml Data

This scenario should be one of the reasons you need this book. As database administrator, you know you can benefit from using XML in combination with the EVENTDATA() function.

Now, if you have to write a trigger every time you want to use the Eventdata collection and in that trigger decompose your XML data into a relational engine to store it inside a log table, you would be wasting a lot of work on rewriting or copying the code data that decomposes the Eventdata results in relational data.

As administrator, you would definitely benefit by combining the decomposition of the XML Eventdata to a user-defined function. In Exercise 8.2 you will implement all these. You are basically able to copy and paste the definition of your user-defined functions into any database and extend its functionality for the valuable data you want to retrieve from an XML column.

What other benefits do you get from defining user-defined functions in which you decompose the XML data? Suppose a future version of SQL Server has a change in the Eventdata collection. You would need to verify every single trigger you defined or every single procedure where you used the XML data collection.

In Exercise 8.2 you will create and use user-defined functions to decompose data gathered from the Eventdata collection that you executed in a DDL trigger.

EXERCISE 8.2

Decomposing XML into Relational Data

1. In SQL Server Management Studio, open a new query window, and connect to the Sybex database.

2. Type and execute the following syntax to create a new schema:

   ```
   CREATE SCHEMA EventFunctions

   GO
   ```

3. After you created the schema, you will create a function that decomposes the Eventdata XML in relational data:

   ```
   -- Create a function that decomposes the eventtype out of Eventdata

   CREATE FUNCTION EventFunctions.fn_Eventtype (@eventdata xml)
   ```

```
returns nvarchar(max)

AS

BEGIN

RETURN @eventdata.value

        ('(/EVENT_INSTANCE/EventType)[1]','nvarchar(max)')

END

GO
```

4. Type the following syntax to decompose the T-SQL statement from the XML collection:

```
-- Create a function that decomposes the TSQLstatement out of Eventdata

CREATE FUNCTION EventFunctions.fn_TSQLStatement (@eventdata xml)

returns nvarchar(max)

AS

BEGIN

RETURN

@eventdata.value

        ('(/EVENT_INSTANCE/TSQLCommand/ CommandText)[1]','nvarchar(max)')

END

GO
```

5. Create a DDL trigger in which you will call the two functions you created:

```
-- create a ddl trigger to test the functionality

CREATE TRIGGER TRG_DDL_event ON DATABASE

    FOR DDL_DATABASE_LEVEL_EVENTS

AS

declare @eventdata xml

set @eventdata = EVENTDATA()

select EventFunctions.fn_TSQLStatement (@eventdata), EventFunctions.
fn_TSQLStatement (@eventdata)
```

6. Test the trigger's functionality by creating a table:

   ```
   CREATE TABLE tbl_test (test int)
   ```

7. This will result in the following result set:

   ```
   CREATE TABLE tbl_test (test int)
   ```

8. Drop the trigger you created:

   ```
   DROP TRIGGER TRG_DDL_event ON DATABASE
   ```

Creating XML Indexes

The XML column in its native datatype provides great capabilities in terms of retrieving data from within the XML column using various query methods. To support the querying of XML data, you can create indexes on these columns.

The start of an XML index is a *primary XML index,* and all other XML indexes will depend upon the primary index. You have the ability to create the following XML indexes to support optimized XML querying:

Primary XML index   This is a shredded and persisted representation of the XML data in the xml datatype column. For each XML binary large object (BLOB) in the column, the index creates several rows of data. The number of rows in the index is approximately equal to the number of nodes in the XML binary large object. Each row stores the following node information:

- Tag name
- Node value
- Node type
- Order information
- Root path
- Primary key of the data row

Path XML index   This improves search capabilities for queries based on path instructions. A path index is a secondary XML index, which means a primary index needs to be created first.

Value XML index   This improves search capabilities for queries based on values. A *value index* is a secondary XML index, which means that a primary index needs to be created first.

Property XML index   Queries that retrieve one or more values from individual XML instances may benefit from this type of index. This scenario occurs when you retrieve object properties using the value method of the xml datatype and when the primary key value of the object is known.

Real World Scenario

Case Study: Implementing XML in SQL 2005

The XYZ company ships orders from pharmaceutical companies to customers all over the world. The company has implemented SQL Server 2005 within its business environment. Some of the products the company ships require different preparations and are composed of several other products that are customized based on the required usage.

Some of the articles the company provides require special handling and have different package shipping requirements. In addition, the company receives prescriptions that require a combination of medicines. The usage of the medicines that are produced will depend on the patient's age, weight, and other factors that have to be considered when taking a variety of medicines in combination with one another. In this environment, the prescription for some of these medicines are simple—take three pills a day—and others are complex prescriptions that are a combination of medicines.

To be able to address the variety of different package units/product compositions and prescriptions, the company created a complex data model using relational storage. The query response when testing all the application functionally ended up having poor performance when large amounts of data were loaded and retrieved from the database.

After optimizing and reviewing the data model, XYZ decided to store any complex structure with unknown properties in an XML format. This allows a less complex query method to retrieve the product information and prescriptions in general and still allows the retrieval of specific data that was initially decomposed in relational data.

One of the key benefits of using the xml datatype instead of a complex model of relational tables is that when the XYZ company needs to represent a prescription that was entered by a doctor, it can now easily retrieve it in its entire structure. To allow the maximum flexibility, the company decided to store the data as untyped XML to allow it for maximum flexibility of structure. To improve query response, the company created a primary XML index on all XML columns. The company's DBA is using SQL Server Profiler to trace the most common XML queries that are sent to the database and will then later create supportive path queries to optimize query response.

By deciding to choose the xml datatype as a storage type, a lot of CPU-intensive relational processing has been resolved.

Summary

In this chapter, you learned about the xml datatype, which is a new and native datatype supported in SQL Server 2005. Using and storing XML data in SQL Server 2005 can be easy or complex, but it is important you understand the benefits of using the xml datatype.

You also learned how SQL Server 2005 works with XML and how you can decompose XML into relational data. However, these are just basic components of the xml datatype and its associated methods.

To query XML data, you learned different methods to use. The nodes and value methods can convert XML data into relational data and therefore are probably the most commonly used methods.

SQL Server supports two types of XML: typed and untyped. When using typed XML, you first need to catalog the XML Schema inside SQL Server using a CREATE XML SCHEMA COLLECTION statement.

Exam Essentials

Be able to identify the data structure.   Understand when to use XML and when another datatype is preferable or usable.

Know how to retrieve XML data.   To retrieve XML data, you can use several methods. It is important to know the query, exist, nodes, value, and modify methods to be able to work with XML data. You need to fully understand how to decompose to XML but also how to convert it.

Know how to modify XML data.   XML data can be modified in the XML column using the modify method, and you don't need to shred out and update the entire XML data in order to replace, insert, or even delete data in an XML column.

Understand how to convert between XML data and relational data.   Since the xml datatype is about the highest in the datatype precedence hierarchy, you will have conversion from and to the xml datatype. It is important to know how to use the CAST and CONVERT functions to support the xml datatype.

Know how to create an XML index.   When optimizing XML querying, you can create multiple indexes, which are the primary starting point for your XML optimization. To support the various types of XML queries, you will create secondary indexes.

Know how to load an XML schema.   SQL Server stores typed or untyped XML; when storing typed XML, you first will need to load an XML schema in the database before you can use it and have schema validation in variables, columns, and expressions. It is important to be familiar with this syntax.

Review Questions

1.   You need to obtain a rowset from an XML document and avoid null results. Which code can you use? (Choose all that apply.)

   A. Use this:
   ```
   DECLARE @doc XML
   SET @doc = '<?xml version="1.0" ?>
   <Order OrderId="1">
   <Product ProductID="110" Quantity="50" />
   <Product ProductID="115" Quantity="40" />
   <Product ProductID="120" Quantity="70" />
   </Order>'
   DECLARE @idoc int
   EXEC sp_xml_preparedocument @idoc OUTPUT, @doc

   SELECT      *
   FROM  OPENXML (@idoc, '/Order/Product',1)
   WITH (ProductID  int,
                 Quantity int)
   ```

   B. Use this:
   ```
   DECLARE @doc varchar(MAX)
   SET @doc = '<?xml version="1.0" ?>
   <Order OrderId="1">
   <Product ProductID="110" Quantity="50" />
   <Product ProductID="115" Quantity="40" />
   <Product ProductID="120" Quantity="70" />
   </Order>'
   DECLARE @idoc int
   EXEC sp_xml_preparedocument @idoc OUTPUT, @doc

   SELECT      *
   FROM  OPENXML (@idoc, '/Order/Product',0)
   WITH (ProductID  int,
                 Quantity int)
   ```

   C. Use this:
   ```
   DECLARE @doc XML
   SET @doc = '<?xml version="1.0" ?>
   <Order OrderId="1">
   <Product ProductID="110" Quantity="50" />
   <Product ProductID="115" Quantity="40" />
   <Product ProductID="120" Quantity="70" />
   </Order>'
   DECLARE @idoc int
   EXEC sp_xml_preparedocument @idoc OUTPUT, @doc
   ```

```
SELECT    *
FROM  OPENXML (@idoc, '/Order/Product',2)
WITH (ProductID  int,
             Quantity int)
```

D. Use this:
```
DECLARE @doc XML
SET @doc = '<?xml version="1.0" ?>
<Order OrderId="1">
<Product ProductID="110" Quantity="50" />
<Product ProductID="115" Quantity="40" />
<Product ProductID="120" Quantity="70" />
</Order>'
DECLARE @idoc int
EXEC sp_xml_preparedocument @idoc OUTPUT, @doc

SELECT    *
FROM  OPENXML (@idoc, '/Order/Product',0)
WITH (ProductID  int,
             Quantity int)
```

2. You have an XML variable declared using the following code:

```
DECLARE @doc XML
SET @doc = '<?xml version="1.0" ?>
<Order OrderId="1">
<Product ProductID="110" Quantity="50" />
<Product ProductID="115" Quantity="40" />
<Product ProductID="120" Quantity="70" />
</Order>'
```

You want to insert the values of the ProductID and Quantity attributes in a table. Which code can you use? (Choose all that apply.)

A. Use this:
```
DECLARE @idoc int
EXEC sp_xml_preparedocument @idoc OUTPUT, @doc

INSERT INTO tblTempOrders(ProductId,Quantity)
SELECT    *
FROM  OPENXML (@idoc, '/Order/Product',0)
WITH (ProductID  int,
      Quantity int)
```

B. Use this:
```
DECLARE @idoc int
EXEC sp_xml_preparedocument @idoc OUTPUT, @doc
```

```
INSERT INTO tblTempOrders(ProductId,Quantity)
SELECT    *
FROM  OPENXML (@idoc, '/Order/Product',1)
WITH (ProductID  int,
      Quantity int)
```

C. Use this:
```
DECLARE @idoc int
EXEC sp_xml_preparedocument @idoc OUTPUT, @doc

INSERT INTO tblTempOrders(ProductId,Quantity)
SELECT    *
FROM  OPENXML (@idoc, '/Order/Product',0)
WITH (ProductID  int '@ProductID',
      Quantity int '@Quantity')
```

D. Use this:
```
INSERT INTO tblTempOrders(ProductId,Quantity)
SELECT
T.c.value('@ProductID','int') AS ProductID,
T.c.value('@Quantity','int') AS Quantity
FROM   @doc.nodes('/Order/Product') T(c)
```

3. One of your tables has an XML column with a primary XML index defined on it. You want to improve the performance of several queries that specify complete path expressions without wildcards on the XML column. Which method is optimal?

   A. Define an additional primary XML index.

   B. Create a path secondary XML index.

   C. Create a value secondary XML index.

   D. Create a property secondary XML index.

4. Which of the following is *not* true regarding XML indexes? (Choose all that apply.)

   A. When you create a primary XML index, the table that contains the XML column (that will be indexed), which is the base table, must have a clustered index on the primary key.

   B. When you create a primary XML index, the table that contains the XML column (that will be indexed) must have a nonclustered index on the primary key.

   C. A primary XML index can be created on a multiple XML-type column.

   D. You can have an XML index and a non-XML index on the same table with the same name.

5. You want to import an UTF-8 encoded XML file. Which of the following options is recommended?

   A. Use this:
   ```
   INSERT INTO tblImport(XmlCol)
   SELECT * FROM OPENROWSET(
   BULK 'C:\Import\XmlDataFile.txt',
       SINGLE_NCLOB) AS xmlResult
   ```

B. Use this:
```
INSERT INTO tblImport(XmlCol)
SELECT * FROM OPENROWSET(
BULK 'C:\Import\XmlDataFile.txt',
    SINGLE_CLOB) AS xmlResult
```

C. Use this:
```
INSERT INTO tblImport(XmlCol)
SELECT * FROM OPENROWSET(
BULK 'C:\Import\XmlDataFile.txt',
    SINGLE_BLOB) AS xmlResult
```

D. Use this:
```
INSERT INTO tblImport(XmlCol)
SELECT BulkColumn FROM OPENROWSET(
BULK 'C:\Import\XmlDataFile.txt',
    SINGLE_NCLOB) AS xmlResult
```

6. You need to import data from a document that contains a Document Type Definition (DTD). Which of the following scripts can be used?

A. Use this:
```
INSERT INTO tblImport(XmlCol)
SELECT CONVERT(xml, BulkColumn, 2)
FROM OPENROWSET(Bulk 'C:\Import\DataFile.xml', SINGLE_BLOB) AS xmlResult
```

B. Use this:
```
INSERT INTO tblImport(XmlCol)
SELECT BulkColumn
FROM OPENROWSET(Bulk 'C:\Import\DataFile.xml', SINGLE_BLOB) AS xmlResult
```

C. Use this:
```
INSERT INTO tblImport(XmlCol)
SELECT *
FROM OPENROWSET(Bulk 'C:\Import\DataFile.xml', SINGLE_BLOB) AS xmlResult
```

D. Use this:
```
INSERT INTO tblImport(XmlCol)
SELECT CONVERT(xml, BulkColumn, 2)
FROM OPENROWSET(Bulk 'C:\Import\DataFile.xml', SINGLE_BLOB) AS xmlResult
```

7. You need to write a query that will return element-centric XML. Additionally, you want null columns to be included in the results. Which code can you use?

A. Use this:
```
SELECT ProductId, Name, ListPrice, Color
FROM Production.Product
FOR XML RAW, ELEMENTS
```

B. Use this:
```
SELECT ProductId, Name, ListPrice, Color
FROM Production.Product
FOR XML RAW
```

  C. Use this:
```
SELECT ProductId, Name, ListPrice, Color
FROM Production.Product
FOR XML AUTO, ELEMENTS XSINIL
```

  D. Use this:
```
SELECT ProductId, Name, ListPrice, Color
FROM Production.Product
FOR XML AUTO
```

8. By default, FOR XML queries return XML fragments. You need to return a well-formed XML document. How can you accomplish this?

  A. Use the XMLSCHEMA directive.

  B. Use the EXPLICIT mode.

  C. Use the TYPE directive.

  D. Use the ROOT directive.

9. You have created an XML Schema collection named ContractSchemas. You want to associate it to an XML column for validation. Both documents and valid fragments should be allowed. Which code can you use? (Choose all that apply.)

  A. Use this:
```
CREATE TABLE HR.Documents(
DocumentId int,
DocumentText xml (DOCUMENT ContractSchemas))
```

  B. Use this:
```
CREATE TABLE HR.Documents(
DocumentId int,
DocumentText xml )
```

  C. Use this:
```
CREATE TABLE HR.Documents(
DocumentId int,
DocumentText xml (ContractSchemas))
```

  D. Use this:
```
CREATE TABLE HR.Documents(
DocumentId int,
DocumentText xml (CONTENT ContractSchemas))
```

10. You try to associate an XML schema collection to an XML column using the following code:
```
CREATE XML SCHEMA COLLECTION ContractSchemas AS '
<schema xmlns="http://www.w3.org/2001/XMLSchema">
        <element name="contract" type="string"/>
</schema>
<schema xmlns="http://www.w3.org/2001/XMLSchema">
```

```
<element name="template" type="string"/>
</schema>'

CREATE TABLE HR.Contracts (
DocumentId int,
DocumentText xml (ContractSchemas)
)
GO
```

You obtained the following error: "Collection specified does not exist in metadata: 'ContractSchemas'." What is the cause of the error?

A. The attribute `targetNameSpace` is not specified.

B. You cannot define multiple XML schemas in a Schema collection.

C. The XML declaration is missing.

D. A Schema collection cannot be referenced in the same batch where it is created.

11. You have declared an XML document using the following code:

```
DECLARE @myDoc XML
SET @myDoc = '<?xml version="1.0" ?>
<booklist>
 <book category="Programming">
  <title>Beginning ASP.NET 2.0
➥E-Commerce in C# 2005</title>
  <authors>
   <author>Cristian Darie</author>
  </authors>
  <year>2005</year>
 </book>
</booklist>'
```

You want to modify the XML document by adding another author after the existing one. Which code can you use? (Choose all that apply.)

A. Use this:
```
SET @myDoc.modify('
insert <author>Karli Watson</author>
as last into (/booklist/book/authors)[1]')
```

B. Use this:
```
SET @myDoc.modify('
insert element author {"Karli Watson"}
as first into (/booklist/book/authors)[1]')
```

   C. Use this:
```
SET @myDoc.modify('
insert element author {"Karli Watson"}
as last into (/booklist/book/authors)[1]')
```

   D. Use this:
```
SET @myDoc.modify('
insert <author>Karli Watson</author>
as first into (/booklist/book/authors)[1]')
```

12. You have declared the following XML document:
```
DECLARE @myDoc XML
SET @myDoc = '<?xml version="1.0" ?>
<booklist>
 <book category="Programming">
  <title>Beginning ASP.NET 2.0
➥E-Commerce in C# 2005</title>
  <authors>
      <author>Cristian Darie</author>
      <author>Karli Watson</author>
  </authors>
  <year>2005</year>
 </book>
</booklist>'
```

You want to replace the category attribute value with ASP.NET instead of Programming. How can you accomplish this?

   A. Use this:
```
SET @myDoc.modify('
replace value of (/booklist/book/@category)[1]
with    "ASP.NET"')
```

   B. Use this:
```
SET @myDoc.modify('
replace value of (/booklist/book/@category)[0]
with    "ASP.NET"')
```

   C. Use this:
```
SET @myDoc.modify('
replace value of (/booklist/book/category)[1]
with    "ASP.NET"')
```

   D. Use this:
```
SET @myDoc.modify('
replace value of (/booklist/book/category)[0]
with    "ASP.NET"')
```

13. You have declared the following XML document:

```
DECLARE @myDoc XML
SET @myDoc = '<?xml version="1.0" ?>
<booklist>
 <book category="Programming">
  <title>Beginning ASP.NET 2.0
➡ E-Commerce in C# 2005</title>
  <authors>
        <author>Cristian Darie</author>
        <author>Karli</author>
        <author>Karli Watson</author>
  </authors>
  <year>2005</year>
 </book>
</booklist>'
```

You want to delete the second author. Which code can you use?

A. Use this:
```
SET @myDoc.modify('
   delete /book/authors/author[2]')
```

B. Use this:
```
SET @myDoc.modify('
   delete /booklist/book/authors/author[2]')
```

C. Use this:
```
SET @myDoc.modify('
   delete /authors/author[2]')
```

D. Use this:
```
SET @myDoc.modify('
   delete /booklist/book/authors/author/[2]')
```

14. Which of the following is not an argument for using the native XML datatype? (Choose all that apply.)

A. You want to modify the XML data.

B. You need XML indexes for faster response time.

C. You need to store exact copies of the XML data.

D. You need to validate your XML data.

15. Which of the following is *not* a characteristic of XML Schema collections?

   A. Schema collections are scoped to the database where they are created.

   B. Schema collections can span databases or instances.

   C. You can assign more than one XML schema to an XML column.

   D. You can load an XML schema using the OPENROWSET function.

16. Which of the following are arguments for using relational storage instead of the native XML datatype?

   A. Your data is hierarchical.

   B. Your data consists of large documents frequently updated.

   C. Your data consists of large documents rarely updated.

   D. Your data is semistructured.

17. You want to store XML documents in SQL Server, and you have to decide what format to use. Considering that you receive the information in XML format and that you need to validate, query, and modify the data, what's the best storage option using the minimum amount of work?

   A. Store the XML documents in tables using the relational model.

   B. Use the native xml datatype.

   C. Store the XML documents in an nvarchar(max) column.

   D. Store the XML documents in a varchar(max) column.

18. You need to retrieve a scalar value from an XML instance. What method can you use?

   A. value

   B. query

   C. exist

   D. nodes

19. You want to obtain information about XML indexes including fragmentation. Which metadata views can be used? (Choose all that apply.)

   A. sys.xml_indexes

   B. sys.dm_db_index_physical_stats

   C. sys.indexes

   D. sys.system_objects

20. You want to convert a string to XML and preserve white spaces. Which code can you use?

A. Use this:
```
SELECT CONVERT(xml, N'<root> <element></element>
</root>', 1)
```

B. Use this:
```
DECLARE @x XML
SET @x = '<root> <element></element>      </root>'
```

C. Use this:
```
SELECT CONVERT(xml, N'<root> <element></element>
</root>')
```

D. Use this:
```
SELECT CAST(N'<root> <element></element>
</root>' AS XML)
```

Answers to Review Questions

1. A, B, D. The partial syntax of OPENXML is as follows:

    ```
    OPENXML( idoc int [ in] ,
    rowpattern nvarchar [ in ] , [ flags byte [ in ] ] )
    [ WITH ( SchemaDeclaration | TableName ) ]
    ```

    To use attribute-centric mappings, only the sample code with a flag's variable value of 0 and 1 will return values. Option C will return only NULL values.

2. A, B, C, D. All options will accomplish the task. Option A and B use attribute-centric mapping, and Option C uses element-centric mapping. However, for Option C the element-centric mapping is overwritten by specifying how the XML nodes should be mapped to the columns. Option D uses the nodes method of the xml datatype with the same result.

3. B. A path secondary index is the best option in this case. Option A is incorrect because you already have a primary XML index defined, and a primary XML index is helpful when you have queries that specify the exist method in the WHERE clause. Option C is incorrect because a value index is helpful when the path is not fully specified or when it includes a wildcard. Option D is incorrect because a property index is helpful for queries that retrieve one or more values from individual XML instances.

4. B, C, D. The base table must have a clustered index on the primary key; a primary XML index can be created on a single XML-type column; and since XML indexes exist in the same namespace as normal indexes, they cannot share the same name.

5. C. It is recommended that you import XML data only using the SINGLE_BLOB option, rather than SINGLE_CLOB and SINGLE_NCLOB, because only SINGLE_BLOB supports all Windows encoding conversions. Additionally, if the text file contains an encoding declaration that you want to apply, specifying the SINGLE_BLOB option will ensure that the XML parser in SQL Server imports the data according to the encoding scheme specified. Option A and D are equivalent and incorrect because the data file will be read as Unicode. Option B will not generate an error but is not optimal.

6. A. To enable DTD support, you must use the CONVERT function with style 2. All other options will generate an error such as "Parsing XML with internal subset DTDs not allowed. Use CONVERT with style option 2 to enable limited internal subset DTD support."

7. C. The ELEMENTS clause returns element-centric XML and includes null columns in the results, and the XSINIL clause should be specified.

8. D. The ROOT directive allows wrapping the fragment returned by a FOR XML query in a specified root element and thus obtains well-formed XML. Option A is incorrect because the XMLSCHEMA directive returns an inline XDR schema. Option B is incorrect because the EXPLICIT mode cannot solve the problem. Option C is incorrect because the TYPE directive is returns an XML value instead of a varchar.

9. C, D. To validate an XML column, you need to associate to it an XML Schema collection. The CONTENT and DOCUMENT keywords specify whether valid fragments are allowed (CONTENT) or just documents (DOCUMENT). CONTENT is the default.

10. D. Inserting GO before a CREATE TABLE statement will solve the problem. The CREATE XML SCHEMA COLLECTION statement must execute as a single batch before you can reference it in a CREATE TABLE statement.

11. A, C. One requirement was to insert the second author after the existing one. Options B and D will insert it in front of the existing one.

12. A. To specify an attribute in the path expression, you need to use @. To select the first book element, you should specify 1 as a value and not 0.

13. B. Only Option B specifies the correct XPath expression.

14. C. To store exact copies of XML data, you cannot use XML datatype. Instead, you can use nvarchar(max), for example.

15. B. Schema collections cannot span databases or instances.

16. B. For frequent updates of large documents, the best storage model is the relational one. All the other options can use the native xml datatype.

17. B. Storing the XML documents in an xml datatype column is the fastest method and satisfies all the requirements.

18. A. To retrieve a scalar value from an XML instance, the best option is the value method. The other methods cannot be used directly to extract a scalar value.

19. A, B, C. The sys.xml_indexes and sys.indexes catalog views can display information about XML indexes. The sys.dm_db_index_physical_stats dynamic management view displays fragmentation information for XML indexes.

20. A. To preserve white spaces, you need to specify the style argument for CONVERT function.

Chapter 9

Working with Service Broker and HTTP

MICROSOFT EXAM OBJECTIVES COVERED IN THIS CHAPTER:

✓ **Implement Service Broker components.**

- Create services.
- Create queues.
- Create contracts.
- Create conversations.
- Create message types.
- Send messages to a service.
- Route a message to a service.
- Receive messages from a service.

✓ **Implement an HTTP endpoint.**

- Create an endpoint.
- Secure an endpoint.

Service Broker is a new feature to SQL Server 2005 and provides a solution to common problems with message delivery and consistency that occur when transferring transactional messages or data from one server to another. The new technology in SQL Server 2005 allows SQL Server to implement its own architecture to create a queue-based message delivery system that guarantees delivery.

In this chapter, you will learn how to implement a SQL Server Service Broker architecture. You'll learn how to do this by investigating all the components of the Service Broker infrastructure. Specifically, you'll implement message types and queues, configure services, and create endpoints, which are the core addressable communication points in this architecture.

Understanding the SQL Server Service Broker Architecture

Before diving into the Service Broker architecture, we'll first cover the technology and demand for a technology like this. Say you want to buy a conference ticket, for example; you don't want to line up at the ticket office to hear that the tickets ran out and you can be added to the standby list.

Wouldn't it be nicer if you could just use an application to formulate your ticket request and then receive a reply that tells you whether you have tickets or are added to a standby list, even when the ticket office is closed and no one is processing your request at that moment?

That is exactly what you can do with Service Broker. The Service Broker technology, which is part of the database engine, provides a message-based communication platform similar to this ticket scenario. The platform enables independent application components to perform as a whole.

Service Broker includes the infrastructure for asynchronous programming that can be used for applications within a single database or a single instance as well as for distributed applications.

Service Broker also makes it easy to scale your application up or down to accommodate the amount of traffic the application receives. When a lot of requests are queued up, you actually can implement more queue readers to process requests. Figure 9.1 shows you how SQL Server Service Broker works with messages, how messages are submitted to a queue, and how messages are processed from a queue.

The nice feature of this queue mechanism is that SQL Server will guarantee that messages will be submitted to and processed from the queue in the correct order. The same thing happens at a ticket desk; when the queue gets too busy, you can add service programs that will read from the queue and process it.

FIGURE 9.1   SQL Server Service Broker

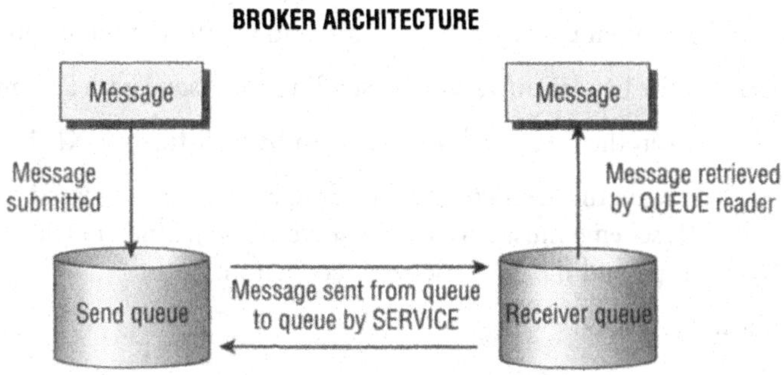

Now, the really nice feature of this service is that you can use any application to read and process messages from a queue. So, integrating and using this architecture over multiple servers and heterogeneous environments provides you with really great features that match closely to technologies such as Microsoft BizTalk Server and Microsoft Message Queuing.

We'll now introduce the components of Service Broker.

Working with Service Broker

Service Broker consists of various components that make up the entire architecture. It is important to understand all these components.

The first step you take when designing a broker architecture is to define what messages you need in the application. You can specify what *message type* can be sent by the initiator and what can be returned by the target or destination. The messages that are sent will be submitted to a *queue* and processed by a *service program*. To communicate from one service to the other, you also have to specify the *route* to get to that destination. What is the protocol you will use to route messages over servers? HTTP, of course; you will define HTTP endpoints and configure them to be used by the broker service. When defining what service can send and receive information from each other, you have to set up an agreement, called a *contract*.

It is important to understand the steps involved in order to configure a broker architecture. We'll cover them in more depth in the following sections.

Creating a Message Type

You can create a message type using the CREATE MESSAGE TYPE statement. In creating those message types, you can define different types, depending on how you structure the message body. Consider this to be the same as an email message where you specify the email subject and then define the body of the message. It's the same for a message type; the subject will be the message type, and you specify what the message body can contain. Sometimes when you read an email message, you know from the subject what the content is about, and you don't need to type a body. The SQL Server Service Broker architecture supports the following message bodies:

None   No validation on the content takes place; you can send whatever you like in the body.

Header only: empty   This is the header only; you are sending a message with an empty body.

Well-formed XML   The data in the message body needs to be well-formed XML.

Schema-bound XML   The data in the message body needs to be schema-validated XML. This means the message body XML schema must exist on the server. You learned in Chapter 8 how to work with the XML datatype and the XML Schema collection.

This leads to the following syntax:

```
CREATE MESSAGE TYPE message_type_name
    [ AUTHORIZATION owner_name ]
    [ VALIDATION = {  NONE
                    | EMPTY
                    | WELL_FORMED_XML
                    | VALID_XML WITH
                      SCHEMA COLLECTION schema_collection_name
                    } ]
[ ; ]
```

Here is an example:

```
-- create message type on initiator and target
CREATE MESSAGE TYPE TicketRequest AUTHORIZATION dbo
    VALIDATION = WELL_FORMED_XML

CREATE MESSAGE TYPE TicketStatus AUTHORIZATION dbo
    VALIDATION = WELL_FORMED_XML
```

Creating a Queue

The next step in configuring a broker architecture is creating the queue. You can specify what should happen to the queue when you submit a message, which you can do by configuring its status and activation properties.

In the following example, you will create the sender *queue* and the recipient queue that will process the send and received messages. Note that you are not putting any automatic activation on the queue so you can see how to manually process a message from a queue. Here's the example:

```
-- Execute this statement on the sender
CREATE QUEUE SenderQUEUE
```

```
-- Execute this statement on the receiver
CREATE QUEUE ReceiverQUEUE
```

Later you will use an ALTER QUEUE statement to specify you are automatically retrieving and processing messages from a queue.

The full syntax to create a queue is as follows:

```
CREATE QUEUE <object>
    [ WITH
      [ STATUS = { ON | OFF }  [ , ] ]
      [ RETENTION = { ON | OFF } [ , ] ]
      [ ACTIVATION (
          [ STATUS = { ON | OFF } , ]
            PROCEDURE_NAME = <procedure> ,
            MAX_QUEUE_READERS = max_readers ,
            EXECUTE AS { SELF | 'user_name' | OWNER }
              ) ]
    ]
      [ ON { filegroup | [ DEFAULT ] } ]
[ ; ]

<object> ::=
{
    [ database_name. [ schema_name ] . | schema_name. ]
        queue_name
}

<procedure> ::=
{
    [ database_name. [ schema_name ] . | schema_name. ]
        stored_procedure_name
}
```

Creating a Contract

In a *contract,* you set up the agreement between the sender of a message and the recipient. This contract will define what message type can be sent by the initiator and what can be returned by the target.

In the ticket service example, you will submit a ticket request from the initiator using a TicketRequest message and receive a status update message from the sender in the form of a TicketStatus message.

The contract defines what messages can be sent to what queue; of course, it is perfectly possible to have various contracts submitting messages to the same queue.

The CREATE CONTRACT syntax is as follows:

```
CREATE CONTRACT contract_name
   [ AUTHORIZATION owner_name ]
      ( {    message_type_name
SENT BY { INITIATOR | TARGET | ANY }
         | [ DEFAULT ] } [ ,...n] )
[ ; ]
```

Here's an example:

```
-- create the contract
CREATE CONTRACT Ticketservicescontract
(TicketRequest SENT BY INITIATOR,
TicketStatus SENT BY TARGET)
```

Creating a Service

Now that you have configured queues, *message types,* and a contract, you can set up the service. In the service you reference to the contract, you can have a single service that runs. Service Broker uses the name of the *service* to route messages, deliver messages to the correct queue within a database, and enforce the contract for a conversation. If you are targeting multiple services to participate in the *broker service,* you need to create the route between them as well.

You can assign multiple contracts to a service as well. Service programs initiate conversations to this service using the contracts specified. If no contracts are specified, the service may only initiate conversations.

In the following example, you will set up the broker services that follow the Ticketservicescontract:

```
-- create the service on the sender
CREATE SERVICE SendTicketingService ON
Queue SenderQUEUE
(Ticketservicescontract)
```

```
-- create the service on the recipient
CREATE SERVICE ReceiveTicketingService ON
Queue ReceiverQUEUE
(Ticketservicescontract)
```

Once the services are configured, you can specify the route between them if you communicate over multiple services. When not configured, you will use the local database service and default service route.

The CREATE SERVICE statement follows this syntax:

```
CREATE SERVICE service_name
   [ AUTHORIZATION owner_name ]
   ON QUEUE [ schema_name. ]queue_name
   [ ( contract_name | [DEFAULT] [ ,...n ] ) ]
[ ; ]
```

Are you ready to go now?

One last thing you need to check is whether the database has the broker service enabled. If not, no broker service communication is possible. You can check whether the database is broker service is enabled by querying the sys.databases view:

```
select name,service_broker_guid,is_broker_enabled from sys.databases
```

If the broker service is enabled, it will return a value of 1; otherwise, you will have to enable the broker service by executing an ALTER DATABASE statement:

```
ALTER DATABASE SYBEX
SET ENABLE_BROKER
```

After creating and configuring the broker service, you can proceed to the next level, performing a test message, and see whether you can get an item in the queue.

Creating a Route

For outgoing messages, Service Broker determines the routing by checking the routing table in the local database.

In a *route*, you specify the communication settings between services. Before creating a route, you should configure the HTTP endpoints used by the CREATE ENDPOINT statement, which is covered later in the "Creating HTTP Endpoints" section.

One of the settings you need to determine is the *broker instance identifier*, which is expressed by a *GUID*. The broker instance you specify must be the identifier of the destination database and can be determined by the following SELECT statement:

```
SELECT service_broker_guid
FROM sys.databases
WHERE database_id = DB_ID()
```

This is an example of how to specify the route:

```
CREATE ROUTE TicketingRoute
   WITH
   SERVICE_NAME = 'SendTicketingService',
   BROKER_INSTANCE =
 'D8D4D268-02A3-4C62-8F91-634B89C1E315',
```

```
      ADDRESS = 'TCP://192.168.10.2:1234' ;
CREATE ROUTE route_name
[ AUTHORIZATION owner_name ]
WITH
    [ SERVICE_NAME = 'service_name', ]
    [ BROKER_INSTANCE = 'broker_instance_identifier' , ]
    [ LIFETIME = route_lifetime , ]
    ADDRESS =  'next_hop_address'
    [ , MIRROR_ADDRESS = 'next_hop_mirror_address' ]
[ ; ]
```

Since in this example you are using services that run on the same database, you don't need to create a route.

Using Service Broker

After successfully configuring the broker service, you can start sending messages over the broker instance. Key components in this process are the queue and the service program.

On a queue you have the ability to add an item to a queue and have the service program automatically pick up the message. You can configure this using the ACTIVATION option on the CREATE QUEUE statement.

Now what is so specific about a queue? Actually, you could consider this as a special, system-created table with certain columns. Table 9.1 displays the entire structure of a queue.

If you consider the queue to be a table, you would be able to insert records (messages) into this table. However, the syntax you will be using is slightly different. Instead of inserting messages and selecting messages, you send and receive messages to and from a queue using SEND and RECEIVE statements.

Multiple messages can be *sent* together, which is expressed in a conversation. In the following section, you will learn how to submit messages to a queue. In the section after that, you will learn how to submit messages to the queue.

Sending Messages

We've already covered that you are submitting messages or sending messages to a queue. To group messages, you initiate a *dialogue conversation*, in which you can group related messages.

To uniquely identify a conversation, you use a unique identifier. By the end of submitting messages to a queue, you have to end the conversation so the messages in the conversation are ready to be processed by the queue.

TABLE 9.1   Queue Description

Column name	Datatype	Description
Status	Tinyint	Status of the message. For messages returned by the RECEIVE command, the status is always 1. Messages in the queue may contain one of the following values: 0=Received message, 1=Ready, 2=Not yet complete, and 3=Retained sent message.
queuing_order	Bigint	Message order number within the queue.
conversation_group_id	Uniqueidentifier	Identifier for the conversation group to which this message belongs.
conversation_handle	Uniqueidentifier	Handle for the conversation for which this message is a part.
Message_sequence_number	Bigint	Sequence number of the message within the conversation.
service_name	Nvarchar(512)	Name of the service to which the conversation belongs.
service_id	Int	SQL Server object identifier of the service to which the conversation belongs.
service_contract_name	Nvarchar(256)	Name of the contract that the conversation follows.
service_contract_id	Int	SQL Server object identifier of the contract that the conversation follows.
Message_type_name	Nvarchar(256)	Name of the message type that describes the message.
Message_type_id	Int	SQL Server object identifier of the message type that describes the message.
Validation	Nchar(2)	Validation used for the message (E=EmptyN=NoneX=XML).
Message_body	Varbinary(MAX)	Content of the message.
Message_id	Uniqueidentifier	Unique identifier for the message.

You begin a conversation from one service to another service like this:

```
BEGIN DIALOG [ CONVERSATION ] @dialog_handle
   FROM SERVICE initiator_service_name
   TO SERVICE 'target_service_name'
       [ , { 'service_broker_guid' |
  'CURRENT DATABASE' } ]
   [ ON CONTRACT contract_name ]
   [ WITH
   [   { RELATED_CONVERSATION = related_conversation_handle

       | RELATED_CONVERSATION_GROUP = related_conversation_group_id } ]
   [ [ , ] LIFETIME = dialog_lifetime ]
   [ [ , ] ENCRYPTION = { ON | OFF }  ] ]
[ ; ]
```

In this example, you will create an easy XML ticket request where you provide the number of requested tickets and the email address of the requestor:

```
-- test and submit an order to a queue
declare @message xml
declare @conversationhandle UNIQUEIDENTIFIER
set @message =
'<TICKETREQUEST><Requestor>dandy@ilikesql.com</Requestor>
    <Requestednumber>5</Requestednumber>
    <RequestedShow>Sybex Book Seminar</RequestedShow>
    </TICKETREQUEST>'

BEGIN DIALOG CONVERSATION @conversationHandle
    FROM SERVICE SendTicketingService
    TO SERVICE 'ReceiveTicketingService'
    ON CONTRACT Ticketservicescontract
   WITH ENCRYPTION = OFF;

-- Send the message on the dialog.

SEND ON CONVERSATION @conversationHandle
  MESSAGE TYPE TicketRequest
  (@message);
END CONVERSATION @conversationHandle
-- End the conversation.
```

Now, let's dive deeply into this example. Before sending a message, you need to initiate a conversation; consider this to be a normal conversation where you first say "hi" to someone before you start asking questions or talking. This conversation handle is unique, which is why you declare it as a UNIQUEIDENTIFIER.

The type of message you'll send is XML; remember, you declared the message type to be a well-formed XML message.

In a conversation, you communicate from one service to the other over an existing contract. Within a conversation it is perfectly possible to submit more than one message. Think about this as requesting some tickets for a show on Broadway and at the same time requesting tickets for the U.S. Open Tennis final.

In the example, you are sending only one ticket request, which you do by using the SEND statement on the existing conversation. As soon as you submit the message and don't have to send any additional messages within the same conversation, you end the conversation by using an END CONVERSATION statement. Of course, in a real-world scenario you would create a stored procedure from this instead of repeating all the T-SQL syntax.

Receiving Messages

Once you have the message submitted to the recipient, you have to retrieve it from the receiving queue. As already mentioned, if the queue is a table, this would be selecting from the table to process the message and, in a next step after processing, delete it from a table.

Retrieving a message from a queue, however, uses the RECEIVE statement, which will process every message. This message retrieval process could be complex because you have the possibility of retrieving messages from the queue one by one or all at once. When processing these messages, it is important to test on the message type and filter informational messages from the message you want to process.

The following example processes messages from a queue:

```
-- retrieve messages from a queue
DECLARE @conversation_handle UNIQUEIDENTIFIER,
        @message_body XML,
        @message_type_name NVARCHAR(128);

    RECEIVE    TOP(1)
        @conversation_handle = conversation_handle,
        @message_type_name = message_type_name,
        @message_body = message_body
  FROM [dbo].[ReceiverQUEUE]
  -- DO SOMETHING with the message
  if @message_type_name = 'TicketRequest'
  BEGIN
        EXEC stp_processticketrequest (@message_body)
```

```
    END
    END CONVERSATION @conversation_handle WITH CLEANUP ;
END
```

In this example, again you declare a conversation handle to define a conversation handle. You also declare an XML datatype to retrieve the message body and use a variable to which you will assign the message type name.

The RECEIVE statement will process the message from the queue and store it in the variables. If the message type received is TicketRequest, you will proceed with executing a stored procedure to which you pass the message. The procedure called will insert the ticket request into a stored procedure and submit an email to the sender using SQL Database Mail. By the end of the processing, you end the conversation to delete the processed message from a queue.

The full syntax for receiving messages from a queue is as follows:

```
[ WAITFOR ( ]
    RECEIVE [ TOP ( n ) ]
        <column_specifier> [ ,...n ]
        FROM <queue>
        [ INTO table_variable ]
        [ WHERE {   conversation_handle = conversation_handle
                | conversation_group_id = conversation_group_id } ]
[ ) ] [ , TIMEOUT timeout ]
[ ; ]

<column_specifier> ::=
{     *
  |  { column_name | [ ] expression }
  [ [ AS ] column_alias ]
     |   column_alias = expression
}      [ ,...n ]

<queue> ::=
{
    [ database_name .[ schema_name   .| schema_name .]
        queue_name
}
```

The WAITFOR statement waits until a message is received in the queue, while the RECEIVE statement with the TOP clause specifies how many messages you are processing at once. In a real-world scenario you would process the messages in the queue using a stored procedure, meaning you would put the RECEIVE statement inside the stored procedure.

Automating the Queue Processing

To automate the queue processing, you can change the status of a queue (or specify this when you create the queue). When making changes to the queue, you execute the ALTER QUEUE statement as shown here:

```
ALTER QUEUE ReceiverQUEUE
WITH ACTIVATION  (STATUS = ON,
                 PROCEDURE_NAME = STP_ProcessQUEUE,
                 EXECUTE AS OWNER)
```

In the example you are activating the stored procedure STP_ProcessQUEUE to fire when an item is submitted to a queue. The content of the stored procedure will of course check the messages submitted and take appropriate action.

In the ACTIVATION property, you specify what stored procedure needs to be called and what security context you will execute on the stored procedure and in what security context the stored procedure will execute.

The stored procedure will look similar to the RECEIVE statement you issued:

```
CREATE PROCEDURE STP_ProcessQueue
AS
BEGIN
DECLARE @conversation_handle UNIQUEIDENTIFIER,
        @message_body XML,
        @message_type_name NVARCHAR(128);


    RECEIVE    TOP(1)
        @conversation_handle = conversation_handle,
        @message_type_name = message_type_name,
        @message_body = message_body
  FROM [dbo].[ReceiverQUEUE]
  -- DO SOMETHING with the message
  if @message_type_name = 'TicketRequest'
  BEGIN
        EXEC stp_processticketrequest @message_body
  END
  END CONVERSATION @conversation_handle ;
END
```

As soon as an item is submitted to the queue, the stored procedure will execute the statement and process it.

In Exercise 9.1 you will set up a broker architecture to send messages—a ticket request—from an initiator queue to a target queue. By the end of the exercise you will have completed the entire process of setting up and configuring a broker architecture.

EXERCISE 9.1

Implementing a Service Broker Architecture

1. Open a new query window, and type the following syntax to enable the broker architecture on the Sybex database:

```
USE MASTER

GO

-- Enable the broker architecture

alter database sybex

set ENABLE_BROKER

GO

USE SYBEX

GO
```

2. Execute the following code to create the message types:

```
-- define broker architecture

-- create message type on initiator and target

CREATE MESSAGE TYPE TicketRequest AUTHORIZATION dbo

    VALIDATION = WELL_FORMED_XML


CREATE MESSAGE TYPE TicketStatus AUTHORIZATION dbo

    VALIDATION = WELL_FORMED_XML
```

3. Execute the following code to create the sender and receiver queue:

```
-- CREATE QUEUES


-- Execute this statement on the sender

CREATE QUEUE SenderQUEUE
```

```
-- Execute this statement on the receiver

CREATE QUEUE ReceiverQUEUE
```

4. Execute the following code to create the contract:

```
-- create the contract

CREATE CONTRACT Ticketservicescontract

(TicketRequest SENT BY INITIATOR,

TicketStatus SENT BY TARGET)
```

5. Execute the following code to initiate the services:

```
-- create the service on the sender


CREATE SERVICE SendTicketingService ON

Queue SenderQUEUE

(Ticketservicescontract)


-- create the service on the recipient

CREATE SERVICE ReceiveTicketingService ON

Queue ReceiverQUEUE

(Ticketservicescontract)
```

6. Execute the following code to submit a message to the queue:

```
-- test and submit an order to a queue

declare @message xml

declare @conversationhandle UNIQUEIDENTIFIER

set @message =

'<TICKETREQUEST>

  <Requestor>dandy@ilikesql.com</Requestor>

  <Requestednumber>5</Requestednumber>
```

```
    <RequestedShow>Sybex SQLTraining</RequestedShow>

    </TICKETREQUEST>' '

BEGIN DIALOG CONVERSATION @conversationHandle

    FROM SERVICE SendTicketingService

    TO SERVICE 'ReceiveTicketingService'

    ON CONTRACT Ticketservicescontract

    WITH ENCRYPTION = OFF;


-- Send the message on the dialog.


SEND ON CONVERSATION @conversationHandle

  MESSAGE TYPE TicketRequest

  (@message);

END CONVERSATION @conversationHandle

-- End the conversation.
```

7. Execute the following SELECT statement to check whether a message is submitted to the queue:

```
-- check the content of the queue

select * from ReceiverQUEUE

GO
```

8. Create a stored procedure to process the messages from the queue:

```
-- CREATE PROCEDURE TO RETRIEVE MESSAGES FROM THE QUEUE

CREATE PROCEDURE STP_ProcessQueue

AS

BEGIN
```

```
DECLARE @conversation_handle UNIQUEIDENTIFIER,

        @message_body XML,

        @message_type_name NVARCHAR(128);


        RECEIVE    TOP(1)

            @conversation_handle = conversation_handle,

            @message_type_name = message_type_name,

            @message_body = message_body

    FROM [dbo].[ReceiverQUEUE]

    -- DO SOMETHING with the message

    if @message_type_name = 'TicketRequest'

    BEGIN

        -- To process from the queue you would write a stored procedure to handle
    the message

        -- EXEC stp_processticketrequest @message_body

        --for exercise purposes we just select the message

        SELECT @message_body

        END

        END CONVERSATION @conversation_handle ;

    END


    GO
```

9. Alter the queue, and enable automatic activation:

```
-- alter the queue for automatic activation

ALTER QUEUE ReceiverQUEUE
```

EXERCISE 9.1 *(continued)*

```
WITH ACTIVATION  (STATUS = ON,

                  PROCEDURE_NAME = STP_ProcessQUEUE,

                  EXECUTE AS OWNER)
GO
```

10. Execute the stored procedure manually to check the queue processing:

```
-- EXECUTE the Stored Procedure Manually

EXEC STP_ProcessQUEUE
```

As you probably noticed, a lot of syntax is required with the SQL Server Service Broker architecture, and SQL Server 2005 does not provide you a graphical interface to configure queues, and so on. However, you can review created queues in and other broker service–related objects in Object Explorer (see Figure 9.2).

FIGURE 9.2   Object Explorer objects

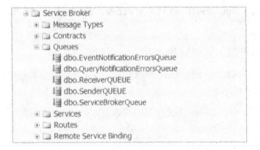

Introducing HTTP Endpoints

An endpoint is the connecting point for two services in the communication architecture and is addressed by a protocol and IP port number. We already mentioned you'll need to specify endpoints when setting up the communication between two broker services. (Remember that Service Broker uses HTTP.)

However, you have many more options with endpoints. One of the great features is that you can create endpoints to provide the user with access to the database objects using a web service, and endpoints are also used as configuration points for database mirroring. These are the types of endpoints you can use:

Service Broker endpoint   SQL Server uses Service Broker endpoints for Service Broker communication outside the SQL Server instance. An *endpoint* is a SQL Server object that represents the capability for SQL Server to communicate over the network, so a *Service Broker endpoint* configures SQL Server to send and receive Service Broker messages over the network.

Service Broker endpoints provide options for transport security and message forwarding. A Service Broker endpoint listens on a specific TCP port number.

By default, an instance of SQL Server does not contain a Service Broker endpoint. You must create a Service Broker endpoint to send or receive messages outside the SQL Server instance.

Mirror endpoints   For database mirroring, a server instance requires its own, dedicated database-mirroring endpoint. *Mirror endpoints* are special-purpose endpoints used exclusively to receive database-mirroring connections from other server instances.

The same as broker instance endpoints, database-mirroring endpoints use TCP to send and receive messages between the server instances in database-mirroring sessions. Each configured database mirror endpoint exclusively uses a TCP-specific port number.

HTTP endpoints   SQL Server exposes native XML web services through the database engine by configuring and creating *HTTP endpoints*. To work enable native calls, SQL Server will request and register with the HTTP listener http.sys, which is available only on Windows Server 2003 and Windows XP Service Pack 2. This means SQL Server uses XML and HTTP to access services and objects regardless of the client software used.

SQL Server uses SOAP message requests to an instance of SQL Server over HTTP to provide the following:

- Access to T-SQL batch statements, with or without parameters
- Access to stored procedures, extended stored procedures, and scalar-valued user-defined functions

The key point to remember is that SQL Server does not use Internet Information Services (IIS) but instead directly registers with http.sys. When setting up a web service that can listen natively for HTTP SOAP request, you have to configure this endpoint using the CREATE ENDPOINT statement.

In the following sections, you will learn how to configure endpoints for the various usages. Also, you will learn how to configure endpoint security.

Configuring HTTP Endpoints

HTTP endpoints can listen and receive requests on any TCP port, regardless of the URL you specified.

Since endpoints register with http.sys, the request will first go to the server identified in the URL, and then the http.sys layer will forward the URL to the instance of SQL Server whilst bypassing IIS. You don't need to have IIS running and configured for this service.

To configure an endpoint, you use the CREATE ENDPOINT statement. You can break this statement into two parts to describe its functionality. The following is the full syntax:

```
CREATE ENDPOINT endPointName [ AUTHORIZATION login ]
STATE = { STARTED | STOPPED | DISABLED }
AS { HTTP | TCP } (
    <protocol_specific_arguments>
        )
FOR { SOAP | TSQL |
 SERVICE_BROKER | DATABASE_MIRRORING } (
    <language_specific_arguments>
        )
```

```
<AS HTTP_protocol_specific_arguments> ::=
AS HTTP (
  PATH = 'url'
      , AUTHENTICATION =( { BASIC | DIGEST |
INTEGRATED | NTLM | KERBEROS } [ ,...n ] )
      , PORTS = ( { CLEAR | SSL} [ ,... n ] )
  [ SITE = {'*' | '+' | 'webSite' },]
  [, CLEAR_PORT = clearPort ]
  [, SSL_PORT = SSLPort ]
  [, AUTH_REALM = { 'realm' | NONE } ]
  [, DEFAULT_LOGON_DOMAIN = { 'domain' | NONE } ]
  [, COMPRESSION = { ENABLED | DISABLED } ]
  )
```

```
<AS TCP_protocol_specific_arguments> ::=AS TCP (
  LISTENER_PORT = listenerPort
  [ , LISTENER_IP = ALL |
(<4-part-ip> | <ip_address_v6> ) ]
)
```

```
<FOR SOAP_language_specific_arguments> ::=
FOR SOAP(
```

```
[ { WEBMETHOD [ 'namespace' .] 'method_alias'
  (   NAME = 'database.owner.name'
    [ , SCHEMA = { NONE | STANDARD | DEFAULT } ]
    [ , FORMAT = { ALL_RESULTS | ROWSETS_ONLY } ]
  )
} [ ,...n ] ]
[   BATCHES = { ENABLED | DISABLED } ]
[ , WSDL = { NONE | DEFAULT | 'sp_name' } ]
[ , SESSIONS = { ENABLED | DISABLED } ]
[ , LOGIN_TYPE = { MIXED | WINDOWS } ]
[ , SESSION_TIMEOUT = timeoutInterval | NEVER ]
[ , DATABASE = { 'database_name' | DEFAULT }
[ , NAMESPACE = { 'namespace' | DEFAULT } ]
[ , SCHEMA = { NONE | STANDARD } ]
[ , CHARACTER_SET = { SQL | XML }]
[ , HEADER_LIMIT = int ]
)
<FOR SERVICE_BROKER_language_specific_arguments> ::=
FOR SERVICE_BROKER (
  [ AUTHENTICATION = {
          WINDOWS [ { NTLM | KERBEROS | NEGOTIATE } ]
    | CERTIFICATE certificate_name
    | WINDOWS [ { NTLM | KERBEROS
| NEGOTIATE } ] CERTIFICATE certificate_name
    | CERTIFICATE certificate_name WINDOWS
 [ { NTLM | KERBEROS | NEGOTIATE } ]
  } ]
  [ , ENCRYPTION = { DISABLED | SUPPORTED | REQUIRED }
     [ ALGORITHM { RC4 | AES | AES RC4 | RC4 AES } ]
  ]
  [ , MESSAGE_FORWARDING = { ENABLED | DISABLED* } ]
  [ , MESSAGE_FORWARD_SIZE = forward_size ]
)

<FOR DATABASE_MIRRORING_language_specific_arguments> ::=
FOR DATABASE_MIRRORING (
  [ AUTHENTICATION = {
          WINDOWS [ { NTLM | KERBEROS | NEGOTIATE } ]
```

```
      | CERTIFICATE certificate_name
    } ]
  [ [ , ] ENCRYPTION = { DISABLED |SUPPORTED | REQUIRED }
      [ ALGORITHM { RC4 | AES | AES RC4 | RC4 AES } ]
  ]
  [,] ROLE = { WITNESS | PARTNER | ALL }
)
```

This is quite a syntax, isn't it? We'll break this syntax down to make it more readable.

Part 1: Configuring the Protocol and Endpoint

This is the protocol and endpoint configuration:

```
CREATE ENDPOINT .. AS

...

FOR
```

In this part, you provide information specific to the protocol being used, which will be TCP or HTTP, depending on whether you use the endpoint for database mirroring and Service Broker or for XML web services.

In this configuration, you also specify the method of authentication and the list of IP addresses you want to permit or restrict connecting to the endpoint.

This is an example of specifying the first part of the CREATE block:

```
CREATE ENDPOINT sql_endpoint
STATE = STARTED
AS HTTP(
    PATH = '/sql',
    AUTHENTICATION = (INTEGRATED ),
    PORTS = ( CLEAR ),
    SITE = 'LOCALHOST'
    )
```

This statement will create an endpoint with the initial state started, using integrated security on port 80 with the virtual path `http://localhost/sql`.

Part 2: Using the *FOR* Clause

After the FOR clause, you specify the payload for the endpoint, which can consist of several supported types:

HTTP SOAP   When using HTTP SOAP, you specify the stored procedures you want to expose in the endpoint as web methods. You can specify a corresponding stored procedure or a user-defined function.

When a client application sends an HTTP SOAP request, the client can call all these exposed methods.

The configuration allows you to provide SOAP configuration information such as the following:

- The allowance of ad hoc queries
- Whether to return the XSD schema for the result set
- The endpoint namespace

A typical FOR clause looks like this:

```
FOR SOAP (
    WEBMETHOD 'CheckTicketStatus'
            (name='sybex.dbo.stp_CheckTicketStatus',
            SCHEMA=STANDARD ),
    WSDL = DEFAULT,
    SCHEMA = STANDARD,
    DATABASE = 'sybex',
    NAMESPACE = 'http://localhost/'
    );
```

Service Broker   Configuring an endpoint for broker allows you to specify the endpoint to which the broker service can connect. A typical configuration looks like this:

```
CREATE ENDPOINT BrokerEndpoint
    STATE = STARTED
    AS TCP ( LISTENER_PORT = 4037 )
    FOR SERVICE_BROKER ( AUTHENTICATION = WINDOWS ) ;
GO
```

Database mirroring   Database mirroring, covered in Chapter 13, is one of the high-availability features you can use with SQL Server 2005. You can configure the endpoint for database mirroring. A typical configuration looks like this:

```
CREATE ENDPOINT endpoint_mirroring
    STATE = STARTED
    AS TCP ( LISTENER_PORT = 5022 )
    FOR DATABASE_MIRRORING (
        AUTHENTICATION = WINDOWS KERBEROS,
        ENCRYPTION = SUPPORTED,
        ROLE=ALL);
```

When registering endpoints, the endpoint will be known by http.sys only when the SQL Server instance is running. To reserve the necessary namespaces in http.sys and prevent them to be overwritten by an IIS configuration when the SQL Server instance is not running, it is advisable to register the endpoint using the sp_reserve_http_namespace stored procedure.

Securing HTTP Endpoints

An endpoint is a securable object, and to be able to connect/create or alter an endpoint, you need to have appropriate permissions.

The following are the most common permissions that can be granted:

- ALTER
- CONNECT
- CONTROL
- TAKE OWNERSHIP
- VIEW DEFINITION

You have the possibility to GRANT/REVOKE/DENY permission on the endpoint in order to provide a database user or role access to the endpoint configuration.

The GRANT permission you have to specify follows this syntax:

```
GRANT permission ON ENDPOINT::endpointname TO user or role
```

So, a typical configuration when you want to allow endpoint access to every user connecting to SQL looks like this:

```
GRANT CONNECT ON ENDPOINT::sqlendpoint TO public
```

Before a user can connect to an endpoint, CONNECT permissions have to be granted.

Summary

In this chapter, you learned how to configure a Service Broker architecture. A Service Broker architecture is useful in an environment where you need a message-based system or a queue-based system.

Since SQL Server 2005 is secure out of the box, you need to enable Service Broker on the database level before you can start using it, which is something people frequently forget.

Because of security reasons, Service Broker by default is able to communicate only on local servers. If you want to allow external access, you need to configure an endpoint for Service Broker. You learned how to do this in this chapter. HTTP can use endpoints for SOAP requests, and endpoints can provide access to the database from any client that can explore and use a web service.

Service Broker works with message types, contracts, queues, and service programs. On a queue you can specify how an endpoint should be activated. The entire configuration of the web service, including the permissions and IP restrictions, are managed within SQL Server. Users will need to get permissions to be able to connect to an endpoint.

Endpoints are not only used by SOAP requests but are also the configurable network addresses for Service Broker and database mirroring. Together with the endpoint you will specify the authentication of the endpoint.

 **Real World Scenario**

Case Study: Implementing a Broker Architecture

The XYZ company wants to automate its process to submit orders to suppliers and also inform distributors about orders that need to be shipped to their customers. Before SQL Server 2005, the company was manually submitting an order by email in the form of an Excel spreadsheet and then was imported by a supplier into an order-entry system. However, the complaint of XYZ was that it took too long before suppliers confirmed the delivery of a certain order. Since all the suppliers already implemented SQL Server 2005, the company's technology design team decided to work out a new solution.

The result of this design translates to SQL Server Service Broker architecture.

When an article reaches its minimum stock, a message for purchase is submitted to a queue. The service program will submit a purchase request to the supplier that will be confirmed by a confirmation that the order is currently processing.

The XYZ company is planning on extending this automated service not only to its suppliers but also to inform distributors about orders that need to be delivered. Also, XYZ is investigating how it can integrate the service on its own delivery trucks; as soon as an order is delivered to the customer, the company will automatically send a delivery confirmation to the central database.

XYZ decided to implement this strategy because it will allow the company to integrate with future customers, and it will also give the company the ability to deliver queued messages to BizTalk Server 2006 by using a data connector that allows BizTalk Server to read from a SQL Server Service Broker service queue.

Exam Essentials

Know how to configure and work with the Service Broker.   Understand the Service Broker architecture and the components it consists of in terms of services, service programs, contracts, message types, and routing.

Understand how to create a service.   Understand how a service is created by identifying what contract is used, and be able to configure and identify the CREATE SERVICE syntax.

Understand how to create a queue.   On a queue you have the possibility to initiate the activation of the queue and specify the service program to use (stored procedure).

Understand how to create a contract.   In a contract, you identify what message types the initiator can send and what can be returned by the sender.

Understand how to create a message type.   Message types can have a message body that can be empty (header only messages) or that needs to be well-formed XML or match an XML schema collection.

Understand how to initiate a conversation.   When submitting messages to a queue, you need to create a conversation. Within a conversation, you can submit multiple messages that relate to each other.

Understand how to send and receive messages.   When sending and receiving messages, you use the SEND and RECEIVE keywords. You need to fully understand the syntax, understand how to retrieve messages from a queue, and know how to close the dialogue by the end of your conversation.

Understand how to create and secure HTTP endpoints.   When creating endpoints, you need to identify the virtual directory or path on the server, as well as configure the methods that can be used by the endpoint. You need to know that all security is managed within the endpoint configuration and that a user needs to have the appropriate permissions in order to connect to an endpoint.

Review Questions

1. You want to expose the sp_who stored procedure as a web method on a Window XP machine with IIS installed and running. You run the following code:

```
1.    CREATE ENDPOINT sql_endpoint
2.    STATE = STARTED
3.    AS HTTP(
4.    PATH = '/sql',
5.    AUTHENTICATION = (INTEGRATED ),
6.    PORTS = ( CLEAR ),
7.    SITE = 'MySERVER'
8.    )s
9.    FOR SOAP (
10.     WEBMETHOD 'ConnectionsInfo'
11.       (name='master.sys.sp_who'),
12.     WSDL = DEFAULT,
13.     SCHEMA = STANDARD,
14.     DATABASE = 'master',
15.     NAMESPACE = 'http://tempUri.org/'
16.     );
17.    GO
```

However, running the code, you get the following error: "An error occurred while attempting to register the endpoint 'sql_endpoint'. One or more of the ports specified in the CREATE ENDPOINT statement may be bound to another process. Attempt the statement again with a different port or use netstat to find the application currently using the port and resolve the conflict." How can you solve the problem? (Select the best option.)

   A. Add the following line of code between line 6 and line 7, specifying any free port: CLEAR_PORT = 7200,.

   B. Uninstall IIS.

   C. Use Basic Authentication.

   D. Change the PORTS argument to SSL instead of CLEAR.

2. You expose the sp_who stored procedure as a web method using the following code:

```
1.    CREATE ENDPOINT sql_endpoint
2.    AS HTTP(
3.    PATH = '/sql',
4.    AUTHENTICATION = (INTEGRATED ),
5.    PORTS = ( CLEAR ),
6.    CLEAR_PORT = 7200,
```

```
7.    SITE = 'YUKON'
8.    )
9.    FOR SOAP (
10.     WEBMETHOD 'ConnectionsInfo'
11.       (name='master.sys.sp_who'),
12.     WSDL = DEFAULT,
13.     SCHEMA = STANDARD,
14.     DATABASE = 'master',
15.     NAMESPACE = 'http://tempUri.org/'
16.     );
```

The query completed successfully. However, your client application receives a "Service Unavailable" error. How can you fix the problem? (Choose all that apply.)

A. Use ALTER ENDPOINT, and specify the STATE attribute with the STARTED value.

B. Use the SQL Server 2005 Surface Area Configuration tool to start the endpoint.

C. Change line 9 to FOR SERVICE_BROKER.

D. Change line 9 to FOR DATABASE_MIRRORING.

3. You create a database-mirroring endpoint that will support both the partner and witness role. You use the CREATE ENDPOINT statement for that. Which attribute will allow both mirroring roles?

A. The AUTH_REALM attribute.

B. The FORMAT attribute. Use the SQL Server 2005 Surface Area Configuration tool to start the endpoint.

C. The MESSAGE_FORWARDING attribute. Change line 9 with FOR SERVICE_BROKER.

D. The ROLE attribute.

4. You need to create a message type TicketIssued that will have an empty message body. What is the syntax you use to accomplish this?

A. Use this:
```
CREATE MESSAGE TYPE TicketIssued VALIDATION = NONE
```

B. Use this:
```
CREATE MESSAGE TYPE TicketIssued VALIDATION = EMPTY
```

C. Use this:
```
CREATE MESSAGE TYPE TicketIssued BODY = NONE
```

D. Use this:
```
CREATE MESSAGE TYPE TicketIssued BODY = EMPTY
```

5. You need to insert a message in a queue and execute the following statements, but for some reason the message was not submitted to the queue. Identify the problem.

```
declare @message xml
declare @conversationhandle UNIQUEIDENTIFIER
```

```
set @message = '<TICKETREQUEST><Requestor>dandy@ilikesql.com</Requestor>
<Requestednumber>5</Requestednumber>
<RequestedShow>Sybex SQL Training</RequestedShow></TICKETREQUEST>'

BEGIN DIALOG CONVERSATION @conversationHandle
    FROM SERVICE SendTicketingService
    TO SERVICE 'ReceiveTicketingService'
    ON CONTRACT Ticketservicescontract
    WITH ENCRYPTION = OFF;

END CONVERSATION @conversationHandle
-- End the conversation.
```

   A. You need to commit the transaction by the end of the statement.

   B. You forgot to insert the record in the queue table using the INSERT statement.

   C. You forgot to send the message on the conversation.

   D. You cannot close the conversation at the end of a conversation message.

6. You need to create the infrastructure for a service. One of the tasks is to create a queue. You don't want the queue to allow receiving messages until you complete all work. What code can you use?

   A. Use this:
```
CREATE QUEUE SalesQueue
```

   B. Use this:
```
CREATE QUEUE SalesQueue WITH STATUS=ON
```

   C. Use this:
```
CREATE QUEUE SalesQueue WITH STATUS=OFF
```

   D. Use this:
```
CREATE QUEUE SalesQueue WITH RETENTION=OFF
```

7. For auditing purposes you want to retain messages sent or received on conversations for a certain queue until conversations ended. What method can you use?

   A. Use this:
```
CREATE QUEUE SalesAuditQueue WITH RETENTION=OFF.
```

   B. Use this:
```
CREATE QUEUE SalesAuditQueue WITH RETENTION=ON.
```

   C. Use this:
```
CREATE QUEUE SalesAuditQueue.
```

   D. Use this:
SELECT statement instead of RECEIVE.

8. You are building the infrastructure for a service. You create a queue, and you need to have the queue active. Service Broker will activate a stored procedure to handle messages. Currently the stored procedure is not finished, and you want to prevent its activation. What method can you use?

   A. Use this:
   ```
   CREATE QUEUE SalesQueue
       WITH STATUS = ON,
   ACTIVATION (
            STATUS=OFF,
   PROCEDURE_NAME = sales_procedure,
   MAX_QUEUE_READERS = 10,
   EXECUTE AS SELF)
   ```

   B. Use this:
   ```
   CREATE QUEUE SalesQueue
       WITH STATUS = OFF,
   ACTIVATION (
        STATUS=OFF,
        PROCEDURE_NAME = sales_procedure,
        MAX_QUEUE_READERS = 10,
        EXECUTE AS SELF )
   ```

   C. Use this:
   ```
   CREATE QUEUE SalesQueue
       WITH STATUS = OFF,
       ACTIVATION (
       STATUS=ON,
       PROCEDURE_NAME = sales_procedure,
       MAX_QUEUE_READERS = 10,
       EXECUTE AS SELF)
   ```

   D. Use this:
   ```
   CREATE QUEUE SalesQueue
       WITH
       ACTIVATION (
   STATUS=ON,
   PROCEDURE_NAME = sales_procedure,
   MAX_QUEUE_READERS = 10,
   EXECUTE AS SELF)
   ```

9. You need to create a contract to send and receive ticket requests and status. Both types can be sent from both ends of the conversation. What method can you use?

   A. Use this:
   ```
   CREATE CONTRACT TicketServicesContract
     (TicketRequest SENT BY INITIATOR,
   TicketStatus SENT BY TARGET)
   ```

   B. Use this:
   ```
   CREATE CONTRACT TicketServicesContract
     (TicketRequest SENT BY ANY,
   TicketStatus SENT BY ANY)
   ```

C. Use this:
```
CREATE CONTRACT TicketServicesContract
 (TicketRequest SENT BY INITIATOR,
TicketStatus SENT BY INITIATOR)
```

D. Use this:
```
CREATE CONTRACT TicketServicesContract
 (TicketRequest SENT BY TARGET,
TicketStatus SENT BY TARGET)
```

10. You need to create a contract to send and receive ticket requests and status. Both types can be sent from both ends of the conversation. Additionally, you want to be able to send messages of the default message type. What method can you use?

A. Use this:
```
CREATE CONTRACT TicketServicesContract
    (TicketRequest SENT BY ANY,
    TicketStatus SENT BY ANY)
```

B. Use this:
```
CREATE CONTRACT TicketServicesContract
    (TicketRequest SENT BY INITIATOR,
    TicketStatus SENT BY TARGET)
```

C. Use this:
```
CREATE CONTRACT TicketServicesContract
    (
    DEFAULT SENT BY ANY,
    TicketRequest SENT BY ANY,
    TicketStatus SENT BY ANY)
```

D. Use this:
```
CREATE CONTRACT TicketServicesContract
    (
    [DEFAULT] SENT BY ANY,
    TicketRequest SENT BY ANY,
    TicketStatus SENT BY ANY)
```

11. You need to change the authorization for an existing contract. How can you accomplish that?

A. Use the DROP CONTRACT statement followed by a CREATE CONTRACT statement.

B. Alter the contract using ALTER CONTRACT.

C. Use the ALTER AUTHORIZATION statement.

D. Use the DROP CONTRACT statement.

12. Which of the following is not true regarding services?

A. You can have multiple contracts for a service.

B. You can use the DEFAULT contract for creating a service.

C. You cannot create a service without a contract.

D. You can add and remove contracts from an existing service.

13. You need to modify an existing service. You want to use a new queue and move the existing messages from the old queue to the new one. How can you accomplish that?

    A. Use the ALTER SERVICE statement and ON QUEUE option.

    B. You cannot move existing messages to a new queue.

    C. Drop the existing service, and re-create it using the new queue.

    D. Move messages manually.

14. You want to create a service that will use the DEFAULT contract and a contract named SalesContract. How can you accomplish that?

    A. Use this:
```
CREATE SERVICE SalesService
ON QUEUE SalesQueue
```

    B. Use this:
```
CREATE SERVICE SalesService
ON QUEUE SalesQueue ([DEFAULT])
```

    C. Use this:
```
CREATE SERVICE SalesService
ON QUEUE SalesQueue ([DEFAULT],SalesContract)
```

    D. Use this:
```
CREATE SERVICE SalesService
ON QUEUE SalesQueue (SalesContract)
```

15. Which of the following is true about conversations and encryption? (Choose all that apply.)

    A. Messages exchanged within services are always encrypted.

    B. Messages exchanged with services in the same instance of SQL Server 2005 are not encrypted.

    C. When the services are in different databases, a database master key is not required.

    D. The ENCRYPTION setting of the BEGIN DIALOG statement specifies whether messages sent and received must be encrypted.

16. You create a conversation between two services. You want to specify 30 minutes as the maximum amount of time that the conversation will remain open. How can you accomplish that?

    A. Use this:
```
DECLARE @dialog_handle UNIQUEIDENTIFIER
BEGIN DIALOG CONVERSATION @dialog_handle
FROM SERVICE SalesClientService
TO SERVICE 'SalesService'
ON CONTRACT SalesContract
WITH LIFETIME = 1800;
```

    B. Use this:
```
DECLARE @dialog_handle UNIQUEIDENTIFIER
BEGIN DIALOG CONVERSATION @dialog_handle
FROM SERVICE SalesClientService
```

```
      TO SERVICE 'SalesService'
      ON CONTRACT SalesContract
      WITH LIFETIME = 1800000;
```

C. Use this:
```
      DECLARE @dialog_handle UNIQUEIDENTIFIER
      BEGIN DIALOG CONVERSATION @dialog_handle
      FROM SERVICE SalesClientService
      TO SERVICE 'SalesService'
      ON CONTRACT SalesContract
      WITH LIFETIME = 30;
```

D. Use this:
```
      DECLARE @dialog_handle UNIQUEIDENTIFIER
      BEGIN DIALOG CONVERSATION @dialog_handle
      FROM SERVICE SalesClientService
      TO SERVICE 'SalesService'
      ON CONTRACT SalesContract;
```

17. You need to remove all messages from one side of an existing conversation. The remote services are owned by another company and have been completely removed. How can you complete your task?

A. Use this:
```
      END CONVERSATION @conversation_handle;
```

B. Use this:
```
      END CONVERSATION @conversation_handle
      WITH ERROR = 1 DESCRIPTION = 'Remote service is unavailable';
```

C. Use this:
```
      END CONVERSATION @conversation_handle
      WITH CLEANUP;
```

D. Do nothing. SQL Server will clean up automatically.

18. Which of the following are true about SEND statement? (Choose all that apply.)

A. To send a message, you need a valid conversation identifier.

B. It's mandatory to specify a message type.

C. You can send a message having the message body empty.

D. You can specify NULL for the `message_body_expression` argument.

19. You retrieve a message using the RECEIVE statement from queue that has the RETENTION setting ON. What is the effect of the RECEIVE statement on the message in this particular case?

A. The RECEIVE statement will remove the message from the queue.

B. The RECEIVE statement will have no effect on the message.

C. The RECEIVE statement will update the status column of the queue for the retrieved message and leave the message in the queue.

D. The RECEIVE statement will update the queuing_order column of the queue.

20. You want to receive all available messages from a specified conversation group. You do not need all columns from the queue. You need just the message body. Which code can you use?

A. Use this:
```
RECEIVE *
FROM SalesQueue
WHERE conversation_group_id = @conversation_group;
```

B. Use this:
```
RECEIVE *
FROM SalesQueue
WHERE conversation_handle = @conversation_group;
```

C. Use this:
```
RECEIVE message_body
FROM SalesQueue
WHERE conversation_ group_id = @conversation_group;
```

D. Use this:
```
RECEIVE message_type
FROM SalesQueue
WHERE conversation_ group_id = @conversation_group;
```

Answers to Review Questions

1. A. The endpoint is in conflict with IIS, which listens on port 80. By default, the CLEAR_PORT attribute is also 80. Uninstalling IIS is not an option, and specifying SSL will generate another conflict if there are web applications that use SSL. Changing the authentication mode will not solve the problem.

2. A, B. By default, the value of the STATE attribute is STOPPED. You have to start the endpoint using either ALTER ENDPOINT or the Surface Area Configuration tool.

3. D. The ROLE attribute with the value ALL allows both mirroring roles.

4. B. The correct statement is specifying an EMPTY message body; VALIDATION = means the message can still have a message body.

5. C. You submit a message to the queue using a SEND message:

    ```
    SEND ON CONVERSATION @conversationHandle
      MESSAGE TYPE TicketRequest
      (@message);
    ```

6. C. A queue in an inactive status would not allow messages to be added or removed from the queue. The default value of a CREATE QUEUE automatically sets the queue to accept messages.

7. B. You can set the retention setting for a queue set using the RETENTION argument. By default retention is turned off, so you have to explicitly turn it on.

8. A. The queue should be active, so its status should be ON. To prevent the activation of the specified stored procedure, the activation status should be OFF.

9. B. Only Option B accomplishes the intended results. When specifying the SENT BY ANY option, you specify that both the INITIATOR and TARGET can initiate the sending of a ticket request.

10. D. Only Option D accomplishes the intended results. The message type DEFAULT must be delimited as an identifier.

11. C. You need to use the ALTER AUTHORIZATION statement to accomplish the intended results. The ALTER CONTRACT statement is not supported yet.

12. C. You can create a service with no contracts (which can be the initiator of a conversation).

13. A. The ALTER SERVICE statement with the ON QUEUE option allows you to specify a new queue and move existing messages.

14. C. You need to specify both types of contract.

15. B, D. Messages exchanged with services in the same instance of SQL Server 2005 are not encrypted (so not all messages are encrypted). However, database master key is required even if messages are not encrypted.

16. A. You can set the maximum amount of time that a conversation will remain open using the LIFETIME parameter that is expressed in seconds. By default, the parameter is the maximum value of the int datatype.

17. C. You need to specify the option WITH CLEANUP in this particular case.

18. A, C. If a message type is not specified when you use the SEND statement, the message will have the DEFAULT type. However, you cannot specify NULL as the message_body_expression argument.

19. C. When the RETENTION setting is ON for a queue, the messages will be kept in the queue until the conversation ends.

20. C. You need to filter using the conversation_group_id column and retrieve the message_body column.

Chapter 10

Maintaining and Automating SQL Server

MICROSOFT EXAM OBJECTIVES COVERED IN THIS CHAPTER:

✓ **Implement and maintain SQL Server Agent jobs.**

- Set a job owner.
- Create a job schedule.
- Create job steps.
- Configure job steps.
- Disable a job.
- Create a maintenance job.
- Set up alerts.
- Configure operators.
- Modify a job.
- Delete a job.
- Manage a job.

✓ **Manage databases by using Transact-SQL.**

- Manage index fragmentation.
- Manage statistics.
- Shrink files.
- Perform database integrity checks by using DBCC CHECKDB.
- Configure the SQL Server DatabaseMail subsystem for an instance.

Throughout this book, we have discussed administrative activities that would best be performed during off-hours. These activities include backing up databases, creating large databases, reconstructing indexes—the list goes on. Most of these activities need to be performed on a regular basis, not just once. For example, you'll need to back up at frequent intervals. Because most administrators would rather not have to stand at the SQL Server to start the task in question, SQL Server has the built-in capability to automate tasks.

First you need to look at maintenance basics—what to maintain and how. You'll learn how to maintain indexes, statistics, and databases. Then we'll discuss the basics of how automation works in SQL Server. We'll explain some of the basic concepts of automation and how the SQL Server Agent service plays a part.

After we discuss the basics of automation, we'll cover Database Mail, SQL Server 2005's new mail-processing functionality. It's essential to configure Database Mail because SQL Server is capable of sending you email when a problem occurs as long as the email functionality is configured properly.

Next we'll explain how to configure operators. An operator is a person who is able to receive messages from SQL Server via email, pager, or Net Send. Configuring an operator tells SQL Server who to contact and when they're available.

After you have operators in place, you can start creating jobs, the heart of automation. Jobs are the activities you need to administer, such as database backups or index reconstructions. We'll discuss each part of a job, the steps required to complete the job, and the schedules that tell SQL Server when to run the job.

Next we'll discuss how to configure alerts, which will warn you of problems or events that have occurred on the server. Not only will we explain how to configure standard SQL Server alerts, but we'll also discuss the methods for creating your own user-defined alerts to cover any possible event that may occur on your server.

After this, we'll discuss the Maintenance Plan Wizard, which automates all the standard database maintenance procedures such as backups, index reconstructions, transaction log backups, and so on. Finally we'll cover the Copy Database Wizard and show how to simplify the process of copying databases.

We'll start this chapter by discussing basic maintenance procedures.

Maintaining Indexes

In Chapter 4, you learned you need indexes on most SQL Server tables to speed up access to the data. Without these indexes, SQL Server would need to perform table scans, reading every record in the table, to find any amount of data. To keep your indexes running at peak efficiency, you must perform periodic maintenance on them.

The primary issue to watch for in an index is page splitting. As described in Chapter 4, a page split is caused when a page of data fills to 100 percent and more data must be added to it. To make room for the new data, SQL Server must move half of the data from the full page to a new page.

Page splitting has a few disadvantages. First, the new page that is created is now out of order. So instead of going right from one page to the next when looking for data, SQL Server has to jump around the database looking for the next page it needs. This is referred to as *fragmentation*. Not only that, but the server also has to take the time to delete half of the records on the full page and rewrite them on a new page.

Although page splitting has advantages in some scenarios, you will most often find you need to recover from the effects of page splitting by rebuilding the index. Before you do that, you need to ascertain whether your index is fragmented badly enough to warrant reconstruction. The way to determine this is by querying sys.DM_DB_INDEX_PHYSICAL_STATS.

Understanding *sys.DM_DB_INDEX_PHYSICAL_STATS*

To overcome the effects of fragmentation of the database, you need to either reorganize or completely rebuild the indexes on the tables. That is time-consuming, so you will want to do it only when needed. The best, and only, way to tell whether your indexes need reconstruction is to perform sys.DM_DB_INDEX_PHYSICAL_STATS.

> In previous versions of SQL Server, you would have used DBCC SHOWCONTIG to find index fragmentation, but that is now deprecated.

You can get information from sys.DM_DB_INDEX_PHYSICAL_STATS using a simple SELECT query. Here is the syntax:

```
Sys.DM_DB_INDEX_PHYSICAL_STATS (
      { database_id | NULL }
    , { object_id | NULL }
    , { index_id | NULL | 0 }
    , { partition_number | NULL }
    , { mode | NULL | DEFAULT }
)
```

The following list explains the arguments:

- *database_id* is the numeric ID of the database. You can substitute the DB_ID() function for this parameter.

- *object_id* is the numeric ID of the table or view to check. You can use the results of the Object_ID() function to get a specific object ID here.

- *index_id* is the numeric ID of the index to check. Use 0 for a heap or Object_ID() for a specific index. NULL returns all indexes.

- *partition_number* is the number of the partition you want to query if the database is partitioned. NULL or 0 returns all partitions; any other non-negative value returns data for a specific partition.

- *mode* is the scan-level mode to use on the database. Valid values are DEFAULT, NULL, LIMITED, SAMPLED, and DETAILED. The default value is LIMITED.

When queried, DM_DB_INDEX_PHYSICAL_STATS returns a table with the columns listed in Table 10.1.

TABLE 10.1   sys.DM_DB_INDEX_PHYSICAL_STATS

Name	Datatype	Description
database_id	Smallint	This is the database ID of the table or view.
object_id	Int	This is the object ID of the table or view that the index is on.
index_id	Int	This is the index ID of an index.
partition_number	Int	This is the 1-based partition number within the owning object, whether it's a table, view, or index. 1 = nonpartitioned index or heap.
index_type_desc	Nvarchar(60)	This is a description of the index type: HEAP CLUSTERED INDEX NONCLUSTERED INDEX PRIMARY XML INDEX XML INDEX
alloc_unit_type_desc	Nvarchar(60)	This is a description of the allocation unit type: IN_ROW_DATA LOB_DATA ROW_OVERFLOW_DATA
index_depth	Tinyint	This is the number of index levels. 1 = HEAP or LOB_DATA or ROW_OVERFLOW_DATA allocation units.

TABLE 10.1 `sys.DM_DB_INDEX_PHYSICAL_STATS` *(continued)*

Name	Datatype	Description
index_level	Tinyint	This is the current level of the index. Use 0 for index leaf levels, heaps, and LOB_DATA or ROW_OVERFLOW_DATA allocation units. Use a number greater than 0 for nonleaf index levels. index_level will be the highest at the root level of an index. The nonleaf levels of indexes are processed when only *mode* = DETAILED.
Avg_fragmentation_in_percent	Float	This is the logical fragmentation for indexes or extent fragmentation for heaps in the IN_ ROW_DATA allocation unit.
fragment_count	Bigint	This is the number of fragments in the leaf level of an IN_ROW_DATA allocation unit. For more information about fragments see Chapter 4.
avg_fragment_size_in_pages	Float	This is the average number of pages in one fragment in the leaf level of an IN_ ROW_DATA allocation unit.
page_count	Bigint	This is the number of index or data pages.
avg_page_space_used_in_percent	Float	This is the average percentage of available data storage space used in all pages.
record_count	Bigint	This is the number of records.
ghost_record_count	Bigint	This is the number of ghost records ready for removal by the ghost cleanup task in the allocation unit.
version_ghost_record_count	Bigint	This is the number of ghost records retained by an outstanding snapshot isolation transaction in an allocation unit.
min_record_size_in_bytes	Int	This is the minimum record size in bytes.
max_record_size_in_bytes	Int	This is the maximum record size in bytes.
avg_record_size_in_bytes	Float	This is the average record size in bytes.
forwarded_record_count	Bigint	This is the number of forwarded records in a heap.

Each scan mode has its own advantages and disadvantages, as listed in Table 10.2.

TABLE 10.2   The Scan Modes

Mode	Description	Advantage	Disadvantage
Limited	Reads only parent-level pages.	This is the fastest mode, it is accurate, and it allows concurrent access during the scan.	Only a subset of statistics is calculated.
Sampled	Reads parent-level pages, and scans indexes with less than 10,000 pages at 100 percent. Otherwise, they are scanned at 1 percent and 2 percent simultaneously. If the difference between the two is close, then the 2 percent scan is reported; otherwise, a 10 percent sample is performed.	This is faster than a detailed scan; this calculates all statistics and allows concurrent access during the scan.	Calculated statistics may not be 100 percent accurate.
Detailed	Reads parent-level and every leaf-level page.	This calculates all statistics based on all available data.	This is the slowest mode, and data modification is prohibited during the scan.

So if you want to find the fragmentation on the Sales.SalesOrderDetail table in the Adventure-Works database, the query might look like this:

```
USE AdventureWorks;
SELECT INDEX_ID, AVG_FRAGMENTATION_IN_PERCENT
FROM sys.dm_db_index_physical_stats
(db_id(),Object_ID(N'Sales.SalesOrderDetail'),
NULL, NULL, 'DETAILED')
```

This would give you the index names in the Sales.SalesOrderDetail table and the corresponding amount of fragmentation. Using this data, you could then decide whether to reorganize or rebuild your indexes.

Reorganizing and Rebuilding Indexes

If the amount of fragmentation on your index is less than 10 percent, you really don't need to do anything. When it's from 10 percent to 30 percent, you should reorganize your index, and anything higher requires a rebuild. To reorganize an index, use the ALTER INDEX REORGANIZE statement. Here is what it would look like if you wanted to reorganize the PK_Product_Product-PhotoID index on the Production.ProductPhoto table in the AdventureWorks database:

```
USE AdventureWorks
ALTER INDEX PK_ProductPhoto_ProductPhotoID
ON Production.ProductPhoto
REORGANIZE
```

You have two effective ways to rebuild indexes on a table. One way is to use the CREATE INDEX statement with the DROP_EXISTING option. The way to reconstruct an index that is being used as a primary key is to use ALTER INDEX REBUILD, which is also used to repair corrupt indexes and rebuild multiple indexes at once. In Exercise 10.1 you will reconstruct the indexes on the Production.Product table in the AdventureWorks database.

As discussed in Chapter 4, the ONLINE option used in this chapter states whether the underlying tables and indexes are available for queries and data modification while indexing operations are taking place.

EXERCISE 10.1

Reconstructing an Index

1. Open a new SQL Server query in SQL Server Management Studio, and execute the following code to find the current amount of fragmentation on the Production.Product table:

```
USE AdventureWorks;

SELECT INDEX_ID, AVG_FRAGMENTATION_IN_PERCENT

FROM sys.dm_db_index_physical_stats (db_id(),

Object_ID(N'Production.Product'),

Default, Default, 'DETAILED');
```

2. Enter and execute the following code to reconstruct the index on the orders table:

```
USE AdventureWorks;

ALTER INDEX ALL

ON Production.Product

REBUILD WITH (FILLFACTOR = 80, ONLINE = ON,

        STATISTICS_NORECOMPUTE = ON);
```

3. Query the sys.DM_DB_INDEX_PHYSICAL_STATS statement to see whether the fragmentation is gone:

   ```
   USE AdventureWorks;

   SELECT INDEX_ID, AVG_FRAGMENTATION_IN_PERCENT

   FROM sys.dm_db_index_physical_stats

   (db_id(),Object_ID(N'Production.Product') ,

   Default, Default, 'DETAILED');
   ```

4. You should see 0 percent fragmentation.

Maintaining Statistics

Whenever you perform a query on your data, SQL Server creates a map of which tables and indexes to use to execute the query as fast as possible. This map is called an *execution plan.* To choose the fastest index for the query, SQL Server must know how much of the data in the index is applicable to the query being run. To get this information, SQL Server reads the index statistics, which tell the database engine what the index holds.

The problem is that indexes change when the data in the underlying table changes. When the index changes, the statistics become out-of-date. This isn't a problem if you created the index with the default value of STATISTICS_NORECOMPUTE OFF, because SQL Server will automatically update statistics for you. But if your server is low on resources and you had to turn this value on, then you will need to update your statistics manually. In Exercise 10.2 you will see how to update statistics manually using the UPDATE STATISTICS command.

Updating Index Statistics

1. Open a new SQL Server query in SQL Server Management Studio.

2. Enter and execute the following code to reconstruct the index on the Sales.SalesOrderDetail table:

   ```
   USE AdventureWorks

   UPDATE STATISTICS Sales.SalesOrderDetail
   ```

Maintaining Databases

Database files are volatile, constantly being changed and updated, so, just like any other volatile file on a system, database files can become corrupt. Because of this, it is important to perform periodic maintenance on database files. You must perform two important tasks, the first of which is running DBCC CHECKDB.

Understanding *DBCC CHECKDB*

You can use DBCC CHECKDB to check the allocation, logical, and structural integrity of objects in the database. This is necessary because databases are in a constant state of flux; in other words, data is always being inserted, updated, and deleted. So, it stands to reason that occasionally something is not going to be written to disk correctly and will need to be repaired.

The syntax of the command looks like this:

```
DBCC CHECKDB
[
(
        'database_name' | database_id | 0
    [ , NOINDEX
    | { REPAIR_ALLOW_DATA_LOSS
    | REPAIR_REBUILD
    } ]
)
]
    [ WITH        {
            [ ALL_ERRORMSGS ]
            [ , [ NO_INFOMSGS ] ]
            [ , [ TABLOCK ] ]
            [ , [ ESTIMATEONLY ] ]
            [ , [ PHYSICAL_ONLY ] ] |
[ , [ DATA_PURITY ] ]
        }
    ]
```

The following list explains the options:

NOINIDEX   This specifies that intensive checks of nonclustered indexes should not be performed. This speeds up execution time. You can use this when you plan to rebuild indexes shortly after running DBCC CHECKDB.

REPAIR_REBUILD   This tries to repair all reported errors as long as such repairs do not result in a loss of data; therefore, you incur no risk of losing data with this option.

REPAIR_ALLOW_DATA_LOSS   This is the most comprehensive repair option. It performs all the checks the previous two options perform, and it adds the allocation and deallocation of rows for correcting allocation errors, correcting structural row and page errors, and deleting corrupted text objects. You incur a risk of losing data with this option (as the name implies). To lessen that risk, you can perform this option as a transaction so you can roll back the changes.

ALL_ERRORMSGS   If this is not used, then only the first 200 errors display. If this option is used, then all errors display. Error messages are sorted by object ID, except for those messages generated from tempdb.

NO_INFOMSGS   This suppresses all informational messages.

TABLOCK   By default, DBCC CHECKBD uses an internal database snapshot to perform its work. This allows users to access data while the command is being run, but it can be a little slow. TABLOCK causes DBCC CHECKDB to obtain locks instead of using a snapshot, which makes it run faster.

ESTIMATEONLY   Displays the estimated amount of tempdb space needed to run DBCC CHECKDB with all the other specified options. The actual database check is not performed.

PHYSICAL_ONLY   This tells DBCC to check only the physical structure of the database file. Using this, DBCC will check only the structure of the page and record headers and the physical structure of indexes (called *B-Trees*), and it will make sure space inside the file is allocated correctly (that is, all pages have 8 bytes). This means DBCC can also detect torn pages, checksum failures, and common hardware failures that can compromise a user's data. Using this option causes DBCC CHECKDB to run much faster than performing a full check, which makes it well suited for frequent use on production systems. PHYSICAL_ONLY always implies NO_INFOMSGS and is not allowed with any of the repair options.

DATA_PURITY   This causes DBCC CHECKDB to check the database for column values that are not valid or are out of range. For example, DBCC CHECKDB detects columns with date and time values that are larger than or less than the acceptable range for the datetime datatype; or DBCC CHECKDB detects decimal or approximate-numeric datatype columns with scale or precision values that are not valid. This is useful only for databases that have been upgraded from previous versions of SQL Server because databases that are created in SQL Server 2005 have column-value integrity checks enabled by default.

In Exercise 10.3 you will try your hand at DBCC CHECKDB by running it on the Adventure-Works database.

EXERCISE 10.3

Using *DBCC CHECKDB* on AdventureWorks

1.   Open a new SQL Server query in Management Studio.

2.   Enter and execute the following code to check the AdventureWorks database for errors:

   ```
   USE AdventureWorks

   DBCC CHECKDB
   ```

3.   You should see the results in the Messages pane.

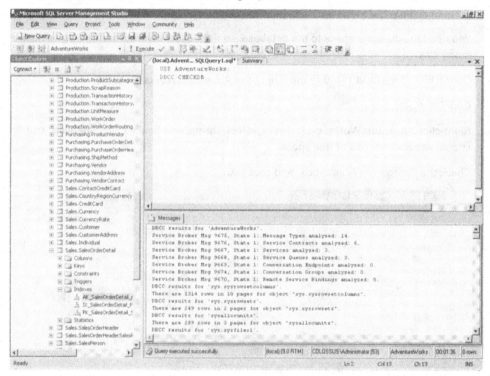

Shrinking Files

When users enter new data into a database, SQL Server may have to expand the size of the data and log files on disk to accommodate the new data. When this happens, the size of the physical file on disk increases, so the hard drive has less space available for other files. When a user deletes data, though, the size of the physical file is not reduced; the file remains the same size. This condition can result in wasted system resources and possibly cause problems for other processes that need disk space.

To combat this problem, you need to occasionally shrink the data and log files so they do not take up too much space. Using SQL Server Management Studio, you can shrink the entire database or just a single file at a time. In Exercise 10.4 you will shrink the entire Adventure-Works database.

EXERCISE 10.4

Shrinking the AdventureWorks Database

1. Open SQL Server Management Studio, and expand your server and then Databases.

2. You need to add some space to the database, so right-click AdventureWorks, and select Properties.

3. On the Files page, add 10MB to the size of the AdventureWorks_Data file.

4. Click OK.

5. Right-click AdventureWorks, go to Tasks, select Shrink, and finally click Database. You should see about 10MB of free space.

6. Check the Reorganize Files... box, and click OK.

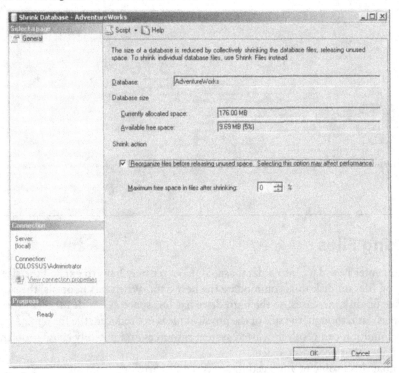

EXERCISE 10.4 *(continued)*

7. Right-click AdventureWorks, go to Tasks, select Shrink, and finally click Database. You should see no free space.

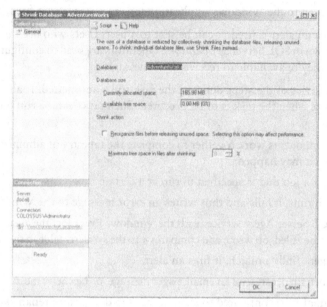

8. Click Cancel to close the dialog box.

Now you know how to keep your databases running at peak efficiency by performing regular maintenance, but you probably don't want to be there after-hours waiting for the best time to perform this maintenance. That is why you need to know how to automate these tasks. You'll start by looking into the basics of automation.

Understanding Automation Basics

You can automate nearly any administrative task you can think of through SQL Server. That may sound like an exaggeration, but look at the features you can automate:

- Any T-SQL code
- Scripting languages such as VBScript or JavaScript
- Operating system commands
- Replication tasks (which you'll learn about in Chapter 12)

This functionality is powerful, so before you start to use automation, you need to know how it works. At the heart of SQL Server's automation capability is the SQL Server Agent service (also referred to as *the agent*). Automation and replication are the sole functions of the service that uses three subcomponents to accomplish its automation tasks:

Alerts   An *alert* is an error message or event that occurs in SQL Server and is recorded in the Windows Application log. Alerts can be sent to users via email, pager, or Net Send. If an error message isn't written to the Windows Application log, an alert is never fired.

Operators   When an alert is fired, it can be sent to a user. Users who need to receive these messages are known in SQL Server as *operators*. Operators are used to configure who receives alerts and when they're available to receive these messages.

Jobs   A *job* is a series of the steps defining the task to be automated. It also defines schedules, which dictate when the task is to be executed. Such tasks can be run one time or on a recurring basis.

These three components work together to complete the tapestry of administration. Here is an example of what may happen:

1. A user defines a job that is specified to run at a certain time.

2. When the job runs, it fails and thus writes an error message to the Windows Event log.

3. When the SQL Server Agent service reads the Windows Event log, the agent finds the error message that the failed job wrote and compares it to the sysalerts table in the MSDB database.

4. When the agent finds a match, it fires an alert.

5. The alert, when fired, can send an email, pager message, or Net Send message to an operator.

6. The alert can also be configured to run another job designed to repair the problem that caused the alert.

For any of this to function, though, you must properly configure the SQL Server Agent service. To begin with, the agent must be running for automation to work. You can verify this in three ways. First, you can open SQL Server Management Studio and notice the SQL Server Agent icon—if it's a red circle with an X, the service is stopped; if it's a green arrow, the service is started. (You can start the service by right-clicking the icon and selecting Start.) Second, you can check and change the state of the service by using the SQL Server Configuration Manager; third, you can use the Services applet in the Control Panel.

Not only should the agent be running, but it's also best to have it log in with a domain account as opposed to a local system account, because using the local system account won't allow you to work with other SQL Servers on your network. This means you can't perform multiserver jobs, carry out replication (discussed in Chapter 12), or use SQL Server's email capabilities. To make sure the agent is logging in with a domain account, open the Services applet in the Control Panel (if you're using Windows 2003, you'll find it in Administrative Tools under Programs on the Start menu), double-click the SQL Server Agent service, and select a domain account by clicking the ellipsis next to This Account.

Once all this is in place, you're nearly ready to begin working with automation. First, though, you should configure SQL Server to send email using Database Mail.

Configuring Database Mail

You can use Database Mail to send email for the SQL Server services using the standard Simple Mail Transfer Protocol (SMTP). It is actually a separate process that runs in the background (called SQLiMail90.exe), so if a problem occurs, SQL Server is unaffected. You can also specify more than one mail server, so if one mail server goes down, Database Mail can still process mail. Database Mail is also scalable because it uses the Service Broker queue, which allows the request to be handled asynchronously and even saves the request if the server goes down before it can be handled (see Chapter 9 for more about the Service Broker).

To top it off, Database Mail provides granular control so you can limit which users are allowed to send mail. You can also specify what file extensions are allowed and disallowed as attachments, as well as the maximum size of those attachments. Everything Database Mail does is logged in the Windows Application log, and sent messages are retained in the *mailhost* database for auditing.

This all sounds great, but how do you use it? First you need an SMTP mail server somewhere on the network with a mail account configured for the SQL Server Agent service account. The topics of setting up and configuring an SMTP server are beyond the scope of this book, but if you have an email account with your Internet service provider (ISP), you can use that. Then you can configure Database Mail using the configuration wizard. To send email to operators, the MSDB database must be a mailhost, so you'll configure MSDB as a mailhost database in Exercise 10.5.

EXERCISE 10.5

Configuring a Mailhost

1. Open SQL Server Management Studio, and connect to your server.

2. Expand Management in Object Explorer, right-click Database Mail, and select Configure Database Mail.

3. On the Select Configuration Task page, select Set Up Database Mail by Performing the Following Tasks, and click Next.

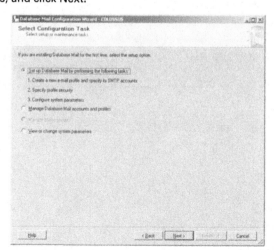

4. If a dialog box opens and asks you whether you would like to enable Database Mail, click Yes.

5. On the New Profile page, create a mail profile, and associate it with a mail server account:

   a. Enter **SQLAgentProfile** in the Profile Name box.

   b. Under SMTP Accounts, click Add.

   c. In the Account Name box, enter **Mail Provider Account 1**.

   d. In the Description box, enter **E-mail account information**.

   e. Fill in your outgoing mail server information using the information provided by your ISP or network administrator.

   f. If your email server requires you to log in, check the SMTP Server Requires Authentication box, and enter your login information.

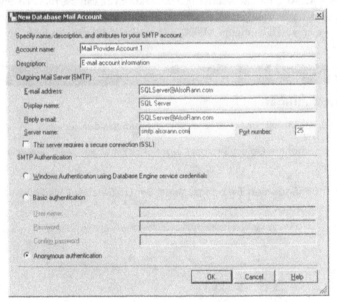

g. Click OK to return to the wizard. Your account should now be listed under SMTP Accounts.

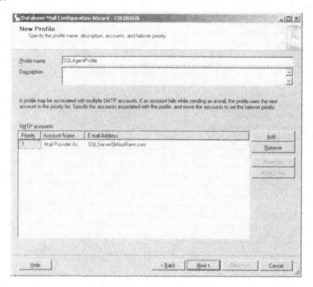

6. Click Next.

7. On the Manage Profiles Security page, check the Public box next to the mail profile you just created to make it accessible to all users. Set the Default Profile option to Yes, and click Next.

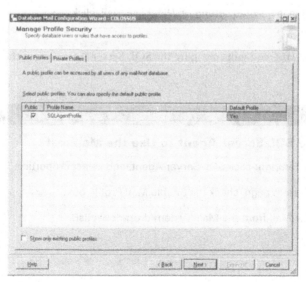

8. On the Configure System Parameters page, accept the defaults, and click Next.

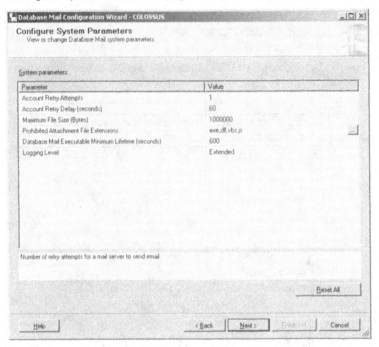

9. On the Complete the Wizard page, review all your settings, and click Finish.

10. When the system is finished setting up Database Mail, click Close.

Now in Exercise 10.6 you will configure the SQL Server Agent to use the mail profile you just created.

EXERCISE 10.6

Configuring the SQL Server Agent to Use the Mailhost

1. In Object Explorer, right-click SQL Server Agent, and select Properties.

2. On the Alert System page, check the Enable Mail Profile box.

3. Select Database Mail from the Mail System drop-down list.

4. Select SQLAgentProfile from the Mail Profile drop-down list.

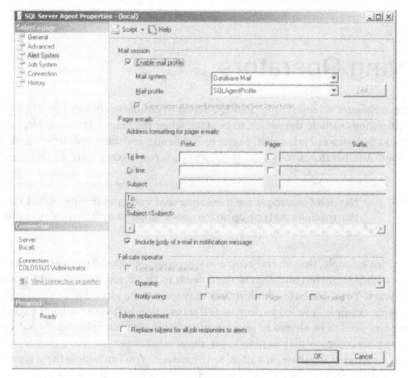

5. Click OK.

6. From SQL Computer Manager, stop and restart the SQL Server Agent service.

You can run the configuration wizard again at any time to make changes to the Database Mail configuration. For example, you may want to do the following:

- Create a new Database Mail database.
- Add or remove accounts or profiles.
- Manage profile security by marking them as public or private.
- View or change system parameters.
- Uninstall Database Mail.

With Database Mail successfully configured, you can create the operators who receive email from SQL Server.

Internet Information Services comes with a built-in SMTP server that you can use with Database Mail.

Creating Operators

You need to configure several settings for SQL Server to be able to contact you when problems occur. Such settings include the person to contact, when the people are available, how those people should be contacted (via email, pager, or Net Send), and what problems should they be alerted about. An *operator* is the object used in SQL Server to configure all these settings.

Net Send messages are messages sent from a source machine to a destination machine that pop up on the user's screen in a dialog box over all the open applications.

Suppose, for example, that several people in your company need to be alerted when a problem occurs with SQL Server, and each of them needs to be alerted for different problems and in various ways. Your database administrator may need to be alerted about any administration issues (for example, a failed backup or full transaction log) via email and pager. Your developers may need to be alerted to programming issues (for example, deadlocks) via email. Managers in your company may need to know about other issues, such as a user deleting a customer from a customer database, via a Net Send message. You can handle these types of users by creating separate operators for each and then configuring the desired settings.

To demonstrate, you'll configure an operator in Exercise 10.7.

EXERCISE 10.7

Configuring an Operator

1. Open SQL Server Management Studio.

2. In Object Explorer, expand your server and then SQL Server Agent.

3. Right-click Operators, and select New Operator.

4. In the Name box, enter **Administrator**.

5. If you configured your system to use Database Mail, enter your email address as the email name. If you didn't configure your system to use email, skip this step.

6. Type the name of your machine in the Net Send Address box. You can find the name by right-clicking the My Computer icon on the Desktop, selecting Properties, and then clicking the Network Identification tab. The computer name is the first section of the full computer name (before the first period). For instance, if the full computer name is instructor.domain.com, the computer name is instructor.

7. If you carry a pager that is capable of receiving email, you can enter your pager's email address in the Pager E-mail Name box.

8. At the bottom of the page, you can select the days and times this operator is available for notification. If a day is checked, the operator will be notified on that day between the start and end times noted under Start Time and End Time. Check the box for each day, and leave the default workday times of 8 A.M. to 6 P.M.

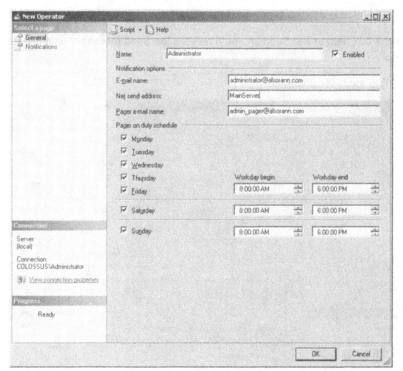

9. We'll discuss the Notifications tab later; for now, click OK to create the operator.

Because you can make operators active at different times, it's possible to accidentally leave a small period of time uncovered. If an error occurs during that window of time, no operator will receive the alert, because no one is on duty. To avoid such a problem, you should create a fail-safe operator who will receive alerts when no one is scheduled to be on duty. You'll create one in Exercise 10.8.

With an operator in place, you're ready to start creating jobs to automate tasks.

EXERCISE 10.8

Configuring a Fail-Safe Operator

1. In SQL Server Management Studio, right-click the SQL Server Agent icon in Object Explorer, and select Properties.

2. On the Alert System page, check the Enable Fail-Safe Operator box.

3. Select Administrator in the Operator drop-down list.

4. Check the box next to Net Send so you'll receive Net Send messages as a fail-safe operator.

5. Click OK to apply the changes.

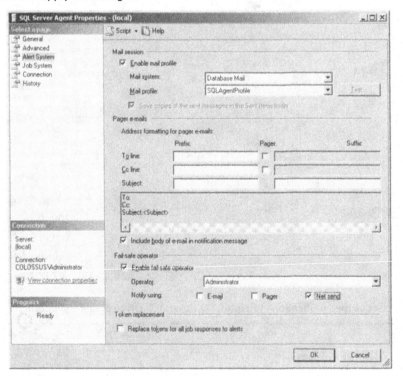

Creating Jobs

A *job* is a series of tasks that can be automated to run whenever you need them to run. It may be easier to think of them as like cleaning your house. Most of us think of cleaning our house as one big job that needs to be done, but it's really a series of smaller tasks such as dusting the furniture, vacuuming the carpet, doing the dishes, and so on. Some of these steps need to be accomplished in succession (for example, dusting before vacuuming); others can happen at any time (for example, the dishes don't need to be done before you can wash the windows).

Any job for SQL Server works in much the same way. Take, for example, a job that creates a database. This isn't just one big job with one step to accomplish before you're finished; several steps need to take place. The first step creates the database. The next step backs up the newly created database, because it's in a vulnerable state until it's backed up. After the database has been backed up, you can create tables in it and then perhaps import data into those tables from text files. Each of these tasks is a separate step that needs to be completed before the next can start, but not all jobs are that way.

By controlling the flow of the steps, you can build error correction into your jobs. For example, in the create-database job, each step has simple logic that states, "On success go to the next step; on failure quit the job." If the hard disk turns out to be full, the job stops. If you create a step at the end of the job that is designed to clear up hard disk space, you can create logic that states, "If step one fails, go to step five; if step 5 succeeds, go back to step 1." With the steps in place, you're ready to tell SQL Server when to start the job.

To tell SQL Server when to run a job, you need to create schedules, and you have a lot of flexibility there. If a job creates a database, it wouldn't make much sense to run the job more than once, so you need to create a single schedule that activates the job after-hours. If you're creating a job that is designed to perform transaction log backups, you want a different schedule; you may want to perform these backups every two hours during the day (from 9 A.M. to 6 P.M.) and then every three hours at night (from 6 P.M. to 9 A.M.). In this instance, you need to create two schedules: one that is active from 9 A.M. to 6 P.M. and activates the job every two hours and another that is active from 6 P.M. to 9 A.M. and activates the job every three hours. If you think that's fancy, you'll love the next part.

Not only can you schedule jobs to activate at certain times of the day, but you can also schedule them to activate only on certain days of the week (for example, every Tuesday), or you can schedule them to run only on certain days of the month (for example, every third Monday). You can schedule jobs to run every time the SQL Server Agent service starts, and you can even schedule them to run every time the processor becomes idle.

You can set schedules to expire after a certain amount of time, so if you know you're going to be done with a job after a few weeks, you can set it to expire—it will automatically be disabled (not deleted, just shut off).

You also have the capacity to be notified about the outcome of a job. When you create a job, you can add an operator to the job that's notified on success, on failure, or on completion (regardless of whether the job failed or succeeded). This comes in handy when the job you're running is critical to your server or application.

With the ability to change the logical flow of steps, schedule jobs to run whenever you want, and have jobs notify you on completion, you can see how complex jobs can become. With this complexity in mind, it's always a good idea to sit down with a pencil and paper and plan your jobs before creating them; doing so will make your work easier in the long run.

To demonstrate this concept, you'll create a job in Exercise 10.9 that creates a new database and then backs it up.

EXERCISE 10.9

Creating a Job

1.   Open SQL Server Management Studio by selecting it from the SQL Server 2005 group under Programs on the Start menu.

2.   Expand your server in Object Explorer, and then expand SQL Server Agent.

3.   Right-click Jobs, and select New Job.

4.   In the Name box, type **Create Test Database** (leave the rest of the boxes on this page with the default settings).

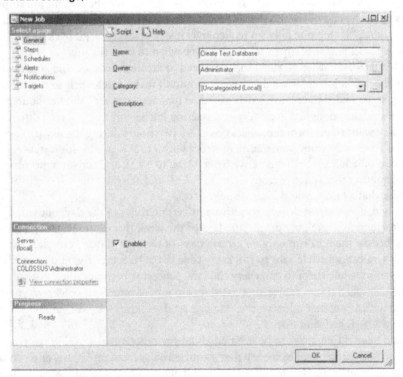

5. Go to the Steps page, and click the New button to create a new step.

6. In the Step Name box, type **Create Database**.

7. Leave Type as Transact-SQL, and enter the following code to create a database named Test on the C drive:

```
CREATE DATABASE TEST ON

PRIMARY (NAME=test_dat,

FILENAME='c:\test.mdf',

SIZE=10MB,

MAXSIZE=15,

FILEGROWTH=10%)
```

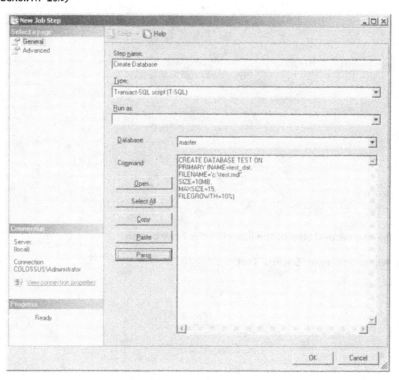

8. Click the Parse button to verify you entered the code correctly, and then move to the Advanced page.

9. On the Advanced page, verify that On Success Action is set to Go to the Next Step and that On Failure Action is set to Quit the Job Reporting Failure. Click OK.

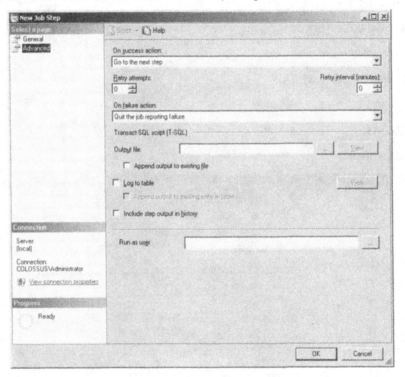

10. To create the second step of the job, click the New button.

11. In the Name box, enter **Backup Test**.

12. Leave Type as Transact-SQL Script, and enter the following code to back up the database once it's created:

```
EXEC sp_addumpdevice 'disk', 'Test_Backup',

'c:\Test_Backup.dat'

BACKUP DATABASE TEST TO Test_Backup
```

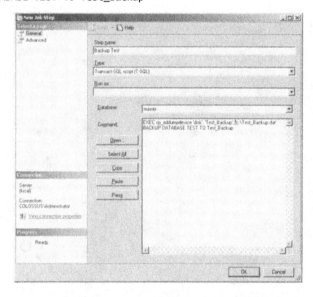

13. Click OK to create the step; you should now have two steps listed on the Steps page.

14. Move to the Schedules page, and click the New button to create a schedule that will instruct SQL Server when to fire the job.

15. In the Name box, type **Create and Backup Database**.

16. Select One Time from the Schedule Type drop-down list. Set the time to be five minutes from the time displayed in the system tray (usually at the bottom-right corner of your screen).

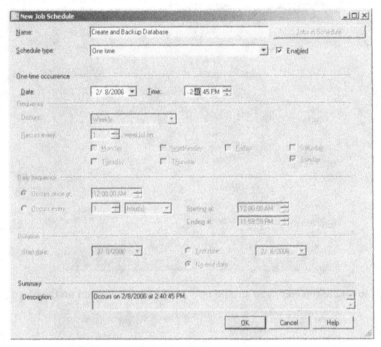

17. Click OK to create the schedule and move to the Notifications tab.

18. On the Notifications tab, check the boxes next to E-mail (if you configured Database Mail earlier) and Net Send, choosing Administrator as the operator to notify. Next to each, select When the Job Completes from the list box (this will notify you no matter what the outcome of the job is).

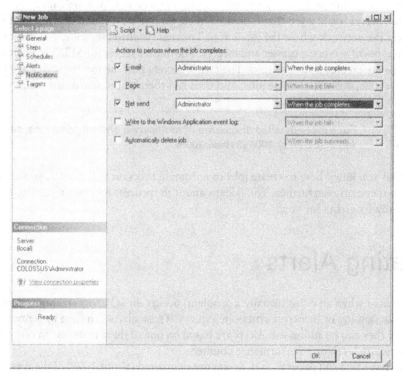

19. Click OK to create the job. Wait until the time set in step 16 to verify completion. You should see a message pop up on your screen, notifying you of completion.

What just happened? You created a job with two steps; the first step created a new database named Test, and the second step backed up the database to a new backup device. This job was scheduled to run only one time and notify you of completion (whether or not it was a success).

> The history of each job is stored in the MSDB database. By default, the database can store 1,000 lines of history, and each job can take up to 100 of those records.

It's not hard to see the value of creating jobs that run T-SQL code, but you can do more. Not only can you schedule T-SQL statements, but you can also schedule any active scripting language: VBScript, JavaScript, Perl, and so forth. This frees you from the boundaries of T-SQL, because scripting languages have features that SQL Server doesn't implement. For example, you can't directly access the file structure on the hard disk using T-SQL (to create a new text file, for example), but you can do so with a scripting language.

You can also create jobs that run on more than one server, which are called *multiserver jobs*. A multiserver job is a job that is created once, on one server, and downloaded to other servers over the network where the job is run. To create multiserver jobs, you must first designate two types of servers: a master and targets. The master server (or MSX) is where the multiserver jobs are created and managed. The target servers poll the master server at regular intervals for jobs, download those jobs, and then run them at the scheduled time.

 For a more detailed discussion of multiserver and scripting jobs, see *Mastering SQL Server 2005* (Sybex, 2006).

Now that you know how to create jobs to automate tasks on SQL Server, you're ready to enhance your system even further. You'll learn about the process for creating alerts, which can automatically fix errors for you.

Creating Alerts

An *alert* is fired when an event (usually a problem) occurs on SQL Server; some examples are a full transaction log or incorrect syntax in a query. These alerts can then be sent to an operator so that they can be addressed. Alerts are based on one of three features: an error number, an error severity level, or a performance counter.

All the errors that can occur in SQL Server are numbered (about 3,700 of them exist). Even with so many errors, there aren't enough. For example, suppose you want to fire an alert when a user deletes a customer from your Customers database. SQL Server doesn't have an alert with the structure of your database or your users' names; therefore, you have the ability to create new error numbers and generate an alert for such proprietary issues. You can create alerts to fire on any valid error number.

Each error in SQL Server also has an associated severity level, stating how serious the error is. Alerts can be generated by severity level. Table 10.3 lists the common levels.

Alerts can also be generated from performance counters. These are the same counters you would see in Performance Monitor, and they come in handy for correcting performance issues such as a full (or nearly full) transaction log. You can also generate alerts based on Windows Management Instrumentation (WMI) events. You'll see these in more detail later in this chapter. To start, you'll create some alerts using the errors and severity levels that are built into SQL Server.

TABLE 10.3   Severity Levels of Errors

Level	Description
10	This is an informational message caused by mistakes in the information that was entered by the user. It isn't serious.
11–16	These are all errors that can be corrected by the user.
17	These errors are generated when the server runs out of resources, such as memory or hard disk space.
18	A nonfatal internal error has occurred. The statement will finish, and the user connection will be maintained.
19	A nonconfigurable internal limit has been reached. Any statement that causes this will be terminated.
20	A single process in the current database has suffered a problem, but the database itself is unscathed.
21	All processes in the current database are affected by the problem, but the database is undamaged.
22	The table or index that is being used is probably damaged. You should run DBCC to try to repair the object. (Alternatively, the problem may be in the data cache, which means a simple restart may suffice.)
23	This message usually means the entire database has been damaged somehow, and you should check the integrity of your hardware.
24	Your hardware has failed. You'll probably need to get new hardware and reload the database from a backup.

Creating Event Alerts Based on Standard Errors

Standard alerts are based on the error messages or severity levels that are built into SQL Server. To create an alert based on one of these events, the error must be written to the Windows Event log, because the SQL Server Agent reads errors from there. Once the SQL Server Agent has read the Event log and detected a new error, the agent searches through the MSDB database looking for a matching alert. When the agent finds one, the alert is fired; it can in turn notify an operator, execute a job, or both.

You'll create one of those alerts in this section—the one that fires from an error number (alerts based on severity work the same, except they're based on the severity of an error, not the number). Then, to fire that alert, you'll use the RAISERROR() command, which is designed specifically for the purpose of firing alerts. You'll begin in Exercise 10.10 by creating an alert based on error number 1 that sends a Net Send notification to an operator.

EXERCISE 10.10

Creating an Alert for a Standard Error

1. Open SQL Server Management Studio, expand your server, and then expand SQL Server Agent.

2. Right-click Alerts, and select New Alert.

3. In the Name box, enter **Number Alert**.

4. Select SQL Server Event Alert from the Type list.

5. Select <all databases> from the Database Name list.

6. Check the Error Number radio button, and enter **14599** in the text box.

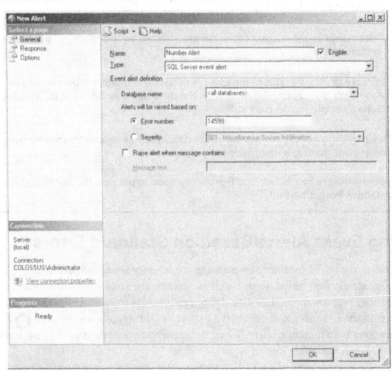

7. On the Response page, check the Notify Operators box, and check the Net Send box next to Administrator.

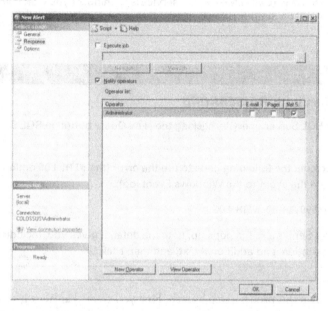

8. On the Options page, check the Net Send box under Include Error Alert Text In, and click OK.

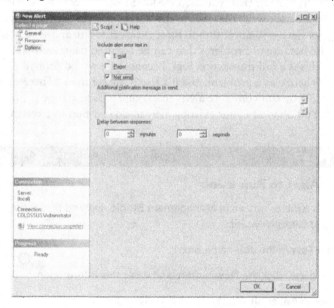

Now that you have an alert that is designed to fire whenever error number 14599 occurs, you'll generate error number 14599 using the RAISERROR() command in Exercise 10.11.

 Make sure your Messenger service is running, or you won't be able to receive the Net Send message.

EXERCISE 10.11

Testing an Alert with *RAISERROR()*

1. Open a new SQL Server query by clicking the New Query button in SQL Server Management Studio.

2. Enter and execute the following code to fire the error (the WITH LOG option forces SQL Server to write the event to the Windows Event log):

   `RAISERROR(14599,10,1) WITH LOG`

3. When the Net Send message pops up, note the detail it gives you, including the error number, description, and additional text, and then click OK.

We'll break down this process, step by step. First you created an alert based on error number 14599. Then you configured the alert to notify an operator (you) via a Net Send message whenever the alert fires. After that, you used the RAISERROR() command with the WITH LOG option to make SQL Server write the error to the Windows Event log (if an error isn't written to the Event log, its alerts will never fire) to force the alert to fire and send you a notification.

Many alerts fire because of problems that can be repaired using minimal T-SQL code (a good example of this is a full transaction log). Because you would probably rather see a message that states, "There was a problem, and it's fixed" rather than "There's a problem; come and fix it yourself," you can configure alerts to execute jobs to fix the problems that caused the alerts to fire. You'll modify your existing alert to do just that in Exercise 10.12.

EXERCISE 10.12

Modifying an Alert to Run a Job

1. First you need a job to run, so in Management Studio, expand SQL Server Agent, right-click Jobs, and select New Job.

2. Enter **Backup Test** in the Job name box.

3. On the Steps page, click the New button, and enter this information:

   a. Enter **Backup AdventureWorks** in the Step Name box.

   b. Enter this code in the Command box:

   BACKUP DATABASE AdventureWorks

   TO DISK='C:\AdventureWorks.bak'

   c. Click OK, and then click OK again to create the backup job.

4. To create the alert, expand Alerts under SQL Server Agent.

5. Right-click Number Alert, and select Properties.

6. Select the Response page.

7. Check the Execute Job box, and enter **Backup Test** in the Job name box.

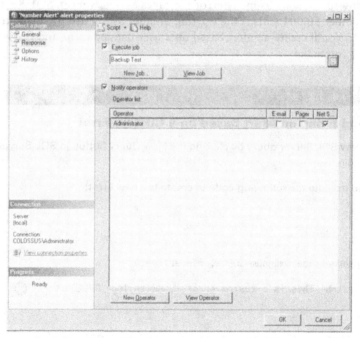

8. Click OK to apply the changes.

9. To test the alert, open a new query, and execute this code:

RAISERROR(14599,10,1) WITH LOG

10. When the Net Send message pops up, note the message at the bottom stating that the Backup Test job has run, and then click OK.

Creating alerts based on built-in errors isn't so rough, is it? Even though SQL Server includes nearly 3,700 such errors, not nearly enough exist to cover all your needs. Therefore, you need to know how to create custom error messages on which to base your alerts.

Creating Event Alerts Based on Custom Errors

Having 3,700 errors may seem like an awful lot, but they don't cover every situation for which you might need an alert. For example, suppose you have a sales department that allows customers to order on credit, and you need to keep track of those credit lines. Your sales managers probably want to be notified whenever a customer with good credit is deleted or a customer's credit limit is decreased, or they may want to know when a customer's credit limit is raised to greater than $10,000. In any event, these error messages don't exist in SQL Server by default; you must create the error message before you can use it to fire an alert.

You're allowed to create as many error messages as you want in SQL Server, starting with error number 50,001 (this is the starting number for all user-defined errors). In Exercise 10.13 you'll create an alert based on a user-defined error and fire it with the RAISERROR() command.

EXERCISE 10.13

Creating and Firing an Alert Based on a Custom Error

1. Open a new SQL Server query by clicking the New Query button in SQL Server Management Studio.

2. Enter and execute the following code to create the new error:

   USE master

   GO

   EXEC sp_addmessage @msgnum=50001, @severity=10,

      @msgtext=N' This is a custom error.', @with_log='TRUE'

   GO

3. In Object Explorer, expand your server, and then expand SQL Server Agent.

4. Right-click Alerts, and select New Alert.

5. In the Name box, enter **Custom Alert**.

6. Select the Error Number radio button, and enter **50001** in the Error Number text box.

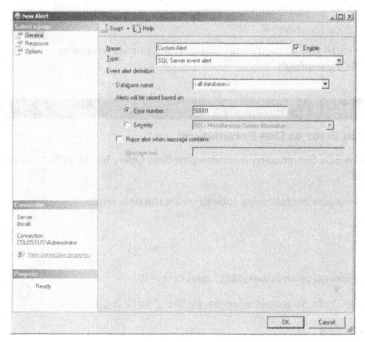

7. On the Response page, check the Notify Operators box, and check the Net Send box next to Administrator.

8. On the Options page, check the Net Send box, and click OK to create the alert.

9. To test the new alert, open a new query, and execute the following code (WITH LOG is not required because you specified that this event is always logged when you created it):

    RAISERROR(50001,10,1)

10. When the Net Send message pops up, note the detail it gives you, and then click OK.

The alert you just created is good but isn't as useful as it could be. What if you need an alert to tell a manager in a customer service department that a customer has been deleted? If you employ the method used in the previous series of steps, you'll have a bland, slightly informative message stating that a customer has been deleted. If you use parameters in your error message, though, you can make the text much more meaningful.

A *parameter* is a placeholder for information that is supplied when the error is fired. For example, "A customer has been deleted" always displays the same static text every time the error occurs; but if you use a parameter such as "Customer %1s has been deleted," you can use the RAISERROR()

command with a parameter that looks like this—RAISERROR(50001,10,1,'Bob Smith')—to create the result "Customer Bob Smith has been deleted." Parameters can be more useful than static text; the parameters you can use are as follows:

- %1s and %s for strings (such as 'Bob Smith')

- %1d and %d for numbers

In Exercise 10.14 you'll modify your customer alert to use parameters and then fire it using the RAISERROR() command.

EXERCISE 10.14

Modifying an Error to Use Parameters

1. Open a new SQL Server query by clicking the New Query button in SQL Server Management Studio.

2. Enter and execute the following code to create the new error:

    ```
    USE master

    GO

    EXEC sp_addmessage @msgnum=50001, @severity=10,

    @msgtext=N' This is a custom error by %1s',

    @with_log='TRUE',

    @replace='replace'

    GO
    ```

3. To fire the error, enter and execute the following code:

    ```
    RAISERROR(50001,10,1,'SQL Guru')
    ```

4. When the Net Send message pops up, note that the description now mentions "SQL Guru," which replaced the %1s in the message text.

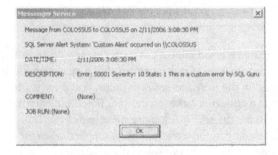

5. Click OK to close the Net Send message.

Now you have a better understanding of alerts that are based on error messages, both standard and custom, but you have more to learn. In SQL Server 2005, you can create alerts that are designed to repair problems before they even become problems; these are known as *performance alerts*.

Creating Performance Alerts

Event alerts are great for tending to a problem after it has occurred, but not all problems can wait that long. You need to discover some problems before they cause damage to your system. You can do this using a *performance alert*.

Performance alerts are based on the same performance counters you may have seen in the Windows Performance Monitor program. These counters provide statistics about various components of SQL Server and then act on them. A good example of when to use such an alert is with a full transaction log error.

When a transaction log fills to 100 percent, no users can access the database, so they can't work. Some companies lose substantial amounts of money every hour their users aren't working, and it could take some time before you can bring the database to a usable state by clearing the transaction log. Therefore, you should find the problem before it happens by clearing the transaction log when it reaches a certain percentage, say 70 percent.

To see the capability of performance alerts in action, you'll create an alert that isn't something you're likely to see in the real world in Exercise 10.15. In this exercise, you'll create an alert that fires when the transaction log for the AdventureWorks database is less than 100 percent full. On your own systems, you would want to set this to fire when the log is about 70 percent full and then fire a job that will back up (and thus clear) the transaction log.

Creating a Performance Alert

1. Open SQL Server Management Studio, expand your server, and then expand SQL Server Agent.

2. Right-click Alerts, and select New Alert.

3. In the Name box, enter **Performance Alert**.

4. In the Type list, select SQL Server Performance Condition Alert.

5. In the Object box, select SQLServer:Databases.

6. In the Counter box, select Percent Log Used.

7.   In the Instance box, select AdventureWorks.

8.   Make sure Alert If Counter is set to Falls Below.

9.   In the Value box, type **100**.

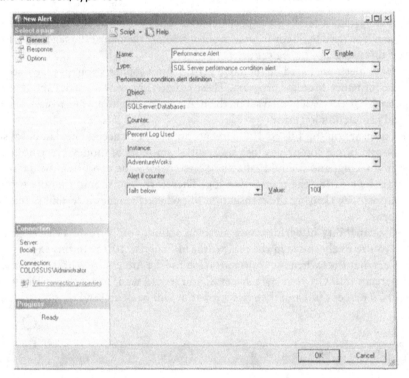

10.   Select the Response tab, check the Notify Operators box, and check the Net Send box next to your operator name.

11.   Click OK to create the alert.

12.   When the Net Send message pops up, note the detail that is provided, and click OK to close the message.

Because you probably don't want that error popping up every few minutes, you need to disable it in Exercise 10.16.

Also, a new type of alert in SQL Server 2005 is sure to come in handy: WMI alerts.

EXERCISE 10.16

Disabling an Alert

1. In SQL Server Management Studio, under Alerts in SQL Server Agent, double-click Performance Alert to expose its properties.

2. Uncheck the Enable box, and click OK to apply the changes.

Creating WMI Alerts

WMI is Microsoft's implementation of web-based enterprise management, which is an industry initiative to make systems easier to manage by exposing managed components such as systems, applications, and networks as a set of common objects. SQL Server has been updated to work with WMI and respond to WMI events. But with all the techno-babble out of the way, what does this mean to you?

Using WMI alerts, you can respond to events that you couldn't even see before. For example, you can create an alert to fire when an ALTER LOGIN command is issued. This can be useful for managing security. In addition, you can create an alert to fire when a CREATE TABLE command is run so you can keep track of storage on your database. The only limitation is your imagination—and you need to know how to create WMI alerts. You'll create a WMI alert in Exercise 10.17 that fires when a DDL statement such as CREATE TABLE is issued on the AdventureWorks database.

EXERCISE 10.17

Creating a WMI Alert

1. Open SQL Server Management Studio, expand your server, and then expand SQL Server Agent.

2. Right-click Alerts, and select New Alert.

3. In the Name box, enter **WMI Alert**.

4. In the Type list, select WMI Event Alert.

5. Make sure Namespace is set to \\.\root\Microsoft\SqlServer\ServerEvents\ MSSQLSERVER.

6. Enter this query in the query box:

    SELECT * FROM DDL_DATABASE_LEVEL_EVENTS

    WHERE DatabaseName = 'AdventureWorks'

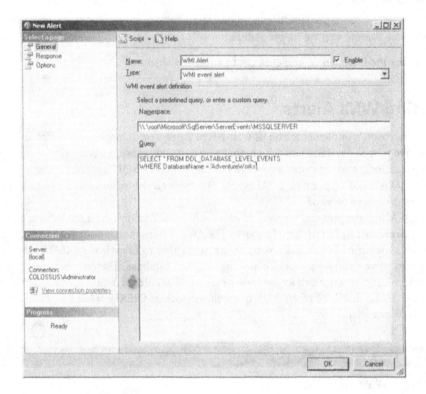

7. Select the Response tab, check the Notify Operators box, and check the Net Send box next to your operator name.

8. On the Options page, check the Net Send box under Include Alert Error Text In, and click OK to create the alert.

9. Open a new SQL Server query in SQL Server Management Studio by clicking the New Query button.

10. Enter and execute the following code to fire the new alert:

```
USE AdventureWorks

ALTER TABLE Person.Address

ADD WMI_Test_Column VARCHAR(20) NULL
```

11. When the Net Send message pops up, note the detail that is provided, and click OK to close the message (it may take a few seconds for the message to open).

12. To return the AdventureWorks database to normal, execute the following command (note that the WMI alert will fire again):

USE AdventureWorks

ALTER TABLE Person.Address DROP COLUMN WMI_Test_Column

13. To disable the alert, open it, uncheck the Enable box, and click OK.

Now you've seen the importance of maintaining your database, and you've seen how to automate those administrative tasks using jobs, operators, and alerts. Wouldn't it be nice if you had a tool that would create these maintenance jobs for you? Microsoft knew you'd ask for that, so it created just such a tool: the Maintenance Plan Wizard.

Using the Maintenance Plan Wizard

You need to perform many tasks to keep your databases running at peak performance at all times. Such tasks as index reorganizations, database file size reductions, and database and transaction log backups all need to happen on a regular basis to keep your server running smoothly. The trick is that most of these tasks should happen off-hours. "No problem," you may respond. "I'll just create jobs for them." That is the proper response, but you'll have to create a number of jobs for each of your databases to keep them all up to par. To avoid all the labor of creating multiple jobs for multiple databases, use the *Maintenance Plan Wizard*.

You can use the wizard to create jobs for all the standard maintenance tasks discussed so far in this chapter. The best way to learn how to use it is to run it, so you'll do that in Exercise 10.18.

Running the Maintenance Plan Wizard

1. In SQL Server Management Studio, expand Management, right-click Maintenance Plans, and select Maintenance Plan Wizard.

EXERCISE 10.18 *(continued)*

2.   On the welcome page, click the Next button.

3.   On the Select a Target Server page, enter **Maintenance Plan 1** in the Name box, enter a description if you'd like, select your local server, and click Next.

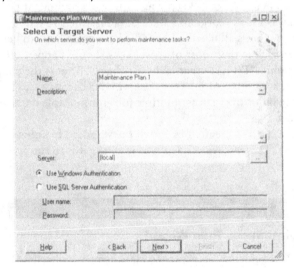

4. On the Select Maintenance Tasks page, check the boxes for all the available tasks, and click Next.

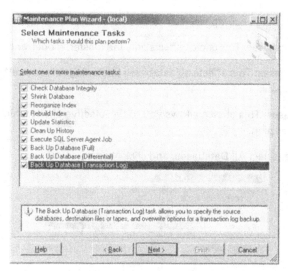

5. On the next page, you can set the order in which these tasks are performed. Leave the default, and click Next.

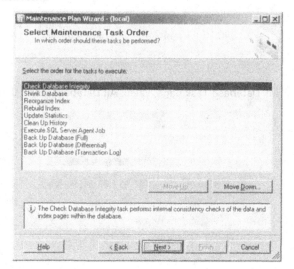

EXERCISE 10.18 *(continued)*

6. The next page allows you to select the databases you want to include in your mainte-
    nance plan. When you click the drop-down list, you're presented with several choices:

    All Databases: This encompasses all databases on the server in the same plan.

    All System Databases: This choice affects only the master, model, and MSDB databases.

    All User Databases: This affects all databases (including AdventureWorks) except the
    system databases.

    These Databases: This choice allows you to be selective about which databases to
    include in your plan.

7. For this exercise, select All Databases, and click Next.

8. On the Define Shrink Database Task page, select All Databases, and then click Next.

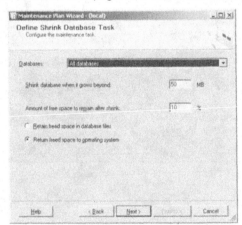

9. On the Define Reorganize Index Task page, select All Databases from the Databases drop-down list, and click Next.

10. The Define Rebuild Index Task page gives you a number of options for rebuilding your indexes:

Reorganize Pages with the Original Amount of Free Space: This regenerates pages with their original fill factor.

Change Free Space per Page Percentage To: This creates a new fill factor. If you set this to 10, for example, your pages will contain 10 percent free space.

11. Again, select All Databases, accept the defaults, and click Next.

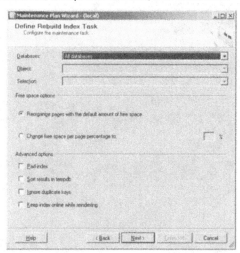

12. Next comes the Define Update Statistics Task page. Again, select All Databases, and click Next.

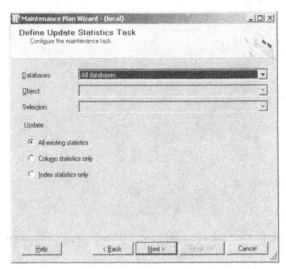

13. Next is the Define Cleanup History Task page. All the tasks performed by the mainte-nance plan are logged in the MSDB database. This list is referred to as the *history*, and it can become quite large if you don't prune it occasionally. On this page, you can set when and how the history is cleared from the database so you can keep it in check. Again, accept the defaults, and click Next.

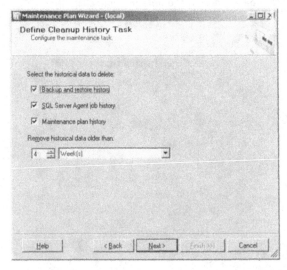

14. On the Define Execute SQL Server Agent Job Task page, you can tell SQL Agent to run a job every time the maintenance plan runs. Because you have to select a job, check the Backup Test job, and click Next.

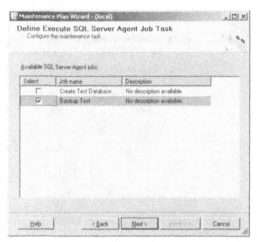

15. The next page allows you to control how full backups are performed. Select All Databases from the drop-down list, accept the defaults, and click Next.

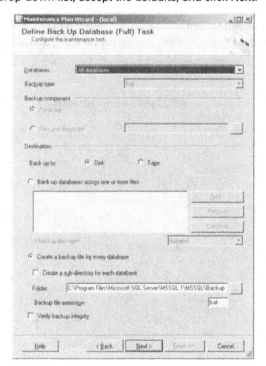

EXERCISE 10.18 *(continued)*

16. The next page allows you to control how differential backups are performed. Select All Databases from the drop-down list, accept the defaults, and click Next.

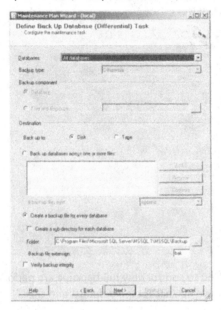

17. The next page allows you to control how transaction log backups are performed. Select All Databases from the drop-down list, accept the defaults, and click Next.

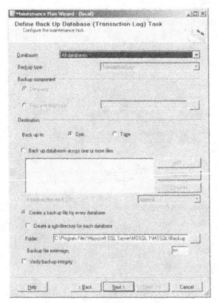

18. On the Select Plan Properties page, click the Change button to create a schedule for the job.

19. Enter **Maintenance Plan 1 Schedule** for the schedule name, accept the rest of the defaults, and click OK to create the schedule.

20. Click Next to continue.

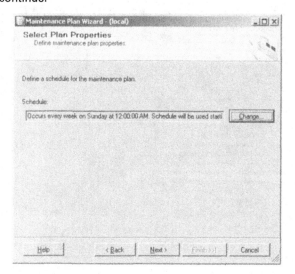

21. On the Select Report Options page, you can write a report to a text file every time the job runs, and you can email the report to an operator. In this case, write a report to C:\, and click Next.

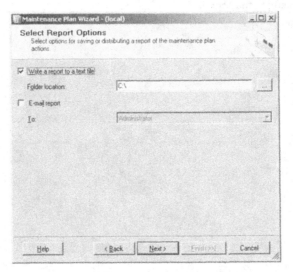

22. On the next page, you can view a summary of the tasks to perform. Click Finish to create the maintenance plan.

23. Once SQL Server is finished creating the maintenance plan, you can click Close.

If you need to change the plan at any time after you've created it, all you need to do is expand Maintenance Plans (which is under Management), right-click the plan, and select Modify. From there you can change any aspect of your maintenance plan from the Properties dialog box. To view the plan's history, just right-click it, and select Maintenance Plan History. This option displays everything the plan has accomplished recently.

As you can see, maintenance plans are helpful in keeping your database running smoothly and efficiently. Now you don't have to worry about staying late to run maintenance jobs or which task should be completed first. The plan does it all for you. One last tool helps automate administration, the Copy Database Wizard.

Copying Databases

One of the handiest tools in the SQL Server arsenal is the *Copy Database Wizard*. You can use this wizard to copy or move a database and all of its associated objects to another server. Why would you want to do that? You might want to do that for a few reasons:

- If you are upgrading your server, the Copy Database Wizard is a quick way to move your data to the new system.

- You can use the wizard to create a backup copy of the database on another server, ready to use in case of emergency.

- Developers can copy an existing database and use the copy to make changes without endangering the live database.

The Copy Database Wizard will prove to be a valuable tool in your administrative functions, so you'll use it in Exercise 10.19 to make a copy of the Test database.

EXERCISE 10.19

Running the Copy Database Wizard

1. Open Management Studio by selecting it from the Microsoft SQL Server group under Programs on the Start menu, expand your server, and expand Databases.

2. Right-click the Test database, go to Tasks, and select Copy Database. You will see the welcome page.

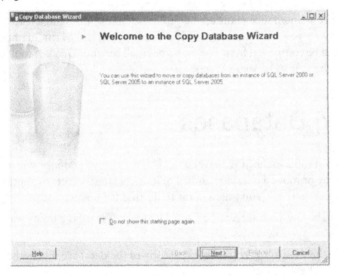

3. Click Next.

4. On the second page, you are asked to select a source server. Select the default instance of your server and the proper authentication type (usually Windows Authentication), and click Next.

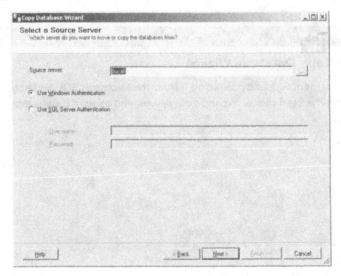

5. On the next page, you need to select a destination. Here you will choose the (local) instance of the server as the destination. Choose the appropriate security, and click Next.

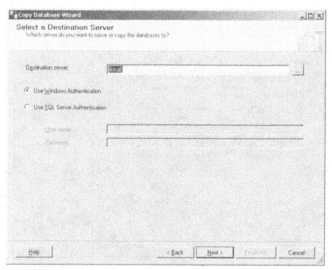

6. Next you are asked which mode you would like to use. Attach/detach is useful for copying databases between servers that are in remote locations from each other and requires the database to be taken offline. The SQL Management Object transfer method allows you to keep the database online and gives you the flexibility to make a copy on the same server, so select the SQL Management Object Method option, and click Next.

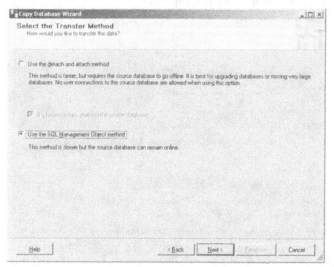

7. Next you are asked which database you would like to move or copy. Check the Copy box next to Test, and click Next.

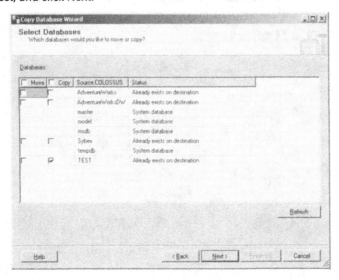

8. On the Database Destination page, you need to make a few changes:

   a. Change the destination database name to **TEST_Copy**.

   b. Change `Test.mdf` to **TEST_copy.mdf**.

   c. Change `Test_log.ldf` to **TEST_log_copy.ldf**.

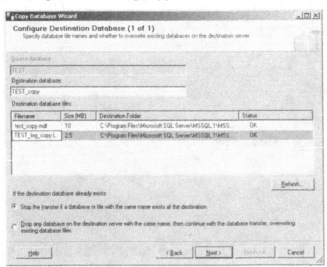

9. Click Next. You now have the option to change the name of the package that will be created; this matters only if you plan to save the package and execute it later. Accept the defaults, and click Next.

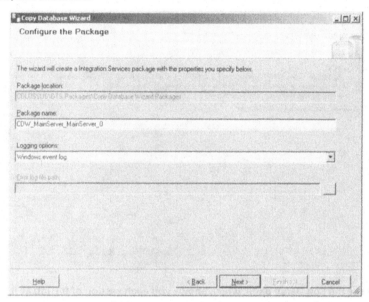

10. On the next page, you are asked when you would like to run the SSIS job created by the wizard. Select Run Immediately, and click Next.

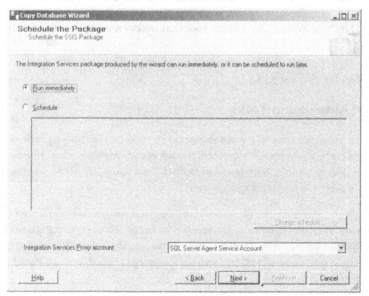

11. The final page summarizes the choices you have made. Click Finish to copy the Test database.

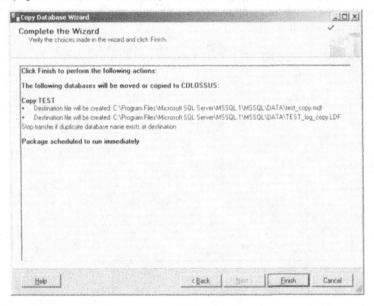

12. You will see the Log Detail page, which shows you each section of the job as it executes. Clicking the Report button will show each step of the job and its outcome.

13. Click Close on the Performing Operation page to complete the wizard.

The Copy Database Wizard is a simple tool that makes a complex task much easier.

 Real World Scenario

Case Study: Automating Tasks

AlsoRann wanted to make sure all the databases on its server were running at peak efficiency at all times. The company wanted to perform the necessary maintenance after-hours, but it also wanted its DBA to be able to go home at night. So the company asked us to come in and automate the regular maintenance procedures.

This was simple and straightforward. All we had to do was run the Maintenance Plan Wizard for the databases. We created one maintenance plan for all the system databases (master, model, and MSDB) and one for each of the user databases. This way, if the plan failed for one database, we could get an email letting us know which plan failed, and we could restart the plan for the database that failed.

After we created the maintenance plans, we found more to automate. It turns out that Also-Rann needed to download a file from one of its vendors via File Transfer Protocol (FTP) and import that file into a database every day. When the company called us in, the DBA was downloading and importing this file manually—an unattractive prospect. If the DBA called in sick or went on vacation, the file sometimes did not get downloaded and imported, so the company's data was out of sync.

To fix this problem, we created a SQL Server Integration Services (SSIS) package that connected to the FTP server, downloaded the file, and imported it into the database. Then we created a job that runs the SSIS package every night. We configured the job to email the DBA if it fails.

Summary

That was a lot of ground to cover, but it will save you a lot of time and effort in server administration and reporting. First we discussed required maintenance. You need to perform many tasks on your server to keep it running smoothly and efficiently. You need to back up databases and transaction logs, reorganize index and data pages inside the database files, check for database integrity regularly, and keep statistics up-to-date.

Then you learned that automation includes three main components: operators, jobs, and alerts. Operators are the individuals who are notified when a problem needs attention; they can be notified via email, pager, or Net Send messages. Jobs are series of tasks and schedules that can be automated to activate at any time; they can include T-SQL code, command executive code, or scripting language code.

After that, we discussed mail support. To configure mail support, you learned you first need create a mailhost database and add a profile and an account. When these are in place, you can start sending email. If you want to send mail to operators, you need to make MSDB a mailhost database.

Then you learned how to create operators and configure them to receive email, pager, or Net Send messages. You can also configure them to be available only at certain times of the day by setting their availability.

In addition, you learned how to create jobs. You can configure jobs to run any type of code at any time, and you can configure them to inform an operator when they complete, when they succeed, or when they fail.

Next we discussed alerts, which are used to notify an operator when an error has occurred. Not all errors fire an event, though—only those that are written to the Windows Event log and have an alert configured fire an alert that notifies someone. You learned how to create alerts that are based on the standard error messages that come with SQL Server as well as how to create your own custom error messages that can be used for any purpose. We then discussed how to create and use performance alerts to stop problems before they start. You also learned how to create WMI alerts so you can be notified when server events occur such as CREATE TABLE or other DDL statements.

After learning the importance of periodic maintenance and how to schedule jobs to run automatically, you learned how to tie all of that together by using the Maintenance Plan Wizard to automate these processes for you.

Finally, we discussed the Copy Database Wizard, because you may occasionally need to copy a database between servers. For example, your developers may need to copy a database from a development server to a production system. The Copy Database Wizard simplifies this task.

Exam Essentials

Know how to find and fix index fragmentation.   When users insert data in a table, SQL Server must make room for the new data in the table and any associated indexes. When an index page gets too full, SQL Server moves half of the data to a new page to make room for more data on the existing page. This is called a *page split*; when it occurs, the pages are no longer contiguous, and a condition called *fragmentation* occurs. You can use sys.DM_DB_ INDEX_PHYSICAL_STATS to find the amount of fragmentation on your indexes. If your index is less than 30 percent fragmented, you can reorganize it; anything higher than 30 percent requires a rebuild to bring the index back into shape.

Know how to update statistics.   SQL Server uses statistics to figure out which index, if any, you can use to speed up a SELECT query. If you created an index and told SQL Server not to automatically recompute statistics for you, then you will need to update them yourself using the UPDATE STATISTICS command.

Know how repair databases.   Because databases are just files on the hard disk, they can become corrupted on occasion. You need to know how to use DBCC CHECKDB to find and fix imperfections in your databases.

Understand Database Mail.   New to SQL Server 2005, Database Mail is used for sending email from SQL Server. This is especially useful for sending notifications for alerts and errors. Make sure you know how to set up a mailhost database and configure the SQL Server Agent to use a profile to send mail.

Understand jobs, operators, and alerts.   SQL Server automation is built on three primary features. *Jobs* are a series of steps that can be run on a set schedule. *Operators* are people or groups of people to be notified by email, pager, or Net Send message when something happens on the server. *Alerts* are fired when something happens on the system, such as an error. Alerts can notify an operator and automatically run a job when fired.

Know the Maintenance Plan Wizard and Copy Database Wizard.   You can automate all the maintenance tasks discussed in this chapter by using the Maintenance Plan Wizard. Just run the wizard, and it will create all the appropriate jobs for you and then run them on a set schedule. The Copy Database Wizard is just as handy. When a developer needs to copy a database from development to production, for instance, or you need to copy a database from a satellite office to the home office, you can use this wizard to simplify the process.

Review Questions

1. You have created an operator with an email address and a Net Send address. You have also created several alerts for which the new operator should be notified. When any of the alerts fire, the operator gets the email but never receives the Net Send message. What should you do to fix this?

   A. Start the Messenger service on the operator's computer.

   B. Start the alerter service on the operator's computer.

   C. Reinstall the SQL Server Agent on the SQL Server.

   D. Reconfigure the SQL Server Agent service to log in using the Network Service account.

2. You are performing maintenance on one of you databases, so you run this query against the database to find the index fragmentation:

   ```
   USE AdventureWorks;
   SELECT INDEX_ID, AVG_FRAGMENTATION_IN_PERCENT
   FROM sys.dm_db_index_physical_stats (db_id(),
   object_id('sales.SalesOrderDetail'),
    1, null, 'LIMITED');
   ```

   You receive this result:

   ```
   INDEX_ID    AVG_FRAGMENTATION_IN_PERCENT
   1                35.17
   ```

   Assuming that index 1 is named PK_IDX_Sales with a fill factor of 80 percent, what should you do to optimize this index?

   A. ALTER INDEX ALL ON Sales.SalesOrderDetail REBUILD WITH (FILLFACTOR = 80, ONLINE = ON, STATISTICS_NORECOMPUTE = ON)

   B. ALTER INDEX PK_IDX_Sales ON Sales.SalesOrderDetail REORGANIZE

   C. ALTER INDEX PK_IDX_Sales ON Sales.SalesOrderDetail REBUILD WITH (FILLFACTOR = 80, ONLINE = ON, STATISTICS_NORECOMPUTE = ON)

   D. ALTER INDEX ALL ON Sales.SalesOrderDetail REORGANIZE

3. You have just had a power surge at your office, and you are concerned that one of your databases may have been corrupted on the hard disk when the power surged. What can you run to find out whether the database's physical structure is still intact?

   A. DBCC CHECKDB WITH ESTIMATEONLY

   B. DBCC CHECKDB WITH PHYSICAL_ONLY

   C. DBCC CHECKDB WITH DATA_PURITY

   D. DBCC CHECKDB WITH STRUCTURE_ONLY

4. You want to be able to send email to operators when alerts are fired or when a job fails. Which database needs to be a mailhost to allow this?

   A. Master

   B. Model

   C. MSDB

   D. Tempdb

5. Your customer service manager wants to be notified whenever a customer service representative adjusts a customer's credit limit to any amount greater than $10,000. How can you create an alert that will fire when a customer service representative adjusts a credit limit?

   A. EXEC sp_addmessage @msgnum=50001, @severity=10, @msgtext=N'Credit increased', @with_log='TRUE'

   B. EXEC sp_addmessage @msgnum=50001, @severity=10, @msgtext=N' Credit increased ', @with_log='FALSE'

   C. EXEC sp_addmessage @msgnum=50001, @severity=19, @msgtext=N' Credit increased ', @with_log='TRUE'

   D. EXEC sp_addmessage @msgnum=50001, @severity=19, @msgtext=N' Credit increased ', @with_log='TRUE'

6. You have a production database named Sales. As an administrator, it is your job to make sure all the tables in your production database do not get modified without a written request on file. You need to be notified whenever a table is modified in each database. What can you do?

   A. Create a performance alert based on the SQLServer:ObjectsModified counter, and set the threshold to any value greater than 1.

   B. Create a WMI alert with this query:

   SELECT * FROM DDL_DATABASE_LEVEL_EVENTS

   WHERE DatabaseName = 'Sales'

   C. Create a standard alert based on error number 14599.

   D. Create a custom error that fires an alert.

7. You have created several alerts and operators on your server. Each of your operators is configured to receive email and Net Send messages. When the alerts occur, though, the operators are not receiving any notifications. What can you do to fix this?

   A. Make sure the SQL Server Agent service is running.

   B. Make sure the SQL Server Agent service is using a valid mail profile.

   C. Make sure the SQL Server Agent service is logging in as the Network Service account.

   D. Make sure the SQL Server Agent service is configured to log alerts to the Event log.

8. You are going to perform some standard maintenance on one of your servers that will take a couple of hours to complete. During this time, you have an alert based on a performance counter that will fire every few minutes until the maintenance is complete. You do not want this to happen, so what can you do to stop the alert from firing?

    A. Disable the custom error.

    B. Disable the alert.

    C. Delete the error, and re-create it when you are done with the maintenance.

    D. Delete the alert, and re-create it when you are done with the maintenance.

9. You are creating a job that copies a file from an FTP server and then imports the data in the file into a table in a database. You do not want the job to import old data if the FTP download fails, so what should you do?

    A. Make step 1 of the job the FTP download. Make step 2 of the job the import task. Have step 1 quit the job on failure.

    B. Make step 1 of the job the FTP download. Make step 2 of the job the import task. Have step 1 retry three times at an interval of five minutes. After the three retries, continue to step 2.

    C. Make step 1 of the job the FTP download. Make step 2 of the job the import task. Make step 3 an ActiveX scripting task that creates a blank file. Have step 1 go to step 3 on failure; have step 3 go to step 2 on completion.

    D. Make step 1 of the job the FTP download. Make step 2 of the job the import task. Have step 2 quit the job on failure.

10. You are performing maintenance on one of you databases, so you run the following query against the database to find the index fragmentation:

    ```
    USE AdventureWorks;
    SELECT INDEX_ID, AVG_FRAGMENTATION_IN_PERCENT
    FROM sys.dm_db_index_physical_stats (db_id(),
    object_id('Sales.SalesOrderDetail'),
     1, null, 'LIMITED');
    ```

    You receive this result:

    ```
    INDEX_ID    AVG_FRAGMENTATION_IN_PERCENT
    1           29.36
    ```

    Assuming that index 1 is named PK_IDX_Sales with a fill factor of 80 percent, what should you do to optimize this index?

    A. `alter index all on Sales.SalesOrderDetail rebuild with fillfactor = 80, online = on, statistics_norecompute = on)`

    B. `alter index pk_idx_Sales on Sales.SalesOrderDetail reorganize`

    C. `alter index pk_idx_Sales on Sales.SalesOrderDetail rebuild with (fillfactor = 80, online = on, statistics_norecompute = on)`

11. One of the developers at your company has just completed development on a database and is ready to move it into production. What is the simplest way to copy the database from development to production?

A. Use the Maintenance Plan Wizard to copy the database from the development server to the production server.

B. Create a job that copies the database using T-SQL code.

C. Use the Copy Database Wizard to copy the database from the development server to the production server.

D. Use DBCC CHECKDB WITH COPY_ONLY to copy the database from the development server to the production server.

12. Your accounting database processes thousands of transactions per day, and you want to make sure it is always online. You need to be alerted whenever the log file reaches 75 percent full. What should you do?

A. Create a WMI alert with this query:

```
SELECT Percent_Log_Used FROM DDL_TLOG_LEVEL_EVENTS
WHERE DatabaseName = 'Sales'
```

B. Create a performance alert based on the Percent Log Used counter of the SQLServer:Databases object.

C. Create a job that runs the sp_spaceused stored procedure every 15 minutes.

D. Create a job that runs the DBCC CHECKLOG function every 15 minutes.

13. You have created a user-defined message that says, "Please call the help desk." It is numbered 50001, and it is configured to post to the Windows Application log. How can you fire the alert that is based on this custom error?

A. ALERT(50001)

B. ALERT(50001, 10, 1)

C. RAISERROR (50001, 10, 1)

D. RAISERROR (50001, 10, 1) WITH LOG

14. You want to make sure someone is always notified of errors when they occur. You have many operators who are all available at different times of the day throughout the week, but you want to make certain no time is left uncovered. What should you do?

A. Make one of your operators available at all times.

B. Create a last-resort operator.

C. Create a fail-safe operator.

D. Create an off-hours operator.

15. You have created an operator with an email address and a Net Send address. You have also created several alerts for which the new operator should be notified. When any of the alerts fire, the operator gets the Net Send messages but never receives emails. You have verified that the MSDB database is a mailhost. What should you do to fix this?

A. Make sure Outlook is installed on the server.

B. Start the Messenger service on the server.

C. Reconfigure the SQL Server Agent service to log in using the Network Service account.

D. Make sure the SQL Server Agent service is configured to use a valid mail profile.

16. You had a systems failure over the weekend; everything seemed to come back up without major issues. However, your users are now complaining they are seeing some strange values in some of the queries they run against a database that was upgraded from SQL Server 2000. It looks like some of the columns now contain larger numbers than expected. What should you run to fix this?

A. DBCC CHECKDB WITH ESTIMATEONLY

B. DBCC CHECKDB WITH PHYSICAL_ONLY

C. DBCC CHECKDB WITH DATA_PURITY

D. DBCC CHECKDB WITH REPAIR_DATA

17. You have just bought a new server, and you need to start moving your databases from the old server to the new server. You cannot take the databases offline at any time because they are always in use. How can you move the databases to the new server while keeping them available?

A. Use the Maintenance Plan Wizard to copy the databases.

B. Use the Copy Database Wizard to copy the databases, and specify the SQL Management Object method for copying.

C. Use the Copy Database Wizard to copy the databases, and specify the attach/detach method for copying.

D. Run DBCC CHECKDB WITH COPY_ONLINE to copy the database.

18. You have a BugTracking database that your developers use to keep track of bugs in their custom software. Your development manager wants to be notified whenever a developer deletes a bug from the database. How can you create an error message that will fire an alert when a developer deletes a bug?

A. EXEC sp_addmessage @msgnum=14599, @severity=10, @msgtext=N'Bug deleted', @with_log='TRUE'

B. EXEC sp_addmessage @msgnum=14599, @severity=10, @msgtext=N'Bug deleted', @with_log='FALSE'

C. EXEC sp_addmessage @msgnum=50001, @severity=10, @msgtext=N'Bug deleted', @with_log='TRUE'

D. EXEC sp_addmessage @msgnum=50001, @severity=10, @msgtext=N'Bug deleted', @with_log='TRUE'

19. Your accounting manager wants to know whenever a record is deleted from the General Led-ger database. She also needs to know the username of the person who deleted the record. How can you create an error message that will fire this alert?

A. EXEC sp_addmessage @msgnum=50001, @severity=10, @msgtext=N'GL Record deleted by %d', @with_log='TRUE'

B. EXEC sp_addmessage @msgnum=50001, @severity=10, @msgtext=N'GL Record deleted by %s', @with_log='TRUE'

C. EXEC sp_addmessage @msgnum=50001, @severity=10, @msgtext=N'GL Record deleted by @d', @with_log='TRUE'

D. EXEC sp_addmessage @msgnum=50001, @severity=10, @msgtext=N'GL Record deleted by @s', @with_log='TRUE'

20. You have an index named idx_SalesOrderDetail on the SalesOrderDetail table of your Sales database. The table is not used heavily, so there are not many changes on it throughout the day. Because it is so lightly used, you decided to save system resources by not having SQL Server auto-matically update the index statistics. What do you need to do to bring the index up-to-date?

A. Run this: UPDATE STATISTICS Sales.SalesOrderDetail

B. Run this: ALTER INDEX idx_SalesOrderDetail

ON Sales.SalesOrderDetail

REORGANIZE

C. Run this: ALTER INDEX idx_SalesOrderDetail

ON Sales.SalesOrderDetail

UPDATE_STATS

D. Run this: ALTER INDEX idx_SalesOrderDetail

ON Sales.SalesOrderDetail

REBUILD WITH (FILLFACTOR = 80, ONLINE = ON,

STATISTICS_NORECOMPUTE = ON)

Answers to Review Questions

1. A. For the operator to receive Net Send messages, the operator's machine must have the Messenger service running. The SQL Server Agent service does not require any special configuration for this to work, and the alerter service does not work with Net Send messages.

2. C. Ten percent or less fragmentation requires no action because it is acceptable. On the other hand, 10 to 30 percent require an index reorganization, and higher than 30 require a rebuild. This is 35 percent fragmented, so it should be rebuilt, but you do not want to rebuild all the indexes—just the one that is fragmented—so ALTER INDEX ALL is not required.

3. B. To check the physical structure of a database that you suspect might be corrupt, use DBCC CHECKDB WITH PHYSICAL_ONLY. The ESTIMATE_ONLY option tells you how much space the operation will consume in tempdb. The DATA_PURITY option checks for column values that are out of range, and the STRUCTURE_ONLY option is not a valid option.

4. C. To email operators using Database Mail, the MSDB database must be a mailhost.

5. A. When you create a custom error, it must be written to the Event log, or it will never fire an alert. The severity level for this error should be left low as well because severity 19 and higher is a severe error that can terminate client communications. So, severity 10 with logging set to true is the best way to create the new error.

6. B. To fire an alert whenever a user modifies an object in the database, you need to create a WMI alert and have it watch for DDL events. Creating a standard or custom alert would not accomplish your goal, and SQLServer:ObjectsModified does not exist.

7. A. Because your operators are not receiving any notifications when alerts occur, then you know it is not because of an invalid mail profile, and the account that the agent logs in as does not matter for Net Send messages. Also, the SQL Server Agent service does not need to be configured to log events to the Event log; that happens automatically when the error is configured to be logged. The most likely cause then is that the agent simply isn't running.

8. B. You do not need to delete anything; you can just disable the alert during the maintenance window. Also, you cannot disable an error; you can delete only the alert based on it.

9. A. The simplest way to accomplish your goal is to have a two-step job; the first step is the FTP download, and the second is the import task. If the FTP download fails, then you do not want to try to import any existing files because they would contain old data; therefore, the best approach is to quit the entire job if the download fails.

10. B. Ten percent or less fragmentation requires no action because it is acceptable. On the other hand, 10 to 30 percent requires an index reorganization, and higher than 30 percent requires a rebuild. This is 29 percent fragmented, so it should be reorganized; however, you do not want to rebuild all the indexes—just the one that is fragmented—so alter index all is not required.

11. C. Even though you could create a job of your own, the simplest way to copy the database is to use the Copy Database Wizard. The Maintenance Plan Wizard does not copy databases, and DBCC CHECKDB does not have a COPY_ONLY option.

12. B. The best method to get an alert when the log reaches 75 percent full is to create a performance alert based on the Percent Log Used counter. Running a job to check the space used every 15 minutes is inefficient, and sp_spaceused won't tell you how much of the log is full anyway. Also, DBCC CHECKLOG is not a valid function; the WMI query is invalid as well.

13. C. This alert can be fired using the RAISERROR statement without using the WITH LOG option because the error was configured to post to the Application log when it was created. Also, ALERT does not exist.

14. C. Making one of your operators available at all times is not going to make that operator happy, and you would have to configure that one operator to receive every alert. The best approach is to create a fail-safe operator who will receive alerts when no other operators are available. Also, the last-resort and off-hours operators don't exist.

15. D. For the agent to send email, it must be configured to use a valid mail profile. Outlook is not required on the server to send email, and the Messenger service is used only for Net Send messages. Also, it does not matter what account the SQL Server Agent service logs in as to send email.

16. C. Because the users are saying they are getting bigger numbers than expected, it is possible the data was corrupted in the database. The DATA_PURITY clause of the DBCC command is especially for fixing problems with tables that are returning unexpected results, such as returning int when it should return smallint. PHYSICAL_ONLY checks the physical structure of a database that you suspect might be corrupt. The ESTIMATE_ONLY option tells you how much space the operation will consume in tempdb. Also, REPAIR_DATA is not a valid option.

17. B. The only way to copy the database and keep them available is to use the SQL Management Object method for transferring the database. The attach/detach method will take the database offline. Also, the Maintenance Plan Wizard does not copy databases, and the COPY_ONLINE clause is not a valid option.

18. D. When you create a custom error message, it must be written to the Event log, or it will never fire an alert. The severity level for this error should be left low as well because severity 19 and higher is a severe error that can terminate client communications, so severity 10 is best. Also, custom error messages must start with numbers higher than 50,000, so you cannot use 14,599 to create the error.

19. B. To create an error message with custom text, you must create the error to accept parameters. The percent sign (%) indicates a parameter. Because you are sending a username as the parameter, you need to use %s for strings and %d ID for decimal values, so it won't work. Also, the @ symbol specifies a parameter in T-SQL code, so it does not work in a custom error message.

20. A. To update statistics for an index manually, you just need to run UPDATE STATISTICS. Altering the index with REORGANIZE or REBUILD would be too resource intensive and would be unnecessary. Also, UPDATE_STATS is not a valid clause of the ALTER INDEX statement.

Chapter

11

Performing Backups and Restores

MICROSOFT EXAM OBJECTIVES COVERED IN THIS CHAPTER:

✓ **Back up a database.**

- Perform a full backup.
- Perform a differential backup.
- Perform a transaction log backup.
- Initialize a media set by using the FORMAT option.
- Append or overwrite an existing media set.
- Create a backup device.
- Back up filegroups.

✓ **Restore a database.**

- Identify which files are needed from the backup strategy.
- Restore a database from a single file and from multiple files.
- Choose an appropriate restore method.

✓ **Move a database between servers.**

- Choose an appropriate method for moving a database.

Of all the maintenance tasks you can perform on your server, performing regular backups is possibly the most important. Without a backup strategy, you can—no, you *will*—lose data. Therefore, you'll want to pay close attention in this chapter as we discuss each of the four types of backup (full, differential, transaction log, and filegroup) and how to use each one.

Of course, backing up is not very useful if you can't restore, so we'll also cover the different types of restores available to you, including piecemeal and point-in-time restores.

Finally, we'll discuss the importance of a good backup strategy, and you'll see what issues to consider when you devise one of your own. To get things rolling, we'll discuss backups in general.

Backing Up Your Data

A *backup* is a copy of your data stored somewhere other than on the hard drive of your computer, usually on some type of tape (a lot like audio cassette tapes); you can also store a backup on a hard drive on another computer connected over a local area network (LAN). Why would you want to keep a copy of your data in two places? You'll want to do this for many reasons.

The first reason for keeping a backup is the possibility of hardware failure. Computer hardware has a Mean Time Between Failures (MTBF) that is measured in hours. This means every 40,000 hours or so, a piece of hardware is going to fail, and you can't do much about it. True, you could implement fault-tolerance by providing duplicate hardware, but that isn't a complete guarantee against data loss. If you don't want to lose your data when a hard disk goes bad, it's best to create a backup.

Another reason for creating backups is the potential for a natural disaster. No matter how much redundant hardware you have in place, you can't assume it will survive the wrath of a tornado, hurricane, earthquake, flood, or fire. To thwart the wrath of the elements, you need to back up your data.

Finally, another reason for creating backups stems from all the injustice in today's world. Many employees are angry with their boss or their company in general, and the way they seek revenge is by destroying or maliciously updating sensitive data. This is the worst kind of data loss, and the only way to recover from it is by having a viable backup.

Now that you have some good reasons to back up your data, you need to know how to do it. Next you'll learn how the backup process works, and then you'll learn about the four types of backup you can perform to protect your data.

Understanding How Backups Work

Some features are common to all types of backup. For instance, you may wonder when you'll be able to get your users to stop using the database long enough to perform a backup. Stop wondering—all backups in SQL Server are online backups, which means your users can access the database while you're backing it up. How is this possible? Well, SQL Server uses transaction logs, which are a lot like a diary for the database. In a diary, you put a date next to everything that happens to you. It might look as follows:

3-21-06	Bought a car.
3-22-06	Drove new car to show off.
3-23-06	Drove car into tree.
3-24-06	Started looking for new car.

Much like a diary, a transaction log puts a *log sequence number* (LSN) next to each line of the log. Every time SQL Server writes the data from the transaction log into the database, it creates a *checkpoint* in the log. SQL Server uses the checkpoint like a bookmark so it will remember where it left off the next time it copies from the log to the database. A transaction log might look as follows:

147	Begin Tran 1
148	Update Tran 1
149	Begin Tran 2
150	Update Tran 2
151	Commit Tran 1
152	Checkpoint
153	Update Tran 2
154	Commit Tran 2

When a backup starts, SQL Server records the current LSN. Once the backup completes, SQL Server backs up all the entries in the transaction log from the LSN it recorded at the start of the backup to the current LSN. Here's an example of how it works:

1. SQL Server checkpoints the data and records the LSN of the oldest open transaction (in this case, 149 Begin Tran 2, because it wasn't committed before the checkpoint).

2. SQL Server backs up all the pages of the database that contain data (no need to back up the empty ones).

3. SQL Server grabs all the parts of the transaction log that were recorded during the backup process—that is, all the lines of the transaction log with an LSN greater than the LSN

recorded at the start of the backup session (in this case, 149 and greater). This way, your users can still do whatever they want with the database while it's being backed up.

To perform any type of backup, you need a place to store it. The medium you'll use to store a backup is called a *backup device*. You'll learn how to create one now.

Creating a Backup Device

Backups are stored on a physical backup medium, which can be a tape drive or a hard disk (local or accessed over a network connection). SQL Server isn't aware of the various forms of media attached to your server, so you must inform SQL Server where to store the backups. This is what a backup device is for; it's a representation of the backup medium. You can create two types of backup devices: permanent and temporary.

Temporary backup devices are created on the fly when you perform the backup. They're useful for making a copy of a database to send to another office so it has a complete copy of your data. Or, you may want to consider using a temporary backup device to copy your database for permanent offsite storage (usually for archiving).

Although it's true you can use replication (discussed in Chapter 12) to copy a database to a remote site, backing up to a temporary backup device can be faster if your remote site is connected via a slow wide area network (WAN) link (such as 56K Frame Relay).

You can use *permanent backup devices* over and over again; you can even append data to them, making them perfect devices for regularly scheduled backups. You create permanent backup devices before performing the backup, and you can store them, like temporary devices, on a local hard disk, on a remote hard disk over a LAN, or on a local tape drive. You'll create a permanent backup device in Exercise 11.1.

If you go to Windows Explorer and search for a file named AdvWorksFull.bak right now, don't be too surprised if you don't find it. SQL Server hasn't created the file yet; it simply added a record to the sysdevices table in the master database telling SQL Server where to create the backup file the first time you perform a backup to the device.

If you're using a tape drive as a backup medium, it must be physically attached to the SQL Server machine. The only way around this requirement is to use a third-party backup solution.

EXERCISE 11.1

Creating a Permanent Backup Device

1. Open SQL Server Management Studio by selecting it from the SQL Server 2005 group under Programs on the Start menu. Expand your server and then Server Objects.

EXERCISE 11.1

2. Right-click Backup Devices in Object Explorer, and select New Backup Device.

3. In the Device Name box of the Backup Device dialog box, enter **AdvWorksFull**. Notice that the filename and path are filled in for you; make sure you have enough free space on the drive SQL Server has selected.

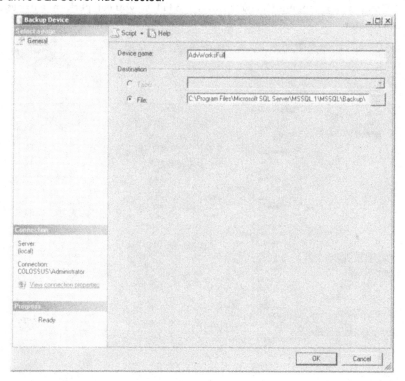

4. Click OK to create the device.

Performing Full Backups

Just as the name implies, a *full backup* is a backup of the entire database. It backs up the database files, the locations of those files, and portions of the transaction log (from the LSN recorded at the start of the backup to the LSN at the end of the backup). This is the first type of backup you need to perform in any backup strategy because all the other backup types depend on the existence of a full backup. This means you can't perform a differential or transaction log backup if you have never performed a full backup.

To create your *baseline* (which is what the full backup is called in a backup strategy) in this chapter's example, you need to back up the AdventureWorks database to the permanent backup device you created in the previous section of this chapter. You'll do that in Exercise 11.2.

EXERCISE 11.2

Performing a Full Backup

1. Open SQL Server Management Studio. Expand your server and then Databases.

2. Right-click AdventureWorks, and select Properties.

3. On the Options page, change Recovery Model to Full so you can perform a transaction log backup later.

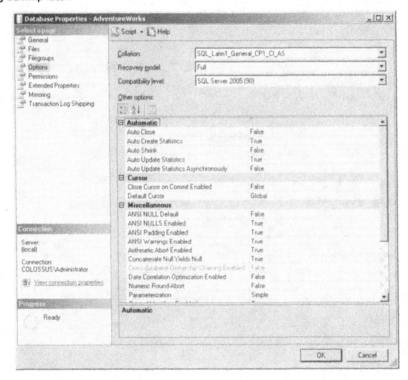

4. Click OK to apply the changes.

5. Right-click AdventureWorks under Databases, point to Tasks, and click Back Up.

6. In the Backup dialog box, make sure AdventureWorks is the selected database to back up and Backup Type is Full.

7. Leave the default name in the Name box. In the Description box, type **Full Backup of AdventureWorks**.

8. Under Destination, a disk device may already be listed. If so, select the device, and click Remove.

9. Under Destination, click Add.

10. In the Select Backup Destination box, click Backup Device, select AdvWorksFull, and click OK.

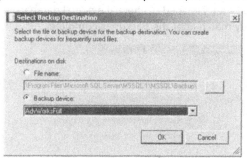

11. You should now have a backup device listed under Destination.

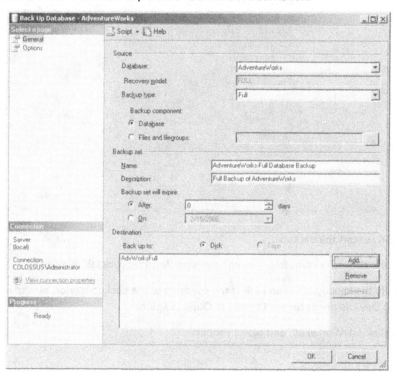

12. Switch to the Options page, and select Overwrite All Existing Backup Sets. This option initializes a new device or overwrites an existing one.

13. Select Verify Backup When Finished to check the actual database against the backup copy and be sure they match after the backup is complete.

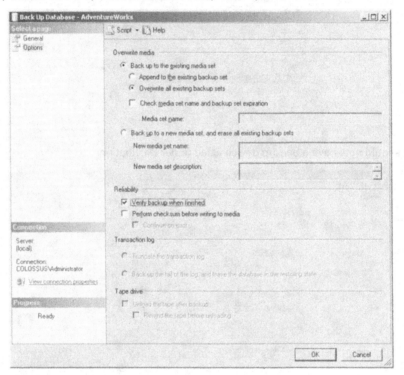

14. Click OK to start the backup.

15. When the backup is complete, you will get a notification; click OK to close it.

16. To verify the backup, you can look at the contents of the backup device, so expand Backup Devices under Server Objects in Object Explorer.

17. Right-click AdvWorksFull, and select Properties.

EXERCISE 11.2 *(continued)*

18. On the Media Contents page, you should see the full backup of AdventureWorks.

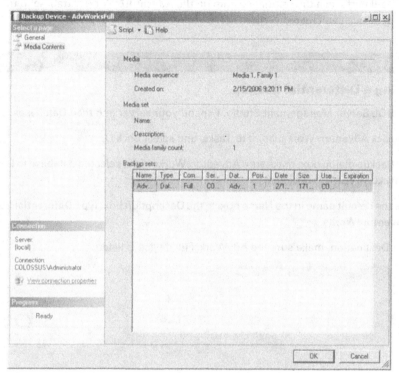

19. Click OK to return to SQL Server Management Studio.

Now that you have a full backup in place, you can start performing other types of backups. You'll learn about differential backups next.

Performing Differential Backups

Differential backups record all the changes made to a database since the last full backup was performed. Thus, if you perform a full backup on Monday and a differential backup on Tuesday, the differential will record all the changes to the database since the full backup on Monday. Another differential backup on Wednesday will record all the changes made since the full backup on Monday. The differential backup gets a little bigger each time it's performed, but it's still a great deal smaller than the full backup; so, a differential is faster than a full backup.

SQL Server figures out which pages in the backup have changed by reading the last LSN of the last full backup and comparing it with the data pages in the database. If SQL Server finds any updated data pages, it backs up the entire extent (eight contiguous pages) of data, rather than just the page that changed.

Performing a differential backup follows almost the same process as a full backup. In Exercise 11.3 you'll perform a differential backup on the AdventureWorks database to the permanent backup device you created earlier.

EXERCISE 11.3

Performing a Differential Backup

1. Open SQL Server Management Studio. Expand your server and then Databases.

2. Right-click AdventureWorks, point to Tasks, and select Back Up.

3. In the Backup dialog box, make sure AdventureWorks is the selected database to back up and Backup Type is Differential.

4. Leave the default name in the Name box. In the Description box, type **Differential Backup of AdventureWorks**.

5. Under Destination, make sure the AdvWorksFull device is listed.

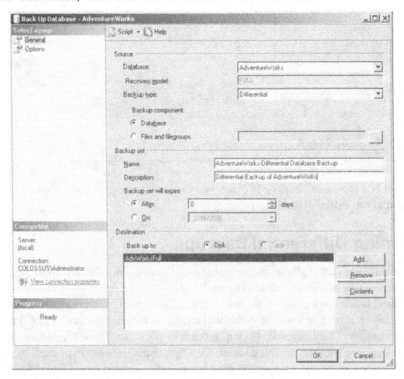

6. On the Options page, make sure Append to the Existing Backup Set is selected so you don't overwrite your existing full backup.

7. On the Options tab, select Verify Backup When Finished.

8. Click OK to start the backup.

9. When the backup is complete, you will get a notification; click OK to close it.

10. To verify the backup, you can look at the contents of the backup device, so expand Backup Devices under Server Objects in Object Explorer.

11. Right-click AdvWorksFull, and select Properties.

12. On the Media Contents page, you should see the full backup of AdventureWorks.

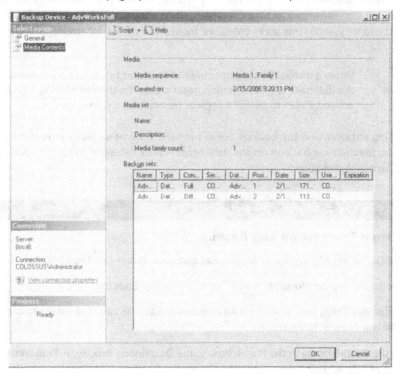

13. Click OK to return to SQL Server Management Studio.

Performing only full and differential backups isn't enough. If you don't perform transaction log backups, your database could stop functioning.

Performing Transaction Log Backups

Although they rely on the existence of a full backup, *transaction log backups* don't back up the database itself. This type of backup records only sections of the transaction log, specifically since the last transaction log backup. It's easier to understand the role of the transaction log backup if you think of the transaction log the way SQL Server does: as a separate object. Then it makes sense that SQL Server requires a backup of the database as well as the log.

The transaction log is an entity unto itself, but you should back it up for another important reason. When a database is configured to use the Full or Bulk-Logged recovery model, a transaction log backup is the only type of backup that clears old transactions from the transaction log; full and differential backups can clear the log only when the database being backed up is configured to use the Simple recovery model. Therefore, if you performed only full and differential backups on most production databases, the transaction log would eventually fill to 100 percent capacity, and your users would be locked out of the database.

 When a transaction log becomes 100 percent full, users are denied access to the database until an administrator clears the transaction log. The best way around this is to perform regular transaction log backups.

Performing a transaction log backup doesn't involve a lot of steps; in Exercise 11.4 you'll perform a transaction log backup on the AdventureWorks database using the backup device created earlier in this chapter.

EXERCISE 11.4

Performing a Transaction Log Backup

1. Open SQL Server Management Studio. Expand your server and then Databases.

2. Right-click AdventureWorks, point to Tasks, and select Back Up.

3. In the Backup dialog box, make sure AdventureWorks is the selected database to back up and Backup Type is Transaction Log.

4. Leave the default name in the Name box. In the Description box, type **Transaction Log Backup of AdventureWorks**.

EXERCISE 11.4 *(continued)*

5.   Under Destination, make sure the AdvWorksFull device is listed.

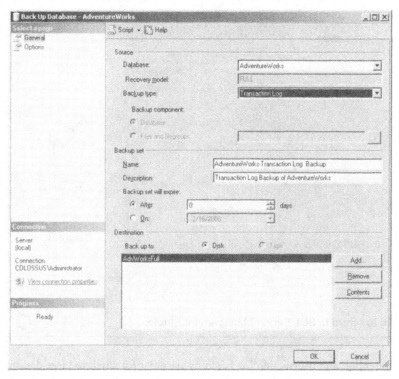

6.   On the Options page, make sure Append to the Existing Backup Set is selected so you don't overwrite your existing full backup.

7.   On the Options page, select Verify Backup When Finished.

8.   Click OK to start the backup.

9.   When the backup is complete, you will get a notification; click OK to close it.

10.   To verify the backup, you can look at the contents of the backup device, so expand Backup Devices under Server Objects in Object Explorer.

11.   Right-click AdvWorksFull, and select Properties.

12. On the Media Contents page, you should see the full backup of AdventureWorks.

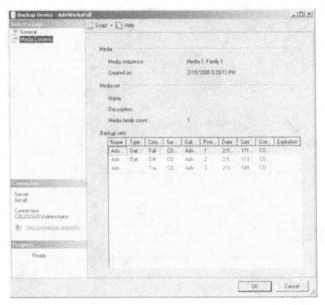

13. Click OK to return to SQL Server Management Studio.

Full, differential, and transaction log backups are great for small to large databases, but another type of backup is specially designed for huge databases that are usually terabytes in size. In the next section you'll look into filegroup backups to see how you can use them to back up huge databases.

Performing Filegroup Backups

A growing number of companies have databases reaching the terabyte range. For good reason, these are known as very large databases (VLDBs). Imagine trying to perform a backup of a 2TB database on a nightly, or even weekly, basis. Even if you have purchased the latest, greatest hardware, you're looking at a long backup time. Microsoft knows you don't want to wait that long for a backup to finish, so it gives you a way to back up small sections of the database at a time: a *filegroup backup*.

We discussed filegroups in Chapters 2, so we won't rehash many of the details here. Essentially, a *filegroup* is a way of storing a database on more than one file, and it gives you the ability to control on which of those files your objects (such as tables or indexes) are stored. This way, a database isn't limited to being contained on one hard disk; it can be spread out across many hard disks and thus can grow quite large. Using a filegroup backup, you can back up one or more of those files at a time rather than the entire database all at once.

However, you need to be aware of a caveat when using filegroup backups to accelerate the backup process for VLDBs. You can also use filegroups to expedite data access by placing tables on one file and the corresponding indexes on another file. Although this speeds up data access, it can slow the backup process because you must back up tables and indexes as a single unit, as shown in Figure 11.1. This means if the tables and indexes are stored on separate files, the files must be backed up as a single unit; you can't back up the tables one night and the associated indexes the next.

FIGURE 11.1   Tables and indexes must be backed up as a single unit if they're stored on separate files.

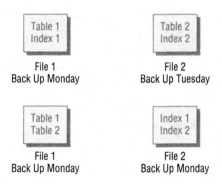

To perform a filegroup backup, you need to create a filegroup. In Exercise 11.5 you'll add one to the Sybex database you created in Chapter 2.

With a second filegroup in place that contains data, you can perform a filegroup backup in Exercise 11.6.

EXERCISE 11.5

Preparing the Sybex Database for a Filegroup Backup

1. Open SQL Server Management Studio. Expand your server and then Databases.

2. Right-click the Sybex database, and select Properties.

EXERCISE 11.5 *(continued)*

3. On the Filegroups page, click the Add button. In the Name text box, enter **Secondary**.

4. On the Files page, click the Add button, and enter this information:

   Name: **Sybex_Data_3**

   File Type: **Data**

   Filegroup: **Secondary**

   Initial Size: **3**

5. Click OK to create the new file on the Secondary filegroup.

6. Now, to add a table to the new filegroup, expand Sybex in Object Explorer, right-click Tables, and select New Table.

7. Under Column Name in the first row, enter **Emp_Name**.

8. Next to Emp_Name, select varchar as the datatype. Leave the default length of 50.

9. Just below Emp_Name in the second row, enter **Emp_Number** as the column name with a type of varchar. Leave the default length of 50.

10. Select View ➢ Properties Window.

11. Expand the Regular Data Space Specification section, and change the Filegroup or Partition Scheme Name property to Secondary.

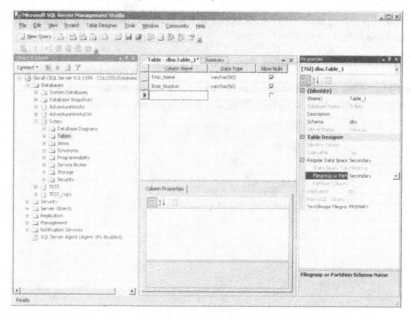

12. Click the Save button (it looks like a floppy disk on the toolbar) to create the new table, and enter **Employees** for the table name.

13. Close the Table Designer by clicking the *X* in the upper-right corner of the window.

14. Now, to add some data to the new table, open a new query, and execute the following code (note that the second value is arbitrary):

```
USE Sybex

INSERT Employees
```

EXERCISE 11.5 *(continued)*

VALUES('Tim Hsu', 'VA1765FR')

INSERT Employees

VALUES('Sue Hernandez', 'FQ9187GL')

15. Close the query window.

EXERCISE 11.6

Performing a Filegroup Backup

1. Right-click the Sybex database in Object Explorer, point to Tasks, and select Back Up.

2. In the Backup dialog box, make sure Sybex is the selected database to back up and Backup Type is Full.

3. Under Backup Component, select Files and Filegroups.

4. In the Select Files and Filegroups dialog box, check the Secondary box, and click OK (notice that the box next to Sybex_Data_3 is automatically checked).

5. Leave the default name in the Name box. In the Description box, type **Filegroup Backup of Sybex**.

6. Under Destination, make sure the AdvWorksFull device is the only one listed.

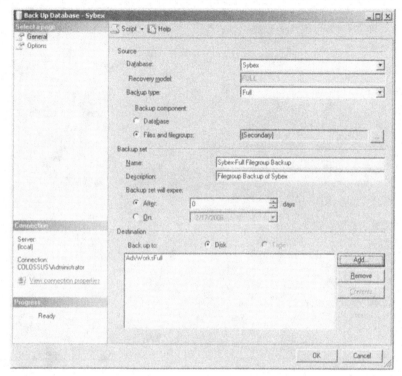

7. On the Options tab, make sure Append to the Existing Backup Set is selected so you don't overwrite your existing backups.

8. On the Options tab, select Verify Backup When Finished.

9. Click OK to start the backup.

10. When the backup is complete, you will get a notification; click OK to close it.

11. To verify the backup, you can look at the contents of the backup device, so expand Backup Devices under Server Objects in Object Explorer.

12. Right-click AdvWorksFull, and select Properties.

13. On the Media Contents page, you should see the full backup of Sybex.

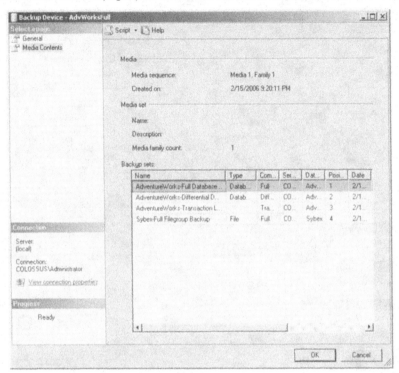

14. Click Close, and then click OK to return to SQL Server Management Studio.

 You could have backed up the Sybex database to another backup device named Sybex; we had you back it up to an existing device so the exercise would move along faster.

That takes care of the mechanics of all four types of backup. Next, you'll look at a technique to make the backups even faster—backing up to multiple devices.

Backing Up to Multiple Devices

Thus far you've seen how to perform backups to a single backup device. If you really want to speed up the process, you can perform backups to multiple devices at the same time. You can perform this type of backup on the hard disk, network, or local tape drive, just like a normal backup.

If you want to do this with tape devices, you need more than one local tape drive in the SQL Server machine.

This type of backup uses multiple devices in parallel and writes the data in stripes across the media. What does that mean? You may expect that you fill one device to capacity and then move to the next, but that isn't what happens. The data is striped across all the media at the same time, which means all the devices are written to at once; this is why it's faster to use multiple devices for backup operations.

There is just one small drawback: once you combine backup devices, you can't use them separately. As shown in Figure 11.2, if you back up AdventureWorks to three devices (BD1, BD2, and BD3), you can't back up another database to just BD3; you must use all three devices for the backup. The three devices are now considered part of a media set and can't be used separately without losing all the backups stored on the set.

FIGURE 11.2   You can't use the backup devices in a media set for individual backups.

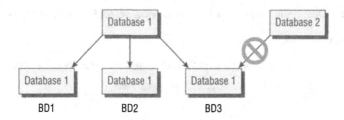

To perform a backup with multiple devices, you need to create two more backup devices and then perform a backup. You'll do that in Exercise 11.7.

EXERCISE 11.7

Backing Up to Multiple Devices

1. Open SQL Server Management Studio by selecting it from the SQL Server 2005 group under Programs on the Start menu. Expand your server and then Server Objects.

2. Right-click Backup Devices in Object Explorer, and select New Backup Device.

3. In the Name box of the Backup Device dialog box, enter **PSDev1**. Notice that the filename and path are filled in for you; make sure you have enough free space on the drive that SQL Server has selected.

4. Click OK to create the device.

5. Right-click Backup Devices in Object Explorer, and select New Backup Device.

EXERCISE 11.7 *(continued)*

6. In the Name box of the Backup Device dialog box, enter **PSDev2**. Again, notice that the filename and path are filled in for you.

7. Click OK to create the device.

8. To start the backup, right-click Model under System Databases, point to Tasks, and click Back Up.

9. In the Backup dialog box, make sure Model is the selected database to back up and Backup Type is Full.

10. Leave the default name in the Name box. In the Description box, type **Full Backup of Model**.

11. Under Destination, a disk device may already be listed. If so, select the device, and click Remove.

12. Under Destination, click Add.

13. In the Select Backup Destination box, click Backup Device, select PSDev1, and click OK.

14. Under Destination, click Add.

15. In the Select Backup Destination box, click Backup Device, select PSDev2, and click OK.

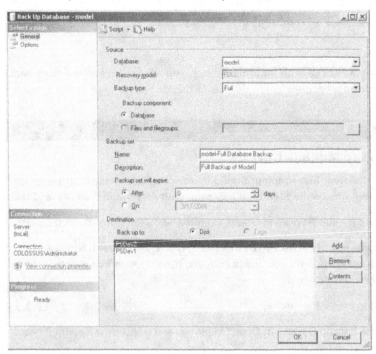

16. On the Options page, select Overwrite All Existing Backup Sets. This option initializes a new device or overwrites an existing one.

17. Check Verify Backup When Finished to check the actual database against the backup copy and be sure they match after the backup is complete.

18. Click OK to start the backup.

19. When the backup is complete, you will get a notification; click OK to close it.

20. To verify the backup, you can look at the contents of the backup device, so expand Backup Devices under Server Objects in Object Explorer.

21. Right-click PSDev1, and select Properties.

22. On the Media Contents page, you should see the first half of the full backup of Model. You should also note that the Media Family Count property is 2, denoting this is part of a multiple-device backup.

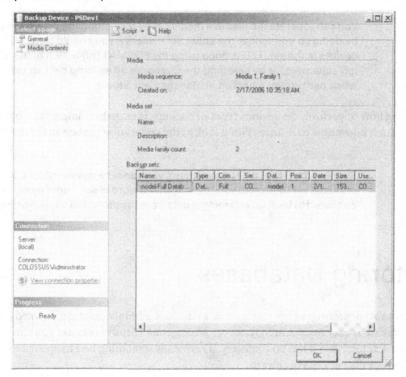

23. Click OK to return to SQL Server Management Studio.

Advanced Backup Options

You can use two slightly more advanced options to help with your database backups:

Copy-only backups Sometimes you'll need to make a special backup of a database outside your normal backup scheme. For instance, you may need to send a copy of your database to an offsite archive for safekeeping. To do this without throwing off the rest of your backups, you can create a *copy-only backup* that backs up the database without affecting the logs or database. You do this using the COPY_ONLY option of the BACKUP statement.

Partial full and differential backups A *partial backup* is a special type of backup that you can use only with filegroups. It backs up only the primary filegroup and all read-write filegroups. Read-only filegroups aren't backed up. You need to back up read-only filegroups only occasionally, because they don't change; thus, partial backups can make backups faster. To perform a partial backup, use the READ_WRITE_FILEGROUPS option of the BACKUP statement.

You can separate the files in a media set by formatting the files in the set, but by doing so you render the entire set useless—you should format all the devices in the set. This is done using the FORMAT [pf] option of the BACKUP [pf] statement, or by selecting the Overwrite all existing backup sets option when performing a backup in Management Studio.

Knowing how to perform the various types of backups is extremely important, but it's useless if you don't know how to restore. You'll look at the restoration process in the next section.

By using the T-SQL BACKUP statement, you can set a password for a backup set or media set to protect your data. If a password is set, users must have the password to back up and restore data from the protected backup or media set.

Restoring Databases

One of the most depressing sights you'll see as a database administrator is a downed database. Such a database is easy to spot in SQL Server Management Studio because you can't expand it in Object Explorer and it has no summary. This means something bad happened to the database; a corrupt disk is a likely culprit.

Suspect or corrupt databases aren't the only reasons to perform restores, though. You may, for example, need to send a copy of one of your databases to the home office or to a child office for synchronization. You may also need to recover from mistaken or malicious updates to the data. These reasons, and many others, make it important for you to know how to *restore* your databases.

Performing Standard Restores

Restoring a database doesn't involve a lot of steps, but you need to understand one important setting before undertaking the task. The RECOVERY option, when set incorrectly, can thwart all your efforts to restore a database. The RECOVERY option tells SQL Server that you're finished restoring the database and users should be allowed back in. You should use this option only on the last file of the restore process.

For example, if you performed a full backup, then a differential backup, and then a transaction log backup, you would need to restore all three of them to bring the database back to a consistent state. If you specify the RECOVERY option when restoring the differential backup, SQL Server won't allow you to restore any other backups. In effect, you have told SQL Server that you're done restoring and it should let everyone start using the database again. If you have more than one file to restore, you need to specify NORECOVERY on all restores except the last one.

SQL Server also remembers where the original files were located when you backed them up. Thus, if you backed up files from the D drive, SQL Server will restore them to the D drive. This is great unless your D drive has failed and you need to move your database to the E drive. You'll also run into this problem if you have backed up a database on a server at the home office and need to restore the database to a server at a child office. In this instance, you need to use the MOVE...TO option. MOVE...TO lets you back up a database in one location and move it to another location.

Finally, before allowing you to restore a database, SQL Server performs a safety check to make sure you aren't accidentally restoring the wrong database. The first step SQL Server takes is to compare the database name that is being restored to the name of the database recorded in the backup device. If the two are different, SQL Server won't perform the restore. Thus, if you have a database on the server named Accounting and you're trying to restore from a backup device that has a backup of a database named Acctg, SQL Server won't perform the restore. This is a lifesaver, unless you're trying to overwrite the existing database with the database from the backup. If that is the case, you need to specify the REPLACE option, which is designed to override the safety check.

With all that said, you're ready to restore a database. You'll now make one of the databases suspect so you can see exactly what SQL Server does to restore it. Specifically, in Exercise 11.8 you'll blow away AdventureWorks and then restore it.

EXERCISE 11.8

Restoring a Database

1. Open the SQL Server Configuration Manager from the Start menu.

2. In the left pane, select SQL Server 2005 Services.

3. Right-click SQL Server (MSSQLSERVER) in the right pane, and click Stop. You'll be asked whether you want to stop the SQL Server Agent service as well; click Yes.

4. Find the file AdventureWorks_Data.mdf (usually in C:\Program Files\Microsoft SQL Server\MSSQL.1\MSSQL\Data\).

5. Rename the file to **AdventureWorks_Data.old**.

6. Find the file AdventureWorks_Log.1df, and rename it to **AdventureWorks_Log.old**.

7. From the Configuration Manager, restart the SQL Server Agent and SQL Server services.

8. Open SQL Server Management Studio, and expand databases under your server name. AdventureWorks cannot be expanded and has no summary; it is now inaccessible.

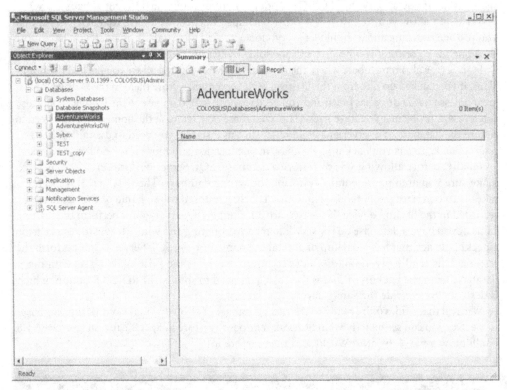

9. To restore the database, right-click Databases, and select Restore Database.

10. In the Restore Database dialog box, select AdventureWorks from the To Database drop-down list box.

11. Under Source for Restore, select From Device. Click the ellipsis (…) button next to the text box to select a device.

12. In the Specify Backup dialog box, select Backup Device from the Backup Media drop-down list box, and click Add.

EXERCISE 11.8 *(continued)*

13. In the Select Backup Device dialog box, select AdvWorksFull, and click OK.

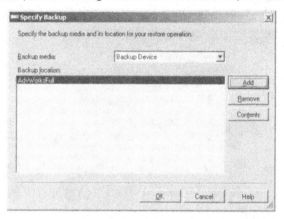

14. Click OK to close the Specify Backup dialog box.

15. Under Select the Backup Sets to Restore, check all three backups (full, differential, and transaction log). Doing so returns the database to the most recent state.

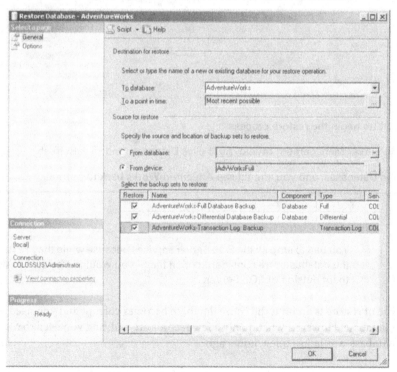

EXERCISE 11.8 *(continued)*

16. On the Options page, make sure the RESTORE WITH RECOVERY option is selected, because you have no more backups to restore.

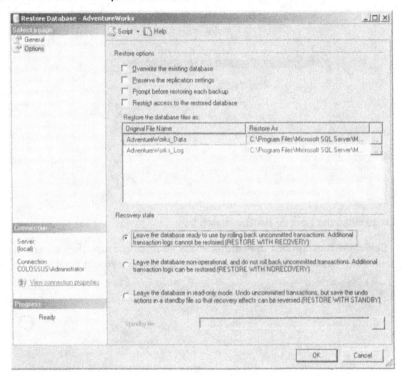

17. Click OK to begin the restore process.

18. In SQL Server Management Studio, right-click Database, and click Refresh.

19. Expand Databases, and you should see AdventureWorks back to normal.

You had to stop all the SQL Server services because while they're running, all the databases are considered open files—you wouldn't be able to work with them outside of SQL Server.

This type of restore is useful if the entire database becomes corrupt and you need to restore the whole database. However, what if only a few records are bad, and you need to return to the state the database was in just a few hours ago?

Performing Point-in-Time Restores

You'll usually get requests to return the data to a previous state at the end of the month, when accounting closes out the monthly books. Most often the request sounds like this: "We forgot to carry a 1; can you bring the data back to yesterday at about 2 P.M?" At this point you remember that accounting signs your paycheck, so you're delighted to help them in any way you can; you tell them you can do it. "How is this possible?" you may ask. If you're performing transaction log backups, you can perform a *point-in-time restore*.

In addition to stamping each transaction in the transaction log with an LSN, SQL Server stamps them all with a time. That time, combined with the STOPAT clause of the RESTORE statement, makes it possible for you to return the data to a previous state. You need to keep two issues in mind while using this process. First, it doesn't work with full or differential backups, only with transaction log backups. Second, you'll lose any changes made to your entire database after the STOPAT time. For instance, if you restore your database to the state it was in yesterday at 2 P.M, everything that changed from yesterday at 2 P.M until the time you restore the database will be lost and must be reinserted. Other than that, the point-in-time restore is a useful and powerful tool. You'll prepare to use it on AdventureWorks in Exercise 11.9.

EXERCISE 11.9

Preparing for a Point-in-Time Restore

1. You need to add a record that will survive the restore. Open a new SQL Server query in SQL Server Management Studio by clicking the New Query button on the toolbar.

2. To create a new record, enter and execute the following code:

    ```
    USE AdventureWorks

    INSERT HumanResources.Shift

    (Name, StartTime, EndTime, ModifiedDate)

    VALUES('Test Shift 1',getdate()+1,getdate()+2,getdate())
    ```

3. Note the time right now.

4. Wait two minutes, clear the query window, and then enter a new record using the following code:

    ```
    USE AdventureWorks

    INSERT HumanResources.Shift

    (Name, StartTime, EndTime, ModifiedDate)

    VALUES('Test Shift 2',getdate()+1,getdate()+2,getdate())
    ```

EXERCISE 11.9 *(continued)*

5. To see both records, clear the query window, and enter and execute the following code:

    USE AdventureWorks

    SELECT * FROM HumanResources.Shift

6. To perform a point-in-time restore, you must perform a transaction log backup. Open SQL Server Management Studio. Expand your server and then Databases.

7. In Object Explorer, right-click AdventureWorks, point to Tasks, and select Back Up.

8. In the Backup dialog box, make sure AdventureWorks is the selected database to back up and Backup Type is Transaction Log.

9. Leave the default name in the Name box. In the Description box, type **Point-in-time Backup of AdventureWorks**.

10. Under Destination, make sure the AdvWorksFull device is listed.

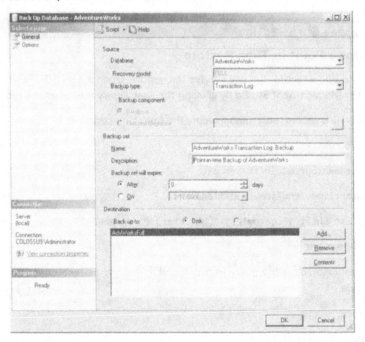

11. On the Options page, make sure Append to the Existing Backup Set is selected so you don't overwrite your existing full backup.

12. On the Options page, select Verify Backup When Finished.

13. Click OK to start the backup.

You have created two new records and performed a transaction log backup. In Exercise 11.10 you'll roll the database back to the point in time just before you added the second record so you can test the functionality of the point-in-time restore.

EXERCISE 11.10

Performing a Point-in-Time Restore

1. Open SQL Server Management Studio. Expand your server and then Databases.

2. Right-click AdventureWorks, point to Tasks, move to Restore, and select Database.

3. Click the ellipsis (...) button next to the To a Point in Time text box.

4. In the Point in Time Restore dialog box, enter the time from step 3 of Exercise 11.9, and click OK.

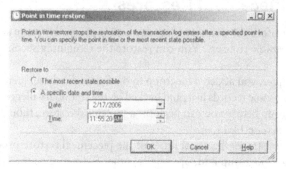

5. Make sure you're restoring from the AdvWorksFull device, select all the available back-ups in the device, and click OK to perform the restore.

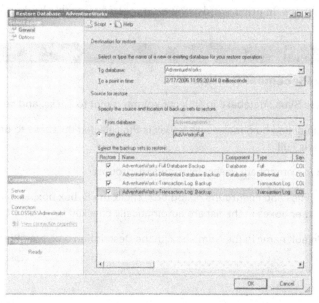

EXERCISE 11.10 *(continued)*

6. To test the restore, open a new SQL Server query in SQL Server Management Studio, and enter and execute the following code:

    ```
    USE AdventureWorks

    SELECT * FROM HumanResources.Shift
    ```

7. Notice that Test Shift 2 is no longer there, but Test Shift 1 remains.

Another type of restore will come in handy for VLDBs: piecemeal restores.

Performing Piecemeal Restores

Piecemeal restores restore the primary filegroup and (optionally) some secondary filegroups and make them accessible to users. You can restore the remaining secondary filegroups later if needed.

Earlier in this chapter, you added a filegroup to the Sybex database; then you added a table to that filegroup, created some records in it, and backed up the secondary filegroup. You need to back up the primary filegroup before you can perform a piecemeal restore, though, so you'll perform another backup in Exercise 11.11.

The exercise demonstrates the capabilities of the piecemeal restore process. You can use it to restore the primary filegroup and, optionally, other filegroups to the same or another database to make the data accessible to users. You can restore the remaining filegroups later.

With the mechanics of backing up and restoring under your belt, you're ready for a discussion of the theory behind backups. You need to know not only how but when to use each of these types of backups. In other words, you need to devise a viable backup strategy.

EXERCISE 11.11

Performing a Piecemeal Restore

1. Right-click the Sybex database in Object Explorer, point to Tasks, and select Back Up.

2. In the Backup dialog box, make sure Sybex is the selected database to back up and Backup Type is Full.

3. Under Backup Component, select Files and Filegroups.

4. In the Select Files and Filegroups dialog box, check the Sybex box, and click OK (notice that all the other boxes in the list are automatically checked for you).

5. Leave the default name in the Name box. In the Description box, type **Piecemeal Backup of Sybex**.

EXERCISE 11.11

6. Under Destination, make sure the AdvWorksFull device is the only one listed.

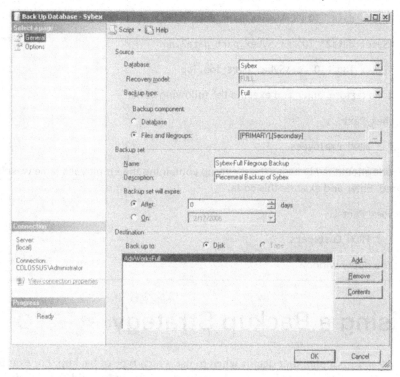

7. On the Options page, make sure Append to the Existing Backup Set is selected so you don't overwrite your existing backups.

8. On the Options tab, select Verify Backup When Finished.

9. Click OK to start the backup.

10. To perform a partial restore of the Sybex database to a new database named Sybex_part, execute the following code in a new query window:

```
RESTORE DATABASE Sybex_part

FILEGROUP = 'PRIMARY'

FROM DISK='C:\Program Files\

Microsoft SQL Server\MSSQL.1\MSSQL\

Backup\AdvWorksFull.bak'
```

EXERCISE 11.11

```
WITH FILE=6,RECOVERY,PARTIAL,

MOVE 'Sybex_data' TO 'C:\Sybex_part_data.mdf',

MOVE 'Sybex_data2' TO 'C:\Sybex_part_data2.ndf',

MOVE 'Sybex_log' TO 'c:\Sybex_part_log.log'
```

11. To test the restore, enter and execute the following code:

```
USE Sybex_Part

SELECT * FROM Employees
```

12. This code should fail because the filegroup containing the Employees table wasn't restored. Enter and execute this code:

```
USE Sybex_Part

SELECT * FROM Customers
```

13. Close the query window.

Devising a Backup Strategy

A *backup strategy* is a plan that details when to use which type of backup. For example, you could use only a full backup, a full with differential, or any other valid combination. Your challenge is to figure out which one is right for your environment. You'll now look at the pros and cons of each available strategy.

Planning for Full Backups Only

If you have a relatively small database, you can perform just full backups with no other type; but you need to understand what we mean by a "relatively small" database. When we're speaking of backups, the size of a database is relative to the speed of the backup medium. For example, a 200MB database is fairly small, but if you have an older tape drive that isn't capable of backing up a 200MB database overnight, you won't want to perform full backups on the tape drive every night. On the other hand, if you have a set of hardware capable of a 1GB backup in a few hours, you can consider a full backups–only strategy. We can't tell you what to do in every situation; we can only present the principles that govern what you should do.

The disadvantage of a full-only strategy is that it gives a comparatively slow backup when compared to other strategies. For example, if you perform a full backup every night on a

100MB database, you're (obviously) backing up 100MB every night. If you're using a differential backup with a full backup, you aren't backing up the entire 100MB every night.

The major advantage of a full-only strategy is that the restore process is faster than with other strategies, because it uses only one tape. For instance, if you perform a full backup every night and the database fails on Thursday, all you need to restore is the full backup from Wednesday night, using only one tape. In the same scenario (as you'll see), the other strategies take more time because you have more tapes from which to restore.

One other disadvantage of a full-only strategy involves the transaction log. As we discussed earlier in this chapter, the transaction log is cleared only when a transaction log backup is performed. With a full-only strategy, your transaction log is in danger of filling up and locking your users out of the database. You can avoid this problem in two ways. First, you can set the recovery model for the database to Simple, which instructs SQL Server to completely empty the log every time it writes to the database from the log (a process called *checkpointing*). This isn't the best solution, though; you'll lose up-to-the-minute recoverability because the latest transactions will be deleted every time the server checkpoints. If your database crashes, you can restore it only to the time of the last full backup.

Another option is to perform the full backup and, immediately afterward, perform a transaction log backup with the TRUNCATE_ONLY clause. This option frees space, but risks possible data loss. After the log is truncated by using either NO_LOG or TRUNCATE_ONLY, the changes recorded in the truncated portion of the log are not recoverable. Therefore, for recovery purposes, after using either of these options, you must immediately execute BACKUP DATABASE to take a full or differential database backup. We recommend that you do not use either of these options.

This option will be removed in a future version of SQL Server. Avoid using it in new development work, and plan to modify applications that currently use it.

The first step you should take in the event of any database failure is to use the NO_TRUNCATE option with the transaction log backup to save the orphaned log.

Planning for Full with Differential Backups

If your database is too large to perform a full backup every night, you may want to consider adding differentials to the strategy. A full/differential strategy provides a faster backup than full alone. With a full-only backup strategy, you're backing up the entire database every time you perform a backup. As shown in Figure 11.3, with a full/differential strategy, you're backing up only the changes made to the database since the last full backup, which is faster than backing up the whole database.

FIGURE 11.3 Differential backups are faster than full backups because they record only the changes to the database since the last full backup.

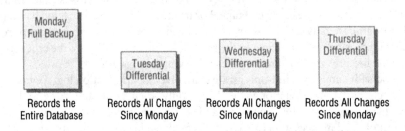

The major disadvantage of the full/differential strategy is that the restore process is slower than with the full-only strategy, because full/differential requires you to restore more backups. Suppose you perform a full backup on Monday night and differentials the rest of the week, and your database crashes on Wednesday. To return the database to a consistent state, you'll need to restore the full backup from Monday and the differential from Tuesday. If your database crashes on Thursday, you'll need to restore the backups from Monday and Wednesday. If it crashes on Friday, you'll need to restore the full backup from Monday and the differential from Thursday.

The only other disadvantage to be aware of is that differential backups don't clear the transaction log. If you opt for this method, you should clear the transaction log manually by backing up the transaction log.

Planning for Full with Transaction Log Backups

Another method to consider, regardless of whether your database is huge, is full/transaction. This method offers several advantages. First, it's the best method to keep your transaction logs clean, because this is the only type of backup that purges old transactions from your transaction logs.

Second, this method makes for a fast backup process. For example, you can perform a full backup on Monday and transaction log backups three or four times a day during the week. This is possible because SQL Server performs online backups, and transaction log backups are usually small and quick (your users should barely notice).

Transaction log backups are also the only type of backup that gives you point-in-time restore capability. "How often will I use that?" you may ask. If you have any people in your company who aren't perfect, you'll probably use this capability quite a bit, so it's best to have it when you need it.

The disadvantage of this strategy is that the restore process is a little slower than full alone or full/differential. This is because you'll have more backups to restore, and any time you add more work to the process, it gets slower. For instance, suppose you perform a full backup on Monday and transaction log backups three times a day (at 10 A.M., 2 P.M, and 6 P.M) throughout the week. If your database crashes on Tuesday at 3 P.M, you'll need to restore only the full backup from Monday and the transaction log backups from Tuesday at 10 A.M. and 2 P.M However, if your database crashes on Thursday at 3 P.M, you'll need to restore the full backup from Monday as well as all the transaction log backups made on Tuesday, Wednesday, and Thursday before the crash. So although this type of backup may have blinding speed, it involves a lengthy restore process. It may be better to combine all three types of backups.

Planning for Full, Differential, and Transaction Log Backups

If you combine all three types of backups, you get the best of all worlds. The backup and restore processes are still relatively fast, and you have the advantage of point-in-time restores as well. Suppose you perform a full backup on Monday, transaction log backups every four hours (10 A.M., 2 P.M, and 6 P.M) throughout the day during the week, and differential backups every night. If your database crashes at any time during the week, all you need to restore is the full backup from Monday, the differential backup from the night before, and the transaction log backups up to the point of the crash. This approach is nice, fast, and simple. However, these combinations do not work well for a monstrous VLDB; for that you need a filegroup backup.

Planning for Filegroup Backups

We discussed the mechanics of the filegroup backup earlier in this chapter, so you know they're designed to back up small chunks of the database at a time rather than the whole database all at once. This may come in handy, for example, with a 700GB database contained in three files in three separate filegroups. You can perform a full backup once per month and then back up one filegroup per week during the week. Every day, you perform transaction log backups for maximum recoverability.

Suppose the disk containing the third file of your database crashes. With the other backup strategies we discussed, you would need to restore the full backup first and then the other backups. With filegroup backups, you don't need to restore the full backup first (thank goodness). All you need to restore is the backup of the filegroup that failed and the transaction log backups that occurred after the filegroup was backed up. If you backed up your third filegroup on Wednesday and then it fails on Friday, you'll restore the filegroup backup from Wednesday and the transaction log backups from Thursday and Friday up to the point of the crash.

 SQL Server is fully capable of determining which transactions belong to each filegroup. When you restore the transaction log, SQL Server applies only the transactions that belong to the failed group.

Whew! Backups are a big chunk of information to assimilate, but they're important. Now you're ready for the next phase of administration and maintenance: maintaining the indexes on your databases.

Summary

In this chapter, we talked about how to back up and restore your databases. The first topic was backups. You have many reasons to back up data: natural disaster, hardware malfunction, and even people with malicious intent. If you perform regular backups, you can overcome these problems.

You can use four types of backups to help thwart the evils that could claim your data. First is the full backup, the basis of all other backups, which makes a copy of the entire database. Next, the differential backup grabs all the changes made to the database since the last full backup. The transaction log backup is useful for implementing a quick backup strategy, performing point-in-time restores, and clearing the transaction log on a periodic basis. Finally, the filegroup backup makes backups of small chunks of very large databases.

After learning how to back up data, you learned how to restore from those backups. First you performed a standard database restore, and then you performed the more advanced point-in-time and piecemeal restores.

Finally, we discussed how to create a backup strategy so that you have a better idea of what to back up and when to do it.

Case Study: Backups for the AlsoRann Company

You may remember from other chapters that AlsoRann started out kind of small, but the company grew over time, and so did some of its databases. One of the best examples is its Ecommerce database that stores product catalog data as well as order and customer information.

When we first started working with AlsoRann, the Ecommerce database was only about 300MB, and it didn't change a lot during the day. AlsoRann was concerned more with having a fast restore than it was with having a fast backup, so we implemented a backup strategy in which we ran a full backup every night. To keep the database reliable, though, we left the recovery model at Full and then cleared the transaction log by running a transaction log backup right after the full backup was done.

Within a few years, though, business was booming for AlsoRann, and its Ecommerce database grew with the company, to about 900MB in fact. To speed up data access and make the backups faster, we suggested splitting the database into three filegroups; the primary filegroup would hold the system tables, the CustomersFG filegroup would hold all the customer data and order information, and the CatalogFG filegroup would hold the product catalog data. With a larger database, the company was concerned with backup speed as well as restore speed. To accommodate this, we changed the backup strategy to a filegroup backup strategy with transaction log backups. We backed up on filegroup each night and performed transaction log backups every three hours during the day. This kept the database safe because we could always restore to the most current state, and the backups were as fast as they could be.

Exam Essentials

Understand backup devices.   SQL Server can store backups on hard disk or tape drive; however, because SQL Server doesn't know about the hardware attached to your machine, you have to tell it, which is what a backup device does. Backup devices are SQL Server objects that represent the available backup media that SQL Server can use for storing backups. These can point to hard disk or tape drives and can be permanent or temporary.

Know your backup types.   Four backup types are available in SQL Server 2005. Full backups back up the entire database. You must perform a full backup before any other type. Differential backups record only the changes made to the database since the last full backup. Transaction log backups back up only the log, which is the only backup that will clear the transaction log. You can use filegroup backups to back up the contents of one or more filegroups.

Know how to restore.   Restoring a database is simple if you are using the standard restore method; you just need to remember which files to restore. If you want to return a database to the most recent content, then you restore the last full backup, the last differential (if any exist), and all the transaction log backups after the last full or differential backup. You can also perform a point-in-time backup that allows you to restore up to a specific point in time, but only if you have performed transaction log backups. You can also perform a piecemeal restore, which allows you to restore the primary and any secondary filegroups to a new database.

Know how to devise a backup strategy.   You need to know how to use all this technology to protect your data, and to effectively do that, you must have a backup strategy. You need to know when to use each type of backup and how to use those backups to restore your data after a disaster.

Review Questions

1. One of your users has discovered some malicious updates to your data that occurred the day before at about 2 P.M How can you return the database to the state it was in just before the update occurred?

    A. Perform a full database restoration with point-in-time recovery.

    B. Perform a differential database restoration with point-in-time recovery.

    C. Perform a transaction log restoration with point-in-time recovery.

    D. You cannot return the database to the previous state.

2. You have a huge database, several hundred gigabytes in size, with the recovery model set to Full. With your current hardware, a full backup of this database takes 15 hours. You cannot have the backup running during working hours because you do not have the system resources available to support users while performing a backup. What backup strategy should you use?

    A. Perform a full backup every night.

    B. Perform a full backup and a transaction log backup every night.

    C. Perform a full backup every weekend and a differential backup every weeknight.

    D. Perform a full backup every weekend, a differential backup every weeknight, and a transaction log backup every night.

3. You have a VLDB with four filegroups (Primary, FG1, FG2, FG3) with the recovery model set to Full. You need to make sure the database is backed up in the shortest time possible while being able to restore in the shortest time possible. Which backup strategy should you use?

    A. Perform a full backup once a month, filegroup backups once a week, and transaction log backups throughout the week.

    B. Perform a full backup once a month, filegroup backups once a week, and differential backups throughout the week.

    C. Perform a full backup once a week and transaction log backups throughout the week.

    D. Perform a full backup every night.

4. You have a database named Sales that is set to use the Full recovery model. This is not a very big database—only about 200MB—so you perform a full backup of this database every night and transaction log backups every two hours during the day starting at 8 A.M. At 12:30 P.M on Tuesday you have a power surge, and the Sales database becomes corrupted. How should you restore the database to get to the most current state?

    A. Restore the full backup from Monday night.

    B. Restore the full backup from Monday night, then restore the 12 P.M transaction log backup, then restore the 10 A.M. transaction log backup, and finally restore the 8 A.M. transaction log backup.

    C. Restore the full backup from Monday night, then restore the 8 A.M. transaction log backup, then restore the 10 A.M. transaction log backup, and finally restore the 12 P.M transaction log backup.

    D. Restore the 8 A.M. transaction log backup, then restore the 10 A.M. transaction log backup, and finally restore the 12 P.M transaction log backup.

5. You have a medium-sized database named Sales that is set to use the Full recovery model. Your users insert, update, and delete data from this database frequently. You perform a full backup on this database every Saturday and differential backups Monday through Friday. One day your users start complaining they cannot update the database any longer. What should you do to get the database back up?

   A. Set the database to use the Simple recovery model.

   B. Set the database to use the Bulk-Logged recovery model.

   C. Back up the transaction log with NO RECOVERY.

   D. Back up the transaction log.

6. Your Sales database is very large, approximately 800GB. You have split this database into four filegroups: Primary, OrdersFG, CatalogFG, and CustomersFG. Each filegroup contains tables and indexes for a group of data; for example, the CatalogFG filegroup contains all the tables and indexes used for storing product catalog data. One of your satellite offices also has a Sales database, but it is not an exact duplicate of yours. However, that office needs a copy of the product catalog tables. How can you send them the product catalog data?

   A. Send them the last full backup of the database, and have them restore it on their server. Then they can copy the product catalog tables from your database to theirs.

   B. Send them the last full backup of your database, and have them do a piecemeal restore of the CatalogFG file group. Then they can copy the data from the new database to the existing database.

   C. Send them the last backup of your Primary and CatalogFG filegroups, and have them do a piecemeal restore to a new database. Then they can copy the data from the new database to the existing database.

   D. Send them the last backup of your CatalogFG filegroup, and have them do a piecemeal restore of the CatalogFG file group. Then they can copy the data from the new database to the existing database.

7. You have three backup devices (BD1, BD2, and BD3) that point to tape drives locally installed on your server. You perform a full backup of your Manufacturing database every night on both of these devices using a parallel striped backup. You have recently created a new, smaller database named Production that you need to back up every night. What should you do?

   A. Back up the Production database to BD1, BD2, and BD3 in a parallel striped backup.

   B. Back up the Production database to BD1 only.

   C. Back up the Production database to BD2 only.

   D. Back up the Production database to BD3 only.

8. You have a large database named Ecommerce that is divided into four filegroups.

   - The Primary filegroup contains only system tables.

   - The OrderTablesFG filegroup contains order information tables.

   - The OrderIdxFG filegroup contains indexes associated with the order information tables.

   - The CatalogFG filegroup contains product catalog information tables and associated indexes.

You need to devise a backup strategy. Which filegroups need to be backed up as a unit?

A. They can all be backed up individually.

B. The Primary and OrderIdxFG filegroups must be backed up as a unit.

C. The Primary, CatalogFG, and OrderTablesFG filegroups must be backed up as a unit.

D. The OrderTablesFG and OrderIdxFG filegroups must be backed up as a unit.

9. You have a huge database that is split up into five filegroups. Two of these filegroups are for archive data, and they are marked as read-only so they cannot accidentally be changed. The other three filegroups are for system tables and current data. You want to perform a full backup of your current data once a week, but you need to back up your archived data only once a month. You want the weekly full backup to be as fast as possible. What should you do?

A. Make the weekly backup a copy-only backup.

B. Make the weekly backup a partial backup.

C. Make the weekly backup a differential backup.

D. Make the weekly backup a piecemeal backup.

10. Your developers are working on a new database on the development system. They do not want to lose the work they are doing on the database, so they need to have it backed up regularly. They are not interested in keeping the data from the database, because it is merely test data; they are interested only in the schema and other database objects. They need to be able to insert new data in the database at all times for testing purposes. This database will never exceed 200MB in size. You also need to spend as little time as possible backing this database up. What backup strategy should you use?

A. Set the recovery model to Full, perform a full backup every night, and then immediately perform a transaction log backup with the TRUNCATE ONLY option.

B. Set the recovery model to Simple, perform a full backup every night, and then immediately perform a transaction log backup with the TRUNCATE ONLY option.

C. Set the recovery model to Simple, and perform a full backup every night.

D. Set the recovery model to Full, and perform a full backup every night.

11. You have a database named Manufacturing that is set to use the Full recovery model. You perform a full backup of the entire database once a week on Saturday. You perform a differential backup every night, Monday through Friday, and perform transaction log backups every two hours starting at 6 A.M. until 6 P.M On Wednesday at 11:15 A.M. your users start complaining they cannot get into the database. You verify the database is down. What order should you restore each backup to bring the database back online? (Choose all that apply, and place them in order.)

A. Restore the differential backup from Tuesday.

B. Restore the 10 A.M. transaction log backup.

C. Restore the 6 A.M. transaction log backup.

D. Restore the 8 A.M. transaction log backup.

E. Restore the full backup from last Saturday.

F. Restore the differential backup from Monday.

12. You have an Accounting database that you use to store payroll and employee information. Your home office has requested you send them a backup copy of this database so they can update their records. You need to send them this copy without affecting the backup strategy you are using. What should you do?

 A. Make a full backup.

 B. Make a copy-only backup.

 C. Make a partial backup.

 D. Make a differential backup.

13. You have a database named Ecommerce that contains product and order information for your company website, so it must be available at all times. How can you back the database up and still make it available to users?

 A. Run the backups with the ONLINE option.

 B. Run the backups using the ALLOW_ACCESS option.

 C. Create a copy-only backup every night, which allows users to access the database while it is being backed up.

 D. Just run your normal backups; nothing special is required.

14. You need to be able to back up your databases to a tape drive. The only tape drive you have is on another server on the network. How can you get SQL Server to use this remote tape drive as a backup device?

 A. Create the backup device using the NETWORKED option.

 B. Create the backup device using a Universal Naming Convention (UNC) path (\\server_name\tape_drive).

 C. Purchase third-party backup software capable of backing up a SQL Server database.

 D. There is no way to use a remote tape drive.

15. You need to be able to restore your Accounting database to any point in time in case an accounting error is saved to the database before it is caught. To accomplish this, you decide to set the recovery model of the database to Simple and perform full backups of the database every night and transaction log backups every three hours during the day. Is this the correct solution?

 A. This is the correct solution.

 B. No, the recovery model should be set to Full.

 C. No, you need to perform differential backups to use a point-in-time restore.

 D. No, you need to back up the transaction logs at least once an hour to use point-in-time restores.

16. You have a database that is approximately 400MB, and you need to be able to recover the database to a specific point in time. Which recovery model should you use for this database?

   A. Full

   B. Bulk-Logged

   C. Transactional

   D. Simple

17. You have a database, which is 350MB in size, that contains sales data. You need to back up this database; however, you do not have enough hard disk space on your server to accommodate the backup device, you do not have a tape drive in the server, and you have no budget for new hardware. What can you do?

   A. Create a backup device on a remote server that has enough disk space to accommodate the device. Use the new backup device to back up your database.

   B. Create a backup device that points to a tape drive on a remote server. Use the new backup device to back up your database.

   C. Stop the SQL Server services, copy the data and log files to a remote server, and then restart the SQL Server services.

   D. There is nothing you can do; you must obtain more hardware.

18. Your developers are ready to create several new tables and modify several existing tables on your production SQL Server so they can accommodate a new application they are nearly ready to release. They have a lot of changes, so they need to do this after-hours, during the same time frame when your backups are scheduled to run. What can you do to allow the developers to modify the databases while the backups are running?

   A. You do not need to do anything special; database modifications are allowed during a backup.

   B. Run a full backup with the DDL_ALLOWED option so the developers can make changes to the database.

   C. Set the database to the Simple recovery model before running your backups that night to allow the developers to make changes.

   D. There is no way to allow schema changes to the database during a backup; you'll need to reschedule the backup.

19. You need to make sure your HumanResources database is available at all times; if it crashes, you need to be able to return it to the most current state. This is a small database that does not change much during the day, so you have decided to perform a full backup every night. What should you do to keep the transaction log from filling to capacity?

   A. Set the recovery model to Full, and perform a transaction log backup every night immediately after the full backup.

   B. Set the recovery model to Simple, and perform a transaction log backup every night immediately after the full backup.

   C. Set the recovery model to Bulk-Logged, and perform a transaction log backup every night immediately after the full backup.

   D. Just set the recovery model to Simple; SQL Server will clear the log for you.

20. You have a database that is used to store customer information and is set to use the Full recovery model. You perform a full backup of the entire database once a week on Sunday. You perform a differential backup every night Monday through Saturday at 9 P.M and transaction log backups every hour starting at 6 A.M. until 6 P.M On Thursday at 8 A.M., as soon as you get to work, you find that the database has been down since 8 P.M Wednesday night. What order should you restore each backup to bring the database back online? (Choose all that apply, and place them in order.)

A. Restore the differential backup from Monday.

B. Restore the differential backup from Tuesday.

C. Restore the differential backup from Wednesday.

D. Restore each transaction log backup since the last differential backup.

E. Restore each transaction log backup since the last full backup.

F. Restore the full backup from last Sunday.

Answers to Review Questions

1. C. You can perform transaction log restorations up to a point in time. This means you can return the database to the state it was in just before the update.

2. D. You can't perform a full backup every night because it would still be running when users came in the next morning. You can perform a full backup on the weekend, though. You can perform differential backups during the week because they are much faster than full backups so they would be complete before users come in the next day. Also, because the recovery model is set to Full for this database, you must perform a regular transaction log backup, or the log will fill to capacity and lock out your users.

3. A. Performing a full backup once a month, filegroup backups every week, and transaction log backups every day is the fastest possible back up strategy for this database. This method gives you the fastest restore because you do not need to perform a restore of the full backup if one of the filegroups becomes corrupt; you restore the corrupt filegroup and restore all the transaction log backups recorded afterward. You do not need to perform differential backups with this backup strategy because they would be too slow to restore.

4. C. To return the database to its most current state, you have to restore the last full backup first and then restore each transaction log backup in ascending order (8 A.M. and then 10 A.M. and then 12 P.M). This will return the database to where you need it.

5. D. When a database is set to use the Full recovery model, only a transaction log backup will clear the log. If the log is not backed up, then it will fill to capacity, and users will not be able to perform updates. When this happens, the only step you can take to get the database back online is to back up the log with TRUNCATE ONLY.

6. C. The fastest way to do this with a backup/restore scenario is to send them the last backup of your Primary and CatalogFG filegroups, from which they can perform a piecemeal restore. You have to send them the Primary filegroup because piecemeal restores require it. You do not need to send the full backup because they do not need all the data.

7. A. Once several backup devices have been combined into a media set, then you cannot use them separately without losing all the data already recorded on them. To keep using the devices as a set, you have to perform a parallel striped backup on the new Production database.

8. D. When your database is configured such that one filegroup contains tables and its associated indexes are in a different filegroup, then those filegroups must be backed up as a single unit. Any other filegroups can be backed up individually.

9. B. A partial backup will back up only the Primary filegroup and all read-write filegroups. Any filegroups marked read-only will not be backed up, which makes a partial backup the fastest possible backup. Copy-only backups record the entire database but do not affect the transaction logs. Differential backups back up only the changes since the last full backup. Piecemeal backups do not exist; they are piecemeal restores.

10. C. With the recovery model set to Simple, the transaction log is truncated every time SQL Server writes the data from the log file to the database (called a *checkpoint*), so the log will never fill up even if you perform only full backups. Because your developers do not need to keep the data, you do not need to worry about keeping any part of the transaction log. So, setting the recovery model to Simple and performing a full backup every night will meet all your goals.

11. E, A, C, D, B. To get this database back online, you need to restore the last full backup first, and then you need to restore the last differential backup. You do not need to restore all the differential backups, only the most recent. Then restore the transaction logs to bring your database back up.

12. B. A copy-only backup is perfect for this situation because it is specifically designed to make a backup without affecting the logs, so it will not affect your backup strategy in any way. A partial backup will back up only the Primary filegroup and all read-write filegroups in a database, so it is not a good choice. Full and differential backups both affect the logs, and differential backups back up only the changes since the last full backup.

13. D. All backups in SQL Server 2005 are online backups; this means no matter what backup strategy you use, the database will be available for use. Also, the ONLINE and ALLOW_ACCESS options are not valid options for a backup.

14. C. The only way to use a remote tape drive is to purchase some third-party software that is capable of backing up a SQL Server database. You can't share a tape drive using a UNC path, and the NETWORKED option is not a valid option.

15. B. You can't back up the transaction log on a database when the recovery model is set to Simple because SQL Server clears the log every time it checkpoints the log. This means there is nothing in the log to back up. If you set the recovery model to Full, then this solution will work fine because there is no time constraint on how often you need to back up the logs to use point-in-time restores, and differential backups cannot be used to run a point-in-time restore.

16. A. The only recovery model that will allow you to back up enough of the log to do a point-in-time restore is the Full recovery model. Also, there is no transactional recovery model.

17. A. You can create a backup device that points to a share on a remote server and then back up the database to that remote device. You cannot point a backup device to a remote tape drive. Option C would technically work, but you don't need to go through all that hassle, Option D is a bad idea because you should always have a current backup of your databases.

18. D. You can't make schema changes during a backup no matter what type of backup you run or what recovery model the database is using, so you'll need to reschedule the backup. Also, DDL_ALLOWED is not a valid option.

19. A. It is true you could set the recovery model to Simple and have SQL Server clear the log on every checkpoint, but then you would not be able to restore the database to the most current state in the event of a crash. The best way to keep the log clear and have complete recoverability is to perform a transaction log backup with the TRUNCATE_ONLY option immediately after the full backup.

20. F, B, D. To get this database back online, you need to restore the last full backup first, and then you need to restore the last differential backup. Since the database went down at 8 P.M and you ran the backup at 9 P.M, you cannot use the Wednesday backup because it didn't happen. Finally, you need to restore the transaction log backups in order since the last differential backup, not the last full backup.

Chapter

12

Achieving High Availability through Replication

MICROSOFT EXAM OBJECTIVES COVERED IN THIS CHAPTER:

✓ **Manage replication.**

- Distinguish between replication types.
- Configure a publisher, a distributor, and a subscriber.
- Configure replication security.
- Configure conflict resolution settings for merge replication.
- Monitor replication.
- Improve replication performance.
- Plan for, stop, and restart recovery procedures.

Replication allows for the distribution of your SQL Server 2005 data to other database engines. This includes both SQL Server 2005 databases and non–SQL Server databases such as Oracle and IBM's DB2 database. This chapter covers a lot of ground regarding replication. We will first look at the publisher/subscriber metaphor that has been implemented in SQL Server 2005's replication strategy. This metaphor includes publishers, distributors, and subscribers and goes a step further by including publications and articles.

We'll discuss the factors that affect replication—transactional consistency, latency, and site autonomy influence your distribution choice, whether it is transactional, merge, or something else. We'll also cover the way in which replication actually works with the various replication agents to move your data from a publisher through the distributor and on to the subscribers.

The administrative concerns involved with replication include security issues, data definition issues, non–SQL Server 2005 database issues, and other SQL Server configuration issues. You can choose from several replication scenarios to implement. These scenarios are important because each scenario has specific advantages and disadvantages for a particular business situation that the replication strategy must address.

In addition, we'll detail how to install and run replication on your SQL Server 2005 computer. We will walk through the process of setting up a distributor, a publisher, and a subscriber. We will then create a publication, subscribe to it, and check whether replication is working properly.

Finally, we'll provide some optimization and troubleshooting techniques specific to replication tasks.

Introducing Replication

You use *replication* to put copies of the same data at different locations throughout the enterprise. You might want to replicate your data for several reasons, but the following are among the most common:

- To move data closer to the user
- To reduce locking conflicts when multiple sites want to work with the same data
- To allow site autonomy so each location can set up its own rules and procedures for working with its copy of the data
- To remove the impact of read-intensive operations such as report generation and ad hoc query processing from the OLTP database

SQL Server 2005 uses two strategies for replication: replication itself and distributed transactions. Whichever strategy you use, the copies of the data are current and consistent. You can also use both strategies in the same environment.

The main difference between replication and distributed transactions is in the timing. With distributed transactions, your data is 100 percent synchronized 100 percent of the time. When you use replication, some latency is involved. It may be as little as a few seconds or as long as several days or even weeks. Distributed transactions require that the replicated databases be connected at all times. If they are not, then the distributed transactions will fail. Replication does not have this requirement.

Introducing the Publisher/Subscriber Metaphor

SQL Server 2005 uses a publisher/subscriber metaphor to describe and implement replication. Your database can play different roles as part of the replication scenario: it can be a publisher, subscriber, distributor, or any combination of these. When you publish data, you do it in the form of an article, which is stored in a publication. Here are the key terms used as part of the publisher/subscriber metaphor:

Publisher   The *publisher* is the source database where replication begins. It makes data available for replication.

Subscriber   The *subscriber* is the destination database where replication ends. It either receives a snapshot of all the published data or applies transactions that have been replicated to itself.

Distributor   The *distributor* is the intermediary between the publisher and subscriber. It receives published transactions or snapshots and then stores and forwards these publications to the subscribers.

Publication   The *publication* is the storage container for different articles. A subscriber can subscribe to an individual article or an entire publication.

Article   An *article* is the data, transactions, or stored procedures that are stored within a publication. This is the actual information that is going to be replicated.

Two-phase commit   *Two-phase commit* (sometimes referred to as 2PC) is a form of replication in which modifications made to the publishing database are made at the subscription database at the same time. This is handled through the use of distributed transactions. As with any transaction, either all statements commit successfully or all modifications are rolled back. Two-phase commit uses the Microsoft DTC to accomplish its tasks. The DTC implements the functionality of a portion of the Microsoft Transaction Server. In this chapter, we will focus on replication as opposed to two-phase commits.

A publisher can publish data to one or more distributors. A subscriber can subscribe through one or more distributors. A distributor can have one or more publishers and subscribers.

Introducing Articles

An article is data in a table. The data can be the entire table or just a subset of the data in the table. Your articles need to be bundled into one or more publications in order for them to be distributed to the subscribers. When you want to publish a subset of data in a table, you must specify some type of partitioning, either vertical or horizontal.

With a vertical partition, you select specific columns from your table. In a horizontal partition, you select only specific rows of data from the table. Figure 12.1 shows an example of both a vertical partition and a horizontal partition. Here, the horizontal partition might be when you want to make specific rows of data available to different regions. More specifically, you could create three separate articles. One article would be horizontally partitioned based on region 1. The next article would be horizontally partitioned on region 2, and the third would be horizontally partitioned on region 3. Each region could then subscribe to only its regional data.

FIGURE 12.1   You can create articles based on subsets of your data.

Horizontal Partition

ReCode	EmpID	Q1	Q2	Q3
1	5	40.1	39.8	37.7
1	7	28.7	33.5	38.2
1	8	39.9	42.2	48.1
1	13	28.8	32.8	33.7

Vertical Partition

ReCode	EmpID	Q1	Q2	Q3
2	2		44.6	
1	5		39.8	
2	3		41.7	
3	11		28.8	
1	7		33.5	
1	8		42.2	
3	22		45.5	
1	13		32.8	

Introducing Publications

Articles must be stored in a publication, which is the basis for your subscriptions. When you create a subscription, you are actually subscribing to an entire publication; however, you can read individual articles. Referential integrity is maintained within your publication because all articles in a publication are updated at the same time.

In SQL Server 2005, you can publish to non–Microsoft SQL Server computers. The replicated data does not need to be in the same sort order or be the same datatype. Although it is possible to replicate to different sort orders and datatypes, we do not recommend it.

Understanding Replication Factors and Distribution Types

Before you can choose a distribution type, you should understand the factors that influence your decision. The three main items to consider are autonomy, latency, and transactional consistency:

Autonomy   This refers to how much independence you want to give each subscriber with regard to the replicated data. Will the replicated data be considered read-only? How long will the data at a subscriber be valid? How often do you need to connect to the distributor to download more data?

Latency   This refers to how often your data will be updated. Does it need to be in synchronization at all times? Is every minute enough? What if you are a salesperson on the road who dials in to the office once a day to update your data? Is this good enough?

Transactional consistency   Although several types of replication exist, the most common method is to move transactions from the publisher through the distributor and on to the subscriber. Transactional consistency comes into play here. Do all the transactions that are stored need to be applied at the same time and in order? What happens if there is a delay in the processing?

Once you understand these factors, you need to start asking yourself the following questions, after which you can decide on a distribution type:

- What am I going to publish? Will it be all the data in a table, or will I partition information?
- Who has access to my publications? Are these subscribers connected or dial-up users?
- Will subscribers be able to update my data, or is their information considered read-only?
- How often should I synchronize my publishers and subscribers?
- How fast is my network? Can subscribers be connected at all times? How much traffic is there on my network?

Each of the several types of distribution you can use has different levels of autonomy, transactional consistency, and latency involved. You can choose from three basic types: snapshot replication, transactional replication, and merge replication.

When you factor in latency, autonomy, and consistency, you end up with seven different distribution types:

- Distributed transactions
- Transactional replication
- Transactional replication with immediate updating subscribers
- Snapshot replication
- Snapshot replication with immediate updating subscribers
- Merge replication
- Queued updating

As shown in Figure 12.2, distributed transactions have the least amount of latency and autonomy, but they have the highest level of consistency. Merge replication has the highest amount of latency and autonomy and a lower level of consistency.

FIGURE 12.2   Distribution types

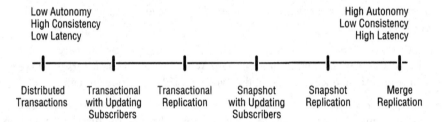

Using Distributed Transactions

When you use distributed transactions (also called *two-phase commit*, or 2PC) to replicate your data, you have almost no autonomy or latency, but you do have guaranteed transactional consistency. With 2PC, either all changes are made at the same time or none of the changes are made. Remember that all the affected subscribers must be in contact with the publisher at all times. This type of distribution is most useful when subscribers must have real-time data, such as in a reservation system.

For example, think of a cruise line that has only so many rooms of a particular type available. If someone in Dallas wants the captain's suite and someone in California also wants the captain's suite, the first one to book the room will get it. The other booking won't be allowed because that location will immediately show that the room is already booked.

Using Transactional Replication

When you use the transactional replication distribution method, transactions are gathered from the publishers and stored in the distribution database. Subscribers then receive these transactions and must work with the data as if it were read-only. This is because any changes made to their local copy of the data might prohibit new transactions from being applied properly, which would destroy the transactional consistency.

Each site, however, has some limited autonomy. You can introduce some latency because the subscribers don't have to be in contact at all times. Transactional consistency can be maintained as long as the subscribed data remains unchanged by the subscribers.

The advantages to this approach include that transactions are relatively small items to move through the system (unlike snapshot replication, which we will look at shortly). The main disadvantage of using transactional replication is that subscribers must treat the data as read-only.

Use this distribution method when subscribers can treat their data as read-only and need the updated information with a minimal amount of latency.

This type of replication would be useful in an order-processing/distribution system with several locations where orders are taken. Each of the order locations would be a publisher, and the published orders could then be replicated to a subscription database at your central warehouse. The central warehouse could then accept the orders, fill them, and ship them.

Using Transactional Replication with Immediate Updating Subscribers

When you use transactional replication with immediate updating subscribers, you are gaining site autonomy, minimizing latency, and keeping transactional consistency. This (in most cases) would be considered the best possible solution.

When you implement transactional replication with immediate updating subscribers, you are essentially working with all the tenets of transactional replication. The major difference is that when you change the subscription data, 2PC changes the publishing database as well. In this fashion, your local subscriber is updated at the same time as the publisher. Other subscribers will have your changes downloaded to them at their next synchronization.

This scenario can be useful for a reservation system that needs to be updated frequently but does not need total synchronization. Let's use a library as an example here. You want to reserve a book about SQL Server 2005. You go to the computer, look up the book you want to reserve, and find that one copy is currently available at the library. When you try to reserve the book, however, you might find that the data isn't 100 percent up-to-date and the book has already been checked out. In this example, when you try to reserve your book, the subscriber automatically runs a 2PC to the publisher. At the publisher, someone has already checked out the last copy, and therefore the update fails. At the next synchronization, your subscriber will be updated with the news that the last copy has been checked out.

Using Snapshot Replication

When you use snapshot replication as your distribution method, you are actually moving an entire copy of the published items through the distributor and on to the subscribers. This type of replication allows for a high level of both site autonomy and transactional consistency because all records are going to be copied from the publisher and because the local copy of the data will be overwritten at the next synchronization. Latency may be a bit higher because you probably will not move an entire snapshot every few minutes.

Online Analytical Processing (OLAP) servers are prime candidates for this type of replication. The data at each subscriber is considered read-only and doesn't have to be 100 percent in synchronization all the time. This allows your IT departments to run their reporting and ad hoc queries on reasonably fresh data without affecting the OLTP server (which is doing all of the order-processing work).

Keep in mind that most people who run ad hoc queries generally don't modify the data. They are looking for historical information such as how many widgets they sold, so the data that is a few hours or even a few days old will generally not make a difference to the results returned by the queries.

Using Snapshot Replication with Immediate Updating Subscribers

The initial portion of this distribution style works just as in snapshot replication, and in addition, it gives the subscriber the ability to update the publisher with new information. The updates use the 2PC protocol as described previously.

This maintains a high level of site autonomy, a high level of transactional consistency, and a moderate level of latency. The data may be downloaded to the subscriber only once a day, but the publisher must first approve any updates the subscriber tries to make to the data.

This type of distribution is useful when you have read-only data that needs to be updated infrequently. If your data needs to be updated often, we suggest you use transactional replication with immediate updating subscribers.

Snapshot replication might be useful when auditing your database, downloading portions of the data, and then double-checking that everything is being updated properly. You could then quickly fix the occasional mistake, and auditing could continue.

Using Merge Replication

Merge replication provides the highest amount of site autonomy, the highest latency, and the lowest level of transactional consistency. Merge replication allows each subscriber to make changes to their local copy of the data. At some point, these changes are merged with those made by other subscribers as well as changes made at the publisher. Ultimately, all sites receive the updates from all other sites. This is known as *convergence*; that is, all changes from all sites converge and are redistributed so that all sites have the same changes.

Transactional consistency is nearly nonexistent here because different sites may all be making changes to the same data, resulting in conflicts. SQL Server 2005 will automatically choose a particular change over another change and then converge that data. To simplify, sooner or later, all sites will have the same copy of the data, but that data may not necessarily be what you want. For example, subscriber A makes changes to record 100. Subscriber B also makes changes to record 100. Although this doesn't sound too bad, suppose the changes that subscriber A made to record 100 are because of changes that were made to record 50. If subscriber B doesn't have the same data in record 50, then subscriber B will make a different decision. Obviously, this can be incredibly complex.

You might wonder why anyone would want to use merge replication. There are many reasons to use it, and with some careful planning you can make merge replication work to your advantage. You can modify triggers to determine which record is the correct record to use. The default rule when records are changed at multiple sites is to take the changes based on a site priority, converge the results, and then send them. The exception to this general rule occurs when the main database as well as all the user databases are changed. In this case, the user changes are applied first, and then the main database changes are applied. For example, say you have a central server that you call Main, and you have 20 salespeople who are using merge replication. If one of your salespeople modifies record 25 and you modify record 25 at the Main server, when the records are converged, the user changes will first be placed in the Main server, and then the Main server changes will overwrite them.

If you design your publishers and subscribers to minimize conflicts, merge replication can be advantageous. Look at the highway patrol, for example. A patrol car might pull over a car and write the driver a ticket for speeding. At the end of the day, that data is merged with data from other officers who have also written tickets. The data is then converged back to all the different squad cars' computers, and now all the police know who to watch for on the roads.

Using Queued Updating

With transactional and snapshot replication, you can also configure queued updating. Like the immediate updating subscribers option, this gives your users the ability to make changes to the subscription database, but unlike immediate updating subscribers, queued updating will store changes until the publisher can be contacted.

This can be extremely useful in networks where you have subscribers who are not always connected or the connection is unreliable. Here is how it works:

1. Updates made on the subscribers are captured by triggers on the subscribing tables and stored in the storage queue.

2. The updates are stored in a table named MSreplication_queue in the subscription database. These messages are automatically sent to the distributor when it becomes available.

3. The queue reader agent applies the changes to the publication.

4. Any conflicts are detected and resolved according to a conflict resolution policy that is defined when the publication is created.

5. Changes made at the publisher are applied to all remaining subscribers.

Here are some things to keep in mind if you plan to use queued updating:

- INSERT statements must include a column list.

- Subscribers using immediate or queued updating cannot republish at the subscriber.

- Once a publication is configured to use queued updating, the option cannot be removed (though subscribers do not need to use it). To remove the option, you must delete and re-create the publication.

- You cannot use transformable subscriptions with queued updating. The Transform Published Data page of the Create Publication Wizard will not be displayed.

- Only SQL Server 2000 and higher servers can subscribe using queued updating.

Understanding Replication Internals

Understanding how the transactions or snapshots are handled is essential to a full understanding of how SQL Server 2005 implements replication.

When you set up your subscribers, you can create either pull or push subscriptions. *Push subscriptions* help centralize your administrative duties because the subscription itself is stored on the distribution server. This allows the publisher to determine what data is in the subscription and when that subscription will be synchronized. In other words, the data can be pushed to the subscribers based on the publisher's schedule. Push subscriptions are most useful if a subscriber needs to be updated whenever a change occurs at the publisher. The publisher knows when the modification takes place, so it can immediately push those changes to the subscribers.

Pull subscriptions are configured and maintained at each subscriber. The subscribers will administer the synchronization schedules and can pull changes whenever they consider it necessary. This type of subscriber also relieves the distribution server of some of the overhead of processing. Pull subscriptions are also useful in situations in which security is not a primary issue. In fact, you can set up pull subscriptions to allow anonymous connections, including pull subscribers residing on the Internet.

 Ordinarily, non–SQL Server databases such as DB2 must use push subscriptions. If you have a real need to pull with another database system, you can write your own custom program using the Replication Management Objects (RMO) programming interface.

In either a push environment or a pull environment, five replication agents handle the tasks of moving data from the publisher to the distributor and then on to the subscribers. The location of the particular agent depends upon the type of replication (push or pull) you are using:

Logreader agent Located on the distribution server, the logreader's job is to monitor the transaction logs of published databases that are using this distributor. When the logreader agent finds a transaction, it moves the transaction to the distribution database on the distributor;

transactions are stored and then forwarded to the subscribers by the distribution agent for transactional and snapshot replication or by the merge agent for merge replication.

Distribution agent   The distribution agent is responsible for moving the stored transactions from the distributor to the subscribers.

Snapshot agent   This agent, which is also used for snapshot replication, is responsible for copying the schema and data from the publisher to the subscriber. Before any type of replication can begin, a copy of the data must reside on each subscriber. With this baseline established, transactions can then be applied at each subscriber, and transactional consistency can be maintained.

Merge agent   The merge agent is responsible for converging records from multiple sites and then redistributing the converged records back to the subscribers.

Queue reader agent   The queue reader agent runs on the distributor and is responsible for reading messages from the queue on the subscribers and applying them to the appropriate publication. It is used only with queued updating publications and subscribers.

You will now see how these different agents work in concert to create the different distribution types.

You do not have to choose a single type of distribution for all your subscribers. Each subscriber can implement a different type of data distribution.

Remote Agent Activation allows you to run a distribution or merge agent on one machine and activate it from another. It can save resources on your servers in a heavy replication environment.

Understanding Merge Replication

When you use merge replication, the merge agent can be centrally located on the distributor, or it can reside on every subscriber involved in the merge replication process. When you have implemented push replication, the merge agent will reside on the distributor. In a pull scenario, the merge agent is on every subscriber.

Walking through the Merge Process

The following steps outline the merge process and how each agent interacts with the other agents:

1.   As shown in Figure 12.3, the snapshot agent that resides on the distribution server takes an initial snapshot of the data and moves it to the subscribers. This move takes place through the `Distribution` working folder. The folder is just a holding area for the snapshot data before it is moved to the subscriber. As stated earlier, you must do this first so you can apply later transactions.

FIGURE 12.3 How the merge replication process works

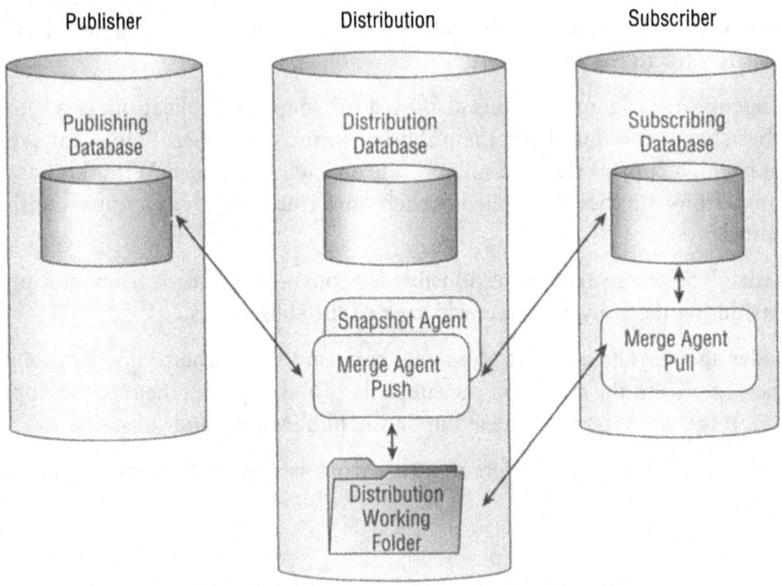

Publisher | Distribution | Subscriber

Publishing Database

Distribution Database

Subscribing Database

Snapshot Agent

Merge Agent Push

Merge Agent Pull

Distribution Working Folder

Subscribers must have the appropriate permissions to access the Distribution working folder on the distribution server.

2. Replication can now begin.

3. The merge agent (wherever it resides) will take modifications from the publishers and apply them to the subscribers.

4. The merge agent will also take modifications from the subscribers and apply them to the publishers.

5. The merge agent will gather any merge conflicts and resolve them by using triggers. Merge information will be stored in tables at the distributor. This allows you to track data lineage.

To track these changes, SQL Server adds some new tables to the publication and subscription databases. The most important of these is the MSmerge_contents table, which is used to track changes to the replicated table as well as possible conflicts. SQL Server also creates triggers on the publishing and subscription servers used for merge replication. These triggers are automatically invoked when changes are made at either of these locations. Information about the changes is stored in the database system tables on the distribution server. With this change information, SQL Server can track the lineage or history of changes made to a particular row of data.

Merge replication is most useful in situations in which there will be few conflicts. A horizontally partitioned table based on a region code or some other
ID is best suited to merge replication.

Performing Conflict Resolution in Merge Replication

Performing updates to the same records at multiple locations causes conflicts. To resolve these
conflicts, SQL Server 2005 uses the MSmerge_contents table and some settings from the publication itself.

When you first create a merge publication, you can choose from three levels of conflict resolution tracking in a merge publication:

Row-level tracking In row-level tracking, any change to an entire row on multiple subscribers is considered a conflict. If one subscriber modifies data in ColA and another modifies data
in ColB on the same row, then SQL Server considers this a conflict.

Column-level tracking In column-level tracking, any change to a single column on multiple
subscribers is considered a conflict. If one subscriber modifies data in ColA and another modifies data in ColB on the same row, it is not viewed as a conflict. However, if they both modify
ColA on the same row, then SQL Server considers this a conflict.

Logical record-level tracking This is new to SQL Server 2005. Using a JOIN statement, you
can create logical records to replicate. This means you can combine data from multiple tables
to replicate as a single, logical table. Using this level of conflict tracking tells SQL Server that
if users at multiple subscribers modify the same data in any of the joined tables, then there is
a possible conflict.

When the publication is created, changes to the data are tracked in the MSmerge_contents
table. If you are using record-level tracking, then the metadata about the changes are stored
in the lineage column; if you are using column-level tracking, then the COLV1 column is also
used. Using this lineage, the merge agent evaluates the current values for a record or column
and the new values to determine whether a conflict exists. If a conflict does exist, SQL Server
considers two more important factors before resolving it.

First, when you create a subscription to the publication, you can also set the priority for the
subscription. When there is a conflict, subscribers with higher priority win out over subscribers with lower priority, and the higher-priority change is replicated to all subscribers. The
lower-priority change is logged to the MSmerge_conflicts_info table and, if there is an INSERT
or UPDATE conflict, the conflict_*publication_article* table.

Second, you have a choice of resolvers to use when creating a new publication. If you use
the default resolver, then SQL Server will automatically resolve the conflict, apply the winning
changes to all subscribers, and notify you of a conflict. If you choose a manual resolver, then
you will have to manually choose the winning changes and apply them yourself. The manual
option works best only if you have a complex merge replication scenario that requires complex business logic.

When you begin to customize the conflict resolution process, we suggest you store both the record that is converged and the conflicting records that were not converged. This allows you to manually test and optimize your triggers. Note that covering how to create and modify triggers is beyond the scope of this book. For more information, see the SQL Server Books Online or *Mastering SQL Server 2005* (Sybex, 2006).

Understanding Snapshot Replication

When you use snapshot replication, an entire copy of the publication is moved from the publisher to the subscriber. Everything on the subscriber database is overwritten, allowing for autonomy as well as transactional consistency because all changes are made at once. Latency can be high for this type of replication if you want it to be. You can schedule your refreshes when and as often as you want (we have found that this normally occurs once a day, at off-peak hours). Keep in mind that snapshot replication occurs on demand. This means no data is transferred from the publisher to the distributor until a subscriber is ready to receive it. The snapshot then moves straight through. Status information is stored in the distribution database; however, the snapshot agent and the distribution agent do all their work at the time the snapshot is initiated.

When you use snapshot replication, there is no merge agent. Snapshot replication uses the distribution agent. If you are using a pull replication, the distribution agent resides on the subscription server. If you are doing a push replication, the agent resides on the distributor. When used in a push scenario, snapshot replication consumes a large amount of overhead on the distribution server. We suggest that most snapshot subscribers use a pull scenario at regularly scheduled intervals. The following steps (see Figure 12.4) outline the snapshot replication process:

1. The snapshot agent reads the published article and then creates the table schema and data in the `Distribution` working folder.
2. The distribution agent creates the schema on the subscriber.
3. The distribution agent moves the data into the newly created tables on the subscriber.
4. Any indexes that were used are re-created on the newly synchronized subscription database.

This works in the same fashion when you are using snapshot replication with immediate updating subscribers. The only difference is that the subscriber will use a two-phase commit to update both the subscription database and the publishing database at the same time. During the next refresh, all subscribers will receive a copy of the modified data.

Understanding Transactional Replication

When you use transactional replication, only the changes (transactions) made to the data are moved. Before these transactions can be applied at a subscriber; however, the subscriber must have a copy of the data as a base. Because of its speed and its relatively low overhead on the distribution server, transactional replication is currently the most often used form of replication. Generally, data on the subscriber is treated as read-only, unless you are implementing transactional replication with immediate updating subscribers. Because the transactions are so small, this type of replication is often set up to run continuously. Every time a change is made at the publisher, it is automatically applied to the subscriber, generally within one minute.

When you use transactional replication, you don't need the merge agent. The snapshot agent must still run at least once; it uses the distribution agent to move the initial snapshot from the publisher to the subscriber. You also use the logreader agent when using transactional replication. The logreader agent looks for transactions in published databases and moves those transactions to the distribution database. The following steps (see Figure 12.5) outline the transactional replication process:

1. The logreader agent reads the published article and then creates the schema on the subscriber and bulk copies the snapshot over to the subscriber. (This happens only when the subscription is created or re-created.)

2. The logreader agent scans the transaction logs of databases marked for publishing. When it finds an appropriate transaction, it copies the transaction to the distribution database. The distribution database will store the transaction for a configurable length of time.

3. The distribution agent will then apply those transactions to the subscribers at the next synchronization. The subscriber then runs the sp_repldone system stored procedure on the distribution database. This marks the newly replicated transactions stored on the distributor in the MSrepl_commands table as completed.

4. When the next distribution cleanup task executes, the marked transactions are truncated from the distribution server.

FIGURE 12.4   The snapshot replication process

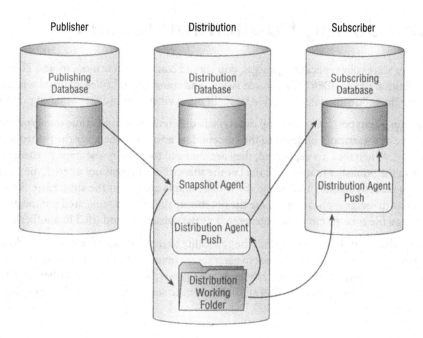

FIGURE 12.5   The transactional replication process

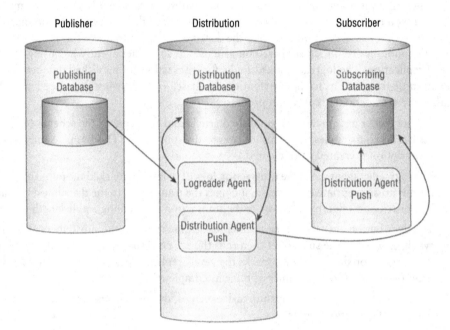

Considering Publication Issues

Before you start your replication process, you should consider a few more topics. This includes data definition issues, IDENTITY column issues, and some general rules involved when publishing. Keep the following data definition items in mind when you are preparing to publish data:

Timestamp datatypes   A timestamp datatype is different than a datetime datatype. Time stamps are automatically updated to the current date and time whenever the record is inserted or updated. When they are replicated, they are changed to a binary datatype to ensure that the data from the publisher matches the data at the subscriber. If it was not altered, the time stamp will automatically update itself when the transaction is applied at the subscriber. This is the opposite with merge replication, where the timestamp datatype is replicated but the data is not. This allows the time stamp to be regenerated at the subscriber and used in conflict resolution.

Identity values   SQL Server 2005 has the capability to replicate identity values. To do this, you must assign a range of identity values to each server involved in the replication at the time the publication is created (for example, the publisher gets 1,000–2,005; subscriber A gets 2,001–3,000; and subscriber B gets 3,001–4,000). When each server runs out of identity values, a new range is automatically assigned.

User-defined datatypes   If you have created your own user-defined datatypes on the publishing server, you must also create those same datatypes on the subscriptions servers if you want to replicate that particular column of data.

Not for replication   Most objects in the database can be created using the NOT FOR REPLICATION option, which prevents the object from being replicated. For example, if you have a constraint on a table that you do not want to be replicated to subscribers, then you would create the constraint using NOT FOR REPLICATION, and it would never be replicated.

You should keep the following publishing restrictions in mind as well:

- If you are not using snapshot replication, your replicated tables must have a primary key to ensure transactional integrity.

- Publications cannot span multiple databases. All articles in a publication must be derived from a single database.

- Varchar(max), nvarchar(max), and varbinary(max) binary large objects (BLOBs) are not replicated when you use transactional or merge replication. Because of their size, these objects must be refreshed by running a snapshot. What will be replicated is the 16-byte pointer to their storage location within the publishing database.

- You cannot replicate from the master, model, MSDB, or tempdb databases.

Considering Distributor Issues

Here are some tips to keep in mind when selecting a machine to be the distributor:

- Ensure you have enough hard disk space for the Distribution working folder and the distribution database.

- You must manage the distribution database's transaction log carefully. If that log fills to capacity, replication will no longer run, which can adversely affect your publishing databases as well.

- The distribution database will store all transactions from the publisher to the subscriber. It will also track when those transactions were applied.

- Snapshots and merge data are stored in the Distribution working folder.

- Be aware of the size and number of articles being published.

- Text, ntext, and image datatypes are replicated only when you use a snapshot.

- A higher degree of latency can significantly increase your storage space requirements.

- Know how many transactions per synchronization cycle there are. For example, if you modify 8,000 records between synchronizations, you will have 8,000 rows of data stored on the distributor.

Introducing Replication Models

You can use one of several models when you implement replication:

- Central publisher/central distributor
- Remote distribution
- Central subscriber/multiple publishers
- Multiple publishers/multiple subscribers

You'll now look more closely at each of these and see what business situations they most accurately represent.

Introducing Central Publisher/Central Distributor

As shown in Figure 12.6, both the publishing database and the distribution database are on the same SQL Server system. This configuration is useful when modeling replication strategies for the following business scenarios:

- Asynchronous order processing during communication outages
- Distribution of price lists, customer lists, vendor lists, and so on
- Removal of administrative activities from the OLTP environment
- Establishment of executive information systems

FIGURE 12.6 The central publisher model

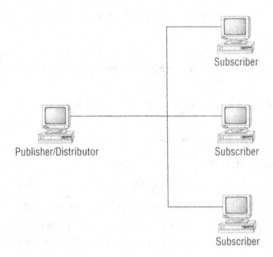

One of the most important aspects of the central publisher model is the ability to move data to a separate SQL Server system. This allows the publishing server to continue handling online transaction processing duties without having to absorb the impact of the ad hoc queries generally found in IT departments.

You can use any type of replication here—transactional, merge, or snapshot. If you do not have to update BLOB objects such as text, ntext, and image datatypes, we suggest you use transactional replication. IT departments generally don't need to make changes to the subscribed data.

> You can further reduce the impact of replication on your OLTP server by implementing pull subscriptions. This will force the distribution agent to run on each subscriber rather than on the OLTP publishing server.

Introducing Remote Distribution

In this model, you remove the impact of the distribution process from your OLTP server, which gives you the best possible speed on the OLTP server. This model is useful in situations in which you need the optimal performance from your OLTP server. As discussed earlier, a single distribution server can work with multiple distributors and multiple subscribers. Figure 12.7 shows a representation of this strategy.

This calls for transactional replication and minimizing the impact of replication on the publishing database. By moving just transactions rather than moving snapshots or attempting to merge data at the publisher, you can gain the most possible speed and have the lowest impact on the publisher.

FIGURE 12.7   The remote distribution model

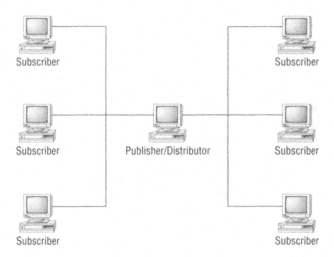

Introducing Central Subscriber/Multiple Publishers

The central subscriber model shown in Figure 12.8 is useful in the following situations:

- Roll-up reporting

- Local warehouse inventory management

- Local customer order processing

You need to keep several issues in mind when you attempt to use this model. Because multiple publishers are writing to a single table in the database, you must take some precautions to ensure that referential integrity is maintained. If your New York office sent an order with a key of 1000 and your Milwaukee office also sent an order with a key of 1000, you would have two records with the same primary key. You could get bad data in your database because the primary key is designed to guarantee the uniqueness of each record. In this situation, only one of those records would post.

To make sure this doesn't become a problem, implement a composite primary key using the original order ID number along with a location-specific code. You could, for example, give New York a location code of NY and the Milwaukee branch a location code of MW. This way, the new composite keys would be NY1000 and MW1000. There would be no more conflicting records, and both orders would be filled from the Denver offices.

This scenario is especially suited to transactional replication because the data at the Denver site is really read-only. Snapshot replication wouldn't work here because that would overwrite everyone else's data. You could use merge replication if the other locations needed to be able to see all the orders placed.

FIGURE 12.8 The central subscriber model

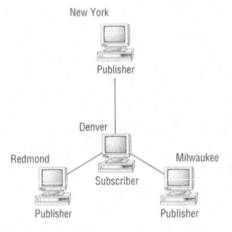

Introducing Multiple Publishers/Multiple Subscribers

Use this model when you need to maintain a single table on multiple servers. Each server subscribes to the table and also publishes the table to other servers. This model can be particularly useful in the following business situations:

- Reservations systems
- Regional order-processing systems
- Multiple warehouse implementations

Think of a regional order-processing system, as shown in Figure 12.9. Suppose you place an order on Monday and want to check on that order on Tuesday. When you call the company, you may be routed to any of several regional order-processing centers. Each of these centers should have a copy of your order so you can go over the order with a salesperson.

We suggest you use transactional replication for this scenario, using some type of region code (as described in the central subscriber/multiple publishers scenario). Each order-processing center should publish only its own data, but it should subscribe to data being published by the other publishers. In addition, each location should update only the data it owns. This scenario is also a good candidate for the transactional replication with an updating subscriber model. In this case, each center could update data owned by another center; however, this update would take place at both servers and therefore maintain transactional consistency.

A variation of this would be central publisher/multiple subscribers where you have only one publisher with a number of subscribers.

FIGURE 12.9   Multiple publishers of one table model

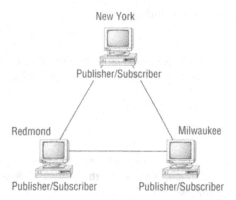

Replicating over the Internet and to Heterogeneous Database Servers

In addition to the replication scenarios already discussed, it is possible to replicate data to non-Microsoft database servers. This is known as *heterogeneous database replication*. You can also replicate to databases across the Internet.

Using Heterogeneous Replication

Heterogeneous replication occurs when you publish to other databases through an OLE DB connection. In special cases, you can even use SQL Server 2005 to subscribe to these OLE DB databases. Currently, SQL Server supports replication to Oracle and IBM databases that conform to the IBM Distributed Relational Database Architecture (DRDA) data protocol. When you publish to these non–SQL Server subscribers, you need to keep the following rules in mind:

- Only push subscriptions are supported.
- You can publish index views as tables; they cannot be replicated as an indexed view.
- Snapshot data will be sent using bulk copy's character format.
- Datatypes will be mapped as closely as possible.
- The account under which the distribution agent runs must have read access to the install directory of the OLE DB provider.
- If an article is added to or deleted from a publication, subscriptions to non–SQL Server subscribers must be reinitialized.
- NULL and NOT NULL are the only constraints supported for all non–SQL Server subscribers.
- Primary key constraints are replicated as unique indexes.

 In previous versions of SQL Server you could replicate using ODBC; this is no longer supported. Replication to Microsoft Access is no longer supported either.

Using Internet Replication

If you want to enable SQL Server to publish to the Internet, you must make some additional configuration changes to your SQL Server 2005 computer. For either a push style or a pull style of replication, you must configure the following:

- TCP/IP must be installed on the computers where the merge agent and distribution agents are running.

- The publishing server and the distribution server should be on the same side of the firewall.
- The publishing server and the distribution server should have a direct network connection to each other (rather than a connection across the Internet). This is for both security and latency concerns.

You need to make some additional configuration changes if you are going to allow pull subscriptions:

- Your distribution server must have Microsoft IIS installed and running.
- Both the merge and distribution agents must be configured with the correct FTP address. You do this through the distribution agent or from a command prompt.
- The working folder must be available to your subscription servers.
- The FTP home folder on your IIS computer should be set to the `Distribution` working folder. This is normally `\\`*ServerName*`\C$\Program Files\Microsoft SQL Server\ MSSQL\REPLDATA\FTP`.

For additional information on how to set up replication for the Internet, refer to the SQL Server Books Online.

Installing and Using Replication

In the following sections, you will learn how to configure your servers for replication. You will then walk through the process of installing a distribution database, a publishing database, and a subscription database. You will finish up this topic by creating and then subscribing to an article and a publication.

To successfully install and enable replication, you must install a distribution server, create your publications, and then subscribe to them. Before any of this can take place, you must first configure SQL Server.

 To install your replication scenario, you must be a member of the sysadmins fixed server role.

Configuring SQL Server for Replication

Before you can configure your SQL Server for replication, the computer itself must meet the following requirements:

- All servers involved with replication must be registered in Management Studio.
- If the servers are from different domains, trust relationships must be established before replication can occur.

- Any account you use must have access rights to the Distribution working folder on the distribution server.

- You must enable access to the Distribution working folder on the distribution server. For a Windows server, this is the *ServerName*\C$\Program Files\Microsoft SQL Server\MSSQL\REPLDATA folder. On Windows XP and earlier computers, you must create the C$ share because it exists by default only on Windows Server–family operating systems.

We suggest you use a single Windows domain account for all your SQL Server Agents. Do not use a LocalSystem account because this account has no network capabilities and will therefore not allow replication. Also, you need to make the account a member of the Domain Administrators group because only administrators have access to the $ shares.

Installing a Distribution Server

Before you can start replicating data, you need to install a distribution server. You'll do that in Exercise 12.1.

Before you can enable a publication database, you must be a member of the sysadmin fixed server role. Once you have enabled publishing, any member of that database's db_owner role can create and manage publications.

EXERCISE 12.1

Installing a Distribution Server

1. Open Management Studio, and connect to your server.

2. Right-click Replication, and click Configure Distribution.

EXERCISE 12.1 *(continued)*

3. You are presented with a welcome page; click Next to continue.

4. The Select Distributor page appears. Select the server that will act as its own distributor option, and click Next.

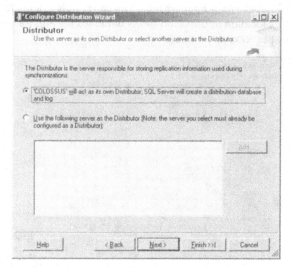

5. You are now asked to specify the snapshot folder. The only reason to change this is if you are replicating over the Internet and need to specify a folder that is accessible via FTP. Accept the defaults, and click Next.

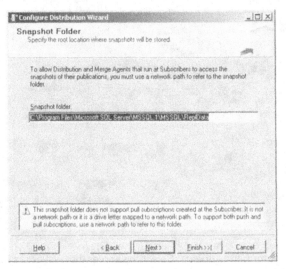

6. The Distribution Database page appears next. You can supply a name for the distribution database as well as location information for its database file and transaction log. Keep the defaults, and click Next to continue.

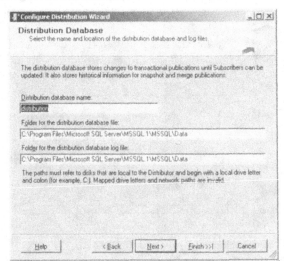

EXERCISE 12.1 *(continued)*

7. Now you are on the Publishers page where you can choose which servers you want to configure as publishers. The ellipsis (...) button allows you to specify security credentials such as login ID and password, as well as the location of the snapshot folder. Be sure to place a check mark next to your local SQL Server system, and then click Next to continue.

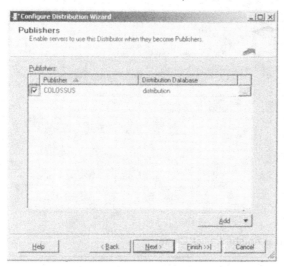

8. On the Wizard Actions page, you can have the wizard configure distribution, write a script to configure distribution that you can run later, or both. Leave the Configure distribution box checked, and click Next to continue.

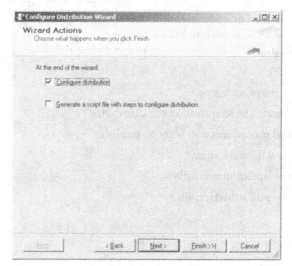

9.   On the Complete the Wizard page, review your selections, and click Finish.

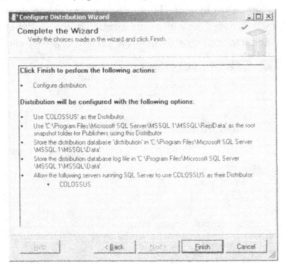

10.   When the wizard is finished, click Close.

Adding a Publication

Now you can add a publication and articles to your server. When you add a new publication, you need to determine the type of replication that will be used, the snapshot requirements, and the subscriber options such as updating subscribers. You can also partition your data and decide whether you will allow push or pull subscriptions.

The Create Publication Wizard allows you to specify the following options:

- Number of articles
- Schedule for the snapshot agent
- Whether to maintain the snapshot on the distributor
- Tables and stored procedures you want to publish
- Publications that will share agents
- Whether to allow updating subscribers
- Whether to allow pull subscriptions

Each publication will use a separate publishing agent by default, but you can override this option.

In the Exercise 12.2 you will create a new publication based on the Production.Product-Category table in the AdventureWorks database.

EXERCISE 12.2

Creating a Publication

1. Connect to your SQL Server system in Management Studio.

2. Expand Replication, right-click Local Publications, and click New Publication. This brings you to the New Publication Wizard welcome page.

3. Click Next to continue.

EXERCISE 12.2 *(continued)*

4. On the Publication Database page, highlight AdventureWorks, and click Next to continue.

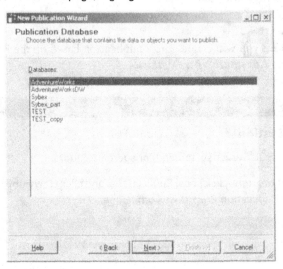

5. On the Publication Type page, you can choose what type of publication to create. For this exercise, choose Transactional Publication, and click Next to continue.

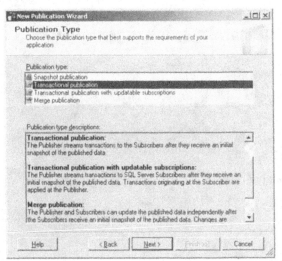

6. On the articles page, you can select what data and objects you want to replicate. Expand Tables, and check the ProductCategory box.

7. You can also set the properties for an article from this page. Make sure ProductCategory is highlighted, click Article Properties, and then click Set Properties of Highlighted Table Article.

8. In the Destination Object section, change the Destination Object name to **Replicated-Category**, change the Destination Object Owner to **dbo,** and click OK.

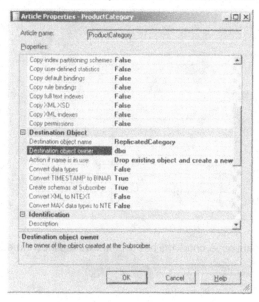

9. Back at the Articles page, click Next to continue.

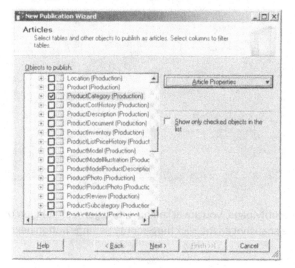

10. On the next page, you can filter the data that is replicated. You do not want to filter the data in this case, so click Next to continue.

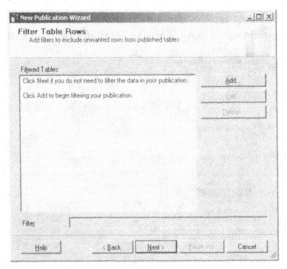

11. On the Snapshot Agent page, check the box to create a snapshot immediately, and click Next.

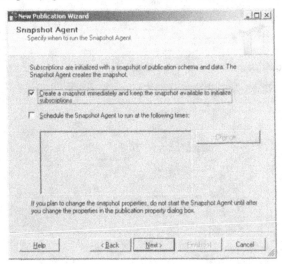

12. On the Agent Security page, you are asked how the agents should log on and access data. To set this for the snapshot agent, click the Security Settings button next to Snapshot Agent.

13. Ordinarily you would create an account for the agent to run under, but to make the exercise simpler, you will run the agent using the SQL Server Agent account, so select the radio button for that option, and click OK.

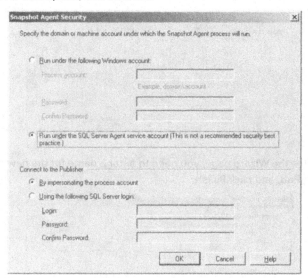

14. Back at the Agent Security page, click Next to continue.

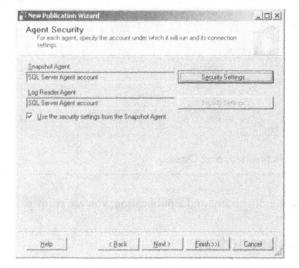

EXERCISE 12.2 *(continued)*

15. On the Wizard Actions page, you can have the wizard create the publication, write a script to create the publication that you can run later, or both. Leave the Create the Publication box checked, and click Next to continue.

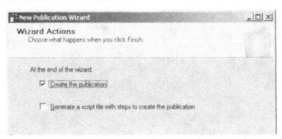

16. On the Complete the Wizard page, you need to enter a name for the new publication, so enter **CategoryPub**, and click Finish.

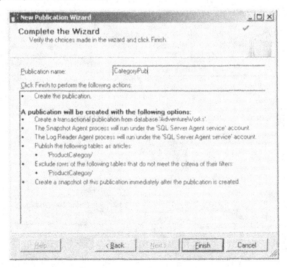

17. When the wizard is finished, click Close.

Now that you have a distributor and a publication, you are ready to create a subscription.

Creating a Subscription

As part of the process of creating a subscription, you will be able to specify the publishers you want to subscribe to and a destination database to receive the published data, verify your security credentials, and set up a default schedule. You will create a pull subscription in Exercise 12.3.

EXERCISE 12.3

Creating a Subscription

1.   Connect to your SQL Server system in Management Studio.

2.   Expand Replication, right-click Local Subscriptions, and click New Subscription. This brings you to the New Subscription Wizard welcome page.

3.   On the Publication page, select your server from the Publisher drop-down list, select CategoryPub from the Databases and Publications list, and click Next to continue.

EXERCISE 12.3 *(continued)*

4.   On the Distribution Agent Location page, you are asked which machine should run the replication agents, at the distributor or at the subscriber. Because you want to create a pull subscription, select the Run Each Agent at Its Subscriber option, and click Next.

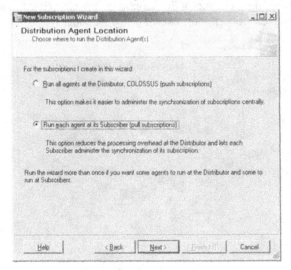

5.   On the Subscribers page, you can choose a subscriber for the publication. Check the box next to your server.

6.   Then the drop-down list is populated with all the available databases on the subscriber. Select the Sybex database (created in Chapter 2), and click Next.

7. On the next page you need to set the distribution agent security. To do so, click the ellipsis (...) button in the Subscription Properties list.

8. Ordinarily you would create an account for the agent to run under, but to make the exercise simpler, you will run the agent using the SQL Server Agent account, so select the radio button for that option, and click OK.

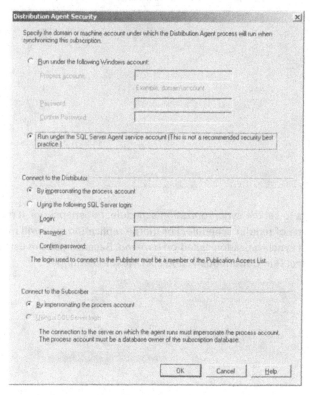

EXERCISE 12.3 *(continued)*

9. Back at the Distribution Agent Security page, click Next to continue.

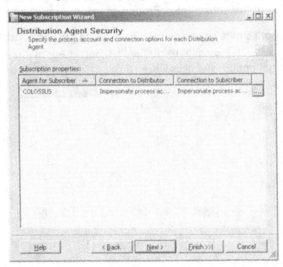

10. The next step is to set the synchronization schedule. For snapshots, it might be wise to set up some type of regular schedule. For merge replication, you will most likely use a manual form of synchronization called *on demand.* Because you are using transactional replication, select Run Continuously, and click Next to continue.

11. On the next page, you can tell SQL Server when to initialize subscription, if at all. If you have already created the schema on the subscriber, then you do not need to initialize the subscription. In this case you should select Immediately from the drop-down list, make sure the Initialize box is checked, and click Next to continue.

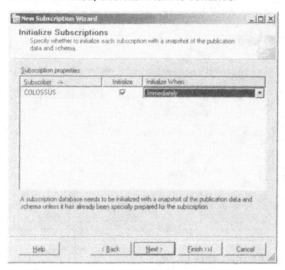

12. On the Wizard Actions page, you can have the wizard create the subscription, write a script to create the subscription that you can run later, or both. Leave the Create the Subscription box checked, and click Next to continue.

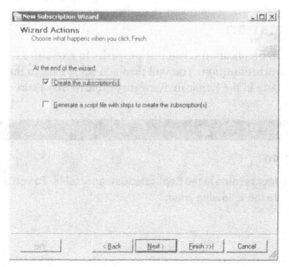

EXERCISE 12.3 *(continued)*

13. On the Complete the Wizard page, you can review your options and click Finish to create the subscription.

14. When the wizard is finished, click Close.

Now, with a subscription in place, you can test replication to make sure it is working as expected.

Testing Replication

You can now verify that replication is running properly. In Exercise 12.4 you will check for the initial snapshot synchronization. You will then add some data to the ProductCategory table and review the data in the ReplicatedCategory table to make sure it was replicated.

EXERCISE 12.4

Testing Replication

1. You should have four records in the ReplicatedCategory table. To verify that, open a new query, and execute the following code:

```
USE Sybex
```

```
SELECT * FROM ReplicatedCategory

GO
```

2. Now add a new record to the ProductCategory table in the AdventureWorks database. Run the following code to add a new record:

```
USE AdventureWorks

INSERT INTO Production.ProductCategory (Name)

VALUES('Tools')

GO
```

3. You should get the message that one row was added. Give the server about a minute to replicate the transaction; then run the following query:

```
USE Sybex

SELECT * FROM ReplicatedCategory

GO
```

4. You should get five records back. The last record should be the new Tools record.

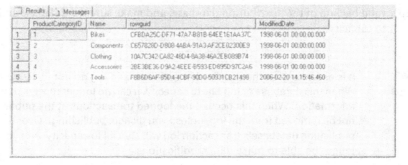

Managing Replication

Managing and maintaining replication can be intensive work for an administrator. Microsoft SQL Server 2005 has included many tools in the Replication Monitor to make this job a lot easier. Before you look at the various tools and methodologies, you'll see some of the administrative issues you should consider.

Considering Administrative Issues

This section provides some tips for optimizing your replication as well as some tips to minimize your administrative duties:

- Use a remote distributor to minimize the impact of replication on your publishing servers.

- Use pull subscriptions to off-load the work from the distributors to each subscriber.

- Use immediate updating subscribers rather than merge replication if possible.

- Replicate only the data you need. Use filters to partition your data.

- Keep in mind that replication increases network traffic. Make sure your network, especially your WAN links, can handle it.

- Use primary keys on replicated tables to ensure entity integrity.

- Using the same SQL Server Agent domain account for all servers involved in replication will minimize the impact of administering security issues.

- Ensure that replication jobs and their agents are running smoothly. Check the agent histories and logs periodically.

- Create and monitor replication alerts.

- Ensure that the distribution database and the `Distribution` working folder have enough space and that they have the appropriate permissions assigned to them.

- Develop a recovery and resynchronization plan. You can use replication scripts for version control as well as a huge part of the recovery process.

- Keep a valid backup of the distribution database, and make sure the database and log do not fill to capacity.

It is essential that the distribution database and log do not fill to capacity. When this database or log fills to capacity, it can no longer receive publication information. When this occurs, the logged transactions at the publisher cannot be removed from the log (unless you disable publishing). Over time, your publishing database's transaction log will also fill to capacity, and you will no longer be able to make data modifications.

Considering Replication Backup Issues

When you perform backups of your replication scenario, you can make backups of just the publisher, the publisher and distributor, the publisher and subscriber, or all three. Each of the strategies has its own advantages and disadvantages. The following list highlights these distinctions:

Publisher only   This strategy requires the least amount of resources and computing time because the backup of the publisher does not have to be coordinated with any other server backups to stay synchronized. The disadvantage is restoring a publisher or distributor is a slow and time-consuming process.

Publisher and distributor   This strategy accurately preserves the publication as well as the errors, history, and replication agent information from the distributor. You can recover quickly because there is no need to reestablish replication. The disadvantages of this strategy are the coordination of the backups and the amount of storage and computing time necessary to perform a simultaneous backup.

Publisher and subscriber(s)   This strategy significantly reduces the recovery time by removing the initialization process (running a snapshot). The main disadvantages of this strategy manifest themselves when you have multiple subscribers. Every subscriber will have to be backed up and restored.

Publisher, distributor, and subscriber(s)   This strategy preserves all of the complexity of your replication model. The disadvantages are storage space and computing time. This scenario also requires the most time for recovery.

Using the Replication Monitor

You can administer your publishers, subscribers, and publications as well as the different replication agents through the Replication Monitor utility. You can also look at agent properties and histories and even set replication alerts with this utility.

The Replication Monitor resides on the computer where the distribution server has been installed and gathers replication information about the different replication agents. This includes the agent history with information about inserts, updates, deletes, and any other transactions that were processed. Through the Replication Monitor, you can also edit the various schedules and properties of the replication agents.

In Exercise 12.5 you'll use the Replication Monitor.

EXERCISE 12.5

Using Replication Monitor

1.   Open the Management Studio on the distribution server.

2.   Right-click Replication, and select Launch Replication Monitor.

3.   Expand your server to view the publications available.

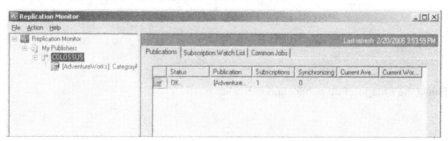

4. Switch to the Subscription Watch List tab. From here you can view reports about the performance of all publications and subscriptions that this distributor handles.

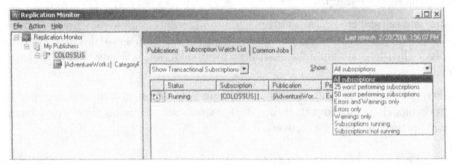

5. Switch to the Common Jobs tab. On this tab you can view the status of replication jobs that affect all publications and subscriptions handled by this distributor.

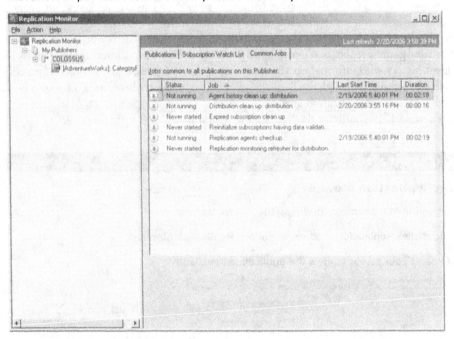

6. Select the CategoryPub publication in the left pane.

EXERCISE 12.5 *(continued)*

7. On the All Subscriptions tab, you can view reports about all of the subscriptions for this particular publication.

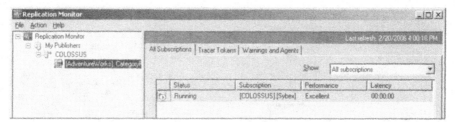

8. Switch to the Tracer Token tab. From here you can insert a special record called a *tracer token* that is used to measure performance for this subscription.

9. To test it, click the Insert Tracer button, and wait for the results.

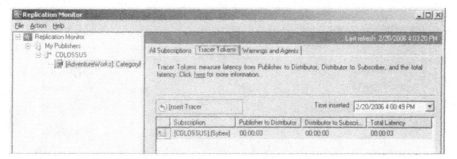

10. Switch to the Warnings and Agents tab. From here you can change settings for agents and configure replication alerts.

11. Click the Configure Alerts button, select Replication: Agent Failure, and click Configure.

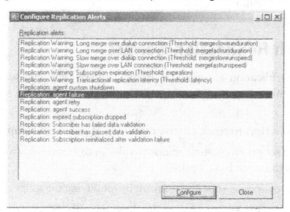

12. Notice that this opens a new alert dialog box (we discussed alerts in Chapter 11). Check the Enable box, and click OK to enable this alert.

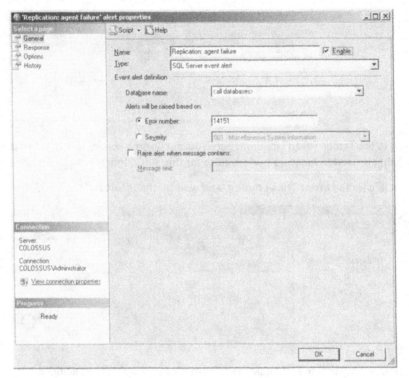

13. Click Close to return to Replication Monitor.

14. Close Replication Monitor.

Working with Replication Scripts

Now that you have replication set up and working properly, you may want to save all your hard work in the form of a replication script. Scripting your replication scenario has the following advantages:

- You can use the scripts to track different versions of your replication implementation.
- You can use the scripts (with some minor tweaking) to create additional subscribers and publishers with the same basic options.
- You can quickly customize your environment by modifying the script and then rerunning it.
- You can use the scripts as part of your database recovery process.

FIGURE 12.10   Generate SQL Script dialog box

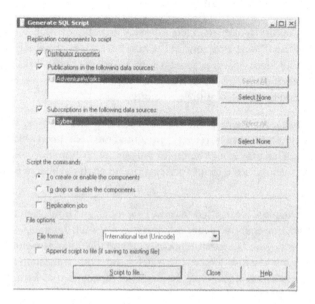

Scripting replication is so simple that it requires only two clicks: just right-click Replication, and then select Generate Scripts. That's it; you'll then be presented with the screen shown in Figure 12.10.

From here you can script the distributor and publications for the various replication items stored with this distribution server. You can also script the options for any subscribers and even the replication jobs. When you have made your choices, just click the Script to File button, and save the script wherever you like.

Enhancing Replication Performance

Replication is, as we call it in the industry, a *resource hog*, meaning it uses quite a bit of memory and processor resources. You can perform a number of tweaks to increase the performance of your replication scheme, though. Here are a few suggestions:

Set a minimum memory allocation limit.   By default, SQL Server dynamically configures the amount of RAM it uses while it is running. The problem is that it may release too much memory and then not have enough when replication starts. True, SQL Server will just allocate more memory, but it is faster if you simply tell SQL Server to always allocate at least enough memory to run replication. In that light, consider allocating a minimum of 16MB of RAM to SQL Server.

Use a separate hard disk for all the databases used in replication.   You should add hard disk arrays for the publication, distribution, and subscription databases if you can.

Use multiple processors.   All the agents involved in replication are multithreaded, which means they can take advantage of multiple processors. Therefore, more CPUs equal faster replication.

Case Study: Deciding on a Replication Model and Type

AlsoRann opened its doors in California, and when the company grew big enough, it opened a regional branch office on the East Coast. Everyone at the new East Coast office had access to the inventory data so they could make sales without having to call the home office to find out whether the parts were in stock. They also needed the capability to update their local copy of the data and have those changes reflected at the home office.

Before anything else, we had to assess the network connections between the offices to make sure they were reliable. If the network was not reliable, we would not have been able to use immediate updating subscribers, so that would be out of the picture. Fortunately, we found that the network was fast and reliable, so we could consider using all the available types of replication.

When it came to the type of replication, we needed to know how much and how often the data would change. If the entire database changed every day and it was a small database, then we might have been able to get away with snapshot replication. But if the database was large, then snapshot was not the answer because it takes too much bandwidth; transactional replication would be better. AlsoRann's data was too big for snapshot replication, so we opted for transactional with immediate updating subscribers.

Next we needed to consider the model. In this instance, we had one publisher in California and one subscriber that was quite some distance away. Because there was only one subscriber, we decided to use the central publisher/central distributor model.

One more question popped up—should the subscription be push or pull? The staff at AlsoRann's headquarters in California wanted to control when data was replicated, so we made this a push subscription so they could have that control.

Publish only the amount of data required.   This may seem like common sense, but it is one of the biggest culprits of slow replication. You should publish only the columns you need to publish. Publishing too many columns adds time at every step of the process and slows down the entire process. Ergo, use vertical partitioning whenever possible.

Place the snapshot folder on a drive that does not have database or log files.   This does not have to be a dedicated disk, mind you; it can have other things on it if necessary. The data and log files are constantly written to and read from, which means if you put the snapshot folder on a disk containing these files, it will have to compete for disk time. If you move it to a disk that is relatively empty, though, it will not need to compete, and snapshots will move faster.

Be sparing with horizontal partitioning.   When you horizontally partition a publication, the logreader agent has to apply the filter to every single row that is affected by the update as it scans the transaction log. This takes extra CPU time that can slow your system down, so if it is not necessary, don't use it.

Use a fast network.   Again, this is common sense. Because replication occurs between two or more database servers, a network is involved at some point. The faster the network, the faster replication will be.

Run agents continuously instead of frequently.   Running agents on frequent schedules, such as every minute, is actually more work for the server than if you just turn on the agent and leave it on. This is because the server has to expend CPU and memory to stop and start the agent regularly. It's better to just leave it on.

Replication also exposes many new and useful performance counters that can be used in your optimization efforts. As you recall, performance counters are grouped into performance objects and are used in the SQL Server Performance Monitor. With all of these new performance counters, you can track how effective your replication strategies are and then fine-tune your scenario.

Summary

Replication is a powerful tool used to distribute data to other database engines in your enterprise, which you need to do so your data will be closer to your users and therefore faster and easier for them to access.

Microsoft uses a publisher/subscriber metaphor to explain replication. The publisher contains the data that needs to be copied. The subscribers get a copy of the data from the publisher, and the distributor moves the data from the publisher to the subscribers. The data is published in groups called *publications*; a publication can contain several *articles*, which are the actual data being replicated.

You can choose from three main types of replication: merge, transactional, and snapshot. Each has its own set of pros and cons, but you should consider three main issues when picking a replication type: autonomy, latency, and consistency. In other words, you need to know whether the data has to be replicated right away or whether it can be late (latency), you need to know whether subscribers can update the data (autonomy), and you need to know whether the transactions need to be applied all at the same time and in a specific order (consistency).

When you have picked the right type of replication, you have a number of physical models to choose from:

- Central publisher/central distributor
- Remote distribution
- Central subscriber/multiple publishers
- Multiple publishers/multiple subscribers
- Heterogeneous replication

Once you have implemented a replication solution, you need to back it up. You should back up all the databases involved in replication but especially the distributor, because if you do not, the transaction log in the distribution database will fill up and replication will stop.

You should also generate replication scripts so that if your server ever suffers a catastrophic failure, you will be able to rebuild the replication solution much faster.

You should also keep in mind all the points for enhancing replication performance. Once you have implemented replication, your users will come to depend on it, and if it doesn't move fast enough, it will not be dependable, and your users will not be happy. If you keep it in top shape, though, users will be able to take full advantage of the power of replication.

Exam Essentials

Know the publisher/subscriber metaphor.   Publishers contain the original copy of the data where changes are made. Subscribers receive copies of the data from the publishers. The data is disseminated to the subscribers through the distributor.

Know the types of replication.   Three basic types of replication exist: snapshot, transactional, and merge. In transactional replication, transactions are read right from the transaction log and copied from the publisher to the subscribers. In snapshot replication, the entire publication is copied every time the publication is replicated. In merge replication, data from the publisher is merged with data from the subscribers, which are allowed to update. With the immediate updating subscribers and queued updating options, subscribers can make changes to data that has been replicated with transactional and snapshot data as well.

Know the replication models.   You also need to be familiar with the various models, that is, who publishes, who subscribes, and who distributes:

- In the central publisher/central distributor model, a single server is both the publisher and distributor, and there are multiple subscribers.

- The remote distribution model has one publishing server, a separate distributor, and multiple subscribers.

- In the central subscriber/multiple publishers model, multiple publishers all publish to a single subscribing server.

- The multiple publishers/multiple subscribers model contains multiple publishing servers and multiple subscribing servers. The number of distributors is undefined.

- Heterogeneous replication describes replication to a third-party database engine, such as DB2 or Oracle.

Understand how publications and articles work.   A *publication* comprises articles that contain the data being replicated. An *article* is actually a representation of a table. The article can be partitioned either vertically or horizontally, and it can be transformed.

Review Questions

1. You are the administrator of a SQL Server 2005 server located in New York City. That server contains a sales database that needs to be replicated to your satellite offices in Berlin, London, and Moscow, which are connected via a partial T1 connection that consistently runs at 80 percent capacity. Your sales associates make changes to the database regularly throughout the day, but the users in the satellite offices do not need to see the changes immediately. Which type of replication should you use?

   A. Merge

   B. Transactional

   C. Snapshot

   D. Transactional with updating subscribers

   E. Snapshot with updating subscribers

2. You are the administrator of a SQL Server 2005 server located in New York City. That server contains a sales database that needs to be replicated to your satellite offices in Berlin, London, and Moscow, which are connected via a partial T1 connection that consistently runs at 80 percent capacity. Your sales associates make changes to the database regularly throughout the day, but the users in the satellite offices do not need to see the changes immediately. Which replication model should you use?

   A. Central subscriber/multiple publishers

   B. Multiple publishers/multiple subscribers

   C. Central publisher/central distributor

   D. Remote distribution

3. You are the administrator of several SQL Server computers that are configured to use replication in a remote distribution configuration with several subscribers. Each of the subscribers requires the ability to update the data they receive, so you implement transactional replication with the immediate updating subscribers option. After several weeks, replication starts to fail intermittently. What is the most likely cause?

   A. The SQL Server Agent has stopped.

   B. The Distributed Transaction Coordinator has stopped.

   C. The network connection is down intermittently.

   D. The distribution database transaction log is full.

4. You are the administrator of a SQL Server 2005 server, and you have just installed a new accounting application that stores its data in a database named Accounting. Users in your satellite office need to access the Accounting database to run reports regularly, but they are connected by a very slow network connection. Most of the reports they run will require data that is accurate up to the last working day. You cannot make any changes to the database. What should you do? (Choose all that apply.)

   A. Implement merge replication.

   B. Implement snapshot replication.

   C. Implement transactional replication.

   D. Schedule replication to run continuously.

   E. Schedule replication to run at off-peak hours.

5. You work for a multinational company where each branch office has its own accounting department. The network connections between the branch offices are reliable, but they are consistently at 80 percent usage during the day. Each of your branch office accounting departments needs a copy of the accounting database that they can update locally, and they need it to be as current as possible. Which replication type best suits your needs?

   A. Merge

   B. Transactional

   C. Snapshot

   D. Transactional with updating subscribers

   E. Snapshot with updating subscribers

6. You have successfully installed and configured replication on your SQL Server 2005 computer. After you create a publication and add a push subscriber to the publication, you notice that the subscriber is not receiving the data. On further investigation you find that the snapshot agent is failing. What is the most likely cause?

   A. The snapshot agent is frozen. Stop and restart it.

   B. A push subscription is being used instead of a pull subscription, so the snapshot agent is running on the distributor instead of the subscriber.

   C. The snapshot agent does not have access to the Distribution working folder.

   D. The transaction log for the distribution database needs to be cleared.

7. You have a company with several sales offices located throughout the country. Headquarters needs an up-to-date copy of the sales offices' databases. When headquarters sends new inventory to the sales offices, they want to update the database at headquarters and have the new data replicated to the respective sales offices. How could you make sure the sales offices are getting only the data that pertains to their particular office?

   A. Create multiple horizontally partitioned articles at headquarters.

   B. Create multiple vertically partitioned articles at headquarters.

   C. Create a single horizontally partitioned article at headquarters.

   D. Create a single vertically partitioned article at headquarters.

8. You have a company with several sales offices located throughout the country. Headquarters needs an up-to-date copy of the sales offices' databases. When headquarters sends new inventory to the sales offices, they want to update the database at headquarters and have the new data replicated to the respective sales offices. Which replication type should you use?

   A. Merge

   B. Transactional

   C. Snapshot

   D. Transactional with updating subscribers

   E. Snapshot with updating subscribers

9. You have a company with several sales offices located throughout the country. Headquarters needs an up-to-date copy of the sales offices databases. When headquarters sends new inventory to the sales offices, they want to update the database at headquarters and have the new data replicated to the respective sales offices. Which replication model should you use?

   A. Central subscriber/multiple publishers

   B. Multiple publishers/multiple subscribers

   C. Central publisher/central distributor

   D. Remote distribution

10. A small automotive parts company has four shops, each with its own inventory database to maintain. The owner wants the shops to be able to share inventory so that employees can pick up a part from another nearby store rather than waiting for a shipment from the manufacturer. To do this, employees at each shop should be able to update their local copy of the inventory database, decrement the other store's inventory, and then go pick up the part. This way, the other store won't sell their part because it will have already been taken out of stock. Which replication type should you use to accomplish this?

    A. Merge

    B. Transactional

    C. Snapshot

    D. Transactional with updating subscribers

    E. Snapshot with updating subscribers

11. A small automotive parts company has four shops, each with its own inventory database to maintain. The owner wants the shops to be able to share inventory so that employees can pick up a part from another nearby store rather than waiting for a shipment from the manufacturer. To do this, employees at each shop should be able to update their local copy of the inventory database, decrement the other store's inventory, and then go pick up the part. This way, the other store won't sell their part because it will have already been taken out of stock. Which replication model should you use to accomplish this?

    A. Central subscriber/multiple publishers

    B. Multiple publishers/multiple subscribers

    C. Central publisher/central distributor

    D. Remote distribution

12. You have just set up a merge replication subscription between three SQL Server machines using a multiple publishers/multiple subscribers topology. The article looks like this:

ProdID	ProdName	ProdPrice	Updated
Int	varchar(200)	money	timestamp

You soon start getting complaints that the updated column is not being replicated correctly. You can change any part of this that you need in order to fix the problem. What can you do to fix this?

A. Alter the Updated column using the NOT FOR REPLICATION option.

B. Alter the Updated column using the REPLICATE AS TIMESTAMP option.

C. Change to a remote distributor topology.

D. Change to transactional replication.

13. You are the administrator of several SQL Servers systems. Your main server is located in the home office in Denver, and you have servers in satellite offices in Orlando, Nashville, San Francisco, and Portland. You have configured the server in Denver as a publisher and distributor, and you need to configure each of the satellite servers as subscribers as quickly as possible with minimal administrative overhead. What should you do?

A. Run the Pull Subscription Wizard on each subscriber.

B. Push the subscription from the publisher to each subscriber.

C. Run the Pull Subscription Wizard on one subscriber, generate replication scripts on that subscriber, and modify and run the scripts on the remaining subscribers.

D. Run the Pull Subscription Wizard on one subscriber, and use DTS to copy the database to the remaining subscribers.

14. When checking the subscriber database in a transactional replication scenario, you notice that updates are no longer happening. When you check the publisher, you notice that the database is working properly but the transaction log seems to be filling up even though you are performing regular backups. What is the most likely cause?

A. The subscriber database does not have access to the Distribution working folder.

B. The distribution database transaction log has filled to capacity.

C. The publisher has lost its network connection to the distributor.

D. The logreader agent has been stopped on the distributor.

15. You are configuring a snapshot replication scenario with a single publisher and almost 100 subscribers. You want to remove as much burden from the distributor as possible. How should you create the subscriptions?

A. Create push subscriptions so that the snapshot agent runs on the distributor.

B. Create pull subscriptions so that the snapshot agent runs on the subscriber.

C. Create push subscriptions so that the distribution agent runs on the distributor.

D. Create pull subscriptions so that the distribution agent runs on the subscriber.

16. You are the administrator of a SQL Server 2005 computer, and you want to set up snapshot replication on the server. You will be publishing 4GB to 5GB of data, and that amount is expected to increase over time. Each of your subscribers will receive a new snapshot every month, so you need to minimize the workload on the publisher/distributor. What should you do? (Choose all that apply.)

A. Store the snapshot in its default folder on the distributor.

B. Store the snapshot in a shared folder on a file server.

C. Create push subscriptions.

D. Create pull subscriptions.

E. Separate the publisher and distributor, each one on its own server.

F. Use heterogeneous replication.

17. You are the SQL Server administrator for a large bank. The bank's customers can access their accounts at the headquarters or at any of the bank's regional offices. The server at headquarters maintains a master copy of the database, so when a customer withdraws funds or makes a deposit at any of the regional offices, the data must be copied to the database at headquarters. The data at headquarters must, in turn, be replicated to all the regional offices. All of this must happen as quickly as possible. What should you do?

A. Implement snapshot replication, and set the snapshot agent to run continuously.

B. Implement merge replication, and configure the conflict resolver to keep transactions from the subscriber.

C. Implement transactional replication with immediate updating subscribers, and configure the logreader agent to run continuously.

D. Implement transactional replication with queued updating subscribers, and configure the logreader agent to run continuously.

18. You are using a transactional replication scenario, and you notice that your varchar(max) type fields are not being updated regularly. Changes are made to the text fields on a weekly basis, but the changes to the text fields are showing up at the subscribers only once a month. Why is this?

A. The varchar(max) fields were created with the NOT FOR REPLICATION option.

B. The publication schedule was set to replicate the varchar(max) fields only on a monthly basis.

C. The subscribers are refreshed with a snapshot on a monthly basis.

D. The subscribers are configured to pull the varchar(max) fields only once a month.

19. You are using a multiple publishers/multiple subscribers scenario with transactional replication in which you do not want users to be able to modify data that comes from another database. To do this, you create a constraint that does not allow users to modify data that does not use their own location code. If this constraint gets replicated, it would prevent users from modifying their own local data. How do you prevent the constraint from being replicated?

   A. Create the constraint with the NOT FOR REPLICATION option.

   B. Use snapshot instead of transactional replication because it does not replicate constraints, triggers, or stored procedures.

   C. Configure the publisher to drop, and re-create the constraints when replicating data.

   D. Do nothing; constraints are not replicated.

20. To use the Replication Monitor to check the status of replication, which server would you connect to?

   A. The publisher

   B. The subscriber

   C. The distributor

   D. Any of the above

Answers to Review Questions

1. B. Because the entire database does not change every day, you do not need to use snapshot. Also, snapshot would use a great deal more bandwidth than transactional. Because the subscribers do not need to update their copy of the data, you do not need the added complexity of merge or updating subscribers. Also, you do not have much network bandwidth to play with, and transactional replication uses the least amount of bandwidth.

2. D. The models that involve multiple publishers obviously won't work here because you have only one publisher. The remote distributor option can save long-distance charges because, instead of making several long-distance calls from New York to the satellites, you can place a distributor in London and let the distributor make less-expensive calls to the remaining satellites.

3. C. Options A, B, and D would certainly stop an immediate updating subscriber from replicating, but they would cause replication to stop all together, not intermittently, so they are not the most likely cause. Remember that the Distributed Transaction Coordinator needs a reliable network connection to do its job. Without a reliable connection, the transaction could not be applied to all subscribers at once, so all of them would be rolled back, and the transaction would fail.

4. B, E. Transactional replication would take up too much of the network bandwidth because there would be constant updates to the subscribers; in addition, the users can withstand a full day's latency, so they do not need the constant updates anyway. They also do not need to make any changes to the data; they just need to read the data to run reports, so they do not need merge replication. The best option is snapshot replication with the agent scheduled to run at off-peak hours so it doesn't overload the network connection.

5. D. Because the network is running close to capacity most of the time, it would not support snapshot replication. Because the users would be updating only their own data, merge replication would be overkill. Transactional with updating subscribers fits your needs because the network usage is lower than snapshot and still allows users to update local copies of the data.

6. C. The snapshot agent has to be able to access the `Distribution` working folder over the network, and the account it runs under must have permissions on the folder. Whether it is a push or pull subscription has no bearing on the snapshot agent failing, and a full distribution log would stop all replication, not just the snapshot agent.

7. A. Horizontally partitioning the data means you would be replicating only a subset of records to the sales offices. In this example, you could replicate only the records where the store ID is equal to the store that is subscribing to the publication. You need to create an article for each sales office because those offices each need to subscribe to a specific subset of the data.

8. D. Because each office needs to be able to update their own inventory databases each time they make a sale and headquarters needs to be able to update the main database, you need to give the sales offices the capability to update. Merge replication would be overkill here because each sales office does not need to update other sales offices data.

9. C. Because you are using transactional replication with updating subscribers, you can use a central publisher at headquarters with each sales office being a subscriber.

10. A. In this scenario, you do not have a central "main" database that each subscriber will update. All of the stores must be able to update data for the other stores' data. The best way to accomplish this is through merge replication.

11. B. Each store will publish its inventory database and subscribe to the other stores' inventory databases. This makes it the perfect scenario for a multiple publishers/multiple subscribers model.

12. D. In merge replication only the schema of `TIMESTAMP` columns are replicated; the data in them is not. So the data in the Updated column would never be replicated to the subscribers. However, `TIMESTAMP` data is replicated in transactional (and snapshot) replication, so changing the replication type will fix the problem. Changing the Updated column to `NOT FOR REPLICATION` would prevent it from ever being replicated by any type of replication, and the topology has no bearing on what data is replicated to subscribers. Also, the `REPLICATE AS TIMESTAMP` is not a valid option.

13. C. Options A and B would work, but they are slower than generating replication scripts. Option D would not work because DTS does not copy subscription information. The fastest method is to generate replication scripts with the subscriber information and run them at each subscriber.

14. B. The most likely cause here is that the distribution database log has been filled to capacity. That stops transactional replication in its tracks. The best thing to do to prevent this is to set up a maintenance plan for the distribution database.

15. D. If you pull the subscription to each of the subscribers, the distribution agent will run on the subscribers and remove some of the processing burden from the distributor.

16. B, D. The best way to relieve stress on the publisher/distributor is to move the snapshot folder to another server from which it can be distributed and create pull subscriptions so that the agents will run on the subscribers instead of the distributor. Just so you know, heterogeneous replication is between SQL Server and a third-party database engine, so it would have no effect on distributor stress.

17. C. To replicate the data as quickly as possible, you want to send the least amount of data possible. That would be transactional replication. You also want the ability to update the data at the subscribers, so you need to configure immediate updating subscribers. Queued updating would take too long to replicate. To move the data as fast as possible, you should also configure the logreader agent to run continuously.

18. C. Varchar(max), nvarchar(max), and varbinary(max) data are replicated only when the snapshot is refreshed. The only thing that is replicated through transactions is the pointer record that tells SQL Server where the data is located in the database.

19. A. To keep a constraint from being replicated, you need to specify the `NOT FOR REPLICATION` option when creating it.

20. C. The Replication Monitor runs on the distributor, where most of the replication process takes place.

Chapter

13

Introducing More High-Availability Methods

MICROSOFT EXAM OBJECTIVES COVERED IN THIS CHAPTER:

✓ **Implement database mirroring.**

- Prepare databases for database mirroring.
- Create endpoints.
- Specify database partners.
- Specify a witness server.
- Configure an operating mode.

✓ **Implement log shipping.**

- Initialize a secondary database.
- Configure log shipping options.
- Configure a log shipping mode.
- Configure monitoring.

✓ **Managing database snapshots.**

- Create a snapshot.
- Revert a database from a snapshot.

SQL Server 2005 provides a set of high-availability methods that you can use to achieve fault-tolerance and to prevent server outages and data loss. You can also implement a cluster, which can be a two-node cluster in Standard Edition or can consist of more nodes in SQL Server 2005 Enterprise Edition.

The high-availability method your company will implement depends on several factors. Clustering is a more expensive high-availability method than database mirroring, but it allows users to failover immediately and provides the failover of both user and system databases. Choosing a high-availability method also affects when failover can occur and affects availability. Some companies need the server to be available 24/7; others can afford an outage of a couple of hours.

In this chapter, we will cover the additional high-availability methods that provide fault-tolerance. You will learn what method to implement and learn how database mirroring and log shipping compare to each other. In addition, you will learn how to prevent user mistakes by implementing database snapshots.

Choosing the High-Availability Features You Need

SQL Server 2005 has the following features available depending on the edition of SQL Server you're using. It is important to understand which features are available in specific editions of SQL Server before you decide to build a business technology around high availability.

You'll get the following high-availability features with Enterprise Edition:

- Failover clustering
- Multiple instances (up to 50)
- Log shipping
- Database snapshots
- Database mirroring

You'll get the following high-availability features with Standard Edition:

- Failover clustering (maximum two nodes)
- Multiple instances (up to 16)

- Log shipping
- Database mirroring (synchronous with automatic failover only)

You'll get the following high-availability features with Workgroup Edition:

- Multiple instances (up to 16)
- Log shipping

You'll get the following high-availability features with Express Edition:

- Multiple instances (up to 16)
- Log shipping
- Can be used as a witness

We'll discuss all of these features throughout this chapter to help you choose the correct edition for your organization.

Implementing Database Mirroring

Database mirroring allows you to create an exact copy of a database on a different server and implement high availability on the user database. Although Microsoft support policies currently do not apply to database mirroring, you can still enable this feature. (This support policy is scheduled to change in SQL Server 2005 Service Pack 1.)

Since Microsoft does not support database mirroring, the feature is currently disabled by default. You can enable it, but it is a general recommendation to use database mirroring only for testing purposes.

If you want to test database mirroring, you first need to enable database mirroring by setting the appropriate trace flags. Trace flag 1400 will enable you to use database mirroring. You can specify this using the following T-SQL statement:

```
DBCC TRACEON (1400)
```

Database mirroring is a software solution, implemented on a database-per-database basis, and involves two copies of a database, with only one accessible by the user. Since database mirroring does not require any additional hardware in terms of clustering support, you can use this as a cheaper implementation instead of clustering a database. Keep in mind, however, that mirroring supports only user databases, and you might need additional requirements in a fault-tolerance scenario.

How does database mirroring work?   Mirroring is a process that looks similar to *log shipping*; however, it involves a direct process between two separate instances of SQL Server. Updates made to a database on the first server, called the *principal*, are copied over, or are *mirrored*, to the target server, called the *mirror*. The process involves applying any transaction from the principal to the mirror.

When an application sends an update to the database, the database engine will also apply the transaction to the *mirror* and receive an acknowledgment that the transaction is committed, or *hardened* into the target database, before the process will be returned to the user application. Figure 13.1 displays this process.

How do you configure database mirroring? Configuring database mirroring involves several steps, covered throughout the following sections. You have to configure the connection between servers and also configure which database you will mirror from one server to the other. We'll cover how to configure this in the "Preparing for Mirroring" section later in this chapter.

FIGURE 13.1 Database mirroring

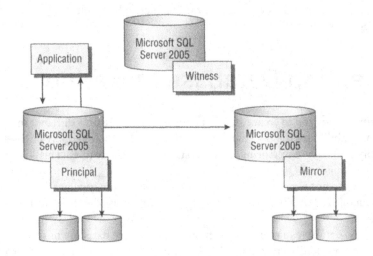

Understanding Database Mirroring Concepts

Mirroring, partners, witnesses…these are some basic concepts you really need to understand in order to start using database mirroring and comprehend where database mirroring fits into the fault-tolerance strategy of your business solutions.

Principal The principal server is your primary database that will be your starting point in a database-mirroring session. Every transaction that will be applied to this database will be transferred to the mirror using a process similar to distributed transactions. When a database-mirroring session starts, the mirror server asks the principal server's transaction log for all transactions, based on the latest log sequence number.

Mirror The mirror is the database that will receive the copies from the principal server; this assumes that a consistent connection between the mirror and the principal exists.

Standby server The process of database mirroring is really maintaining a *standby server* (which means the mirrored database is not accessible by users) that you can easily switch over to in case of the principal server failing.

Synchronous/asynchronous Database mirroring can work in twos different ways: synchronous or asynchronous:

Synchronous mode In synchronous mode, every transaction applied to the principal will also be committed (or hardened) on the mirror server. You can consider this to be similar to distributed transactions, which means a transaction on the principal will be released only when it is also committed on the mirror. Once it receives an acknowledgment from the mirror server, the principal will notify the client that the statement has completed.

Asynchronous mode In asynchronous mode, the principal server sends log information to the mirror server, without waiting for an acknowledgment from the mirror server. This means transactions commit without waiting for the mirror server to commit, or harden, the log file. This mode allows the principal server to run with minimum transaction latency and does not allow you to use automatic failover.

Preparing for Mirroring

To prepare for database mirroring, you need to perform three configuration steps:

1. Configure the security and communication between the instances.

2. Create the mirror database.

3. Establish a mirror session.

Configuring Security and Communication between Instances

To establish a database mirror connection, SQL Server uses endpoints to specify the connection between servers. This means you have to create the endpoints for the database mirroring. And just like with SQL Server Service Broker, you have to use a CREATE ENDPOINT statement, as covered in the "Creating Endpoints" section.

Of course, in this communication, SQL Server performs authentication over the endpoints (mirror endpoint services), and you can achieve this by using Windows Authentication or certificate-based authentication.

If you are configuring a *witness server*, you also need to specify the communication and authentication between the principal and the witness and between the mirror and the witness.

Creating the Mirror Database

To create a mirror database, you have to restore the full backup of a principal including all other types of backup (transaction logs) you created on the principal before you can establish a session. It is important, however, that you use the NORECOVERY option when restoring from backup so the backup database will remain in a nonusable state. The mirror database needs to have the same name as the principal database.

Establishing a Mirror Session

Your next step in setting up database mirroring is to set up the mirror session on the database by identifying the mirroring partners. On the principal database and on the mirror, you need to identify what partners are involved in database mirroring.

You can do this from within SQL Server Management Studio; however, as a general rule in configuration, we recommend you script this using T-SQL syntax instead. Refer to the "Specifying Partners and Witnesses" section for more information.

Creating Endpoints

Because you already learned about endpoints in Chapter 9, it won't be too difficult to configure endpoints for database mirroring. Database mirroring requires you to define TCP endpoints in the same way as you configured HTTP endpoints for Service Broker.

In an endpoint configuration, you identify TCP as the core protocol, and you specify the following options:

- Authentication
- Encryption
- Role

A typical configuration looks like this:

```
CREATE ENDPOINT endpoint_mirroring
    STATE = STARTED
    AS TCP ( LISTENER_PORT = 4099 )
    FOR DATABASE_MIRRORING (
        AUTHENTICATION = WINDOWS KERBEROS,
        ENCRYPTION = SUPPORTED,
        ROLE=ALL);
```

Setting the Authentication

Let's take a closer look at the authentication for database-mirroring endpoints. Database mirroring supports Windows Authentication or certificate-based authentication.

Windows Authentication   The authentication mechanism is specified in the FOR_DATABASE_ MIRRORING part of the CREATE ENDPOINT statement, as shown here, and has configurable options:

```
<FOR DATABASE_MIRRORING_ language_specific_arguments> ::=
FOR DATABASE_MIRRORING (
   [ AUTHENTICATION = {
            WINDOWS [ { NTLM | KERBEROS | NEGOTIATE } ]
       | CERTIFICATE certificate_name
```

```
    } ]
    [ [ , ] ENCRYPTION =
{ DISABLED |SUPPORTED | REQUIRED }
        [ ALGORITHM { RC4 | AES | AES RC4 | RC4 AES } ]
    ]
    [,] ROLE = { WITNESS | PARTNER | ALL }
```

For your authentication options, you can specify WINDOWS authentication, and you need to choose the authorization method (using NTLM or KERBEROS). By default, the NEGOTIATE option is set, which will cause the endpoint to negotiate between NTLM or Kerberos:

```
<authentication_options> ::=
WINDOWS [ { NTLM | KERBEROS | NEGOTIATE } ]
```

However, if you specify an authorization method, whether it is Kerberos or NTLM, that method will be used as the authentication protocol.

Certificate-based authentication   You can specify that the endpoint has to authenticate using a certificate by specifying the CERTIFICATE keyword and the name of the certificate, like this:

```
CERTIFICATE certificate_name
```

This means the endpoint must have the certificate, with the matching public key in order to match the private key of the specified certificate. Using the CERTIFICATE option, you put the certificate as a mandatory requirement, and you can authenticate using certificates only.

The authentication options also allow you to specify that you first check certificate authentication, and if the certificate cannot be found, it should use Windows Authentication. You do this by using the CERTIFICATE keyword in combination with the WINDOWS keyword:

```
CERTIFICATE certificate_name
 WINDOWS [ { NTLM | KERBEROS | NEGOTIATE } ]
```

If you prefer to first try Windows Authentication and then, if that fails, try with the certificate, you basically have to revert the keyword to the following syntax:

```
WINDOWS [ { NTLM | KERBEROS | NEGOTIATE } ] CERTIFICATE certificate_name
```

Setting the Encryption

The next part of the mirror endpoint is the encryption you want to use when sending data over a connection. By default, database mirroring uses RC4 encryption:

```
[ , ] ENCRYPTION = { DISABLED |SUPPORTED | REQUIRED }
      [ ALGORITHM { RC4 | AES | AES RC4 | RC4 AES } ]
```

Table 13.1 lists the possible encryption options you can use.

When specifying that you are using encryption, you can also specify what encryption mechanism to use, as listed in Table 13.2.

TABLE 13.1   Encryption Options When Mirroring Endpoints

Option	Description
DISABLED	The data sent over the connection is not encrypted.
SUPPORTED	The data is encrypted if the opposite endpoint is set to REQUIRED or SUPPORTED.
REQUIRED	The connections to this endpoint must use encryption.

TABLE 13.2   Encryption Algorithm Options When Mirroring Endpoints

Option	Description
RC4	The endpoint must use the RC4 algorithm (which is the default behavior).
AES	The endpoint must use the AES algorithm.
AES RC4	The endpoint will first negotiate for the AES algorithm.
RC4 AES	The endpoint will first negotiate for the RC4 algorithm.

Setting the Role

In the role part of the statement, you specify the endpoint's role:

- Partner
- Witness
- All

Using the ALL keyword as the role, you identify that the mirroring endpoint can be used for the witness as well as for a partner in a database-mirroring scenario. However, you need to keep in mind that a server instance cannot have a mirror of a database that is configured as the principal database.

 Database mirroring can use only TCP and does not have a predefined port number, which means you have to configure the port.

> **WARNING**   You must configure an endpoint on each of the partnering nodes in a database mirror. Also, the login you specify to authenticate with needs to have GRANT CONNECT permission on the endpoint.

Specifying Partners and Witnesses

After specifying the endpoints, you need to establish the mirror session. You can do this by following these steps:

1. Configure the principal as a partner on the mirror.
2. Configure the mirror as a partner on the principal.
3. Optionally configure a witness.

Configuring the Principal as a Partner on the Mirror

You have to configure the mirror to point to the principal database. You have the ability to achieve this from within SQL Server Management Studio, but it is preferable to use the ALTER DATABASE syntax.

A typical configuration syntax looks like this:

```
ALTER DATABASE <database_name>
SET PARTNER = <server_network_address>
```

For example:

```
ALTER DATABASE Sybex
    SET PARTNER =
    'TCP://SQL.SYBEX.COM:4999'
```

Configuring the Mirror as a Partner on the Principal

When you configure the mirror as a partner on the principal, you will initiate at that moment for the database-mirroring session to be established. Just like with specifying the principal as a partner in the previous step, you will use the ALTER DATABASE statement.

A typical configuration syntax looks like this:

```
ALTER DATABASE <database_name>
SET PARTNER = <server_network_address>
```

For example:

```
ALTER DATABASE Sybex
    SET PARTNER =
    'TCP://REMOTE.ILIKESQL.COM:4999'
```

Configuring a Witness

If you care about automatic failover, you should enable a witness server. The witness server does nothing but monitor the status of the principal; in our opinion, it is sad that you need to have SQL Server for that. But the good news is that you can have SQL Server Express Edition participate as a witness in database mirroring. To enable a witness, you merely need to set the witness option on the principal database and point to the already created witness server (that is the endpoint, of course). Here's the syntax:

```
ALTER DATABASE <database_name>
SET WITNESS = <server_network_address>
```

   For example:

```
ALTER DATABASE AdventureWorks
   SET WITNESS = 'TCP://WITNESS.SYBEX.COM:4999'
```

In the previous examples, the TCP port we used is 4999. Keep in mind that this port number is not a requirement; you can basically configure any port. Also, instead of using the IP address, it does make sense to configure a DNS name as in these examples.

Configuring the Operating Mode

To support database mirroring, you have different operating modes for specifying a transaction safety level. The mode you use will impact how transactions are managed between the principal and mirror; also, you can choose whether to have automatic or manual failover with a potential loss of data. Specifically, database mirroring works in three modes:

High availability   In this mode, the database *transaction safety* is set to FULL, and you will use a witness server to monitor the availability of the principal and mirror. In this mode, every transaction applied to the principal will also be applied to the mirror. When the connection to the principal fails, clients will be reconnected to the mirror automatically, after an automatic role transfer occurs.

High protection   In the absence of a witness server, database mirroring will run in high-protection mode, which still allows every transaction applied to the principal to be applied to the mirror as well. If the principal goes down, you can then force to switch roles to the mirrored server, and data loss can occur.

High performance   High-performance mode is also called *asynchronous mode*. The chance of data loss is high since it is not guaranteed that the transactions that are applied to the principal are applied to the mirror at the moment the principal fails.

You can specify transaction safety to be FULL or OFF. When specifying transaction safety to FULL, you are running in synchronous mode, which of course will impact your transaction performance but should be considered to be a low impact, given that you are implementing a nice failover method.

A synchronous operation implies that transactions will be committed and acknowledged after they are also committed and hardened on the mirrored server. So, having a reliable and high-performing network connection to the mirrored database is mandatory.

When switching transaction safety to OFF, you configure database mirroring to run without waiting for the transaction to complete on the mirrored database, which causes potential data loss.

Switching Roles

A mirror database is a failover database for the principal, and that is what database mirroring is about. So, when the principal server fails, you want to switch roles over to the mirror and from then on specify that the mirror should become the primary.

This concept is called *role switching*. You have three options for role switching:

Automatic failover   When you're using a witness server, automatic failover will occur when the principal database is not available and when the witness server confirms this. At that moment, the mirror will be automatically promoted to the principal, and whenever the principal comes back on, it will automatically take the role of a mirror.

Manual failover   You can perform manual failover only if the both the principal and the mirror are live and in a synchronized status. This is the operation you will use most frequently to perform maintenance tasks on the principal. You have to initiate the failover from the principal, and of course later you will again revert roles after you do database maintenance.

The statement used to switch database roles (manual failover) is an ALTER DATABASE statement, as shown here:

```
ALTER DATABASE SYBEX SET PARTNER FAILOVER
```

Forced service   When you are not using a witness server, your principal might go down unexpectedly. In that case, you'll want to initiate manual failover to the mirror. Because at that time you have no idea whether the actual transactions that were committed on the principal but might not have made it to the mirror (asynchronous mode), you'll want to switch roles, with the possibility of losing data.

To achieve this, you need to invoke an ALTER DATABASE statement, as shown here:

```
ALTER DATABASE SYBEX
SET PARTNER FORCE_SERVICE_ALLOW_DATA_LOSS
```

WARNING When forcing a service to switch the mirror to become the principal server, you are losing data.

Database Mirroring Implementation

As the cost of bandwidth falls lower and lower, it could be interesting to combine a clustered environment with database mirroring on specific user databases.

In a perfect scenario, a company would then be able to keep its business running from a remote location when an entire region or area goes down. One of the key problems with clustering is that a company is stuck to a geographical location that requires servers to be close to each other because of the cluster heartbeat.

In previous editions of SQL Server, a lot of companies used a similar method via replication. They would replicate an entire user database to a remote server, which was hosted in an external data center that would allow them to switch over to the remote server in case of a server or database outage. This, however, caused a lot of implications once the "principal" server came up again, since they needed to resynchronize and basically break the replication.

Implementing Log Shipping

Log shipping has existed in several releases of SQL Server. It started as a manual process in SQL Server 7.0 and became an automated process in SQL Server 2000.

Log shipping is relatively easy: you take a backup of a transaction log and restore that onto another server, thus maintaining a standby server that can be used as a read-only server for different purposes, such as for Reporting Services or as your data engine to populate a data warehouse running SQL Server Analysis Services.

These are the steps involved in setting up log shipping, as shown in Figure 13.2:

1. Back up the transaction log on the primary database.

2. Copy the log files to the secondary database, which should reside on a separate server.

3. Restore that log file onto the secondary server.

It's as simple as that, right? Now, of course we'll cover how to configure and initialize these servers and how to configure log shipping.

FIGURE 13.2   Log shipping

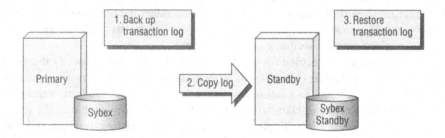

Log shipping consists of two servers:

- The *primary server* in a *log shipping* configuration has the primary database you want to back up and restore on another server. You configure the log shipping on the primary server/database.

- The *secondary server* hosts the database that maintains a copy of your primary database, and of course it is common that a server can maintain and host multiple copies of primary databases coming from multiple servers. A secondary database is usually initialized by taking a backup from the primary database.

Monitoring the Server

Monitoring the server in log shipping is more or less similar to the process of using a witness server in database mirroring; you have to configure a monitor server that will keep track of when the last backup was taken and applied to the secondary server in order to have automatic failover.

In the next section, you will learn how to configure log shipping and monitor the log shipping process.

Configuring Log Shipping

You can configure log shipping from within SQL Server Management Studio, and in our opinion it is much easier to configure using Management Studio than using the corresponding stored procedures.

To initialize log shipping, right-click the database you want to use as the primary database, and from the Tasks menu, select the Ship Transaction Logs option, as displayed in Figure 13.3.

Then, click the Enable This As a Primary Database in a Log Shipping Configuration, as displayed in Figure 13.4.

The next step is to specify the transaction log backup location and backup settings, as displayed in Figure 13.5.

After you configure the backup log and backup locations, you are then ready to create transaction log backups and configure the primary database for log shipping. The failover and redundancy between the primary database and the secondary database will be affected by the number of transaction log backups you take on the primary database and the frequency of the restore operations onto the secondary database.

As soon as you have specified the primary database, you have to specify the secondary server and database in order to initiate the failover database. Connect to an instance of SQL Server that you want to use as a secondary server by clicking the Add button under the Secondary Server Instances and Databases options. In this window, you have the option to specify a new database for log shipping, or you can pick an existing database and configure how the database needs to be initialized. If you create a new database, you also have the option to specify its file locations as well the data file's and the log file's locations, as shown in Figure 13.6.

FIGURE 13.3   Configuring log shipping

FIGURE 13.4   Enabling log shipping

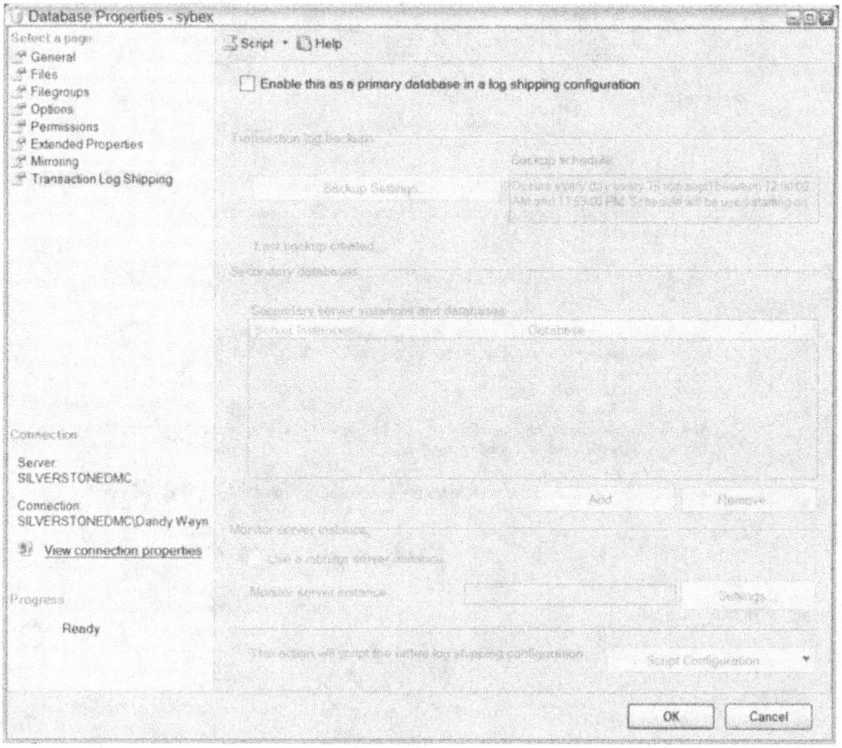

FIGURE 13.5   Specifying a log shipping backup

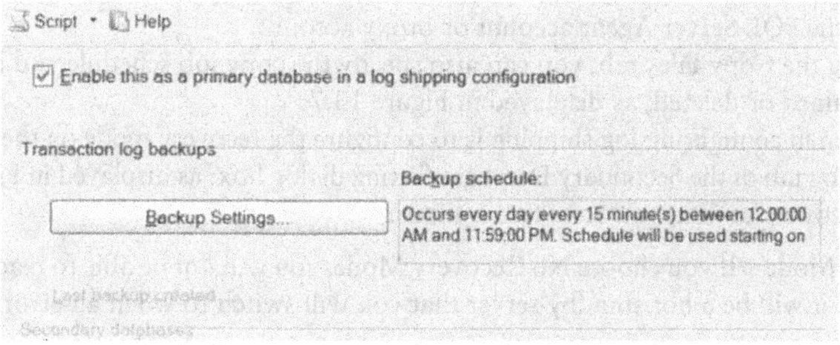

FIGURE 13.6   Specifying the secondary database

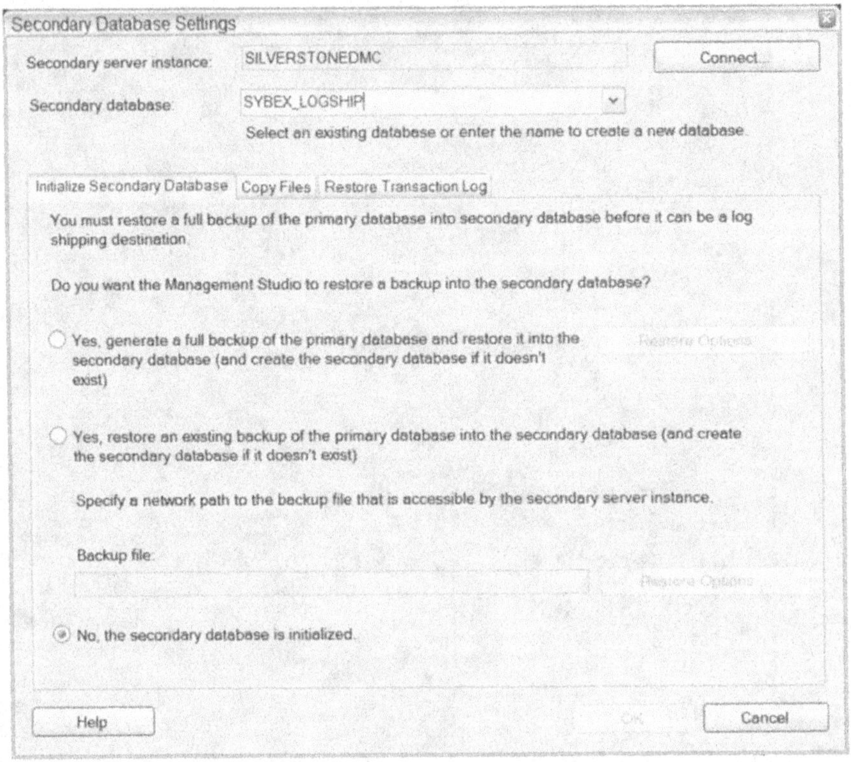

After you select the target database, you will then specify the destination folder for the backup log files to be copied to on the target server (secondary server). This means you have permission to both read from the primary and write to the target, which depends on the configuration of the SQL Server Agent account or proxy account.

By selecting the Copy Files tab, you can also specify the copy job schedule and how files should be retained or deleted, as displayed in Figure 13.7.

The last step in configuring log shipping is to configure the recovery mode on the Restore Transaction Log tab of the Secondary Database Setting dialog box, as displayed in Figure 13.8.

For this recovery option, you have two options:

No Recovery Mode   If you choose No Recovery Mode, you will not be able to read from the database, and it will be a hot standby server that you will switch to when an error occurs.

Standby Mode   If you choose the Standby Mode option, you will disconnect users from the secondary database while you perform a restore. In this mode, the database will return in a read-only mode after a restore operation is completed, and the database would then be accessible, for example, for you to perform the population of your data warehouse environment or reporting services.

FIGURE 13.7   Configuring the copy log operation

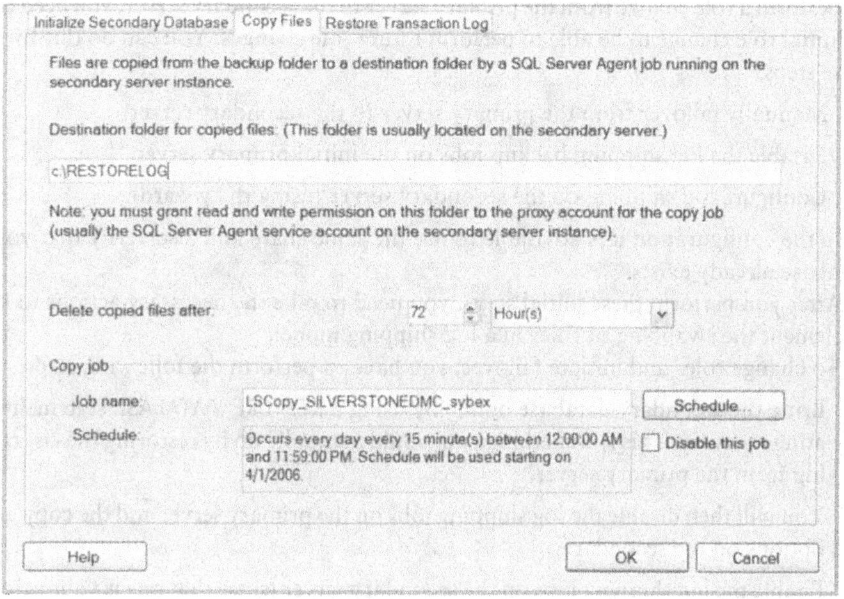

FIGURE 13.8   Configuring the restore operation

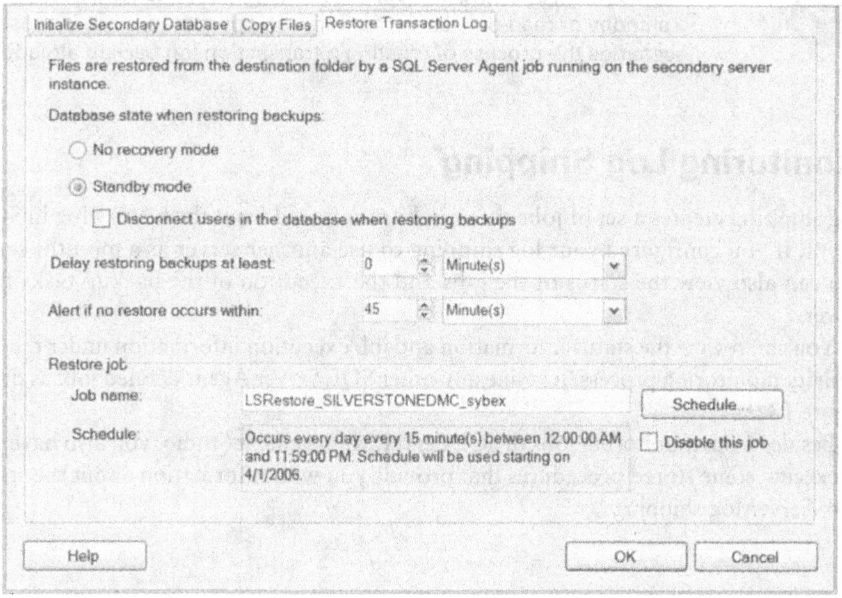

Changing Roles

To perform a role change from the primary server to the secondary server, you need to perform an initial role change to be able to perform future role changes. You can do this by following these steps:

1. Manually failover from the primary server to the secondary server.

2. Disable the log shipping backup jobs on the initial primary server.

3. Configure log shipping on the secondary server (using the wizard).

In the configuration it is advisable to use the same share and also verify that your initial database already exists.

After you perform these initial steps, you need to take the necessary actions to be able to implement the swapping of roles in a log shipping model.

To change roles and initiate failover, you have to perform the following steps:

1. Bring the secondary database online by using a RESTORE DATABASE statement and initiating recovery. This is something you would manually do by restoring the last transaction log from the primary server.

2. You will then disable the log shipping jobs on the primary server and the copy and restore options on the secondary.

3. Enable the log shipping jobs on the secondary server (since that one is your primary now) and also enable the copy and restore jobs on the former primary server.

Although log shipping is a fault-tolerant method, often it is used just to create a standby or read-only server for reporting purposes, since in most database scenarios the process of creating a transaction log backup already exists.

Monitoring Log Shipping

Log shipping creates a set of jobs that can be monitored from the history log in SQL Server Agent. If you configured your log shipping to use another server as a monitor server, then you can also view the status of the jobs and the execution of the backup tasks from that server.

You can review the status information and job execution information under the Agent Job Activity monitoring process, just like any other SQL Server Agent defined job, as displayed in Figure 13.9.

Besides from monitoring jobs in SQL Server Management Studio, you also have the ability to execute some stored procedures that provide you with information about the status of the SQL Server log shipping.

FIGURE 13.9 Log shipping monitoring

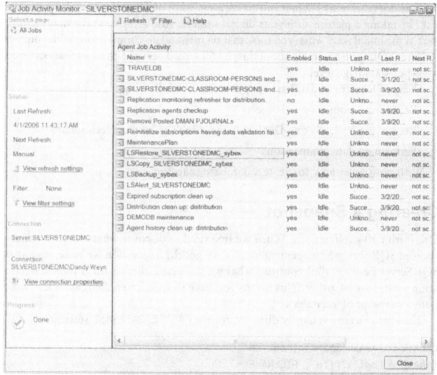

In SQL Server 2000, you can implement transaction log shipping as part of a database maintenance plan. Since there are so many changes in SQL Server 2005 regarding the structure and definition of a database maintenance plan, unfortunately the feature to perform log shipping no longer exists in the Maintenance Plan Wizard.

Managing Database Snapshots

It is tough to hide our excitement about this feature of SQL Server since we were excited about it even before it was released. How many times has a user (or a DBA who is not awake) made a mistake and you needed to recover from backup? One of the key problems of recovery is that SQL Server doesn't provide a way to back up a single table unless you force it to be created on its own filegroup. With a *database snapshot,* you have the ability to create a snapshot of your data, even before users start playing with the data.

How does this work? When you create a snapshot of a database, it takes a moment in time, just like taking a picture with your digital camera. And after you take that picture, you can look at the initial state when you took that picture and do comparisons with your current data.

Now, SQL Server is smart about this; it will record only the changes that occurred on a data page–per–data page level.

The cool features of database snapshots are the following:

- Recovering from dropped objects
- Recovering basically any DML statement such as insert/delete/update
- Performing data comparisons

We'll now cover how to create a database snapshot.

Creating a Snapshot

OK, it isn't all good news…. When we first tried to discover where to create database snapshots in SQL Server Management Studio, we got the impression we were missing something. SQL Server Books Online confirms what we suspected: there is no graphical interface for creating a database snapshot. This means you have to switch to a database query window to initiate a snapshot of a database.

The syntax to use is hardly different from a CREATE DATABASE statement:

```
CREATE DATABASE Snapshotname ON
( NAME = Logicalfile , FILENAME =
'Physicalfilename' )
AS SNAPSHOT OF SnapshotThisDatabase;
```

You use the AS SNAPSHOT keyword on the CREATE DATABASE statement, but that is not the only requirement. You also need to provide the same logical filename as named in the database used to create the snapshot.

The following statement should help you see the logical filename:

```
use sybex
select name,physical_name from sys.database_files
where type_desc = 'ROWS'
```

This results in something similar to this:

```
  name          physical_name
  -----------------------------
Sybex         C:\Program Files\ Microsoft SQL Server\MSSQL.1\MSSQL\DATA\sybex.mdf
```

So the CREATE DATABASE snapshot created is as follows:

```
CREATE DATABASE Sybex_snapshot ON
( NAME = Sybex , FILENAME =
'C:\SybexSnapshot.mdf' )
AS SNAPSHOT OF Sybex;
```

Please note that the CREATE DATABASE statement does not include, and should not include, a log file.

Now, what does SQL Server do when you create a snapshot? It reserves the disk space on the hard disk, but it also uses much less space since it uses the same behavior as Volume Shadow Copies on the file system. As mentioned, only the changes to the actual data page are recorded, meaning that a snapshot initially will not take a lot of disk space, as displayed in Figure 13.10.

As you review the file properties in Figure 13.10, you can see that the size on disk is definitely less than the size of the actual database. This is because no changes have occurred since creating the snapshot database.

FIGURE 13.10   File properties of a snapshot file

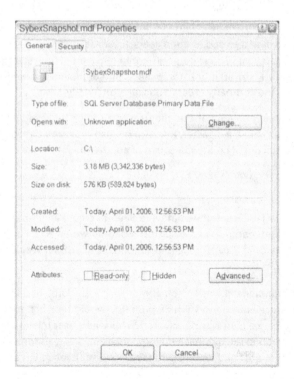

SQL Server allows you to create multiple snapshots of a database. Of course, the snapshot database will have the changes only since the moment you took the snapshot. Think of this as taking a picture of a group of friends. If you take a picture of three people, the initial picture contains three people. When someone leaves and you take a new picture, the initial picture will still contain the three people, even though the actual situation has changed. If then the group grows to 20 people and you take another picture, this picture will contain the 20 people but will not affect your other pictures.

 Real World Scenario

Implementing a Database Snapshot

The XYZ company could have prevented a disaster by creating a database snapshot; however, the company was not using SQL Server 2005 yet. Later the company decided to switch over to SQL Server 2005 for this specific feature.

XYZ had data collected from different machines with PLC interfaces to save log data into a database. After data was collected over a period of three years, a user started a manual T-SQL command and initiated it on the database. The statements contained a lot of SQL statements that heavily modified the data values stored in the database. Using database maintenance plans created on every database, the company created backups on a daily basis.

After performing the batch processing on a database, the user realized he had executed the script in the wrong database. This caused a disaster, because he also discovered that on the database the maintenance plan was never created because of another user mistake.

So, the XYZ company had a situation where they had no valid data, but even worse…no recovery.

If one of the first statements in the T-SQL script would have been to create a database snapshot before the data processing and manipulation occurred, not only would XYZ have been able to prevent the data loss but it would also provide the company with an easy way to revert the situation without restoring from backup.

Now, what can you learn from situations like this? You should create backups or use a database snapshot strategy and also use automation, which probably would be a better choice. Why was it that the initial maintenance plan was not created? This was a user mistake, which also could be avoided by implementing the database maintenance plan in an automated way through, for example, a trigger that fires and creates a database maintenance plan on every database that is created.

Reverting from a Snapshot

The key benefit of working with snapshots is that you are able to compare a "before" and an "after" status of your data when you want to perform certain data-intensive actions. Another key benefit is that you can recover from malicious deletes, so you have quite a few opportunities here.

The following are some of the key features of working with database snapshots:

Recovering from an update   When a database has a snapshot, the old value of the data will be stored in the snapshot database. Suppose you perform the following update in the Sybex database, on which you just created an initial snapshot:

```
update tbl_countries
set countryname = 'BelUSA'
where countrycode = 'BE'
```

When selecting from the snapshot database, you will get the following:

```
select * from sybex_snapshot.dbo.tbl_countries

countrycode countryname
----------- -----------------------------------------
BE          Belgium
CA          Canada
US          USA
FR          France

(4 row(s) affected)
```

To review your changed records, you can perform the following query:

```
select new.countrycode, old.countryname,
new.countryname
from sybex_snapshot.dbo.tbl_countries old
join sybex.dbo.tbl_countries new
➥on new.countrycode = old.countrycode
and new.countryname <> old.countryname
```

This will allow you to revert from the update by performing the following query:

```
update tbl_countries
set countryname = old.countryname
from sybex_snapshot.dbo.tbl_countries old
join sybex.dbo.tbl_countries new
on new.countrycode = old.countrycode
```

Recovering from a delete   Say someone accidentally deleted all your records in the countries table. You will be able to revert from the data loss by inserting from the old status that was saved in the snapshot database:

```
insert into tbl_countries
select * from sybex_snapshot.dbo.tbl_countries
```

Recovering from a dropped object   When you want to recover from a dropped object, the problem is that the object will no longer exist in the database but will still exist in the snapshot. Therefore, you will be able to script the object in the other database and then use one of the previous methods to recover from a delete.

As you can see, snapshots can be useful in a database recovery strategy, although you should not view them as a high-availability solution but rather as "preventing human mistake."

In Exercise 13.1 you will create a database snapshot, perform modifications to the actual database, compare those with the database snapshot, and recover from a deleted object.

EXERCISE 13.1

Implementing Database Snapshots

1.   Connect to SQL Server Management Studio, and open a new query window.

2.   In the new query window, type the following syntax to create a database snapshot. If you have multiple files, you need to list each logical name and filename separately. See How to Create a Database Snapshot in Books Online.

```
CREATE DATABASE Sybex_snapshot ON

( NAME = Sybex_data , FILENAME =

'C:\SybexSnapshot.mdf' )

AS SNAPSHOT OF Sybex;
```

3.   After you created the snapshot, insert a record into the actual database:

```
USE SYBEX

insert into tbl_countries values ('ES', 'Spain')

Review the data stored in the snapshot

USE SYBEX_SNAPSHOT

SELECT * FROM tbl_countries
```

4. This will result in the following:

```
countrycode countryname

----------- ----------------------

BE          Belgium

CA          Canada

US          USA

FR          France


(4 row(s) affected)
```

5. Update a record in the Sybex database:

```
USE Sybex

update tbl_countries

set countryname = 'BelUSA'

where countrycode = 'BE'
```

6. Review the data stored in the snapshot:

```
USE SYBEX_SNAPSHOT

SELECT * FROM tbl_countries
```

7. This will result in the following:

```
countrycode countryname

----------- ----------------------

BE          Belgium

CA          Canada

US          USA

FR          France


(4 row(s) affected)
```

EXERCISE 13.1 *(continued)*

8. Drop the table in the Sybex database:

```
USE SYBEX

DROP TABLE tbl_countries
```

9. Review the table existence in the Snapshot database.

```
USE SYBEX_SNAPSHOT

SELECT * FROM tbl_countries
```

10. This will result in the following:

```
countrycode countryname

----------- -----------------------

BE          Belgium

CA          Canada

US          USA

FR          France


(4 row(s) affected)
```

11. Perform a bulk insert to re-create the object in the Sybex database:

```
USE Sybex

Select * into tbl_countries

from sybex_snapshot.dbo.tbl_countries
```

12. You have now successfully re-created a dropped object using database snapshots.

Case Study: Using Other High-Availability Methods

The XYZ company ships orders from pharmaceutical companies to customers all over the world. To provide fault-tolerance on their production servers, the company decides to implement a clustered environment. However, the database administrator as well as the company management is concerned about potential data loss in case of a disaster such as a plant explosion, earthquake, or flooding.

The general requirement is not to have this recovery method implemented on all databases but as a general implementation for mission-critical databases.

To support the needs of the company, the network administrator and database department decide to use an external data center to which they will implement database mirroring on their mission-critical databases. This will allow them to immediately switch over and keep their industry running in case of a disaster at the local plant.

Because of the highly secure environment the company runs in, they enforced encryption on the database mirror and also included certificate-based authentication.

Some of the processes the company runs invoke extensive manipulation of data. In case of a process failure, XYZ wants to be able to compare the status before initiating the process to the current status because it was calculated and stored in the database. Here the company decides to implement database snapshots.

To minimize the creation of large snapshots, the company decides to create and manage multiple snapshots.

Summary

In this chapter, you learned about several high-availability options and how to implement them.

Database mirroring uses TCP communication to allow you to create an exact copy of a database at a remote location. It also allows you to automatically switch over when implemented with a witness that monitors the connection and initiates the mirror to take over from the principal database.

You also learned how to work with log shipping, which takes a copy of the transaction log and "ships" it to a remote destination. To switch over to the remote standby server, you manually need to perform certain steps to perform the switch. The standby server, however, has the ability to be used as a read-only server that you can use to populate a data warehouse, use for ad hoc querying, or use for reporting capabilities.

Another nice method to implement is database snapshots; this creates pictures of data and saves only the changes to the snapshot from the moment you initiated the creation of a snapshot. These snapshots allow you to revert from user mistakes but do not provide fault-tolerance.

Exam Essentials

Understand database mirroring concepts.   Familiarize yourself the concept of database mirroring, and know general terms such as *principal*, *mirror*, and *witness server*. If you want to have automatic failover, you can achieve this only by having a witness. Database mirroring uses endpoints that communicate with each other using TCP. You also need to know how you can manually force a mirror to take over the role of the principal server.

Understand log shipping.   Understand the implementation and usage of log shipping on a database, and keep in mind that this is implemented using transaction log backups. The ability to specify the schedule on the transaction log backup and when to restore initially determines the latency between the recovery and failover strategy. Log shipping is a manual failover process and allows you to have a hot standby server or a read-only server that can be used for different purposes.

Understand database snapshots.   In a database snapshot, it is important to understand that the snapshot does not implement high availability but merely records the changes of the data to a snapshot database. When retrieving data from a snapshot, the data will be partially read from the production database and will get only the changed data pages from the snapshot.

Review Questions

1. What protocol is used by database-mirroring endpoints?

   A. HTTP

   B. SMTP

   C. TCP

   D. SOAP

2. What technologies allow you to avoid user mistakes and prevent malicious deletes on a database? (Choose all that apply.)

   A. Database mirroring

   B. Clustering

   C. DDL triggers

   D. Database snapshots

3. You need to create a snapshot of the database ILIKESQL. What is the correct syntax to use?

   A. Use this:
   ```
   CREATE DATABASE ILIKESQL_snapshot ON
   ( NAME = ILIKESQL_Data , FILENAME =
   'C:\IlikeSQL_Snapshot.sss' )
   AS SNAPSHOT OF ilikesql;
   ```

   B. Use this:
   ```
   CREATE DATABASE ILIKESQL_snapshot ON
   ( NAME = ILIKESQL_Data , FILENAME =
   'C:\IlikeSQL_Snapshot.sss'
   LOG ON 'C:\IlikeSQL_Snapshot_log.sss')
   AS SNAPSHOT OF ilikesql
   ```

   C. Use this:
   ```
   CREATE DATABASE SNAPSHOT  ILIKESQL_snapshot
   AS SNAPSHOT OF ilikesql
   ```

   D. Use this:
   ```
   CREATE DATABASE SNAPSHOT  ILIKESQL_snapshot
   AS SNAPSHOT OF ilikesql ON
   ( NAME = ILIKESQL_Data , FILENAME =
   'C:\IlikeSQL_Snapshot.sss' )
   ```

4. A database snapshot has been created. Now because of a user mistake, you need to restore a table and its indexes from the snapshot database. How can you achieve this with the least administrative effort?

   A. Use the Copy Database Wizard.

   B. Script the creation of the objects in the snapshot database, and run the script in the user database.

   C. Use a SELECT statement to reinsert the table.

   D. Rewrite the entire statement.

5. You have a database mirror in place without a witness server and notice that the principal database is down. What statement should you execute to promote the mirror server to take the principal role?

A. ALTER DATABASE databasename SET PARTNER FAILOVER

B. ALTER DATABASE databasename SET PARTNER SWITCH_ROLE

C. ALTER DATABASE databasename SET PARTNER FORCE_SERVICE_ALLOW_DATA_LOSS

D. ALTER DATABASE databasename SET PARTNER FORCE_SERVICE_ALLOW_NO_DATA_LOSS

6. You are configuring an endpoint for database mirroring but are not sure about the correct syntax to use. What lines would you insert on the following statement?

```
CREATE ENDPOINT endpoint_mirroring
    STATE = STARTED
  --- insert line here
(     AUTHENTICATION = WINDOWS KERBEROS,
      ENCRYPTION = SUPPORTED,
      ROLE=ALL);
```

A. Use this:
```
    AS TCP ( LISTENER_PORT = 5022 )
    FOR DATABASE_MIRRORING
```

B. Use this:
```
    AS HTTP ( LISTENER_PORT = 5022 )
    FOR SERVICE_BROKER
```

C. Use this:
```
    AS HTTP ( LISTENER_PORT = 5022 )
    FOR DATABASE_MIRRORING
```

D. Use this:
```
    AS HTTP ( LISTENER_PORT = 5022 )
    FOR SOAP
```

7. You implemented database mirroring; however, when a connection to the principal fails, you need to manually switch over to the mirror. What can you do to avoid this?

A. Start SQL Server Agent.

B. Review the Event log for error details.

C. Break the mirror, and install a witness first.

D. Configure a witness.

8. You configured database mirroring; however, the principal does not seem to be able to connect to the mirror. You verified that you created the mirroring endpoints on both the mirror and the principal using the following script on both the principal and the mirror:

```
-- on principal and mirror you executed the script below
CREATE ENDPOINT endpoint_mirroring
    STATE = STARTED
```

```
     AS TCP ( LISTENER_PORT = 5022 )
     FOR DATABASE_MIRRORING (
         AUTHENTICATION = WINDOWS KERBEROS,
         ENCRYPTION = SUPPORTED,
         ROLE=ALL);


-- on mirror you executed the script below
ALTER DATABASE Sybex
     SET PARTNER =
     'TCP://PRINCIPAL.SYBEX.COM:4999'


-- on principal you executed the script below
ALTER DATABASE Sybex
     SET PARTNER =
     'TCP://MIRROR.SYBEX.COM:4999'
```

What could be the problem?

A. The mirror and principal communicate on the same port.

B. The mirror and principal endpoint have a wrong port setting.

C. The mirror has the wrong port setting.

D. The principal should connect to port 5022.

9. You configured database mirroring; however, the principal does not seem to be able to connect to the mirror. You verified that you created the mirroring endpoints on both the mirror and the principal using the following script on both the principal and the mirror:

```
-- on principal you created the following endpoint
CREATE ENDPOINT endpoint_mirroring
     STATE = STARTED
     AS TCP ( LISTENER_PORT = 5022 )
     FOR DATABASE_MIRRORING (
         AUTHENTICATION = WINDOWS KERBEROS,
         ENCRYPTION = REQUIRED
         ALGORITHM RC4,
         ROLE=PARTNER);


-- on mirror you created the following endpoint
CREATE ENDPOINT endpoint_mirroring
     STATE = STARTED
     AS TCP ( LISTENER_PORT = 5022 )
     FOR DATABASE_MIRRORING (
         AUTHENTICATION = WINDOWS KERBEROS,
```

```
        ENCRYPTION = REQUIRED
        ALGORITHM RC4,
        ROLE=WITNESS);


-- on mirror you executed the script below
ALTER DATABASE Sybex
        SET PARTNER =
        'TCP://PRINCIPAL.SYBEX.COM:5022'


-- on principal you executed the script below
ALTER DATABASE Sybex
        SET PARTNER =
        'TCP://MIRROR.SYBEX.COM:5022'
```

What could be the problem?

A. You need to set SAFETY TO FULL on the database option.

B. You need to change the encryption mechanism to SUPPORTED.

C. You need to set the ROLE option on the principal to ALL or PARTNER.

D. You need to set the ROLE option on the mirror to ALL or PARTNER.

10. What should you do to centralize the results of a log shipping job to one server?

A. Centralize the location of the transaction log backup to that server.

B. Configure the server to be a monitoring server.

C. Open Windows Event Viewer to remotely review log shipping details.

D. You are unable to centralize log shipping details to one server.

11. When trying to implement log shipping, you noticed that the backup jobs run successfully, but the secondary database fails to retrieve the transaction log files. What should you do?

A. Check the file permissions on the log backup location.

B. Reinitialize log shipping.

C. Start SQL Server Agent on the secondary database.

D. Check that SQL Server Agent runs in the same security context on the primary as on the secondary database.

12. After a primary database fails, you want to bring the secondary database online. What should be your first step?

A. Try to take a backup from the last transaction log on the primary database.

B. Restore the secondary with the RECOVERY option.

C. Stop the SQL Server Agent on the primary server.

D. Disable the log shipping jobs on the secondary server.

13. You created two database snapshots, one at 2 P.M. and one at 4 P.M. At 5 P.M. a user warns you he accidentally dropped an existing table. The user was certain that he dropped the table somewhere between 3 P.M. and 4 P.M. What should you do?

A. Inform the user you cannot recover the table.

B. Inform the user you can restore the table from the first snapshot.

C. Inform the user you can restore the table from the second snapshot.

D. Inform the user you will combine the 2 P.M. and 4 P.M. snapshot to recover both the table and data.

14. You created two database snapshots, one at 2 P.M and one at 4 P.M. At 3 P.M. a user issued an UPDATE statement to a table without specifying a WHERE clause. What can you do to bring the data back to the state it was in before the user issued the statement? (Choose all that apply.)

A. Update the database with the stored information in the 2 P.M. and 4 P.M. snapshots.

B. Update the database with the stored information in the 2 P.M. snapshot.

C. Drop the table, and retrieve all information from the 2 P.M. snapshot.

D. Inform the user you will combine the 2 P.M. and 4 P.M. snapshots to recover both the table and data.

15. You created two database snapshots, one at 2 P.M. and one at 4 P.M. At 5 P.M. a user warns you he accidentally dropped a table he created around 3 P.M. The user was certain he dropped the table somewhere between 3 P.M. and 4 P.M. What should you do?

A. Inform the user you cannot recover his table.

B. Inform the user you can restore the table from the first snapshot.

C. Inform the user you can restore the table from the second snapshot.

D. Inform the user you will combine the 2 P.M. and 4 P.M. snapshots to recover both the data.

16. You are planning on integrating snapshots on an hourly basis. However, you want to perform maintenance and retain a snapshot only from the last eight hours. How can you accomplish this with the least administrative effort?

A. Create a job that will automatically drop the database snapshots after eight hours.

B. Manually drop database snapshots.

C. When you create a new database snapshot, specify the WITH DROP_EXISTING option.

D. You can create only one database snapshot at a time.

17. You have a SQL Server report server that is currently generating reports with data coming from your production database. The company has a log shipping database, and you also use database snapshots. Recently there has been a heavy workload on the production database. What can you do to minimize the impact of database querying on the production database?

A. Point the report data sources to retrieve data from the snapshot.

B. Point the report data sources to retrieve data from the secondary log shipped database.

C. Set up replication to replicate data from the production database to the report server.

D. Create another instance of SQL Server, and set up log shipping.

18. You need to implement a fault-tolerance method that will allow you to automatically switch over to a standby server when an error occurs with the primary production database. What options can you choose to implement?

A. Clustering

B. Database snapshots

C. Database mirroring

D. Log shipping

19. You have only two servers in place and want to implement fault-tolerance. What can you do to provide fault-tolerance on two important user databases that you have?

A. Implement a cluster.

B. Implement database mirroring.

C. Implement database snapshots.

D. Implement log shipping.

20. What is one of the disadvantages of database mirroring?

A. You need to have the same hardware.

B. The database you mirror to will be in an unused standby state.

C. You cannot have automatic failover.

D. You need to have at minimum three servers.

Answers to Review Questions

1. C. Database mirroring and Service Broker endpoints use TCP as their communication protocol.

2. C, D. Both database snapshots and triggers allow you to prevent user mistakes and malicious deletes on a database. By implementing a trigger, you can log the old status of a record in a log table and retrieve from that log table. By implementing database snapshots, snapshot data will record every change made to the database.

3. A. The correct syntax is to use a CREATE DATABASE statement and specify a data file location for every logical data file without specifying a log file (which invalidates Option B).

4. A. When re-creating the object in the snapshot database, you can also script the indexes and triggers. After you create the script, you can rerun the script in the database.

5. C. You can use SET PARTNER FAILOVER only when the actual principal and mirror are both in sync. This means you are allowing data loss by forcing the roles, so the only option here is Option C.

6. A. Database mirroring uses TCP. In the protocol definition, you initiate the protocol and port number and specify where the endpoint is.

7. D. To have automatic failover, you need to implement a witness. You should do this after you establish the connection between the principal and mirror.

8. B. Both the mirror and principal endpoint are configured on port 5022. In communication between the principal and mirror when setting up the partner, you need to identify the port number. This port number should be the same connecting port number as you specified on the endpoint but can be the same for both endpoints.

9. D. The role of the mirror is wrongly configured; it is set to take only a witness role instead of PARTNER or ALL. If the endpoint should be used for only mirroring and not playing the role of a witness, you should change this to PARTNER.

10. B . To centralize but also review logging job execution, you can set up a monitor server that monitors the execution of log shipping jobs.

11. A. You need to check that the job agent has permission to read the files from the file system in order to be able to transfer them to the secondary database.

12. A. The first step you should try is to take a transaction log backup of the primary server to prevent from potential data loss. This will allow you to recover on the secondary database by applying the backups that did not get restored automatically, using the NORECOVERY option. On the last restore, you then initiate recovery.

13. B. Since the user dropped an existing table, the table was in the 2 P.M. snapshot. This means you can recover both the table and data from the first snapshot.

14. B, C. Although it sounds strange, you can do either B or C. When you drop a table, the entire table will still be available in the snapshot as it was at the moment you took the snapshot. In this case, it means the initial state is still there, and you are able to recover from that. Another option would be to perform an UPDATE statement against the live data, with data coming from the snapshot database.

15. A. You cannot recover since the table was created after the first snapshot was taken and before the second snapshot was taken. This means at the moment the user created a table, the snapshot 2 P.M. data did not record the creation of the table, since it did not exist at 2 P.M. Since the user was sure he dropped the table before 4 P.M., the table will not be in any of the snapshots.

16. A. You need to create a job that will drop the older database snapshots. You could also manually drop the snapshots, but you want to accomplish this with the least administrative effort.

17. B. When you point the data source to the log shipping database, you will reduce the stress load on the production server. Querying on a snapshot database will still go to the underlying production database, since a snapshot contains only the changed data pages.

18. A, C. Database snapshots do not provide fault-tolerance, and log shipping does not automatically failover. Your only option is to implement a SQL Server cluster or a database mirror with a witness server in place.

19. A, B, D. To provide fault-tolerance, you can implement clustering as well as database mirroring or log shipping since they require you to have only two servers. Database snapshots do not provide fault-tolerance.

20. B. Database mirroring can be implemented with automatic failover if you have a witness server. One of its benefits is that it does not require you to have the same hardware. The only disadvantage is that database mirroring does not support read-only status, which would be a nice feature to have.

Chapter

14

Monitoring and Optimizing SQL Server 2005

MICROSOFT EXAM OBJECTIVES COVERED IN THIS CHAPTER:

✓ **Gather performance and optimization data by using the SQL Server Profiler.**

- Start a new trace.
- Save the trace logs.
- Configure SQL Server Profiler trace properties.
- Configure a System Monitor counter log.
- Correlate a SQL Server Profiler trace with System Monitor log data.

✓ **Gather performance and optimization data by using the Database Engine Tuning Advisor.**

- Build a workload file by using the SQL Server Profiler.
- Tune a workload file by using the Database Engine Tuning Advisor.
- Save recommended indexes.

✓ **Monitor and resolve blocks and deadlocks.**

- Identify the cause of a block by using the sys.dm_exec_requests system view.
- Terminate an errant process.
- Configure SQL Server Profiler trace properties.
- Identify transaction blocks.

✓ **Diagnose and resolve database server errors.**

- Connect to a nonresponsive server by using the dedicated administrator connection (DAC).
- Review SQL Server startup logs.
- Review error messages in event logs.

✓ **Monitor SQL Server Agent job history.**

- Identify the cause of a failure.
- Identify outcome details.
- Find out when a job last ran.

Imagine for a moment you are the chief operating officer of a sizable company. It is your job to make sure the company runs smoothly and that everything gets done efficiently. How will you do this? You could just guess at it, randomly assigning tasks and then assuming they will get done. Imagine the chaos that would ensue if you used this approach. Nothing would get done. Some departments would have too much to do, and others would have nothing to do—and your company would go bankrupt.

A better approach would be to ask for reports from the various department managers and base your decisions on those reports. You might discover, for instance, that the accounting department has too much work and could use some help. Based on this report, you could hire more accountants. You might find that the production department has little to do because the sales department has not been doing a good job; based on this report, you could motivate sales to get to work so that production would have something to do.

Now, instead of being in charge of the entire company's operations, you are in charge of your SQL Server. Here too, you need to make certain everything is getting done efficiently. Again, you could just guess at this and randomly assign tasks, but that is an invitation to disaster. You need to get reports from your department managers—and in this case, the department managers are the CPU, the disk subsystem, the database engine, and so on. Once you have these reports, you can assign tasks and resources accordingly.

Many system administrators don't perform monitoring functions because they think they don't have the time. Most of their time is spent on firefighting—that is, troubleshooting problems that have cropped up. It's safe to say that if the system administrators had taken the time to monitor their systems, those problems might never have arisen in the first place. That makes monitoring and optimization *proactive* troubleshooting, not *reactive*, as is the norm. To that end, in this chapter we'll discuss the various methods and tools for getting the reports you need from SQL Server.

But, no matter how diligent you may be in monitoring your system, problems will arise from time to time. To deal with these problems, you need to have some troubleshooting skills, so we will cover some methods for troubleshooting common problems.

As is best with most subjects, you'll start at the bottom and work your way up; we'll discuss the tools (System Monitor, the Management Studio Query Editor, and SQL Profiler) and then move on to troubleshooting.

Using System Monitor

To ensure your company functions properly, you need to make certain the foundation of the company is doing its job. You need a management group that works well together and gets tasks done—a group where each member pulls their own share of the load.

With SQL Server, this management group is the computer system itself. SQL Server cannot function properly if it does not have available system resources such as ample memory, adequate processor power, fast disks, and a reliable network subsystem. If these systems do not work together, the overall system will not function properly. For example, if the memory is being overused, the disk subsystem slows down, because the memory has to write to the pagefile (which is on the disk) far too often. To keep such things from happening, you need to get reports from the subsystems; you can do this using System Monitor.

System Monitor comes with Windows and is located in the Administrative Tools section of the Start menu (the tool is labeled Performance). Four views are available for your use:

Graph   This view displays a graph of system performance. As values change, the graph will spike or dip accordingly.

Report   The report view looks like what you might get on a piece of paper, except that the values here change with system use.

Alert   With alert view, you can tell System Monitor to warn you when something bad is looming on the horizon, perhaps when CPU use is almost—but not quite yet—too high. This type of warning gives you time to fix potential problems before they become actual problems.

Log   The log view is for record keeping. With log view, you can monitor your system over a time period and view the information later, as opposed to viewing it in real time (the default).

With each of these views, you monitor objects and counters. An *object* is a part of the system, such as the processor or the physical memory. A *counter* displays the statistical information about how much that object is being used. For example, the % Processor Time counter under the Processor object will tell you how much time your processor spends working. Table 14.1 lists common counters and their recommended values.

TABLE 14.1   Common Counters and Values in System Monitor

Object	Counter	Recommended Value	Use	Recommendations
Processor	% Processor Time	Less than 75%	The amount of time the processor spends working	If this is too high, you should off-load some processes to another server or purchase a multiprocessor machine.

TABLE 14.1   Common Counters and Values in System Monitor *(continued)*

Object	Counter	Recommended Value	Use	Recommendations
Memory	Pages/Sec	Fewer than 5	The number of times per second that data had to be moved from RAM to disk, and vice versa	If this is too high, it means your system is compensating for a lack of RAM by paging to disk. You should add more RAM if this is too high.
Memory	Available Bytes	More than 4MB	The amount of physical RAM available	This number should be low, because Windows uses as much RAM as it can grab for file cache.
Memory	Committed Bytes	Less than physical RAM	The amount of RAM committed to use	If this is higher than the physical RAM, then you should consider adding more RAM.
PhysicalDisk	% Disk Time	Less than 50%	The amount of time the disk is busy reading or writing	If this is higher than 50%, you should consider off-loading some processes to another machine or adding disks to your array.
Network Segment	% Network Utilization	Less than 30%	The amount of network bandwidth being used	If this is too high, then you should consider segregating your network with a router or bridge to decrease broadcast traffic.

To see the Network Segment: % Network Utilization, you must install the Network Monitor Agent on the Services tab of the Network Control Panel.

Now you'll get some practice with System Monitor in Exercise 14.1.

EXERCISE 14.1

Working with System Monitor

1. Log on to Windows as Administrator.

2. From the Start menu, select Programs ➢ Administrative Tools ➢ Performance. Notice that the graph is already populated with counters.

3. On the toolbar, click the Add button (it looks like a + sign) to open the Add Counters dialog box.

4. In the Performance Object box, select Memory.

5. In the Select Counters from List box, select Available Bytes, and click Add.

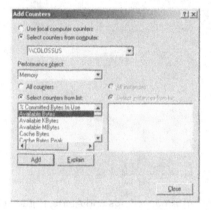

6. Click Close, and notice the graph being created on the screen.

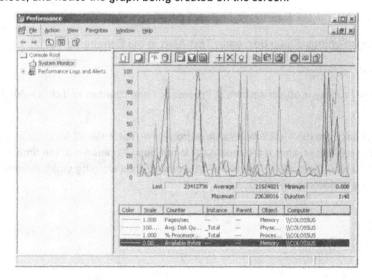

EXERCISE 14.1 *(continued)*

7.   Press Ctrl+H, and notice the current counter turns white. This makes the chart easier to read.

8.   On the toolbar, click the View Report button (it looks like a sheet of paper), and notice how the same data appears in report view.

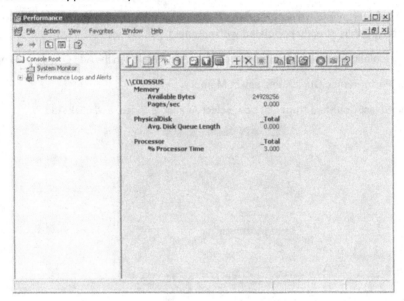

9.   In the left pane, expand Performance Logs and Alerts, right-click Alerts, and select New Alert Settings.

10.   Enter **Test Alert** in the Name box, and click OK.

11.   In the Alert Settings dialog box, enter **Test Alert** in the Comment field.

12.   Click Add.

13.   Select the Processor object and the % Processor Time counter, and click Add; then click Close.

14.   Select Under from the Alert When Value Is drop-down list, enter **70** for Limit, and click OK. This will generate an alert if the processor is not busy 70 percent of the time. In the real world, you would set this to more than 70 percent, thus warning you just before it becomes a serious problem.

EXERCISE 14.1 *(continued)*

15. Click OK to create the alert.

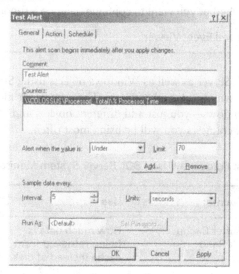

16. To view the alerts, open Event Viewer, and look for them in the Application log, then double-click the event to view its properties.

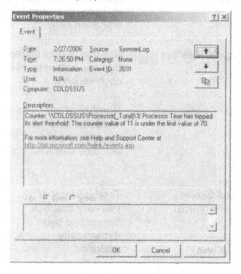

17. Watch the alerts generated for a short time, then select the alert, and finally press the Delete key. If asked whether you want to continue deleting a running alert, click OK.

18. Exit System Monitor and Event Viewer.

You can monitor SQL Server as well as Windows objects using System Monitor, because SQL Server provides its own objects and counters. The process for monitoring SQL Server is the same as it is with Windows—you just add different objects and counters. Table 14.2 describes the SQL Server counters you will be using most often.

TABLE 14.2 Most Frequently Used SQL Server System Monitor Counters

Object	Counter	Use	Recommendations
SQLServer: Buffer Manager	Buffer Cache Hit Ratio	How much data is being retrieved from cache instead of disk.	This should be in the high 90s. If it is too low, then you may need to add more RAM to your system.
SQLServer: Buffer Manager	Page Reads/Sec	Number of data pages that are read from disk each second.	This should be as low as possible.
SQLServer: Buffer Manager	Page Writes/Sec	Number of data pages that are written to disk each second.	This should be as low as possible.
SQLServer: General Statistics	User Connections	Number of user connections. Each of these connections will take some RAM.	Use this to predict how much memory you will need for your system when you add new users.
SQLServer: Memory Manager	Total Server Memory (KB)	Total amount of memory that SQL Server has been dynamically assigned.	Use this when determining whether you have enough RAM to add more processes, such as replication, to a SQL Server.
SQLServer: SQL Statistics	SQL Compilations /Sec	Number of compiles per second.	This should be as high as possible.

Now that the system resources are working together, you need to make sure SQL Server is working the way you want it to work. To monitor SQL Server, you need to know how to use SQL Server Profiler.

Monitoring with SQL Profiler

When running a company, once you have the management team working in harmony, you can focus your attention on the rest of the workforce. As in any company, the employees need to be monitored to make sure they are doing their fair share of work. In this analogy, the queries that are run on SQL Server would be the employees that need to be monitored, and Profiler is the tool you need to do the work.

Profiler allows you to monitor and record what is happening inside the database engine. This is accomplished by performing a *trace,* which is a record of data that has been captured about events. Traces are stored in a table, a trace log file, or both, and they can be either shared (viewable by everyone) or private (viewable only by the owner).

The actions you will be monitoring, called *events*, are anything that happens to the database engine, such as a failed login or a completed query. These events are logically grouped into *event classes* in Profiler so that they will be easier for you to find and use. Some of these events are useful for maintaining security, and some are useful for troubleshooting problems, but most of these events are used for monitoring and optimizing. The following event categories are available:

Cursors   A *cursor* is an object that is used to work with multiple rows of data by moving through them one row at a time. This event class monitors events that are generated by cursor usage.

Database   This is a collection of events that monitor automatic changes in size for data and log files.

Errors and Warnings   The events in this class monitor errors and warnings such as a failed login or a syntax error.

Locks   When users access data, that data is locked so other users cannot modify data someone else is reading. This class of events monitors the locks placed on your data.

Objects   Monitor this class of events to see when objects (such as tables, views, or indexes) are opened, closed, or modified in some way.

Performance   This collection of events displays Showplan event classes as well as event classes produced by data manipulation operators.

Scans   Tables and indexes can be *scanned*, which means SQL Server must read through every single entry in the object to find the data for which you are looking. The events in this class monitor these object scans.

Security Audit   These events monitor security. Such things as failed logins, password changes, and role changes are contained in this category.

Server   This category contains classes that monitor server control and memory change events.

Sessions   When a user connects to SQL Server, that user is said to have "started a session" with the server. This event class monitors user sessions.

Stored Procedures   A *stored procedure* is a collection of T-SQL code that is stored on the server, ready to be executed. This event class monitors events that are triggered by the use of stored procedures.

Transactions   A *transaction* is a group of T-SQL commands that are viewed as a unit, meaning either they must all be applied to the database together or all of them fail. This event class monitors SQL Server transactions (including anything that happens to a transaction log where transactions are recorded) as well as transactions that go through the DTC.

TSQL   This event class monitors any T-SQL commands that are passed from the client to the database server.

User Configurable   If the other events in Profiler do not meet your needs, you can create your own event to monitor with these user-configurable events. This is especially handy for custom applications you may create.

OLEDB   OLEDB is an interface that developers can use to connect to SQL Server. This event class monitors OLE DB–specific events.

Broker   Service Broker is a new component in SQL Server 2005 that provides asynchronous message queuing and delivery. The Broker event class monitors events generated by Service Broker.

Full Text   Full-text indexing gives you flexibility in querying SQL Server by letting you search for phrases, word variations, weighted results, and so on. These indexes are controlled by a separate service (`msftesql.exe`). Using this event class, you can monitor events generated by the full-text index service and its indexes.

Deprecation   Over the years, many commands have been deprecated in SQL Server. One such example is the `DUMP` statement, which was used in earlier versions of SQL Server to back up databases and logs but is no longer a valid command. The Deprecation event class helps you track down procedures and programs that are using deprecated functions and commands so you can update them.

Progress Report   This class of events helps you monitor the progress of long-running commands, such as online index operations.

When you create a trace, it is based on a *trace template*. A template is a predefined trace definition that can be used to create a trace out of the box, or you can modify it to fit your needs. You can choose from several templates:

Blank   This template has no configuration at all. It is a blank slate that you can use to create a completely unique trace definition.

SP_Counts   You can use this template to see how many stored procedures are started, what database ID they are called from, and which server process ID (SPID) called the stored procedure.

Standard   This template records logins and logouts, existing connections (at the time of the trace), completed remote procedure calls (RPCs), and completed T-SQL batches.

TSQL   This records the same events as the Standard template except that this template displays only the EventClass, TextData, SPID, and StartTime data columns. This is useful for tracking which queries are being run, when they are being run, and who is running them.

TSQL_Duration   This tracks what queries are being executed and how long those queries take. This is especially useful for finding queries and stored procedures with poor performance.

TSQL_Grouped   You can use this template to discover what applications are being used to connect to SQL Server and who is using those applications. This template tracks queries that are being run and groups them by application name, then Windows username, then SQL Server username, and then process ID.

TSQL_Replay   Trace files can be replayed against a server, meaning that every action in a trace file can be executed as if it were coming from a user. This template is especially useful for replaying against a server to find the cause of a crash or some other unexpected event.

TSQL_SPs   You can use this template to find out who is running stored procedures and what those stored procedures do.

Tuning   You can use this specifically for creating a trace file for the Database Tuning Advisor, which we will discuss later in this chapter.

In Exercise 14.2, you'll get some hands-on experience with Profiler by creating a trace that monitors the opening and closing of objects.

When the Server Processes Trace Data box is checked, SQL Server processes the trace. This can slow server performance, but no events are missed. If the box is unchecked, the client processes the trace data. This results in faster performance, but some events may be missed under a heavy server load.

EXERCISE 14.2

Creating a Trace with Profiler

1. From the Start menu, go to Programs ➢ Microsoft SQL Server 2005 ➢ Performance Tools ➢ SQL Server Profiler.

2. From the File menu, select New Trace.

3. Connect to your default server instance using the proper authentication; this opens the Trace Properties dialog box.

4. In the Trace Name box, type **Monitor**.

5. Use the TSQL_Replay template (we'll replay this later).

6. Check the Save to File box, and click Save to accept the default name and location. Leave the Enable File Rollover box checked and the Server Processes Trace Data box unchecked.

7. Check the Save to Table box, log on to your default server instance, and fill in the following:

   Database: **AdventureWorks**

   Owner: **dbo**

   Table: **Monitor**

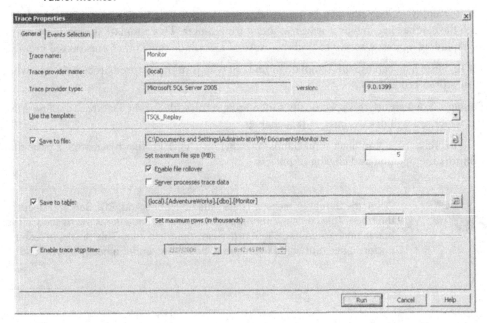

8. Click the Events Selection tab, and check the Show All Events box toward the bottom of the tab.

9. In the Events grid, expand Security Audit (if it is not already expanded), and check the box to the left of Audit Schema Object Access Event. This will monitor the opening and closing of objects, such as tables.

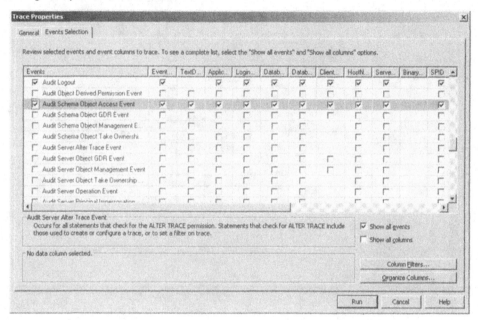

10. Click Run to start the trace.

11. Leave Profiler running, and open a new SQL Server query in Management Studio.

12. Execute the following query:

    USE AdventureWorks

    SELECT * FROM Person.Contact

13. Switch to Profiler, and click the Pause button (double blue lines). In the Profiler, notice the amount of data that was collected.

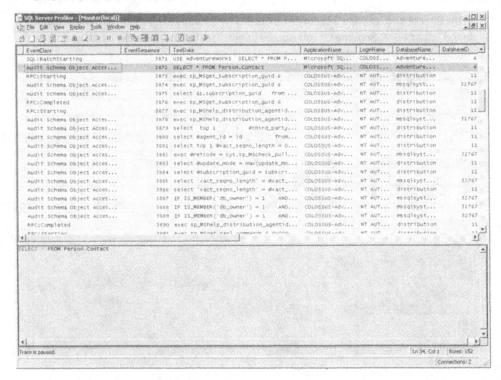

14. Close Profiler and Management Studio.

If you look toward the end of the results in the trace, you should see the SELECT query you executed in step 12 in the previous exercise. Once a trace has been recorded, everything in the trace can be executed as if it were coming from a user. This is a process called *replaying*.

Replaying a Trace File

When a detective is trying to solve a crime, one of the first steps is to re-create the action as closely as possible. This helps find specific clues that cannot be found any other way. In the same way, when something bad happens to SQL Server (such as a server crash), you need to be able to re-create the circumstances that led up to the event as closely as possible, which you can do with Profiler by replaying a trace.

Loading your saved traces into Profiler allows you to replay them against the server and, in this way, figure out exactly where the problem occurred. An especially nice touch is that you don't have to play the whole trace all at once; you can take it step by step to see exactly where the problem lies, and you can even play the saved traces against a different server so you don't crash your production server in the process. You'll try this in Exercise 14.3.

Replaying a Trace

1. Open Profiler; from the File menu, select Open and Trace File.

2. In the Open dialog box, select `Monitor.trc`, and click OK.

3. On the toolbar in the trace window, click the Execute One Step button (a blue arrow pointing to a gray line). This will execute a single step at a time.

4. Log on to your default instance of SQL Server.

5. On the Replay dialog box that opens, you can choose to create an output filename, which will store all error messages and output for later review. Leave this blank.

6. Under Replay Options, you can opt to enable debugging by replaying events in the order they were recorded or disable debugging by replaying multiple events at the same time. Select the option to replay events in the order they were recorded, enable debugging, and click OK.

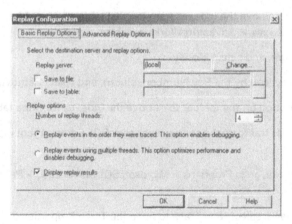

7. Scroll down, and select the first line you find that contains `SQL:BatchCompleted`.

8. On the toolbar, click the Run to Cursor button (an arrow pointing to double braces). This will execute all steps between the current position and the event you have selected.

9. Click the Start Execution button (a yellow arrow) to finish replaying the trace.

10. Close Profiler.

Profiler is a wonderful tool for monitoring database activity and reporting problems, but that is not all it can do. Profiler comes with yet another wizard that will help you even further improve the performance of your queries—the Database Engine Tuning Advisor.

Using the Database Engine Tuning Advisor

If one musical instrument in an orchestra is out of tune, the entire symphony sounds bad, and the performance is ruined. In the same way, if even one SQL Server database were out of tune, it could slow down the entire system. Perhaps an index was created using the wrong columns, or maybe users have started querying different data over time, which would require the creation of new indexes. If any of this is true, your databases need tuning. To do that, you need to use the *Database Engine Tuning Advisor*.

Before you can run the Database Engine Tuning Advisor, you need to create a *workload*. You get this by running and saving a trace in Profiler (usually by creating a trace with the Tuning template). It is best to get this workload during times of peak database activity to make sure you give the advisor an accurate load. First you need to create a workload file to use with the advisor, which you'll do in Exercise 14.4.

EXERCISE 14.4

Creating a Workload File

1. First you need to remove the indexes from the test table, so open Management Studio, and expand Databases ➢ AdventureWorks ➢ Tables.

2. Right-click Monitor, and select Modify.

3. Right-click the key icon by the RowNumber column, and select Remove Primary Key.

4. Click the Save button on the toolbar to remove the indexes from the table.

5. To stop any excess traffic on the server, right-click SQL Server Agent in Object Explorer, and select Stop.

6. From the Start menu, go to Programs ➢ Microsoft SQL Server 2005 ➢ Performance Tools ➢ Profiler.

7. From the File menu, select New Trace to open the Trace Properties dialog box.

8. Connect to your default server instance using the proper authentication.

9. In the Trace Name box, type **Tuning**.

10. Use the Tuning template.

11. Check the Save to File box, and click Save to accept the default name and location. Leave the Enable File Rollover box checked and the Server Processes Trace Data box unchecked.

12. Click Run to start the trace.

EXERCISE 14.4 *(continued)*

13. Leave Profiler running, and open a new SQL Server query in Management Studio.

14. Execute the following query:

    USE AdventureWorks

    SELECT textdata FROM monitor

    WHERE DatabaseName = 'AdventureWorks'

15. Switch to Profiler, click the Stop button (red box), and then close Profiler.

Exercise 14.5 will show you how to run the Database Engine Tuning Advisor using the workload file you just created.

EXERCISE 14.5

Using the Database Engine Tuning Advisor

1. From the Start menu, go to Programs ➤ Microsoft SQL Server 2005 ➤ Performance Tools ➤ Database Engine Tuning Advisor.

2. Connect to your server using the appropriate authentication method. This will create a new session in the advisor.

3. In the Session Name box, enter **Tuning Session**.

4. In the Workload section, click the browse button (it looks like a pair of binoculars), and locate the Tuning.trc trace file created earlier.

5. In the databases and tables grid, check the box next to AdventureWorks.

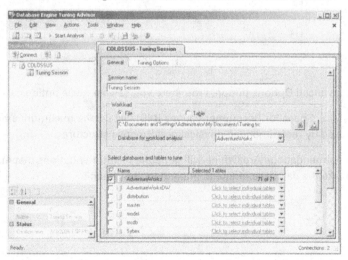

6. Switch to the Tuning Options tab. From here you can instruct the advisor what physical changes to make to the database; specifically, you can have the advisor create new indexes (clustered and nonclustered) and partition the database.

7. Leave the Limit Tuning Time option checked and set for the default time; this prevents the advisor from taking too many system resources.

8. Leave the default options for Physical Design Structures (PDS) Options to Use in Database, Partitioning Strategy to Employ, and Physical Design Structures (PDS) to Keep in Database.

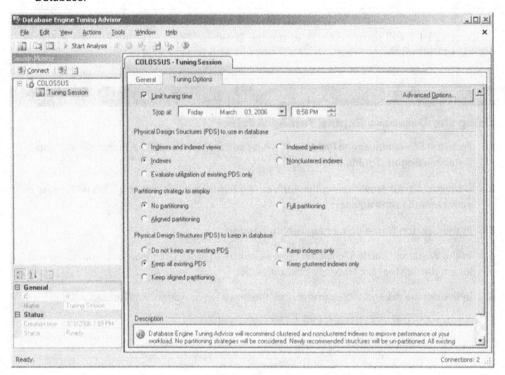

9. Click the Advanced Options button. From here you can set these options:

Define Max. Space for Recommendations (MB) will set the maximum amount of space used by recommended physical performance structures.

All Recommendations Are Offline will generate recommendations that may require you to take the database offline to implement the change.

EXERCISE 14.5 *(continued)*

Generate Online Recommendations Where Possible will return online recommendations even if a faster offline method is possible. If there is no online method, then an offline method is recommended.

Generate Only Online Recommendations will return only online recommendations.

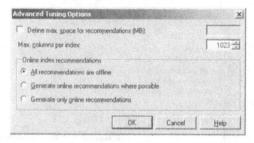

10. Click Cancel to return to the advisor.

11. Click the Start Analysis button on the toolbar.

12. You should see a progress status screen during the analysis phase.

13. After analysis is complete, you will be taken to the recommendations screen; you should see a recommendation for creating an index on the monitor table.

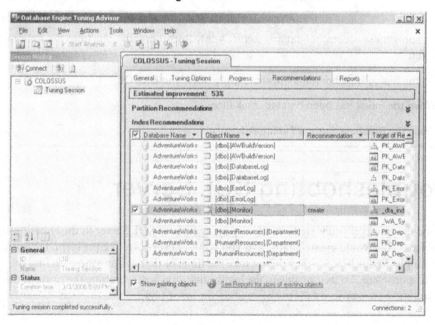

EXERCISE 14.5 *(continued)*

14. You can also check the reports screen for more detailed information on the analysis process.

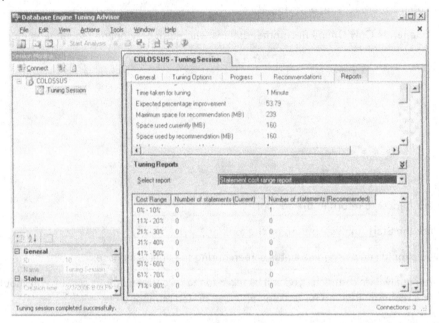

15. To apply these recommendations, select Apply Recommendations from the Actions menu.

16. On the dialog box that pops up, click Apply Now, and click OK.

17. When the index has been created, click Close.

18. Close the Database Engine Tuning Advisor.

Troubleshooting SQL Server

Imagine the results if you were to randomly apply fixes to SQL Server in the hopes of solving a problem. This would create chaos, and you would never solve the problem. Surprisingly, some people do this because they do not take the time, or do not know how, to find the actual cause of a problem. To fix a problem, the logical first step is determining the cause of the problem, and the best way to do that is by reading the *error logs*.

Reading Error and Event Logs

Error logs in SQL Server 2005 are stored in two places—the first is the SQL Server error logs. You'll access the SQL Server 2005 error logs in Exercise 14.6.

Reading SQL Server Error Logs

1. Open Management Studio.

2. In Object Explorer, expand your server and then expand Management.

3. Under Management, expand SQL Server Logs.

4. Under SQL Server Logs, you should see a current log and up to six archives; double-click the current log to open it.

5. In the Log File Viewer, you should see a number of messages. Many of these are informational, but some will be error messages. To find the errors, just read the description at the right of each error.

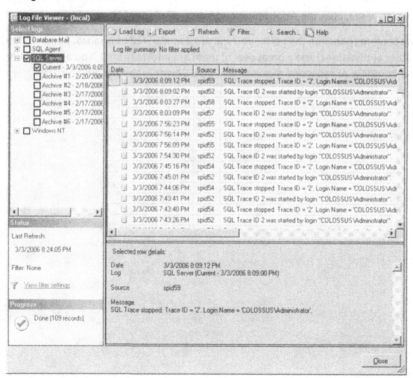

EXERCISE 14.6 *(continued)*

6. Click one of the errors to read more detail in the lower half of the right pane.

7. To view archive logs from here, check the box next to one of the logs.

8. To view Windows event logs, check the box next to an event log.

9. To filter the logs, click the Filter button on the toolbar, enter your filter criteria, and then click OK.

The second place you will find SQL Server error messages is in the Windows Application log, which you will access in Exercise 14.7.

EXERCISE 14.7

Reading Windows Event Logs

1. Select Event Viewer from the Administrative Tools group on the Start menu.

2. In Event Viewer, click the Application Log icon.

3. In the contents pane (on the right), you will see a number of messages. Some of these are for other applications, and a great deal of them are informational. You are primarily interested in yellow or red icons that mention SQL Server in the description.

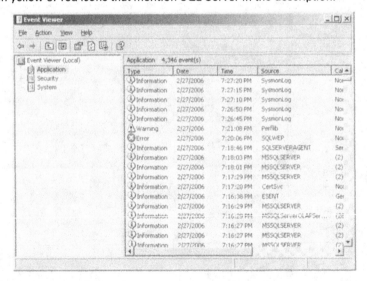

EXERCISE 14.7 *(continued)*

4. Double-click one of the messages to get more details about it.

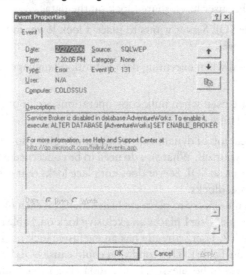

5. Close Event Viewer.

Once you have the information you need, you can begin the troubleshooting process. You'll start by looking at a common problem area: blocks.

Troubleshooting Blocks and Deadlocks

Obviously, you do not want other users to be able to make changes to data while you are reading or modifying it yourself. This would cause confusion and inaccuracies in your database, and your system would soon go from being a database server to being a large paperweight. To keep this from happening, SQL Server automatically places *locks* on the data that is being accessed to limit what other users can do with that data. SQL Server has several types of locks; shared locks and exclusive locks are the most important to understand:

- *Shared locks* are placed on data that is being accessed for read purposes. In other words, when a user executes a SELECT statement, SQL Server places a shared lock on the data requested. Shared locks allow other users to access the locked data for reading but not modification.

- *Exclusive locks* are placed on data that is being modified. This means when a user executes an INSERT, UPDATE, or DELETE statement, SQL Server uses an exclusive lock to protect the data. Exclusive locks do not allow other users to access the locked data for any purpose; the data is exclusively available to the user who placed the lock.

You won't deal with other locks as often (if ever), but it is good to know they are there:

- *Update locks* indicate that a user may want to update data. This prevents a type of deadlock where two users are trying to update data but neither of them can get an exclusive lock because the other user has a shared lock on the data.

- *Intent locks* indicate SQL Server wants to place a lock lower in the database hierarchy, such as at the table level.

- *Schema locks* are used when executing data definition language statements, such as ALTER TABLE.

- *Bulk update locks* are used when bulk copy operations are in progress or when the TABLOCK hint is used on a query.

SQL Server does a great job of dynamically setting these locks, so you don't need to be concerned with setting them yourself. What you do need to be concerned with is making sure your queries are properly written so SQL Server does not place locks that get in the users' way. The primary cause of this is deadlocks.

Deadlocks occur when users try to place exclusive locks on each other's objects (as shown in Figure 14.1). For example, User1 places an exclusive lock on Table1 and then tries to place an exclusive lock on Table2. User2 already has an exclusive lock on Table2, and User2 tries to put an exclusive lock on Table1. This condition could cause SQL Server to enter an endless loop of waiting for the locks to be released, but fortunately an algorithm built into SQL Server looks for and rectifies this problem. SQL Server picks one of the users (called the *victim* in SQL Server terminology) and kills their query. The user whose query was killed will receive an error message stating they are the victim of a deadlock and should try their query again later.

FIGURE 14.1   Deadlocks degrade system performance.

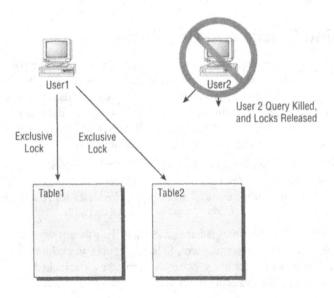

This can cause aggravation among the users because it slows their work. You can avoid deadlocks by monitoring SQL Server using one of three methods:

- Use Profiler to monitor the Locks:Deadlock and Locks:Deadlock Chain events in the Locks event category.

- Check the `Current Activity` folders under **Management** in Enterprise Manager.

- Use the `sp_lock` stored procedure to find out what locks are in place.

When you find the cause of the deadlock, you can have your developers rewrite the offending queries. Of course, that takes time, and you need to get your users running again right away. You can find which user is blocking other users by querying the `sys.dm_exec_requests` system view. Once you find the offending session, you can terminate it with the KILL command. You'll see how to do that in Exercise 14.8.

EXERCISE 14.8

Using *sys.dm_exec_requests* and *KILL*

1. To start a locking session, open a new query in Management Studio, and execute this command:

   ```
   BEGIN TRAN

   SELECT * FROM monitor WITH (TABLOCKX, HOLDLOCK)
   ```

2. Now to create a blocked session, open a new query, and execute this code:

   ```
   UPDATE monitor SET textdata = 'test'

   WHERE rownumber = 1
   ```

3. Notice that the second query does not complete because the first query is holding an exclusive lock on the table. To find the session that is doing the blocking, open a third query window.

4. In the third query window, query the `sys.dm_exec_requests` system view for any session that is being blocked with this code:

   ```
   SELECT session_id, status, blocking_session_id

   FROM sys.dm_exec_requests

   WHERE blocking_session_id > 0
   ```

5. The blocking_session_id is the session causing the problem. To end it, execute the KILL command with the blocking_session_id value. For example, if the blocking_session_id is 53, you would execute this:

   ```
   KILL 53
   ```

6. Switch to the second query (from step 2); it should be complete with one row affected.

Troubleshooting Jobs

You can use jobs to automate tasks in SQL Server. *Jobs* are actually a series of steps that occur, one after the other, to accomplish a task. If one or more of your jobs are not working, check the following:

- The SQL Server Agent service must be running for jobs to work. If it is not, start it.

- Make sure the job, each step of the job, and each schedule of the job is enabled.

- Make sure the owner of the job has all the necessary permissions to run the job.

- Check the logic of your job—make sure all the steps fire in the correct order.

   You can easily tell whether a job has run successfully by looking at the history to find out when the job last fired. You'll do that in Exercise 14.9.

EXERCISE 14.9

Find Out When a Job Last Fired

1.   Open Management Studio.

2.   Make sure your SQL Server Agent is started by right-clicking it in Object Explorer and selecting Start. Click Yes on the dialog box that opens.

3.   To create a job to run, expand SQL Server Agent, right-click Jobs, and select New Job.

4.   Enter **Test History** in the Name box.

5.   Go to the Steps page, and click the New button.

6.   Enter History Step in the Step Name box.

7.   Select AdventureWorks from the database drop-down list.

8.   Enter this code in the command box:

   SELECT * FROM Person.Contact

9.   Click OK, and then click OK again to create the job.

10.   When you return to Management Studio, right-click the Test History job, and click Start Job.

11.   When the job has finished, click Close.

12.   To find out when the job last ran, right-click the Test History job, and click View History.

13. In the Log File Viewer, expand the log file entry by clicking the + sign. This will show you when the job last ran and which step last completed.

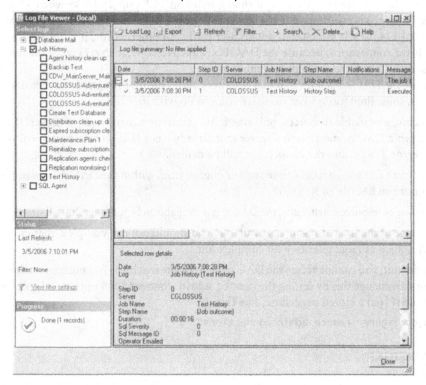

14. Close the Log File Viewer.

Using the Dedicated Administrator Connection

It is a rare occasion, but SQL Server can stop responding to normal queries and appear to be frozen. How could this happen? Consider that when you bought the system that houses SQL Server, you likely planned for future growth and usage. No matter how much time and effort you put into this plan, though, some companies just outgrow their servers too quickly, and the servers can't handle the workload. In a scenario like this, it is possible that SQL Server might stop responding to normal queries. To troubleshoot this issue, or any kind of problem where SQL Server just isn't responding to normal calls, you need the *Dedicated Administrator Connection* (DAC).

The DAC is a special diagnostics connection that is always available for connection, even under normal operating circumstances. As the name implies, only administrators (members of the sysadmin server role) can connect to the DAC to run diagnostic queries and troubleshoot problems. So, how does it work?

By default, SQL Server listens for normal queries on TCP port 1433, so when a user runs a SELECT query, it is transmitted to the server over port 1433. The DAC listens, by default, on TCP port 1434, so it is not cluttered with user traffic. In other words, it is always free and available for connections. Because the DAC is always available, it always consumes some system resources, but these are kept to a minimum.

Because the DAC consumes minimal resources and is meant to be used only for diagnostic functions, some limitations exist on what you can do with it:

- To ensure available resources, only one DAC connection is allowed per server. If you try to open a DAC connection to a server that already has a DAC connection open, you will get error 17810, and the connection will be denied.

- You can't run any parallel commands or queries from within the DAC. For example, you cannot run BACKUP or RESTORE.

- Because of resource constraints, the DAC is not available in SQL Server 2005 Express Edition.

- Because of the limited resources available, you should not run complex queries in the DAC, such as large queries with complex joins.

- By default, you cannot access the DAC from a remote machine; you must be on the server. You can change this by setting the remote admin connections option to 1 by using the sp_configure stored procedure, like this:

```
sp_configure 'remote admin connections', 1
GO
RECONFIGURE
GO
```

That seems like a lot of restrictions, so you may be wondering what you *are* allowed to do. The DAC is especially good for these tasks:

- Querying dynamic management views:
  - You can query sys.dm_exec_requests to find blocking queries.
  - You can query sys.dm_os_memory_cache_counters to check the health of the system memory cache.
  - You can query sys.dm_exec_sessions for information about active sessions.
- Querying catalog views
- Running basic DBCC commands:
  - You can use DBCC FREEPROCCACHE to remove all elements from the procedure cache.
  - You can use DBCC FREESYSTEMCACHE to remove all unused entries from all caches.

- You can use DBCC DROPCLEANBUFFERS to remove all clean buffers from the buffer pool.
- You can use DBCC SQLPERF to retrieve statistics about how the transaction log space is used in all databases.
- Using the KILL command to end an errant session

You can see that this is a powerful weapon in your troubleshooting arsenal, but how do you use it? You'll fire up the DAC in Exercise 14.10.

EXERCISE 14.10

Connecting to the DAC

1. Open a command prompt on your server.

2. The following command connects to the server specified with the -S parameter using a trusted connection as specified by the -E parameter. The -A parameter specifies the DAC, or an administrative connection. Run the following command now:

   Sqlcmd -S (local) -A -E

3. You should see a 1> prompt. From here you can enter a query. Type the following, and hit Enter:

   SELECT session_id, status, blocking_session_id

   FROM sys.dm_exec_requests

4. You should now see a 2> prompt. Type **GO**, and hit Enter to execute the query.

5. You should now be back at the 1> prompt. Type **Exit**, and hit Enter to exit the DAC.

 You can also open a DAC in Management Studio by typing **admin:** in front of the server name in the connection dialog box.

Summary

This chapter has stressed the importance of monitoring and optimizing. Monitoring allows you to find potential problems before your users find them; without monitoring, you have no way of knowing how well your system is performing.

You can use System Monitor to monitor both Windows and SQL Server. Some of the more important counters to watch are Physical Disk: Average Disk Queue (which should be less than two) and SQLServer:Buffer Manager: Buffer Cache Hit Ratio (which should be as high as possible).

Case Study: Monitoring Counters

The AlsoRann company bought an excellent system when it first started using SQL Server. It was top of the line with resources to spare. Over time, though, the company saw performance start to drop; it was a slow but steady decrease. After a few months of this, it seemed that the server wasn't responding at all. That's when the company asked for our help.

The first information we needed to know was how many new users had been added since the server was first put in place. As it turns out, about 100 new users were added. That led to the next question: how heavily did they use SQL Server? It turns out that all the new users accessed the server regularly throughout the day. This got us thinking.

First, we opened the Windows System Monitor and added a few counters:

- Processor: % Processor Time

- Memory: Committed Bytes

- Memory: Pages/Sec

The results were no real surprise. The Processor: % Processor Time counter was only about 15 percent maximum, well below the 75 percent upper limit. The Memory: Pages/Sec was at a sustained average value of 10, which is twice the acceptable limit. The Memory: Committed Bytes was about 300MB higher than the installed physical RAM. The solution here was simple: the processor was fine for the load on the server, but there was not enough RAM. The company forgot to consider that as new users were added to the system, more RAM would be consumed. We added more RAM to the system, and performance returned to acceptable levels.

You can use Profiler to monitor queries after they have been placed in general use; it is also useful for monitoring security and user activity. Once you have used Profiler to log information about query use to a trace file, you can run the Database Engine Tuning Advisor to optimize your indexes.

You also learned about troubleshooting problems, which is important because all systems will eventually have problems. You first learned where to find the SQL Server error logs in Management Studio and how to read them. You then saw how to find errors in Windows Event Viewer.

Next you learned about troubleshooting blocks using the `sys.dm_exec_requests` system view. This is a valuable skill because when a session is blocked, it will never execute, and your users will not be able to get their work done.

After that, you learned how to find out when a job last ran in Management Studio. It may seem simple, but this can save a lot of time when troubleshooting problem jobs.

Finally, you learned about a new tool in SQL Server 2005, the DAC. This is a special connection that is always open and listening on TCP port 1434. It allows a single member of the sysadmins server role to connect to an unresponsive SQL Server to run simple diagnostic queries.

Exam Essentials

Know SQL Server counters, and understand how to use them.   Know the counters available in SQL Server and the acceptable values for each of them. There are quite a few, so we won't rehash them here, but review Tables 14.1 and 14.2 to find the counters and values that are important to know.

Familiarize yourself with Profiler.   Profiler displays what is happening in the database engine by performing a trace, which is a record of data that has been captured about events that are logically grouped into event classes. There are a large number of events, most of which can be used in optimization.

Get familiar with the DAC.   The DAC is a special diagnostic connection that is always available for administrators to connect with. This special connection uses limited resources on the server and is useful for running simple diagnostic commands. You can use either `sqlcmd` with the -A switch or Management Studio with `admin:` in front of the server name to connect to the DAC. Only one administrator at a time can connect.

Know the error logs and locations.   SQL Server logs errors in two places on the server: the SQL Server error logs and the Windows event logs. To find SQL Server errors in the Windows logs, you need to use Event Viewer and look in the Application log. The SQL Server error logs are best viewed in Management Studio.

Know how to use `sys.dm_exec_requests` to troubleshoot blocks.   Blocks occur when one session has an exclusive lock on an object that another session needs to use. If the blocking session does not let go of the lock, then the second session will never complete. This causes problems for your users, so to find the blocking session, you can query the `sys.dm_exec_requests` system view and specifically look at the session_id, status, and blocking_session_id columns.

Review Questions

1. You are the administrator of a SQL Server 2005 computer that has been running fine for some time. Your users started complaining of poor performance, which started when your company hired about 150 more people, each of them having access to the SQL Server computer. When you monitor the system, you notice that the Pages/Sec counter is consistently at 6 and the Buffer Cache Hit Ratio counter is sustained at 75. What should you do to increase performance?

   A. Add another SQL Server computer to the network, and replicate the database to the new server.

   B. Add another hard disk to the server, and implement RAID-5.

   C. Add more RAM to the server.

   D. Set the Query Governor to 2.

2. When performing routine maintenance on your server, you notice that the % Processor Time counter has been at 82 percent consistently since you added about 50 new users to the system. What should you do to remedy this without impacting the users?

   A. Nothing; 82 percent is an acceptable threshold for this counter.

   B. Purchase a faster processor.

   C. Move some of the users' databases to another SQL Server computer.

   D. Replace the current SQL Server computer with a faster server.

3. You are the administrator of a SQL Server 2000 computer that contains your company's inventory-tracking database. Each day more than 100 operators make approximately 5,000 changes to the database. Your accounting and sales departments generate monthly and daily reports against the database as well. Your developers need to analyze the activity against the database to see whether they can do anything to accelerate the generation of these reports. What should you do to get a valid analysis?

   A. Run Profiler on a client computer, configure it to monitor database activity, and log the data to a table in the inventory database.

   B. Run Profiler on the server, configure it to monitor database activity, and log the data to a table in the inventory database.

   C. Run Profiler on a client computer, configure it to monitor database activity, and log the data to a .trc file.

   D. Run Profiler on the server, configure it to monitor database activity, and log the data to a .trc file.

4. One of your users is complaining that whenever she runs a certain query, she loses her connection to SQL Server and does not receive the results of the query. She is forced to reconnect to the server when this happens, and it is slowing her down in her work. What can you do to find the problem?

   A. Run the query yourself on your own machine to see whether it crashes your system.

   B. Run the query in Query Editor with the Set Statistics IO option set.

   C. Run a trace while the user is performing the query, and replay the trace against a test server to find the exact step that is causing the problem.

   D. Run a trace while the user is performing the query, and replay the trace against the production server to find the exact step that is causing the problem.

5. After adding about 100 new users to your server, you notice that the Average Disk Queue counter is at about 3 on a consistent basis. You need to fix this, so you decide to add more disks to the subsystem, but the counters are still too high. What should you do?

   A. Add more RAM.

   B. Add more disks to the array.

   C. Purchase a faster processor.

   D. Remove the users from the system, and add them to another SQL Server computer.

6. You are the administrator of a SQL Server 2005 system with an order-tracking database. You have about 325 users who are constantly updating this database. Shortly after updating the stored procedures that your users use to modify the data in the database, many of your users have started complaining they are getting errors and that their updates are not taking place. What should you do to correct this?

   A. Run a trace, monitor the Locks:Deadlock object, and have the developers rewrite the offending query.

   B. Rewrite your application so that the queries run from the client systems instead of the server.

   C. Rewrite your application so that the queries run from the server instead of the client systems.

   D. Increase the size of the tempdb database so that SQL Server has more room to perform any necessary calculations on the query.

7. You want to monitor the percent of network utilization because your users have been complaining about slow response times, but you cannot find the proper counter to do this. What do you need to do?

   A. Run the command `netcounters -install` at the command prompt to start the network counters.

   B. Start the Windows System Monitor in network monitor mode.

   C. Install the Network Monitor Agent.

   D. Install TCP/IP; the counter will be installed automatically.

8. Your users have been complaining about slow response times since your company hired about 125 people within the last 2 months. Not all of these users have access to the SQL Server computer, but they do all have access to the network. When you start monitoring to find the problem, you notice that the network usage is at about 45 percent on a sustained basis. What should you do?

   A. Remove TCP/IP, and use NetBEUI instead.

   B. Remove TCP/IP, and use NWLink instead.

   C. Segment the network with a router or bridge.

   D. Nothing; 45 is an acceptable range for this counter.

9. You want to be warned when the processor reaches 70 percent utilization so you can monitor the system closely and make sure this does not develop into a more serious problem. What should you do?

   A. Create an alert that sends you a message whenever the % Processor Time value is greater than 70.

   B. Create an alert that sends you a message whenever the % Processor Time value is less than 100.

   C. Create a trace log that fires whenever the % Processor Time value is greater than 70.

   D. Create a Counter Log that fires whenever the % Processor Time value is greater than 70.

10. You have a SQL Server system that has been running fine for several months, but now the system does not seem to be responding to user queries. You need to troubleshoot the problem so your users can access the system again. What can you do?

   A. Reboot the server, and read the logs when it comes back up.

   B. Access the DAC, and run some diagnostic commands to find the problem.

   C. Run a trace in Profiler, and look for errors in the trace.

   D. Open Management Studio in debug mode, and run diagnostic commands to find the problem.

11. One of your users is complaining that an update query they are trying to run has been running for an excessively long time without completing. You suspect that the query may be blocked. How can you verify that the query is blocked?

   A. Query the `sys.dm_blocked_sessions` system view.

   B. Query the `sys.dm_exec_sessions` system view.

   C. Query the `sys.dm_blocked_requests` system view.

   D. Query the `sys.dm_exec_requests` system view.

12. One of your users is complaining that an update query they are trying to run has been running for an excessively long time without completing. You have investigated and found that the query is being blocked by session 135. What command can you use to terminate the errant session?

   A. `STOP 135`

   B. `END 135`

   C. `KILL 135`

   D. `TERMINATE 135`

13. You are one of several SQL Server administrators in your company. One day you receive a complaint that one of your SQL Server machines does not seem to be responding to normal queries, so you try to connect to the DAC to troubleshoot the problem, but you are denied access and given error 17810. What is the problem?

   A. The server has stopped responding to DAC requests and must be rebooted.

   B. The DAC has not been enabled for the server to which you are trying to connect.

   C. The SQL Server Agent service is not running and must be started.

   D. Another administrator has already made a connection to the DAC, and only one connection is allowed at a time.

14. You created a database several weeks ago, and now users have really started putting it to use. You want to make sure it is running as fast as possible so you decide to run the Database Engine Tuning Advisor against it. What do you need to do first?

   A. Create a workload after-hours on the production system.

   B. Create a workload during working hours on the production system.

   C. Create a workload in a test environment using a duplicate of the production database.

   D. Create a workload in a test environment using a database filled with test data.

15. Your database server has suffered a serious problem and is no longer responding to normal commands. You connect via the DAC and find that one of your databases is now corrupt. You decide to restore the database using the RESTORE command to bring the database back online. Does your solution work?

   A. Yes, the solution works, and the database is restored.

   B. No, the RESTORE command cannot be run in the DAC because it modifies a database, which is not allowed.

   C. No, the RESTORE command cannot be run in the DAC because it runs in parallel, which is not allowed.

   D. No, the RESTORE command cannot be run in the DAC because it accesses the disk drive or tape drive to read the backup device, which is not allowed.

16. You need to be able to connect to the DAC from remote machines on your network. What command should you run to configure this?

   A. None; you can access the DAC remotely by default.

   B. Use sp_configure 'remote connections', 1.

   C. Use sp_configure 'remote admin connections', 0.

   D. Use sp_configure 'remote admin connections', 1.

17. You have just configured your SQL Server to allow remote DAC connections, and you need to make sure your company firewall allows access through the correct port. What port does your network administrator need to open to allow remote DAC access?

    A. 1433

    B. 1434

    C. 1435

    D. 1343

18. You have a Windows XP desktop machine running SQL Server 2005 Express Edition. The desktop has 1GB of RAM and a 3GHz processor. Can you access the DAC on the desktop machine?

    A. Yes, you can use the DAC.

    B. No, you cannot use the DAC because you do not have sufficient RAM.

    C. No, you cannot use the DAC because you are running Windows XP and the DAC requires a server operating system such as Windows Server 2003.

    D. No, you cannot use the DAC because you are running SQL Server Express Edition, which does not include the DAC.

19. You have a SQL Server with 4GB of RAM, a 3GHz processor, and a RAID-5 disk array with five disks. When looking at the Windows System Monitor you notice that the Memory: Committed Bytes counter is at 4.2GB. What should you do to fix this?

    A. Nothing; this is an acceptable value for the Memory: Committed Bytes counter.

    B. You should add another disk to the RAID-5 disk array.

    C. You should consider adding more RAM.

    D. You should purchase a faster processor.

20. You are testing a new application and you need to be able to re-create any problems that may arise from the new code running against your SQL Server. You decide to run Profiler to capture all the activity on the server, but what template should you use to create the new trace?

    A. TSQL

    B. TSQL_SPs

    C. TSQL_Duration

    D. TSQL_Replay

    E. Tuning

Answers to Review Questions

1. C. The key here is the value of the counters. The Pages/Sec counter should be at 5 or less. If it is greater than 5, you know that data is being swapped to disk too often. Also, the Buffer Cache Hit Ratio should be at 90; any less tells you that there is not enough RAM for SQL Server to maintain a large enough buffer in RAM.

2. B. The acceptable threshold for the % Processor Time counter is 75 percent. To fix this without affecting the users, you can purchase a faster processor and upgrade the current system after hours.

3. C. The best way to monitor the server without placing excess load on the server is to run Profiler on a client system and save the data on the client system in a .trc file. If you run the trace on the server or save the trace in a table on the server, you will throw off the trace with the excess activity generated by Profiler.

4. C. The best way to find the problem is to run a trace while the user is performing the query. And, if you know that a query is going to crash the client, it will definitely cause some problems at the server as well. You should run the replay against a test server to avoid affecting other users.

5. A. If you do not have enough RAM on your system, it must write to the page file excessively. This will cause the disk queue to exceed acceptable limits even though you have added more disks to the array. The way to stop this excessive paging is by adding more RAM.

6. A. The most likely cause of this error is a deadlock, where two users are trying to access each other's objects at the same time. This is likely because of poorly written queries that need to be rewritten. The machine where the queries run has no bearing on whether those queries are blocking objects. The size of the tempdb database would also not stop some user transactions from being applied; they would simply take longer.

7. C. You need to install the Network Monitor Agent to see the % Network Utilization counter. There is no network monitor mode for the Windows System Monitor, and the counter is not installed with TCP/IP; in fact, TCP/IP is installed automatically, so you do not need to install it. Also, `netcounters -install` is not a valid command.

8. C. When the network utilization gets to be greater than 30 percent on a sustained basis, you need to segment the network to get rid of some of the broadcast traffic that is affecting it. Changing to NWLink would only make the problem worse because it adds more broadcast traffic than TCP/IP (plus, it is no longer available in SQL Server 2005), and NetBEUI is no longer available in server operating systems.

9. A. An alert will send you a message; trace and counter logs do not. Also, you need to send the alert when the value is greater than 70 percent; otherwise, you will receive an alert the entire time the processor is less than 70 percent, which would be annoying.

10. B. The best way to troubleshoot an unresponsive SQL Server is to connect to the DAC and run diagnostic commands to find the problem. Running a trace on the server won't work because the server will not respond to Profiler and because rebooting the server unnecessarily can damage open files. Also, Management Studio doesn't have a debug mode.

11. D. To find out whether a session is being blocked, you can query `sys.dm_exec_requests` and look at the blocking_session_id column. If this has a value greater than 0, then the query is being blocked by another session. For example, if the blocking_session_id column has a value of 135, the session 135 is blocking the query.

12. C. The command to terminate an errant session is `KILL process_id`, so `KILL 135` will terminate the errant session. The other commands are not valid SQL Server commands.

13. D. Only one DAC connection can be made to a server at a time. If more than one administrator tries to connect, they will get the 17810 error code. Also, the DAC is always enabled and always responds, and the SQL Server Agent service has no effect on it.

14. B. The best time to get an accurate workload is during normal business hours on the production system. Running Profiler to get the workload does not generate enough overhead to impede user progress, and trying to get a workload at any other time or on a test system will yield inaccurate results.

15. C. Because the DAC consumes limited resources on the server, it is not capable of running commands that execute in parallel, such as `BACKUP` and `RESTORE`. You can run commands that modify databases in the DAC.

16. D. By default, the DAC is not available over the network; you must set the `remote admin connections` option to 1 by using the `sp_configure` stored procedure. Setting it to 0 will disable remote connections. Also, `remote connections` is not a valid option.

17. B. The SQL Server database engine listens for connections, by default, on port 1433. The DAC listens on port 1434, so that port needs to be open for remote DAC connections. SQL Server does not use ports 1435 or 1343 by default.

18. D. SQL Server Express Edition does not include the DAC because Express Edition is designed to consume as little resources as possible. The DAC does not depend on a specific operating system or amount of RAM.

19. C. When the Memory: Committed Bytes counter is higher than the physical RAM installed on your server, it means you do not have enough RAM and your system will start paging excessively soon. You should add more RAM or consider moving some processes to a different server.

20. D. If you need to re-create any activity that you record in Profiler, then you should use the TSQL_Replay template because it captures all the necessary data to replay a trace. None of the other templates captures the necessary data.

Glossary

@@error   @@error is a variable that returns the last error number in a T-SQL batch. It is preferable to use ERROR_NUMBER() in SQL Server 2005.

A

alert   An alert is an error message or event that occurs in SQL Server and is recorded in the Windows Application log. Alerts can be sent to users via email, pager, or Net Send.

application role   This is a special type of role that requires activation using the sp_setapprole stored procedure. This is primarily used to keep users from accessing a database with anything other than a custom application.

article   In replication an article is a table, or part of a table, that is being replicated.

authentication mode   This dictates how SQL Server processes usernames and passwords.

B

backup   This is a copy of a database that can be used to bring the database back to a stable condition in the event of a disaster.

backup device   This is a pointer to a file or tape drive where backup files are stored.

backup strategy   This is a plan that the database administrator devises stating what types of backup to perform and when.

bcp   This is a command prompt utility to extract or load data from/into SQL Server using bulk insert methods.

broker instance identifier   This identifier is assigned to an instance of Service Broker.

broken ownership chain   This is a condition that occurs when dependant objects are owned by different users.

broker service   A broker service communicates over database endpoints and uses a message-based system with guaranteed delivery. It consists of message types, contracts, and services.

built-in functions   Built-in functionality in T-SQL represents data. Functions are defined in several categories.

bulk insert   A bulk insert, or BULK INSERT statement, loads data into SQL Server without logging it as single transactions in the transaction log.

Bulk-Logged recovery model   The database recovery model is set to log minimal information about BULK INSERT statements and is used to minimize logging in the transaction log.

B-Tree   Short for *binary-tree*, this is the structure of an index in SQL Server. It's called this because it resembles a tree when drawn. Starting with a root page, it expands into leaf pages where data is stored.

C

catalog   This is an object in a database that is used to organize full-text indexes.

checkpoint   This is an entry that SQL Server records in a transaction log when it copies transactions from the log to the datafile.

CLR functions   These manage code functions written in Visual Studio and cataloged in SQL Server as T-SQL stored functions out of a cataloged assembly.

CLR procedure   These manage code procedures written in Visual Studio and cataloged in SQL Server as T-SQL stored procedures out of a cataloged assembly.

clustered index   This is an index that physically rearranges the data that is inserted into your tables.

COLLATE   This keyword is used within T-SQL to return a different collation type or data sort order.

collations   Collations represent different types of character sets as case sensitive/case insensitive but also are used to represent non-ASCII character sets.

collation designator   If you use Windows Collation, then this setting designates how characters are stored.

collation setting   This designates how characters are stored and sorted.

column   See *field*.

COMMIT TRANSACTION   This statement is executed at the end of a T-SQL batch to harden a transaction in the transaction log.

contract   This is an agreement used within Service Broker that specifies what messages can be sent between multiple instances.

convergence   In replication, when all articles in a merge replication scenario contain the same data, they are in convergence.

Copy Database Wizard   This is a wizard that copies a database from one server to another.

copy-only backup   This is a special type of backup that allows an administrator to make a backup of a database without affecting other active backup types.

counter   This is an object in Windows that provides statistics about system objects, such as memory or the processor.

CREATE ENDPOINT   This T-SQL statement is used to define an endpoint and is used for database-mirroring endpoints, Service Broker endpoints , or even HTTP endpoints (XML web services).

cursor   Queries in SQL Server return a block of rows called a *recordset*. A cursor is a subset of a recordset with the added ability to move back and forth through the records.

custom database role   These are special groups that can be created in a database and have custom permissions applied to limit the permissions that a user has inside the database.

D

Database Mail   This is a special program (called `SQLiMail90.exe`) that is used to send email for SQL Server using the standard Simple Mail Transfer Protocol (SMTP).

database mirroring   This high-availability feature mirrors a database onto another server to have a standby failover mechanism on user databases.

database snapshot   A database snapshot is a moment-in-time recording of a database and keeps track of every change made to a database from the moment the snapshot was taken. This method often prevents user mistakes as an add-on to fault-tolerance.

Database Tuning Advisor   This is a tool that helps administrators tune databases by analyzing a workload and suggesting possible indexes.

DDL triggers   DDL triggers are T-SQL triggers that execute the trigger code when a DDL statement is issued.

decompose XML   This is way to transform XML into relational data.

Dedicated Administrator Connection   This is a special connection that allows administrators to run diagnostic commands in case SQL Server stops responding to normal queries.

default constraints   This is a constraint that is used to automatically fill in fields that are left blank in an INSERT statement.

DENY   This is a permission state that prevents a user from using a permission even if the user is a member of a group that has been granted that permission.

deterministic Deterministic functions return the same value each time they're invoked with the same arguments.

dialogue conversation Dialogue conversations are used by Service Broker to initiate communication on a queue (to send or receive messages).

differential backups This is a type of backup that backs up changes to the database only since the last full backup was made.

distributed query This is a query that returns result sets from databases on multiple servers.

distributed transaction A distributed transaction is a transaction that spans multiple servers and has to execute as one single batch statement.

distributor In replication, this is the server that receives data from publishers and transfers it to subscribers.

DML This stands for Data Manipulation Language and is used in T-SQL to insert/update/delete data.

DML triggers T-SQL triggers execute the trigger code when a DML statement is issued. DML triggers are fired after the actual event occurs or can replace the statement by using an INSTEAD OF TRIGGER.

E

error logs These are files in Windows or SQL Server that contain information about errors that have occurred.

event classes These are a logical grouping of events.

event notifications These are methods used in SQL Server 2005 to generate events and submit the event to a queue. Events can be any DML/DDL statement but can also consist of database-level or server-level events, including audit and login.

Eventdata function This is a function that returns the collection information gathered within a trigger execution. Eventdata returns an xml datatype with event information.

events This is any action that happens with the database engine, such as a failed login or a completed query.

exist method This is a method used by XML querying to check for the existence of a certain XML node.

extent This is a group of eight data pages totaling 64KB in size.

F

field   Fields are objects in a table that contain a certain type of information of the same datatype.

filegroup   This is a logical grouping of files used to segregate database objects for storage and performance reasons.

filegroup backup   This is a type of backup that backs up one or more filegroups in a database.

fill factor   The fill factor of an index indicates how much space to leave open for new data when the index is reorganized during maintenance.

fixed database roles   These are special groups in each SQL Server database that already have permissions applied and are used to limit the permissions that a user has inside the database.

fixed server roles   These are special groups in SQL Server that are used to limit the amount of administrative access that a user has once logged on to SQL Server.

fragmentation   When a page fills with data, SQL Server must take half of the data from the full page and move it to a new page to make room for more data. When a new page is created, then the pages inside the database are no longer contiguous. This condition is called *fragmentation*.

full backup   This is a type of backup that backs up the entire database, but not the transaction logs.

full-text index   This is an index that can be queried for large amounts of text. This is maintained by the full-text search service.

full-text search   This is a program that runs as a service and can be used to index large amounts of text from multiple sources.

G

grant   This is a permission state that allows a user to use a permission.

guest user   This is a catchall database user account for people who have a SQL Server logon but not a user account in the database.

GUID   This stands for Global Unique Identifier, a uniquely generated string on SQL Server.

H

heap   This is a table with no clustered index in place.

heterogeneous replication   This is the process of replicating data from SQL Server to a third-party database system, such as IBM DB2.

HTTP endpoints   An endpoint is expressed by an IP address and port number that hosts web services on SQL Server 2005.

http.sys   This is an operating system file on Windows Server 2003 and Windows XP used by Internet Information Services but also used by SQL Server to register endpoints and operate over endpoints without needing IIS.

I

included columns   These columns are used to extend a nonclustered index to include nonkey columns.

INSTEAD OF   This is a trigger action that executes instead of the actual statement (see *DML triggers*).

intermediate-level pages   This term describes all index pages between the root page and the leaf-level pages.

J

job   A job is a series of steps that define the task to be automated. It also defines schedules, which dictate when the task is to be executed.

K

key values   This is a list of all the values in an indexed column.

L

leaf pages   These are the pages in a B-Tree index structure that contain the actual data.

linked login   This is a special login that linked servers use to gain access to remote servers when performing distributed queries.

linked servers   This is the remote servers in a distributed query.

locks   SQL Server uses locks to prevent multiple users from modifying the same data at the same time.

log sequence number   This is part of a transaction log entry that is used to track when a transaction begins and ends in the transaction log. This is used in restoring a database so that transactions are restored in order.

log shipping This is a method used to ship log data information from one server to a standby server.

login This is an object that allows a user to connect to SQL Server. This contains information about whether the login is Windows or SQL Server, about fixed server role membership, and about database access.

M

mailhost This is any database that is configured to process mail for Database Mail.

Maintenance Plan Wizard This is a wizard that creates jobs for defragmenting, repairing, backing up, reindexing, and regenerating statistics for databases.

managed procedures See *CLR procedures*.

message type A message type is a definition of a message that can be sent by Service Broker. They are defined and used within a contract to determine the type of messages that can be sent. Message types can be header only, XML, or binary.

mirror See *database mirroring*.

modify method This method is used by XML in SQL Server to replace and modify data in an XML column.

multiserver job This is a job that is created on a central server and downloaded to other servers over the network where the job is run. Job log information is returned to the initiating or master server.

N

named instance Named instances allow you to run multiple copies of SQL Server on a single machine. Each instance shows up on the network as a distinct instance of SQL Server.

nesting This process is used within triggers when one triggers fires another.

nesting transactions This transaction is started within another transaction and will create a nested transaction.

.NET CLR SQL Server hosts the .NET common language runtime in order to support the usage of extended functionality written in Visual Studio or any .NET Framework–supported language.

.NET Framework This is a framework used by Microsoft to provide common functionality to the operating system and application layers.

nodes method This method is used by XML to retrieve nodes in an XML structure.

nonclustered index   This is an index that does not physically rearrange the data that is inserted into your tables. This index contains pointers to the data that is stored in the table or clustered index.

nondeterministic   Nondeterministic functions return different values when they're invoked with the same arguments.

nontrusted   A type of connection in which SQL Server does not trust Windows to verify a user's password and must verify the password itself.

O

object   In Windows System Monitor, this is a part of the system, such as the processor or the physical memory.

object permissions   Object permissions regulate a user's ability to work with the data contained in the database.

OPENROWSET   This statement is issued to connect to external databases or sources and retrieve data.

operator   Operators are objects that configure who receives alerts and when those people are available to receive these messages.

ownership chain   This is a series of owners for each object in a group of dependent objects. For example, when a view is based on a table, the ownership chain is the owner of the view and the owner of the table.

P

page   Databases are divided into 8KB blocks of storage called pages. This is the smallest unit of data storage in SQL Server.

page split   This is the process of moving half of the data from a full data page to a new, empty data page to make room for new data to be inserted.

parameter   This is a placeholder for information that is supplied when an alert is fired.

partial backup   This is a type of backup that contains all the data from the primary filegroup and each read-write filegroup. Read-only filegroups are not backed up.

partition function   This is a special function that SQL Server uses to divide the data in a table into multiple partitions for storage and performance reasons.

partition schema   This maps the partitions of a partitioned table or index to physical file or filegroup.

path index   This is an index used on an xml datatype to optimize XQuerying.

performance alert   This is an alert that is based on the same performance counters used in the counters used in Windows System Monitor.

piecemeal restore   This is a type of restore that allows administrators to restore a database that consists of multiple filegroups in stages instead of restoring all filegroups at the same time.

point-in-time restore   This is a type of restore that allows an administrator to restore a database to the condition it was in at a specific point in time.

precision   This is the total number of digits that can be stored in an object that uses the decimal datatype.

primary data files   This is the first data file created for any database. It has an .mdf extension.

primary key   This is an index that ensures that each of the records in your table is unique in some way.

primary XML index   A primary XML index is created as a starting point entry index on an xml datatype.

principal   This identifies the primary database in database mirroring.

property index   This is an index used on an xml datatype to optimize XML querying on the value property.

publication   In replication, this is a logical grouping of multiple articles from a single database.

publisher   In replication, this is the server that contains the original copy of the data to be replicated.

Q

Query Optimizer   This is the component in SQL Server that analyzes your queries, compares them with available indexes, and decides which index will return a result set the fastest.

queue   This is a sort of internal table used by Service Broker to submit messages to and retrieve messages from.

R

RAID   This is short for Redundant Array of Inexpensive Disks. This is a grouping, or array, of hard disks that appear as a single, logical drive to the operating system.

RAISERROR   This is a T-SQL function used to generate an error message. The error message can be user-defined or predefined in SQL Server.

RECEIVE   This is a statement issued to retrieve items from a SQL Server message queue.

recompile   The process that occurs when a stored procedure is translated into binary executable code is called *compilation*. When an application forces a procedure to recompile, it will regenerate the executable code.

record   This is a group of related fields containing information about a single entity.

recursive triggers   Triggers are recursive when one trigger causes the same trigger to be fired and thus enables recursion. These are blocked by default on SQL Server 2005.

replication   This is a process that copies data from one database to another.

restore   This is the process of bringing a database back to a stable condition after a disaster.

revoke   This is a permission state that neither permits nor prevents a user from using a permission.

rollback   Rolling back a transaction means you are undoing the actual transaction you are currently in.

ROLLBACK TRANSACTION   This is a statement issued to roll back a transaction instead of committing and hardening the data in the log file.

rollforward   When SQL Server stops unexpectedly or when a restore from backup is done, a rollforward will occur, meaning that SQL Server will apply the committed records from the log file to the actual data file.

root page   This is the first page in a B-Tree index structure. All searches of the index begin with the root page.

route   This is a destination defined by endpoints to specify how to communicate from one service to the other.

row overflow data   This is a special area in the database that is used to store data for variable-length columns when the length of the row they are in exceeds 8,096 bytes.

row   See *record*.

S

scalar functions   These are functions in SQL Server that return a scalar datatype.

scale   This is the total number of digits that can be stored to the right of the decimal point in an object that uses the decimal datatype.

schema validation   This is validation done on an XML column to verify the structure of an XML datatype with an XML schema; the schema itself needs to be cataloged first in SQL using CREATE schema collection.

secondary data files   Secondary files can be created to store database objects if more than one file is needed. These have an `.ndf` extension by default.

securable   This is any object to which SQL Server regulates access.

selectivity   This is a term used to describe the number of duplicate values in a column.

SEND   This is a T-SQL command to submit items to a queue in the Service Broker architecture.

service   A service consists of a contract and message types in Service Broker and is used to send and receive messages from/to.

service account   This is a special user account that gives service access to the machine and network with the privileges granted to the user account.

Service Broker   This is a message-based queuing architecture within SQL Server 2005 used to transfer related messages over HTTP.

service program   This is a program or procedure that automates the processing of queues inserted into a Service Broker queue.

severity level   This is the status level of an error message and is used to indicate how severe a certain error is.

sort order   If you use Windows collation, this setting defines how SQL Server sorts and compares your data during queries or indexing.

SQL injection attacks   This is a way that hackers can bring a database down. SQL injection attacks can be avoided by using stored procedures with the appropriate configured parameters.

SSIS   This stands for SQL Server Integration Services and replaces DTS on SQL Server 2000. It is used to transfer data from any source to any destination. It is a separate service that comes with a package designer integrated into Business Intelligence Development Studio.

standby server   This is a server that can be switched over to provide fault-tolerance in a log shipping implementation or database-mirroring fault-tolerance implementation.

statement permissions   These are permissions that regulate a user's ability to create structures that hold data, such as tables and views.

stored procedure   This is a batch of SQL commands that are precompiled and saved as a procedure in SQL Server.

subscriber   In replication, this is the server that receives a copy of the data contained on the publisher.

T

table scan   This is the process of scanning each extent of a table for a needed record.

tables   These are the objects in the database that hold all the data.

trace   This is a record of data that has been captured about events in Profiler.

table-valued functions   This is a function that returns a result set because it returns a SELECT statement from a table.

traceflag   This is an option that can be set to set SQL Server–specific tracing or to provide and enable certain SQL Server configuration features such as database mirroring.

trace template   This is a predefined trace definition that can be used to create a trace using SQL Server Profiler.

transaction log   Transactions in SQL Server are written to the transaction log before they are written to the database. This log information is used primarily for database recovery in the event of a disaster.

transaction log backups   This type of backup makes a copy of all transactions in the transaction log, and it can clear all the inactive transactions from the log, thus giving the log more space to hold new transactions.

transaction safety   This is a mode to specify in what context database mirroring should be configured—asynchronous or synchronous.

trusted   This is a type of connection in which SQL Server trusts Windows to verify a user's password.

TRY-CATCH   This is an error handling message block, new to SQL Server 2005.

two-phase commit   This is a special transaction involving two servers in which the transaction must be applied to both servers, or the entire transaction is rolled back from both servers.

typed XML   This is XML that matches a schema validation.

U

unique index   This is a special index that prevents users from inserting the same value into a column (or columns) more than once.

untyped XML   This is XML that is well-formed but not schema validated.

V

value index   See *property index*.

value method   This is an XML method to return scalar data from an XML expression

views   These are virtual representations of a table whose contents are defined by a query.

W

Windows Management Instrumentation   This is Microsoft's implementation of web-based enterprise management, which is an industry initiative to make systems easier to manage by exposing managed components as a set of common objects.

witness server   This is a server that facilitates automatic failover. Its only role is to monitor the status of the principal server.

workload   This is a special trace that is used by the Database Tuning Advisor to determine which indexes may enhance database performance.

X

XML datatype   A native datatype is stored in SQL Server to support the direct querying and storing of XML data.

XQuery   This is a standard method of querying XML data using XML query expressions.

Index

Note to the Reader: Throughout this index **boldfaced** page numbers indicate primary discussions of a topic. *Italicized* page numbers indicate illustrations.

The Best MCTS Book/CD Package on the Market!

Get ready for the new Microsoft Certified Technology Specialist SQL Server 2005 Implementation and Maintenance (70-431) exam with the most comprehensive and challenging sample tests anywhere! The Sybex test engine includes the following features:

- Chapter-by-chapter exam coverage of all the review questions from the book.

- Challenging questions representative of those you'll find on the real exams.

- Two bonus exams, available only on the CD.

Search through the complete book in PDF:

- Read the entire MCTS: *Microsoft SQL Server 2005 Implementation and Maintenance Study Guide (70-431)* book, complete with figures and tables, in electronic format.

- Search the MCTS: Microsoft SQL Server 2005 Implementation and Maintenance Study Guide (70-431) chapters to find information about any topic in seconds.

Use the 150 electronic flash cards for PCs or Palm devices to jog your memory and prep for the exam at the last minute:

- Reinforce your understanding of key concepts with these hard-core flash card–style questions.

- Download the flash cards to your Palm device, and go on the road. Now you can study anywhere, anytime.

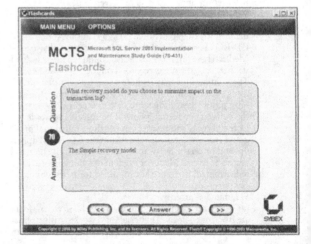

MCTS: Microsoft Certified Technology Specialist: SQL Server 2005 Study Guide

Exam 70-431: Microsoft SQL Server 2005—Implementation and Maintenance

Sybex®
An Imprint of
WILEY

OBJECTIVE	CHAPTER
CREATING AND IMPLEMENTING DATABASE OBJECTS	
Implement a table.	3
Specify column details.	3
Specify the filegroup.	3
Assign permissions to a role for tables.	3
Specify a partition scheme when creating a table.	3
Specify a transaction.	3
Implement a view.	3
Create an indexed view.	3
Create an updateable view.	3
Assign permissions to a role or schema for a view.	6
Implement triggers.	5
Create a trigger.	5
Create DDL triggers for responding to database structure changes.	5
Identify recursive triggers.	5
Identify nested triggers.	5
Identify transaction triggers.	5
Implement functions.	5
Create a function.	5
Identify deterministic versus nondeterministic functions.	5
Implement stored procedures.	5
Create a stored procedure.	5
Recompile a stored procedure.	5
Assign permissions to a role for a stored procedure.	6
Implement constraints.	3
Specify the scope of a constraint.	3
Create a new constraint.	3
Implement indexes.	4
Specify the filegroup.	4
Specify the index type.	4
Specify relational index options.	4
Specify columns.	4
Specify a partition scheme when creating an index.	4
Disable an index.	4
Create an online index by using an ONLINE argument.	4
Create user-defined types.	5
Create a Transact-SQL user-defined type.	5
Specify details of the data type.	5
Create a CLR user-defined type.	5
Implement a full-text search.	4
Create a catalog.	4
Create an index.	4
Specify a full-text population method.	4
Implement partitions.	2, 3, 4
Create a partition scheme.	4
Create a table on a partition scheme.	4
Create a partition function.	3
Work with schemas to create table objects.	3

MONITORING AND TROUBLESHOOTING SQL SERVER PERFORMANCE

Sybex®
An Imprint of
WILEY

Exam objectives are subject to change at any time prior to notice and at Microsoft's sole discretion. Please visit Microsoft's web site (www.microsoft.com/learning) for the most current listing of exam objectives.

Sybex®
An Imprint of
WILEY